W9-BRV-722

Growing Up Gifted

To my beautiful mother, who started it all,
   my son, who allowed me to live with giftedness,
      my daughter, who taught me the gentleness of special gifts,
         my husband, who believes in growing and miracles,
            my dearest father, who loves us all.

Barbara Clark
California State University, Los Angeles

Growing Up Gifted
Developing the Potential
of Children
at Home and at School
SECOND EDITION

Charles E. Merrill Publishing Company
A Bell & Howell Company
Columbus   Toronto   London   Sydney

Published by
Charles E. Merrill Publishing Company
A Bell & Howell Company
Columbus, Ohio 43216

Cover photo by Charles J. Quinlan
Cover design by Tony Faiola

International Standard Book Number: 0–675–20060–1
Library of Congress Catalog Card Number: 82–62500

2   3   4   5   6   7   8   9   10—90   89   88   87   86   85   84   83

Printed in the United States of America

TABLE OF CONTENTS

PHOTO CREDITS

The remaining photographs were taken jointly by Barbara Clark, Carmela Del Duca, Christine Cenci, and Patricia Belohovek.

References for Chapter Opening Quotations

Chapter 1	A. Perone and D. Pulvino
Chapter 3	Walter B. Barbe
Chapter 4	Sidney Marland, 1972, p. 23
Chapter 5	Elizabeth Monroe Drews, 1976, pp. 27–28
Chapter 6	Alfred North Whitehead
Chapter 7	J. Krishnamurti, 1964
Chapter 8	Anonymous
Chapter 9	Kahil Gibran, *The Prophet*. New York: Alfred A. Knopf, 1960 (© 1923), p. 62.
Chapter 10	James Fadiman, 1976

Figures 4.3 (p. 153), 4.4 (p. 154), and 4.5 (p. 155) courtesy of Kay S. Bull, Oklahoma State University.

PREFACE TO THE SECOND EDITION

How giftedness begins, the demands it makes on our children, and how a gifted child's development can be enhanced are important and exciting challenges for all of us. Since the first edition of *Growing Up Gifted* was published, the interest in how individuals become highly intelligent has increased. This interest has been pursued by those in early childhood education, biology, psychology, and to a lesser extent by those in gifted education. Yet, in the emerging data lie the roots of giftedness; the hope for the children we wish to serve. This area of inquiry is of primary importance to those involved in educating gifted children. We must understand how infants develop intelligence as well as how we as educators may nurture its growth.

Events in these past few years have allowed us a far deeper understanding of intellectual development. The fields of psychobiology and brain/mind research, among others, have added to our knowledge of human learning and added dimensions to our view of human capability. In this edition, we will explore these new data and discover their fascinating implications for the classroom and the home. These ideas and discoveries will, I believe, allow us to provide a better, more effective educational experience for our children. Of greater importance, it can assure our children of more fully developing their vast capabilities; more effectively using the potential with which they were born.

As I updated the material on the exploration of giftedness and synthesized the progress made during the last few years, I was surprised and pleased to find that a lot of the ideas and research previously considered "amazing possibilities" could now become an integral part of the book. For example, discoveries from the field of brain research not only provide clues to the future, but could be used presently in developing classroom curriculum and strategies. Other amazing possibilities continue to open before us.

We discuss the emotional and social aspects of growing up gifted and the role that attitudes and support from the home and the school play in nurturing this development. Being gifted affects both the children who are gifted and those around them. We will look at the emotional impact on the child and on the environment and suggest ideas for promoting positive attitudes and ways to meet the needs of the total child.

Once gifted children enter school, they must encounter appropriate educational experiences to ensure their continuous growth. Current models for providing these programs are presented with guides for organizing such programs to meet the needs of the gifted. The steps necessary to provide a quality, differentiated program —from identifying the students to be served to implementing the written plan—are discussed and helpful examples presented. The most common expressions of giftedness are examined: cognitive, academic, leadership, creative, and visual and performing arts abilities.

Of great interest are the activities and strategies which can be used in the gifted classroom. This material has been organized by the use of framework and by func-

tion. The secondary educator will find a discussion of the special problems encountered with older gifted youth and a presentation of activities and strategies which
have been used successfully in secondary classrooms. Curriculum based on brain/
mind research has been developed and is presented as part of the Integrative Education Model. This edition presents the model's rationale and format and details strategies that have proven effective in implementation.

Research is continuing in a variety of areas important to those concerned with
educating gifted individuals. A summary of the research now available in many of
these areas is presented with the hope of stimulating continued inquiry in this area,
so that with increased knowledge more of these special needs may be met.

Finally, we look at possibilities that show promise of significantly affecting the
future of our children and through them all of us. We continue to live in times of
great change, times of beckoning promise, times that challenge us to be the most of
who we can be, to take joy in the human possibilities. In this book it is my hope that
you will find much that will aid you to discover the excitement and pleasure of being with these special children as they share the process of growing up gifted.

A special note: While working on the second edition, I met Nhut Ha, a most talented
young man age 13. I invited him to submit some of his work for publication in this
book. You will find two of his drawings illustrating the discussion of the brain in
Chapter 1. I'm sure you will find his contribution as exciting as I do. I did not want
you to miss the opportunity to know the work of my young friend, who has now received the status of a professional illustrator.

Barbara Clark
October 1982

Growing Up Gifted

SECTION ONE

Understanding the Gifted Individual

CHAPTER ONE

Who Are
the Gifted?

The information in this chapter provides for the reader

- an assessment of beliefs and understandings of gifted children.
- a rationale for a definition of the term *gifted*.
- a discussion of interactive intelligence and its relationship to giftedness.
- an awareness of the nature and the limitations of measuring intelligence.
- an overview of the historical development of the concept of intelligence.
- a discussion of the importance of brain function to the concept of intelligence.
- a model of creativity showing integration of the four major areas of human function.
- information on each category of creativity as identified in the literature, its definition, characteristic population, and conditions for development.

Assessment Instrument

Before you begin reading this text, you may find it helpful to try the following questionnaire. These questions allow you to look at your beliefs and understandings regarding gifted children. Before each statement place the number that you feel most closely represents your present position. At the end of this exercise the results are discussed. Be as open as you can. You may discover some new insights about yourself.

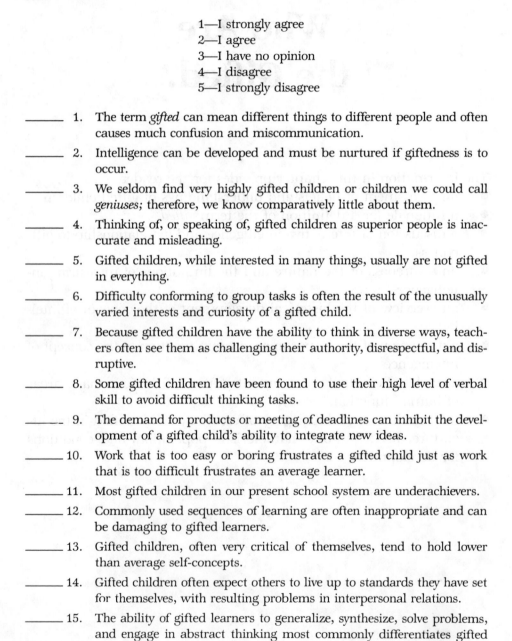

> 1—I strongly agree
> 2—I agree
> 3—I have no opinion
> 4—I disagree
> 5—I strongly disagree

_____ 1. The term *gifted* can mean different things to different people and often causes much confusion and miscommunication.

_____ 2. Intelligence can be developed and must be nurtured if giftedness is to occur.

_____ 3. We seldom find very highly gifted children or children we could call *geniuses*; therefore, we know comparatively little about them.

_____ 4. Thinking of, or speaking of, gifted children as superior people is inaccurate and misleading.

_____ 5. Gifted children, while interested in many things, usually are not gifted in everything.

_____ 6. Difficulty conforming to group tasks is often the result of the unusually varied interests and curiosity of a gifted child.

_____ 7. Because gifted children have the ability to think in diverse ways, teachers often see them as challenging their authority, disrespectful, and disruptive.

_____ 8. Some gifted children have been found to use their high level of verbal skill to avoid difficult thinking tasks.

_____ 9. The demand for products or meeting of deadlines can inhibit the development of a gifted child's ability to integrate new ideas.

_____ 10. Work that is too easy or boring frustrates a gifted child just as work that is too difficult frustrates an average learner.

_____ 11. Most gifted children in our present school system are underachievers.

_____ 12. Commonly used sequences of learning are often inappropriate and can be damaging to gifted learners.

_____ 13. Gifted children, often very critical of themselves, tend to hold lower than average self-concepts.

_____ 14. Gifted children often expect others to live up to standards they have set for themselves, with resulting problems in interpersonal relations.

_____ 15. The ability of gifted learners to generalize, synthesize, solve problems, and engage in abstract thinking most commonly differentiates gifted from average learners. Therefore, programs for gifted children should stress utilization of these abilities.

_____ 16.   The persistent goal-directed behavior of gifted children can result in others perceiving them as stubborn, willful, and uncooperative.

_____ 17.   If not challenged, gifted children can waste their ability and become mediocre, average learners.

_____ 18.   Gifted children often express their idealism and sense of justice at a very early age.

_____ 19.   Not all gifted children show creativity, leadership, or physical expertise.

_____ 20.   People who work with, study, and try to understand gifted children have more success educating the gifted than those who have limited contact and have not educated themselves as to the unique needs of these children.

_____ 21.   I would be pleased to be considered gifted, and I enjoy people who are.

The questionnaire you have just completed should give you some indication of opinions of gifted children that are supportive to their educational growth. The more "1—I strongly agree" answers you were able to give, the more closely your opinions match those who have devoted their energy to understanding gifted children. In the pages to follow, we examine these issues and others that augment our understanding and ability to better educate gifted children.

> The key to understanding how people interact in their environment may be in knowing how the brain works, what behavioral actions are coupled with specific brain functions and how brain processes can be assessed in educational institutions.
>
> Perone and Pulvino

Who Are the Gifted? A Definition

Who are the gifted has been answered in many ways. Some have chosen to say they are the 2 percent who score highest on a test of intelligence (Terman, 1925); some equate them with creative/productive accomplishment and speak of the necessary clusters of characteristics that define them (Renzulli, 1978). Definitions range from general ones, such as the definition postulated by Witty (1940) describing them as children "whose performance is consistently remarkable in any potentially valuable area" (p. 516), to the specific though broad definition used in P.L. 97-35, the Education Consolidation and Improvement Act, passed by Congress in 1981.

> Gifted and talented children are now referred to as, "children who give evidence of high performance capability in areas such as intellectual, creative, artistic, leadership capacity, or specific academic fields, and who require services or activities not ordinarily provided by the school in order to fully develop such capabilities," (Sec. 582)

With the new research in brain/mind function, a different definition for giftedness becomes possible. The research data give us a much better understanding of the brain processes involved in learning and in the development of high levels of intelligence. Intelligence can no longer be confined to cognitive function, but clearly must include all of the functions of the brain and their efficient and integrated use. Intelligence is defined in this text as total and integrated brain functioning, which includes cognition, emotion, intuition, and physical sensing. We now have a better idea of the biological differences that will be found in very intelligent or gifted learners. It is now possible to speak of the gifted as having at least three areas of advanced or increased brain growth: the growth of dendritic spines, increases in the complexity of networks of synaptic connections among neurons, and the division of neuroglial cells (Wittrock, 1980).

Such brain development may partially manifest itself in outstanding cognitive ability, academic aptitude, creative behavior, leadership ability, or ability in visual and performing arts. How giftedness will be expressed depends on the genetic patterns and anatomical structure of the individual and the support and opportunities provided by that individual's environment. As we will see, it is not only the genetic endowment that results in giftedness; it is also the opportunities the environment provides to develop those genetic programs that will allow some children to enhance their abilities to the point of giftedness while others will be inhibited in their development, some even to the level of retardation. The growth of intelligence depends on the interaction between our biological inheritance and our environmental opportunities to use that inheritance. High levels of intelligence or giftedness are, therefore, the result of a dynamic, interactive process.

Such advanced brain growth, regardless of how it is expressed, will manifest itself in more effective and efficient use of brain function. This may be seen as accelerated thought processing, complex problem identification and solution, use of abstract thought that is often unusual and diverse, and insights of a useful and profound nature. Intellectual development will include the possibility for advanced and integrated growth of all the basic human functions identified by Jung (1964): cognitive, affective, intuitive, and physical sensory.

Given the advance in brain research and our understanding of the learning process, we can now discuss with more precision the nature and development of intelligence and, therefore, of giftedness. The following definition of giftedness encompasses this knowledge and provides an integration of earlier definitions.

> Giftedness is a biologically rooted concept, a label for a high level of intelligence that results from the advanced and accelerated integration of functions within the brain, including physical sensing, emotions, cognition, and intuition. Such advanced and accelerated function may be expressed through abilities such as those involved in cognition, creativity, academic aptitude, leadership, or the visual and performing arts. Therefore, with this definition of intelligence, gifted individuals are those who are performing, or who show promise of performing, at high levels of intelligence. Because of such advanced or accelerated development, these individuals require services or activities not ordinarily provided by the schools in order to develop their capability more fully.

This definition of giftedness relies on evidence of advanced or accelerated development of brain function. Such development can be considered synonymous with high levels of intelligence when intelligence is seen as whole brain function. When understood in this way, the term gifted refers to those persons who have developed high levels of intelligence or who show promise of such development.

Giftedness may be identified through many channels: (1) observation of processes used in learning in any content area, in or out of the classroom; (2) observation of performance or products from any content or problem-solving encounter; (3) results of a wide array of psychometric instruments including tests of intelligence, achievement, and creativity; (4) self-report and reporting from others such as parents, teachers, and peers. Truly, any data that give evidence of accelerated or advanced brain development should be considered.

In the discussion of giftedness, let us distinguish between the typical or most commonly found person we call gifted and the rare genius, sometimes labelled *highly gifted*. Most of our discussion relates to the typically gifted, for they are as different from the more highly gifted as they are from the average learner. The highly gifted seem to have different value structures, which usually allow them to cope with the dissonance they find between their perception of life and the average person's. They tend to be more isolated by choice, more invested in concerns of a metanature. They seldom seek popularity or social acclaim. Typically, schools offer these children little; some educators suggest that tutoring with eminent authorities would be far more productive as an educational plan. For further insight into this group, the reader may consult Hollingworth (1942), keeping in mind that we need new data in this area.

One further clarification would aid our definition of *giftedness*. Human beings differ in ability in all human traits. Each of us, in numerous ways, is totally unique, and in no way are we identical. Admission of difference need not, however, necessarily imply superiority. Only the history of our culture can indicate which traits are requisites for human survival and actualization. In earlier times, dinosaurs grew larger in size than all other living creatures; however, this very quantitative difference led to their extinction in the events that were to follow. Having a measurably larger quantity of one trait in this case meant nothing about superiority. People of high intelligence do cope better with the demands of today's society. Rather than consider possession of the attribute as superior, wouldn't it be more profitable in the long run to view it as being further along the way to being all a human can be? If a person on a trip is only 40 miles from the destination while another person on the same trip is 60 miles away, is the first person superior to the second? Admittedly, they see different things, they discuss with a different perspective, and depending on their capability, may even end their journey at entirely different points. Superiority does not adequately differentiate their experience. So it is with this discussion of giftedness. The gifted person does display many differences from others not so developed. While this analogy breaks down quickly when we examine complex relationships, it still allows us to see difference without claiming superiority.

The Concept of Intelligence

The terms *intelligence* and *intellectual ability* express many different ideas. In our discussion we will acknowledge intelligence as the result of the development of all functions of the human brain. To communicate the complexity of this development, we will use the definition developed by Cattell. *Intelligence* is a composite or combination of human traits, which includes a capacity for insight into complex relationships, all of the processes involved in abstract thinking, "adaptability in problem solving, and capacity to acquire new capacity" (Cattell, 1971, p. 8). This last phrase brings out the marvelous ability human beings have to actually change, in this case to increase, their own capacity. We can become more than we were at birth; not more in the sense of exceeding the limits of our inborn characteristics or physical structure, but most certainly more in our ability to use those characteristics and structure. In some cases we may modify the total to become more efficient, more powerful than these limits seemingly dictated. We have not properly appreciated the ability of our organism to expand or contract as it interacts with the environment.

High intelligence, advanced or accelerated brain function—whether in cognitive abilities such as the capacity to generalize, to conceptualize, or to reason abstractly, or in specific academic ability, leadership, creative behavior expressed through visual and perfoming arts—results from the interaction between inherited and acquired characteristics. This interaction encompasses all of the physical, mental, and emotional characteristics of the person and all of the people, events, and objects entering the person's awareness. As no two people have identical physical, mental, or emotional properties, neither do they have the same environment. Our reality is unique to each of us. Even so simple a perception as color vastly differs between individuals. We view color differently because our eye structures differ; we respond to color uniquely because our own emotional pattern causes us to develop a personal meaning for each color as our experiences with objects of each color give us additional information. The wonder is not that we all experience our environment so differently, but that we can communicate our experience to each other at all.

We could not from this interactive point of view say which is more important: the inherited abilities or the environmental opportunities to develop them. A restriction on either would inhibit high levels of actualized intellectual ability. As Dobzhansky states, "The genotype and the environment are equally important, because they are indispensable. There is no organism without genes, and any genotype can act only in some environment" (Dobzhansky, 1964, p. 63). *Genotype* means any constellation of genes that an organism receives from its ancestors. *Phenotype* means any combination of characteristics of an organism that can be observed and measured at any point in its development. A phenotype is always in the state of becoming. Prescott (1979) calls this interaction *ecobiology*, explaining it in this way, "The influence of the environment seems to be imprinted on the structure of the brain, which in turn, shapes the environment."

Genes cannot be thought of as causing particular attributes; rather, they have a wide range of effects in different environments. Vernon (1979) considers the nature-nurture controversy sterile and insoluble, since neither heredity nor environment can be held constant in order to discover its effects in isolation. Cancro (1971) comments that it is misleading to think of either genes or environment as being more important: genes can only express themselves in an environment, and an environment has no effect except by evoking genotypes already present. Any reference to "high-IQ genes" must be seen as a misnomer since the nature of the phenotype always depends on the particular environmental history (Rose, 1972). It would be equally incorrect to regard genetic endowment as "setting the limits" (Lerner and Libby, 1976).

Interaction between genetic and environmental contributions is complex and interdependent. Although all of the results are not yet understood, our exploration of this interaction will focus on the environment. We proceed with the knowledge that a one-sided focus reflects our ability as educators to influence growth and development only in the environmental realm. We fully recognize the importance of the genetic endowment and leave it to others to pursue the advancement of human intelligence by interventions from that side. Further, it must be noted that as we change the environment, we affect the genetic or biological structure of the organism. Education deals with using environments for learning; we must be aware that the decisions for environmental intervention do, in fact, change the neurological and biological structure of the living organism (Rosenzweig, 1966). The only way not to become involved in this dramatic interaction is to disavow being an educator in any form. Those of us who choose to remain in this profession or who parent children must be aware of the total impact of our decision. We investigate this concept further in the next chapter as we discuss early stimulation.

Environmental interaction with the genetic program of the individual occurs whether planned or left to occur by chance. By conservative estimates, this interaction can result in a 20-point difference in measured intelligence; some allow for a 40-point variation or even more (Bloom, 1964; Skeels and Dye, 1959; Hunt in Pines, 1979). For example, two individuals with approximately the same genetic capacity for developing intelligence, as a result of the environment with which they interact, could be regarded as high achieving, as potentially gifted, or as educably retarded.

Figure 1.1a.   Expanded Potential   **Figure 1.1b.**   Restricted Potential

Mild retardation, constituting one of the largest categories of handicapping conditions found among children and adults, stems in large part from deprived environments (Tarjan, 1970). Such environments are apparently caused by far less than optimal prenatal and perinatal conditions in interaction with deleterious factors after birth (Birch and Gussow, 1970).

McCandless (1964), among others, concludes that at least 85% of those now functioning as educably retarded do so as a result of deprived, nonsupportive environments. We already know enough about supportive environments to prevent this type of retardation from occurring, enough to assure most of our children a level of functioning that would actualize far higher levels of intellectual ability. Yet, because of society's priorities, social dilemmas, and lack of parental training, we do not use what we know.

Those who work with gifted children must acquire an understanding of the power of this interaction. What we believe about how people become intelligent will very much influence the way we plan for their educational development. If we believe that individuals come to us already gifted, that they were born that way, we will probably feel that we can do little to affect their development. We may believe enrichment will be sufficient for people at this ability level to "get by on their own." If, however, we consider giftedness as a dynamic process in which a person's innate ability is in constant and continuous interaction with the environment, and if we believe that the strength of that interaction will determine just how much ability this person will be able to develop, we will accomplish far more. We will become highly sensitive to the person's level, to the needs he or she expresses, and we will know how to support and challenge this developing intellect continually. Without such efforts, intellectual abilities will be wasted and untold potential will never be realized. A discussion of how intelligence develops is far more than an academic pursuit. For our children, it is a matter of who they are and who they may become.

Measuring Intelligence

Measuring intelligence has, up to now, been mostly dependent on paper and pencil tests. The limited tasks of performance tests narrowly reflect few of the possibilities for human growth. Some of our leading researchers (Hunt & Kirk, 1971; Sternberg, 1981) perceive a need for a different way of assessing intellectual development. They feel that our reliance on tests comparing people against a standard or norm (decided upon by taking the average of what many people can do and assigning a score to it) prevents us from developing more useful measures. We must discover which activities and skills include both cognition (thinking ability) and motivational development and in what sequence these activities or skills usually appear. From that information, we could set up criterion measures that would tell us not only the present level of a child's development, but also which experiences would best challenge further growth. Sternberg (1981) states that the tests used today are little better than tests used three decades ago, and are, in many cases, the same tests. He believes that the weakness of these tests is not the kind of items that they contain, but rather their lack of a viable theory base.

Sternberg and several others at Yale University are working on a theoretical base for intelligence. Setting their work in an information-processing framework, these researchers believe that such a theory base will prove more useful than has the factor-analytic, psychometric base previously used for measuring, understanding, and nurturing intelligence. By delineating the components of giftedness and their functions, all of which point to specific abilities found in learners with high levels of intelligence, we may better understand how to program for the development of advanced and accelerated brain development; that is, giftedness.

Until more productive measures of intelligence are developed, we will continue to use available measures, but would be well advised to supplement their use with other evaluative tools such as observation of the processes, performance, or products of learning; the results from a variety of measures of achievement and creativity; self-report and reports from parents, teachers and peers.

The most commonly used test of intelligence is the Stanford-Binet Intelligence Scale. This scale was developed to test general intellectual ability, including verbal adroitness, ability to perceive analogies and abstractions, capacity for problem solving, ability to find causal relationships, and classification aptitude. It gained wide acceptance because it did just what was expected of it. Those judged intuitively to be highly intelligent did well on the test, while those who exhibited subnormal ability did, in fact, do poorly on the test. The test was never based on an exact definition of intelligence, nor did it reflect any commitment to a rationale for how we develop intelligence. It was based, rather, on relative performance. Large numbers of people have taken the test, lending stability to it, but its predictive nature is limited to performance on similar activities. The predictive validity of such tests ranks highest on performance of school-related tasks, especially for those tested after the age of five years. Some claim the reliable prediction of adult occupational status from test data obtained after the age of nine years (Jensen, 1969).

A person's score on intelligence tests is usually given as an Intelligence Quotient (IQ). In developing the intelligence test, variations in test performance caused by age differences were taken into account. This adjustment led to the idea of IQ, which is computed by the mental age divided by the chronological age times 100. Standardized on the general population, the test developed with the average IQ at any age set at 100. The middle 50 percent of the population falls between 90 and 110 IQ. On the Stanford-Binet, an IQ of 132 reflects the beginning of the upper 2 percent of the population, and a score of 68 IQ reaches the top of the lower 2 percent.

While other tests of intelligence, such as the Weschler Intelligence Scale for Children (WISC), are used, they tend to measure the same general abilities with the same limitations on predictability. (For further information on individual and group intelligence tests, see Appendix.)

Another possible explanation may exist for the high correlation among intelligence test scores, academic success or failure, and later occupational status. McClelland (1974) suggests that high correlation may only show that those who control economic and social opportunities, the standards for values and language by which all are judged, are also those who can assure their offspring educational advantage. By knowing the right people, they can influence job selection. McClelland claims that there is no direct evidence to prove that higher test scores can guarantee any person the ability to do the higher status job. While that may be so, the predictive validity, for whatever reason, does exist as society now functions.

Regardless of the "fairness" of intelligence testing, according to the interactive concept of intelligence, any subculture or family pattern that does not support but, in fact, restricts the growth of intelligence will cause its members to receive low test scores (IQs). We could then find fault not with the test, but rather with the subculture or family patterns that brought about such low performance. The environment was unfair, not the test. Scarr-Salapatek (1974) reports this interesting finding: genetic differences account for almost half of the IQ differences among middle-class children, but for practically none of the IQ differences among lower-class children. We must provide poor children who are truly disadvantaged by their family pattern and members of various subcultures who are limited by their inculturation with more growth-producing alternatives. In so doing, we must guard against changing cultural and family patterns just because they are different. Diversity is the cornerstone of developing potential and only patterns that are inhibiting to the development of that potential need modification.

Today these tests of intelligence are being looked at very critically while tests sampling other human abilities are being developed. We may soon have a way of knowing more about how a person develops and be able to apply these measures appropriately to a wider range of our human population, but until then we must be cautious about how we use current tests. If added as only one bit of information to many other observations and types of data (case studies, peer reports, parent interviews), intelligence tests have value. By themselves, as a sole criterion for selecting educational experiences for children, they are unnecessarily damaging.

Unfortunately many people, including too many educators, believe that the IQ score gives an accurate description of a person's capacity. It does not. We now have no tests of capacity. The most any test will tell us is how well a person can handle certain problems on the test. Because the tests resemble the material covered in formal schooling, performance on these tests will very likely predict how well the child will do in school-related activities. We must be sure to understand the strengths and weaknesses of each test before making any inferences or predictions about any person. Much more must be known before any decisions can be made about that person's future.

There is another way to discover growing ability. If from the beginning of their educational experience children were allowed to learn at their own rates, to pursue ideas and activities to whatever depth possible for their ability, and if they were encouraged to be curious in a rich, responsive environment, those children with special needs would begin to emerge very early. An educational program designed to meet each person's needs from the beginning of school can better show us those children with high intellectual ability than any single test instrument. Such a program could also be advantageous in building on these strengths continuously. Thus, the problems usually encountered in traditionally group-oriented programs would be less inhibiting to the child's development. Later we discuss in detail programming for the gifted, but we might think about this possibility now as it relates to identification of gifted children.

At this time, with so many of our schools moving in lock-step, using only a group approach to instruction and authoritarian modes of organization, we could not possibly rely on this approach for identification. However, I do believe that it has many advantages and that the possibility of moving in this direction exists. We can begin to encourage those involved in education for the gifted to consider approaches and programs that will allow for this type of natural selection.

An Historical Overview

Although the concept of intelligence as interactive has gained wide acceptance, many still are either unaware of recent data or are convinced of another view. Let us look back at how the concept of intelligence has developed over the past century.

Over 100 years ago, Charles Darwin (1859) began his investigation of the origin of the species. His cousin, Francis Galton (1869), had great interest in the hereditary factors that Darwin was investigating, and Galton began asking important questions regarding the heritability of human intelligence. The importance of his investigation into intellectual differences must not be minimized for, prior to Galton, no one had investigated the individual differences of human beings. The very success of this investigation, however, locked us into a limited concept of intellectual development for nearly a century. Because Galton, influenced by Darwin, admired and pursued the heritability issue to the exclusion of environmental effects, he established a pattern that remains a part of the inquiry into intelligence to this day. This resulted in the theory of fixed intelligence. People believed that the amount of intelligence at birth would remain intact until the day the person died. Nothing could add or subtract or in any way change this amount. Galton was the first to attempt an intelligence test based on scientific data. His test assumed a relationship between sensory acuity and general intelligence. Though this later proved an inadequate base for such testing, his efforts nevertheless served to begin the search for functional intelligence testing. As testing for intelligence became popular, the belief prevailed that if we could find a test powerful enough, we could predict from infancy exactly what the individual would become. The seeming unreliability of infant testing was thought to be a problem of the testing procedure, not of any change in the actual intelligence.

During this period of belief in fixed intelligence, many significant events occurred. In France, in 1905, the government asked Alfred Binet to develop a way to separate a group of slow learners from other school children for the purpose of creating a special curriculum and methodology that would aid in their learning. Unlike those who later utilized his intelligence scales and concept of mental age, Binet did not agree with the theory of fixed intelligence or with the unitary factor of intelligence. He believed intelligence to be educable, a belief not again heard until the 1960s. The articles and speeches of Binet would be considered quite radical even today. Many of the educational problems he spoke out against during his day still need change (Binet, 1969). Today in our country, Binet is best known through a revision of his intelligence scale, originally made by Lewis Terman at Stanford in 1921. This test, the Stanford-Binet Intelligence Scale, originated when no one questioned the belief in fixed intelligence. Later revisions are still based on this assumption.

Testing became very popular during the 1930s and 1940s. For a time in the United States we tested everyone for everything. There were tests for career placement, for various kinds of aptitude, for scholastic ability, for personality factors, and even for predicting success with a future marriage partner. Armies of men and thousands of school children were tested. During this period the test became the ultimate authority. Intelligence testing went to the extreme that a test score placed on a school cumulative record could be used for educational decision making without stating the availability of the protocol or even the name of the test. Parents were not permitted to know the IQ of their children, as the belief prevailed that this number gave evidence of capacity for mental development. So powerful a piece of information could not be trusted to the lay public. Some school districts and classrooms still are reluctant to share this information.

During this period of belief in fixed intelligence, the most extensive study of the characteristics and behaviors of gifted individuals was undertaken. Lewis Terman at Stanford University, working under a grant from the Commonwealth Fund of New York City, began in 1921 by choosing over fifteen hundred students with an average age of eleven years and IQs over 140, the average being 150. He collected extensive personal and educational data on them. The stereotype of a gifted person at that time pictured a bespectacled, frail youngster, ill at ease socially, lost in a world of books and lofty thoughts, usually isolated in some corner tenuously holding onto sanity. "Early ripe, early rot," the motto of the day, described the gifted person. No clear-thinking parent would ever desire to have such a child. Any attempt to encourage this type of development would be unthinkable. Terman's data went far to dispel these myths. Although his sample was limited culturally, socioeconomically, and racially, his findings were significant in influencing those who held extreme ideas about gifted individuals. His data allow a more realistic opinion and a more accepting view of the gifted. While conceived and mostly conducted during a period of belief in fixed intelligence, Terman's longitudinal work (lasting thirty years during his life and recently updated by some of his colleagues) added to the data disputing fixed intelligence as a viable concept (Terman, 1925).

In the first half of the twentieth century, a student of Galton, G. Stanley Hall, introduced another idea about human development that was a logical outgrowth of the concept of fixed intelligence. This view of development as predetermined was largely made popular by the work of Arnold Gesell (Gesell et al., 1940), a disciple of Hall. Again, a man who made many valuable contributions to our understanding of children became instrumental in solidifying misconceptions about how children grow and develop. Predeterminism assumes that the human organism is programmed in a sequentially time-controlled way, and that regardless of events or environments the program will prevail. Maturation and learning were seen as distinct and separate processes, with maturation controlled by heredity, and learning controlled by the environmental conditions. Maturation was thought to lead necessarily to learning. This idea was carried to such an extreme that avant-garde schools saw any attempt to guide the growth of youngsters as a grievous fault. The abuses that followed inevitably limited growth and demeaned the human beings involved. Parents were advised to allow each child to "flower" unrestrained. Permissive patterns were extolled.

Into this climate of nonintervention and nonstimulation some dissonant information began to appear. At first, any ideas that varied from the norm were disputed, rationalized away, or simply ignored. The work of Maria Montessori exemplifies the reception offered educational methodology based on opposing ideas (Standing, 1966). Although Montessori's work was highly successful, it assumed the educability of intelligence and therefore the inconstancy of the IQ. Not until decades later could the techniques and ideas of Montessori be incorporated into our educational practices. Such ideas were lost until years of evidence began to accumulate. Determined and courageous researchers and practitioners in education and psychology risked their professional reputations to share findings in direct conflict with the concept of intelligence as "fixed." Even today some consider this area of inquiry controversial.

Beth Wellman and her colleagues at Iowa University began to question the premise of fixed intelligence. In 1938, this group began an experiment that later caused them to become part of a professional controversy (Skeels et al., 1938; Wellman, 1940). The group established a model nursery school on the grounds of an orphanage. The operation of the orphanage was efficient in that the basic needs of the children were provided, but little time was spent in stimulation or educational activities. The nursery school was highly successful. In fact it seemed to change the intellectual behavior exhibited by the children in attendance. After measuring their progress on achievement and intelligence tests, Wellman reported her findings to the academic community in what must have been a mood of optimistic enthusiasm. In a time when information such as changes in intelligence scores and environmental intervention could only be received with suspicion, when women professors were themselves not taken seriously, small wonder that the following storm of protest became a humiliating experience for the educator.

Not until years later did another team, some of whom had worked on the original project, conduct a similar study after carefully redesigning their approach to meet the criticisms leveled at the Wellman data. This study and subsequent follow-up studies finally made an impact on the academic community. Their findings were intriguing. Children removed from the orphanage to a more stimulating environment (an institution for retarded girls where they received much attention, stimulation, and affection) gained over 20 IQ points when retested, while the control group left at the orphanage lost between 13 and 45 IQ points (Skeels and Dye, 1959). A follow-up study (Skeels, 1966) further dramatized the findings by reporting that the experimental group had become productive, functioning adults, while the control group, for the most part, had been institutionalized as mentally retarded. Few were productive adults. Whatever one might think of the research design or sampling methods used, the results were, at the very least, provocative.

In 1960, another event occurred that again raised questions that the prevailing theory of intelligence could not answer. Dennis (1960), while observing deprived conditions in Teheran orphanages, found twelve-month-old babies who could not sit by themselves (although maturational theories assured this behavior by eight months at the latest). Other four-year-olds were unable to walk alone, although development scales showed one year of age to be the appropriate time schedule. Why? How could the maturational development of these children be so far off the norm? Do environments affect maturation after all? To answer these questions, Dennis conducted a series of experiments. The resulting data, combined with earlier data, showed the concept of fixed intelligence and its natural extension, predeterminism, to be untenable (Dennis and Dennis, 1935; Dennis and Najarian, 1957).

Data such as those produced by the researchers Wellman, Skodak, Skeels, and Dennis made the formulation of a new theory for looking at intelligence necessary. An important new concept of the structure of the intellect now appeared with the factor-analytic work of J. P. Guilford (1956). Guilford felt that psychology had overly restricted its view of human intelligence. His model expanded the factors seen as part of human intelligence and showed their interrelatedness. Guilford, too, discussed intelligence as educable. He drew attention to creativity as an important function of the human mental process.

Not until well into the 1960s did the challenge against fixed intelligence reach significant proportions. A veritable cadre of intelligent men and women now faced the issue. Armed with data resulting from their work, they proceeded from an examination of the dissonance between accumulating information and the old theoretic framework, through the postulation of a new theory of intelligence, to the collection of evidence to support the new hypothesis. The sequence, difficult to assess, affected the literature and theory. Let us mention only a few of the milestone events, knowing that sheer quantity of activity makes the delineation of a chronology of importance impossible.

Work done in the 1920s in Russia had just begun to reach the American academic community. The work of the Russian researcher Vygotsky, which was suppressed during his lifetime, finally became known and discussed. With data received in Europe and finally translated for use in the United States, educators could no longer deny the possibility that learning might lead and direct the quality and speed of maturation. Vygotsky's contributions provided data for the areas of language development, educational remediation, early stimulation, and remediation of physical disability (Vygotsky, 1962).

Also from Europe, in varying quality of translation, came the work of Jean Piaget (1952). This man influenced educational theory and practice to an unprecedented degree. He began his inquiry in a most unscientific manner, one that no scientist would consider sound as a research design. Without objectivity, he selected only three subjects to observe and no control group. The subjects were his own children. However, he described so clearly and in such detail what he observed that his evidence enabled him to evolve principles of growth and development. Later examination of data from a multitude of studies testing respectable numbers verified his principles as viable and useful.

Piaget was among the first to ask about intellectual development during the first few years of human life. Drawn from his background in marine biology, his work emphasized the principles of assimilation and accommodative interaction. He believed that intellectual growth resulted from the learners' active participation in the learning process, invariably sequenced into stages. Although he set no strict time lines on the stages of development, he considered the order unalterable, with mastery of the lower stages preceding learning in the higher stages of cognition. Piaget stated that the age at which a child passes from one stage to another depends upon both the genetic endowment and the quality of the environment. He espoused one of the first interactive theories of intelligence. Researchers around the world later honored him with awards.

The work of Benjamin Bloom (1964) made another important contribution to educational practice, particularly to the growing concern for the years of early intellectual development. A reexamination of previously published data allowed Bloom to suggest a startling hypothesis. People had long assumed (and intelligence testing norms complied with the assumption) that between birth and eighteen years of age humans learn in a regularly ascending line. At age eighteen they level off to a plateau effect until around forty-five, the age when a gradual decline to senility begins. Bloom used the reassessed data to show a very different pattern. Although he looked at many human characteristics, just the findings from the area of intelligence will receive comment here. Between birth and four years of age children accomplish 50 percent of the deviation in IQ that they will acquire by eighteen years of age. By six years of age another 30 percent will have been added. With the data showing 80 percent of the deviation in adult IQ actualized by age six, educators developed a new awareness of preschool years as an essential time for learning. As society's concern for compensatory education also gained a following, many programs were then established to take advantage of the important early years.

The educational community began to focus on the early years of development as educators became aware of the limitations and deceptions caused by the theories of fixed intelligence and predeterminism. Reliance on these older concepts had left us with a near void in understanding how infants and young children develop intellectually. In chapter 2 we look at the amazing and exciting knowledge that begins to fill this void. Bloom made an important contribution to classroom organization for learning with the publication of his *Taxonomy of Educational Objectives, Handbook I: Cognitive Domain* (Bloom, 1956) and his work with Krathwohl and Masia (1964) in the *Taxonomy of Educational Objectives, Handbook II: Affective Domain.*

For readers nearing or past the magic age of forty-five, let me hasten to add that subsequent studies done by the Fels Foundation (Kagan and Moss, 1962), the Berkeley Growth Studies (Bayley, 1968; Bayley and Schaefer, 1964), and the Terman data itself (Terman and Oden, 1947) give us a very different view of the "off to senility" phenomenon. Those studies indicate that we do *not* plateau intellectually at eighteen years of age; we continue to move either upward or gradually downward depending on the intellectual challenges we engage in and largely upon our personality characteristics. Aggressive, inquiring, active, independent, sensitive people who seek new ideas and adapt comfortably to change tend to continue upward; passive, docile, dependent people who follow set patterns and seek security and repetition gradually lose intellectual facility. Data collected from the Terman studies show that growth patterns continue as people reach their sixties and seventies. Data on aging further support these possibilities.

The constancy of the IQ received a final blow from the work of Sontag, Baker, and Nelson (1958) and Kagan and Moss (1962). Their longitudinal studies followed 300 children from prenatal development through adulthood, with data collected at regular intervals. The results showed consistent change in IQ scores, especially at the extreme ends, with more variation evident for boys than for girls.

Jerome Bruner, J. McV. Hunt, Nancy Bayley, and many others began the task of establishing and supporting a new theory of intelligence. Bruner hypothesized that the young deal with information in three ways—action, imagery, and symbols. He believed that the preschool experience should work toward translating one into the other. Bruner (1964) stated, "The significance about the growth of the mind in the child is to what degree it depends not upon capacity but upon the unlocking of capacity" (p. 14). He saw that the process of translating or unlocking depends upon interaction with the environment of the culture. He attempted to give us a method of implementation as he set forth his new theories on instruction (Bruner, 1960, 1968).

Hunt (1961) brought out the problem of the match, that is, finding the most stimulating circumstances for children at each point in their development. To him, the major challenge of our time was to discover a way to govern the encounters children have with their environment, especially during the early years of their development. With such a match of ability and experience, children could be expected to achieve a substantially higher adult level of intellectual capacity.

Nancy Bayley (Bayley and Schaefer, 1964; Bayley, 1968) gave us a look at the behavioral correlates of mental growth during a thirty-six year period. Here we get more information on genetic and environmental interaction in the growth of intelligence.

Further support for this new interaction theory of intelligence must be noted in the recent renorming of the Stanford-Binet Intelligence Scale. An analysis of the standardization results showed a dramatic rise in the IQ level, especially among the preschool population. We might assume that the higher education of parents and richer earlier environments—television, higher mobility, wider use of educational toys and books, better nutrition—have helped foster this change. Later studies indicate that the observed change in a genuine phenomenon and not a research error (Thorndike, 1975). This information is even more impelling as evidence when one considers that the new standardization population purposefully included minority representation that had been omitted from the previous samplings.

The interactive theory of intelligence seems now to best describe the data available. For the development of giftedness this theory brings into question a new area of inquiry: How do humans become gifted? In chapter 2 we examine the evidence in that area.

Intelligence: The Importance of Brain Function

In our definition of giftedness, a high level of intelligence is viewed as advanced and accelerated brain function. The data allowing this relationship make an exciting addition to our understanding of the development of giftedness.

Neurobiologist T. Teyler explains,

> The fabric of the brain is set down as a result of the interaction of genetic blueprints and environmental influences. While the basic features of brain organization are present at birth (cell division is essentially complete), the brain experiences tremendous growth in neural processes, synapse formation, and myelin sheath formation, declining around puberty. These processes can be profoundly altered by the organism's environment. Furthermore, it has been shown that brain processes present at birth will degenerate if the environmental stimulation necessary to activate them is withheld. It appears that the genetic contribution provides a framework which, if not used, will disappear, but which is capable of further development given the optimal environmental stimulation (Teyler, 1977, pp. 31, 32).

To understand how some individuals become gifted and others do not, we need to become familiar with the basic structure and function of the human brain. As we seek to understand how we might nurture giftedness, such knowledge will prove invaluable.

At birth the human brain contains some 100–200 billion brain cells (Teyler, 1977). Each neural cell is in place and ready to be developed, ready to be used for actualizing the highest levels of human potential. With a very small number of exceptions, all human infants come equipped with this marvelous, complex heritage. While we never develop more, it is hardly necessary, as those we have, if used, would allow us to process several trillion bits of information in our lifetime (Sagan, 1977). At present it is estimated that we actually use less than 5 percent of this capability (Ferguson, 1973). How this complex system is used becomes critical to the development of intelligence and personality, and to the very quality of life experienced by the growing individual.

The Neuron

The nerve cell, or neuron, is the basic unit of the brain. It is composed of the cell body, dendrites, and an axon. Inside the cell body are the nucleus and the biochemical processes that maintain the life of the cell. The neuron is a tiny system for information processing that receives and sends thousands of signals. No two cells are exactly alike nor are any two brains alike. We are as different from one another as snowflakes. The dendrites are short fibers that extend from the cell body, branching out to form the pathways for receiving information from nearby nerve cells. The axon is one long nerve fiber that extends from the cell body and serves as a transmitter, sending signals that are picked up by the branches of the neighboring dendrites. The activity between neurons is carried out by the dendrites of one cell in contact with the axon of another. The end of the axon does not actually touch the dendrite of the other cell but transmits the information chemically across a region where the cells are particularly close. This junction across which impulses travel from one nerve cell to another is called the *synapse*. The transmission of a nerve impulse is an electrochemical process. At the synapse, the electrical impulses that travel through the cell convert into chemical signals, then back to electrical impulses. It is this synapse that is thought to be the most likely site for neural mechanisms of learning and memory (Thompson, Berger, and Berry, 1980).

Incoming Axon

Dendrites

Myelin Sheath

Cell Body
Nucleus

Dendrites

Node of Ranvier

Axon

Surrounding the neurons are special cells known as *glia*. These cells outnumber the neural cells ten to one and can be increased by stimulation from the environment (Rosenzweig, 1966). The glial cells provide the brain with nourishment, consume waste products, and serve as packing material actually gluing the brain together. They also insulate the nerve cell, creating myelin, a special coating that protects the axon and amplifies the signal leaving the cell. Myelin has an important function, in that it allows the coated axon to conduct information away from the neuron at a much faster rate than unmyelinated axons (Thompson et al., 1980). As we increase the glial cells in the brain, we accelerate the speed of learning. It is rather like the difference that can be seen between electrical conduction through insulated and noninsulated wiring: the speed and power of the charge increases by the use of insulation.

We influence the rate of glial cell production by the richness of the environment we provide (Rosenzweig, 1966). The more glia, the more accelerated will be the synaptic activity and the more powerful will be the impulse exchange from one cell to the next, allowing for faster and more complex patterns of thinking, two characteristics we find in gifted children. The speed of thought is amazing. If a nerve pathway is used often, the threshold of the synapse falls, so that the pathway operates more readily. A wave front is started that may sweep over at least 100,000 neurons a second (Brierley, 1976).

Another way of increasing synaptic activity is by strengthening the neuron's cell body. While we cannot increase the quantity of neural cells, we can increase the quality (Rosensweig, 1966; Krech, 1969, 1970). This quality enhancement allows again for information to be processed more quickly and for more power to be conducted, resulting in the availability of more complex neural networks. Interaction in an enriched environment changes the chemical structure of the neural cell, thereby strengthening the cell body.

It is by increasing the strength and the speed of transmission or synaptic activity that we can affect the process of learning. We can through changes in teaching and learning procedures affect the growth of dendritic branching, increase the complexity of the network of connections among neurons, and the quantity of glial cells. These are the differences we see in brains that show advanced and accelerated development. By the environment we provide, we change not just the behavior of children, we change them at the cellular level. In this way gifted children become biologically different from average learners, not at birth, but as a result of using and developing the wondrous, complex structure with which they were born. At birth nearly everyone is programmed to be phenomenal.

As an aid to understanding the organization and structure of the brain I would like to borrow from Paul MacLean (1978) an analogy he used that has helped me in my thinking and teaching. Would you make a fist with each of your hands so that you can see the fingernails and then place your hands together with the fingernails touching? As you look down at your hands they now form a very respectable model of the human brain. Wiggle your little fingers and you have identified the area through which vision enters the brain. Move your middle finger and you have located the motor area. The language area is just below the middle knuckle on the left hand, though please note that it is connected to the right hemisphere (hand) by way of the touching fingernails, which now represent the corpus callosum. This connector has within it more neural connections joining the right and left hemispheres of the brain than there are in any other part of the body. Clearly the interconnection or integration of the right and left hemisphere specializations is biologically intended. With this model we can explore the organization and structure of what MacLean (1978) and others refer to as our *triune brain*.

The Triune Brain

The human brain is organized into three formations or three systems with radically different structures and chemistry. This hierarchy of three brains in one may be called the *triune brain* (MacLean, 1978). Educationally this organization presents some important considerations. Two of the three brains have no system for verbal communication. Given that it is the integration of total brain function that gives us intelligence, a test that measures primarily verbal communication as its sampling of intelligence may be seen as limited.

Now again using our hand/brain analogy, look at just one hand/hemisphere. We will begin with the arm-wrist area, which represents the most primitive, or what MacLean refers to as the *reptilian brain*. Here we have the simplest and oldest system that we share with many life forms. In the lower brain stem and the innermost areas of the cerebrum we find the seat of autonomic (i.e., automatic) function. It is this system that relieves us of consciously processing each breath and each beat of our heart. Within recent years those working in the area of biofeedback have shown us that while most autonomic functions remain just that, we can, if we choose, bring the awareness of these functions to consciousness, allowing us to monitor or change the process if it has become destructive or inefficient. For example, those with high blood pressure can use biofeedback techniques to monitor and change the inappropriate rate of distribution of blood, consciously helping the body to better regulate this usually automatic function (Taylor and Bongar, 1976; Taylor et al., 1981). Here we find the neural pathways for many higher brain centers. Here too are nuclei concerned with motor control and the communication link between the rest of the brain and the cerebellum located at the very base of the brain. The reticular formation is located in this area. It is, in essence, the physical basis for consciousness and plays a major role in keeping us awake and alert.

The second system of the triune brain is known variously as the *old mammalian brain*, the *limbic system*, and the *emotional mind*. It is located at *midbrain* and contributes significantly to the learning process. It can be symbolically viewed by partially unclenching your fist and looking at the palm of the hand. One can see the ventricles of the brain that hold the cerebrospinal fluid, as well as the mounds and depressions of the limbic system itself. Here are the biochemical systems that are activated by the emotions of the learner. Here too are the interactions that enhance or inhibit memory. This area affects such diverse functions as anxiety, rage, sentimentality, and attention span. In addition, our feeling of personal identity and uniqueness depends on this area of the brain to combine internal and external experience. It is in this limbic area that the affective feelings provide the connecting bridge between our inner and outer worlds and provide us with our construct of reality, our model of a possible world. This system is often referred to as the gateway to higher thought, to the cortical and neocortical functions. It is in this regard that it is of such importance to educators, especially to those who would understand gifted development. By the release of neurotransmitters from the limbic system, the cells of the cortex are either facilitated or inhibited in their functioning. One of the activators for growth of function in this area is novelty (Restak, 1979). Feelings of pleasure and joy have been noted for their increased stimulation to this area (Sagan, 1977). Levels of touch and movement that are too low profoundly affect this area and may result in an increase in violent behavior (Prescott, 1979).

The exposed surface of your fingers and thumb held tightly together represent the convoluted mass known as the *new mammalian brain*, the *neocortex*, or the *cerebrum*. It is the largest brain, comprising five-sixths of the total, and envelops the two previously mentioned, the lower brain stem and the midbrain, or limbic system. It is here that sensory data are processed, decisions made, and action initiated. The neocortex is necessary for language and speech. Its most overriding functions involve the reception, storage, and retrieval of information.

The most recently evolved section of the neocortex, the prefrontal cortex, which is represented by the thumbs, provides for behaviors associated with planning, insight, empathy, introspection, and other bases for intuitive thought (MacLean, 1978). It is engaged in firming up intention, deciding on action, and regulating our most complex behaviors (Restak, 1979). It is, in fact, the area that energizes and regulates all other parts: it houses our purpose.

Goodman (1978) more specifically places the following functions in the area of the prefrontal cortex, which he believes develops most fully between twelve and sixteen years of age.

1. Foresight—ability to see patterns of change, to extrapolate from present trends to future possibilities. This process uses imagination, prediction, and behavioral planning.
2. Self-regulation—of bodily processes through insight, internal commands, and generation of visual images. This is the basis for meditation and biofeedback strategies.
3. Analytic systems thinking—high form of creativity, complex analysis of input requiring formal logic and metaphor.
4. Holos—social sense, rational and emotional; the foundation of altruism.

From this perspective we do have three, somewhat different, brains in one: the smallest and oldest, the brain stem; surrounded by the larger, newer brain, the limbic system; and above and around it, the cerebrum or neocortex, the largest brain, consisting of the newest, most sophisticated structures. Under stress this largest, most complex system begins shutting down, turning over more and more functions to the lower, limbic system brain. While rote learning can be continued, higher and more complex learning is inhibited (Hart, 1981). Creating opportunities for the effective operation of this total triune brain is our responsibility as educators and parents. A program model and curricular approach for the development of these total brain processes will be discussed later in this text in the sections on the Integrative Education Model (chapter 4) and strategies for an integrative curriculum in chapter 6.

The Hemispheres of the Brain

Another way of looking at the organization of the brain that is productive to understanding learning and the development of intelligence is to become aware of the asymmetry of the brain hemispheres. An investigative area already proving useful in understanding learning explores the idea that each hemisphere of the brain specializes in a particular type of function. This identification of specialized functioning points to the necessity for different types of educational experience if we are to use the potential each of us possesses. Schools have concentrated their focus on the cognitive, left brain type of learning while devaluing and, in some cases, actually suppressing any use of the more holistic right brain function.

The cerebral cortex of the brain is divided into two hemispheres joined by a large bundle of interconnecting fibers called the *corpus callosum*. The right side of the cortex primarily controls the left side of the body, and the left side of the cortex largely controls the right side of the body. While much is yet to be learned, many now feel that the left and right hemispheres of our brain are responsive to different types of experience and respond in unique ways. While it seems that the entire brain is capable of performing all the activities exhibited by any of its divisions, each does, under normal conditions, assume specific duties.

Wittrock (1980) states that hemispheres may specialize in the strategy of coding they use rather than in the type of information they code. The left brain is most responsible for linear, sequential, analytic, rational thinking. Reading, language, the computational aspects of mathematics, the inquirer, and the critic are located in this hemisphere. Thought of a metaphoric, spatial, holistic nature is the province of the right hemisphere. Here we find involvement with the creation of art, music, the concepts of mathematics, synthesizing, intuitive knowing, and a more coherent perceptual style. The right brain seems better at passive comprehension, the left at active articulation. Some ways of differentiating functions of the left and right brain that have been suggested follow:

Left	Right
math, history, language	self, elaborates and increases variables, inventive
verbal, limits sensory input	nonverbal perception and expressiveness
sequential, measurable	spatial
analytic	intuitive
comparative	holistic
relational	nonreferential
referential	integrative
linear	Gestalt
logical	imagery
digital	better at depth perception, facial recognition
scientific, technological	mystical, humanistic

Emotions of affect are found in both halves of the brain. This description of left/right brain function is true of all right-handed people and over 60 percent of those who are left-handed. In fewer than 40 percent of left-handers, the positions appear to be reversed.

Doktor and Bloom (1977) believe that the right/left brain specialization concept may explain the apparent lack of understanding between people in business and academicians. They found that top executives tend to use intuitive, right brain processing for tasks, while academicians use left brain analytic processing. Consequently, executives pay little attention to the complex mathematical problem-solving models created by the researchers.

Edwards (1976) reports an interesting use of the right brain perceptual difference. She teaches her art students to "turn off" the left side of the brain and tune in, or focus on, the right side when they draw. After finding that the analytic, sequential activity of the left brain interferes with the holistic, spatial right brain function, she developed certain methods to stimulate right brain involvement. First she gives verbal instructions to draw attention to the overall Gestalt of what is to be drawn and the negative space surrounding it. Then she presents the object or picture to be drawn upside down. The left hemisphere refuses to process the incoherent picture, leaving the right hemisphere free to copy the overall impression. Her success using these techniques with high school and adult students has been remarkable, bringing about unusual artistic growth in her students in a short span of time.

Samples (1975) has shown that when the processes and functions of the right brain are facilitated, the self-esteem increases, the performance of skills typical of left brain functioning is enhanced, and the students choose to explore greater numbers of content areas in greater depth.

Sex Differences in Brain Lateralization

The lateral organization of the brain seems to develop differently for girls than it does for boys. Greater lateralization or specialized activation of spatial function to the right hemisphere seems to give males superior ability on tests of spatial skills. However, male lateralization of language to the left hemisphere seems to work against them and result in a more narrow though precise ability in language (Witelson, 1976). More important, functionally, seems to be not the rate of lateral differentiation, but how soon the strategies particular to each hemisphere become mature and competent to integrate function. Maturation of the left hemisphere seems to occur earlier and to be more pronounced in girls, which may allow their apparent superiority in verbal learning (Kimura, 1967; Bryden, 1970; Pizzamiglio and Cecchini, 1971; Van Duyne and D'Alonzo, 1976; and Reid, 1980). Boys surpass girls on tests of spatial function by four years of age (Levy, 1980) and maintain this superiority at least through middle-age (Porteus, 1965; Davies, 1965). Language develops earlier in girls than in boys (Moore, 1967; Clarke-Stewart, 1973) and it remains into middle-age as a superior function (Stevenson et al., 1968; Rosenberg and Sutton-Smith, 1969; Backman, 1972). These tendencies seem to hold across cultures (Porteus, 1965). It seems then to be a function of the brain that the left hemisphere of girls and the right hemisphere of boys mature earlier and that biological differences are largely responsible (Levy, 1980).

It should not be concluded that hemisphere specialization, though it exists, is a simple issue. The following review of data from University of Chicago psychologist Jerre Levy (1980) and Stanford neuropsychologists Diane McGuinness and Karl Pribram (1979) may give us clues as to how we may best develop optimal learning experiences for our children. These differences are not specific to use of just one hemisphere and could not occur without both hemispheres functional and working in integration.

Females excel in—

  perception of fine visual detail;

  understanding the meaning of facial expression, face recognition, and identifying the affective implications of tone of voice;

  reading affective and motivational states of others;

  night vision;

perceiving subliminal messages;

verbal skills of fluency, grammar, reading (language consists of total meaning including tone, context, expression, etc.);

sensitivity to odor, taste, touch, and the presence and variation of sound, particularly in high ranges;

manual dexterity and fine muscle coordination;

speed of processing information, especially in tasks that require rapid choices;

interest in people, social responsiveness, and empathy.

Males excel in—

using maps and solving mazes;

spatial skills, perception of depth in space, perception of three-dimensional objects in two-dimensional representations;

daylight vision;

gross motor movements;

exploratory behavior;

math, especially geometry and trigonometry;

observation of objects;

use of language as a tool for logic and mathematical reasoning (the denotative meaning of language overrides all other information);

mastering the underlying principles, which are retained and applied in a tightly organized conceptual system;

independence of situational variables.

The cognitive differences cited above suggest that the organization within hemispheres of the brain is significantly different between males and females, with diffuse organization within and between hemispheres more typical of females, strongly lateralized organization more typical for males. It is not to be assumed that such biological differences rule out effects of the environment. The environment reinforces and magnifies those aptitudes considered sex appropriate by our society. Nor do all males or females fit these data. As with any generalized data, we have only the dominant trend. Tradition and stereotypic roles defined by our culture of what masculine and feminine behaviors are still serve to limit a full range of function for both boys and girls.

While the hemispheres of the brain do show specialization, the entire brain is capable of performing all the activities exhibited by any of its divisions (Pribram, 1977). It would therefore be more accurate to speak of one hemisphere leading the other during certain tasks rather than viewing a person as right-brained or left-brained. The goal would be to have available the leadership from the hemisphere whose processes would be most appropriate to the effective solution in any situation. The ability to use the strategies from either hemisphere would be ideal.

Most of us do have a dominant style that we are most comfortable in using. Herrmann (1981) has developed an instrument for assessing these preferences. Some of his results indicate that when we use our left brain mode we show preference for written directions, structured places, organized tasks, lists that can be crossed off when things are accomplished, successful results, control, and closure. When we are using our right-brain mode we can more easily tolerate a lack of closure and large amounts of ambiguity, desire lots of space, see the whole problem or situation, appreciate an artistic and aesthetic focus, and enjoy spontaneity. Herrmann believes that we can teach our whole brain to work together and that we must do so if we are to have the advantage of our full ability and creativity. If we are concerned about the optimal growth of intelligence, we must provide within the environment the opportunities for the use of both right- and left-brain processes. As Wittrock (1980) explains, "It seems clear that the sophistication and variety of cortical brain function cannot be reduced to any single dichotomy. The cortex of the brain performs a myriad of different functions within and across its hemispheres" (p. 393).

It is most important that we recognize not only the specialization of the hemisphere but also the evidence of the need for interaction and intersupport between the hemispheres. For example, trained musicians listen to music with both left and right brain. More nerve connections exist between the halves of the brain than from the brain to the rest of the body. To actualize the potential we possess, we must develop both types of function and integrate our learning experiences. If we continue to focus all our attention on the rational, cognitive functions of our brain, we will paradoxically limit these very functions. Without the support of a well-developed right hemisphere, such left-brain growth will be inhibited. For years, good teachers and parents have intuitively used both right- and left-brain functions in their teaching. The evidence for specialization now validates their teaching ideas. The teacher or parent who has been unaware of the need for such integration and who has felt that the only valid learning comes from rational inquiry will consider this information new and perhaps even controversial.

As already mentioned, the specialization of the hemispheres is not absolute. All parts of the brain are interdependent and support all functioning. Such an investigation does allow us to view from another perspective the human qualities we have often overlooked and undervalued. Those of us who work with gifted children can find exciting implications for our learning and that of our students in this area of inquiry. As Nebes (1975) comments,

> If there is any truth in the assertion that our culture stresses left hemispheric skills, this is especially true of the school systems. . . . If the right hemisphere does indeed process data in a manner different from the left, perhaps we are shortchanging ourselves when we educate only left-sided talents in basic schooling. . . . Many problems can be solved either by analysis or synthesis, but if people are taught habitually to examine only one approach their ability to choose the most effective and efficient answer is diminished (p. 16).

It is important, therefore, that we do not overemphasize the separate functions of the hemispheres. For most activities, both mental and physical, the human requires both hemispheres to function in close integration, allowing thereby the understanding of both the computation and the conceptualization of mathematics, the structure and the melody of music, the syntax and the poetry of language. "The existence of so complex a cabling system as the corpus callosum must mean, it is important to stress again, that the interaction of the hemispheres is a vital human function" (Sagan, 1977, p. 175).

Brain Waves

An activity of the brain that seems to have important implications for learning is the production of different brain wave frequencies. Through measurement we learn that a variety of activity levels can be correlated with the various frequencies. There are also some data that indicate that the coherence of these frequencies in various parts of the brain are facilitating to different types of learning. Houston (1977b) introduced the idea of coherence of brain waves as a force in maximizing the use of human energy. The ability to focus energy from the entire brain is seen to result in accelerated learning, healing, and higher levels of consciousness.

The value and implications of brain wave training are still being investigated, with many findings and claims being openly disputed. One such debate centers on the "alpha state." People can slow the rhythm of the brain down to eight to twelve cycles per second, as compared to the twelve to twenty-eight cycles per second common to beta wave production. Some have claimed that by slowing down the brain waves, a pleasant floating state of consciousness, similar to the relaxed states that allow body/mind integration and heighten the ability to focus brain energy occurs. The even slower four to seven cycles per second of theta waves were claimed to allow deeper relaxation and a state conducive to creative thought and use of psi abilities (see p. 405). One to three cycles per second typify the slowest wave, delta, that infrequently occurs and barely maintains body functioning. This issue remains under controversy due to the extremely complex nature of the brain. Even the alpha state is not a single phenomenon, but a conglomerate of perhaps some 600, with equally numerous correlated characteristics that are dependent on the location, form, appearance, and movement pattern of the alpha wave. Also involved in the complexity may be the influence of the body's circadian rhythms, the changes in the atmospheric environment, or even the rhythmic activities of the universe (Brown, 1974).

A British physicist, Maxwell Cade, is conducting a very interesting exploration of the differing states and correlated behaviors of alpha. For several years, Cade has been developing instrumentation that will identify and illustrate complex EEG patterns and their related hierarchy of subjective physical states. His "Mind Mirror" shows the left-right symmetry and the relative amounts of beta, alpha, theta, and delta rhythms operating. He has identified and described five, possibly six, major states and their "shapes." He reports in the *Brain/Mind Bulletin* (Ferguson, 1977) the states as—

1. The unilateral pattern of an untrained individual.
2. Alpha rhythms bilateral; calm, detached alertness, no thinking, no images.
3. Alpha blocking; passive awareness, symmetrical beta and theta.
4. "Meditation"; calm detached, inward and outward awareness.
5. Lucid awareness; higher amplitude alpha than in State 4, invariably symmetrical. Subjects can open eyes, converse, move around, solve problems, read and comprehend, all without disturbing this state. Healers have been observed in this state when "sending healing energy."

The possible sixth pattern, appearing egg-shaped, seems to be associated with the subjective impression that one is creating one's own reality.

Research in the area of brain waves and their meaning is the least easily validated of the areas of brain research, due to inadequate data from as yet limited tools of measurement such as those used to record the EEG patterns. As our skills of investigation increase, the possibilities for learning about ourselves and our relationship to our world should prove very exciting.

The Brain as a Hologram: A Holographic Model of Reality

Pribram (1971, 1977) postulates a holographic theory of the mind and believes that the brain is a hologram that stores all information in each part.

> A hologram is a record of a process of optical information processing that stores light from every point in the scene that is distributed or scattered throughout the hologram's surface. When placed in a coherent light source, the hologram can regenerate the original wave pattern from any point on its surface, resulting in what appears to be a three dimensional object. The hologram has a fantastic capability to retrievably store information.

To produce a hologram, the single wavelength light of a laser beam is split with a mirror. Half of the beam is aimed directly at the photographic plate; the other half rebounds from the object to hit the plate. Instead of recording an image, the plate records interference patterns of the colliding light waves. To reconstruct the image, a laser is directed at the plate at the same angle as the original laser. The hologram appears as a three-dimensional image that can be turned and studied from different angles (Fincher, 1981).

Pribram was attracted to the holographic theory of the brain because the hologram is a unique storage device in which every bit of information is distributed over the entire surface and the retrieval process is reconstructive, two properties he believed could be found in the brain. Pribram also believes that the hologram is a model for consciousness. A brain stores information in a variety of ways, can use either linear or spatial modes, and projects space and time, qualities of the holographic process. Pribram agrees with Bohm (Ferguson, 1977a) that reality is the result of our own construction that we make by interpreting frequencies from another dimension, a universe that itself is holographic and transcends time and space. The implications of such a theory change the concept of reality and affect every aspect of our lives. Our potential for affecting our own life is infinite, and the importance of our perception of reality is awesome. Further possibilities of this theory will be discussed in chapter 10. For educators, acceptance of such a theory will lead to teaching methods that seek to reduce anxiety and foster activities that create harmony, coherence, connectedness, and recognition of individual differences in learning style.

Giftedness: A Biological Difference

From animal and human brain/mind research, we can now postulate that individuals with high levels of intelligence, gifted individuals, show the following measurable biological differences:

1. There is, by means of an increase in neuroglial cell production, accelerated synaptic activity that allows for more accelerated thought processing (Thompson, Berger, and Berry, 1980).
2. The neurons become biochemically richer, allowing for more complex patterns of thought (Rosensweig, 1966; Krech, 1969).

3. More use is made of the activity of the prefrontal cortex of the brain. This allows more future planning, insightful thinking, and intuitive experiences (Restak, 1979; MacLean, 1978).

4. More use is made of alpha wave activity within more areas of the brain. The gifted individual can move into this state more quickly and stay in it longer than average learners. Such a state allows more relaxed and concentrated learning, higher levels of retention, and more integration of hemispheric modalities (Lozanov, 1977; Martindale, 1975).

5. There is more coherence and synchronicity of brain rhythms more often, allowing heightened concentration, focused attention, and in-depth probing and inquiry (Millay, 1981).

In addition to the references given for further information in the area of brain/mind research, see Asimov (1965), Bogen (1975), Chall and Mirsky (1978), Eccles (1973), Ferguson (1973), Fincher (1981), Hart (1975), Isaacson (1974), Koestler (1968), Krashen (1975), Levy and Reid (1975), Ornstein (1973, 1974), Oyle (1975), Pietsch (1981), Pribram (1971, 1977), Restak (1979), Sagan (1974, 1977), Samples (1976), Samples, Charles, and Barnhart (1977), *Scientific American* (1979), Springer and Deutsch (1981), Wittrock (1980), and Wittrock et al. (1977).

Creativity: The Highest Expression of Giftedness

Creativity is a very special condition, attitude, or state of being that nearly defies definition. Over the years, scholars and researchers, artists and musicians, and philosophers and educators have tried to use words to communicate this amazing phenomenon. Probably the most unexplainable part of creativity lies in the fact that, even though few agree on a definition, when we say the word, everyone senses a similar feeling. We may not be able to explain what it is rationally, but we know it just the same. When we are being creative, we are aware of its special excitement.

Over and over in discussions of creativity, we find statements to the effect that everyone has a great deal of creativity as a child, but that very few retain it as adults. My favorite expression of this idea can be found in a flyer advertising a creativity training program, *New Directions in Creativity* by Renzulli (1973). He says, "Creativity is as common in small children as runny noses and yet is quite rare in adults." All who comment on this state of affairs go on to ask, "Why must it be so? How does it happen?"

Inside of me I believe that everyone who has defined or discussed creativity is right, though their positions sound disparate. And at the same time, they are wrong because they speak of only the part of creativity that they see or that fits their belief system. Such a limited view of creativity has caused us to recognize only a portion, an isolated part of what, in fact, is a far more complex, more integrated, whole. It is as though we have viewed and discussed only a small, exposed segment, the rational part, while we have only hinted at the most important part.

Some have used creativity synonymously with giftedness; some have limited it to feelings and affective development. It seems incorrect to use it in either of those ways, as it has none of the limitations of those concepts; creativity includes far more. It is the highest expression of giftedness.

An Integrated Concept of Creativity

Looking again at the basic functions of thinking, feeling, sensing, and intuiting (Jung, 1964), we find that we must now develop another dimension, for the integration of these functions releases creativity (see figure 1.2). Restrict any one of the functions and you reduce creativity. Creativity involves the synthesis of all functioning, and yet it is still more. It includes a spark from another dimension.

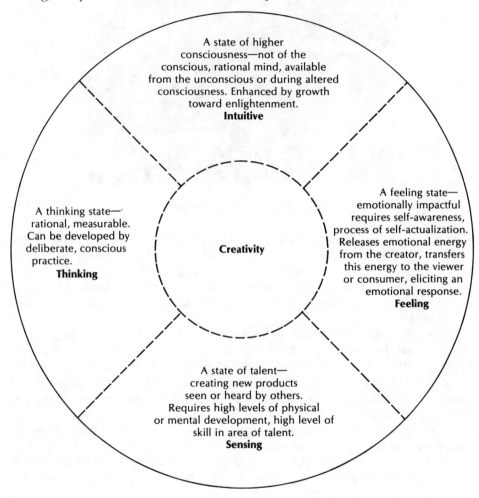

A state of higher consciousness—not of the conscious, rational mind, available from the unconscious or during altered consciousness. Enhanced by growth toward enlightenment.
Intuitive

A thinking state—rational, measurable. Can be developed by deliberate, conscious practice.
Thinking

Creativity

A feeling state—emotionally impactful requires self-awareness, process of self-actualization. Releases emotional energy from the creator, transfers this energy to the viewer or consumer, eliciting an emotional response.
Feeling

A state of talent—creating new products seen or heard by others. Requires high levels of physical or mental development, high level of skill in area of talent.
Sensing

Figure 1.2.   Creativity Circle

Previous reviews of creativity delineated various categories to organize the information known and the diverse points of view. They seem to lack a common base in the organizations used. When one categorizes with areas as diverse as curiosity, measurements, relationship to intelligence, personality, and motivation as components of the same system, no base remains for comparing the results of research or the differing viewpoints. To provide a common system of categorizing that results in clearer understanding of the information about creativity, the material could be organized according to human function. All research, characteristics, discussions of

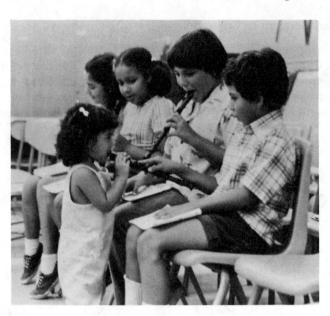

Allowing creativity to grow.

enhancing practices, and so on are grouped in one of four areas, depending on the definition the author or researcher gives creativity and which function that definition uses. In some cases, the confusion in the literature results directly from the fact that the author neglects to state a point of view on creativity and uses the term as though everyone agrees on a single definition. This is the source of contradictory research results.

The following model coincides well with the Integrative Model described in chapter 4, not by coincidence. The categories of creativity incorporate these functions: (a) rational thinking; (b) high levels of emotional development or feeling; (c) talent and high levels of mental and physical development; and (d) higher levels of consciousness, resulting in use of imagery, fantasy, and breakthroughs to the preconscious or unconscious states.

When viewed from this common base, instead of describing different phenomena or even different types of creativity, all of these perceptions may be only fragments of the total; creativity includes all of these ideas and more. Thinking, feeling, sensing, and intuiting unify to become creativity. With only one function operating alone a person could not create.

The definition of giftedness used earlier in this chapter now aids in our understanding of creativity. As giftedness is the result of total integrated functioning of the human brain, so creativity, the highest expression of giftedness, can be viewed from the biological brain/mind base. All of the functions of the human brain/mind system are involved at higher and higher levels when creativity occurs. Gowan (1981) discusses the relationship between giftedness and creativity by first distinguishing between personal and cultural creativity. He believes that anyone can be taught personal creativity, but that giftedness is necessary for cultural creativity, the form that produces major discoveries and ideas which significantly add to and inevitably change the future of humankind. He sees giftedness only as the potential for creativity.

It is my belief that only as the functions combine and interact, drawing from and giving to each other, can creativity occur. A belief in this unity underlies this discussion of the different perceptions of creativity. Although researchers and authors may define creativity from a one-function viewpoint, they draw from other functions to discuss or develop it; for example, although a population may be identified by tests of fluency or flexibility, they may use self-awareness to increase creativity. A few authors do acknowledge the holistic nature of their work, but nearly all treat creativity more holistically than they define it.

Creativity: A Rational Thinking Function

The rational view of creativity has accumulated the most literature and nearly all of the testing. To get an idea of how researchers view this aspect of creativity, look at a few definitions proposed by advocates of the rational thinking position:

> Torrance (1962)—"the process of sensing gaps or disturbing missing elements; forming new hypotheses and communicating the results, possibly modifying and retesting the hypotheses" (p. 16).

> Parnes (1967)—"Creativity is a function of knowledge, imagination, and evaluation" (p. 6). He sees the processes involved as fact finding, problem finding, idea finding, solution finding, and acceptance finding.

> Williams (1968)—An act of creativity is a conscious act of human intelligence. Operationally, he defines it as including knowledge, mental processes based on cognition, divergent-productive, and associative thinking, evaluative behaviors, and communicative skills.

> Guilford (1959)—"aptitude traits that belong most clearly logically in the area of creativity . . . fluency of thinking and flexibility of thinking, as well as originality, sensitivity to problems, redefinition and elaboration . . . classifiable in a group of divergent thinking abilities" (p. 160).

> Taylor (1959)—Interested most in scientific creative ability, he discusses five levels of creativity: expressive, productive, inventive, innovative, and emergenative. He views the steps in the process as mental labor, incubation, illumination, and deliberate effort.

The criterion for selecting and evaluating creative students from the view of creativity as rational is usually a high score on a test designated as a creativity measure, such as the Minnesota Test of Creative Thinking (MTCT) (Torrance, 1962); Torrance Tests of Creative Thinking (TTCT) (Torrance, 1966); and Remote Associates Test (RAT) (Mednick and Mednick, 1967). In fact, most instruments for measuring creativity come from this rational approach. Other ways to select and evaluate creative students congruent with this point of view have been tried:

— Honor point ratios and achievement test scores: Results are quite poor (Yamamoto, 1964).
— Teacher nomination: Also found to be quite inaccurate, identifying less than one-third (Ellinger, 1964; Holland, 1959).
— Peer nomination: Results unproductive (Torrance, 1962).

— Intelligence tests: Torrance (1962) shows that if you use only an intelligence test and identify the upper 20 percent as gifted, you will miss 70 percent of those who would fall into the upper 20 percent of a test of creative thinking ability.

Tests of creativity (defined as a rational function), such as the MTCT, may test some of the same abilities as intelligence tests (Wodtke, 1964; Yamamoto, 1965). However, Torrance (1962) found a low correlation between the two types of measures in unselected populations. He found practically no correlation in high-ability populations. He reports correlations that are slightly higher for girls than for boys and that high scores on the MTCT were usually obtained by children with IQ scores of at least 115.

Guilford (1967) found the relationship between divergent-production test scores and IQ scores generally low; he suggested that, although a high IQ did not guarantee doing well, being above average in IQ was almost a necessity. Others have found the same relationship. However, an IQ of 120 is often mentioned as the lowest score possible to establish a base of knowledge broad enough to use the analytic, synthetic, and evaluative thinking necessary for rational creative production (Getzels and Jackson, 1962; Smith, 1965). When production of associations (naming instances, alternative uses, similarities, pattern meanings, and line meanings) is used as the criterion for creativity, the correlation with intelligence measures is even lower (Wallach and Kogan, 1965).

Criticisms of tests of creativity range from Yamamoto's challenge to their validity to Barron's report of the viewpoint of creative individuals. Yamamoto (1964) warns us against assuming that the factor-analytic model of creative thinking abilities satisfactorily explains high scores (or even low) on these traits and thinking of the test items as representative samples of these traits. He believes we need more evidence for these assumptions.

Barron (1969) presents an interesting view by suggesting that highly creative individuals become very annoyed with the above types of tests. These individuals reportedly consider the tests too superficial, for they fail to engage the deeper levels of a person involved in creative work. Further, the fragmentation of the factor-analytic model provides no opportunity for the more holistic quality of creativity. Finally, the tested students felt that "short and closely timed tests do violence to the very essence of the creative process" (p. 37).

Thorndike (1963) finds that tests of creativity lack internal consistency and that they do not seem to test any common characteristic. He believes it essential that measured creativity, potential creativity, and achieved creativity show an approximate relationship.

With a belief system that assumes creativity to be measurable, educators and researchers who adhere to the rational definition of creativity continue to look for adequate tests to identify and evaluate creative individuals. Part of the problem may be that the contributions of the sensing, feeling, and intuitive functioning of these individuals, although probably far more important, are less easy to measure.

Characteristics of the Rationally Functioning Creative Individual

Those who subscribe to the rational viewpoint of creativity (Hughes, 1969; Kurtzman, 1967; Stein, 1962) find the following attributes common to those they designate as creative:

Self-disciplined, independent, often anti-authoritarian

Zany sense of humor

Able to resist group pressure, a strategy developed early

More adaptable

More adventurous

Greater tolerance for ambiguity and discomfort

Little tolerance for boredom

Preference for complexity, asymmetry, open-endedness

High in divergent thinking ability

High in memory, good attention to detail

Broad knowledge background

Need think periods

Need supportive climate, sensitive to environment

Need recognition, opportunity to share

High aesthetic values, good aesthetic judgment

Freer in developing sex role integration; lack of stereotypical male, female identification

In a study with creative adolescents, Halpin, Payne, and Ellett (1973) found significant differences between females and males.

Females	**Males**
Liked school, especially courses in sciences, music, and art	Disliked school
Liked their teachers	Disliked their teachers and thought they were uninteresting
Regularly read news magazines and other nonrequired reading and special reports	Did little homework
Were active in dramatics and musical productions	Disliked physical education and seldom engaged in team sports
Did not go out on dates as often	Were regarded as radical or unconventional
Were daydreamers	Often wanted to be alone to pursue their own thoughts and interests

Development of Creativity—The Thinking Aspect

Most writers and researchers agree that all people have the ability to be creative, at least while they are young. However, the growth of creativity defined by test performance is not continuous, but rather increases from three to four and one-half years of age and then takes a small drop. It begins to rise again, making a sharp drop at the fourth grade. The scores in fluency, flexibility, originality, and elaboration drop so significantly that some students have lower scores in the fifth grade than they had in the third grade. The scores begin to rise again and continue through the junior year except for a slight drop at seventh grade (Torrance, 1962,

1968). These studies showed that as early as third grade, girls were more reluctant to think creatively than were boys. Torrance believes girls have, by this time, been conditioned to be more passive and accept things as they are, rather than to try to manipulate or change things. He also found that contributions made by boys were more highly valued by their peers.

What conditions can facilitate development of this aspect of creativity? The following compilation comes from the research of Anderson and Anderson (1965); Domino (1969); Drevdahl (1956); Eisenman and Schussel (1970); Gowan (1981); Hautz, Rosenfeld, and Tetenbaum (1978); Landry (1968); MacKinnon (1964); Nichols (1964); and Torrance (1962, 1966). Factors facilitating development include—

situations that present incompleteness, openness;

allowing and encouraging lots of questions;

producing something, then doing something with it;

granting responsibility and independence;

emphasizing self-initiated exploring, observing, questioning, feeling, classifying, recording, translating, inferring, testing inferences, communicating;

bilingual experiences resulting in development of greater potential creativity due to the more varied view of the world, a more flexible approach to problems, and the ability to express self in different ways that arise from these experiences;

birth order (first born males more creative (on tests of creativity) than later born males);

predisposing and focusing of the child's interests and attention by parents, the stimulation of the school environment, and by self-motivation.

Factors that inhibit development include—

need for success, limiting risk taking or pursuit of unknown;

conformity to peer group and social pressure;

discouragement of exploration, using imagination, inquiry;

sex role stereotyping;

differentiation between work and play (e.g., learning is hard work);

adherence to "readiness" viewpoint for learning;

authoritarianism;

disrespect for fantasy, daydreams.

The schools could make important contributions toward advancing creativity, for this aspect of development is considered learned behavior and, therefore, is capable of improvement through instruction. Skills such as those measured on the MTCT have significantly increased through special programs (Crutchfield, 1969; Davis, Manske, and Train, 1967; Parnes, 1963; and Torrance, 1960). If schools are to do this job, there must be a change in their focus. Cole (1969) makes the point in an interesting analogy: If people were computers, schools are "programming" to receive, store, retrieve, and reproduce information only. We must also "program" other processes involved in the processing, organization, efficient utilization, and application of information. Williams (1968) believes that all learning involves creative organization of the culture's knowledge with the individual's experience. This creativity will then produce new and unique perceptions of the culture.

While the process may differ slightly from program to program, most agree with Wallas (1926) that it must include: preparation, incubation, illumination, and verification.

The teacher becomes the facilitator, the arranger of appropriate experiences, the encourager, the skill builder. Effective teachers tend to have common behaviors. Those listed here come from the work of Anderson (1968); Cole (1969); Ellinger (1964); Hughes (1969); Kneller (1965); Parnes (1963); Torrance (1962); and Williams (1968). Teachers who successfully develop creativity—

do more thinking activities (convergent, divergent, evaluative);

use fewer memory activities;

use evaluation for diagnosis, not judgment; rewarding correctness of spelling, punctuation, grammar, neatness, handwriting, or quantity inhibits the production of original ideas;

give opportunities to use knowledge creatively;

encourage spontaneous expression;

provide an atmosphere of acceptance;

provide a wealth of stimulation from a rich and varied environment;

ask provocative questions;

value originality;

encourage students to examine new ideas on their merit and not dismiss them as fanciful;

provide for unevaluated practice and experimentation;

teach skills of creative thinking, such as originality, fluency, flexibility and elaboration, deliberate idea finding, deferred judgment, forced relationships, alternative thinking, hypothesis setting;

teach skills of researching, such as self-initiated exploring, observing, classifying, questioning, arranging and using information, recording, translating, inferring, testing inferences, representing experience and observations, communicating, generalizing, simplifying.

Another clue: creative teachers have proved more effective at teaching creativity than those who are not themselves creative.

Frierson (1965) raises an interesting question: Do students who improve on problem-solving skills become more effective in their pursuit of personal and occupational goals than noncreative problem solvers, or do they merely learn strategies that enhance scores on these types of creativity tests? Longitudinal research with students in programs for developing productive and creative thinking skills will need to answer this query; however, if this is only one aspect of the total phenomenon of creativity, there will be other important factors to consider.

With so much research energy focused on this aspect of creativity, a picture emerges of the antecedents incorporating data about parent and peer relationships of students included in this population.

In line with the facilitating conditions already mentioned, parents of creative children tend to be less authoritarian. The entire family stresses openness and expresses an enthusiasm for life. Parents value the expression of feelings and individual divergence. Permissive parents have more spontaneous, original, self-initiating, and independent children. These children also seem less hostile, more outgoing and friendly. Their parents allow them more freedom in decision making and in exploring the environment. Their parents read more to them and often take them to the library. The parents prefer guidance over punishment and seldom use physical punishment.

The parents are themselves creative and show self-assurance and initiative. Comfortable with change, they prefer unstructured demands. They value their own autonomy and independence, but are conscientious and dependable toward their children. Clearly, they serve as role models for their children (Domino, 1969, 1979; Drevdahl, 1964; Dreyer and Wells, 1966; Ellinger, 1964; Getzels and Jackson, 1961; Gowan, 1965; Holland, 1961; MacKinnon, 1964; Nichols, 1964; and Watson, 1957).

Torrance (1981) reported interesting results from an investigation of the patterns of various cultural groups in an attempt to understand the universality of the slump in creative development at the fourth grade level. Looking at seven different cultural groups—advantaged U.S.; disadvantaged, minority U.S. (black); primitive, Western Samoa; West German; Western Australian; East Indian; and Norwegian—he came to the following conclusions:

> Cultural factors strongly influence the course of creative development, the level of creative functioning, and the type of creativity that is most evident.
>
> In most cultures there are discontinuities in creative development, in some around the fourth grade, in some not until the sixth grade.
>
> Such discontinuities occur whenever the children of that culture are confronted with new stresses and demands.
>
> General rankings can be made among cultures of the level of creative functioning, with the children within the advantaged cultures showing a higher creativity index than children of less advantaged cultures.

Peers in the school climate influence learning; in the case of creative students, their peer interactions do not seem to facilitate creative growth. In grades two through six, peer sanctions operate against the most creative children, and few are credited for their contributions to the group. They develop, therefore, a tendency to work alone. In the sixth grade, highly creative children encounter open hostility, aggression, criticism, and rejection. Their peers use organized efforts to limit their scope of operation and to impose sanctions. By junior high school, creative students who are not intellectually gifted are discounted, with their ideas being considered wild and their behavior deviant and wrong. Creative boys gain more acceptance from their peers when engaging in divergent behavior than creative girls. Is it any wonder that the more creative the students, the less they like school (Kurtzman, 1967; Liberty, Jones, and McGurie, 1963; Torrance, 1963)?

For those who develop this aspect of creativity, we can picture a warm, affectionate family background with stimulation and encouragement to be unique and to value that uniqueness. Creative individuals who have learned independence of thought and deed can become intrinsically motivated and set their own standards.

Placing such people in the traditionally oriented, conformist setting of school leads to growth inhibition, frustration, and often the denial and abandonment of creative potential. Creative students fare somewhat better with creative teachers. Consider this: we have just looked at those who are creative thinkers, those who are creative in the one function our schools value most. How then do those creative in other aspects fare?

Creativity: A Function of Feeling

Those who view creativity from the feeling perspective focus on the emotional well-being and self-actualizing qualities of the human being. For them, creativity forms more of an attitude or belief system that permeates all the life choices and activities of the creative person. It is a concept of health, naturalness, intunedness, and development of unique potentials. Here are some definitions of this aspect of creativity:

Maslow (1959)—"Self-actualizing creativeness . . . sprang directly from the personality, which showed itself widely in ordinary affairs of life and which showed itself not only in great and obvious products but also in many other ways (p. 85) . . . a tendency to do anything creatively . . . expressive of being quality . . . rather than its problem-solving or product-making quality . . . a defining characteristic of essential humanness" (p. 94).

Fromm (1959)—"Creativity is the ability to see (or to be aware) and to respond" (p. 44). He views it as an attitude for living.

Anderson (1959)—Creativity in human relations; "relating to others which admits one's own uniqueness and dignity and at the same time respects a uniqueness and dignity in others" (p. 120).

Moustakas (1967)—"To be creative means to experience life in one's own way, to perceive from one's own person, to draw upon one's own resources, capacities, roots. . . . Only from the search into oneself can the creative emerge" (p. 27). He believes that in true experience every expression is creative, the creation of the person one is and is becoming.

Rogers (1959)—"The mainspring of creativity . . . man's tendency to actualize himself, to become his potentialities" (p. 72).

Krishnamurti (1964)—"Creativeness has its roots in the initiative which comes into being only when there is deep discontent . . . One must be wholly discontented, not complainingly, but with joy, with gaiety, with love" (pp. 47, 48).

May (1959)—"Creativity is the encounter of an intensively conscious human being with his world" (p. 68).

Taylor (1976)—Transactional motivation (the person shapes the environment rather than being shaped by the environment) and environmental stimulation (behavior is initiated toward unpredictable but creative outcomes) combine to form a system he calls creative transactualization that is in continuity with self-actualization.

Hallman (1963)—"Creativity is defined as a way of conducting one's life rather than in terms of the number and kinds of objects which one may have produced" (p. 132).

According to this view, a measure of self-actualization is the criterion for selecting and evaluating creative students. The Personal Orientation Inventory (POI)

(Shostrom, 1964) has been developed as such a measure. The relationship between measures of creativity defined as a thinking function (e.g., TTCT) and self-actualization measures is seen only in the elaboration trait. Murphy, Dauw, Horton, and Friedian (1976) speculate that "self-actualization may be a larger, global concept whereas creativity measured by the TTCT may be a more clearly defined trait in the realm of intellectual abilities" (p. 43). In Damm's (1970) study, the groups of students who obtained high scores on both intelligence (as measured by the California Test of Mental Maturity) and creativity (as measured by the Remote Associates Test) were superior in self-actualization (as measured by the POI) to those who had obtained a high score in only intelligence or creativity or low scores on both.

Other ways of selecting and evaluating self-actualizing creative persons are limited. Maslow, from as early as 1950, studied people who were self-actualizing. He began by choosing people who, in his opinion, were the most healthy and the most self-fulfilling. He felt they were motivated by growth needs (trends toward self-actualization, i.e., ongoing actualization of potentials, such as the fulfillment of mission, a fuller knowledge and acceptance of one's own intrinsic nature, an unceasing trend toward unity, integration, or synergy from within) rather than the basic needs of safety, belongingness, love, respect, and self-esteem. Maslow (1959) reports these common attributes in his population of self-actualizers:

A special kind of perception

More spontaneous and expressive

Unfrightened by the unknown, the mysterious, the puzzling; often attracted to it

Resolution of dichotomies: selfish and unselfish; duty and pleasure; work and play; strong ego and egolessness

Able to integrate

More self-accepting, less afraid of what others would say, less need for other people, lack of fear of own emotions, impulses, and thoughts

Have more of themselves available for use, for enjoyment, for creative purposes; they waste less of their time and energy protecting themselves against themselves

Involved in more peak experiences, integration within the person and between the person and the world, transcendence

Fromm (1959) believes the following characteristics are necessary for creativity to occur:

Capacity to be puzzled

Ability to concentrate

Ability to experience self as creative, as the originator of one's acts

Willingness to be born every day

Ability to accept conflict and tension from polarity rather than avoiding them

Courage to let go of certainties, to be different, to be concerned with truth, to be certain of one's own feelings and thoughts and trust them

Others have found that creative persons have the ability to identify closely with the feelings and expectations of others (Taylor and Williams, 1966).

To develop creativity from the feeling aspect, the following conditions have been suggested (Anderson, 1968; Drews, 1965; Fromm, 1959):

Provide an environment rich and varied in stimulation.

Teach with materials and methods harmonious with each other and with the teacher.

Delineate clearly and repeatedly the aims of this type of program.

Allow free interplay of differences.

Make environment and materials friendly, nonthreatening, thereby allowing disagreement and controversy without hostility (this allows children to engage freely in behavior underlying creativity).

Reduce anxiety in classroom, especially that created by the teacher.

Handle differences as confrontations, not as conflicts.

Find integrative elements in differences.

Emerge unifying concepts.

Allow individuation and differentiation within the unity.

Foster positive change in directions congruent with student's predilections in cognitive and affective areas.

Drews (1964–1966) successfully used ten half-hour films (the *Being and Becoming* series, Drews and Knowlton, 1963) dealing with the life styles and value systems of creative and socially concerned adults. By presenting an anthology of heroic characters, ideas, and issues, she was able to make significant changes in the direction of greater motivation to learn, openness, and the valuing of self-actualization.

A very provocative finding by Anderson (1959) indicates that "socially integrative behavior in one person tends to induce socially integrative behavior in others" (p. 130). This says a lot to teachers and parents about their techniques and modeling behaviors.

Although in the past people assumed that those who are highly creative are less emotionally stable, less mature, and more childlike, the data seem to counterindicate such an assumption. High creativity does not seem to result in neuroticism; in fact, no relationship was found (Feldhusen, Denny, and Condon, 1965; Flescher, 1963; Ohnmacht, 1966). Gowan (1981) observes that creative people have a great fund of free energy that seems to result from a high degree of psychological health.

In addition to creating the conditions and allowing the freedom to develop the feeling aspect of creativity, no one set of skills can be taught. Unlike the rational aspect of creativity, this area does not develop by asking the learner to try consciously to be more creative. Creativity, in this respect, is enhanced by the absence of trying. The more one strives to succeed, the more anxious or competitive one feels and the more out of tune and insensitive one becomes. Feelings of self-confidence, self-acceptance, and self-esteem provide the basis for growth in this area of creativity. Creativity as a feeling function interrelates and supports all of the other aspects. Rational functioning alone produces predictable associations. However, add emotions, and the original associations increase. Emotions are also inseparably involved in creative activity, inspiration, and intuition.

Fearn (1976) has developed a very interesting and useful model for teaching the feeling aspect of creativity. He suggests that creativity is the process of persons, limited and confined by what is known in their cultural space and time, reaching out beyond their limits to grasp ideas or concepts that already exist, but that are not presently known. His model, *Individual Development: Creativity,* is concerned with two basic processes, involvement with data and involvement with self. Data involvement includes collecting necessary knowledge and follows the assumption that creativity does not occur in a vacuum. Awareness, fluency, and flexibility are parts of the collection process that then depends upon self-discipline, elaboration, and complexity preferences for further development. At this point, the personal ability to risk, question, imagine, and perform originally become important. He sums up the model with this statement of the final process:

> Individual reaching out is the process whereby the person who is (a) sufficiently aware of the task and its parameters, (b) willing to risk the known and unknown consequences of stepping beyond the established, and (c) sufficiently disciplined to see a task through to self-satisfaction and who arranges creative behaviors appropriately manages to bring into his or her space (and perhaps the spaces of millions of others) an arrangement or a definition that increases consciousness by contributing to a total collection of possibilities (p. 62).

This model has been used successfully in inservice teacher workshops.

Simonov (1970) discusses the relationship of emotions to creativity. He believes positive emotions are far more productive than negative ones. To develop creativity from this view requires more than "the simple elimination of unpleasant feelings" (p. 54). Without stimulation, positive emotions do not arise. Increasing the amount of information available to a person enriches positive emotions. How emotions interrelate with rationality is shown in Simonov's statement: "strengthening of rationality in a modern person leads not to weak emotions, but rather to richer and more complicated emotions" (p. 55). Positive emotions, rationality, and intuition all seem to lead to creative actions, the talent aspect.

Creativity: The Talent Aspect

The talent aspect of creativity includes the product, the art form, and the realm of the talented creator:

> Maslow (1959) calls this aspect special talent creativeness; he defines it as a production that results from activity, control, and hard work.

> Rogers (1954) in recognizing this type of creativity states, "emergence in action of a novel rational product, growing out of the uniqueness of the individual on the one hand and the materials, events, people or circumstances of his life on the other" (p. 71).

> May (1959) also sees this area when he says, "Creativity is bringing something new into birth . . . the expression of the normal man in the act of actualizing himself . . . as the representation of the highest degree of emotional health" (pp. 57, 58).

> Simonov (1970) sees the product the artist has created as "a model of the artist's attitude toward a phenomenon. He creates the model with the aim of getting to know, checking and specifying his attitudes" (p. 55).

Rhodes (1963)—"the birth of an idea and its embodiment in form recognizable by someone or society as valuable" (p. 305).

The criterion for evaluating creativity in this aspect is how original, inventive, or imaginative the product is. Simonov sees the criterion as that of social consumption. He believes that the longer a work survives, the closer the creator has come to "perceiving and presenting an essential truth of human existence" (p. 77).

How can this aspect of creativity be developed? Many of the conditions for facilitating growth of the talent aspect are the same as we found necessary for the two previously discussed aspects. Furthermore, Cole (1969) has found that "the creative process is very similar among different people regardless of the diverse nature of the products" (p. 247). The inner conditions or characteristics of the creator are (May, 1959; Maynard, 1970; Rogers, 1959)—

openness to experience, new ideas;

an internal locus of evaluation;

an ability to toy with elements and concepts;

perceiving freshly;

concern with outside and inside worlds;

ability to defer closure and judgment;

ability to accept conflict and tension;

skilled performance of the traditional arts;

high theoretical and aesthetic values.

To facilitate creative and artistic production externally:

Treat the child with respect and allow freedom to explore the universe.

Create an atmosphere with really good music, books, and pictures as a natural part of the child's world.

Treat ideas and questions respectfully.

Respect the child's privacy.

Value the unusual, the divergent.

Help the child learn by mistakes.

Avoid sex role stereotyping.

Encourage self-expression.

Teach the child to look and really see.

Help the child learn to trust the senses.

Permit the child's own creativity to emerge.

Rogers (1959) writes of the psychological safety and freedom needed to carry out a creative act. Psychological safety can be created by "accepting the individual as of unconditional worth . . . providing a climate in which external evaluation is absent . . . and by understanding empathetically (pp. 78–80). By *psychological freedom*, he means the complete freedom of *symbolic* expression with responsibility only to one's self.

In Schaefer's (1970) study, the parents of creative (as defined by number and quality of creative products) adolescent girls were well-educated, and most mothers worked outside the home. Both parents had more interest in cultural-intellectual pursuits than in social-civic organizations or sports. The parents read far more than average, engaged in creative hobbies, and played musical instruments. They provided their children with role models for creative people.

When one is involved in a creative act, there is likely to be first the "aha" or "Eureka!" feeling, then an anxiety of separateness, and finally a strong desire to communicate. At this point the product begins to emerge (Rogers, 1959).

Again, we see the interdependence of the different views of creativity. No one view fully explains either the process or the emerging product. The area least explored and yet probably most indispensable to the act or attitude of creativity is our next area for discussion, the higher levels of consciousness, the intuitive aspect.

Creativity: A Function of Higher Levels of Consciousness

Our society places so much value on the rational, analytic type of thinking that recent researchers of the human brain claim an unbalanced focus on one half, the dominant left hemisphere.[1] Although both sides seem to receive similar information, they process the information differently. The left concerns itself more with verbal forms and uses logical, analytic processing, while the right side reacts more nonverbally and uses more of a holistic synthesis in its operations.

Differentiation and emphasis on left hemisphere functions have led many researchers to look toward the right side of the brain as a pathway to creativity. It may be that through our contact with the right hemisphere, we will find ways to understand the unconscious or preconscious state, believed by some to contain the roots of creative acts. Researchers have begun to explore altered states of consciousness as possible areas of information on creativity. They examine the use of drugs, trances, hypnotism, meditation, chanting, dreams, fantasies, and daydreams for clues to lead us to the intuitive, creative spark (Bogen, 1975; Ferguson, 1973; Krashen, 1975; Krippner, 1968; Nebes, 1975; Ornstein, 1972, 1973; Oyle, 1975).

As we examine the higher levels of consciousness aspect of creativity, we must be aware that much of what happens can only be understood experientially and that rational, verbal explanations dilute the events, for the essence of the experience may be changed by its description. With this difficulty in mind, let us look at yet another view of the meaning of creativity:

> Anderson (1962)—indicates that a creative product is never completely a product of one's rational, everyday state of mind.

> Taylor (1963)—"There is reason to think that much of the creative process is intuitive in nature and that it entails a work of the mind prior to its arising to the conscious level and certainly also prior to its being in expressible form. It is most likely preconscious, nonverbal or preverbal, and it may involve a large sweeping, scanning, deep, diffused, free and powerful action of almost the whole mind" (p. 4).

---

[1]The left hemisphere dominates in nearly all right-handed people and in all except approximately one-third of the left-handed people. For them, the location of functions seems to be reversed.

Krippner (1968)—"Without access to alternative levels of awareness, creative behavior may be stifled or blocked" (p. 149). He further indicates that it is "essential to the individual's well-being and creative development."

Koestler (1964)—"The temporary relinquishing of conscious controls liberates
the mind from certain constraints which are necessary to maintain the disciplined routines of thought but which may become an impediment to the creative
leap. . . . The creative act, in so far as it depends on unconscious resources, pre-
supposes a relaxing of controls and a regression to modes of ideation which are
indifferent to the rules of verbal logic, unperturbed by contradiction, untouched
by the dogmas and taboos of so-called common sense. At the decisive stage of
discovery the codes of disciplined reasoning are suspended (p. 178). . . . Language can become a screen which stands between the thinker and reality. This is
the reason why true creativity often starts where language ends" (p. 177).

MacKinnon (1965)—gives being more intuitively perceptive as one of the major
conditions for creativity.

Characteristically, those who would be identified as creative from this view
(Koestler, 1964; Krippner, 1968; Martindale, 1974; Schaefer, 1970) would—

have their energy field accessible;

have ability to tap and release unconscious and preconscious thought;

be able to withstand being thought of as abnormal or eccentric;

be more sensitive;

have a richer fantasy life and greater involvement in daydreaming;

be more enthusiastic and impulsive;

often show abilities of synesthesia (e.g., tasting color, seeing sound, hearing
smells);

show different brain wave patterns than the less creative, especially during creative activity;

when confronted with novelty of design, music, ideas, get excited and involved
(less creative people get suspicious and hostile);

when given a new solution to a problem, get enthused, suggest other ideas; overlook details and problems (less creative students analyze the defect rather than
explore potentials).

In an interesting study, Martindale (1975) found that creative people show a
pattern of brain wave production during creative activity and creativity testing that
is the reverse of those less creative. Most people produce alpha waves (slower than
average brainwaves) while relaxing and reduce alpha production while working on
a problem. Creative people produce fewer alpha waves when relaxing and increase
them when working on an imaginative problem. The creative seem to have higher
resting levels of brain wave activity, resulting in fewer alpha waves than average
people. "Creativity and intellectual ability require two different thought processes:
the former calls for low cortical arousal and defusing one's powers of concentration,
the later calls for higher cortical arousal and focused attention" (pp. 48–50). Martindale concludes that the creative do not consciously control their alpha; they view the
world differently because they process information differently and have different
brain wave patterns.

When discussing how to develop creativity as a function of consciousness, several components need to be mentioned. The ability to relax is the first skill needed. The skills of imagery and imagination also facilitate creativity and the development of higher levels of consciousness. We will later discuss strategies for acquiring these skills in Chapter 6.

Griffiths (1945) defines imagination as a mode of thinking concerned with fantasy and daydreams. *Imagery* is defined as a type of sensory experience in which images arise independent of external stimulation. Eidetic imagery, a type of three-dimensional imagery, often occurs in children, but tends to disappear as we get older. It persists in only a few highly imaginative adults and is associated with the sudden flash of insight. The decline is due to the predominance of verbalism and conscious control, claims Rugg (1963). While one is very young, linguistic vocabulary increases, verbalizing is limited, and concept formation takes place slowly. In adulthood, if home and school have been "successful," the reality-mind has taken over. Andrews (1930) reports that the more uncommon types of imagination (personification, fantastic stories, etc.) were found to be most prevalent at age three and one-half, although they occur in few children. By five years of age, they were on the wane. Girls seem to peak one year before boys.

Society, and schools in particular, have expectations that block creativity. Krippner (1967) lists ten assumptions guaranteed to stop creativity in all but the hardiest:

1. Everything must be useful.
2. Everything must be successful.
3. Everything must be perfect.
4. Everyone must like you.
5. You shall not prefer solitude to togetherness.
6. You must have concentrated attention.
7. You must not diverge from culturally imposed sex norms.
8. Do not express excessive emotional feeling.
9. Do not be ambiguous.
10. Do not rock the cultural boat.

Griffiths (1945) found that a limited environment also restricts the level of creative performance.

The criterion for evaluation in the higher level of consciousness aspect of creativity is the availability of the preconscious or unconscious state to the person. Krippner (1968) asserts that the ability to operate simultaneously at different levels of consciousness is characteristic of this type of creative person and those "individuals who spend all their waking hours in rational, everyday consciousness are functioning below their optimal level and perhaps demonstrating signs of emotional disturbance" (p. 148).

As of now, with the exception of the researchers mentioned, few have looked at consciousness and its relationship to creativity. It seems clear from the recent data coming to us from neurophysiology, brain research, dream research, anthropology, drug therapy, and other fields that such investigation is necessary and would prove to be quite productive in helping us to understand the total meaning of creativity.

The Integrative Approaches to Creativity

A number of individuals have recognized the limitations of focusing on only one aspect of creativity and have combined several of these areas in their work. They view creativity from process and product, from skill development and use of intuition. Personality, verbal skill, and talent expressed through achievement are the elements of a study by Callaway (1969). He concludes:

> The complete creative act, as depicted by those who have probed its process as well as by the subjective analysis of the creators themselves is seen to involve much more than "divergent thinking." Socially useful creativity demands the synergistic cooperation of the entire personality, including all physical mechanisms and modes of thought. Affective and conative dimensions are as essential as the cognitive ones (pp. 240–241).

Gowan (1972) also points out the holistic nature of creativity. In his discussion, he groups the investigations of creativity into the areas of (a) cognitive, rational, and semantic; (b) personal and environmental; (c) mental health and openness; (d) Freudian and Neo-Freudian; and (e) psychedelic, existential, and irrational. He views these subdivisions on a continuum. His organization brought about my concern for a more integrated approach. The clarity of his categorization aided my students and me for many years as we moved to the model presented in this chapter. He presents helpful overviews of all of the areas and of their relationship to the total concept. Later work expands his involvement with the irrational aspect (Gowan, 1974, 1975). He states:

> Creativity is a characteristic not only of individual human behavior, but also of the species in general. What is true of the development of the superior individual is also true of the developing aspects of mankind. The emergence of creative abilities is a triumph not only of individual development, but as Bucke (1929) points out, the harbinger of evolutionary progress for all men (p. 70).

Others who view creativity from this integrated vantage point are Leonard (Ferguson, 1973):

> A brain composed of such neurons obviously can never be "filled up." Perhaps the more it knows the more it can know and create. Perhaps, in fact, we can now propose an incredible hypothesis: *The ultimate creative capacity of the brain may be, for all practical purposes, infinite* (p. 308).

and Ferguson (1973):

> There is a strong likelihood that creativity does not need to be developed in man but simply liberated. . . . The view of creativity as a nonintellectual activity fails to take into account the dynamic, unitary and coherent nature of the brain. Emotion and intellect, freedom and discipline, reason and intuition, the precise and the gossamer, primary and secondary processes, chaos and order—all of these apparent opposites can exist in creative harmony in the human brain (pp. 308, 315).

Earlier in this chapter we have discussed the holographic functions of the brain. The brain may indeed be a hologram interpreting a holographic universe. Viewing this possibility with its exciting implications for expanding our view of the reality in which we live, which we may even create, Gowan (1981) suggests that far more attention must be paid to the development of our creative abilities. At the very least he believes we should: (1) study creativity directly in high school and university classes; (2) help young children learn techniques of relaxation, stress reduction, and the incubation of creative thought; (3) help children practice use of imagination and imagery, and (4) encourage creative production appropriate to their developmental phase.

Trowbridge (1978) discusses creativity in terms of a dynamic balance between the processes associated with the three substrates of the brain, the primary reticular brain stem (action), the limbic system (affect), and the cortical areas (cognition). Creativity depends on the balance between action, emotion, and cognition with the addition of insight or intuition, the ability to synthesize the components of a situation into a meaningful whole.

Harrington (1980) argues for the inclusion of kinesthetic and muscular modes of representation and expression in the creative process. He believes that such involvement facilitates creativity by encouraging the analogical and metaphorical transformation of information.

Herrmann (1981) suggests a view of creativity that allows for this synthesis by comparing the steps of creativity directly to brain function. The first step he suggests is using the learner's interest, which he believes to be whole-brain-derived. At the preparation stage, the left brain would take the leadership position. During the incubation and illumination stages, the right brain processes would be dominant as the "aha" experience occurs. The critical left brain analytic process of verification follows. Finally the emerging product or solution is put into use and the application again requires the whole brain to act in synthesis. Creativity must include feelings, rational thinking, intuitive thinking, and physical actions. It is the extension of giftednesss, a truly integrative function of our efficient effective human brain. The art of creating allows us to become more than we could have imagined.

Andrews (1975), in a study involving scientists who had been project directors, found the following:

A lack of relationship between creative ability and innovativeness
A lack of relationship between verbal intelligence and either innovativeness or productiveness
Creative ability accomplished more when the scientist had:
1. A perception of self-initiation of the activity
2. Substantial power and influence in decision making
3. A feeling of professional security
4. Freedom to conduct the activity without inhibiting administrative supervision
5. A project small in scope, time, and personnel requirement
6. Other activities to engage in
7. High motivation

Under favorable conditions high creative ability correlates with innovativeness of output. In unfavorable conditions the reverse is true. It was strongly urged that the social and psychological setting of the creative process be considered most seriously.

The impact of the above mentioned factors was cumulative and only with several factors evident did positive correlation occur.

Barron (1969) has been one of the researchers to look at the creative person for answers to the creative process. To use data from this source effectively requires an integrative approach. Even among those who identify themselves primarily with one aspect of creativity, there is considerable overlap with other aspects. It is hoped that this trend will continue as we learn more about creativity as the synthesis of all human functions.

In summary, we have begun our exploration of gifted individuals by establishing a common base of understanding of the terms and concepts that we will use throughout our discussions. The term *gifted* refers to individuals who are functioning at, or who show promise of functioning at, high levels of intelligence. Intelligence is defined as advanced or accelerated development of brain function. It is a composite of human functions of cognition, emotion, intuition, and physical sensing and can be expressed through outstanding cognitive ability, academic aptitude, creative behavior, leadership, or ability in visual and performing arts. Intelligence includes the capacity for insight into complex relationships and for the processes of abstract thinking, adaptability in problem solving, and capacity to acquire new capacity.

The concept of intelligence used is based on the principle of interaction, regarding both heredity and environment as necessary components of the concept. The interactive concept of intelligence is seen as critical to an understanding of the devel-

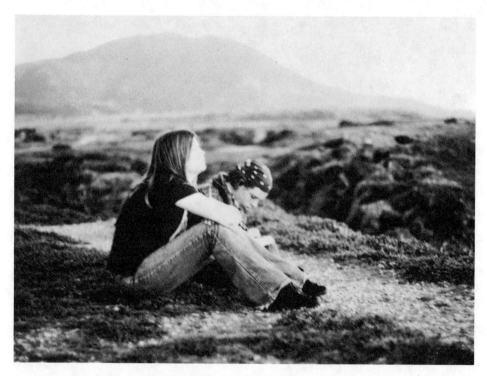

The gifted may seek moments of privacy for intense concentration.

opment of gifted individuals, and an overview of the evolution of the concept was presented to aid in this understanding. A look at current research seems to indicate that the interactive concept best explains the known data. *Interactionism* regards the fertilized ovum as an organism in adaptive interaction with its environment and states the belief that physical conditions surrounding the embryo may alter the direction of development. The genotype appears to provide controlling directives for development and set limits for the range of phenotypic variation, but we are unable to know the full range possible. While genes provide programs for individual potential, they do not guarantee this potential will be achieved.

In this chapter, we have looked at the concept of creativity from a holistic point of view. A model was presented using the four human functions as a base and synthesizing the important aspects of creativity: the rational, the emotional, the talent, and higher consciousness. While the research is often unclear as to the area of creativity it is investigating, this model and the accompanying definitions and population characteristics should allow us to draw more useful comparisons with other areas of creativity or with less creative individuals. The conditions favoring development of each aspect should allow teachers and parents to provide better for creative individuals and encourage a more complete and balanced experience in developing creativity.

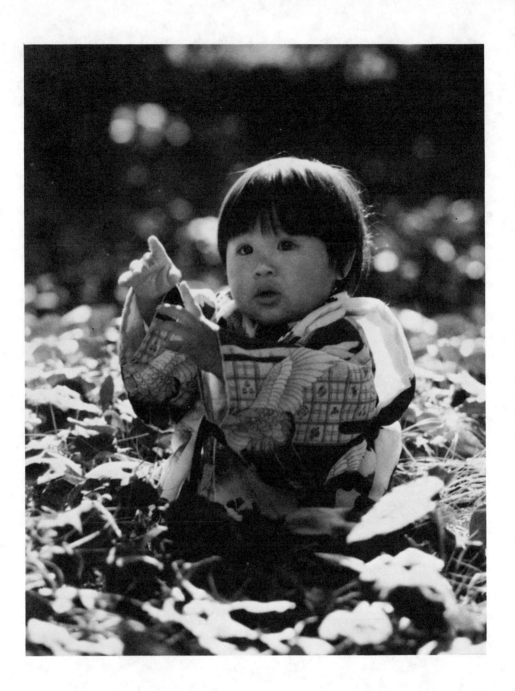

CHAPTER TWO

Becoming
Gifted

The purpose of this chapter is to provide the reader with

- an understanding of the importance of early learning to the development of giftedness.
- an awareness of some of the environmental influences on cognitive development during prenatal, perinatal, infancy, and early childhood periods.
- an awareness of the concept of sensitive periods and their importance to optimal development.
- specific suggestions for developing a nurturing environment for optimal intellectual growth: birth through three months; four through ten months; ten months through two years; two through four years of age.
- many of the characteristics that are unique to gifted learners, the needs that these characteristics may cause, and some of the concomitant problems.

We now begin our inquiry into an area that has been omitted in the literature of gifted education. As a student and now with my students, I found it necessary to study the fields of biology, psychobiology, neurobiology, medicine, and linguistics to bring together data that are crucial to the understanding of how giftedness occurs. Though we have begun to collect data on the origin of giftedness, we know little of the phenomenon we call *highly gifted* or *genius*. However, as information becomes available at a geometrically progressive rate, the excitement of events to come can surely be glimpsed.

As early as 1955, Pressey admonished educators and parents to create genius. Pressey's plan for developing genius is still thought-provoking today (Pressey, 1964). He studied the careers of eminent European musicians in the past century and American athletes in the 1950s. He suggests that the following factors are important to their development and possibly to the development of all special talent or ability: (a) excellent early opportunities for ability to develop with encouragement from family and friends; (b) superior early and continuing guidance and instruction; (c) frequent and continuous opportunity to practice and extend their special abilities and to progress as they are able; (d) close association with others of similar ability; (e) opportunities for real accomplishment within their capabilities, but with increasing challenge; (f) provision for strong success experiences and recognition of these successes. While genius may not result, we have every reason to believe that a level of giftedness may be attainable for a great many children. Although Pressey's comments grew from logical theorizing, we now have evidence to support his conclusions. The new knowledge comes from data showing us the responsiveness of the central nervous system (CNS) including the brain to environmental demands and from new discoveries concerning the sensitivities and propensities inherent in the CNS.

As the brain researcher Elio Maggio (1971) writes, "Experience, in other words, molds neurophysiological mechanisms, even those which appear more stable and closely depending upon genetic and biochemical factors." McCall (1979) believes that the potential for change remains, "although naturalistic circumstances typically conspire to favor stability" (p. 189). He points to the fact that experience is cumulative and that children are a dynamic force in the selection and creation of their own environments that tends to promote environmental stability. By living in the same family until adulthood and as adults selecting experiences that are similar to the intellectual environment they experienced in childhood, we further contribute to the stability of the environment on our intellectual growth. The evidence tends to support the possibility of change in such growth, however, if circumstances and environments are changed. For that reason, McCall believes that although naturalistic circumstances favor environmental stability, mental capability is not essentially imprinted by age six. The plasticity of the system responds to the impact of the environmental experience.

Even before data supported these theories, clues to the importance of the earliest years as the nurturing point for eminence had been found. Goertzel and Goertzel (1962) reported on the lives of a host of eminent people and found that, without exception, these individuals had grown up in early stimulating environments. Colvin (1915) states that all the prodigies he studied were educated from the first months of their lives. Fowler (1962), Hollingworth (1942), and Terman (1925) reported no cases of high ability who had not been exposed to early stimulation. Ausubel (1967) even contended that failure to stimulate in the early years was irreversible. Young genes display more plasticity than adult genes. Educators have long believed in early achievement, especially in speech and reading, as a sure sign of giftedness. Let us now ask a question that I find as optimistic as it is fascinating: Can early opportunity for achievement and early stimulation create giftedness? More accurately, can such opportunity allow the developing child to actualize more of the potential available that may well fall within the range of performance we call gifted?

Early Learning: The Importance of Developing Potential

Lipsitt, Mustaine, and Zeigler (1976) compare the use of the findings of infant studies to the phenomena now being observed in athletics: Increased knowledge of human systems and their nurture, human aspirations and motivations, and opportunities for individual performance combine to bring out higher levels of excellence year after year. The first four years of life are the most critical for human development. Not only is physical survival tenuous, but patterns for both the personality and the actualization of learning ability have begun. The personality established and the type of learning opportunities available will facilitate or inhibit the development of inherited intellectual capacity. Again we have the choice. We may either plan to provide the most nourishing environment that is possible within our current knowledge, or we may allow this important interaction to occur by chance. Regardless of how we choose to approach these formative years, interaction will occur and intelligence will develop. Whether that development leads to actualization or loss of human potential depends on us.

Prior to the 1960s, relatively few studies viewed the developing infant as more than a biological entity. The earlier picture of the infant showed a reflexive organism unable to see or hear, who was only partially aware of being alive. People believed that pain, pleasure, and perception came about much later, as the neural structure completed its development. No logical person would have spoken of stimulation. For that reason parents, mostly mothers, were given instructions on bathing, feeding, and other physical concerns related to infant care. Motherhood became very clean, sterile, and convenient, as disposable bottles, disposable diapers, and ever-increasing amounts of expensive equipment made mother and child more safe and hygienic. Classes on child rearing were held, again largely for mothers, but no one considered the mental development of the new person.

Then a few researchers began to observe and publish what many intuitive mothers already knew. Infants were far more capable than anyone had believed. From the moment of birth their world was available to them. Some researchers even began looking at the pre- and perinatal periods of development. The findings are exciting! From 1960 until today we have witnessed an explosion of information about these periods and about the early childhood years that follow. We can no longer "just let children be children" without our awareness that we are inducing events that will have permanent effects on their lives. Many of our children have been fortunate; many others have not. We can do something about ameliorating development. We now have the knowledge that will allow more potentially gifted children to actualize their potential. We may find that most children could be functioning at the level we now called *gifted*; for some there will be further reaches of development as yet unknown. Let us look at some discoveries we have made about our own human infants. We have only begun to understand; there is still much to learn.

Animal studies provide answers to some very important questions. At the level of gene action and cell development, it is possible to generalize animal results to humans. Comparison is less useful at the level of behavior. In the first instance, the patterns of action are the same. At their brain research laboratories at the University of California at Berkeley, Krech (1969), Rosenzweig (1966), and their colleagues sought to discover the effect experience has on learning. Specifically, they questioned whether differential experience could modify the brain in measurable anatomical and chemical terms. Their initial study involved two groups of rats from the same genetic strain. One group was reared in a nonstimulating environment. They placed each animal in solitary confinement in a small cage situated in a dimly lighted, quiet room. These rats received no attention, but they had unlimited access to the same standard food provided both groups. The other group was environmentally enriched by living together in large, wire mesh cages in a well-lighted, noisy, busy laboratory. The cages were equipped with toys, and the rats were allowed to explore freely the environment outside of the cage thirty minutes each day. Upon later examination of these rats, the researchers found that the brain cortexes of those rats had significantly expanded and had grown thicker and heavier than those of the deprived group!

Of greater importance, the researchers found an increase in the number of glial cells (which seem to play a vital function in the nutrition of the neurons and in the learning capability of the animal), an increase in the size of the neuronal cell bodies and their nuclei, and an increase in diameter of the blood cells supplying the cortex. Chemical changes had also occurred. Enriched brains showed more acetylcholinesterase, the enzyme involved in the transsynaptic conduction of neural impulses, and cholinesterase, the enzyme found in glial cells.

Later experiments showed that, in the brains of rats sacrificed after stimulation had ceased for a period of time, the weight and size changes were no longer apparent, but the chemical changes remained. These changes correlate with changes in problem-solving ability; stimulated rats rank as superior problem solvers. A later experiment will prove quite thought-provoking for anyone concerned with disability. In this experiment they blinded two groups of rats and studied them along with two groups of sighted rats. They stimulated one group of sighted and one group of blind rats and they left the other two groups unstimulated. The results showed that in learning ability the sighted, stimulated rats were, of course, significantly more capable. Interestingly, they found that the blind, stimulated rats were significantly better learners than either the sighted or blind nonstimulated groups. It would seem from these results that stimulation is critical even to damaged organisms (Rosenzweig, 1966).

As a result of other experiments conducted to examine the effect of early stimulation on animals, Seymour Levine of Stanford University declared: "Minimal changes in the early environment have proved to have profound effects on the subsequent performance of the developing organism" (1957, p. 405). He discovered that other very significant effects were derived from lack of stimulation. Being undisturbed, even in a warm, sheltered environment with a nourishing mother, could not provide the experience needed for later coping and learning behavior. Animals provided with early experience that was stimulating, even at times traumatic, seemed to be more emotionally stable, more curious, and more able to learn and to display appropriate coping behavior. Too much aversive stimulation reverses the effects; anxiety can be debilitating (Levine, 1957, 1960).

In work done to learn more about the functioning of the human brain, Scheibel and Scheibel (1964b) found far more complexity than previously supposed. In addition to the millions of cells found in the human brain, each individual cell has hundreds of branches called dendrites. The dendrite, the structure that forms part of the connection (called a synapse) with another nerve cell, makes possible the transmission of impulses from one cell to another. The Scheibels discovered that each dendrite seems to have a different function. To complicate the picture further, each dendrite has thousands of spines that may further differentiate functions. The number of possibilities for individual learning differences and levels of intelligence could be enormous. Early environmental experiences appear to be the key determinants to the density and quantity of spines.

Cooper and Zubek (Bodmer and Cavalli-Sforza, 1970) at the University of Manitoba found that when rats from "bright" and "dull" strains had been raised for one generation in a restricted environment, a difference in learning ability could no longer be perceived. When raised in a stimulating environment, they did almost equally well. Another researcher, James L. McGaugh (Krech, 1969) of the University of California at Irvine, tested chemical stimulation of mice. He found that mice showing hereditarily superior learning ability can be surpassed by mice who are hereditarily dull, but chemically enriched. Krech (1970) suggests that chemical changes from rich environmental interaction have a similar effect.

Along with these research trends came research directed at exploring the specific factors within the environment that interact with the characteristics of human infants to promote or facilitate development, such as home qualities, patterns of mother-child or father-child interaction, forms of communication, and others (Beckwith, 1971; Clarke-Stewart, 1973; Lewis and Rosenblum, 1974; White and Watts, 1973; Yarrow et al., 1975). While there are still many unanswered questions, there is a substantial amount known on the cognitive-affective-social capabilities of infants and the mechanisms that contribute to their development.

One question continued to concern early childhood educators: Can learning, or rather the benchmarks for development, be accelerated, or is it dependent solely on maturation? Among types of learning, physical control seems most clearly affected by maturation. Haynes, White, and Held (1965) conducted an experiment on newborns in a nursery to answer the above question. The researchers placed mobiles in the babies' cribs, replaced plain sheets and bumpers with patterned ones, changed positions of the infants, and provided other forms of sensory enrichment. When compared with other babies, the enriched group accelerated the first major event in the developmental motor sequence, fisted swiping, by several weeks. More importantly, Haynes et al. concluded that once children operate at a higher level, they assimilate more information to allow their cognitive development to proceed even more rapidly. Techniques to accelerate infant development include those that make available more color, more complex patterns, and more accessibility to the world around them. Dr. Hunt (Pines, 1979) tells us that development does not come just from exposure to stimulating environments. The child must be allowed to cope, to interact with the environment. Acting on things, interacting with people, and having the people and the environment be responsive is critical.

These studies and other similar findings mean to the educator that by early stimulation we may affect deprivation that has occurred over past generations. Of course, we could equally restrict an environment to the degree that a leveling effect takes place regardless of the genetic advantage enjoyed at birth. We can no longer leave early stimulation to chance. While genetic differences between human beings do exist, such differences are insufficient to explain differences in intellectual ability. Early experience can validate or invalidate the genetic contribution to our intellectual growth. To use the environment as a powerful interacting agent, we must know more about our children and their capabilities. Environmentally produced individual differences begin at birth, possibly before. We must provide an environment rich in opportunities and responsive to each individual. We must allow ourselves to be effective observers in order to assure optimal growth. If even such less complex animals as rodents show individual differences and require differential treatment and programming, and if such programming can make such critical differences, what must infants require? Can we dare to neglect the implications of these findings?

Prenatal and Perinatal Interaction

Interaction with the environment begins to affect the infant significantly during the prenatal period. Some researchers investigating this area of growth warn that the history of the mother governs occurrences during this period. Drugs, alcohol, and cigarettes used prior to conception by the mother will affect her ability to conceive a healthy fetus. Her diet and health habits, her anxiety and mental health will all be reflected in the child she bears. Even more dramatic effects can be noted during the fetal period. Researchers have shown a cause-and-effect relationship between diseases, malnutrition, and drug use by the mother and the damage to the growing fetus.

Factors affecting the health of the mother and, therefore, the child she is carrying were found by the Preschool Nutrition Survey (Owen at al., 1974). Very young mothers have less adequate nutritional reserves, as they are still growing themselves. Further, teen-age mothers are less likely to have adequate diets during gestation. Lower class mothers tend to have far more first time pregnancies before they are seventeen (42 percent) than do upper class mothers (4 percent). The nutrition and overall health of the mother directly affects the intellectual as well as the more obvious physical growth of her infant. We are also aware of genetic problems that can now be detected in utero. There are, however, very few acceleration studies available to show the same causal relationship in humans.

Ockert S. Heyns (1963), of the University of Witwatersrand in Johannesburg, South Africa, conducted one study that raises some interesting speculation. Heyns became aware of a vast number of children born with brain damage presumably because of forced passage through the bony pelvic area of the mother during birth. In 1954, Heyns devised a vacuum chamber to fit over the abdomen. He believed the device would relax the uterus and the abdominal muscles during labor, thus reducing the pain of childbirth and allowing for easier delivery. Pregnant patients used the chamber for thirty-minute periods the last ten days prior to and throughout delivery. Heyns was very pleased with the results, finding deliveries easier and of shorter duration. He could bring the women into the final stages of birth in a more relaxed and vigorous state.

Some months later Heyns began receiving reports of unusually advanced behavior and growth in the infants of mothers he had used in his experiment. After many favorable reports, Heyns decided to test these infants against physical and mental norms. What he found caused him to bring his procedure to the attention of the London University Hospital for verification. Infants using the decompression chamber scored 18 percent higher than norms on tests of the landmarks of infant development; 16 percent scored 48 percent higher. Children at twelve months appeared as physically and behaviorally developed as normal two-year-olds.

After replication and study, the hospital researchers made an announcement about the advanced mental and physical development. Use of the vacuum chamber seemed to allow for an increase in oxygen available to the fetus at a decisive point in the physiological and neural development of the infants. While many countries have since used this delivery method, doctors in the United States have not adapted its use on any wide scale. It is still considered experimental. Along this same line, however, natural childbirth and many techniques for relaxation during fetal development and birth are becoming quite widespread today. Concern has even been raised over birth trauma; procedures for insuring the infant a less painful and shocking beginning are being used more commonly (Lamaze, 1970; LeBoyer, 1975). Verny (1981) gives evidence to show that how children are born, how painful, smooth, or violent, will largely determine who they become and how they will view the world around them. The only reason we may not consciously recall our birth experience may be the effect of the hormone oxytocin, which is secreted by the mother during labor and birth and which has an amnesic effect. We can be deeply affected by the experience without consciously remembering it.

Bonding

An issue that may affect our ability to optimize human development is that of bonding, the intimate, emotional attachment between mother and infant. Poor bonding may contribute to psychological and social disorders throughout childhood and shows a high correlation with unsocial, unproductive adult behavior, even violence. The quality of the bonding may be determined by at least three variables: hormones, physical contact, and timing. The increase in estrogen levels experienced by the mother just prior to birth provides a triggering for the bonding response but is not sufficient to establish it; physical contact within moments of the birth experience seems to be required (Kennell and Klaus, 1979). Says Dr. Kennell, "The hours after birth seem to comprise a sensitive period for maternal-infant attachment" (Marano, 1981, p. 66). In ways that are physiologically measurable, bonding buffers both mother and child from the effects of stress. Breast feeding, frequent verbalizing with the infant, holding, and rocking all are factors in good bonding.

The results of ten studies (Kennell et al., 1974) show a significant difference between the behavior of mothers who had early contact (i.e., those who had their baby with them for one hour during the first two hours after delivery and for an extra five hours on each of the next three days) with their babies from those who followed the usual hospital routine (i.e., a brief glimpse of the baby at birth and visits of twenty to thirty minutes for feeding every four hours). At one month the babies of early-contact mothers handled stress more easily and received more support from their mothers. Their relationship with the mother evidenced more intimacy and more eye contact. At one year the early-contact mothers spent more time supporting and caring for their babies. At two years the linguistic patterns of the early-contact mothers were more supportive of the development of complex linguistic skills. Desmond et al. (1966) observed that the newborn is in a very alert and active state for approximately one hour immediately after birth. Infants have their eyes wide open, and are able to follow objects with their eyes and head. After this period the infant falls deeply asleep for three to four hours. The early responsiveness of infants to their environment and their ability to interact with their parents makes this an optimal period for the formation of affectional bonds. Verny (1981) contends that children who learn most quickly and seem happiest have bonded with their mothers after birth. "By joining mother and child, bonding supplies not only someone who understands and loves the baby but also an ally who can provide the infant with the stimulation he needs to expand emotionally and intellectually" (p. 153).

Most of the data regarding pre- and perinatal environmental interaction come from the deprivation studies or from animal research. While findings from animals cannot provide unquestioned generalizations about human fetal development, some interesting possibilities have been raised. In a study involving fertilized eggs, an old wives' tale gets some support. The researchers (Grier, Counter and Shearer, 1967) played a melody repeatedly to an experimental group of developing chicks while the eggs hatched. After hatching, all chicks tended to creep toward sounds emitted, but the experimental group showed a preference for the melody heard during incubation. We can only speculate on what this means to the in utero environment of the human fetus.

Genetic-Environmental Interaction during Infancy (Birth Through Two Years)

Much of the research with humans has attempted to discover all that infants are capable of doing. We will not be able to make decisions about what children should do until we know what they *can* do. We have only begun to explore this period of growth. Already many different experiences can be suggested to allow infants to explore their world more easily and facilitate their opportunities for interaction. We now know that infants from birth are active, perceiving, learning, and information-organizing individuals. With our present knowledge, we could best provide the optimal interactive environment by relying on the human resources of the infant to select, from the large quantity of activities available, only those events or experiences that are stimulating. This would provide the best match for the infants' point in development. As we understand the period of infancy with greater clarity, we will have clues available to aid us in providing the proper stimulation at the proper time for each infant. Making optimal use of this important learning period may not be too far beyond us.

The Preschool Nutrition Survey (Owen et al., 1974) produced some interesting clues to early facilitation or inhibition of growth in infants. Reported by socioeconomic class, the survey discovered that food was used as an extrinsic motivator (re-

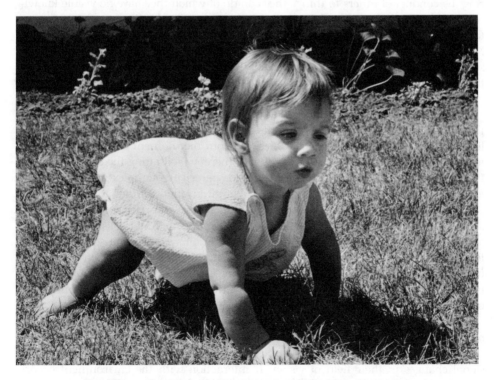

Early exploration is important to later development.

ward) for children of all classes, but while 54 percent of the lower class parents used food in this way with their children, only 23 percent of the upper class did so. Nearly one-fourth of the lower class parents used the withholding of food as a punishment, but only 4 percent of the upper class parents did so. Such practices do not encourage good nutritional habits in children. Nor do they contribute to the balance of nutrients needed to support the growing intellect, i.e., advanced and accelerated brain development.

Brazelton (1979) has shown that at birth babies orient themselves to sound and prefer the human voice, especially the high pitch of the female voice. They can imitate facial gestures and synchronize their body movements to rhythm. Klaus (1978) finds that newborns born to unmedicated mothers spend nearly forty minutes of their first hour in a state of rapt attention, eyes bright, wide open, capable of focusing and fixating on objects.

A number of studies in the past decade have shown abilities of infants that are at variance with models of development previously accepted, such as that of Piaget (1954). Meltzoff and Moore (1977) have found that infants as young as twelve to twenty-one days old can imitate movements that they cannot see themselves perform, such as sticking out the tongue, grimacing, mouth opening, etc. Infants can not only copy the behavior of others selectively, but seem to have a means of referring the conduct of others to things they can do of which they have no visible knowledge. Bower et al. (1971) and Gardner (1971) report that by five months of age infants are able to track moving objects visually in the sense of object permanence. Not only do they anticipate the reappearance of an object that moves behind a screen, but, if a different object emerges, they will look back to the screen to find the missing object. Such evidence indicates that infants are far more capable than we have assumed.

The classic study conducted by Fantz in 1961 added much to our knowledge of the learning capability of human infants. By using measures of attention, he established a fact unknown to science: Babies see from the moment of birth. They seem to have an innate ability to perceive patterns, thereby facilitating the development of form perception. They develop their ability for perceiving complex forms to a high level of discrimination by two months. When given opportunities to interact with patterns of varying degrees of complexity, infants seem to prefer more complex designs. In their order of preference, the complexity of printed matter is second only to a preference for the human face. This information allowed the first sensitive period for learning to be delineated from birth to two months as the time when the human infant can most easily acquire form perception. It is critical that the environment provide patterns to be viewed during this sensitive learning period if the ability is to be optimally used (Fantz, 1961).

When we consider the amount of stimulation usually available to the infant, we recognize that far more could be done to take advantage of this sensitive learning period. Most infants kept in a basket or enclosed crib are provided with only occasional changes in their field of vision. If interaction with the environment occurs from birth, repetition of this limited view must indeed be boring. For the infant reaching out visually without the ability to change body positions, the world of ruffled canopies, ceilings, pastel sheets, and occasional mobiles must be quite limiting. Fortunate is the child who during this period experiences different areas of the home, the out-of-doors, and various objects and people. The utilization of complexity seems to become cumulative with early experience because form and complex patterns result in a preference by the infant for more and more complex forms and patterns (Fantz, 1965). We must note that if this period is not used, the infant will still need to develop these visual skills. A delay will only retard development and may result in less than optimal use of the child's potential. Ideas for more adequate cultivation of this period will be given at the end of this chapter.

We can already by three months of age begin to see evidence of the limitations the environment may be creating on intellectual growth. Researchers have observed that tests administered during this period can predict to a certain extent future language development, quality of interaction with the environment, and personality characteristics that help determine future learning patterns. One researcher calls this first three-month period a deprivation period for many children. The growing child cannot possibly assume responsibility for the quality of environmental interaction during this time. The infant depends almost totally on others for any intellectual stimulation that occurs.

Not only does the quantity of stimulation seem to influence intellectual development, but the quality of interaction as well. Children from homes crowded with other children and/or an abundance of sights and sounds often exhibit deprived growth patterns (Kagan, 1968; Murphy, 1972; Wachs, 1969). Differentiated, meaningful interaction is necessary. The infant must be responded to directly; what the baby does must be the cause of the resulting action. Not only is cognitive stimulation necessary but emotional involvement is shown to be predictive of later intellectual development. Birns and Golden (1972) found pleasure in the task to be a better predictor of later cognitive performance than early cognitive measures. Early laughter at complex events is probably one of the best predictors because it taps the motivational, attentional, affective, and cognitive ability of the infant. Sroufe (1979) contends that emotion is necessarily integrative. It is as accurate to say that emotional experience and expression facilitate cognitive growth as it is to say that cognitive factors are involved in emotional development.

Further, adults must get involved. In an interesting study, Carew (1976) reported that children prior to two years of age require demonstrations and modeling behaviors on the part of the caregiver. The person in charge of the infant needs to provide a variety of language patterns, visual encounters, and other sensory opportunities for the growing infant. However, such interaction must be responsive to the child. Fear of overstimulation is unnecessary if you center the learning plan on responses to the infant and the expressed needs of the infant. Simply stopping an activity if the child shows discomfort or in any way indicates a dislike for it benefits the child. In a study conducted at the Harvard Pre-School Project, too much stimulation (in this case pinwheels spinning while mobiles jumped overhead) made the infants cry. I doubt if infants will allow themselves to be overstimulated without giving some indication to the offending adult. In this context, consider the response some thoughtless parents get when they take tired infants into restaurants or public meetings. We can all vouch for the unmistakable messages the infant is sending.

In the study reporting the need for demonstration prior to two years of age, Carew (1976) indicated that a change occurs at this age. The nurturing caregiver must then pull back, allowing discovery behavior to become the dominant mode of operation for the child. To be most facilitative in developing a child's potential, direct guidance is advisable and necessary prior to two years of age, while opportunities for discovery and encounters within a rich environment are preferred after that age. Guidance will, of course, still be necessary.

Sensitive and Critical Periods for Learning

Some researchers have labeled the first twenty-four hours after birth a human sensitive period for the normal maternal reaction to the newborn (Salk, 1973). There is evidence of qualitative and quantitative differences in later maternal behavior dependent on the amount of contact during this period (Kennell and Klaus, 1979). Visual complexity is best learned during the intellectually sensitive birth-to-two-month period. Discovery of other sensitive periods is necessary for optimal development to be realized. Bloom's major hypothesis proposed that the environment in which the individual develops will have the greatest effect on a specific characteristic in its most rapid period of change (Bloom, 1964). The definition of the *sensitive period* reflects this hypothesis. During this period all systems, visual, mental, and motor, are ready to be used. If activated by the environment, they will be used together at peak efficiency. The time when an organizational process proceeds most rapidly is a *critical period* for the resulting organization, if failure to use a process during this time results in loss of the process or function (Vygotsky, 1974). Epstein (1978) comments

> The role of intellectual experience or learning is to select among existing networks created by the genetic apparatus during brain development. If the complete spectrum of needed experience is not available to the organism, it loses forever the possibility of having those functions that are operated by the lost networks (p. 354).

He shows evidence that human brain growth occurs primarily during age intervals of three to ten months, two to four years, six to eight years, ten to twelve or thirteen years, and fourteen to sixteen or seventeen years. The sensitive period concept tells us that intensive and novel intellectual inputs to children may be most effective during these brain growth stages.

While we had previously believed that the plasticity of the brain was only available to the very young, Buell and Coleman (1981) have made a remarkable discovery. In their study comparing a normal aged population (ages sixty-eight to ninty-two) with adults (ages forty-four to fifty-five) and population showing Senile Dementia (SD) (ages seventy to eighty-one), they found that the normal aged persons had longer and more branched dendrites than did either the adults or the SD group. These data suggest a model in which the aging cortex contains both regressing, dying neurons and surviving, growing neurons. This was the first demonstration of plasticity in the adult human brain. The field of biology has long accepted the theory of sensitive periods. The first trimester of fetal growth is seen as a critical period for physical growth. Now milestone events are just beginning to be uncovered for sensitive or critical periods in mental development. Animal studies of the imprinting phenomenon hint that such mental developmental periods do exist, but only a few as yet have been documented in humans (Lorenz, 1969; Scott, 1962).

Creating a Responsive Environment for Early Learning (Birth Through Two Years)

In the process of developing intelligence, young children have a great need for a responsive environment. Both people and objects in the environment can be growth-producing only if they have some meaning or use for the child. Jeffrey (1980) reminds us that it is not the stages or sequence of development that is our most important focus, but rather the individual differences that appear with that development, differences in ability to perform as well as to profit from the experiences provided. Age is an inadequate index of neurological and physical maturation, as both are changed by the environment of the child and by that child's genetic program.

Earlier theories on how children develop suggested that both parents and teachers should wait until the children ask for an activity. In that way we could be sure that children were ready to learn. Now this seems far too wasteful of their resources, an unnecessary barrier to their developing potential. As we become aware of children's ability to choose only those activities or objects for which they are ready among a variety of activities or objects, our skill in structuring a rich environment becomes more necessary. The better we know a child, the less difficult is our task. However, we do not have to wait until we know what children need. We need only make available a large variety of objects and activities and then observe and respond as the children interact. The availability of many resources, including the parent and teacher, will allow children to stretch beyond known areas, to experiment with new materials and ideas, and to develop at their own pace and in their own-style. Dubos (1969) states that human potential has a better chance of developing when the social environment is sufficiently diversified to provide a variety of stimulating experiences. He comments:

> The total environment affects individuality through the influences it exerts on the organism during the crucial phases of development, including the intrauterine phase. These early influences affect lastingly and often irreversibly practically all anatomical, physiological, and behavioral characteristics throughout the whole life span (p. 6).

It is true, as Krech reminds us, that "each species has species-specific experiences that are maximally enriching and maximally efficient in developing its brain" (Krech, 1970, p. 373). The most effective way to create a learning environment for the young child would be to take advantage of those experiences that most enrich human growth. Unfortunately at this point in time, we do not yet know enough about the timing or detail of these experiences. We must continue to explore this area and develop this all-important learning curriculum. Until this is done, and probably even then, responsiveness to the child interacting with a rich and varied environment will be our best guide to optimal development. Parents have for years approached the cognitive areas of learning cautiously for fear of harming their child or teaching something in the "wrong" way that would need to be unlearned at a later time. With a responsive-environment approach, there can be no wrong way of learning. In a situation where the child and the parent or teacher respond sensitively to each other, only growth and pleasure in learning can be the outcome. Sroufe (1979) comments, that "caregivers may be so effective in promoting development because they help create the appropriate affective climate and tune their behaviors to the infant's tension level, catching it at the peak of organized engagement, rather than simply because they respond to its behavior in a reliable, mechanical fashion" (p. 507).

Birth Through Three Months

The optimal environment for an infant must include attention to all of the basic needs, physical and psychological. The needs for security, safety, nutrition, belonging, and love are basic to all infants. Only as these needs are met, can the infant give any attention to self-concept and intellectual development at optimal levels. Indeed, how the basic needs are met will critically affect and influence how self-concept and intellectual ability develop. According to reports, infants who are gratified much of the time and who experience tension infrequently show more capacity for handling stress than infants more often subjected to frustration. Infants in an environment characterized by frequent and exuberant expressions of positive feelings tend to develop a high degree of initiative (Yarrow, 1963). Other books deal in detail with how to provide for the basic needs. While they cannot in reality be separated from intellectual growth, we artificially make that separation. Here we assume that attention to the basic needs is given, as we explore means of optimizing the growth of intellectual ability.

During the first two months infants are referred to as *newborns* and, though they are responsive to external stimuli and able to learn from the environment, they are dependent on biological states and inborn dispositions (Karmel and Maisel, 1975; Emde and Robinson, 1976; Parmelee and Sigman, 1976). Some researchers (Meltzoff and Moore, 1977) have found that newborns, some only one hour old, can mimic or imitate the behavior of adults with whom they are interacting. Such studies convince Verny (1981) that "the presence of well developed thinking, including handling of abstract ideas, is found in the newborn" (p. 171).

The first three months of postnatal life may be the most critical for the infant's developing brain, since the first trimester of intrauterine fetal life. During this period the infant has no mobility and must depend upon the caregiver for all intellectual stimulation. We have a baby who we now know can see, hear, and smell, and who can do all these things with discrimination. Here is a baby ready to interact with the environment, ready to learn. In too many cases this interaction is severely limited—so much so that some researchers have called this period the greatest deprivation period for human infants. Little is known about how we may best enrich this period. Some clues do exist about activities that have proven enriching for some infants. They could, in a responsive environment, be made available to all newborns.

From birth, innate programs facilitating usage of language, hands, eyes, etc. seem to be available to the human infant. Unlike any other animal, the human infant has the ability to pick up logical rules. This important competency is basic and available from birth. Bruner (1964) found that not only do infants notice more detail in the environment than we believed, but they actively invent rules or theories to explain what they observe. Even at three weeks, an infant will have complex hypotheses about the world and will react if proven wrong. One experiment supporting this observation used the baby's caregiver and a stereo sound system. The baby responded happily to the caregiver standing by when the sound of the caregiver's voice came from the same location. However, when the caregiver's voice came from a different part of the room than the location of the caregiver, the baby became solemn and then upset.

The best rule for stimulating an infant during this period is to maintain a responsive environment. Over and over in the literature on development of intellectual capacity we find reference, usually in italics, to the importance of responding to an infant's cues or signals of distress. In times past it was thought that picking up babies when they cried would "spoil" growing children. The results of not attending, ignoring, or allowing infants to "cry it out" are now viewed as far more damaging. One of the differences between institutionalized infants and home-reared infants is that institutions do not attend to crying behavior. The results indicate that institutionalized infants lose their sense of control over the environment and become passive, externally motivated children. This does not produce optimal intellectual growth (Provence and Lipton, 1962). The quantity and timing of the caregiver's responses to the infant and the degree of consistency of the responses play important roles in developing and reinforcing the infant's belief that his or her behavior can affect the environment (Lewis, 1972). This belief regarding inner locus of control seems to be learned early in life.

Parents should be advised to respond to infants when they cry and to look for what might be causing the discomfort. If nothing appears wrong, consider the cry a call for loving attention. Rocking and cuddling infants will reassure them and allow them to feel wanted and loved. Parents should also respond to babies' coos and giggles. In this way, infants learn that they can influence the world and they they really matter. The infant will learn that actions other than crying bring attention. However, you need not wait for these signals. Playing regularly with babies and enjoying them and displaying spontaneity and affection will establish a basis for loving that will last a lifetime and will allow infants to develop into trusting, loving, warm human beings. White (1975) believes that infants fail to learn not because they are not bright enough but rather because they have not been properly shown. Parents can provide all the right things but they must do so with their child's rhythms and abilities in mind if they are to succeed. There is an almost geometric progression between the amount of meaningful time spent with a child and that child's intellectual growth. Ainsworth (1974) asks that caregivers see the world from the baby's point of view. It is then not possible to be rejecting, interfering, or ignoring because all responses, even refusals, acknowledge the baby and provide specifically for that baby's needs.

It is important to know that, for a few days after birth, an infant seems able to cope with only one activity at a time. Between three and five weeks, the infant can do one thing, such as nurse, while looking at another source of interest. However, when the viewed activity becomes more interesting, the first activity stops. Between two and four months, an infant will continue the first activity while involved in the second, but with less intensity, almost as though the shift can more easily be made between the two if participation in the first activity is at least superficially maintained.

The infant under three months does not have to touch or manipulate in order to learn something about structure; the infant's attention suffices. Probably the infant learns much about the environment through merely attending to it. Although action is not necessary, it can facilitate learning because activity is accompanied by an increased alertness and, therefore, a greater likelihood of noting differentiating attributes of an object. However, active involvement is clearly an effective aid to acquiring cognitive structures (Kagan, 1971).

This period of the infant's development is important because it holds an initiating place in the child's learning system. What first goes into the system in the way of

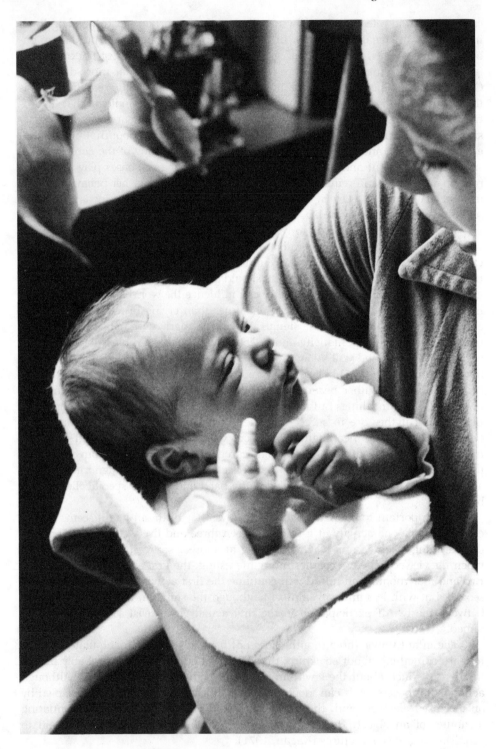

Baby's learning environment.

skills, beliefs, and ideas will set up a resistance to future dissimilar patterns of learning. Initial learning is far more difficult to unlearn. In the following activities, it must be stressed that the caregiver is the most critical factor in the child's learning. A responsive environment can occur only through an aware adult who responds to signals initiated by the child. Stimulation and demonstration of language and skill are available only if the adult provides them.

Be aware that 90 percent of all social interaction with a child from birth to eighteen months occurs during caregiving activities, such as changing diapers, dressing, bathing, and feeding. These activities should be treated not as chores to get out of the way as quickly as possible but as learning opportunities and as times to communicate with the child. Parents must be encouraged to smile and talk a lot even if they feel the baby cannot understand. These are the most important moments of the baby's life. A major factor to the success of parents of competent infants is the parents' belief that they can influence their child's mental development (Kagan, 1971).

Table 2.1 gives specific suggestions to parents for activities most appropriate to this age group:

Table 2.1.   Birth through Three Months.

Caregiver Activities:	Because:
Respond to infant's activity and signals, e.g., awakening and looking—offer objects for baby to look at.	This establishes feeling of inner locus of control, ability of child to affect the environment.
Respond to distress signals (crying) and give attention to cause. Crying it out is definitely *not* recommended.	This establishes a code of mutual expectancy.
When bottle feeding, change positions for each feeding, e.g., right arm holding baby, then left.	This encourages development and coordination of both eyes.
Change position of crib in room.	This increases visual stimulation.
Place mobiles over crib, patterned with a variety of shapes, colors (make your own); Use patterned sheets; clear bumpers; change position and surroundings of infant.	This develops visual complexity skills, nourishes growth of intelligence through heightened interaction with the environment, stimulates curiosity.
Rock infant while held next to chest for ten-minute periods; pick up infant and place on the shoulder; rocking chairs are most useful at this age.	Infants handled in this manner show more visual attention than other infants (White and Castle, 1964; Korner and Grobstein, 1966).
Allow bare skin cuddling, yours and baby's; rub baby's skin with nubby towel when drying; tickle, squeeze, and pinch a little in games; give baby "feely" objects, put them in hand, e.g., velvet, silk, sponge.	This stimulates sensory development; baby learns about feeling.

Table 2.1.   Birth through Three Months. *(continued)*

Caregiver Activities:	Because:
Turn lights on and off for visual stimulation.	Infants are normally overly sensitive to bright sunlight; care must be taken not to create discomfort.
Provide a variety of sounds and speech patterns (music box, radio, variety of rhythms, voices).	These are important prelanguage experiences.
Play vocal games, imitate baby's cooing, introduce real words by naming body parts and toys.	Familiar sounds are of high interest to infants; builds vocabulary, initiates conversation, establishes babies' perceived control of their lives (Hunt, in Pines, 1979).
Allow lots of different smells.	This stimulates olfactory sense.
This is the time for the playpen, or a hard, broad surface, not carpeted. It allows baby to move from room to room with you. Cover the floor with a plastic mat and turn baby loose on tummy. Keep temperature up so that baby can play without restrictive clothing (85°). Play on floor with baby, be near; encourage movement, e.g., rolling over, creeping.	This allows intellectual stimulation.
Provide toys that are patterned, manipulative, textured (rattles are not very interesting toys).	This stimulates self-initiated activities.
Toward the end of this period, use crib devices the baby can bat and play with. They should be brightly colored, have complex shapes, and be strong enough to take abuse. The parts should be hung with semirigid attachment (not string) so that motion can occur, but not too much motion; no sharp or loud sounds or any abrupt changes in stimulation such as flashing lights.	This develops hand-eye coordination.

From Four Through Ten Months

Much physical activity begins here that will remain a dominant factor from now through all of infancy. During this period, interest in active exploration will also be noticeable: exploring with touch, by mouthing, with sounds, by reaching, and always visually. The amount of visual experience, the decor and colorfulness of the home, the presence of a variety of responsive play objects, and the freedom to explore the environment were seen to have a significant relationship with performance on infant testing from five to thirty-six months (Bradley and Caldwell, 1976; Wachs, 1976; Yarrow et al., 1972). The infant enjoys people now more than before and develops obviously affectionate ties. This can be a delightful period for both child and caregiver.

Table 2.2. From Four through Ten Months.

Caregiver Activities:	Because:
Use playpen only until baby becomes mobile, if used later only for very short periods (five to ten minutes).	This restricts environmental interaction, creates limit to intellectual development.
Provide toys of interest: mirrors (very appealing to baby now; be sure they are safe, unbreakable); stacking toys, moderately small objects for dropping, throwing, banging; moving and pop-up toys are interesting late in this period. Be cautious about expensive "educational toys"; it is not necessary to buy toys; homemade toys with your baby in mind are often far better.	This provides intellectual stimulation.
Play games with fingers and toes, stroking legs, patting back; talking and identifying parts of baby can also be added. Encourage baby to pat caregiver, touch fingers, pat-a-cake; allow to play unrestrained by clothing.	These activities contribute to the baby's perception of self and the beginnings of cognitive experience (Murphy, 1972).
Play peek-a-boo games.	This provides visual, auditory, problem-solving stimulation; encourages cognitive anticipation.
Play, talk, interact with infant during all caregiving activities.	This is the most important language for development and motivation.
Encourage new games invented by baby such as drop toy—caregiver picks it up—baby drops toy.	Baby develops beginnings of inner locus of control, senses an active influence on environment, increases motivation.
Play games using eyes and language in games, e.g., "Look at Daddy, look at Mommy, look at baby's foot, look at kitty, look at . . ." (Include things above, below, to right, to left.)	This promotes eye coordination and focus, language experience, coordinating sight and sound, words with things.
Trips to the grocery store, drug store, department store (take baby only when rested, *not* during usual nap time). On trips talk about what is being seen.	These alert attention to varied environments, allow enrichment of sensory experience.

Table 2.2. From Four through Ten Months. *(continued)*

Caregiver Activities:	Because:
Cook and talk to baby, talk at meals, encourage baby to use words (infant seats are useful on trips or to have baby nearby as you work).	This is an important language experience.
Look at books and talk, read to baby.	Symbols of language become familiar, important, a source of fun and pleasure.

From Ten Months through Two Years

During the ten-month to two-year period, the baby experiences real mobility. The major driving force seems to be curiosity. At this stage, the infant's curious nature establishes roots and begins to flower into what will later be experienced by the learning child as motivation. Unreasonably applied limits and controls can cause frustration, leaving an aimless, internally unmotivated child as a result. Let us stress that allowing a baby to explore the environment (made safe by having dangerous items placed out of reach) freely is the single most important action to insure intellectual growth. The environment need not be filled with expensive toys. Any small, manipulatable, visually detailed articles, objects to climb on, objects to move on, all easily accessible, will provide much stimulation. As the baby increasingly experiments and interacts with the environment, guidance, of course, is necessary. Whenever possible, the natural environment should be used to provide correction for the baby's misjudgments. In this way natural consequences can themselves become teachers, and the baby can learn to change or adapt in his or her own way.

A toddler I observed waiting for a plane with his mother was engaged in exploration of the airport environment. Suddenly, as the baby was walking along a railing, he came to a hinged gate that opened into the area behind the counter. The hinge was fairly strong, but the child could swing the gate open a short way before it returned to a closed position on its own. The toddler pushed open the gate over and over, intent upon watching the hinge and the automatic return of the gate. He was hurting no one nor was he bothering anyone. Even if the gate had closed on his hand it would have caused little discomfort and would have provided a lesson the child would likely have incorporated into his schema for swinging doors. However, his mother saw him moving the gate and rushed to scold and spank, hurting him far more than the gate would have. Noisy crying followed, accompanied by more spanking. What should have been a useful learning experience became a power struggle ending with a frustrated, sobbing little boy commanded to sit in an overly large adult chair until his mother felt he could "behave himself."

This happened in contrast to a mother I observed on a ferry one afternoon cautiously monitoring her toddler's actions while appearing unconcerned. Only when the child approached a dangerous situation, such as open ventilation ducts, did the mother move up to him to distract him to some new interest. She never interfered with his dignity nor attempted to be overly controlling. Both the mother and the little boy were enjoying the trip.

Babies are remarkably curious from ten months to two years about things adults would find totally uninteresting, such as hinged doors, cellophane wrappers, tiny pieces of dust, and plant leaves. Parents should expect fascinated repetitions and allow for them. They should be extra alert to keep dangerous items out of the environment. In this way children can begin their own self-initiated, autonomous learning.

White (1975, 1980), in his work at the Harvard Pre-School Project, has established this period as the most decisive for intellectual development. White thinks it essential to nurture balanced development in many areas, including children's interests, people (noticeably the primary *caregiver*), exploration of the world, and use of their own bodies (for instance, motor skills). This period will bring essential development in language, curiosity (leading to motivation), social development, and intelligence (table 2.3).

Table 2.3.   From Ten Months through Two Years.

Caregiver Activities:	Because:

Organize and design a safe physical environment that allows for a variety of sensory experiences; family living areas and outdoor areas should be available for exploration of the senses:
  Visual: plants, fish in bowls, pictures, patterned objects, mirrors
  Auditory: exposure to many types of music, voices, rhythms, singing, bells, drums, shakers, music boxes, animal sounds
  Tactile: a variety of textures to feel (soft, hard, rough, smooth), sculpture, finger food, mud play, finger paints, painting with jello
  Olfactory: bakery smells, flower smells, farm and field smells
  Gustatory: snacks of differing tastes and textures
	Toddlers spend most of their time gaining information, building concepts, and observing.

Provide a variety of toys and household objects to play with: for stringing, nesting, digging, pounding, screwing; construction toys (pieces not too small), peg boards, record players, magnets, magnetic letters, alphabet blocks, prisms, water toys, flashlights, spin tops, jigsaw puzzles, magnifying glasses, dolls, collections of small objects, toy animals, various household tools, books, and art materials.	This gives intellectual stimulation, support for later learning, strengthens perception and problem-solving abilities.
Play games like hide-n-seek, treasure hunts, guessing games, matching and sorting, finger games, circle games; encourage and provide materials for imitative play, such as "I do what you do."	This facilitates concept development, practice in planning and carrying out complicated projects, anticipating consequences, developing skills of problem solving.

Table 2.3.   From Ten Months through Two Years. *(continued)*

Caregiver Activities:	Because:
Teach child to be aware of and name objects in the environment (including baby's own body parts). This can be done by playing games with the caregiver, giving names to objects as they are used.	This provides language experience.
Look at scrapbooks with child, read books to child, make books familiar.	This provides symbolic language experiences.
Make scrapbooks with the child of pictures of animals, cars, trips. These can become the child's own books.	This gives language experience.
Talk to baby during all caregiving activities: bathing, dressing, eating; use patterns of speech with baby that you use with other members of the family; short twenty to thirty second "conversations" are important.[1]	This helps baby to understand more complicated sentences, increases language background and experience.
Take neighborhood walks to library, stores, playgrounds, on collection excursions, out to feed birds; always discuss what is seen and experienced.	This provides a background of experiences for future concept building.

[1]Note. When engaging children in "conversation" try to talk about what they are doing from their perspective. Try to understand their meaning for the activity and what they may be learning from it. Then try to give them something new and interesting to think about along the same lines. Allow children to initiate the activity and then respond enthusiastically, but be careful not to insist on doing it only your way.

Also use language to heighten curiosity and develop interest. Teach children vocabulary words to express their interests by engaging them at the point of interest. This will further help children see adults as valuable resources. Talk to your child even before you are sure the child understands what you are saying. It is important to use a variety of speech patterns and normal conversational intonations. Remember, you are the model. While the act of repeating sounds the baby makes is fun and can be enjoyed by both adult and baby, the child needs good speech models and language patterns. Babytalk does not provide a useful model for children to emulate. Children do create unusual patterns for their own use. However, repetition of these patterns by the adult limits children to those unique patterns.

In order to develop the goal-directed behavior so important to learning activity, children from ten months through two years of age must experience rewards for their efforts, response to their actions, support for reaching out, safety, acceptance, and trust. Only as these are made a part of children's life will they begin to explore and move cognitively toward mastery of more complex skills. If deprived of these experiences, their motivation for learning and potential for wonder and discovery is stunted. Creativity as well as competence will suffer.

During this period children become more mobile. Children need most to interact with the environment for optimal intellectual development to occur. Accessibility to the living area and outdoor areas enhances discovery and self-initiated activities by children. The caregiver must carefully prepare these areas to make them safe and rich in sensory experiences. Lots of objects and materials, not only toys but common household items and junk, all help to construct responsive learning environments. Overuse of playpens and walkers at this stage can be detrimental to intellectual development. The caregiver should continue with trips, reading, and other activities enjoyed by the child in earlier stages. Now more activities of a physical, manipulative nature should be included. Demonstration and modeling behavior by the caregiver are still important.

During this period of beginning mobility the pattern for discipline will be established. While each child responds differently to various methods of discipline, keep in mind that your actions teach far more than your words and that each action has long-term as well as short-term consequences.

In the past, punishment was seen as necessary to teach children proper behavior. Positive guidance has proven far more productive of good behavior than punishment. Misbehavior should indicate to the caregiver that some guidance is needed. If at all possible, find out what preceded the incident. Preventing the next problem may be as simple as changing the cause. For example, when a child begins crying and throwing things out of the shopping basket, everything within reach of the child's seat is fair game. In retrospect, the caregiver had taken the child out during the morning and had stopped to do shopping on the way home. The child had not eaten lunch. Nap time had been invaded by the shopping trip. Rather than punishment, acknowledgment of the child's discomfort and an attempt to remedy the situation as soon as possible would be appropriate. These considerations may be more productive of good behavior than reprimands and physical abuse. Meanwhile, make the child as comfortable as possible by picking him or her up and talking soothingly.

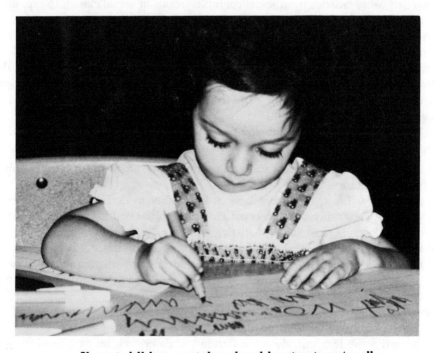

Young children acquire visual language naturally.

After all, the caregiver is at fault. We must guide children in finding better solutions to frustration, but timing is important. Choose a time when they are not tired or hungry.

When we hit a child we are conveying the rule that this behavior solves problems. When we yell at a child we teach that yelling is an appropriate way of interacting to gain attention. While at times a slap on the hand or bottom most effectively halts further misbehavior, physical punishment should be used only as a very temporary solution with a verbal follow-up as soon as possible. Exploration of the cause of misbehavior, explanation of the rules violated and consequences of the action will clarify the need for punishment. Rather than watch children make an error and then punish them, try anticipating the error and warning them that they are approaching a decision point. We can prepare the child to look ahead. We should encourage reflection, give practice in alternative thinking, and share our knowledge of the consequences.

Children must also have some alternative coping techniques. If screaming is all we know how to do when our wishes are frustrated or we need attention, then we'll scream. If we can be assured of getting notice by spitting our food or throwing toys, then we will continue these behaviors. Helping children find better techniques for releasing frustration and getting attention works far better. This requires effective guidance, not punishment. We will produce the same type of behavior we model. The golden rule of "do unto others" never fit better. We should point out that children may encounter damaging behaviors much worse than physical abuse. Lack of acceptance, disregard, and the worthlessness children feel from being ignored by those important to them have far more devastating and long-lasting effect.

Research in child development, especially relating to the area of atypical children, often uses statistics from socioeconomic groups or social classes to explain acceleration or limitations. With increasing evidence we know that we must look beyond the group or class and into the family pattern for our data. In the area of cognitive development, knowledge of such patterns has proven most beneficial. The answer to how children can develop the ability to think in consequences and alternatives, to build rationales, and become good problem solvers and good choosers can be found within the family experience (Hoffman and Hoffman, 1964, 1966; Stone, Smith, and Murphy, 1973).

The following characteristics commonly accredit families that produce children with highly actualized potential and self-esteem.

Parents accept their children as individuals, are loyal sources of support, openly express acceptance.

Parents set clear limits based on each child's ability to understand consequences; goals are clear; success is expected as a right of the child, not of the parent.

Parental guidance is reasonable, realistic, and appropriate to each child.

The family tends to be liberal and flexible, but not permissive.

The family is aware of the environment and relates to the environment in a caring, protective way. Children are helped to see their part in the natural order and to respect this unity.

Parents are relatively self-assured, are on good terms with one another; they accept the responsibility for their own actions.

Parents lead active lives outside of the family and do not rely on their families as the sole or necessarily major source of gratification and esteem.

Children with high self-esteem more often acquire a sense of independence, exhibit exploratory behavior, assert their own rights, develop a strong inner locus of control, and express more self-trust. These traits lead them to personal happiness and more effective functioning.

Low self-esteem results in higher levels of anxiety, more frequent psychosomatic symptoms, less effectiveness, and more destructive behavior. Children with low self-esteem find it hard to believe that any personal action can have favorable outcomes. Instead, they believe themselves powerless and unworthy of love or attention.

Money, education, social class, time spent with the child (quality, not quantity), physical attractiveness, and socioeconomic group identification will influence how society treats a child. However, family acceptance and the child's response to that acceptance are critical factors in developing self-esteem and intellectual potential during this period (Coopersmith, 1967).

An environment controlled by rules rather than attention to individual characteristics of a specific situation produces children who relate to authority rather than to rationality. Although often compliant, these children have never learned to find appropriate solutions to problems. The consequences of their actions are regarded in terms of immediate reward or punishment rather than future effects and long-range goals (Hess and Shipman, 1965).

As much as we want to provide an environment where our children can actualize their intellectual capacity, our society wants and needs good, fully human beings. These persons can establish a more nurturing, good society. While each of us would add our own criteria to the term *good*, I believe we would agree on all factors that allow humans to be more caring, responsible, and growth-producing for both themselves and others. With these ultimate goals in mind, we must foresee the relationship between what occurs in the home, reflecting on the child, and the adult the child will become. Children become what they live. If fear is used for control, the child will learn fear and the use of fear as a controlling technique. Violence fosters violence; abuse teaches abuse; disrespect brings forth disrespect. Mature, loving people must be the responsible caregivers for our future generations. Our homes must establish an environment of trust by respecting and trusting each family member from the oldest to the youngest. You can generate trust by using affirmative behavior, as opposed to judgmental behavior, as follows:

> Child: Cries (He broke his toy.)
>
> Caregiver: I can see you're really unhappy. What can we do?

Rather than:

> Caregiver: Stop that crying! You did it yourself and you know boys don't cry. Crybaby! Now you'll be more careful. Go play and leave me alone!

Caregivers must guide children to see both the strengths and the weaknesses in their personalities. A growing, sincere person who can say "I was wrong" or "I'm sorry" to a little child, who can admit hurt or anger as well as joy and affection, makes the best teacher for someone learning to be human. Empathic understanding is valuable and should be used often, but probably the most critical behavior a child can experience is total acceptance as a person. The behavior of the child may not be acceptable. Ways may be sought to change that behavior. Always accepting the child and letting the child know of that acceptance is the most growth-producing gift that can be given. Effective guidance and personal acceptance are essential to the development of a child's potential.

Intellectual Development During Early Childhood (Two Through Four Years)

Another sensitive period, in addition to the one mentioned for form complexity, exists for language development. Linguists have theorized that between eighteen months and four years of age every human has available an innate ordering device for learning language, referred to as the Language Acquisition Device (LAD) (Chomsky, 1966; McNeill, 1966). During this LAD period, the environment of the child must be rich in language experience. Never again will the child have the ability to learn language-related activities with such ease. Learning is cumulative. If we are to optimize the learning opportunities of our children, we must take advantage of those periods when learning proceeds most rapidly and efficiently (Lenneberg, 1967). Young children will acquire language effortlessly if language is around them, but the kind of language they acquire, whether an instrument of clarity, precision, and imagination or only a tool to handle biological and social exchanges, will depend on the linguistic environment supplied by adults (McKenna, 1978).

Reading as a visual language experience is analogous to speech as an auditory language experience. Both represent receptive language, and both may present similar cognitive problems to the learner. Possibly the eighteen-month- to four-year-old language acquisition period presents the child with an advantage in organizing visual language input (reading) as it does for other language experiences (Moore, 1961, 1967; Chukovsky, 1966). Callaway (1970) presents a further conjecture that reading experiences could enhance cognitive performance through physiological changes in brain cells.

In an attempt to understand better how the LAD period affects young children, I conducted an early reading experiment with children two through four years of age (Dunn, 1969). My goal was to discover the effectiveness of teaching two- through four-year-olds several basic reading skills, names of letters, letter sounds, and a few basic words by televised presentations. This was prior to *Sesame Street*. From my background in preschool television programming, I was convinced that this medium could give large numbers of children the opportunity to explore the world of symbolic language.

For fifteen minutes once a week for sixteen weeks, forty-five mothers brought their children to the campus to watch in small groups the televised antics of a feline puppet and me. Using songs, games, and stories, we involved the children in basic reading experiences. Our two- to four-year-old boys and girls had IQ's ranging from 74 to 134 and represented several racial and ethnic groups and socioeconomic levels.

I found the results exciting yet frustrating. All children reached mastery on all items tested. Their growth was statistically significant at the .001 level over the growth of the control group. Neither IQ, age, nor any other variable we looked at seemed to influence the results except for a slight time advantage evidenced by those children whose parents read to them. This was exciting, as it supported results of other early childhood reading experiments. The frustration came from the low expectation level that I had set as the researcher. Halfway through the experiment my concern regarding too much material presented too quickly became instead too little presented too slowly. Children began leaping ahead, and by the end of the four-month period, over half had taken the tools offered by the program and they began to read. I had not pretested for reading, so I could comment only briefly on this fact in the results. A follow-up study a year later showed that, of those children responding, all had continued to develop their reading skill; several had been accelerated in school placement and identified as gifted children.

Before leaving this study, I would like to mention one unplanned event. Several of the mothers were unable to locate baby sitters for their younger children and were allowed to bring them to the campus. One younger brother, who at the end of the experiment was one year, six months old, came every week. While the student watched the televised presentation, his younger brother could be seen through the one-way glass of the observation booth wandering about the room, sometimes watching, sometimes participating, and often seeming to be interested in play of his own design. During the posttesting he again accompanied the family and, just out of curiosity, I asked if he would like to be tested too. He joined in with gusto. At his own private testing session I found that this child, whose chin could barely clear the table to see the cards and test items, knew several letters, could identify several letter sounds, and had a reading vocabulary of five words.

While not reported with the experimental group, this finding made me wonder just how capable our young children are. How much could they learn if the opportunity were presented? With our group of forty-five I had the pleasure of sharing a whole new world of activities. Some obtained library cards, although mother had to sign for them. One young man discovered that writing could be a useful tool and used his basic skills to print a note declaring his annoyance with the behavior of his little friend next door. Billboards became wonderful adventures. As one three-year-old informed me, when she couldn't find anything else fun to do, she could read her baby a book.

I found with my group the same confidence and joy Fowler (1962) expresses in his research on the outcome of early reading activity. I am convinced that reading is a natural, happy event if introduced during this LAD period. What we do at six years of age may be remedial reading. If you were to force someone to remain immobilized during the nine-through-twelve-month period and only allow walking activity later, around three or four years of age, you would find it necessary to teach balance, left-right sequencing, how to place one foot in front of the other, shifting weight, and other incremental skills. Let us make an analogy to our approach to reading. Children I have known and those reported in the literature (Durkin, 1966; Fowler, 1962) learn with ease and pleasure during the LAD period. At six years of age learning to read becomes quite a different matter. We must later deliberately teach what is incidentally learned during the earlier period. Few children are allowed the opportunity to interact with symbolic language during this early period. Professional education has done an excellent job of convincing parents that they cannot teach reading. And yet, if allowed the opportunity to play with words, if read to or shown any of the ways letters can be used to represent sound, children find their own way to learn. In an environment that responds as the children direct, that is rich in good language experiences, children enjoy learning in their own way. Learning to read would be no exception.

Some years ago educators informed parents that early learning was a waste of time. People accepted the notion that children who learned later would catch up anyway. Too many people, without looking at new data, still believe this to be true. The work of Durkin (1966) has given us a different view of children who read early. Her research shows that children who enter school already reading have a learning advantage that continues to accelerate during the school years. By sixth grade, far from "catching up," the late readers (those learning in first grade) were increasingly outdistanced by the performance of the early readers. Fowler (1963) found much the same to be true and linked the results of early reading to the higher intellectual development of his children. He found reading not only easily accomplished by younger children, but felt that it enriched their play life and resulted in happier, more well-rounded children.

My interest in the benefits of early reading was piqued when I first met Ragan Callaway at UCLA in 1968. I had been working in a clinic for problem learners, trying to develop a remedial program for four nonreaders who were eleven years old and possessed measured intelligence of over 130 IQ on the Binet. As I wondered how such a problem could have occurred, I began a search for prevention. At that point I met Dr. Callaway. He came from a background in biology, having studied to the doctoral level, when he noted occurrences that seemed even more interesting than his studies in biology. His first child began to show a great interest in symbolic language. As Callaway followed and abetted that interest, he found his son was capable of learning to a degree traditionally held as impossible.

Pursuing his son's experiences in learning convinced Callaway of the fallacies to traditional thought. After another young son also read prior to his second birthday, Callaway's interest in education grew. He became principal of a school where he initiated a program of preschool reading that resulted in all of the children reading prior to school entry. Ultimately, he made a change in curriculum for the primary grades. After completing a doctorate with Elizabeth Drews at the University of Michigan, Callaway came to UCLA and conducted research in early reading in the Los Angeles area.

All of this experience and vast exploration of literature led to the publication of his monograph *Modes of Biological Adaptation and Their Role in Intellectual Development* (1970). This work links the biological aspects of growth to learning and intellectual development. He brought out in the monograph the ideas of general plasticity of the human genetic and cellular structure and the special sensitivity of the organism to early experience. These ideas underscore the sensitive or critical period concept.

Callaway's work, having drawn praise from geneticists, educators, and psychologists all over the world, provides guidelines and a solid rationale for educational programs that could take advantage of these important learning periods. He sees reading activity with the young as a triggering device, perhaps the best available, that turns on the genetic potential of the child. "There is very little of the brain not finally involved in the relatively simple act of seeing a letter and pronouncing its label" (Jeffrey, 1980).

We have long known that gifted children read early. Could it be true that children are gifted because they read early? Could this activity and other types of stimulation set into motion structural changes in the organism that result in high-level intellectual development? The data now available support this possibility.

To understand how a person's capacity for learning is affected by the early environment, especially during critical or sensitive periods, we must return to the principles of interaction. Experience affects gene production by making demands on the cell's metabolic resources in such a way that the organism is able to meet similar learning demands in the future more easily. If these demands are made early and repeated, they make lasting changes in the neural structure of the organism. Increased activity increases the amount of transmitter fluid produced at a synapse, the point where there is firing from one brain cell to another during thinking. Nerve cells and fibers become larger through use as does the capillary network. As we have seen before, the thickness and weight of the entire cortex increase by environmental enrichment. There is evidence that experience does lead to maturation. Callaway points out that we have had evidence available for over thirty-five years that myelinization of the optic tracts is accelerated by stimulation. He points out that the assumption that genetic material is completely preprogrammed, and therefore contributes to a stable inheritable mental capacity, cannot be supported in light of more recent evidence.

Creating the Responsive Environment (Two Through Four Years)

We now have a child who is interested in the world and other children. This child has outgrown the baby stage. During the two- through four-year period, the child's mental powers show rapid growth. Speech, mobility, increasing social involvement all add to the fast-paced intellectual development. All of the play materials from previous periods are useful, but in different ways. This child creates, draws, pretends, and imagines, but only if allowed to and if provisions for these activities have been made. Space to explore his or her own way and time to "do it myself" are needed. The child is now a thinker. Cognitive psychologists such as Jean Piaget (1952) and Jerome Bruner (1960, 1964, 1968) have helped us to understand how thinking develops.

Development of the Rational Mind   Piaget, an eminent Swiss psychologist honored by educational groups throughout the world, believed that there were qualitative as well as quantitative differences between the thinking of adults and children. It was not only how much they knew, but the way they knew. The mind, he believed, is always trying to balance between assimilation, bringing in new information that fits our belief system and accommodating our belief system or thought structure to allow for new information, for change. As we grow, ever more complex structures are needed to understand our world and we require more elaborate schemes.

Development of the thought processes involved in such schemes was thought by Piaget to occur in four discrete and qualitatively different stages. The first stage relies primarily on the senses and bodily motion to develop a few simple schemes. This stage is, therefore, called the *sensorimotor stage* and includes the period of infant development (birth to eighteen months). The second stage, called *preoperational*, includes the years from about two to seven. Children now begin to develop an understanding that symbols can represent objects, words can replace and communicate reality. At stage three, children can classify things and think with some logic; they are aware of and can formulate laws of logic. This is the stage of *concrete operations*, occurring around seven to eleven years of age. Finally somewhere around twelve years of age, a person reaches the stage of *formal operations*. Now we find future thinking, critical and alternative thinking, creative problem solving, idealism, and comprehension of metaphors.

While Piaget's theory uses age only as a guide, not as immutable delineations of norms of behavior, it should be noted that he was not interested in accelerated development. Others were. While not disputing the sequential nature of the stage theory, Webb (1974) concluded that the rate of maturation to a new stage depended on IQ. High IQ children between six and eleven achieved maturation in a few months while normal IQ children took a year or two. While not bound to age limits, Piaget felt that the stages were developmental, proceeding sequentially one after the other. His framework allows for an understanding of the variability of learners, as it shows the differences that can be seen in the structure of thought and does not view levels of intelligence as just an acquisition of knowledge. He looked at what was observable with the children he studied, not what was possible or even preferable. Podgoretskaya (1979) believes that what was observed did not reflect age linked characteristics, but rather gave evidence for the types of problems that occur in the thinking process when its development is left to chance. His thesis is that such defects can occur at any age if thinking is allowed to develop spontaneously and unsupported by a responsive environment.

Development of the Metaphoric Mind   It has been pointed out that what Piaget is really describing is the development of only one of our mind styles, the linear-logical style of the left hemisphere (Samples, 1977). Also that the descriptors he uses are valid only in cultures that have placed their emphasis on linear-logical thought processes. What of our other mind, the metaphoric, intuitive, holistic mind valued by Einstein, Bruner, Da Vinci, Salk, and a myriad of other creative thinkers who have changed our culture? Samples suggests a hierarchy of metaphoric modes within which students at any age have the ability to perform. Through use of these modes students were found to develop more comfort and ability in exploring concepts, ideas, and processes in rational ways. The first, the Symbolic Metaphor Mode, exists when either an abstract or visual symbol is substituted for an object, process, or condition. By making the visual symbolism available, understanding can be achieved even by those who are not as adept at deriving meaning from abstract symbolism; that is, by drawing or sculpting an idea, one may understand the meaning and express it through the written word.

Next, the Synergic Comparative Mode, when "two or more objects, processes or conditions are compared in such a way that the both are synthesized into a greater whole as a result of the comparison" (Samples, 1977, p. 690) occurs. Here lie the roots of holistic cyclic thought, the true beginnings of the power of the other mind. While the linear-logical mind would view by seeing the differences, the holistic mind views by seeing the connections allowing an extension or expansion of the original idea. "The petal of the flower looked like white velvet" gives you two unlike objects that serve, by the connection, to extend and enhance your view of the flower.

The Integrative Metaphoric Mode exists when the person experiences objects, processes, or conditions directly with all of their physical and psychic being. This would require the involvement of all of the functions of the human being, feelings, rational thinking, intuitive thinking, and physical sensing in the learning process.

This is what we later will refer to as Integrative Education, engaging total brain function as we learn.

Finally, the Inventive Metaphoric Mode begins at any time an individual creates a new level of awareness or knowing through a self-initiated exploration of objects, processes, or conditions. Samples emphasizes the process of creating. This is to the metaphoric modes of intelligence what discovering is to the linear-logical modes.

While the growth of the metaphoric, holistic mind is available throughout our life space—and, when used, can be shown to result in higher feelings of self-confidence, self-esteem, and compassion; a wider exploration of traditional content and skills; and higher levels of creative invention—current teaching strategies, environments, and curriculum neglect its use. Allowed at the beginning stages of the young child's learning experiences, the acceptance of this mind style disappears as we progress in school. Samples assures us that though his data show this disappearance, he and his colleagues have found that the metaphoric mind does not disappear. In my work I too have found that the children understand and respond to any encouragement to use the other way of knowing. Both parents and teachers can, by valuing this equally important part of each of us and by accepting, encouraging, and creating spaces for its use, allow the development of both mind styles, optimizing the actualization of our fullest potential.

The Preschool Curriculum

During this time of rapid growth for the young child it is important that all modes of learning be nurtured. Many of the characteristics of giftedness may already be evident and should be supported. Throughout this chapter we have looked at how we might optimize growth for our children, and the results of that rich interaction now begin to be evident. Rather than just identifying giftedness, the activities of the years prior to and including this period can be said to produce giftedness.

Curriculum for all preschool children must be rich in variety and stimulating in process. For those who are developing faster and who show higher levels of intelligence, such variety and stimulation is even more necessary. In their experiences we can include more activities allowing self-direction, exposure to more abstract concepts, and more involvement with the tools and skills for operating in the areas of reading, mathematics, science, research, art, music, writing, and the world in which they live. A home or classroom that seeks to optimize growth in young children will incorporate the same elements found in chapter 6 for organizing responsive, individualized learning environments. The differences will be in timing, strategies, and the amount of support needed. Decentralization is appropriate with centers or areas for academic and artistic activities. Choice making can be developed and used by children as young as two and gives the child a sense of competency and achievement, as it does to children further along in their learning. Even very young children can learn to manage their own choice of centers or areas in which to participate, their use of time, and other experiences leading them toward becoming independent learners—such as voluntary adherence to limits on numbers of children who can participate in a given center at a certain time, signals as to when and where activities are most appropriate, etc. It takes more complex planning and structuring to allow the necessary freedom and independence that develops high levels of interaction for young children and ultimately produces higher levels of intelli-

Curriculum for preschool children must be rich in variety and stimulating in process.

gence. However, the results are so valuable and so important to the future of the child that any parent or teacher would be well advised to expend this extra effort.

Language patterns and vocabulary can be very important teaching tools. The choice of words can make a child feel suppressed and helpless or supported and competent. For instance, in situations where the child is involved in an activity that is not allowed, the parent or teacher could use language allowing an alternative choice, e.g., "You can't do this, but you can do this," directing the child to a more appropriate activity. This language produces choice and allows the child to begin to develop alternative thinking skills. Set up situations where the child can be invited to explore and test hypotheses. When a child encounters an obstacle, ask "How can we do that?" If the child encounters something too risky or too scary, suggest "I'll go with you and then you can go all the way through that tunnel. Next time you can do it yourself if you want to." Be sure to use lots of verbal reminders of the child's worth just for being who he or she is, not just when something was done well. As you pass by, say briefly "I really like you." Do be sure that you also share your negative human feelings clearly. Children notice when things are unpleasant. It would be better to state your feeling, such as "What you are doing makes me angry," rather than leaving to chance the interpretation of what is happening. You then have given them the opportunity to change and they need not misinterpret your feelings into a negative concept of themselves. Always with gifted children use lots of humor; they delight in it.

The curriculum for gifted young children must play to the ages and stages of growth by always stretching just a bit beyond the normative expectations. Viewing each stage of development as an exciting opportunity for growth will allow a far more appropriate learning situation, e.g., the "terrible twos" are seen as a time for testing the limits, for risk taking; the threes begin real involvement with opportunities to build social skills; the fours see the child move from me to others; and the fives give endless possibilities for developing independence. A responsive environment allows the organic needs of the child to be met.

When selecting a preschool for their gifted children, parents can improve the possibility of choosing an appropriate program by carefully observing the following:

1. *The teacher* interacting with the children: Do the teachers genuinely like children? Are they being authentic, showing their real feelings, letting the children know them as people? The research on programs for young children indicates that no one program can be shown to be the best. All models investigated were effective when teachers were committed to the model and dedicated to the children (Roedell, Jackson, and Robinson, 1980).
2. *The environment:* Is it nourishing for children? Is it pretty, colorful, thoughtfully organized? Is it flexible, pleasant, and inviting? Does the environment change to stay interesting? The involved, caring parent or teacher who is providing ways that children can learn things that both they and the children find interesting produces the most effective environment for learning.
3. *The activities:* Are there lots of different activities at different levels of difficulty? Are there activities to challenge and stretch the child's thinking? feelings? intuition? physical sensing? Can the children go as far as they want with an activity? Are there lots of skills for the child to master creatively?

Academic subjects can be introduced in an integrative way, that is by combining cognition with feeling, physical sensing, and intuition, as will be described for older children in chapter 6. The following are two examples:

Science

Purpose: To develop the concept of action/reaction

Time involved: Little children will enjoy this activity for long periods of time. As with all activities in a preschool curriculum, the time must be flexible and responsive to the interest of the child.

Material needed: Balloons, one round and one elongated balloon for each child; twenty to thirty feet of string for each child; masking tape; a straw for each child.

Organizational pattern: One or a small group with the teacher

Teaching function: Demonstrator, facilitator

Procedure: Blow up the round balloon and explain how every action has reaction, demonstrate by showing that as the air comes out of the back of the balloon the balloon moves forward. Discuss rockets and how this same principle allows them to fly. Ask the children to close their eyes and see a rocket taking off and flying. Now attach one end of the string to a wall with masking tape while the child holds the other end. Blow up one elongated balloon and attach a straw to the side with masking tape. Run the string through the straw, pointing the balloon toward the wall. Have the child hold the end of the blown up balloon, which is now attached to the string running through the straw. Count down as when a rocket takes off. At blast off the child releases the open end of the balloon and it jets toward the wall along the string (figure 2.1).

Figure 2.1.   Balloon Rocket

Evaluation: Discuss the understanding of the concept action/reaction. Do other things work that way?

Reading

Purpose: To introduce letters and their sounds to children through a game

Time involved: Flexible: Some children will want to play for an hour or more and repeat the activity again and again.

Materials needed: Pencil or small rod with small horseshoe magnet attached by string. Construction paper cutouts of fish with paper clips attached. Print *A,a, B,b, C,c, D,d, E,e, F,f* on fish. Place them in shallow box. (figure 2.2)

Procedure: Child uses pole with magnet to "catch" paper-clipped fish. If he or she can name the letter (or make the sound, if you are using it for sound learning), the child may keep it; if not, it must be thrown back to be caught later.

Figure 2.2.   Fishing Apparatus.

Other caregiver activities that can be used either at home or at school are presented in Table 2.4.

Development of Giftedness and Talents

From an important study Bloom (1982; Pines, 1982) reports results that validate and extend the thesis of Pressey (1964) mentioned at the beginning of this chapter; that giftedness and high levels of talent are created. By interviewing individuals who had attained "world class" status in a variety of fields, their parents and their teachers, the conditions and determinants of their success were elicited. Just as Pressey sug-

Table 2.4. Preschool Curriculum

Caregiver Activities	Because
Organize an environment that allows choice and a high degree of variety and novelty. Organize so that the child can follow through on an activity to its conclusion, e.g., when writing a story, illustrate it and bind into a book; when planting seeds, water and care for plant as it grows.	It helps develop an independent autonomous learner, inner locus of control, intellectual stimulation, developing sense of responsibility.
Centers or areas where children can discover basic concepts, e.g., in math, science, etc.; specific school skills, e.g., writing, hole punching, use of ruler; and develop awareness of themselves.	They provide intellectual stimulation, cognitive skill, problem-solving abilities.
Provide inspiration and materials for children to write their own books and poems, with the help of an encouraging adult who will write as the story/poem is dictated.	This is useful in developing creativity, basic reading skills, language experience, developing intuitive skills.
Provide a variety of art materials, e.g., glue, colored paper, scissors, beans, bits of yarn, ribbon, scraps of wood, crayons, large sized paper, marking pens, water paints, clay, etc.; materials that will stretch them beyond where they have gone, e.g., "Find something inside the clay and let it come out with your hands."	This facilitates developing creativity, sensory skills, artistic and intuitive abilities.
Provide sharing times and social outings with other children; organize group games and cooperative activities. Allow opportunities to settle differences with other children, guiding only when necessary.	Research shows that young children can increase their cooperative social interactions, ability to overcome obstacles and to talk with peers, and decrease negative behavior (Roedell, Jackson, and Robinson, 1980). This allows children to grow in social problem solving.
Make use of the community and the surrounding areas for field trips and explores.	This develops a sense of competency, autonomy, deeper understanding and appreciation of nature.
Provide opportunities to establish a relationship with a significant adult friend.	This allows children to get another point of view on issues; acquaints them with other interests, language patterns, and vocabulary; allows them to be guided and listened to when they feel parents cannot.

gested, these gifts and talents could not have been actualized without the encouragement, support, and environmental opportunities provided by the parents and teachers. Genius indeed cannot "will out" in spite of circumstances, but must be developed, perhaps even created. Whatever the original "gifts," "without extremely favorable supporting and teaching circumstances over more than a decade they would not have been likely to reach the levels of attainment for which they were selected. . . . The most striking finding in talent development is the very active role of the family, selected teachers, and sometimes the peer group in supporting, encouraging, teaching, and training the individual at each of the major stages in his or her development" (p. 511).

As we have seen, and Bloom confirms, data show that most human beings are born with enormous potential. However, three characteristics seem to be necessary to achieve at high levels: unusual willingness to do great amounts of work, a determination to do one's best at all cost, and the ability to learn rapidly. These traits appear to emerge from the early socialization and attitudes in the home and the early training provided by teachers. The evidence that learning rates can be altered by appropriate educational and environmental conditions suggests that very favorable learning conditions provided in the early years can markedly influence learning rate. As the rate of learning is an expression of advanced and accelerated brain development, this evidence relates to our discussion of developing intelligence.

Of major interest is the power of the parents' belief in the child. If the parents believe that a particular child has special ability they will hold different expectancies, allow more opportunities to develop the ability, and treat this child differently. Even if, in fact, the child was not significantly more able than others in the family these beliefs and expectations and what they caused parents, teachers, and the child to do, Bloom found, seem most important to the early and resulting later development of the given ability in reaching an outstanding level. Only one child in each family tended to be chosen for exceptional development in a given ability—not necessarily the most able, but the one with the greatest desire to excel.

It was further discovered that it is "the values and interests of the parents that will determine which traits and qualities will be given great encouragement and further cultivation and which traits and qualities will be ignored" (p. 520). Contrary to previously held belief, Bloom found that the children received opportunities and encouragement first and only later were seen to possess special ability. The following factors seem to be most important in the identification and development of special ability:

Parents who greatly value and enjoy either music, arts, sports, or intellectual activity
    and view it as a natural part of life so that the child learns to speak its language
Parents who believe in the work ethic
A first teacher who is warm and loving, who makes lessons seem like games, instructs on a one-to-one basis, and includes parental interest
A second teacher who emphasizes skills and self-discipline and continues to individualize instruction
Access to a master teacher who opens doors

From this study we find more evidence for the importance of early learning, for opportunities and encouragement to be available. It seems even more evident that children develop their ability because of instruction and attention, not the other way around.

It should be noted that parents are natural teachers. No one else can equal their knowledge of the child, their concerns and responsiveness. With a few learning tools at their disposal, parents can play a major part in their child's early education. Attitude lends the most important ingredient to any learning situation. The child must approach learning with a spirit of adventure and playfulness. Learning should be a joy, not a punishment; a favor, not a duty. Parents can ensure this attitude if they allow the child's natural curiosity to guide the task. Falbo and Cooper (1980) found that the amount of time parents spend playing with their preschoolers is directly related to an increase in verbal intelligence test scores. Parents should view teaching as a pleasure to be shared with their child. Parents need not worry if their child seems reluctant to learn at any given moment. Given opportunities by parents flexible to a variety of responses, chances are that the child will learn faster than expected. If not, the child must be allowed to set the learning pace. Most importantly, remember to foster the excitement of learning. Parents can be assured that—

young children are capable of a great deal of learning,
their children will enjoy learning,
they can be their child's most responsive teacher,
they will enjoy sharing this experience with their child.

Among the many books to guide parents toward more specific activities to stimulate and enrich their child's environment, I would suggest Beadle, 1970; Beck, 1967; Cass-Beggs, 1978; Domain, 1964; Ellis and Scholtz, 1978; Engelmann and Engelmann, 1966; Fine, 1964; Goldstein-Jackson, 1978; Gordon, 1970; Hendricks, 1979; Lehane, 1976, 1979; Levy, 1975; Marzollo and Lloyd, 1972; Painter, 1971; Weiss, 1972; White, 1975, 1980; and White and Watts, 1973; Yarrow et al., 1973.

The gifted may be curious and interested in abstractions.

Characteristics of Gifted Learners

Now that we have discussed giftedness and intelligence and how the interaction of heredity, environment, and the uniqueness of the child develop such high levels of ability, let us look at the demands such development may make on the gifted learner.

As a human being develops higher levels of functioning, many unique patterns and traits emerge. For that reason, the education of groups of gifted individuals is not an easy task. They are not a homogeneous group. The more gifted a person becomes, the more unique that person may appear. There are, however, many characteristics that often recur in groups of gifted individuals. While an individual may not exhibit all of these characteristics, knowledge of all the characteristics may avail our attempts to optimize learning environments and understand the demands higher levels of intelligence make on individuals within our society. To show more clearly examples of these characteristics, their resulting needs, and concomitant problems, we borrow from an organization developed by Hagen and Clark (1977).

As we look more closely at the characteristics and needs of gifted learners, we should mention a common problem in identifying these children. Teachers often attribute a high achiever with giftedness. While there can be no certainty as to clear distinction in every instance, gifted children usually exhibit the ability to generalize, to work comfortably with abstract ideas, and to synthesize diverse relationships to a far higher degree. The high achiever generally functions better with knowledge and comprehension-level learning. While high achievers get good grades and accomplish much, they lack the range and diversity of the gifted. Some need only increased opportunity; others become frustrated by more complex opportunities. The responsive environment is the teacher's best guide. This chapter has discussed in detail the responsive environment. Briefly, it is an environment rich in opportunities for interaction where children can participate in their own learning, select the types of inquiry most appropriate for their learning style and pace, and have additional experiences available ahead of their observed need.

Tables 2.5–2.9 are organized into cognitive (thinking, table 2.5), affective (feeling, table 2.6), physical (sensation, table 2.7), intuitive (table 2.8), and societal (table 2.9), closely approximating the functions available in the human brain. With each characteristic, there is a delineation of possible concomitant problems. This format is an extension of the work of Seagoe (1974) and incorporates her suggestions.

Throughout this chapter we have seen evidence of the importance of optimizing the early learning periods if we are to actualize a child's potential. It seems increasingly clear that the roots of intelligence can be found not only in the genetic endowment of the individual but also within the earlier experiences the individual has with the environment. It is doubtful that even the finest, most richly endowed brain can function at its optimum without an equally enriched environment.

Researchers are finding clues to competent functioning in the prenatal, perinatal, and postnatal periods of human development. Some feel parenting for optimal development must include the health and living habits of the mother-to-be even prior to conception. We can no longer ignore the critical periods for development throughout the fetal period and the early years of life. The use of critical and sensitive periods for learning may make the difference between average and gifted per-

Table 2.5.   Differential Cognitive (Thinking) Characteristics of the Gifted.

Cognitive development rests on the analysis, integration, and evaluation of a vast quantity of experiences of the environment and understandings of those experiences. Educational programs should provide for an array of such experiences and encourage the processes of understanding, analyzing, organizing, integrating, and evaluating. Qualitatively different planning for the gifted implies recognition of the ways in which their differential cognitive characteristics affect this process.

Differentiating Characteristics	Examples of Related Needs	Possible Concomitant Problems
Extraordinary quantity of information, unusual retentiveness	To be exposed to new and challenging information of the environment and the culture, including aesthetic, economic, political, educational, and social aspects; to acquire early mastery of foundation skills	Boredom with regular curriculum; impatience with "waiting for the group"
Advanced comprehension	Access to challenging curriculum and intellectual peers	Poor interpersonal relationships with less able children of the same age; adults considering children "sassy" or "smart alec;" a dislike for repetition of already understood concepts
Unusually varied interests and curiosity	To be exposed to varied subjects and concerns; to be allowed to pursue individual ideas as far as interest takes them	Difficulty in conforming to group tasks; overextending energy levels, taking on too many projects at one time
High level of language development	To encounter uses for increasingly difficult vocabulary and concepts	Perceived as a "show off" by children of the same age
High level of verbal ability	To share ideas verbally in depth	Dominate discussions with information and questions deemed negative by teachers and fellow students; use of verbalism to avoid difficult thinking tasks

Table 2.5. Differential Cognitive (Thinking) Characteristics of the Gifted. *(continued)*

Differentiating Characteristics	Examples of Related Needs	Possible Concomitant Problems
Unusual capacity for processing information	To be exposed to ideas at many levels and in large variety	Resents being interrupted; perceived as too serious; dislike for routine and drill
Accelerated pace of thought processes	To be exposed to ideas at rates appropriate to individual pace of learning	Frustration with inactivity and absence of progress
Flexible thought processes	To be allowed to solve problems in diverse ways	Seen as disruptive and disrespectful to authority and tradition
Comprehensive synthesis	To be allowed a longer incubation time for ideas	Frustration with demands for deadlines and for completion of each level prior to starting new inquiry
Early ability to delay closure	To be allowed to pursue ideas and integrate new ideas without forced closure or products demanded	If products are demanded as proof of learning, will refuse to pursue an otherwise interesting subject or line of inquiry
Heightened capacity for seeing unusual and diverse relationships	To mess around with varieties of materials and ideas	Frustration at being considered "off the subject" or irrelevant in pursuing inquiry in areas other than subject being considered; considered odd or weird by others
Ability to generate original ideas and solutions	To build skills in problem solving and productive thinking; opportunity to contribute to solution to meaningful problems	Difficulty with rigid conformity; may be penalized for not following directions; may deal with rejection by becoming rebellious

Table 2.5. Differential Cognitive (Thinking) Characteristics of the Gifted. (*continued*)

Differentiating Characteristics	Examples of Related Needs	Possible Concomitant Problems
Early differential patterns for thought processing (e.g., thinking in alternatives, abstract terms, sensing consequences, making generalizations)	To be exposed to alternatives, abstractions, consequences of choices, and opportunities for drawing generalizations and testing them	Rejection or omission of detail; questions generalizations of others, which may be perceived as disrespectful behavior
Early ability to use and form conceptual frameworks	To use and to design conceptual frameworks in information gathering and problem solving; to seek order and consistency; to develop a tolerance for ambiguity	Frustration with inability of others to understand or appreciate original organizations or insights; personally devised systems or structure may conflict with procedures of systems later taught
An evaluative approach to themselves and others	To be exposed to individuals of varying ability and talent, and to varying ways of seeing and solving problems; to set realistic, achievable short-term goals; to develop skills in data evaluation and decision making	Perceived by others as elitist, conceited, superior, too critical; may become discouraged from self-criticism, can inhibit attempting new areas if fear of failure is too great; seen by others as too demanding, compulsive; can affect interpersonal relationships as others fail to live up to standards set by gifted individual; intolerant of stupidity
Persistent, goal-directed behavior	To pursue inquiries beyond allotted time spans, to set and evaluate priorities	Perceived as stubborn, willful, uncooperative

Table 2.6.   Differential Affective (Feeling) Characteristics of the Gifted.

High levels of cognitive development do not necessarily imply high levels of affective development. The same heightened sensitivities that underlie gifted intelligence can contribute to an accumulation of information about emotions that the student needs to process. The affect-based information comes from sources within and without the child. Gifted children need to learn that their cognitive powers applied to this material will help them to make sense of their world. Their educational program must provide opportunities to bring emotional knowledge and assumptions to awareness, and to apply verbal ability and inquiry skills in the service of affective development.

The early appearance of social conscience that often characterizes gifted children signals an earlier need for development of a value structure and for the opportunity to translate values into social action. This can occur in the context of the society of the classroom and should then be extended into the larger world, as appropriate to the child's increasing competence and widening concerns.

Differentiating Characteristics	Examples of Related Needs	Possible Concomitant Problems
Large accumulation of information about emotions that has not been brought to awareness	To process cognitively the emotional meaning of experience, to name one's own emotions, to identify one's own and others' perceptual filters and defense systems, to expand and clarify awareness of the physical environment, to clarify awareness of the needs and feelings of others	Information misinterpreted affecting the individual negatively
Unusual sensitivity to the expectations and feelings of others	To learn to clarify the feelings and expectations of others	Unusually vulnerable to criticism of others, high level of need for success and recognition
Keen sense of humor—may be gentle or hostile	To learn how behaviors affect the feelings and behaviors of others	Use of humor for critical attack upon others resulting in damage to interpersonal relationships
Heightened self-awareness, accompanied by feelings of being different	To learn to assert own needs and feelings nondefensively, to share self with others, for self-clarification	Isolate self, resulting in being considered aloof, feeling rejected; perceive difference as a negative attribute resulting in low self-esteem and inhibited growth emotionally and socially

Table 2.6.   Differential Affective (Feeling) Characteristics of the Gifted. *(continued)*

Differentiating Characteristics	Examples of Related Needs	Possible Concomitant Problems
Idealism and sense of justice, which appear at an early age	To transcend negative reactions by finding values to which he or she can be committed	Attempt unrealistic reforms and goals with resulting intense frustration (Suicides result from intense depression over issues of this nature.)
Earlier development of an inner locus of control and satisfaction	To clarify personal priorities among conflicting values To confront and interact with the value system of others	Difficulty conforming; reject external validation and choose to live by personal values that may be seen as a challenge to authority or tradition
Unusual emotional depth and intensity	To find purpose and direction from personal value system To translate commitment into action in daily life	Unusual vulnerability; problem focusing on realistic goals for life's work
High expectations of self and others, often leading to high levels of frustration with self, others, and situations Perfectionism	To learn to set realistic goals and to accept setbacks as part of the learning process To hear others express their growth in acceptance of self	Discouragement and frustration from high levels of self-criticism; problems maintaining good interpersonal relations as others fail to maintain high standards imposed by gifted individual; immobilization of action due to high levels of frustration resulting from situations that do not meet expectations of excellence
Strong need for consistency between abstract values and personal actions	To find a vocation that provides opportunity for actualization of student's personal value system, as well as an avenue for his or her talents and abilities	Frustration with self and others leading to inhibited actualization of self and interpersonal relationships
Advanced levels of moral judgment	To receive validation for nonaverage morality	Intolerance of and lack of understanding from peer group, leading to rejection and possible isolation

Table 2.7. Differential Physical (Sensation) Characteristics of the Gifted.

People of highly developed intellectual ability may be unusually vulnerable to a characteristic "Cartesian split" between thinking and being; a lack of integration between mind and body. During school years, when the gifted student is experiencing large discrepancies between physical and intellectual development, the school may be unintentionally encouraging the student to avoid physical activity. If a child's intellectual peers are physically more advanced so as to make him or her feel physically inadequate, while physical peers are less intellectually stimulating and not within his or her friendship group, the usual competitive playground games may be neither inviting nor satisfying to the gifted child. If the physical development of the gifted child is to be encouraged, programs should provide experiences that develop integration between mind and body in children with nonnormative development patterns.

Differentiating Characteristics	Examples of Related Needs	Possible Concomitant Problems
Unusual quantity of input from the environment through a heightened sensory awareness	To engage in activities that will allow integration and assimilation of sensory data	Attention moving diffusely toward many areas of interest; overexpenditure of energy due to lack of integration; seeming disconnectedness
Unusual discrepancy between physical and intellectual development	To appreciate their physical capacities	Result in gifted adults who function with a mind/body dichotomy; gifted children who are only comfortable expressing themselves in mental activity, resulting in a limited development both physically and mentally
Low tolerance for the lag between their standards and their athletic skills	To discover physical activities as a source of pleasure; to find satisfaction in small increments of improvement; to engage in noncompetitive physical activities	Refuse to take part in any activities where they do not excel; limiting their experience with otherwise pleasurable, constructive physical activities
"Cartesian split"—can include neglect of physical well-being and avoidance of physical activity	To engage in activities leading to mind/body integration; to develop a commitment to own physical well-being; to extend this concern to the social and political realm	Detrimental to full mental and physical health, inhibiting to the development of potential for the individual

Table 2.8. Differential Intuitive Characteristics of the Gifted.

This area of the human experience is involved in initiating or insightful acts and in creative activity. While this is the least well-defined area of human endeavor, it is probably the area that promises the most for the continuance and fulfillment of humankind. All other areas provide support for and are supported by this area of function. As each area evolves to high levels, more of the intuitive and creative are available.

Differentiating Characteristics	Examples of Related Needs	Possible Concomitant Problems
Early involvement and concern for intuitive knowing and metaphysical ideas and phenomena	Opportunities to engage in meaningful dialogue with philosophers and others concerned with these ideas; to become aware of own intuitive energy and ability; guidance in developing and using intuitive energy and ability	Ridiculed by peers; not taken seriously by elders; considered weird or strange
Open to experiences in this area; will experiment with psychic and metaphysical phenomena	Guidance in becoming familiar with, analyzing, and evaluating such phenomena; should be provided a historical approach	Can become narrowly focused toward ungrounded belief systems
Creativity apparent in all areas of endeavor	Guidance in evaluating appropriate uses of creative efforts; encouragement for continued development of creative abilities	Seen as deviant; becomes bored with more mundane tasks; may be viewed as troublemaker

Table 2.9.   Differential Societal Characteristics of the Gifted.

Society has unique needs for the services of unique individuals. While we would not wish that education for the gifted focus on societal needs at the expense of the needs of these individuals, neither can education of the gifted disregard the importance of their mature social roles. Gifted students need direction in exploring all the opportunities society has to offer them and the ways of contributing what they have to offer to society. They need conceptual frameworks to organize their experience of society (e.g., Maslow's (1968) hierarchy of needs), and they need opportunities to develop those skills that will make it possible for them to affect society. Educational programs should provide for the options, conceptual frameworks, and skills that will underlie effective social involvement of gifted students.

Differentiating Characteristics	Examples of Related Needs	Possible Concomitant Problems
Differential Societal Characteristics of the Gifted		
Strongly motivated by self-actualization needs	Opportunities to follow divergent paths, pursue strong interests, help in understanding the demands of self-actualization	Frustration of not feeling challenged; loss of unrealized talents
Advanced cognitive and affective capacity for conceptualizing and solving societal problems	Encounters with social problems, awareness of the complexity of problems facing society, conceptual frameworks for problem-solving procedures	Tendency for "quick" solutions not taking into account the complexity of the problem; young age of gifted person often makes usable alternatives suspect; older, more experienced decision makers may not take the gifted person seriously.

Table 2.9. Differential Societal Characteristics of the Gifted. (*continued*)

Differentiating Characteristics	Examples of Related Needs	Possible Concomitant Problems
Differential Social Expectations for the Gifted		
Leadership	Understanding of various leadership steps and practice in leadership skills	Lack of opportunity to use this ability constructively may result in its disappearance from child's repertoire or its being turned into a negative characteristic, e.g., gang leadership.
Solutions to social and environmental problems	Meaningful involvement in real problems	Loss to society if these traits are not allowed to develop with guidance and opportunity for meaningful involvement
Involvement with the meta-needs of society (e.g., justice, beauty, truth)	Exploration of the highest levels of human thought; application of this knowledge to today's problems	

formance. At the very least, we can use current information to guide our children toward becoming healthier, more intellectually able, more sensitive, and more motivated, self-directed learners. If each parent of each child were to use even what is now known about nurturing human bodies and minds, how very different our world would be. As a result of advanced and accelerated brain function, gifted individuals often exhibit many similar characteristics. Although no one individual would exhibit all or even the same cluster of these characteristics, they help us to understand gifted individuals and the demands high levels of intelligence make upon them better. There is much yet to learn. Many questions remain unanswered, but already we can change our world; we can create a miracle. The amazing thing is we need not wait—we already know how.

CHAPTER THREE

Growing Up Gifted

Within this chapter the reader can find

- a discussion of social-emotional development and its relationship to the gifted.
- a view of the importance of self-concept.
- a discussion of moral development and the developing personality.
- a discussion of attitudes as they relate to the growth of gifted children.
- ideas for encouraging integrative growth of gifted individuals in the home and in the school and for providing for the cooperative involvement of both.

The characteristic most readily identifiable in gifted children, varying both in kind and degree, is sensitivity. Whether the sensitivity is to one or more particular areas of learning, sensitivity to discovering or solving problems, or sensitivity to the feelings of one's fellow man, it is so much a characteristic of giftedness that it can almost be said that the two terms are synonymous.

Walter B. Barbe

In order to develop our potential intellectual abilities, we must understand and nurture our cognitive, social-emotional, physical, and intuitive selves. A limit to any one function limits all functioning. To approach maximum intellectual capacity, one's cognitive, social-emotional, physical, and intuitive development must be highly operable and well-integrated.

Social-Emotional Development and Giftedness

Children who, by fortunate circumstances, develop more of their potential seem to meet a different set of social and emotional consequences than will the more typical child. In the 1920s, people assumed that these children were emotionally borderline neurotics or even psychotics (Terman, 1925). Their advanced performance was viewed with great suspicion. A child prodigy was thought to become an adult imbecile. Parents who found their preschoolers reading would discourage such activities and encourage "playing with little friends" as an antidote. The fear that a neighbor, or worse yet a teacher, would discover precocious behavior in their child led many parents to adopt drastic and punitive actions when they observed any advanced behavior. Although attitudes have changed, some of this type of response to advanced development still lingers.

In that climate of suspicion and rejection of advanced development, Terman (1925) began his study at Stanford mentioned in chapter 1. Terman collected data for thirty-five years on the emotional and social characteristics of children he identified as gifted. They are now adults, and researchers still collect data on them. What Terman found did not support the prevalent view of his day. The majority of children in his 140+ IQ group were physically more attractive than the more typical children. Later studies have linked this finding to better nutrition among children of his population and to the early experiences of most optimally developing children (Laycock and Caylor, 1964). Far from being the misfits and drudges people called them, the gifted youngsters in his population became leaders, organizers, football captains, and class officers. They enjoyed a significantly greater popularity, and their classmates viewed them positively. They showed marked superiority in moral attitudes, as measured by tests of character. Terman found that their moral judgment developed earlier than that of the average population. These children seemed well-rounded and achieved well in most school subjects. Later data showed this population to be socially more able to adjust. They suffered less as adults from social problems such as divorce, alcoholism, and suicide than the average population. This group also had less ill health, insanity, and a lower mortality rate than the average population (Terman and Oden, 1947).

Terman's group not only completed higher levels of schooling in larger numbers than the typical population, they also received more honors and awards while doing so. Professional accomplishments were measured only among the men, as women of that time period were not encouraged to seek careers. This gifted group had an outstanding record of achievement and made a far higher than average number of contributions to society. While the limitations of this study must be noted as we view the accomplishments of the group (e.g., the overloading of higher socioeconomic-level participants), we must recognize it as a major accomplishment in the field of gifted education. As Terman himself remarked, "I take some pride in the fact that not one of the major conclusions we drew in the early 1920s regarding the traits that are typical of gifted children has been overthrown in the three decades since then" (Terman, 1954, p. 223). While his profile of the gifted child has been expanded as we study broader based populations, his statement remains essentially true.

It is as difficult to speak of the social-emotional characteristics of gifted individuals as of any other of the characteristics we have looked at before. Discussions of generalizations will bring out characteristics often found in the population, but all are seldom applicable to any one gifted individual. For the most part, given the opportunity for healthy development, the social-emotional adjustment of gifted children tends to proceed better than among the more typical population. Hollingworth (1926) found a strong positive correlation between intelligence and the desirable traits of character and temperament. Boehm's (1962) study of the development of moral judgment shows that brighter middle- and working-class children make moral judgments earlier; bright middle-class children show the most advanced development. Newland (1976) warns us to assure the gifted that we are concerned with their social interaction *with* others, not just their social adjustment *to* others.

In compiling the studies of the social-emotional characteristics of gifted children, a very positive profile emerges:

> Young gifted children, when compared with chronological peers, feel more comfortable with themselves and with their interpersonal relationships. They perceive themselves to have greater personal freedom than do their average classmates. They value cooperative and democratic forms of interaction though they are less willing to compromise. They report more positive feelings regarding themselves and others (Lehman and Erdwins, 1981).

> Gifted children undergo better emotional adjustment than average children (Lightfoot, 1951; Mensch, 1950; Ramaseshan, 1957), although some studies indicate a closer relationship to socioeconomic differences than to intellectual differences.

> Bright children tend to be more independent and less conforming to peer opinions, more dominant, more forceful, and more competitive than typical learners (Lucito, 1964; Smith, 1965).

> The gifted often show leadership ability and become involved in community projects and concerns. Concern for universal problems and the welfare of others begins much earlier than with more typically developing children. The gifted also become aware of issues of morality and justice very early (Cox, 1926; Martinson, 1961). When involved in group leadership, they emphasize parliamentary procedure and minimize the use of more autocratic or laissez-faire approaches to governance (Cassel and Haddox, 1959).

> Gifted children seem to prefer their intellectual peers to their chronological age peers, resulting in a social preference for older children and adults. They lack interest in children of lower mental age, and they choose friends among children like themselves (Barbe, 1965; Mann, 1957).

Studies repeatedly show that the social status of bright children is high, and their classmates prefer them as companions. This factor seems to diminish at the secondary level, especially if other preferred factors of popularity, e.g., athletic ability, are not also evidenced (Coleman, 1962; Gallagher, 1958; Grace and Booth, 1958; Johnson and Kirk, 1950; Martyn, 1957; Miller, 1956; Purkey, 1966; Tannenbaum, 1962).

Although the very nature of being different in a society that does not value difference, even positive difference, brings more adjustment problems to the individual who is gifted, the very ability that creates the problem can supply the solution. A direct relationship between educational opportunities and adjustment does exist for the gifted (Martinson, 1972). Hunt (Pines, 1979) believes that when parents place demands on their children without giving them the means to meet such demands and when they fail to respect the child's intrinsic motivation their children can grow up to be very unhappy people. The gifted need help in learning to accept themselves as they are, to appreciate the ways in which they are both similar to and different from others. We must create opportunities for them to experience and value themselves as unique persons.

For the highly gifted child, the question of social adjustment takes on an added dimension. These few children have even more problems finding other children to whom they can relate. They become bored with school work, and they find fewer mental challenges within the school setting. Among groups of fellow students and teachers alike, those of lesser ability often display mediocrity and poor decision making. The gifted child ends up feeling disrespect for the judgment and actions of

More autonomous and self-directed, intrinsically motivated.

those in authority (Hollingworth, 1942). In special schools, highly gifted children experience fewer problems of adjustment by working with mental age peers (Gallagher and Crowder, 1957).

In a study conducted in the Chicago public schools (Leaverton and Herzog, 1979) regarding the overall adjustment of highly gifted children, it was found that those tested scored in the twenty-fifth percentile on Social Confidence and the thirty-second percentile on Self Acceptance subtests of the Self-Observation Scales. The conclusion from this study was that these children are in need of counseling to help them reach an adequate social and emotional adjustment. It was noted that very low priority had been given to the problems of this group, only 13 of the 113 tested had been seen by the school psychologist, and that referral was essentially for the purpose of testing only.

Origins of Social-Emotional Development

One of the first people to look at the healthy emotional development of human beings was the psychologist Abraham Maslow. Neither satisfied with the view that humans need control, nor content with the focus of most psychologists on pathology and remediation, Maslow (1971) believed that "well" individuals could become even healthier. He called the pursuit toward developing one's potential, *self-actualization.* Maslow identified a group of people whom he felt exhibited outstanding health, both physically and emotionally. He then collected data coalescing the characteristics they had in common. While the concept of *self* was far from new (in fact, many psychologists, philosophers, and researchers had referred to it), Maslow first listed identifying characteristics that could indicate a high level of development in the social-emotional domain.

From his work, Maslow (1971) identified the following traits among his examples of self-actualizers. He found them often:

1. More aware, more in touch, more perceptive, more realistically oriented.
2. More accepting of self, others, and the natural world.
3. Spontaneous, natural, authentic.
4. More autonomous and self-directed; largely free of the need to impress others or to be liked by everyone; resistant to conformity.
5. Intrinsically motivated; having meta-motivations (e.g., actualization of potentials, capacities, and talents; fulfillment of their life's mission or purpose; knowledge of self; self-acceptance; growth toward unity and synergy).
6. Seeking unity, oneness, integration, increased identification with humanity.
7. Working for a cause, devoted to a task or calling, viewing work and play as one.
8. Holding universal values (beauty, justice, truth) that are important to well-being. Working toward fulfillment of meta-needs (see #5, meta-motivations).
9. Capable of rich emotional reaction and freshness of appreciation.
10. Enjoying a high frequency of peak experiences (moments of highest happiness or fulfillment) and frequent mystic, natural, or cosmic experiences.
11. Capable of deep empathy and profound relationships with others; great ability to love and to enjoy sexuality.
12. Seeking privacy on occasion for periods of intense concentration.
13. Creative, less constricted in thought processes; using a sense of humor that is not hostile.

14. More democratic in character structure.
15. Continually wondering about life; treating each day as new.

Remarkably many of these characteristics can be identified with gifted children.

The Self-Concept

As work in the area of understanding and facilitating emotional growth developed, it soon became apparent that the concept of *self* was central. Researchers and practitioners such as Allport, Aspy, Brookover, Combs, Coopersmith, Jersild, Jourard, May, Maslow, Purkey, Rogers, and Snygg, to name but a few, have, within recent years, brought the concept of self back to psychology and education after abandonment for years by the behaviorists. (Contributions made by each person named are cited in the bibliography at the end of this book.) As interest in the concept of self increased, researchers found that the view of self determines achievement and enhances or limits the development of a person's potential.

The self may be defined as a complex and dynamic system of beliefs that individuals hold to be true about themselves. The concept is organized and can be modified (Purkey, 1970). It is, in part, constructed by us as a result of the interactions we have with others. The beliefs we have about ourselves literally determine our actions and our perceptions of the world and other people. We construct our own reality from these beliefs and often operate as though this is the only view possible (Combs and Snygg, 1959; May, 1967; Rogers, 1961). Growth of self-esteem makes the self-actualizing, integrated person possible. With that in mind, let us look at one especially unexpected finding. Gifted individuals often have lower self-concepts than their more typical peers (Trotter, 1971). One reason for this could be associated with the unusually high expectations the gifted have for themselves. Parents of gifted children, sometimes accused of "pushing" their children, are actually more concerned because their children seem to push themselves unrealistically. This pressure can be far more demanding than any external pressure. Parents and teachers need to be aware of self-expectation so that they can provide help for the gifted child in acquiring more realistic goals and more adequate coping behavior. The frustration of never living up to your own standards and expectations can be very self-defeating and interfere with mental and emotional growth.

Perfectionism, common among the gifted, can become compulsive behavior. At least as painful for the gifted individual is the way this characteristic may be used against others. Not only must gifted persons meet high standards and attain specified levels of performance, but often their acceptance of other people is based on the other person's ability to meet these standards. These expectations of others can seriously interfere with interpersonal relationships, the view the gifted have of their world, and, certainly, how other people view them. Unfortunately, unless someone helps gifted children to understand the dynamics of this problem and provides some alternative behaviors, it can continue throughout their lives.

If the quality of our life depends on our level of self-esteem, why do we find so many who lack adequate levels? As we have seen, the concept of self develops quite early. The following story will illustrate how information from the environment begins to affect the development of self-esteem.

A small boy about two years of age was sitting in a garden watching a little "bug" move slowly across the ground. The child was fascinated by the fact that the little thing had so many legs yet still was able to move without falling down. It wasn't long ago since he had a lot of trouble just managing to move around on his own two legs. He still got them mixed up occasionally. Now as he looked closely at the "bug," he noticed other strange things. There was hair all over its legs. And when he looked really closely, the "bug" really wasn't black. There were some purple and green and even some red and orange colorings on its body. The funny things that came out of its head were really neat, too.

Just then an amazing thing happened. The bug jumped. It jumped up onto a nearby leaf and, of all things, it spit threads out of its back end. The child had seen people spit, but never had he seen anything spit out of its back end. He watched this happen again and again. Then, to his disbelief, the thing walked on its *own spit!* Well, this was getting to be too much. Someone in the house was missing all of this. She was such a nice, fun person, and he loved her very much; yet she couldn't see and share it all with him. He knew she wouldn't be able to come out there into the garden because, actually, that was why he was there. Earlier she had suggested that he spend the morning outside because she had so much work to do. But, maybe . . . if he was very careful . . . he could get his hands together like a little cup and very carefully lift the bug up and carry it into the house. Oh, he wouldn't leave it there. He would bring it right back. And he wouldn't hurt it. He just wanted her to see it, just for a minute. Happily, he picked it up and started toward the house. The door to the kitchen was pretty hard to maneuver, especially when he had to use both hands to keep the bug safe, but he managed. As soon as he was inside he went right to his mother and held his treasure up high for her to see. What followed was not at all what he expected! As he left the house to return the "nasty, dirty, horrible, ugly spider" to its place in the garden, he thought about what she had just said. She must be right, she was always right; he knew that. Well if she was right, then he must be wrong.

Situations such as this give little people messages about their ideas, their competence, and their image of who they are very early in life. Even children from very nurturing homes find their lives filled with individuals, groups of people, and institutions ready and very willing to show them how they are wrong—to acquaint them, often forcibly, with the "right way."

Experiences such as this begin the formation of the concept of self. We are born with a center core—our essence—that is unique to us and is our real self. Tiny babies have no problem communicating to us the real needs or desires they feel. Expressing the real self is never a problem at the beginning. But, as the child in the garden discovered, it does not take long before other information causes us to doubt the messages from our center core. After enough dissonant information enters our awareness, a shell begins to build around this lovely, real center, and it is made up of all the "crummy" stuff we feel and believe about ourself after encounters such as these.

At some point, however, it becomes far too difficult to present ourselves to the world as the "crummy" person this shell leads us to believe we are. So at around ten to thirteen years of age, we begin to look around for another image to adopt. Often we completely forget the inner core of our real self and remember only the "crummy" shell as the definition of who we are. This second shell is formed from all of the nice and enjoyable things we find in other people. "There is someone who smiles a lot," we say; "people seem to like that so I'll smile a lot." "That person wears clothes a certain way that others find attractive; I can do that!" And the second shell builds. Soon we have an image to present to the world that is really great; our image is filled with nice ways of doing things and an agreeable appearance. Unfortunately this image of self is phony, and we know it. Now we must spend time and energy to keep other people far enough away that they do not see through our image. We are sure that if we let them in too close they will find out about the "real" person we are—the crummy, inept, incompetent person we know we really are—the person we know from the first shell. We now accept this shell as us. We have forgotten the beautiful, unique center core, our essence, our real self.

No matter how loving or how caring our family is, we all experience this shell-building phenomenon. Parents must find ways to recognize, accept, and support the center core. Educators can establish classrooms that allow self-discovery and support for individual and unique development. As growing people, we must keep in touch with this essence, accepting ourselves and allowing others to know us as the unique people we are. Work in this area shows us that, from the earliest days of our lives and as long as we live, our awareness and understanding of who we are will have the most effect on determining the quality and direction of our existence (Briggs, 1970; Satir, 1972).

A young woman around twenty years of age, who was in one of my first classes at the university, came up to me after we had been discussing the common characteristics and problems associated with being gifted. Hesitantly and with much confusion, she began to relate how she personally identified with the concepts we had been discussing. She stated that she knew she could not have been gifted because she remembered always having questions when everyone else had been satisfied with the information given. She was often told that she spent too much time investigating a subject when the class needed to move on. Other students often groaned audibly at her remarks or shared insights, a happening that she interpreted as proof of her stupidity. She had, since junior high school, changed most of these "bad" habits and had withdrawn into her own world of interests, accepting some B's, mostly C's, and occasional D's as appropriate representation of her ability as a student. She was, however, intrigued by a number of ideas we discussed that seemed personally applicable. After sharing her bewilderment later that evening, she decided to call her parents in Pennsylvania. At our next class session she shared the news that her parents had been told when she was in the third grade that she was highly gifted, around 165 IQ, but did not mention it to her on the advice of the school personnel. What started as the natural curiosity and expectations of a very bright mind, because of inadequate information about the reasons for her differences, turned into self-doubt and self-criticism to the point that her actual performance was inhibited and her growth arrested. She later used this information to reexamine the attitudes she had developed about herself and her abilities. She began to take more risks, to become more aggressive in pursuing academic and personal knowledge. She will never compensate for the lost years, but she made remarkable progress.

The first step toward intervening in low self-esteem is to acknowledge and clearly affirm what appears to be occurring. For example, the response to a frustrated attempt to complete perfectly a project still beyond the skill of the child would be simply, "You really would like that to be finished perfectly, wouldn't you?" or "It just isn't quite the way you want it yet, is it?" From statements such as these, if open communication exists with the child, a discussion of this need will usually follow.

Unrealistic self-expectations can result in another way of behaving. When others know that children are gifted, they may expect their work to have the aura of quality. Sometimes this results from a heterogeneously grouped regular classroom environment where, indeed, the work of the gifted child is outstanding compared to that of others in the room. In such cases, gifted children become used to being "best." They begin to consider everything they attempt to be exemplary. They may put forth small amounts of effort to achieve success. Many gifted children under these circumstances learn poor study habits, develop disrespect for efforts of others, and bluff their way through educational experiences using their advanced verbal ability or their facile and nimble brain for guessing answers and outcomes. They may seldom need to develop their skills or integrate their abilities. When finally challenged to academic thought or called upon for synthesis and evaluative processing, they become lost. Such sudden loss of power may cause them anger or frustration. Again, good communication of realistic expectations based on the assessed needs and abilities of the child can prevent this situation.

Children do not need to know their IQ score, but they must understand the behaviors associated with a high level of development. Becoming aware of the needs and responsibilities of giftedness will allow gifted children to examine their actions and the expectations they have of themselves and others. They will view their own progress more realistically and be able to clarify their beliefs and motives (Dubrowsky, 1968). These children must have adequate feedback on how others feel when their expectations are placed on them. Experience with the outcomes resulting from nonacceptance of those who do not meet personal standards is necessary for more effective and fulfilling interpersonal relations between the child and others.

Another contributor to the self-doubt often felt by the gifted individual is the lack of recognition from others. Parents and teachers often praise and show appreciation for the performance of those who are obviously just gaining skills, while they expect such performance from the gifted person. Because a person seems to accomplish a difficult task with ease or is able to do many things very well, the others in the environment soon come to expect such behavior and seldom show any appreciation for the quality of performance or effort involved. Without appropriate comments, it becomes difficult for gifted persons to develop a realistic idea of the quality of their contributions. The parent or teacher who only communicates constructive criticism can damage the child's developing self-concept. Sharing genuine appreciation or admiration for excellence is never inappropriate.

For gifted people, the pattern of shell building described earlier is intensified. Both self-imposed and external expectations are so much greater that the gifted often develop and maintain the second shell in desperation. Focus on the second shell may result in children who try to meet everyone's expectations and become perfect children, never allowing themselves to disappoint parents, teachers, or any other significant person knowingly. These children have an impossible task. They may try to meet their parents' needs and find that these differ from the teacher's needs; both may conflict with peer ideals and pressures. The gifted often attempt a trade-off with varying degrees of satisfaction for themselves. Barbe (1954) found that, in a society such as ours that does not value mental precocity, gifted children tend to take one of three patterns for adjusting to their world. They may choose to withdraw, to isolate themselves from the group. This occurs most often when the situation offers no challenge. Or they may become the class clown, showing off in an effort to be accepted and to gain favorable attention. This behavior may be carried to the point that teachers and peer group alike reject their attempts as being inappropriate or silly, or they may view the child as a nuisance. Finally, they may seek conformity through pleasing others, or the child may pretend not to know answers in an effort to seem like everyone else, to hide a superior intellect. This dangerous game of nonuse may result in loss of function; growth cannot be nurtured through this subterfuge. In this way, gifted children may find themselves becoming role players or what our educational system calls "underachievers." Chapter 8 delves into this problem further.

A child may choose to become what the parents value, then shift to perceived teacher values. How closely these are aligned will determine the energy expended. Then the child discovers peer values. A girl from a middle class family may discover that, if she wishes to be considered feminine and gain acceptance, the perfect papers required by parents and teachers become a liability. The challenge of inquiry into unusual subjects "for girls" becomes less rewarding. For boys, the masculine ideal of athletic competence may dictate refocus in that direction. Again, peer values may cause reordering of accepted parental and teacher values. In either case children may discover the use of giftedness to appear not at all gifted. As we have seen from the dynamic nature of intelligence, such denial and disuse can have the long-lasting consequences of diminished intellectual development.

Moral Development

For those who want to guide the development of the gifted child, moral development is another important concern. The level of intellectual power indicated by giftedness could be used against the person or society in general just as it could be used toward positive goals. Even if not used negatively, inadequate moral development would allow intellectual power to be inhibited by external validators, keeping gifted individuals from contributing their innovation and re-creation needed by society.

For over twenty years Lawrence Kohlberg of Harvard has studied, hypothesized, and tested his theories that seek to explain how we acquire moral character. His work is very important to gifted education, for he believes, as does Piaget (1932), that maturity in the intellectual realm influences a person's maturity in moral development (Kohlberg, 1964, 1972; Lickona, 1977).

Kohlberg uses the term *moral development* to indicate the level of internalization of principles that regulate one's conduct in human relations. The data that he has amassed came from longitudinal studies following fifty individuals for some twenty years. These studies of many cultures and countries are designed to show how moral development can be stimulated. He believes that all humans must pass though five stages sequentially, though not necessarily at the same age. He believes that the majority of adults in our culture never reach the fifth stage of principled morality. He clearly believes that we can establish moral climates and that these climates will most benefit development in the moral area. While some short-term benefits may arise from direct teaching of moral principles, the overall environment and interactions of the child within that environment have far more significance in later life.

Let us look briefly at the stages of moral development as Kohlberg identifies them. At stage one authority figures dictate the child's actions. Children follow moral rules to avoid punishment. During the first five to eight years of life, most children find this belief reinforced regularly.

At stage two the child gradually becomes aware of the idea of reciprocity: "If I do something for you, you will do something for me." There is a concern for rewards: "What's in it for me?" Throughout both these stages, which generally continue through the primary grades, the emphasis is on external control and on concrete consequences.

Stage three finds the child seeking to meet the expectations of others, being a "good" child. Being "nice" is now seen in a broader context. The ability to see situations from the position of other persons helps determine the action a child will take.

At stage four, this concern for others now encompasses more of society. The law, rules of the social system, and a desire to do one's duty gain consideration. Avoidance of guilt and social disapproval motivate the child. These last two stages bring us through adolescence. Kohlberg estimates that only 10 percent of the adult population go beyond this externally controlled level of development. With stage five comes the maturity of internal commitment to principles of one's own conscience. At this stage, responsibility, the rights of others, and human dignity are also truly understood. Avoidance of self-condemnation is now important. Notice the reminiscence of Maslow's self-actualized person at this level.

Kohlberg (1964, 1972; Munson, 1979) offers a very interesting conclusion resulting from his studies with members of differing cultures, social classes, races, socioeconomic groups, and both sexes. He believes that the differences in moral development between groups are not related to any cultural values or beliefs, but to the amount of social participation and responsibility they have been allowed. The more interaction, the more maturity. The sense of participation and involvement in an overall moral environment heightens the growth of moral conduct much more than direct teaching from the family or other institutions. Kohlberg has some specific suggestions for heightening that involvement.

Favored as a way of fostering progress through the stages is the provision of opportunities for "role taking." This technique allows the child to assume the viewpoint of others or to act out a situation, taking the part of one of the other participants. This can be used in the family or in the classroom. The situations can be real or imagined problems. Acting on the basis of moral reasoning is an important step for children. The sharing of responsibility for decision making and the evaluation of that decision allow moral growth. Adults who use only authority unilaterally teach children that morality is not for everyone, thereby retarding the youth's movement to higher levels of development.

Throughout his work, Kohlberg often mentions the establishment of a moral climate or environment. This could be the most critical factor to the child in both the home and in school. By establishing a just environment, one can teach justice. If a child experiences moral, humane behavior from others, he progresses in moral development. One component of this environment is discipline.

In a review of the literature on outcomes of styles of discipline, Becker (1964) supports Kohlberg's position that the actions of adults and their chosen method of discipline greatly influence moral behavior. The goal is to help children take responsibility for their own behavior. Again, authoritarian or power-assertive techniques fall short of the goal and can create uncooperative, aggressive behaviors. Warm, love-oriented discipline making use of acceptance, understanding, frequent explanations, and reasoning results in internalization of moral concepts and cooperative, nonaggressive behavior. Even when authoritarian discipline through fear of physical punishment succeeds in squelching overt hostility, the child's anger remains and is only suppressed temporarily. In establishing a moral environment, adults do not give up their authority; rather, they change it. Instead of authority based on fear, threat, punishment, or rewards, the basis becomes the ability to mediate conflict fairly, to guide and facilitate successful solutions to problems, and to help discover alternatives for evaluation.

Vare (1979) cites unique emotional needs and cognitive developmental potential as the rationale for developing a program of moral education for the gifted. By including both cognitive goals (logical, rational evaluation; critical, analytical thinking) and affective goals (empathy, openness and trust, tolerance or acceptance), Vare builds a confluent model that she believes to be more appropriate to the gifted than other previously used programs. She includes a variety of discussion, action, and investigative strategies and sets them in the classroom, which itself must be a model of a democratic atmosphere of openness, tolerance, and concern for others. The goal of such a program is the development of morally autonomous individuals who will not show the discrepancy between intellectual ability and developed moral reasoning found by Tan-Willman and Gutteridge (1981) in their study of academically gifted adolescents.

Another element important to producing a moral climate is good, open communication. Children can be taught to communicate respectfully and clearly with others. Again, the example of the adults in their environment will have most impact, but there are games and strategies that can be directly taught (see chapter 6, the section called Strategies for the Feeling or Affective Function, p. 256). The family or class meeting described later in this chapter (p. 126) can give interactive opportunities for all group or family members.

Recent findings by Yarrow and Zahn-Waxler (Pines, 1979) indicate that with the appropriate environment and experiences children as young as one year can exhibit behaviors that show concern and empathy for others. Yarrow refers to the behaviors she is researching as altruistic. According to the data, all children seem to have the capacity for early development of altruism, but there are enormous individual differences in their development that increase between eighteen and twenty-four months of age. The most powerful factor in producing altruistic behavior was the intensity with which mothers conveyed the message that their children must not hurt others. Physical restraint or punishment without an explanation of how the children had hurt another did not lead to altruism and was actually counterproductive. The other factor that was related to development of this trait was the mother's altruistic behavior toward the child and others in the family. In a later study it was noted that the patterns of altruism set in this early period remained consistent at least through the age of seven.

A responsive environment permits social-emotional growth.

Paul MacLean (1978), the brain researcher whose work we reviewed in chapter 1, believes that altruism and empathy are related to the function of the prefrontal cortex, the newest part of the human brain. He states that if these neural circuits are not brought into play at the critical time of development they may never function properly. Providing a responsive learning environment for our children can now be seen as important to their biological, mental, and emotional growth.

Though Kohlberg and other affective educators have much more to say about creating such an environment, one more element must be included here. Children grow morally only as much as their self-esteem allows. Earlier, this chapter considered the importance of self-esteem. Low self-esteem seems to limit growth in moral development, which in turn affects the child's view and treatment of others (Briggs, 1975; Lickona, 1977; Purkey, 1970; Satir, 1972). The social-emotional growth of our gifted children must be considered by every parent and teacher not only because such growth can sharpen intellect, but even more importantly because such growth becomes the basis for use of that intelligence.

The Developing Personality

Another important theorist in the area of social-emotional development is Erik Erikson. Erikson (1950, 1964) also delineates stages or periods of life to express his view of a growing personality. His eight stages encompass all ages of human life and represent periods during which experiences dictate major adjustments to the social environment and the self. The way each adjustment is handled will affect the way the person adjusts or handles the next stage of development. While these experiences may be present during most of a person's life, the focus or critical stage is believed to proceed in the following order.

1. Trust vs. mistrust—Here we find the roots of inner and outer locus of control. If as infants children experience affection and consistency, they form the belief in a secure world wherein they are effective, they matter. If instead their experience is threatening, unpredictable, stressful, or apathetic, they will believe their world to be untrustworthy, unmanageable, one in which they have no control.

2. Autonomy vs. shame or doubt—Toddlers who are allowed to feel pride and success in their experiences of learning to care for themselves gain a sense of self-confidence and self-control. If they are continually limited, criticized, or punished they will believe themselves to be inadequate or bad and experience shame and self-doubt.

3. Initiative vs. guilt—As four- or five-year-olds begin to explore the world beyond themselves, they discover how the world works and how they affect it. If this exploration is challenging and effective, they learn to deal with people and things in positive ways and gain a strong sense of initiative. If, however, their efforts are always criticized and punished they will feel guilty for self-initiated actions.

4. Industry vs. inferiority—From six to eleven years of age, children develop numerous skills at home, at school, and in the outside world. An evaluation of competence when compared with peers is important at this time. Mistakes must be viewed as growth experiences if further inquiry and exploration are not to be limited.

5. Ego identity vs. ego diffusion—The adolescent explores and affirms belief systems and basic values. If all the roles and beliefs found in their lives cannot be resolved into an integrated identity, the result is what Erikson calls ego diffusion.

6. Intimacy vs. isolation—In late adolescence and young adulthood the focus is on developing the ability to share one's self with another and still retain the essential self. The success one has in doing this reflects the success of the previous five areas of experience.

7. Generativity vs. self-absorption—As adults with the problems of earlier stages at least partially resolved, individuals can now direct their focus toward assisting others, one's own children, social issues, etc. Unsuccessful resolution of earlier issues can result in overconcern for one's health, comfort, and psychological needs.

8. Integrity vs. despair—As one views one's life from the perspective of age, the evaluation may reflect meaning, purpose, and satisfaction or a series of bungled attempts, unresolved efforts, and lost opportunities. The attitude of worth will be affected by this evaluation.

Erikson has given us a map of clues we might look to as we work to understand our gifted children. While the intensity with which they approach each of these stages and the resources they bring to bear on meeting the conflicts presented in each developmental period may be of a larger scope, the focus remains. If we are to optimize their development, we must become aware of these points of focus.

Attitudes

The gifted individual faces another problem while growing up, the area of attitudes. This is a little like discussing the age-old problem of the chicken and the egg— Which came first? Do the attitudes of others result from the actions of the gifted person, or is the gifted individual's behavior the result of other people's attitudes and prejudices? A little of both is probably true.

The moral teachings of nearly all cultures contain the idea that what you give forth will be returned to you in like kind: those who view life positively will have positive experiences; those who give generously will receive generously from others; love begets love. This seems to be quite true of attitudes of groups toward each other. Since the literature on attitudes tends to agree that attitudes are learned and therefore educable, we need to be more aware of the attitudes that we and others communicate toward the gifted.

In a thought-provoking article, Margaret Mead (1954) reveals the plight of the gifted child in the American culture of 1954. Her observations are, unfortunately, just as applicable to American culture of today. She observes that Americans have a narrow competitive range; like must compete with like; all success, to be approved, must result from effort, abstinence, and suffering. The very term used to label children who exhibit high intellectual ability, *the gifted*, indicates that their success has been given, not earned. Therefore, giftedness is to be viewed with suspicion, if not outright hostility.

American society also tends to grade or rate attributes rather than allow uniqueness and incomparability. Therefore, we reduce giftedness to an IQ score. By our refusal to recognize special ability in intellectual areas, we waste the ability of uncounted numbers of gifted children.

> If they learn easily, they are penalized for being bored when they have nothing to do; if they excel in some outstanding way, they are penalized as being conspicuously better than the peer group . . . The culture tries to make the child with a gift into a one-sided person, to penalize him at every turn, to cause him trouble in making friends and to create conditions conducive to the development of a neurosis. Neither teachers, the parents of other children, nor the child's peers will tolerate a Wunderkind (p. 213).

As a remedy for such outcomes Mead suggests,

> The more diversified, the more complex the activities within which children are encouraged to play a role the better the chance for . . . the gifted child to exercise his special talent . . . much more than rewards and praise, the gifted child needs scope, material on which his imagination can feed, and opportunities to exercise it. He needs inconspicuous access to books, museums, instruments, paints, ideas, a chance to feed himself with the accumulated heritage from the genius of other ages. He needs a chance for contact, however fleeting, perhaps only on television or in a special movie, with those who are masters in the abilities with which he has been specially endowed. And within our sternly Puritan tradition, he may well need also a special sense of stewardship for the talents which he has been given, and explicit moral sanction against selling his birthright for a mess of pottage (p. 214).

Newland (1976) points out that sensitivity to the educational needs of the gifted is at a disturbingly low level among educators in general. The Advocate Survey appended to the Marland (1972) Report to Congress described pupil personnel workers as apathetic to hostile in their attitudes toward gifted students. Lack of preparation for working with or understanding the needs of this population may account, in part, for this attitude. The negative attitudes of this group must be changed because of their influence on the attitudes of administrators and teachers through inservice and counseling contacts (Martinson, 1972). Through national projects such as the National/State Leadership Training Institute for Gifted and Talented and the resulting state and local commitment, this seems to be changing.

Attitudes of Teachers

The work of Rosenthal (1968) and others gives us a clear picture of how important the teacher's attitude is to the performance of the student. The level of expectation communicated by the teacher can so easily lead to self-fulfilling prophesies. David Aspy's results readily show the power of the teacher to affect the achievement and growth of the child. He found that the perception teachers have of their own ability and worth most significantly relates to the success of their students (Aspy and Bahler, 1975).

To emphasize the importance of teacher attitude to the achievement and well-being of gifted students, we might share the experience of a very bright young man I have known for several years. After about four years of participation in an excellent gifted program modeled after the cooperative learning environment, the young man began a new experience as a high school student. The "program for the gifted" at this high school provided enrichment whenever the teacher found it possible within the context of the regular class. This student found little enriching, but he tried to cope with the new situation as well as he could. Rare were his challenges; he made his grades without much effort. In one course insisting on the memorization of many details, he had to spend extra time prior to any exam so that the details could be reproduced accurately and in proper order.

After one particular exam in which the student felt he had done well, his exam was returned with the failing grade, F. Not used to such outcomes and feeling that something had to be wrong, as he still believed his answers were correct, he approached the teacher. There followed a rather one-sided inquiry into the reasons for the failing mark, and the student became increasingly frustrated and upset as the teacher sat smiling at his discomfort. Finally, the young man demanded to know why he had failed, and the teacher's response was, "Oh, you didn't really get an F." At this point he showed the student an A + recorded in his grade book—the highest mark in the class. "I just wanted to see how you would take it if you got an F," the teacher commented. The response he got from his student was sharp and alienating. The boy began looking for other ways to meet his needs from that moment on. His high school experience had become, with this last indignity, disappointing to say the least. He completed high school by attending university classes arranged for him by the teacher of his former gifted class.

If perception or attitude so powerfully affects students, it would be fruitful to examine the data on attitudes of school personnel toward the gifted. In general, the attitudes held by the majority of school personnel toward gifted individuals are not positive. Although early entry to school is often sought as a solution for precocious children and such early entrants have a record of performing well academically, this practice is favored neither by school administrators nor by teachers (Braga, 1971; Hobson, 1979). In a study to assess the attitudes of kindergarten and first grade teachers toward academically talented early entrants it was found that these children were assigned the lowest ranks of all candidates to be considered for these classrooms (Jackson, Famiglietti, and Robinson, 1981).

The perception improves, however, among those who have more direct experience and among those who have had courses aimed at understanding and educating gifted children (Justman and Wrightstone, 1956). The Pegnato and Birch study (1959) shows the inability of teachers to identify gifted children accurately. The School Staffing Survey done by the U.S. Office of Education (1969) reveals that 57.5 percent of school administrators in American schools stated that they had no gifted children. These three studies indicate a lack of awareness toward the needs of the gifted and suggest a need for a greater availability of gifted education courses.

Specifically, Weiner and O'Shea (1963) found that the higher the level of education attained by university students, teachers, or administrators, the more accepting they were of the gifted individual. Attitudes of teachers who work with the gifted are more favorable than those who do not. Also, university students who had attended lectures on the gifted displayed more favorable attitudes. In another study, Weiner (1968) reported that school psychologists and psychometrists experienced with the gifted favored them significantly more than those with no experience. An attitude survey administered to faculty of five major universities indicated a strong positive attitude toward gifted education, with those identifying themselves as previous participants in programs for the gifted being the most positive (Weiss and Gallagher, 1980).

Attitudes of Peers

While the attitudes of peers, at least during elementary school, are usually positive, teachers, parents, and administrators fear elitism and snobbishness. In a study by Mills (1973), experience with the gifted and a background in gifted education again related to attitudes of acceptance. Younger respondents from ten to twenty-nine years of age were less sympathetic than those thirty to thirty-nine years old. Blacks and Chicanos were less favorable than Caucasians. The higher people rated themselves in mental ability, the more favorable they tended to be toward gifted children. Teachers of regular classes, education administrators, community leaders, and lay public all showed significantly unfavorable attitudes toward the gifted. Instruction and experience seem to be the most successful ways to improve attitudes. The impact these attitudes have on gifted individuals makes it necessary to consider these results seriously.

Newland (1976) feels that the gifted need to be taught attitudes of commitment, service, continuous learning, and discovery or truth seeking. He believes that these attitudes come naturally to the gifted, but that they have been inhibited or actually blocked by the structure of the schools toward conformity and their toleration of underachievement.

It seems, then, that the power of attitudes in society and specifically within the educational community may be a prime force in furthering or denying educational opportunities for our gifted children.

Integrating Cognitive, Social-Emotional, Physical, and Intuitive Growth

While we cannot be assured that persons with high levels of cognitive development develop equally well socially, emotionally, physically, and intuitively, we can make use of their cognitive ability to facilitate the other skills and thereby strengthen their intellect. The degree to which the other abilities have been nurtured determines the ability to think at high levels. The integration of these functions is necessary to actualize the potential of any one function.

Brain researchers recognize hemispheric specialization. That is to say, the left side of the brain is primarily responsible for logical, analytic, linear thought including language, while the right side is primarily involved in spatial, holistic, more analogous, or intuitive types of functions. If necessary, each hemisphere could replicate the functions of the opposite side. But unless such a need exists, and retraining occurs, the specialization pattern will be followed. Although the majority of the population has left-right brain functioning operable as cited, in some cases, as evidenced by left-handedness or ambidexterity, the reverse may be true. In all cases, when the brain functions normally regardless of the side of functioning, specialization does occur (Bogen, 1975; Gazzanega, 1975; Krashen, 1975; Nebes, 1975; and Ornstein, 1972).

This apparent separation is the strongest argument for integration of the cognitive/physical and the affective/intuitive functions. For, while specialization exists, there are more connectors between brain hemispheres than from the brain to any other part of the human body. The obvious need for integration is apparent even in the structure of the brain itself. According to brain research, mammalian sensory systems must be used in facilitating environments if normal development is to occur (Blakemore, 1974). Haggard (1957) found that early exclusive emphasis or focus on cognitive (left brain) performance can have noticeable attitudinal consequences as well. Such children developed competitive, hostile attitudes toward their peers and disdain for adults in order to maintain their position of intellectual superiority.

In order to optimize the development of all individuals, that they might truly realize their potential and discover their authentic selves, we must look for an integrated approach both at home and at school.

Assuring Integrated Growth

The family plays an important role in creating integrated growth. Newland (1976) comments that all social traits reflect family patterns. Satir (1972) found that, as problem children come from problem families, healthy, open, growing children come from nurturing families. While her work began with therapeutic counseling for problem families, she has developed a framework to guide families who seek to develop family structures that can enhance the growth of each family member. Such families are productive of highly functional, well-integrated children.

In her ideal family, Satir summarizes,

> We have adults who clearly show their own uniqueness, who demonstrate their power, who clearly show their sexuality, who demonstrate their ability to share through understanding, kindness and affection, who use their common sense, who are realistic and responsible (p. 228).

She believes such a family is an open system. This is in opposition to a closed system where self-worth is secondary to power and performance, where rules are created and enforced by the boss (usually father), who knows what is best for all, and where change is resisted for there is only one way to do things—the right way. Satir believes that human beings cannot flourish in a closed system; they may barely exist. We are concerned with more than just existing. We are discussing optimizing human potential to help our children become self-actualizing.

In his study of self-actualizing people, Maslow (1968) conceptualized a hierarchy af human needs that he used to explain how emotional development is facilitated or inhibited. According to this hierarchy, human energy is used to provide for needs at six levels. If needs at any one level remain unmet, energies will be drained off at that level, inhibiting further progress and causing overemphasis on that need level. Such limitation would make attainment of the integrated person difficult. Awareness of need levels can provide parents with a model for directing family and home efforts toward healthy, integrated development. It is important to note that as growth occurs individuals may be operating on several levels at the same time with more or less emphasis. Under certain circumstances and under differing conditions, one may regress or progress through the various levels of need. As the six need levels identified by Maslow may provide a framework for working with integrated development in the home, they should also be introduced into classrooms. While the goal of self-actualization has not been actively sought in most school systems, it has for decades been a declared goal in most public schools' philosophical statements of purpose. Through the work of educators such as Brown at the University of California at Santa Barbara, the implementation of such goals becomes a reality (Brown, 1971).

Let us look at how such a program might be structured to assure integrated growth for gifted individuals. As their ability in cognitive areas develops to higher levels, the potential for development of feeling and intuitive areas also grows.

Level 1—Basic Physical Needs

At Home.   The first level is the provision for the basic physical necessities to support life. Human survival depends primarily on food, clothing, and shelter. Most families clearly provide for these necessities, and modern societies attempt to subsidize those who cannot. During inadequate provision for survival, energies focus totally at this level until such needs are at least minimally met.

At School.   These basic physical needs are usually met, at least minimally, by the home. In some low socioeconomic areas, however, such provisions for basic needs may not be available. In these cases the school, as an agent of society, has instituted free lunch programs and subsidized nutrition periods. Although not always successful, nor sensitive to the population they seek to serve, such programs aim to meet needs at this primary level.

Teachers may wish to examine their classrooms for opportunities to meet needs at this level. Some children have more energy to spend on learning when provided additional nourishment. There are those in every classroom who can accomplish more, with a higher level of concentration, if they can munch on a handful of raisins or a few carrot sticks in the process. Such additions to classrooms need not be treated as rewards or wasted by misuse if children have proper explanations of purpose and need. When classrooms model respect for individual needs and concern for growth, proper use of healthy "treats" can be self-directed.

Level 2—Safety Needs

At Home.   The second level does not so clearly concern all families. At this level we find provisions for safety needs. By this we mean physical, as well as psychological or emotional, safety. Most will agree on the need for physical safety in a family. When this is missing, the results are obvious, and intervention is seen as desirable. However, the lack of emotional safety for a family or family member is not so clearly recognizable. Some families use threat and fear as control strategies. They regulate behavior by such tactics. In some cases the "different" member of the family becomes the scapegoat, and the safety needs of this individual go unfulfilled. Unless this deficit results in physical problems (e.g., psychosomatic illness) or in acting out or antisocial behavior, modern society does not allow intervention. A significant number of people find it necessary to focus an unproductive quantity of their energy on the safety needs level.

At School.   Classrooms most often offend the safety needs level. The reward-punishment-competition model used by so many educators to elicit student motivation toward school-related tasks forces children to spend a great deal of energy insuring their own psychological safety. According to the work of Feldhusen and Klausmeier (1962), superior mental ability may make it possible for a child to assess more adequately the real danger in any threatening object, situation, or person. Children of low and average IQ may show greater anxiety and generalized fear because of their limited intellectual capacity to evaluate the threat or danger. Possibly a more anxious low or average IQ child is less free to respond to the teacher, the learning material, and the learning situation. Whether the child is bright or less able, this study shows that, rather than providing drive or motivation to learn, anxiety in the classroom is debilitating and interferes with the learning process.

Add to these factors the attitudes previously discussed that educators often hold toward gifted children. Include the sensitivity of these atypical learners to their environment, and we have a picture that points clearly to an expenditure of energy at this level that gifted children can ill afford.

To insure your program against such wasteful and unnecessary practices, consider these steps that can be taken: Provide inservice on educating the gifted child for *all* teachers within your school setting. The more teachers or administrators know about gifted children and their special needs, the more favorable will be the attitudes and actions directed toward them. Provide accessible information on alternatives for classroom organization and management. It is likely that we will continue to teach as we have been taught unless we become familiar with other approaches. We have now developed strategies and patterns of organization that are exciting and nurturing for human growth that were not available ten years ago. As these ideas are perfected, they must be made known to classroom teachers and building administrators. All educators in decision-making positions must seek out information to aid in the establishment of more powerful, more humane learning environments. We look at some of these strategies in chapter 6 (p. 231).

Level 3—Love and Belonging Needs

Human beings need to love and to feel loved, to be in physical contact with one another, to associate with others, and to participate in groups and organizations.

At Home.   This level establishes a foundation of love and caring that influences how each family member views the others and operates in the world. Feeling affection is important: affection felt and shared is even more fulfilling for human needs. Boys and girls will benefit from learning about themselves and others as loving beings. Families model this love and caring. While gifted children may be able to analyze the problems within family patterns lacking strong love relationships, they, as much as the more typical individual, still establish patterns for themselves similar to those the family displays. Families must provide sufficient opportunities for development of this level. Nurturing families fit quite naturally into this area. All humans must feel that they matter, that there is a group or a person with whom they can identify. Belonging is a reciprocal arrangement. It does not occur simply by proximity. There must be give and take, respect, and appreciation, as well as some degree of opportunity to share in movement toward a common goal. Many families fail to give adequate time or concern toward providing experiences for all members to meet their needs at this level. Group activities, as well as respect for individual pursuits, must be provided. On occasion, individuals attempt to meet belonging needs outside the family. This can be a positive growth process if not used just to compensate for family deficits. Some ways of insuring growth beyond this level would be—

> involvement in planning and carrying out family trips or activities.
>
> accepting each person as worthy, listening to each, responding to each.
>
> expressing pleasure for accomplishments of each member without comparison.
>
> cooperative planning and decision making in so far as each member is able.
>
> open communication between family members.
>
> cooperative action with each person's contribution seen as valuable to the whole family.
>
> allowance of time to develop understanding and empathy among family members.

At School.   Here again schools can contribute significantly to meeting human belonging needs. Every classroom would certainly benefit through establishment of a wealth of various resources. What better resource than the children themselves? Gifted children often bring to the learning situation a vast quantity and diversity of knowledge and comprehension. They can often contribute highly creative ways to apply such knowledge. The teacher loses out as much as the children if these resources remain untapped.

To assure a rich learning environment, teachers should establish a climate of trust within the classroom that allows each child to see each other child as a person instead of the object a stranger becomes. Where such a climate exists, learners can learn from each other and from the environment as well as from the teacher.

Belonging does not just occur. Children, as adults, easily establish categories for people. "He is my friend," "They are different than we are," "She is stuck-up," "They're just too stupid," "She thinks she's so smart" represent some of the unfortunate labeling activities that form categories. People then become objects within the category, and they lose their uniqueness. Newland (1976) comments that when gifted and nongifted children are taught together, we cannot expect that grouping alone will insure knowledge and understanding of each for the other. There must be interpersonal interaction. And this must be a priority for the teacher. It becomes as important to acknowledge and respect the differences between these groups as it does to look at the similarities. Newland urges that democracy not be seen as egalitarian conformity. To counter a movement toward exclusion or conformity, the teacher must take deliberate action to set up situations in which children can experience each other as unique individuals and as contributing, valuable people. Where teachers do not value these activities enough to include them in their daily classroom routine, children will spend a great deal of unnecessary energy seeking fulfillment of level 3 needs.

Level 4—Needs for Self-Esteem

At Home and At School.   Children need positive responses from others to provide a sense of well-being and self-satisfaction. When lower level needs are met, the child can deal with more abstract thinking skills, release more creativity, and become more self-directed. While this area will require expenditure of energy throughout our lifetime, attention to needs in this area makes the cognitive activities of learning and the affective activities of healthy living possible. Classrooms do not play the same role as the home in this need area. At this level different facets of the child will be revealed and perfected. With gifted children this can be critical. Forced to restrict their inquiry and experiences to already known areas of competence for fear of loss of esteem or even love, their wasted potential will be extensive. By encouraging diverse pursuits, internal validation, and the idea that mistakes provide learning experiences, teachers will furnish the opportunity for fulfillment at this need level.

At this level energy can also be released to engage in the risk taking required for learning. Teachers and parents alike expect children to enter classrooms ready to learn. Only if the needs at the previous three levels have been adequately met will this be possible. Energy too heavily focused in survival, safety, or belonging areas will make energy for learning or creative activity at this fourth level unavailable.

Level 5—Self-Actualization

At Home and at School.   The fifth level relates to the self-actualization needs of humans. At this level Maslow's research makes its greatest contribution. While we may work in several levels simultaneously or focus on different levels at different times, we ultimately reach our highest potential development at this level. Gifted children have tremendous potential toward self-actualization. Our society benefits from their progress toward self-actualization as do they themselves. The greatest contributions to our culture have come from individuals who developed their potential at all levels of functioning, allowing them to integrate all ways of knowing, to risk taking unknown or unpopular stands, and to implement the insights their expanding beliefs made possible. The classroom that values, encourages, and provides opportunity for diversity, self-exploration, introspection, interaction, and quiet contemplation is the classroom where self-actualization will likely occur.

In addition to the characteristics of the self-actualizing person from Maslow's work mentioned at the beginning of this chapter, the concept expands with Morris's (1966) description of *awareness of self*: (a) self as a choosing agent unable to avoid choosing his or her way through life; (b) self as a free agent, free to set the goals for his or her own life; (c) self as a responsible agent, accountable for the choices made and how he or she lives those choices. Communicating these propositions becomes the major task of educators if they desire to nurture self-actualization. Teachers must arrange learning situations so that the truth of these ideas is experienced by each individual. For gifted individuals with heightened awareness and greater capacity for growth, this educational opportunity becomes critical.

Maslow suggests these clues for the development of self-actualization:

1. Experience each moment fully, vividly, and with full concentration.
2. Think of life as a process of choices, your choices.
3. Listen to your Self; trust your inner voice.
4. Take responsibility for yourself.
5. Dare to be different, nonconforming, real.
6. Do what you do with joy, and do it well.
7. Set up conditions that will allow more peak experiences; perceive the world and life positively.
8. Open up to yourself, identify your defenses, and find the courage to give them up.

The goal is to have access to all of your life, all of your potential, to be who you are.

Level 6—Transcendence

Had Maslow lived another decade, he would have added a sixth level. He had already begun an inquiry into the need and meaning of this next level, which he called *transcendence*. He saw it as "the very highest and most inclusive or holistic level of human consciousness, behaving and relating, as ends, rather than as means, to oneself, to significant others, to human beings in general, to other species, to nature, and to the cosmos" (Maslow, 1971, p. 279). While Maslow could not complete his work at the sixth level, many others have now begun to explore this apex—possibly the level that reflects the true meaning of human existence.

The transcendence level includes the nurture of intuitive abilities. To create a world where the oneness of all being is understood and practiced, where the unity with and interdependence of all parts of the cosmos are valued and provide the basis for action, is a noble undertaking. We can live most effectively if we transcend the self by becoming the most each of us can be and recognizing and valuing this in others while, underlying the uniqueness, we experience the connectedness.

At Home.   From the clues we have, families in which individual members seek growth toward transcendence provide the most impact on the development of this level of growth. Allowing the expression of ideas and observations of unusual physical or psychic nature is important. Providing an open forum for discussion and experience with such events will nurture the transcendence level.

In working in the area of transcendence, each family member will likely have a personal commitment toward a particular path, but some areas available for group exploration might be concentration exercises, meditation, and biofeedback training. Any family activity that puts the child in close communication with nature, such as sailing, hiking, or camping, can be used as a transcendence experience. While in the peaceful beauty of nature, we should take time to sit quietly, observe, appreciate, and sense the unity with all life that such places and moments can bring. Leading children to discover their transcendence level can be a joyous process, beginning with the attitudes the parent shares.

High levels of developed cognitive ability do not guarantee high levels of affective or emotional development. While the capabilities exist, opportunities to develop them must be made part of the child's experience. One very early trait in the emotional growth of gifted children is their intense sense of justice and unwavering idealism. The parent of a gifted child will soon experience the futile effort of explaining why injustice so often exists. In attempting to convince my children that "the world just isn't fair," I had limited success. "If it isn't, it should be, and why aren't you (the adult) doing something about it?" they responded. To try to discuss with a three-year-old how one person could affect only a limited amount of inequity was frustrating for both of us. My reasons were not acceptable to my son's world view. The sense of justice is tremendously valuable to society and beautiful in its motivating power for humanistic action. We must guide the idealism of children so that they do not become so frustrated that they lose it early and replace it with cynicism or the sense of being powerless. Parents need to be alert in seeking alternatives with the child when solutions that seem inequitable are posed. A real sharing of problem solving at the child's level of understanding cannot begin too early. Hollingworth (1926) points out that gifted children may be readily disciplined by appeals to reason, presentation of alternative views, modeling, and consistency of expressed values. With this approach, gifted children may keep their sense of justice intact.

Some families have a trying situation to overcome in order to maintain family unity. This situation occurs when one sibling is identified gifted while another is not. It may be very difficult for the more typical child to understand the difference, and special consideration of the needs of both should prevail. The situation is analogous to having one child recognized for athletic ability or artistic talent while the other child is seen as only average in these abilities. The family must clearly recognize the ability of the identified child and just as clearly recognize whatever abilities the other child shows in other areas. A family that values intellectual functions over other human abilities will communicate that bias to less able children. The human and interpersonal consequences will be difficult for all concerned. Give all family members a chance to be respected and valued for their own unique abilities.

In our family, we organized family councils to provide the arena for exposing perceived inequities perpetrated by either parents or siblings. There we sought alternative solutions that could better meet the needs of all concerned. At first, we held council once a week, but later we found that calling council on demand of any fam-

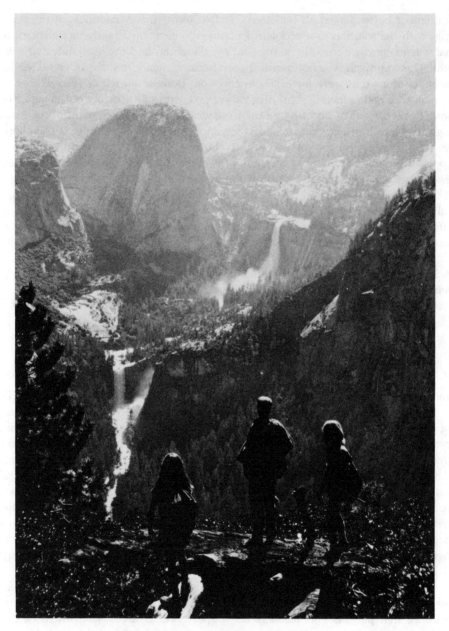

Transcendence: A joyous process.

ily member better served all our needs. I often went to our meetings, at the beginning, with the solution to a problem I planned to clear up already thought out. My goal was to convince the others, my son, my daughter, and my husband, that I was right. This approach was not useful. I soon became aware that the others often had better solutions that were far easier to carry out because all felt committed toward the plan they had helped design. All kinds of problems came before our group, from mother's need for neat and tidy rooms to sister's perceived harassment at the hands of an unaware brother. Questions of allowance, homework, bedtime, house chores, teacher attitudes, and comfort of visiting relatives all were handled with serious and cooperative planning. Through the years the council served to lessen the powerlessness, to increase the comfort level of family members, and generally to provide us all with excellent practice in developing our problem-solving skills, creative thinking abilities, and feelings of caring. Family councils became a meaningful way to communicate and share within the family. I highly recommend them, especially for families who live with gifted children.

At School.   Establishing this sense of unity in a classroom begins with what Weinhold (1976) calls transpersonal communication.

> Transpersonal communication is designed to help people to trust the validity of their personal experiences and accept what they learn from these experiences as their best source of wisdom and truth. This includes both thinking and feeling processes. It teaches people to play hunches, use their intuition and follow their thoughts and feelings rather than direct them in predetermined ways (p. 124).

Any of the strategies for open communication offered in chapter 6 (p. 257) can begin this process. Remember that the attitudes and beliefs a teacher has about teaching and learning have even more effect than the techniques used. A teacher must first believe in self-evolving education—that the process of self-discovery is central to any learning. As is true for parents, teachers teach more from who they are and what actions stem from their beliefs than from what they know. Combs (1969) finds that certain belief systems relate to effective teachers. Among these are beliefs about the nature of people, themselves and their ability, what their purposes are, their area of knowledge, and their approaches to teaching. We discuss this information in chapter 9 (p. 365), Teachers of the Gifted—at School. The teacher has the most influence on creating the climate in the classroom, and a favorable climate must exist for growth toward transcendence to occur.

The development of an integrated person is clearly a complex process. In cases where home and school lend support in the same areas, growth will be significant. To insure that parents and teachers do support similar areas, each must be conscious of the environment the other creates for the child. With this knowledge, they will both be able to provide support and experiences when they are needed. A teacher can initiate this type of communication more easily than a parent. Providing deliberate contact points, meetings, and conferences for parental involvement in the school program assures both the teacher and the parent that the child's development will proceed effectively. The extra effort made to encourage parent involvement or at least the opportunity for contact will pay off handsomely from the educational standpoint. Many gifted programs have survived only because of adamant parent support. Many are dramatically enriched by parent participation.

A parent who does not receive communication from the school has ways to seek involvement. Becoming informed about the community, the district, and gifted education in general could be the first step. Seeking other parents for support and for sharing resources will be valuable to both the parent and the children. Offering informed support to the children's program can do more to improve the quality of their experience than any criticism the parent may offer. Most school personnel have the same goals for the children as the parents. A cooperative effort may help both succeed in providing the quality educational program all desire.

This chapter has focused primarily on the social-emotional and integrative growth of gifted children. The origins of social-emotional development are to be found very early in the child's interaction with the world. The child's evolving self-concept critically influences social-emotional development. We found that both the concept of self and moral development can facilitate or inhibit intellectual growth. For gifted children, the social-emotional aspects of growth present special problems.

Our concern for optimal development and appropriate educational opportunities for gifted children requires that we consider the effect of attitudes on this process. The attitudes of both gifted people and those who work and live with them were seen to affect their development significantly. It is important to integrate growth in all of the human functions if we are to optimize the development of intelligence. Even cognitive function is limited if integration of the other areas is left to chance. Both homes and schools have an important part to play in this integration. Later chapters will present strategies to aid in making this process more effective.

In the following Section II, the concerns and involvement of schools in educating gifted children now become the major focus. Although the information will be most useful in the classroom, administrative offices, and by those educators who are concerned about educational services for gifted individuals, the parent as a cooperative, supportive resource remains a critical factor in the process of growing up gifted.

SECTION TWO

The School
and the Gifted
Individual

A Rationale for Gifted Education

So many times those who believe that gifted children do not need special provisions confront those of us who are concerned about the education of the gifted. Many sincerely feel that truly gifted children will remain gifted and fulfill their educational needs on their own. Others feel that if teachers are doing their job, the gifted should be able to get by without the special attention that other atypical learners need. How do we answer those people who refuse to consider special education for the gifted, who block any attempt to provide programs as undemocratic, elitist, or wasteful? There are several ideas we must ask them to consider:

1. Giftedness arises from an interactive process that involves challenges from the environment stimulating and bringing forth innate capabilities and processes. Although they are most easily affected during the early years, these innate mechanisms require challenge throughout the individual's lifetime for high levels of actualization to result. As we saw in chapter 2, we either progress or regress; stability is not possible. Just to retain giftedness, not to mention furthering the potential, gifted children must participate in programs appropriate to their level of development.

2. Jefferson once said, "There is nothing more unequal than equal treatment of unequal people." Our political and social system is based on democratic principles. The school, as an extension of those principles, purports to provide an equal educational opportunity for all children to develop to their fullest potential. It is then undemocratic to refuse to allow gifted children the right to educational experiences appropriate to their level of development. We do not ask retarded children to work in the same programs and to progress through the same curricula as the more typical learners. How, then, can we justify holding back the gifted student? It would be unjust to require all individuals to perform the same tasks at the same level. Offering all individuals opportunities at only one level with the assumption that this level will meet all their needs is just as unfair. For truly equal opportunity, a variety of learning experiences must be available at many levels so that all youths can develop those skills and abilities they choose to their level of ability.

   We would not ask children who are not yet advanced to the normative level to work there, limiting their growth by creating a situation from which they cannot gain understanding or advance educationally. Neither should we ask advanced students to bide their time and limit their growth by working at a normative level. Each person has the right to learn and to be provided opportunities and challenges for learning at the most appropriate level where growth proceeds most efficiently.

3. When human beings are limited and restricted in their development, when they are not allowed to move, or to reach beyond, they often become bored, frustrated, and angry. There is physical and psychological pain in being thwarted, discouraged, and diminished as a person. To have ability, to feel power you are never allowed to use, can become traumatic if continued. Terman (1925) viewed the gifted as the largest group of under-achievers in education; subsequent research shows that gifted children still lack educational care. At present, fewer

than one-third of the possible gifted learners in the United States are reported receiving education appropriate to their needs (Mitchell and Erickson, 1978).

4. In the past there has been much reference to the term *elitism* when referring to education for gifted individuals, but I believe the problem lies in the meaning of the word. If one means "the chosen ones or the select group," as though the existence of giftedness came only as a bestowing of riches or honor from a higher authority, we might justifiably treat such individuals as an already accomplished population who need only try, and their every wish or thought will be fulfilled. Such individuals would, of course, need no help. They could get along quite well with their already fully functioning gift.

    However, if we mean "a group chosen because of some special skill or ability, which, if fostered, could become truly outstanding (such as athletic prowess, musical talent, or business acumen)," I believe elitism to be entirely justifiable and proper for the benefit of society as a whole. To be superior to others in physical abilities (e.g., boxers, runners, skaters, tennis players) or artistic abilities (e.g., pianists, photographers, conductors, actors) is valued and rewarded in our society. Everyone accepts the idea that such athletes and artists work or train continuously; they, therefore, earn their prestige and status. Not so with intellectual ability. Often viewed with suspicion, considered by some a threat, assumed by many to derive ability from mystical sources, those who possess giftedness are accused of trying to develop elitism even when appropriate educational opportunity is all they seek. Society does not feel personal threat from those accomplished in physical or artistic areas, but often exhibits this reaction in the presence of intellectual ability. Can we continue to justify elitism for some as beneficial to our society, while we fear it in others? Does our society have more need for physical and artistic ability than for intellectual ability? Curiously, the establishment of adequate programs for the gifted results not in the type of snobbishness feared, but in improved social relations and better attitudes of the gifted toward themselves and others (Gallagher, 1966).

    I support the advancement of all abilities. I believe society gains from the highest development of all of its members, whatever their strengths. That which nurtures and actualizes each individual nourishes us as a society.

5. Gifted youngsters very soon discover that their ideas and interests are quite different from their age-mates. They usually enter school having already developed many of their basic skills. Almost at the beginning of school, they begin to sense isolation, for others consider them different. As the roots of a poor self-concept become established, the school often does nothing, for its curriculum and organization are not sufficiently individualized. Most schools seek to develop skills that allow participation in society, not the recreation of that society. Traditional education must be modified. A colleague once said, "Intellectually, they need someone to play chess with, while emotionally they may need someone with whom they can climb trees."

6. When the needs of the gifted are considered and the educational program is designed to meet these needs, these students make significant gains in achievement, and their sense of competence and well-being return. Gifted children in special programs learn to work more efficiently; they develop good problem-solving skills and see solutions from many viewpoints. They experience concepts

and materials in a dynamic relationship, and they can use their vast amount of knowledge to serve as a background for unlimited learning.

7. Contributions to society in all areas of human endeavor come in overweighted proportions from this population of individuals. Society will need the gifted adult to play a far more demanding and innovative role than that required of the more typical learner. We need enough integrated, highly functioning persons to carry out those tasks that will lead us to a satisfying, fulfilling future. Section II proceeds from this view of individual and societal needs.

CHAPTER FOUR

Programs for the Gifted

This chapter will provide the reader with

- a discussion of the organization of programs for gifted learners.
- information on the status of gifted programs and the support they receive.
- goals of a gifted program.
- the role of the administrator, coordinator.
- information on the advantages and disadvantages of traditional programs for the gifted: ability grouping, acceleration, and enrichment.
- a presentation of the Integrative Education Model as an alternative to traditional programming for the gifted.
- resources and ideas for using the community in a program for gifted learners.
- a discussion and planning guide for evaluating gifted programs.
- a guide for a written plan.

The relatively few gifted students who have had the advantage of special programs have shown remarkable improvements in self-understanding and in ability to relate well to others, as well as in improved academic and creative performance. The programs have not produced arrogant, selfish snobs; special programs have extended a sense of reality, wholesome humility, self-respect and respect for others. A good program for the gifted increases their involvement and interest in learning through the reduction of the irrelevant and redundant.

Sidney P. Marland

Gifted Programs Yesterday and Today

Organizing a program that will deliver educational services to gifted learners is one of the most complex, most researched, and least clarified areas of gifted education. The administrative structure is critical to the success of the gifted program. It will reflect the commitment of the school to either expand or inhibit the opportunities for learning experienced by the gifted individual.

We have seen the importance of continuous stimulation to optimal development and have discussed some of the unique learning needs of this population. Let us look at how the school program deals with these needs.

In most traditional classrooms, the teacher groups the students into several ability groups. The educational achievement of any normal, chronological age-grouped class ranges over four to eight years, depending on the grade level. The range broadens as children progress from kindergarten to sixth grade. Because the range of achievement can be so vast, the teacher plans the instructional program for the average, at-grade-level learner. Some modification is made for the bottom group and for the top group, but most instruction falls within the normal range. For the very slow learners, remediation programs, often mandated by the state and well-financed, are available in most schools. Classes for the learner found at the bottom 2 percent of the intelligence scale will provide special educational modifications for those students whose needs for a different learning program are obvious. This provision is accepted and expected by both parent and educator alike.

For the slow student, part-time resource rooms will be available, as well as special tutors or special classrooms where these students receive appropriate educational programs until they are able to keep pace with the average learner. The time spent in the special educational facility is dependent on the level of need the student exhibits. In either case, the regular classroom is expected to provide for only part of the program this atypical learner needs.

On the other end of the scale, the school's organization may be quite different. The learners in the upper 2 percent of the intelligence scale need as much special instruction to continue their growth as the students at the lower end. Yet seldom are special classes provided, or resource personnel made available. Since all students must adjust to the average classroom program, the gifted student loses most (figure 4.1).

This situation leads to loss of ability especially among girls and minority students, as regression toward a more average ability level is the observed outcome. This loss can be prevented.

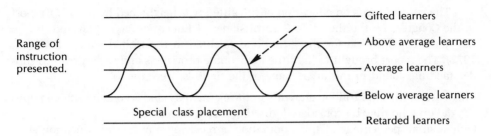

Figure 4.1.   Range of Traditional Classroom Instruction

Programming by Level of Involvement

Using the atypical learning model in the same way at the upper end of the intelligence scale as at the lower end may provide a solution to this problem. Could we not consider three types of gifted learners as we already consider three levels of handicapped learners? These would be the mildly gifted, the moderately gifted, and the highly gifted. The educational modifications could then be provided partially on the basis of how much need the student has for a differential program. The focus here is on the different needs of gifted learners, not on IQ scores.

The mildly gifted student could be provided with a regular, integrated classroom and with a gifted resource room and resource teacher to supplement the program provided by the regular classroom. This would, of course, require assessment, individualized instruction in at least the strength areas, and the availability of a knowledgeable resource person.

Special grouping within the classroom, more time spent in the resource room, or special core subject placement might be programming solutions for the moderately involved gifted student.

The most highly gifted students are found far less often. Many educators have suggested that schools, as they are now organized, have little to offer these individuals and that funds should be provided for private tutoring, acceleration, mentor programs, and very individualized instruction.

While the idea of differentiating within the gifted population following the model used by other atypical learning populations may not solve our problem for providing appropriate experiences for these students, it does suggest a more thoughtful approach. Differentiation quite clearly points to the parallel need these students have with other atypical learners for modifications in educational programs that will allow them to optimize their potential.

Education of the Gifted

During several periods of recent American history, programs for educating gifted learners were encouraged. Terman's study during the 1920s brought on one such period. The dramatic accomplishments of the Russian space program in the late 1950s and early 1960s, which became a concern for the United States with the public launching of Sputnik, heralded another. We are now again involved in a revaluing of our educational system in general with more than usual national attention being directed toward education of the gifted.

The current focus on education of the gifted was heightened by the 1971 report to the Congress by the then U.S. Commissioner of Education, S. P. Marland, Jr., on the status of education for the gifted and talented in the United States (Marland, 1972). The report brought to light the inadequate provisions and widespread misunderstandings found in this area. Some of the findings were the following:

There are at least 2.5 million students in the elementary and secondary school population who may be considered gifted and/or talented.

Only a small percentage of this population is receiving any special education services.

Differential education for the gifted and talented receives very low priority at the federal, state, and most local levels of government and educational administration.

The cost, both individual and social, is enormous when this population goes unserved, for these students cannot excel without assistance.

The apathy and even hostility among teachers, administrators, guidance counselors, and psychologists make even identification of these students difficult.

While programs can provide significant outcomes, lack of services results in psychological damage and permanent impairment of the ability of gifted and talented students.

The report also called attention to the fact that, at that time, the federal government had no role in the leadership or delivery of services for gifted and talented individuals.

The data comprising the report were collected from four major sources: the Advocate Survey, a questionnaire designed to elicit responses to major issues in gifted education from 239 experts in the field; the School Staffing Survey, in which school principals reported data concerning staffing and services to elementary and secondary gifted and talented students in their schools; Project Talent, a longitudinal study of four hundred thousand gifted and talented students made in 1960; and the State Survey, designed to be used by the fifty State Departments of Education as a part of the ten regional hearing procedures. All of these documents, results of which are appended to the Report to Congress, make interesting, though rather less than encouraging, reading for all persons involved in education for the gifted. Some information gathered from these sources follows:

Of all schools surveyed, 57.5 percent reported no gifted individuals among their students.

What services exist are located mostly in the cities and suburbs, although even these programs are generally isolated, experimental, and temporary.

One-third or more of the known gifted receive no special instruction.

Fewer than 2 percent of the known gifted at the high school level are given opportunities to work with specialists or in other school settings. These students are at a level of knowledge that requires such opportunities if they are to learn.

No gifted students are served in twenty-one states.

At least five hundred thousand gifted students in the United States receive no special instruction.

With these facts making the needs of gifted and talented students so apparent, the report put forth several recommendations and, through them, put into motion the first federally supported effort to improve education for the "most neglected and potentially productive groups of students" (Marland, 1972, p. ix).

One outcome to the Marland report was to name one Office of Education staff member in each of the ten Regional Offices of Education throughout the United States as an advocate for education of the gifted. Another was the creation of an Office of Gifted and Talented, housed under the jurisdiction of the Bureau of Education for the Handicapped. This office and its staff have been an important force in developing state and national programs for the gifted and talented. In 1974, another step forward was taken when federal funds were allocated under the Special Projects Section of P.L. 93-380 to state departments of education and local districts. During the first year, 1975, the government allocated approximately 2.5 million dollars to spend on improvement of programs for the gifted population. Also from the Office of Education has come the Presidential Scholars Program. One hundred twenty-one gifted and talented students, at least two from each state, are to be chosen each year to receive a medal presented in Washington, D.C. by the President of the United States. In the third year, the amount of federal support rose to 6.4 million dollars. In 1976 the Office of Gifted and Talented awarded a contract to the Council of Exceptional Children to conduct a national survey to identify current policies, resources, and services for the education of gifted and talented children in the United States and its territories (Mitchell and Erickson, 1978). From the report it was evident that the status of G/T education had improved since the Marland report in 1972.

The findings were reported in five major categories:

1. Gifted and Talented Children—Using the Office of Education definition, it was estimated that 3 percent of the school aged population could be gifted and talented, some 1,352,915 children and youth. The survey found that in the thirty-two states reporting, 437,618 gifted and talented children were provided some type of special educational service in 1976–77: it showed a range of .06 percent to 4.5 percent per state served, with twenty-three states identifying and providing service to 1 percent or less of their school population, and only two states providing for more than 3 percent of their school age population.
2. State Policy—Some type of written policy providing for service to G/T children was reported in forty-three of fifty-one states (84 percent); a definition of G/T was included in the policies of thirty-eight states; identification procedures were described in thirty state policies; guidelines for service in twenty-seven. Only eighteen states had an officially approved state plan.
3. State Personnel—At least one full-time person was assigned to G/T education in twenty-seven states, while fourteen others had at least one part-time person. Ten states had less than a half-time position assigned, and four states had no one at all. In all, 48.18 positions had been allotted to persons assigned to G/T programs.
4. Federal and State Funding—Federal and state appropriations totaling $27,384,316 were reported by fourteen states; 93.1 percent of this amount came from the state funds. Federal funds totaling $3,219,162 were utilized by nineteen states, and twenty-three states utilized state funds totaling $47,076,154. State funds accounted for 95 percent of the total amount expended on programs for G/T education, with eight of the thirty states reporting responsible for 91.8 percent of this expenditure.

5. Preparation of Personnel—One or more courses in G/T education were offered by 177 institutions of higher education in forty-five states. State sponsored in-service training in G/T education was reported by forty-two states.

The conditions identified in the Marland Report as deterrants to development of programs for G/T were still operative in 1977, including lack of adequate funding, trained personnel, and training opportunities, problems in identification, and lack of evaluative data on program effectiveness, especially with special subpopulations.

With a change of administration at the federal level, a new philosophy regarding federal support of education began to take form; and during 1981, PL 97-35, the Education Consolidation and Improvement Act, was passed by Congress. This act placed programs for gifted and talented into a block grant with thirty-two other programs and projects, with appropriations for the block to be sent directly to the states for administration. As a result of this block funding, the Office for Gifted and Talented was removed from the Division of Special Education and Rehabilitative Services whose programs were not in the block, and placed in the Division of Elementary and Secondary Education, where it was then reduced to the position of consultant. The future of the federal involvement remains in question, though paradoxically the interest and commitment to education of gifted and talented children throughout the nation has never been higher. Many of those concerned are turning to the private sector for possible support.

An update of the 1978 study (Mitchell, 1982) shows that only two states reported no programs for G/T learners. Total state department funding rose to $126,530,674. The problems most frequently mentioned by the state directors surveyed were lack of adequate funding, training qualified teachers, and development of a comprehensive K–12 program.

The Commerce Technical Advisory Board of the U.S. Department of Commerce expressed in its report and recommendations, Learning Environments for Innovation, (Branscomb, 1980) concerns shared by many educators of the gifted:

> What we fear is that the basic educational philosophy is far too biased in the direction of remedial learning and fails to identify, much less foster the development of special talents or unique skills. The United States educational system is better at preserving convention than sparking invention, developing logical rather than conceptual thinking, promoting risk aversion rather than acceptance of change, specialization rather than multiple skills, conformity rather than distinctive talents, independent rather than joint responsibility (pp. 23, 24). Moreover, we are concerned that the present trends of back to basics and dispense with the frills more and more eliminate the "hands on" experience which may be necessary to develop right brained skills which we believe are essential to innovative technologists and managers as well as creative artists (pp. 24, 25).
>
> A gifted child has only one chance in twenty to be identified by the school system; for the gifted disadvantaged child the chances are a factor of ten worse—less than one chance in 200.
>
> Even if the unusually talented are lucky enough to be identified, the amount of money available to enrich their academic programs can only be described as shocking (p. 25).

Therefore, one of the major recommendations in this report was,

... that immediate steps be taken by federal, state, and local officials to give programs for the identification and training of gifted students their immediate attention and priority (p. 37).

While in the 80s the United States federal government has all but abolished its role in supporting or even encouraging the appropriate education of its most able children, a group has begun to form in an attempt to meet some of these needs. The National Business Consortium for the Gifted and Talented, under the directorship of Gene Dewey, is soliciting support and funding from major private corporations in the country to sponsor and fund projects that will educationally benefit gifted children. The success of such groups and the continued support of state and local educational agencies is crucial to the future of gifted education in this country.

Worldwide there is an interest in the education of the gifted and talented that is steadily growing. In 1975, the World Council for Gifted Children was formed and through its international conferences and newsletters it is attempting to develop a worldwide network and support system that can benefit gifted children and those who work with them.

As the movement continues to make more and more people aware of the needs of gifted children and to find ways to meet those needs more appropriately, let us look now specifically at your community and how it may best serve the gifted in your local area.

Planning the Gifted Program

The planning necessary to develop a gifted program that will provide the best match for the needs of your students, the expectations of the parents, the philosophy of the school administration, the resources of the community, and the resources and commitment of the school staff is a bit like orchestrating a symphony. There are the homework to do and skills to perfect, there are personnel and materials to collect, beliefs and abilities to assess, cooperation to solicit. To put it all together the timing is crucial.

Components of a Gifted Program

Renzulli (1975) identified seven key features that experts in the field of gifted education agreed were basic to a successful program. The seven were: (1) the selection and training of teachers; (2) a curriculum designed to evoke and develop superior behavioral potentialities both in academic areas and the arts that is both systematic and comprehensive; (3) multiple appropriate screening and identification procedures; (4) statements of philosophy and objectives that support differential education for the gifted; (5) staff orientation to promote a knowledgeable and cooperative attitude; (6) a plan of evaluation; (7) a delineation of administrative responsibility.

With these elements in mind, let us look at the steps we may take and the information we must have to make our program a reality. We have already discussed a rationale for the need to educate gifted individuals. A planning committee composed of teachers, administrators, parents, community representatives, and gifted students should be asked to develop the philosophy statement and goals for the program.

Goals of the Gifted Program

> What do you want schools—even families—to accomplish? Do you want to shape
> adults who will simply repeat what has been done by previous generations? Or
> do you want individuals who are capable of invention? Those are the real ques-
> tions. If you want to produce conformists, then the traditional school is perfect.
> But, if you want original thinkers, you need methods that will permit invention,
> not simply external reinforcements (Piaget in Weinheimer, 1972, pp. 118, 120).

The primary goal of the gifted program is to provide opportunities for gifted
learners to meet the needs that cannot be met in a regular classroom program,
whether those needs are found in content, process, enrichment, or in all three. With
these provisions we believe we will enable gifted students to grow as integrated people toward their full potential. What we will do specifically for each child will depend on our assessment data. Programs for the gifted do not begin with different
curricula or different structures for learning, but with the different needs of each
gifted learner. The gifted program is different only because, and in the same way
that, the gifted learner's needs are different. With this understanding, we may say
that, generally, a gifted program should—

> provide opportunities and experiences particularly suited to the needs of the
> gifted learners and through which they can continue developing potential;
>
> establish an environment that values and enhances intelligence, talent, affective
> growth, and intuitive ability;
>
> allow active and cooperative participation by the gifted students and their par-
> ents;
>
> provide time, space, and encouragement for gifted students to discover them-
> selves, their powers and abilities, and to become all that they can be;
>
> provide opportunities for gifted students to interact with children and adults of
> various abilities, including the bright and talented, to be challenged to know and
> revere humanity for its uniqueness and its connectedness;
>
> encourage gifted students to find their place in human evolution by discovering
> what abilities and in what areas they wish to contribute.

Educational programs for gifted students cannot just be different; they must
be qualitatively different. These programs must have the same goals for gathering
knowledge and developing skills as we find in the regular program. Programs for
the gifted share many of the same strategies and concerns as the regular programs.
But unless the gifted program goes beyond fact gathering and process development,
toward providing opportunities for gifted students to find their own areas of interest
and ability, to experience the problems of their chosen areas, and, through personal
effort, to develop real solutions that affect others, we do not have a program for the
qualitatively different learner we call gifted.

The next step will be to assess the resources and needs of the school, the staff,
the parents, and the community. Knowledge of the discrepancy between what you

want to happen ideally and what is available and presently exists will allow you to plan more realistically what you may accomplish now and what you must develop for future implementation.

It would be well at this point to establish the role of the administrator in designing and maintaining varied and appropriate programs for the gifted in your community. The committee will need to assemble all policy materials that affect the implementation of the program.

A Coordinator Model

Once we have decided on the type of program we want for our gifted students, how do we organize to provide it? Some districts give the responsibility to the school principal, others to the Special Education Director. Some add it to the responsibilities of the school counselor, and some hire a part-time teacher for the assignment. In all of these cases, the most well-meaning people will find it difficult to succeed. Adding such a program to an already overloaded administrator or counselor merely admits its low priority in the district and insures both the organizer and the program of inadequate energy for the job. The teacher will find the part-time status detrimental to any relationship with full-time personnel, with parents, and with the students. There is not enough time to develop the personal contacts, the assessment materials, and the necessary type of continuous program. In many cases, teachers in this position find themselves working full time for part-time pay. While such a situation is common in this profession, because of the lack of closure inherent in any work with growing people, it should not be encouraged. Planning a program based on this type of professional commitment is unfair and can lead to poor programs.

It has been found that in states where the total time of at least one person is devoted to gifted education, far more students have been adequately served. What is true for state levels can be also said for local levels. Whatever monies are allotted to educating the gifted students in your district would be best spent on a full-time person. If your district is small, cooperate with other surrounding districts to establish the position of Coordinator of Gifted Programs. I have heard some people, especially parents, say that the money should not be spent on administering the program; it should be spent on the kids. Ultimately, the gifted students will gain more in educational services with a full-time coordinator. When monies are "given to the kids," they are usually spent on materials or experiences that may or may not fit into a planned program. Sometimes undirected money ends up buying library books or reading kits or sometimes lab equipment or cameras. None of these does any harm in itself, but does it bring the gifted students closer to meeting their needs? How do these materials or experiences provide a continuing program? Who decides which materials or experiences are appropriate? Again, the full-time coordinator seems the best buy. The Coordinator for the Gifted Program in your district would do the following:

1. Plan the overall structure of the district gifted program in consultation with teachers, administrators, and parents.
2. Take care of all administrative paper work inherent in the district program (such as writing proposals for funding, evaluating data, etc.).

3. Interview and recommend teachers for the program for either integrated classes or special classes.
4. Conduct teacher inservice in gifted education for identification and implementation of programs.
5. Conduct parent meetings for inservice in gifted education and encourage active participation in the district program.
6. Establish case studies on all students who have been screened for gifted identification.
7. Conduct assessments of all students identified as gifted and establish profiles.
8. Chair the selection committee for identification of students for the gifted program.
9. Organize a mentor program as a part of the opportunities available to the gifted in the district.
10. Arrange for field trips that are needed for the gifted program.
11. Contact local colleges, universities, and museums for educational experiences available to gifted students advanced in areas not available within the local school.
12. Provide support and resources for teachers with gifted students in their classrooms.
13. Teach special classes for gifted students in small districts or occasionally in large districts.
14. Evaluate the district program and individual school programs to strengthen service to gifted students by obtaining data from teachers, students, and parents.
15. Provide a liaison between parents and the school; regular teachers and special teachers; the administration, the program personnel, and the community at large. Communicate regularly with the school board.
16. Serve on administrative committees with general education responsibilities to provide advocacy for the gifted learner (textbook selection committee, etc.).
17. Attend workshops and meetings to stay informed about current ideas and practices in gifted education.

As you can see, anything less than a full-time position would restrict the program. There are many opportunities appropriate to gifted students throughout the community that cost very little, but which require someone to ferret them out and make them available. A good coordinator can insure a successful gifted program. Of course, the selection of the coordinator is critical. Choosing a person with teaching or counseling experience who is open, excited about learning, enjoys gifted individuals, and has a very positive view of life would be wise. Additional training in gifted education would greatly benefit the position. An experienced educator from the same district would provide a lot of strength, although certainly that criterion is not as important as the person's attitudes and background.

The Coordinator Model for delivery of services in educating the gifted has many advantages. Potential contributions to the entire district's educational system are endless.

You are now ready to consider the many options for the structure you will use for the delivery of service to the gifted individuals to be selected for your program.

Traditional Administrative Organizations for Educating the Gifted

A number of administrative provisions have been tried through the years to help the schools meet the needs of gifted learners. Three of the most commonly used are ability grouping, acceleration, and enrichment. In our discussion we will include provisions at the elementary and secondary levels.

Ability Grouping

Ability grouping is a provision that allows some students to be separated from the more typical students by some given criterion, in this case, the level of measured intelligence. Ability grouping may be implemented as special classes or schools, special groups meeting prior to or after school, pullout programs during school hours where gifted students are separated for a given period of time and then returned to the regular program, or summer workshops. At the secondary level, a tracking system is often used to group students into classes based on academic ability.

Flexible grouping has many advantages. In the 1971 hearings held by the U.S. Department of Health, Education, and Welfare, gifted students expressed preference for programs where they are separated for part of the day, but not totally segregated from other students. They asked for flexibility in their program and in their curriculum (Marland, 1972).

When considering total separation, we might look at the level of involvement. All gifted students need to interact with those who can challenge them. For the highly gifted, ability grouping would justifiably comprise the major part of their educational experience. The moderately gifted and the mildly gifted would need less specialized grouping if classrooms could be individualized. In non-graded, individualized classrooms, a cluster group of five to seven gifted students would be adequate to meet their need for peer challenge. When this type of clustering is done in a classroom that is not organized to meet individual needs, where flexible grouping cannot occur, or where different types of ability are not valued and nurtured, the gifted student does not flourish.

Educational decision makers are often concerned that ability grouping will be detrimental to students left in the regular classroom. Teachers are sometimes concerned that their slower children will have no incentive, that the "spark" will be gone. In an attempt to measure the effects of ability grouping on gifted and nongifted learners, Goldberg and Passow (Passow, 1980) conducted a study in which they compared achievement gains between classes heterogeneously grouped with gifted students and classes comprised of nongifted students only. In science there were small differences evident, with the presence of gifted students contributing an upgrading effect. However, in social studies only the very bright students gained from their presence and then only if less able students were involved also. When the class had only bright and above average students, the attendance of the gifted had an inhibiting effect. In math there was found to be a downgrading effect when nongifted and gifted were grouped together, and in all other areas there seemed to be no consistent or significant trend. In this study as in others, we find that grouping in and of itself is insufficient to have significant effects on achievement among

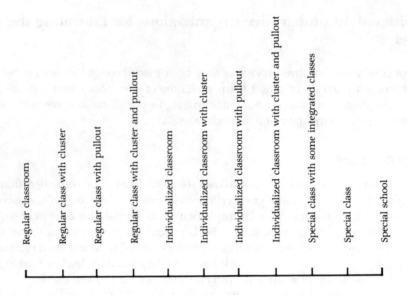

Figure 4.2.   Continuum Model for Ability Grouping

the gifted: the curriculum content and processes must change to become more appropriate to the gifted learner. When this is the case, the longer the gifted are allowed to be in special programs, the greater will be *their* gain (Martinson, 1972).

In planning the gifted program, you must consider the limitations as well as the strengths of your particular setting. The attitudes and beliefs of the school administration and the community, as well as the skills of the teacher, will shape your program. Let us look at several ways of grouping with the idea that you would use the one most suited to your particular situation. By being aware of the difficulties that the model could present because of its structure, you will try to prevent as many of the problems as possible. The continuum will range from ability grouping in regular classrooms to special schools.

1. Regular Classroom and Regular Classroom with Cluster   The regular class when traditionally organized (see p. 142) is not adequate for gifted education. These classrooms rely on group instruction and a set curriculum. The instruction is usually by subject, with similar experiences for everyone. Whitmore (1980) comments, "It seems likely that future research could prove that the regular classroom is the most restrictive environment for the gifted child. . . . This finding will be most probable if teachers are not helped to become more able to effectively individualize instruction" (p. 68).

2. Regular Classroom with Pullout
Advantages: Gifted students may have an opportunity to work at their level of ability and in their area of interest and to interact with other gifted students for at least part of their school time. Upon leaving the regular program, the student may experi-

ence a seminar, a resource room, a special class, a field trip, or other unique learning situations.

Disadvantages: The major part of the school week is still not an appropriate learning experience. Often gifted students are asked to do the regular classroom work missed when pulled out, in addition to the special class work. Also, the special class has little time for meeting all of the gifted needs; teachers may resent interruption of their program; other students in the regular classroom may envy and isolate the gifted child because of the special class. Teachers in pullout programs must establish good working relations with the regular class teachers if this plan is to benefit the gifted learner.

3. Regular Classroom with Cluster and Pullout   The same advantages and disadvantages as above except for the additional advantage of having the possibility for more interaction with gifted peers and better follow-through with the gifted program. The quality of this program will depend on the pullout teacher and class.

4. Individualized Classrooms   Make use of individual, team, and flexible small group instruction. Assessments are used to determine the curriculum and materials for each student. The classroom is decentralized and gives access to many types of learning. In most cases such classes are ungraded, with students from several age levels. Learning centers are often found in these classrooms.

Advantages: In this setting, gifted students are more likely to work at their own level and pace. The learning experience is continuous.

Disadvantages: If there are only one or two gifted students, they may feel isolated and have no one with whom to share ideas. This type of classroom requires a highly competent teacher, or it can become unstructured or only partially individualized. The teacher may not have enough resources available to keep up with a gifted learner and thirty-five others.

5. Individualized Classrooms with Cluster   Same advantages and disadvantages as above without the disadvantage of the isolation of being the only gifted learner.

6. Individualized Classrooms with Cluster and Pullout   Same advantages as above with the additional advantage of more resources available to both the gifted learner and the teacher. In this situation, the problems created by the pullout program in #2 will not be evidenced. If all students are valued and allowed to meet their needs, no students will feel that they must do what every other person does. The gifted can meet their needs without envy from others. Such a program has continuity and allows each student's needs to be met all through the week.

7. Special Class with Some Integrated Classes   Especially appropriate to intermediate and secondary schools that are organized by subject.

Advantages: Programs and environments can be designed to meet gifted needs. By moving into integrated (gifted and nongifted) classes for subjects that stress talent rather than giftedness, the students can learn to appreciate other students for their abilities. The mildly and moderately gifted would find this helpful.

Disadvantages: Such a class requires a specially trained teacher, or it can be just as inhibiting as no program. Often these classes are different only in the population attending them and in the added quantity of assignments. It is important to individualize in this setting, for the gifted are quite different from each other. Although gifted students are not highly advanced in every discipline, many secondary schools use tracking across all areas.

8. Special Class   Has the advantages and disadvantages of #7 without the involvement with other groups that may be talented in other areas. The special class is most appropriate for the highly gifted. In the special class, gifted students can be challenged to their full potential in every area. They are stimulated and not tempted to hide their gifts in order to be accepted.

9. Special Schools   Used most often for highly gifted or talented students, this plan has the advantages and disadvantages of #7 and #8 in a more intensified form.

Ability Grouping for Elementary Students

All of the nine models mentioned could be used with gifted elementary students. One example of the use of ability grouping in elementary gifted programming can be seen in Renzulli's (1978, 1979) Revolving Door Identification and Programming Model (RDIM). Supporting the recommended use of multiple criteria for identification, the model uses standardized tests and subjective evaluation of student performance and potential through teacher, peer, parent, and self-nomination. RDIM allows a rather large group of children who meet the criteria of above average academic ability, creativity, and task commitment to receive special enrichment opportunities on a rotating basis. Underlying this model is the belief that this type of "giftedness" is shown only at certain times, in certain areas of study and under certain circumstances. When behavior showing evidence of such creative, productive accomplishment becomes apparent, the student is allowed to pursue such accomplishment in a resource room setting through independent or small group work. Those using the model like the inclusion of larger numbers of children, the provision for individualized education while the child is in the resource room and the stress on practical application of products (Delisle, Reis, and Gubbins, 1981).

Ability Grouping for Secondary Students

Once the organization of the school moves to departmentalization, the flexibility of ability grouping available to the elementary teachers disappears. It is far more common to find provision for gifted made (if indeed any is made) in the form of special classes, as described in 7 and 8 above. These might be formed through tracking gifted students into designated classes in a few or all of their academic subjects: advanced placement classes, core curriculum plans, independent study groups, or group seminars. Some special schools have been formed at the secondary, like Governor's Schools and the special talent schools in New York. For more detailed information on programs at the secondary level see chapter 7.

Not included in the continuum for ability grouping are the special groups the student may experience as adjunct programs. These would meet before or after school or during summers. The student experience can range from special interest groups or classes with a single subject content to an open, varied approach. Disadvantages special groups have, if used as the total gifted program, are that they do nothing about the student's gifted needs during the entire day and they usually lack continuity. If used only as enrichment experiences with other parts of the program occurring within the regular school day, these adjunct experiences can provide a joyful, worthwhile part of the program for student and teacher alike.

A summary of research on ability grouping with gifted students presents a contradictory picture. The following conclusions recur in several of the studies (Barbe, 1955; Borg, 1964; Breidenstine, 1936; Findley and Bryan, 1971; Goldberg et al., 1965; Justman, 1954; Simpson and Martinson, 1961; Sumption, 1941):

1. Significant academic gains result when programs are adjusted to student abilities. Grouping alone is insufficient to show differences in achievement of grouped over nongrouped gifted students.
2. Attitudes of parents, teachers, and gifted students are generally favorable toward special groups or classes, especially if such grouping is flexible and not totally segregated.
3. Positive development in self-concept and a sense of well-being result from special group placement.
4. The amount of time spent in special groups or classes relates positively to achievement gains of gifted students.
5. Attitudes of other parents and teachers are reported as more negative toward grouped learners.
6. There is more opportunity for individual expression, in-depth study, acceleration, and freedom from regimentation in ability grouped classes.
7. There are more high achievers and fewer underachievers reported in ability grouped classes.

While ability grouping may provide a partial answer to the question of appropriate education for the gifted, other modifications must be made for the program to succeed. When ability grouping is used, the research recommends the following:

1. Recognize that there will still be individual differences. There is a tremendous range found within the gifted group; they are not homogeneous. Assess and plan for individualized instruction.
2. Avoid complete segregation.
3. Select secure, specially trained teachers.
4. Encourage growth in all functions, not just the intellectual.
5. Communicate with all teachers and parents.
6. Be informed on research, evaluation, and curriculum for this population.

Acceleration

Acceleration can take many forms. It can mean early entrance to formal schooling, moving through a primary area in two rather than three years, grade skipping, advanced placement, or moving through material at an accelerated rate. However it is implemented, it will result in student completion of formal schooling in less time than is usually required.

Research reported on acceleration is almost uniformly positive in its results (Anderson, 1960; Alexander and Skinner, 1980; Bish and Fliegler, 1959; Braga, 1969; The Fund for the Advancement of Education, 1957; Gallagher, 1966; Justman, 1953; Lehman, 1953; Lucito, 1964; Morgan, Tennant and Gold, 1980; Plowman and Rice, 1967; Pressey, 1955; Reynolds, 1962; Terman and Oden, 1947; Worchester, 1955). Some of the rationale and advantages reported are as follows:

1. Gifted students are inclined to select older companions because their levels of maturity are often more similar. Neither the method nor the age of acceleration appears to be of consequence.
2. Acceleration can be used in any school.
3. Acceleration allows capable students to enter their careers sooner, resulting in more productivity.
4. Because of their spending less time in school, the gifteds' educational costs are lowered.
5. Accelerated students do as well as or often better than the older students in their classes.
6. There is less boredom and dissatisfaction for the bright student.
7. Social and emotional adjustment are generally high, in most reports above average, when accelerated.
8. In general, teachers and administrators are opposed to acceleration, while parents and students, especially those who have experienced acceleration, are for it. Some possible reasons given for the negative attitudes of some educators are: convenience of lockstep, chronological grade placement, ignorance of research, discredited belief in social maladjustment, state laws preventing early admission.
9. To be successful, acceleration must be continuous and coordinated.

While acceleration should not be used as the total plan for a gifted program, the literature shows very few disadvantages to this provision when used on an individual basis. For the highly gifted, opportunities for acceleration are essential. The work of Stanley of Johns Hopkins University (Nevin, 1977) validates its importance. In a project begun in 1971, Stanley gave students highly gifted in mathematics an opportunity to develop their ability at an accelerated pace. His program has not only met with success among the students, but the results—their contributions to our society—have already been evidenced.

Over the past ten years the Study of Mathematically Precocious Youth (SMPY) has developed educational opportunities in several areas of radical acceleration. An eight-week, fast-paced accelerated mathematics program was begun in 1977 for seventh graders (Fox, 1981). Algebra II and plane geometry were offered. These classes differed from most homogeneously grouped programs for the gifted in several ways: students were selected from measures of specific aptitude in mathematics; they were allowed to self-select into the program after being told that the work load was heavy; there was maximum use of academic learning time, that is the real time in which a student is actually engaged in learning (Berliner, 1979); the material was fast paced and used a high level of abstraction and complexity; no class time was spent on drill or practice; and activities were kept to a minimum. The program was not individualized and demanded intensive self-study.

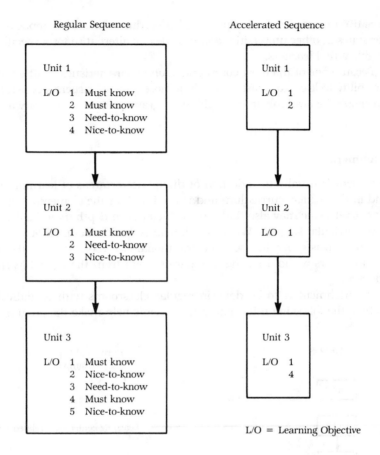

Regular Sequence   Accelerated Sequence

Unit 1

L/O   1   Must know   Unit 1
      2   Must know
      3   Need-to-know   L/O   1
      4   Nice-to-know   2

Unit 2

L/O   1   Must know   Unit 2
      2   Need-to-know
      3   Nice-to-know   L/O   1

Unit 3

L/O   1   Must know   Unit 3
      2   Nice-to-know
      3   Need-to-know   L/O   1
      4   Must know   4
      5   Nice-to-know

                                              L/O = Learning Objective

Directions: Test the student for competency on the must-know L/Os. Start at the one he or she doesn't know. Present only the must-know objective if straight acceleration is the objective.

Figure 4.3.   Acceleration Scope and Sequence

In addition to the fast-paced math, a program for accelerated language arts was begun in 1978 at Johns Hopkins University (Durden, 1980), and a tutorial program based on diagnostic testing, followed by prescriptive instruction in math and verbal ability, was piloted in the summers of 1979 and 1980. Stanley (1979) admits that these programs are designed to serve highly able, achieving, and motivated students. He states

> With more than 2,000 mathematically able boys and girls already identified, we do not have time and facilities to look for latent talent or potential achievers, worthy though that pursuit surely is. We leave that to the many persons who prefer to specialize in identification and facilitation of underachievers, 'late bloomers,' and the 'disadvantaged gifted.' Aside from some concern about sex differences in mathematical precocity, we have not tried to screen in a set percent of any group. From socioeconomic and ethnic standpoints, however, the high scorers have been a varied lot (p. 101).

The SMPY Program, its principles, and procedures have been replicated in several other states at other universities and provide one alternative for a specific population of highly gifted learners.

Because one of the most commonly found characteristics of gifted individuals is their ability to learn at a faster rate than more typical learners, acceleration in some form should be available in every gifted program, both at elementary and secondary levels.

Enrichment

Enrichment is usually the addition of disciplines or areas of learning not normally found in the regular curriculum and is used both at the elementary and at the secondary levels. One may also find more difficult or in-depth material available on the typical curricular subjects. While enrichment is feasible at any time in any organization model, it is generally used in a traditional classroom to meet the needs of advanced learners without having to separate them from the typical learners at their grade level.

If enrichment is to be done in regular classrooms without individualized instruction, the following minimum requirements help make the program effective:

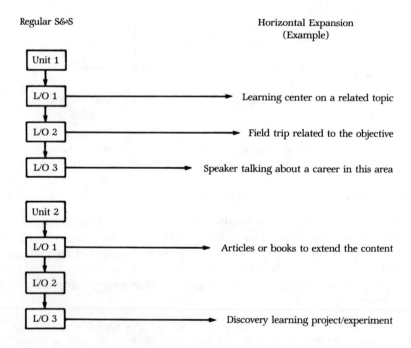

You do not have to plan horizontal expansion (H.E.) for every unit or objective. Use of H.E. activities is optional for the G/T student, based on student interest.

Figure 4.4.   Horizontal Expansion Scope and Sequence

1. The teacher must be able to identify and list the students who are gifted.
2. The teacher must be able to show the specific curriculum modifications being made for the gifted learners.
3. There must be one person with supervisory responsibility over the entire program (such as the Coordinator of Gifted Programs) to help provide resources for the regular teacher (Kough, 1960, p. 147).

Enrichment, the administrative provision most used in programs for gifted, must be well-planned and enhanced by other modifications or it will meet few of the gifted student's needs. By a total focus on enrichment, growth in content and process needs may be overlooked. From the research, we find that this idea has seldom been carefully implemented, and it causes the least change in the opportunities

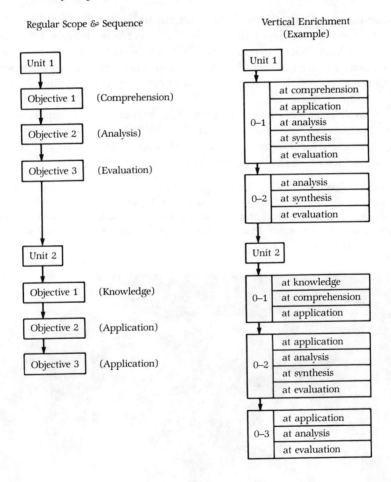

Note: Students **do not** have to complete all levels of every objective. Choice chould be based on student interest in the topic. Objectives do not have to have every higher level represented, this is up to the curriculum designer.

Figure 4.5.   Vertical Expansion Scope and Sequence

provided for the gifted learner. Enrichment in many classrooms often means just more work, sometimes more of the same work.

When enrichment is used, Gallagher (1964) recommends including activities that develop—

the ability to associate and interrelate concepts;

the ability to evaluate facts and arguments critically;

the ability to create new ideas and originate new lines of thought;

the ability to reason through complex problems;

the ability to understand other situations, other times, and other people; to be less bound by one's own peculiar environmental surroundings (p. 80).

Enrichment may appeal to district administration and school boards as the most inexpensive way to meet gifted needs. If the problems of limited teacher time, lack of teacher knowledge in every area, limited availability of resources, and individualized planning are not met, this provision may be, by far, the most expensive in waste of human potential. Enrichment is most effective when combined with other provisions and modifications.

An example of an enrichment program can be found in the implementation of Renzulli's Enrichment Triad Model (Renzulli, 1976). As an answer to criticism regarding enrichment programs that are not differentiated and indeed seem to be good education for all students, the model has two objectives.

Program Object No. 1—For the majority of time spent in the gifted programs, students will have complete freedom to pursue topics of their own choosing to whatever depth and extent they so desire; and they will be allowed to pursue these topics in a manner that is consistent with their own preferred style of learning (p. 307).

Enrichment activities can provide exciting learning.

Program Objective No. 2—The primary role of each teacher in the program for gifted and talented students will be to provide each student with assistance in (1) identifying and structuring realistic solvable problems that are consistent with the student's interests, and (2) acquiring the methodological resources and investigative skills that are necessary for solving these particular problems (p. 312).

The Model identifies three types of enrichment. The first two types, General Exploratory Activities and Group Training Activities, are considered to be appropriate for all learners and provide the basis for the overall enrichment of gifted and talented students. They are intended to provide strategies for expanding student interests and developing the thinking and feeling processes. Type III enrichment, Individual Investigations of Real Problems, is the only one mainly appropriate for gifted students. In Type III enrichment, the student is to focus on real work methods of inquiry to provide first hand experience in that particular field of interest. The teacher is responsible to provide the resources for meeting program objective No. 2, and to provide appropriate outlets for the resulting products. Caffee (1981) describes how the Enrichment Triad Model can be implemented in a secondary gifted and talented program.

Mentors

Another option that you can make available for enrichment, which often provides acceleration, is a mentors' program. Mentors are people with expertise to share with gifted learners who are interested in their field and are at a point of development in that field where they can benefit from involvement with an expert. Mentors can be found in many places. Older students can become mentors for younger students especially if a structure is provided for their contact and some prior training in interpersonal relations is made available. Retirement communities are an excellent resource for mentors, as many retired persons have the experience and record of achievement to share and the time to share it. Parents of gifted students may provide mentorship for other students. Also, don't overlook the practicing professionals in your community. Though their time may be at a premium, they will often make time for that one bright, inquiring student who finds their field fascinating.

Mentors should not be considered the same as another traditional teacher with a need to evaluate, report, and record the progress of the student. There is in this relationship a more equal partnership involved, with more emphasis on the guidance aspect of learning. Mentors provide a social contact, a sponsorship into the world of the profession being shared. Mutual interest and trust will be necessary components of successful mentorships. As you organize to provide a mentors' program, you may want to review programs like the Mentor Academy Model (Runions, 1980), which has developed a procedure for implementing this valuable alternative for enrichment.

Another unique mentors' program is reported by Szekely (1981) and involves the artistically gifted child. The Art Partnership Networks enlist college students, majors in every field of art, as mentors to elementary school children who show interest and ability in art. The college artists are introduced as visiting artists after completing a series of workshops designed to acquaint them with a philosophy of giftedness. The college artist then comes into the elementary classroom to work with one child or a small group who have expressed and demonstrated interest. The results of the program are encouraging and have gained the support of teachers, parents, the PTA, and school personnel.

Independent Study

Although this provision can include acceleration of material and concepts and can be carried out in a variety of settings, it is most often used to provide enrichment. The outcome of independent study should be a self-directed learner who can investigate real problems; but too often teachers expect students, because they are gifted, to be self-directed learners from the start. They often have the curiosity, the interest, and the motivation to pursue a study of their own choosing; but all too often they do not have the skills, skills such as how they can search for primary sources, use professional methods of inquiry, collect and organize raw data, analyze and evaluate data, and form conclusions. These skills often need to be taught if the student is to be successful. Doherty and Evans (1981) suggest a three phase process for using independent study. Phase 1 is teacher led and incorporates learning centers, experimentation, and simulation as the student explores the depth and breadth of the academic area. Phase 2 is the independent study and is a nine step process involving locating and using data, producing new ideas and developing a product that is examined by experts.

Step 1: The student selects a topic that is issue-oriented.
Step 2: The student establishes a schedule.
Step 3: The student develops five or more questions (first objectives) to direct the research.
Step 4: The student secures references and seeks sources or raw data.
Step 5: The student researches the topic, collects raw data, and takes notes.
Step 6: The student develops five final objectives using Bloom's Taxonomy.
Step 7: The student has a conference with the teacher, who evaluates the depth of knowledge and the idea production.
Step 8: The student makes a product showing some of his or her new ideas.
Step 9: The student's product is displayed, evaluated with a friend, and examined by an expert.

The final phase is a culminating seminar. This process allows students to build the skills necessary to carry out an investigation that will satisfy their intellectual curiosity and truly enrich their academic lives.

The use of independent study for gifted learners is supported by a study (Stewart, 1981) that reports that when compared to learning styles of more average students, there was an apparent preference among the gifted students for instructional methods emphasizing independence, i.e., independent study and discussion. The general population within the study preferred more structured methods, i.e., lecture and projects. For a selection of enrichment activities to be used at home and at school you may want to consult Kanigher's book, *Everyday Enrichment* (1977).

All of these provisions have been and are currently being used in various combinations and with varying degrees of success. Research shows that none is without merit, nor do any answer all the needs of gifted students. In light of the extensive literature, further research and modification of these program provisions would seem unnecessary. Possibly adherence to only these models for so long has limited the ability of schools to meet the needs of the gifted individual.

In using any of the traditional program models, as we have in the past, we are left with some uncomfortable problems. Programs often exist for only minimal periods of time throughout the gifted students' educational experience. This results in little continuity of learning experiences. Often gifted students are faced with having their needs met only during the allotted special program time (e.g., one half-day a week, a few weeks a year, or a six-week summer program). Not only are they asked to give up their free time so that their special learning needs can be attended, but there is an assumption that, during the rest of their school time, such needs do not exist, or if they do, they can be sublimated until the allotted period arrives.

Other problems, such as labeling, social integration, and interpersonal relationships, often result from these part-time provisions. It therefore becomes important to find a way to individualize school learning experiences so that gifted individuals can have their atypical needs met continuously throughout their school career. Their differences must become strengths, not the handicaps they often are in a traditional setting. The gifted have a right to pursue learning at their own pace to their level of capability, with challenges available on a full-time basis and progress encouraged by their learning environment.

Rural Programs

In addition to the possibilities for programming for gifted learners already mentioned, those planning for rural areas may want to consider: mobile enrichment vans, independent study "hot lines" (access to mentors through a telephone system), itinerant teachers, correspondence courses, summer seminars followed by monthly meetings, residential summer institutes (Silverman, 1980). Witters and Vasa (1981) consider the most important task in the provision of educational opportunities for rural gifted to be the selection and training of teachers who work with these students.

Birnbaum also emphasizes the teacher need and adds others to be considered. Problems with access to resources, from transportation to material, are seen as inhibiting to cultural and intellectual development. Continuous and assertive leadership is necessary to change a number of other factors inhibiting to the development of quality gifted programs: poor general community understanding, teacher/administrator hostility, and logistical and organizational problems. Cooperatives, consortia of districts, summer programs, and mobile services are suggested by Freehill as possible solutions. For information on a model project for implementing a program for G/T in rural schools, contact M. Humphrey, Shasta County Superintendent of Schools Office, 1644 Magnolia Avenue, Redding, California 96001.

The Integrative Education Program Model—For Elementary or Secondary Settings

Most of the traditional program structures focus on the cognitive area of the intellect and provide avenues to enhance the growth of cognition in the curriculum. However, as we have seen (chapters 1 and 2), within the past two decades findings have been reported from a variety of disciplines that dramatically affect our concepts of teaching and learning. Intelligence can no longer be defined as only a rational process. For over thirty years we have known intelligence to be interactive (Hunt, 1961); now we find it to be integrative (p. 22). It requires not just the use of the rational thinking function, but depends on the integration of the feeling or emotional function, the physical or sensing function, and the intuitive thinking function as well. While we can speak of and experience these functions separately, it is the integration of these functions that creates high levels of intelligence and optimal development of human potential.

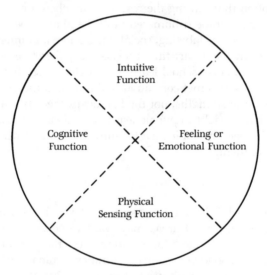

Figure 4.6.   Integrative Education
A model for developing human potential

The Rational Thinking Function (Cognition)

This is the analytic, problem solving, sequential, evaluative function of our brain/ mind. Gifted learners find this function enhanced by their accelerated synaptic activity, the density of their dendritic growth allowing them to establish complex networks of thought more easily. The biochemical changes that result from stimulating environments are expressed in the advanced capacity to generalize, to conceptualize, to reason abstractly, and to problem solve that is found in gifted learners.

The Feeling or Emotional Function (Affect)

This is the function that is expressed in emotions and feelings and, while affecting every part of the brain/mind system, it is primarily regulated from the limbic area by biochemical mechanisms housed there. This function more than supports cognitive processes; it does, in fact, provide the gateway to enhance or inhibit higher cognitive function. To provide for optimal learning, our program must include opportunities to integrate emotional growth.

The Physical or Sensing Function

This function includes all of the sensorium: sight, hearing, smell, taste, and touch. The access to our world is through the physical senses and our level of intellectual ability, even our view of reality, will depend on how our brain organizes and processes this information. We know that gifted learners have a heightened ability to bring in information from their environment and process this information in ways that expand their view of reality. They do, however, often define themselves by their cognitive ability. They may recognize their value through this ability alone, and they may focus more and more energy toward the pursuit of cognitive excellence. They may ignore their physical growth and development. Although we are aware of the above-average physical development of many gifted children, we must also notice how they value and share physical pursuits far less than cognitive endeavors. It is common for gifted learners to develop a Cartesian split, which, if unrecognized and left to intensify, can limit the cognitive growth they so value. Integration of the body and the mind becomes an essential part of an integrated program.

The Intuitive Thinking Function

According to Jung, intuition "does not denote something contrary to reason, but something outside the province of reason" (Jung, 1933, p. 454). He considered intuition vital to understanding. This function, which we all have but use in varying degrees, represents a different way of knowing. We use this ability when we feel that we know, but we cannot tell how we know. It is a sense of total understanding, of directly and immediately gaining a concept in its whole, living existence. People often repress and devaluate it because it does not operate in the rational manner our western mind has been taught to expect. Activating intuition gives a person a sense of completeness, of true integration. This powerful tool leads to the understanding of concepts and people and to an expansion of the human reach.

The physicist, Capra (1975), tells us that rational knowing is useless if not accompanied and enhanced by intuitive knowing. He equates intuition with new creative insights, and he states:

> These insights tend to come suddenly and, characteristically, not when sitting at a desk working out the equations, but when relaxing in the bath, during a walk in the woods, on the beach, etc. During these periods of relaxation after concentrated intellectual activity, the intuitive mind seems to take over and can produce the sudden clarifying insights which give so much joy and delight to scientific research (p. 31).

Many of those working to include the development of intuition in the educational setting believe that the ability to concentrate, to work at complex tasks with unusual clarity, results from the intuitive function. Identified now as a part of the function of the prefrontal cortex, intuition becomes a part of the planning, future thinking, and insight so necessary to the intelligent person.

By the use of integrative education and strategies incorporating this construct, students can expect to make impressive gains in areas of cognition, self-concept, and social-emotional development. Among the cognitive gains will be accelerated learning, higher levels of retention and recall, and higher interest in content. In other areas improvement will be seen in how competent the student feels, pleasure derived from learning, interpersonal relations, and teacher-student rapport (Balevski and Ganovski, 1975; Bordan and Schuster, 1976; Galyean, 1977–80; Galyean, 1978–81; Galyean, 1979; Lozanov, 1977; Mostofsky, 1978; Prichard and Taylor, 1980; Samples, 1975).

The Integrative Education Model uses all of the modifications previously mentioned including ability grouping, acceleration, and enrichment. The strategies for implementing integrative practices will be discussed in chapter 6. In its ability to use more of the brain/mind system, focusing narrowly on neither the cognitive nor any other single component, the Integrative Education Model presents a truly supportive, powerful learning model. By combining previously used structures with the new brain/mind information, we can come far closer to the optimal learning experience we all desire.

Within the structure of the Integrative Education Model, learners of all levels of ability and interest can be served. Because of its decentralized and personalized organization and its concern for total brain function, giftedness, regardless of how it is expressed, can be nurtured and enhanced. We will discuss implementation of the Integrative Education Model in chapter 6. The Model has been successfully implemented in a variety of settings, including self-contained classes both homogeneously and heterogeneously grouped at elementary and secondary levels; resource room settings; and a special-school setting.

Using the Community

Many gifted programs have stretched their resources by using community facilities and people as part of the teaching process. Using the Coordinator of Gifted Programs as the organizer, have you thought of—

equipping a van or bus as a mobile laboratory to take your students into the field for an integrated experience in science, geography, social science, language, mathematics, and interpersonal relations?

contacting your nearest retirement community for experts who could serve as mentors to students who are ready for advanced challenges? Some people who would be uncomfortable teaching in a larger group may be willing to work with one or two youngsters.

contacting parents to give lessons on their area of interest at their place of business or before groups in your classroom?

using the business facilities close to your school (stock exchanges, real estate offices, stores, hospitals, pharmacies, insurance companies, etc.) for learning opportunities? Not to be used as a one-time-only field trip, but as an ongoing or more in-depth contact. This would be especially meaningful to the few students who have special interest in a related field.

using tape recorders to direct teams of students on independent searches or explorations of the surrounding area (its history, its geography, its climate, its economic or cultural nature, etc.)?

The community can also be an amazing source of free materials for the asking. Have you tried contacting—

the telephone company? They have old telephone poles, used equipment, cable spools, and storage containers; some will even set up a communication system in your room as a public relations service.

electronic companies? They have obsolete electronic parts that can be used for great experiments.

construction projects, lumber, and hardware stores? Besides the obvious, in their scrap bin they may have old fencing, paint, rope, bricks, and other treasures.

billboard companies? Their throwaways are great for signs and displays.

rug stores or rug cleaners? If they know it's for kids at school, they often have odds and ends to make a van or classroom really livable.

nurseries, agricultural schools, park departments? They may have plants to donate to science projects and botany buffs.

meat packers or meat markets? Check for spare parts the biologists and anatomists could use.

The list is endless; once you and your students start thinking this way, you will add many, many more. Be sure to check your district or state surplus warehouse. For very little money, you can get a lot of useful items—everything from typewriters and computers to paper cups and newsprint. Check your local community college or university warehouse. Don't forget your school's storage room. Hidden treasures are everywhere. If the school will value the items and write a letter specifying that any materials contributed were donated, the donor can use this as a tax deduction. This practice tends to encourage contributions.

Commitment and Community Involvement

Community involvement does not just happen by chance. A person has to believe that effort spent in community-related activities will indeed make some difference. Gifted students often have a high degree of idealism and, if allowed to use their abilities to make needed changes in the school or community, such activity will foster future commitment to societal goals. Some possible activities are:

Conduct a survey in the school or community that will provide information needed to change something. Then use it.

Make a place in the school or community more beautiful. Be sure to obtain agreement on what you consider more beautiful.

Work with community groups or organizations for civic improvement.

Plan a money raising project for a worthy charity or to buy needed materials for the school.

Class projects can often be made more meaningful by involving students in the larger community.

Evaluating the Program

The word *evaluation* is, for many people, anxiety-producing. It has come to mean a judgment: the act of validating or invalidating a person or thing. Often the word is mistakenly used to mean examination or testing. If used properly, it would mean "to ascertain the value of or to get to know about someone or something." Evaluation goes far deeper than testing, although tests may be used as part of the data collection process. In this discussion, we will consider evaluation as the process of collecting a variety of data to help us understand the student or the program: data that can be used to improve program planning and implementation.

When planning your program evaluation, the first question should be "Who needs to know what?" What persons are interested in, involved in, or responsible for the gifted program? Included in this group would be, at least, the student, the teacher, the administrator(s), the board members, and the parents. Find out what each of these persons or groups needs or expects to find out from an evaluation. They will all want some information (e.g., data on academic progress, social-emotional growth, gains in decision-making ability and leadership). Some of the groups will need information the others will not need. For example, parents would want information on the effects of home involvement, and the board members would need data on finances.

Make a list of what each group wants to know; don't assume you know what they want; ask them orally or in writing. Then you are ready to put together the tools and instruments that will give you the data. You might choose to use standardized or specially constructed tests, rating scales, questionnaires, interview schedules, or observation techniques. Look at the program goals; these are expectations that, ideally, the teacher, the student, the administration, and the parents cooperatively delineated. To discover which of these goals have been reached, you might include the student's file of work completed, teacher observations, parent questionnaires, and the student's self-reports and testing records. Have some of the interested groups visit the program for the purpose of reporting their impressions. After reviewing the information, you may wish to develop new procedures for meeting your goals, or you may find that rethinking and changing the goals would be desirable.

If your assessment procedures (discussed in chapter 5, p. 187) are used regularly, data collection is relatively easy. Assessment should be ongoing throughout the year. When you find additionally needed data that your assessment overlooks, expand the assessment procedure to include such information. When used properly, evaluation data become part of the total assessment package.

In addition to information about pupil progress, be sure to evaluate the learning situation. Are the structure, the time allowed, and the classroom atmosphere conducive to meeting the needs of the gifted students and the goals of the program? Collecting this kind of information will tell you not only if the program is working, but why. An interesting instrument to use for this purpose is the Class Activities Questionnaire (Steele, 1969). It assesses five areas of the learning environment: *lower and higher thought processes* (based on Bloom's taxonomy); *classroom focus* (the role of the teacher and whether the students play a passive or active role); *the classroom climate* (attitudes and feelings); *student opinions* (about class, about things to change, etc.). Others are useful, such as the Flanders' interaction analysis procedures (1960), or you could devise a questionnaire specifically to meet your needs.

Be careful in your evaluation to view the students' growth individually, in comparison with their own past achievements and developed criteria only. The student and the teacher could decide together what form the evaluations should take to show achievement when the learning goal has been completed most effectively.

Gifted students do not necessarily show growth against group norms because they are already near the ceiling of many tests. To expect gifted students to raise their test scores or percentile ranks is not appropriate to measuring their progress.

To make the program evaluation as effective and efficient as possible, set out a plan that allows you to cycle information throughout the year. Make sure you—

1. Know clearly what each person or group involved in your program needs to know.
2. Choose instruments and tools to give you that information.
3. Set up collection points throughout the year in addition to your assessment procedure.
4. Collect only useful data. If you find state or district forms or procedures that require the collection of irrelevant data, discuss them with people at that level. Tell them what data you have, and inquire into their need for the data they are requesting. You may find that they will be willing to change their procedures into a more meaningful model. Sometimes procedures become institutionalized and continue as they always have only because no one questions their purpose.
5. Communicate your information to all concerned persons and groups. It is impossible to get the kind of support your program needs if key people remain unaware of what you are doing. From the student to the board member, keep all persons informed.
6. Use your evaluation data to produce growth in the program and with the gifted students. If done properly, evaluation will never be a final judgment.

For information on specific program evaluations and sample evaluation designs, you may wish to consult the Association for the Gifted's booklet on sample instruments (Renzulli, 1979b), the National/State Leadership Training Institute on Gifted/Talented *Guidebook for Evaluating Programs* (Renzulli, 1975b), the *Diagnostic and Evaluative Scales for Differential Education for the Gifted* (Renzulli and Ward, 1969), and the *Administrator's Handbook on Designing Programs for the Gifted and Talented* from CEC/ERIC, chapter 11 (VanTassel, 1980).

The Written Plan

We have now discussed the rationale for gifted programs, the selection of a planning committee, the philosophy and goals of a gifted program, the assessment of resources needed, the role of the administrator and the coordinator, a variety of traditional and exemplary program structures for the delivery of services to the gifted learner, and the importance of evaluation on these programs. We are now ready to develop a written plan. Kaplan (1974) suggests that the written plan must communicate the program clearly and be able to serve as a reference for any questions regarding its implementation and what it is intended to accomplish. It should also be a guide for evaluating the program goals. In the case of a change of personnel, the plan should be detailed enough to provide for continuity for the new staff. The following are eleven elements that Kaplan (p. 199) considers essential to a written plan:

1. Population, enrollment
2. Descriptive summary
3. Philosophy, goals, and objectives
4. Identification procedures
5. Organization patterns: prototypes, facilities, time allocation
6. Curricular opportunities: activities, techniques, materials
7. Differentiation from regular school program
8. Accountability of personnel
9. Supportive services: inservice, consultants, auxiliary personnel
10. Budgetary allocations
11. Evaluation processes

We have discussed many of these elements. We will look at the strategies for a differentiated curriculum in the pages to follow.

In summary, if we are to meet the needs of gifted learners, we must have a planned, coordinated, continuous program. This program must be open and responsive to the changing individual, while providing continuous challenge and an adequate diversity of content and process. While we may draw from more traditional gifted education models, our own community, our parents, students, and staff must make the decisions of structure and intent. While some goals can be generalized, others must be specifically set by the teacher, the student, and the parent in a cooperative effort.

A gifted program is difficult to implement without a person who will be responsible, one who will give it full-time support. Money spent on a qualified enthusiastic coordinator will be wisely spent, for the returns are abundant. Continuous evaluation to adjust the gifted program is only one of the tasks involved in assuring its effectiveness. Society needs the establishment and maintenance of challenging programs for gifted students. Our job is not easy. As Drews (1976) comments,

> Clearly, we shall never meet the needs of the gifted by systems of prescribed programming, by behavioral objectives and accountability. The prime characteristic of the gifted is their individuality. The precondition of creativity is spontaneity. The creative moment is an intuitive flash. Those of our students who have this potentiality cannot be made to fit into neat sequences of stages of development, whether of intellect or character, as Piaget or Kohlberg suggests (p. 27).

But be of courage. Important things are seldom easy.

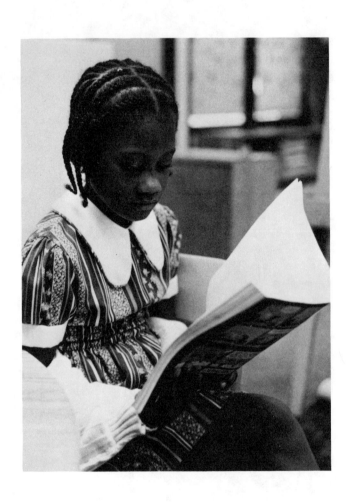

CHAPTER FIVE

Finding the Gifted within the School Setting

This chapter provides for the reader

- information on the need for identifying gifted individuals in schools.
- methods and uses of screening for gifted students.
- a tool for identification of gifted students by teachers.
- procedures for identification of cognitive, academic, creative, leadership, and arts abilities.
- a discussion of identifying the culturally different, handicapped, or educationally atypical gifted individual.
- ideas for assessment of individual needs in content, process, and enrichment.

> The creative and gifted students reach out beyond the amassing and recall of facts. They are at home with the overarching concepts involving the great unitive themes. They strive for a coherent view of themselves, of the world, and of human destiny. Indeed it is by this quality, more than by standardized tests, that we can identify them, for they are ever seeking the interrelations that lead to a higher synthesis.
>
> Elizabeth Monroe Drews

To provide educational experiences that lead a child to the next level of development, we must be aware of what that learner has already accomplished. In schools that provide individualized learning opportunities, that observe, evaluate, and assess as a part of the growth experience, and that make available access to many levels and types of learning simultaneously, identification is not viewed in the same way that it must be viewed in the more traditional school organization. In schools that use discrete grade placement, primarily determined by chronological age, and that use group instruction almost totally, it may even be necessary to label and isolate atypical learners for at least part of the time. In secondary schools where departmentalization by subject is the most common way to present the world to a learner, this will certainly be necessary. Advanced Placement classes and Honors sections are often used to meet this need. Such provisions do not take the place of individual assessment, and planning for appropriate experiences for each learner is still necessary.

When public education began in our country, years before testing became available, students often moved through their educational program as their ability allowed. Fewer pupils studied in smaller, multigraded classrooms. Bright children in classrooms where materials were available over a range of grade levels, often as many as eight, could easily learn from older children and become involved in work beyond their own age group. The early system not only made it possible for students to complete eight grades of schoolwork in a shorter time period, but encouraged them to do so. The ability to pursue any higher levels of education depended on the financial support available to the student. Only bright students had these opportunities, as most families could not economically support the less able students. This was a time when much education stemmed from the home, and experience was viewed as a good teacher. It was possible for eminent people such as Thomas Edison, Jessie Benton, and Albert Einstein to be educated by their families when they, for one reason or another, could not remain in the public educational system.

There are numerous advantages to a more integrated approach to education. For now, let us look at those that affect the educational experience of the gifted child today. Some years ago I taught a cross-graded class of gifted youngsters in a rural area of one of the plains states. The children were all gifted learners, and the school was committed to providing any resources necessary to further their educational growth. It was possible to develop a program that allowed the children to work at their own level of ability and interest. The program used group instruction, individual conferencing, contracts, and group projects. It made much use of peer and cross-grade tutoring and small group projects. Students worked with a variety of levels of materials; at times, second graders worked in eighth-grade material for some subject areas and in third-grade materials for others. This was true of the third graders and the fourth graders as well. They soon lost sight of what "grade" they were in and dealt with material as they were ready for it. Those exceptionally accomplished in one area dealt with very advanced materials in that area while they worked at less advanced levels in other areas of learning. Some recreation or project work included the entire class, for learning many skills was a joint venture. We had an exciting time.

As a child became ready or approached a new level or interest area, appropriate learning opportunities were available. Their abilities did not need to be identified; they could just "bubble up." We could use materials and school and community resources, including a variety of people, to insure continued growth. Later, in a similar plan in Illinois, classes of kindergarten children were observed, and those who showed ability in any particular area were given the opportunity to expand their skills and talents as they "bubbled up." Provisions for advanced learning became a normal part of these classroom situations. In both cases, the schools were committed to providing for individual needs and encouraging unique growth. Identification was a continuous occurrence. Special grouping and specialized instruction were normal parts of the classroom routine.

A few years later, working in another area of the country, I experienced a different and, unfortunately, more common way of instructional organization. This classroom had children all at one grade with a range of ages not more than 2 years apart. However, their learning abilities were extremely divergent. The IQ's ranged from 80 to 180, with only three children above 130. Several spoke only Spanish. It seemed obvious that this would have to be a very individualized program that would need a wide variety of experiences and an even broader range of materials and learning opportunities. To my dismay, I was expected to teach third-grade reading, to use the state-adopted text at grade level, and to give standardized tests at regular intervals. Using any of the tests to diagnose was not allowed. Whether appropriate to the learner or not, they had to be administered and turned in for scoring. Just a printout of the stanines achieved by the students was returned for classroom use. The administration then used the results to compare schools within the district and to make decisions on these comparisons. The room was regularly visited to see that the furniture was in place (fire rules) and that the children were seated and quiet. My final defeat came with the declaration that teachers in first through third grade (this was a third grade room) would be prohibited from using materials from the upper grade bookroom, and that it would be locked with keys issued only to eligible staff members. This was to prevent children from going ahead of their grades so that they would not be bored when they were given material the following year.

In educational settings such as this, identifying atypical learners becomes a concern. In such rigid situations, the energy to meet the needs of the school administration and still provide meaningful individualized learning for such diverse students becomes too overwhelming. Of course one can try, against all odds, to enrich the learning of children such as the three with bright minds. More likely, the push for conformity will prevail, and any extra energy will be spent trying to bring the slow children up to the pace and norms the school expects. One way to insure a gifted learner's growth in this situation is by identification and at least partial segregation. We discussed the possibilities of programming for the gifted in the last chapter.

Because not all children and teachers find themselves in situations where the "bubble-up" method can work and because, even in ideal situations, assessment, profiles, and case studies are extremely valuable, let us look at alternative procedures for finding gifted children.

Screening and Identification Procedures

What do we know about discovering the gifted in large populations of students? This is indeed a difficult task, for although one can generalize certain characteristics within this population, individuals may not possess the same characteristics as other gifted individuals or exhibit them in quite the same way. They may not appear to have any physically observable differences. The gleam in their eye and that extra energy level they seem to possess does not show in many educational situations. Depending on how their previous life experiences have dealt with their giftedness, they may even actively attempt to appear quite "ungifted." They may, too willingly, go along with the classroom program.

To confound the issue, not all gifted children cooperate in a classroom. Many resist routine, exhibit nonconformist behavior, and may be classified as behavior problems. Others may be labeled slow learners because they are bored, uninterested in material learned long ago, and nonresponsive to classroom activities. Unless observation of activities of their own choosing is involved, they may even appear to be educationally retarded or emotionally disturbed. Many gifted youngsters are discovered only after their frustration leads them, by teacher request, to the office of a counselor for testing for a learning handicapped program. They are just as likely to withdraw into the "good" child syndrome, passively doing only what is required and drawing attention to themselves only for excessive participation in school-approved activities such as reading. This is especially common among girls. Because the very qualities that cause a person to be gifted can be successfully used to hide giftedness, we need to be aware of some identification procedures.

Let us look again at our definition. Gifted children are those who have developed or show evidence of developing high levels of intelligence, with intelligence being defined as advanced or accelerated whole brain function. Such children may exhibit any of the characteristic behaviors we discussed in chapter 2. We will be especially concerned about gifted children who show their intelligence through high performance in abilities in the cognitive, specific academic, creative, leadership areas, or ability in the visual and performing arts, when such ability cannot be furthered in the program ordinarily provided by the schools. We will further concern ourselves with children who show the potential for high performance.

Were it not so expensive, the quickest way to find a large percentage of cognitively gifted youngsters would be the administration of individual intelligence tests. If you have access to the protocol, the original copy of the test with the actual responses recorded, you have a good diagnostic tool. If tests are used properly, they provide much information. Test scores alone give very limited data; without a protocol they can be nearly valueless. On some groups of children, the more commonly given intelligence tests may not provide enough information. For some, the child-rearing practices of their parents, the language they use most, and their past experiences are not reflected in these tests. The scores may give a false picture of their abilities. Although Binet (1973), in originating the intelligence scales in 1906, and Terman (1916), in revising and popularizing these scales, both warned that they were to be used as only one piece of data along with other important information about the student in any process of educational decision making, such was seldom the case. Even now, the intelligence test looms very large as a selection tool for gifted individuals. Earlier we discussed some of the limits of the intelligence test, and we will look specifically at its use in the Appendix (p. 412) because the influence of testing as it relates to the identification of gifted children is so significant.

Even the weaknesses mentioned are not the main reason that individual intelligence tests are not used as screening devices. The expense of having such a test administered by a licensed school psychologist is prohibitive. Only after the school has some assurance that the child will perform successfully on such tests can they be scheduled. How, then, can we provide that assurance?

For children who express their intelligence through creative thinking, other tests and activities will be indicated. To identify leadership or arts abilities will take observation and judgment of products or events. What procedure can be devised to find those who are ready to advance in all these areas?

It should be evident that to find and serve children from each of the areas of ability will take varied and numerous resources. It would be well for a school advisory committee to make some initial recommendations prior to the implementation of any identification procedures:

1. What resources (material and personnel) does the school or community have for providing programs for advanced learners?
2. Are they adequate to provide for all five areas of ability?
3. If not, which areas should be included?

It will be assumed that the cognitive and specific academic ability areas would be included, for these are usually the primary focus of the school. Very probably creative ability should also be included, as abilities in these areas are supportive to the cognitive functions and are not totally separable. Leadership may become an important subcomponent of the gifted program in which the learners could choose to participate. Visual and performing arts talent take very special resources significantly different than the other ability areas. The school may need to enlist professional artists, musicians, actors, and dancers from the community to supplement the program in this area.

Dirks and Quarfoth (1981) compared two multiple criteria models for identifying gifted children, one developed for depth (scoring well on one area) and the other for breadth (scoring well on several areas). Children selected for breadth had high classroom grades and were well thought of by their teachers. Those selected for depth included more children and more promising underachievers than the breadth model. The authors of this study believe the depth model to be more valuable in identification.

Screening

Begin by screening for children who show need for a different quality of educational experience. Screens that could be used for all areas of ability are:

1. Nomination forms—from teachers, principal, counselor, psychologist, and others
2. Teacher reports of student functioning—including intellectual, physical, social, and emotional functioning; learning style and motivation
3. Family history and student background—provided by parents, this will include historical and developmental data on the student; health and medical records of student and family; educational and occupational background of parents; description of family unit; anecdotes of the student in the home that indicate unusual capacity and early development; family activities and interests; and the child's out-of-school activities and interests
4. Peer identification
5. Student inventory—of self, values, interests, and attitudes toward school and out-of-school activities
6. Student work or achievements
7. Multidimensional Screen Tests

For best results, none of the above should be used alone, but in combination, for screening and later as part of the data in the identification process. The actual identification of a child as gifted requires the judgment of a selection committee. Screening should be done as early as possible in the child's school career. Identification at kindergarten level allows the child to have appropriate education throughout the school experience. Early screening can prevent the waste of talent we now find all too prevalent.

The most commonly used screen is teacher observation and selection of those nominated for testing. Logically we would believe the teacher to be the one most familiar with the child and best qualified to make such a recommendation. But let us look at the usual situation. One teacher works with thirty-five to forty-five children during the day; at secondary level the number can be six times greater. The curriculum aimed at the norm may not challenge any obviously brilliant performance. Depending on how many years the child has been in the system, the child may have developed adaptive skills to "fit in." We know that much of this "adjustment" has already occurred by the third grade, especially among gifted girls.

We must consider the particular beliefs and attitudes of the teacher. How does the teacher imagine a gifted child? In a study by Pegnato and Birch (1959) done at the junior high school level, they found that teachers most often choose children like themselves as gifted. Whatever the teacher values will be the criterion for selection. That is understandable. How can we select those aspects that we do not experience as valuable or good? Often the quiet, well-behaved, well-dressed youngster who gets good grades is a prime target for teacher selection. In their study, Pegnato and Birch found that teachers identified only 45 percent of the children in their classes who were cognitively gifted, actually missing 55 percent. Further, of the children they named, only 26 percent actually tested high enough to qualify; 74 percent of the students selected for testing did not. This problem exists to an even greater extent in lower grades. According to Jacobs (1971), the effectiveness of teacher identification drops from the 45 percent identified at junior high to 10 percent in kindergarten.

We cannot assume that even the highly gifted are easily identified. Barbe (1965) reports that, through teacher selection, 25 percent of the most gifted students went undetected. Unawareness of the gifted causes this problem: If teachers cannot recognize enough of the gifted in their classes, there may be waste of human potential.

However, administering individual intelligence tests is expensive; if teachers select too many students who do not qualify as gifted when tested, the teachers' errors can waste the often limited monetary resources designated for the gifted. The dilemma is then to select enough students not to miss those who are gifted, and yet not to select too many who will not test as gifted. Teachers must be both effective (correctly nominating a high percentage of children who are the gifted in their class, that is, not missing a lot who are gifted) and efficient (having a high percentage of those they nominate identified for the gifted program, that is, not nominating a lot of children who are not gifted). Gear (1978) found that the effectiveness of teacher selection was improved without any loss in efficiency by a five session training program. The teachers completing the program were, in fact, twice as effective as were untrained teachers. A study by Borland (1978) showed that teachers can improve their efficiency in selecting cognitively gifted students when they are given a list of specific behaviors to rate. Their ability to predict academic achievement was quite high.

Unfortunately, too few teachers know how to identify the characteristics of gifted learners. One way to help those who are screening to improve their accuracy in selecting children who do, in fact, have unusual ability does exist. By distributing a list of common characteristics found among gifted children, we can encourage people to look for those they might otherwise miss.

Looking for Children Who May Be Gifted

If you observe a child showing some of the following behaviors, you may want to look more closely. That child could be gifted. In the classroom does the child—

ask a lot of questions?
show a lot of interest in progress?
have lots of information on many things?
want to know why or how something is so?
become unusually upset at injustices?
seem interested and concerned about social or political problems?
often have a better reason than you do for not doing what you want done?
refuse to drill on spelling, math facts, flash cards, or handwriting?
criticize others for dumb ideas?
become impatient if work is not "perfect"?
seem to be a loner?
seem bored and often have nothing to do?
complete only part of an assignment or project and then take off in a new direction?
stick to a subject long after the class has gone on to other things?
seem restless, out of seat often?
daydream?
seem to understand easily?
like solving puzzles and problems?
have his or her own idea about how something should be done? and stay with it?
talk a lot?
love metaphors and abstract ideas?
love debating issues?

This child may be showing giftedness cognitively.

Does the child—
show unusual ability in some area? maybe reading or math?
show fascination with one field of interest? and manage to include this interest in
all discussion topics?
enjoy meeting or talking with experts in this field?
get math answers correct, but find it difficult to tell you how?
enjoy graphing everything? seem obsessed with probabilities?
invent new obscure systems and codes?
This child may be showing giftedness academically.

Does the child—
try to do things in different, unusual, imaginative ways?
have a really zany sense of humor?
enjoy new routines or spontaneous activities?
love variety and novelty?
create problems with no apparent solutions? and enjoy asking you to solve them?
love controversial and unusual questions?
have a vivid imagination?
seem never to proceed sequentially?
This child may be showing giftedness creatively.

Does the child—
organize and lead group activities? sometimes take over?
enjoy taking risks?
seem cocky, self-assured?
enjoy decision making? stay with that decision?
synthesize ideas and information from a lot of different sources?
This child may be showing giftedness through leadership ability.

Does the child—
seem to pick up skills in the arts (music, dance, drama, painting, etc.) without instruction?
invent new techniques? experiment?
see minute detail in products or performances?
have high sensory sensitivity?
This child may be showing giftedness through visual or performing arts ability.

It is important for teachers to be a part of the selection process. First, they have
data to offer that are not available to other members of the identification team. Sec-
ondly, they need to become aware of, understand, and support the program for
gifted if it is to succeed. Without some involvement in the selection process, they
would be unlikely to cooperate or contribute to any further planning.

Two other screening procedures have yielded results. Interviews with parents of
young children reveal a great deal. Parents are very aware of the behavior of their
child. When asked relevant questions, they can provide information that is clearly
indicative of potential giftedness. In a study, Jacobs (1971) discovered that parents

could identify 76 percent of the gifted children in a kindergarten classroom. This was significantly higher than the teacher's ability at that level—4.3 percent.

Peers have been extremely helpful in identifying other potentially gifted children for screening. Questions such as "Whom would you choose to help you if you were having difficulty with your arithmetic?" or "If you were planning a learning center on (*subject*), whom would you choose to be in your group?" or "Who is the smartest person in our room?" form part of a list of identifying questions that can produce important, and often otherwise unnoticed, information about the students in a class. Gold (1965) suggests sociograms for peer screening. A similar device was used at fourth-grade level with success by Granzin and Granzin (1969).

The work of a student can be very useful in the screening process. Both school and extracurricular activities should be considered. Often the work done on a hobby or toward solving a unique problem at home will indicate advanced thinking and creative ability. The more information that can be obtained, the more chance that the screening will be effective in locating gifted students.

Some of the screening tools that have been used successfully by districts for some of the areas they wish to serve are: The Bella Kranz Multidimensional Screening Device (1978); The Baldwin Matrix (Baldwin, 1980); and the scale developed by Renzulli and Hartman (1971). Perrone and Male (1981) have developed the GIFTS Talent Identification Procedures, which consist of one or more behavior rating sheets plus scoring and interpretation materials. Raters are asked to rate the child only in the areas of talent that they have had the opportunity to observe. Some of the areas that could be assessed are: mathematics, English, music, science, reading, interpersonal relations, art, etc. Whitmore (1980) reminds us that "The effective use of behavioral characteristics in the identification process is dependent upon an appropriate environment for observation of superior mental abilities and awareness that a gifted child may excel only in very specific areas or may be underachieving in one or more of the basic skills" (p. 67).

Cognitive

To the Generic screen add group intelligence tests (for examples see figure 5.1). Group intelligence testing may be useful as part of the screening procedure; however, a cutoff score of 115 IQ should be used. A higher cutoff will result in many gifted students' being missed. By using this cutoff, Pegnato and Birch (1959) found that 92 percent of the gifted, who then scored 135 IQ on an individually given test of intelligence, could be located.

Martinson (1974) suggested the possibility of multiple, abbreviated tests as a possible screen. Such testing seems to reduce the cost of identification, can be administered by untrained examiners, and lacks cultural bias. The pupils also enjoy the tests. While having advantages as a screen, this abbreviated testing approach should not replace individual testing for identification.

Specific Academic

To the Generic screen add group achievement tests. Functional assessment of just what the child can do would also be most useful here. Often knowledge of achievement in subject matter areas is limited within a curricular range deemed appropriate for a particular grade level. If the child has never had an opportunity to show you how high he or she can achieve in reading or math, planning for continuous progress becomes impossible.

Figure 5.1. Suggestions for Screening and Identifying Gifted Learners

Expression of Giftedness	Screening	Identification
Generic	Nomination forms	
	Reports of student functioning	
	Family history and student background	
	Peer identification	
	Student inventories	
	Student work and achievements	
	Multidimensional tests, e.g. Kranz; Baldwin; Renzulli and Hartman; Perrone and Male	
Cognitive	Group intelligence tests, e.g., California Test of Mental Maturity; Lorge-Thorndike Intelligence Test; Henmon-Nelson Tests of Mental Ability; Otis-Lennon Mental Ability Tests; Pinter General Ability Tests; Primary Mental Abilities Test; Kuhlmann-Anderson	Stanford-Binet Intelligence Scale
		Wechsler Intelligence Scale for Children
		Cognitive Abilities Test
		Differential Aptitude Test
	Individual intelligence tests, e.g., Peabody Picture Vocabulary Test; Slosson Intelligence Test; SOI tests	
Specific Academic	Student's work	Tests in specific areas of content
	Functional assessment of content areas	
	Group achievement tests, e.g., California Achievement tests; Metropolitan Achievement Tests; Stanford Achievement Tests; Iowa Tests of Basic Skills	
Creative	Personality Inventories, e.g., Alpha-Biographical Inventory; Adjective Checklist; Group Inventory for Finding Creative Talent; Khatena and Torrance Creative Perception Inventory; Torrance Test of Creative Thinking; Observation of problem solving	Creativity Tests for Children
		Creativity Assessment
		Creativity Perception Inventory
		Something About Myself

Figure 5.1.   Suggestions for Screening and Identifying Gifted Learners *(continued)*

Expression of Giftedness	Screening	Identification
Leadership	Observation in and out of the classroom	No formal standardized tests available
	Scales on leadership from Kranz; Renzulli and Hartmann; Perrone and Male	
Visual and Performing Arts	Observation and recommendations from professional artists	Seashore Measures of Musical Talents
	Peer nominations	Standardized Tests of Musical Intelligence
		Horn Art Aptitude Inventory
		Meier Art Tests
		On site task completion
		Juried student work

Creative

To the Generic screen you may wish to add a personality inventory such as the Alpha-Biographical Inventory (Institute for Behavioral Research in Creativity, 1968) or the Adjective Check List (Gough and Heilburn, 1965), either of which would be appropriate for high school students, and the Group Inventory for Finding Creative Talent (Rimm and Davis, 1980). For all students the Torrance Tests of Creative Thinking (Torrance, 1966) would be appropriate. Observation of the child in an open-ended problem solving situation should provide useful anecdotal material. For other examples of screening see figure 5.1.

Leadership

Observation of leadership skills in and out of the classroom will provide anecdotal material for screening in this area. The multi-dimensional scales mentioned in the generic area include sections related to leadership abilities.

Visual and Performing Arts

Observation and recommendations from professional artists would provide excellent additional screening material. Peer nominations have been highly reliable in this area (Kavett and Smith, 1980).

Identification

Actual identification for the purpose of placement in a gifted program is best done by a group of professionals representing a variety of areas of expertise, such as the principal, a teacher, a counselor or psychologist, and the program coordinator. They should develop a case study or profile to aid in the identification decision and also later in program planning for the individual. One of the major purposes of identification is to obtain information that will help educators provide the program that will be best suited to the development of the gifted student's potential. The report should provide enough information to make good educational planning and placement possible.

All of the materials developed for the screening process now become a part of the data that provide a background for the identification decision. In addition you will need data that discriminate in the areas you have chosen to serve. Care must be taken to use tests and procedures that are valid measures of the skills you are seeking and for the population you are testing. In a survey of identification practices now used in gifted and talented education (Alvino, McDonnel, and Richert, 1981), it was noted that "many tests/instruments are being used for purposes and populations completely antithetical to those for which they are intended and were designed" (p. 128). Such data may only serve to confuse the identification process and the program planning to follow.

Cognitive Ability

Hagen (1980) states, "The standardized tests for individual administration that are most useful in identifying the potentially gifted are those that appraise scholastic aptitude of general cognitive development, such as *The Revised Stanford-Binet Tests of Intelligence* and the *Wechsler Intelligence Scales for Children—Revised*" (p. 18). Shortened versions of individual intelligence tests have been published; while they may be useful for screening, Hagen warns that they are not suitable for identifying gifted or potentially gifted individuals. She believes that by changing the time limits, content, or directions of the test the data on reliability, validity, and norms for that test are no longer applicable. The number and variety of cognitive skills appraised by the shortened test is limited also.

Two tests suggested for inclusion in the identification process are *The Cognitive Abilities Tests* (1979) and *The Differential Aptitude Test*. These tests give scores on verbal, quantitative, and nonverbal reasoning. The Otis-Lennon Mental Ability Test gives but one score, cannot be differentiated and does not appraise high level thinking skills well (Hagen, 1980). The Appendix will discuss these tests further.

Specific Academic Ability

The best single indicator of future academic achievement is the present level of achievement in the area of interest; therefore, data should be obtained on "(1) the level of achievement in general academic skills; (2) the level of achievement in skills and knowledge related to a specific academic area; (3) the level of development of general verbal, quantitative, nonverbal and spatio-visual problem-solving skills; (4) originality; (5) persistent long-term interests; (6) out-of-school time spent on activities related to an academic area; and (7) the trend in complexity of activities that an individual undertakes on his or her own initiative" (Hagen, 1980, p. 10). Some tests suggested are: *Iowa Tests of Basic Skills* (SRA); the *Stanford Achievement Test* (Kelley et al., 1965); see Appendix for tests in specific academic areas.

Creativity

Measures of creativity that emphasize divergent thinking, e.g., the *Creativity Tests for Children* (Guilford, 1973), correlate very modestly with tests of intelligence, and most creativity tests correlate just as little with each other. While tests of creativity may be only assessing a small part of what creativity is about (see chapter 1), some you may find helpful in addition to those used for screening are the *Creativity Perception Inventory* (Torrance and Khatena, 1976); and the *Creativity Assessment* (Williams, 1979).

Leadership

According to Alvino et al. (1981), the most significant identification deficiency of gifted individuals is in the area of leadership. Informal, subjective measures are most commonly used. The sections of the Kranz and Renzulli/Hartman scales mentioned in the screening give data in this area.

Visual and Performing Arts

We know very little about the early indicators of gifted performance in these areas. At present the best indicator of giftedness in visual and performing arts is the ability to perform in the specific area chosen. A panel of experts should be assembled to judge such performances. It is believed that the general level of cognitive skills and achievement in the academic areas should receive no weight in these decisions, as there is no evidence that such measures are predictive of artistic achievement (Rubenzer, 1979; Hagen, 1980). Even tests of creativity have no demonstrated and proven validity as measures of artistic and musical talent (Hagen, 1980), although Torrance has found that those students who major in speech, drama, and art attain higher scores on these tests than do other students (Barbe and Renzulli, 1975).

When used with other data, the *Seashore's Measures of Musical Talents* has been found useful (Kavett and Smith, 1980; Rubenzer, 1979) as has the *Horn Art Aptitude Inventory* and the *Meier Art Tests* (Rubenzer, 1979). While Saunders (1982) indicates that the Meier Art Test can be used to determine levels of aesthetic awareness, he reports that Alexander (1981) has found the Meier Art Tests to be culture bound and of doubtful value for children under twelve years of age. Saunders suggests several ways to secure artistic screening and identification data including the process of assigning a variety of tasks to twenty-five to thirty applicants at a time, asking them to complete the tasks on site in one sitting. The tasks tested were two-dimensional and three-dimensional organization and art problem-solving abilities. Other suggestions for gathering data were:

> Take a number from 0 to 9, make an art work from it. Think of as many ideas as possible, save them, and bring all notes and sketches (to the interview).

> Record a dream you remember that had great impact. It does not have to be a recent dream. Draw it in a cartoon form. Include as many elements of the dream as possible, but do not use words.

> Using six to ten different found objects (such as screws, a broken wheel, a soda can), construct a three-dimensional portrait of yourself at age 85. Try to use the materials in unusual ways. Try to show not only how you look at that age, but

how you might feel. Don't worry about the details, but instead try to suggest the general characteristics, use glue, string, or wire to hold your piece together. The whole piece should be no bigger than 1½ feet by 1½ feet.

Fold a large piece of paper in half. Using a pencil, charcoal or crayons do a drawing of the sun on one half, and do a drawing of the moon on the other. Think carefully about their differences and similarities (p. 9).

Ellison et al. (1976) has researched and developed a procedure for using biographical information as a predictor of artistic talent and claims it to be superior to more traditional measures.

The Case Study

Once the data on a child who is being considered for the gifted program have been collected, they must be put into a usable form for the selection committee. A number of plans have been suggested for ranking or quantifying the results of the screening and identification process. For examples of such plans see Gowan (1967), Hagen (1980), Baldwin (1980), and Vermilyea (1981). Information to include in the data for the committee that will comprise the student's case study should incorporate:

1. Family History and Student Background   Provided by parents, this will include historical and developmental data on the student; health and medical records of student and family; educational and occupational background of parents; description of family unit; anecdotes of the student in the home that indicate unusual capacity and early development; family activities and interests; and the child's out-of-school activities and interests.

2. Teacher Report of Student Functioning   includes intellectual, physical, social, and emotional functioning; learning style; and motivation

3. Nomination Forms   from teachers, principal, counselor, psychologist, and others

4. Student Inventory   of self, values, interests, and attitudes toward school and out-of-school activities

5. Test Protocols   (individual and group tests). Include scores and psychologist's interpretation. If other criteria in lieu of scores are to be used, they should be included. For students on separate criteria such as special populations (e.g., disadvantaged gifted, handicapped gifted), include all data necessary for decision making regarding selection and placement (an annotated listing of useful tests will be found in the Appendix, p. 412).

6. Student's Work or Achievement Awards   After the student has been identified, the parents must be informed of the decision and asked for permission to place their child in whatever program the school provides. The signed permission form will then be placed in the permanent case study file. Administrators should explain to the parents the concept of giftedness and the purpose of the program and then ask for any suggestions they may have, clearly inviting their participation.

Problems of Identifying the Culturally Diverse, Handicapped, or Educationally Atypical Gifted Individual

As we saw in chapter 2, giftedness results partially from an early interaction with a stimulating environment. Family patterns or persons who provide such stimulating interaction can be found in any culture, at any socioeconomic level, and in spite of many disabling conditions. Such differences, however, may make traditional identification procedures ineffective for discovering such ability.

Problems of Traditional Intelligence Tests for Culturally Diverse Learners

The very way that IQ tests are constructed has built-in limitations and assumptions that can be quite unfair to groups who are not closely identified with the dominant culture. First, one assumption of most intelligence tests is that intelligence is a single, unvariable factor. More current data indicate that intelligence is neither a single factor nor is it a constant one (see chapter 1). Although our belief about the reality of intelligence has changed, our measuring tools still proceed from our previous beliefs.

Another problem results from the choice of items on the tests. Out of an infinite number of human accomplishments and interests, the items have been restricted to concepts and skills found in school curricula, especially the more basic abilities: reading, language arts, and arithmetic. For this reason, of course, IQ tests tend to be good predictors of success within the school environment. A wide variety of other human activities and abilities that could be well developed in our atypical learners (e.g., fluency, originality, problem solving in other than academic areas) are not even represented. To make sure the variation of the growing intellect from younger to older children did not disturb the IQ scores, all items that did not fit the smooth growth pattern that the tests assumed were deleted. Items that displayed any bias for either sex were also deleted. By such limited selection procedures, the tests became very narrow in their focus.

The population modeled for standardization of any test is important to measuring its usefulness. The standardization of most commonly used IQ tests has been done within the major culture. For example, the Stanford-Binet was standardized and its scores for success established on white children of English speaking parents. It has become known as the "Anglo test." Many believe that such bias makes this test inappropriate as a measure of ability for children outside the Anglo culture.

These restrictions have led many educators and psychologists to call for the construction of "culture free" tests. Although many have tried (Cattell, 1949; Davis and Eells, 1953; Leiter, 1951), the results have been disappointing. Jensen (1969) found that blacks not only score higher on conventional tests such as the Stanford-Binet and Weschler than they do on "culture free" tests, but that they also score higher on verbal than on nonverbal subtests. In fact, Jerison (1977) contends that a nonverbal test of intelligence may be a contradiction in terms because even if words are avoided, the language and language-related functions of the brain are inevitably dominant in most human performance.

In studies reported by Christiansen and Livermore (1970), Holland (1960), Johnson (1962), and Mercer and Smith (1972), Mexican American children performed significantly better on nonverbal than on verbal intelligence tests. The higher performance more adequately reflected the school grade point average of these children than did the scores received on verbal scales.

Another possible problem of obtaining valid test results seems to be in the test administration. Katz, Robinson, Epps, and Wally (1964) and Katz, Roberts, and Robinson (1965) report that, in several experiments, the race of the tester had an effect on the test results of black students. He believes that the white environment in general may be stressful and threatening to black children. It can create a situation that predicates against accurate test results. The effect of examiner variables (bilingualism, ethnic group membership, and style of test administration) on the test performance of Spanish speaking children was reported by Bordie (1970), Palomares and Johnson (1966), and Thomas, Hertzig, and Fernandez (1971). In a review of experimenter effects in bicultural testing, Sattler (1970) concludes that they play a critical role in any cognitive performance.

Torrance (1969) believes that testing culturally diverse children should include a concern for mood setting or for providing activities that will awaken the creative processes. He states that they should not have imposed time limits, and that ways should be provided for the examiner to record the children's responses. He found these procedures quite effective in eliciting hidden verbal abilities.

In considering the problem of finding hidden ability in this population, Renzulli (1973) suggests that we need to develop non-language-dependent identification strategies that do not require written production. He believes it important to make the identification process a continuous one among the disadvantaged.

Alternative Identification Procedures

Many suggestions for finding ability in culturally diverse people lean heavily toward the identification of noncognitive skills. Much of the investigation has centered on creative abilities, with discussion under the label of gifted and talented—talented here designating creative ability. This practice needs close examination. We do not for the most part use tests of creativity to identify the major population of cognitively gifted children. How, then, can we use such identifiers for other children we include in this population? Some data indicated that children with creative ability may be a different population, that they may or may not be gifted cognitively. In an attempt to find tests that would discover intellectual promise among minority children, Hilliard (1976) used several types of testing. While additional students were discovered, those who excelled in creativity were not the same students who showed cognitive promise. If we are including the gifted and the talented in all of our identification and programming procedures, this seems a justifiable practice; however, if we are using only measures of cognitive intelligence on the majority, while including tests of creativity for only a few, we may be developing an unfair situation. Programs developed for highly cognitive students may not meet the needs of the creative student.

There are, however, many alternatives that you may find useful. Bruch (1971) has been concerned with the problem of finding members of subcultures, primarily southeastern black students, who have potential not evidenced on traditional tests. She hypothesized that, by looking at patterns of strength other than those required for the usual IQ test, we can find otherwise untapped black, disadvantaged, gifted children. Some areas of strength she feels need to be considered are: visual and auditory figural content (e.g., art and music); memory; convergent production in practical problem-solving situations; awareness of details in descriptions; fluency of ideas; spontaneous categorization and classification of spacial items; and awareness of natural relationships or systems. Her work has led her to the development of a form of the Binet that she feels favors southeastern black students and allows the gifted among them to be identified. Her instrument, an abbreviated version of the Stanford-Binet, is known as *The Abbreviated Binet for Disadvantaged* (ABDA).

Another test that has been developed to correct the problems found in traditional testing is the *System of Multicultural Pluralistic Assessment (SOMPA)*. The SOMPA utilizes three assessment models: the medical model, a deficit model that focuses on pathology; the social system model, which compares the behaviors of the child to the behaviors of those in the social system to which he or she belongs; and the pluralistic model, which assumes that only if factors such as exposure to skills and materials, motivation, and learning experiences, etc. are held constant, can learning potential be assessed. This use of adaptive behavior and estimated learning potential to identify gifted children from culturally diverse or disadvantaged backgrounds is a new approach that shows promise but has not yet been validated (Mercer and Lewis, 1978).

Bernal (1978) suggests three techniques for identifying gifted Chicano students: culturally pluralistic assessments such as Mercer discusses above; Piagetian measures for K–3, that is, looking for advanced schema used in problem solving on a test such as the Cartoon Conservation Scales, which are available in English or Spanish; and bilingual language proficiency scales where rapid and advanced growth in language would provide a good indicator of high intelligence. *The Raven's Progressive Matrices Test* (Raven, 1947) has been found to be helpful for mass screening (Wescott and Woodward, 1981).

Another alternative, behavioral identification, is being used with success by Malone (1974) and Malone and Moonan (1975). Their results indicate that selected combinations of behavioral characteristics can be made to categorize gifted and nongifted kindergarten children correctly. They find that this procedure in no way restricts inclusion of culturally diverse children.

Another way of using behavior as an identifier was reported by Childs (1981). This is the use of the Adaptive Behavior Inventory for Children (ABIC) (Mercer and Lewis, 1977). The ABIC is a structured parent interview covering family, community, peer relations, nonacademic school roles, earner/consumer, and self-maintenance. In the study gifted children do more activities related to independence and social responsibility and do them earlier than their chronological peers. Childs found the gifted children consistently superior to normal children in adaptive behavior as measured by ABIC and feels that adaptive behavior can and should be used as part of the identification process. Childs points out that ABIC showed no significant differences among races or cultures in its standardization sample. Torrance (1977) believes that by use of his "creative positives," more talent can be discovered and developed among the culturally diverse and economically disadvantaged. He has developed a system for using his data for nontest ways of identifying the creative among the gifted in these populations.

Some teachers have found that the math concept scores of disadvantaged students on standardized tests are good predictors of the ability to succeed in gifted programs.

Gear (1976) has successfully used a training program she designed, Identification of the Potentially Gifted, to improve the teacher's effectiveness in identifying intellectually gifted students.

There are many new directions now being explored to make identification fairer and more useful. The decade of interest in the work of Jean Piaget has begun to stimulate researchers to move in the direction of development of tests based on his theories. The current interest in brain research evokes numerous attempts to use the new knowledge of brain function as a measure for intelligence. Ertl (1968) has designed a comparison measure of the relationship between the electrical activity of the human brain and intellectual measurement in psychological testing. Results of his experiment show a strong relationship between superior intelligence and response time to sensory stimulation. The use of Ertl's Brain Wave Analyzer has been shown to discriminate more accurately between academically gifted and academically handicapped students (ages twelve through fourteen) in combination with the Primary Mental Abilities tests or the Sequential Tests of Educational Progress (STEP) than do these tests used alone. While it cannot substitute for paper and pencil tests, it can make a valuable contribution to the understanding of learning potential (Fischer, Hunt, and Randhawa, 1978).

Also of interest is the work of Schafer and Marcus at Sonoma State Hospital (1973) on measuring the electrical discharge from a person's brain when a stimulus is presented unexpectedly. They believe that the difference between the electrocortical response of a surprised brain and a prepared brain may be related to intelligence. Much interest has also been shown in the work of E. Roy John and his team at New York Medical College's Brain Research Laboratory. Their test of brain function, the Quantitative Electrophysiological Battery (QB), is both quick and sensitive, and it presents a more accurate picture of learning than a battery of traditional tests (Goleman, 1976). Such techniques may aid not only in the identification of culturally diverse children but of the handicapped gifted as well.

Identifying the Handicapped Gifted

One of the major problems in finding the gifted among the handicapped is a function of the expectation that is the result of labeling. Because most special education programs in schools have far more fiscal and human resources at the disposal of the handicapped child, identification will usually be for that program. Once labeled, teachers expect the child's needs and behavior to fall within those normally found in the identified group. Needs for these children are so often deficit needs that remediation will be the primary concern. In this climate, evidence of giftedness is often missed. So few teachers in the handicapped setting have been exposed to the characteristic behaviors of gifted children that they may interpret any observed deviations from the norm as being unique to the handicapping condition. Even when giftedness is suspected, it is often difficult for a child receiving special services to find a place in a gifted program. The disability teacher may not wish to disrupt the program in the primary area. The teacher in the gifted program may be so limited in time and resources that finding a place for the child may be too difficult. The administration may be under restrictions as to financial and program qualifications. A child who is gifted and also blind, deaf, or physically disabled may find it almost impossible to experience any opportunities for enhancing that ability at school.

The child labeled learning or educationally handicapped has an even more complex problem. Often such a child has extreme ability in one or two areas and remedial needs in others. Such a child may also be a behavioral problem and find working with groups quite difficult. The tests given because of hyperactivity, disruptive classroom conduct, or extreme withdrawal are often the very tests that spot gifted ability. The excessive energy that creates problems may also be behind the student's achievement in a few areas of interest. Unfortunately, it is not rare to find children in a learning handicapped class who were only unable to cope with the structures of a rigid regular classroom. We have previously discussed the importance of self-concept to the success of the student. You can clearly see the results of a negative view in this situation.

Recognizing these special problems, the Bureau of Education for the Handicapped (BEH) funded two projects in 1975, whose goals were to develop and demonstrate models for identifying and programming for young gifted and talented children. One project is located in the public schools of Chapel Hill, North Carolina. The Chapel Hill project has developed a package for training teachers in the identification of potential candidates for the gifted-handicapped program. The techniques suggested for identification are structured and unstructured observations, checklists, and sociometric measures (Blancher-Dixon and Turnbull, 1978).

The other project is located at the Institute for Child Behavior and Development at the University of Illinois, Champaign-Urbana campus. In a report of this project, Karnes and Bertschi (1978) found two levels of identification to be necessary. Some children could be identified during program placement procedures; others required some remediation of the handicapping conditions before their talents emerged.

The training program of all special educators should include some information regarding gifted children. A recent credential requirement in California provides all special education trainees with a generic core of experience that allows them to be involved with and learn about all exceptional learners. The students at our university now have an increased awareness of the needs of gifted children and a growing interest in course work that will provide them with more information on how to identify and serve these handicapped gifted children.

Most of the identification strategies for culturally diverse, disadvantaged, and handicapped gifted individuals have focused on the cognitive abilities, a few on the creative behaviors. Is there a need for measures of academic, leadership, or arts abilities that take into consideration the effects of being atypical? Is leadership expressed differently in disadvantaged or culturally diverse surroundings? Would an arts audition be different if the artist were culturally diverse or handicapped? Perhaps these special talents can be seen when skills of creativity, leadership, and the arts are evaluated; perhaps there is no need for special measures—only a change of attitude and more open-minded observation. While these are not easy questions to answer, the answers will help us to include in our identification all of the ways giftedness can be expressed. This area definitely bears investigation.

Assessment

Having identified those children who require differential education, we must now discover what each child's individual needs are. In the area of education for the gifted, a strange phenomenon occurs. Usually the major part of the differential experiences provided for gifted individuals is provided within a minimum amount of time, often outside the classroom. The advisability of such programming was examined in the last chapter, but the existence of such practices presents us with a dilemma.

In most special education settings, the word *need* has a connotation of deficiency. In gifted education it means quite the opposite. When gifted individuals are assessed for "needs" for special provisions, these denote areas of strength that cannot be properly nurtured in a regular classroom setting. This is not to say that gifted students would have no need for remedial help in some academic areas, nor does it imply that the gifted individual is equally gifted in all areas. Such is just not the case. However, where special attention or funding is found to meet gifted needs, it is the nurture of advanced ability that is intended and not the remediation of deficits. If attention must be given to deficit needs, the regular school program assumes the role. Remediation becomes part of a gifted program only if such a program comprises the major portion of the student's educational experience, such as full-day special class placement. When limited part-time programs are used for remediation, children have no opportunity to grow in their areas of gifted need. These are the areas for which no provisions are made in the regular classroom setting and for which these children have been identified. Programs for the gifted learner must focus on these areas. With this in mind, let us look at the problem of assessing gifted needs.

Gifted needs may be found in areas of content, process, and enrichment. Once such needs are identified, appropriate programs can be planned. Assessment is not, however, only a beginning to the year's activity. To be effective, assessment must continue throughout the year. While some assessment tools have infrequent use, others should be continuous with the student's program as it changes, to reflect the growth such assessment procedures bring to light.

In developing any assessment package, information from both students and parents needs inclusion. Both have unique contributions that will add to the data bank from which good educational decisions can be made. It is inadequate to get such information only once or even yearly. Frequent planning and reporting conferences that include parents and students will additionally aid in establishing communication, gaining support for the program, and insuring the success of the student's educational goals.

Content Assessment

There are at least three major ways to assess the student's level of capability in content areas:

Norm Referenced Tests   standardized or specially constructed; intelligence or achievement; individual or group. Norm referenced measures use the performance of other individuals as the standard by which the student is compared.

Criterion Referenced Tests   tests of specific content skills, teacher written or published. These measures have a predetermined standard or criterion of performance against which the student is compared.

Functional Assessment   observations of a student working to determine level of functioning.

Information on standardized tests should be found in the child's case study and should include the test protocol or booklet and the report from the psychologist with an interpretation of the test results. When only the score is recorded without interpretation, the specific areas of strength and weakness shown on each test disappear. Two children scoring exactly alike could have very different areas of strengths. They would therefore require quite different provisions in their educational program. Meeker (1969) devised a technique that helps teachers to use templates to analyze the Stanford-Binet in areas designated by the Guilford Structure of Intellect (Guilford, 1967). This information may be synthesized into a profile of strengths and weaknesses for a program of specific skill-building activities developed and researched by Meeker. Without the protocol information, the diagnostic value of the test is wasted, eliminating the value of the test score when recorded alone.

Both criterion referenced and norm referenced assessments may be functionally and informally given. Classrooms that use centers or learning activity packages as part of their program can use these approaches to gain assessment information. Allowing students to correct criterion referenced tests as pretests for skill areas and then providing self-instructional materials for areas not yet understood allows the teacher a greater amount of time to direct higher-level learning. Parents in the classroom can act as monitors for final posttest recording that will give additional useful data to the assessment procedure. Be sure that all content ratings are based on age or grade expectations and not on class norms or the achievement of other gifted children. (For more information on specific tests, see Appendix, p. 412.)

Process Assessment

How the student learns is as important as what the student learns. Once we know what content should be available, we must discover the ways in which our students process information. What learning styles or sensory modalities do they use? How independent or self-directed are they? What skills of leadership or initiative do they possess? What research or learning-how-to-learn skills have they already developed? How much of their creativity do they use? We need to ask questions such as these.

There are a number of tests available to help you develop a profile of the major affective characteristics of your learners, such as their values, interests, locus of control, anxiety levels, and their self-esteem. The Appendix has information on a variety of tests in these areas that you will find useful. Detailed information on conducting affective assessment has been compiled by Anderson (1981).

In addition to the information available from published tests of creativity (e.g., Torrance, 1966), the *Taxonomy of Educational Objectives* (Bloom, 1956) can be used to examine which process skills gifted students have developed and which need further development. The processes of analysis, synthesis, and evaluation are all within the capability of gifted students, but they do not reach their most effective level without provision of opportunities for development. Again, it should be noted that these students possess the ability to work with abstracts, concepts, and diverse and integrative thought patterns. The students will need to be familiar with conceptual frameworks such as Bloom's (1956) or Suchman's Inquiry Model (Suchman, 1962) in order to meet this differential need. These models are discussed in chapter 6.

One important way to assess process skills is to observe a student's involvement in problem-solving situations. This can be done individually or even quite successfully in groups. The Inquiry Training sessions discussed by Suchman (1962) can provide these group situations. Approximately ten students are presented a dissonant event by verbal or visual means. They are asked to inquire into the circumstances of the event to discover what caused the results they observed to occur. In a formal inquiry session (described in chapter 6, p. 244), students begin to ask questions, formulate hypotheses, test their hypotheses, and evaluate their ideas. Through observation of such sessions, teachers may become aware of the mental processes their students use to problem solve and the effectiveness of such techniques. Teachers can learn a great deal by careful observation.

Another observational technique to provide process assessment is the contrived problem for group focus. For example, a small group could be given a simulated plot of land to develop as a community. The community should become the place where they would most like to live. Given a house, a business of their choice, and a vote on all development within the community, they must first place their house and business to everyone's satisfaction and then provide for any other facilities they feel necessary to the welfare of the community. With few rules and only the physical materials to manipulate (e.g., simulated lakes, trees, hills, houses, stores, roads) the group must organize, provide its own leadership, develop group communication, and set its own limits. All of these processes can be observed, and the "game" becomes a rich source for assessing process skills.

Gorman (1974) provides formats for student inventories of study habits and skills, personal profiles, learning styles, leadership abilities, and other areas that can add significant data to your process assessment.

Assessing for Enrichment

Enrichment needs, probably the easiest to gain information about, are the most commonly assessed. For the gifted learner, the world seems filled with an overwhelming abundance of exciting things to learn about. Most gifted individuals will be pursuing interests in a large variety of subjects at any given time. The educator will need to learn what those interests are and may ask both the student and the parents for that information. In addition to the interests already being investigated by the student, opportunities should be provided to open up new areas not yet known. Not all gifted students will be interested in all areas; assessing the level of interest after exposure to new experiences will be important.

Once assessments have begun to give information on the gifted student, a profile should be developed and the case study file updated. We can now include recommendations for programming and placement both on content and process and suggest some areas of enrichment. This will allow the teacher to develop a far more effective and meaningful gifted program. Regardless of the model or program followed for delivery of educational services, assessment is essential to meet the needs of gifted students successfully. The profile of gifted learners will usually show areas of relative strength and weakness. Most gifted students show at least average ability in all areas of school-related activity. It is important, however, to assess the strong areas carefully and not to assume strength and ability in all areas. Some educators plan programs for the gifted on the assumption that these learners are gifted in everything. This is not the case. Of all the atypical populations of learners, this group will show the highest degree of uniqueness and a definite need for individualized planning.

Within this chapter we have looked at the rationales and procedures for selecting gifted children who need special educational provisions to continue their growth. Screening procedures and the problems of screening have been discussed. We have viewed identification from a variety of perspectives, including the importance of assessment and case studies. We have looked at the special problems encountered in identifying the atypical, the handicapped, and the culturally diverse gifted learner. But all of this would be meaningless if we did not then look at programming to meet these special needs when they are made evident. The main purpose for identification is to provide educational experiences that can enhance the continuous growth of every gifted child.

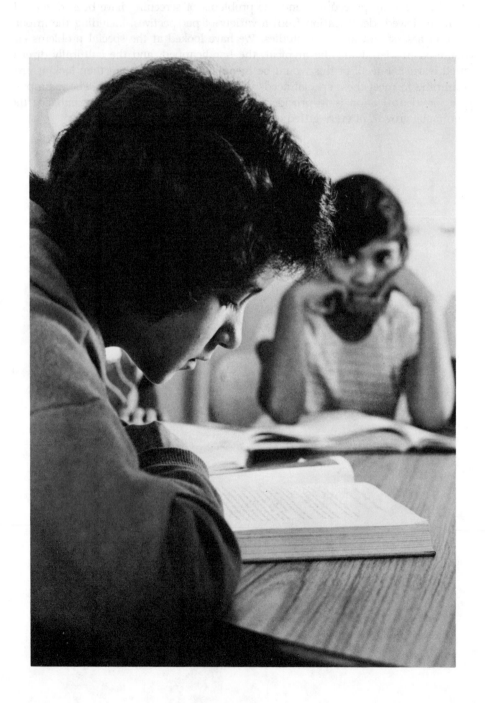

CHAPTER SIX

Meeting the Needs of the Gifted:

Strategies for Teaching in Elementary and Secondary Schools

Presented in the chapter for the reader are

- an overview of the relevant characteristics and needs of gifted learners, accompanied by suggested organizational patterns and sample strategies for meeting these needs.
- a discussion of differentiating curriculum and its importance in gifted education.
- a plan for individualizing a classroom.
- models of learning and teaching often used with the gifted.
- a curriculum criteria checklist.
- a rationale, the time involved, the materials needed, organizational pattern, teaching function, procedure, evaluation, and resources for sample strategies in the integrated approach to educating the gifted including
  - cognitive development
  - affective development
  - physical integration
  - using intuitive abilities
  - enhancing learning through enrichment.
- a discussion of how integrative curriculum can be used in the areas of cognitive, academic, creative, leadership, and visual or performing arts abilities.

> After you understand about the sun and the stars and the rotation of the earth,
> you may still miss the radiance of the sunset.
>
> Alfred North Whitehead

You have organized and established a program that will allow your gifted learners to continue to develop their abilities and interests. You have identified the ways in which your gifted learners express their giftedness. Now we will look again at giftedness as a total brain function, as a level of advanced and accelerated development that causes special needs that are seldom met in the regular school program. High levels of intelligence make demands on the gifted learner that can be seen in characteristic behaviors. These demands create special needs. In this chapter we will begin from these characteristics and needs and suggest specific strategies to meet the needs of elementary and secondary students and the ways in which these needs may be expressed (cognitively, academically, creatively, through leadership, or through the visual or performing arts). Finally we will explore the Integrative Model and its promise for developing a more holistic view of gifted education, where through individualization and differentiation all expressions of giftedness may be served and nurtured.

An Overview of Organizational Patterns and Strategies for Gifted Programs: An Integrative Approach

As an overview of organizational patterns and sample strategies showing their relationship to the characteristics and needs of gifted individuals in each of our four areas of brain function, the following model is presented. In the original development of the model by Hagen and Clark (1977), the intuitive function was omitted. This area of function has been added to the original that included a societal component. The overview now discusses the Cognitive Domain, the Affective Domain, the Physical Domain, the Intuitive Domain, and the Societal Domain and becomes the basis for integrative education for the gifted and its implementation within society.

The special educational needs of gifted pupils result from those characteristics that differentiate them from typical learners. An analysis of those characteristics can provide us with a model for organizing educational programs. Programs that relate clearly to the differentiating characteristics of this population can most effectively meet the educational needs and nurture the high-level abilities of gifted pupils.

While all students have unique needs, some generalizations about needs that result from highly developed intelligence can be made. These generalizations can serve as a starting point for program planning.

The model presented here extends earlier work of Ward (1961) and others by analyzing the characteristics and needs of the gifted into five domains: cognitive, affective, physical, intuitive, and societal. Organizational patterns and classroom teaching strategies are suggested for each identified need. Each domain is divided into a hierarchy, with examples provided for appropriate program provisions at each level.

I. The Cognitive Domain

Cognitive development rests on the analysis, integration, and evaluation of a vast quantity of experience of the environment and on an understanding of those experiences. Educational programs should provide for an array of experiences and for encouraging the processes of understanding, analyzing, organizing, integrating, and evaluating. Qualitatively different planning for the gifted implies recognition of the ways in which their differential cognitive characteristics affect these processes.

Differential Cognitive Characteristics of the Gifted

Extraordinary quantity of information; unusual retentiveness
Advanced comprehension
Unusually varied interests and curiosity
High level of language development
High level of verbal ability
Unusual capacity for processing information
Accelerated pace of thought processes
Flexible thought processes
Comprehensive synthesis
Early ability to delay closure
Heightened capacity for seeing unusual and diverse relationships
Ability to generate original ideas and solutions
Early differential patterns for thought processing (e.g., thinking in alternatives, abstract terms, sensing consequences, making generalizations)
Early ability to use and form conceptual frameworks
An evaluative approach to themselves and others
Persistent goal directed behavior

Each of these characteristics creates related educational needs that make demands upon school programs in terms of modifications in classroom organization and methodology. Table 6.1 presents some examples of appropriate modifications related to cognitive characteristics and needs of gifted pupils. The examples given are only representative of possible patterns and strategies. Addition of alternate organizations and materials is encouraged.

Program provisions implied by the special characteristics and needs of gifted pupils can also be thought of in terms of the categories of a taxonomy of cognitive objectives. Bloom (1956) and his colleagues have classified educational objectives in the cognitive domain into a hierarchy, using the following categories: knowledge, comprehension, application, analysis, synthesis, and evaluation. The educational planner who wishes to emphasize a particular category of objectives will need to provide for appropriate educational experiences. The needs of the gifted might be met by such provisions as the following:

Sample program provisions in the cognitive domain

A. *Knowledge*

1. Exposure to the environment and the culture, including esthetic, economic, political, educational, and social aspects
2. Exposure to peers, adults, and other students with expertise in the student's interest areas
3. Advanced and/or unusual subject matter
4. Experience in identifying data needs and establishing data organization

B. *Comprehension*

1. Opportunities to communicate and exchange ideas, information, and opinions in a variety of ways
2. Experience in data collection

C. *Application*

1. Opportunities to work with peers, adults, and students who have expertise in student's interest areas
2. Instruction in developing original applications of knowledge and understandings, including hypothesizing and hypothesis testing

D. *Analysis*

1. Opportunities to examine and/or to change or alter existing patterns physically and mentally
2. Instruction in, and opportunities to analyze, their own processes of learning, decision making, and communication, and then to compare these processes with the processes used by others

E. *Synthesis*

1. Opportunities to integrate knowledge from various areas of their lives into new, divergent, and/or convergent physical and mental structures

F. *Evaluation*

1. Opportunities to identify and clarify standards of comparison and evaluation
2. Instruction in, and opportunities to develop, data evaluation skills
3. Instruction in, and opportunities to develop, decision-making skills
4. Opportunities to evaluate personal choices in terms of available data, individual needs and goals, and choice consequences

II. The Affective Domain

High levels of cognitive development do not necessarily imply high levels of affective development. The same heightened sensitivities that underlie gifted intelligence can contribute to an accumulation of more information relating to emotions than the student can process. This affect-based information comes from sources both within and outside of the child. Gifted children need to learn that applying their cognitive powers to this material will help them to make sense of their emotional world. The educational program must provide them with opportunities to bring emotional

Table 6.1. The Cognitive Domain.

Differentiating Characteristics	Examples of Related Needs	Organizational Patterns	Sample Classroom Strategies
Extraordinary quantity of information, unusual retentiveness	To be exposed to new and challenging information about the environment and the culture: aesthetic, economic, political, social aspects To acquire early mastery of basic skills	Individualized learning: out of classroom experience	Information organized at levels of difficulty with self-checking pre- and posttests available, and a variety of methods for learning available at each level
Advanced composition	Access to challenging curriculum and intellectual peers	Self-selected flexible groupings; opportunity to enroll in advanced classes on other campuses, if appropriate ones can be found	Group discussion on mutually selected topics; work on advanced topics of interests; advanced materials available
Unusual curiosity and variety of interests	To be exposed to varied subjects and concerns To be allowed to pursue ideas as far as their interests take them	Integrated curriculum Flexible scheduling	Mentor program; simulations
High level of language development	Opportunity to encounter and use increasingly difficult vocabulary and concepts	Work with academic peers	Edit and publish a book, journal, play, or TV script
High level of verbal ability	To share ideas verbally and in depth	Self-selected flexible grouping	Work on projects of student's choosing that involve communication and exchange of opinions in a variety of ways

Table 6.1. The Cognitive Domain. (continued)

Differentiating Characteristics	Examples of Related Needs	Organizational Patterns	Sample Classroom Strategies
Unusual capacity for processing information	To be exposed to a large variety of ideas of many levels	Learning centers available at many levels in a variety of subjects	Projects involving hypothesizing and hypothesis testing, for development of research skills
Accelerated pace of thought processes	To be exposed to ideas at rates appropriate to individual pace of learning	Individualized curriculum, advanced placement	Brainstorming; speed reading; opportunities for acceleration of content; self-paced instructional materials
Flexible thought processes	To be allowed to solve problems in diverse ways	Cooperative student-teacher-parent planning for learning objectives and experiences	Teacher acceptance of unusual products; open-ended assignments; opportunities to examine and/or alter existing patterns physically and mentally
Comprehensive synthesis	To be allowed a longer incubation time for ideas	Flexibility in assignment of deadlines; cooperative instructional planning; individual conferences	Continuous assessment of progress; individualized deadlines for products
Early ability to delay closure	To be allowed to pursue ideas and integrate new ideas without forced closure or products demanded	Integrated curriculum and activities for which no product or judgment is required over a large block of time, mutually agreed upon	Present dissonant events for solution; create a classroom climate of respect for ideas; provide opportunity for reflection
Heightened capacity for seeing unusual and diverse relationships	To "mess around" with varieties of materials and ideas	Integrated curriculum	Unstructured periods of time for exploring materials; teacher acceptance of unusual approaches

Table 6.1. The Cognitive Domain. *(continued)*

Differentiating Characteristics	Examples of Related Needs	Organizational Patterns	Sample Classroom Strategies
Ability to generate original ideas and solutions	To build skills in problem solving and productive thinking; to contribute to the solution of meaningful problems	Small group experiences; access to data throughout the community; opportunity to move out into the community for information	Plan and implement solutions to community problems
Early differential patterns for information processing; thinking in alternatives and abstract terms, sensing consequences, making generalizations	To be exposed to alternatives, abstractions, the consequences of choices, and opportunities for drawing generalizations and testing them	Small group activities; opportunities to interact with adult experts in areas of the students' interest	Activities promoting the development of inquiry skills; instruction in and opportunities to analyze their own learning processes, communication, and decision making, and to compare them with the processes used by peers and adults
Early ability to use and form conceptual frameworks	To use and design conceptual frameworks in information gathering and problem solving	Individual contracts; learning centers; access to the community	Individualized projects integrating knowledge from various areas of life into new divergent, and/or convergent physical and mental structures; designing learning experiences for others
	To seek order and consistency		Simulations and other activities that emphasize the social cost of various solutions
	To develop a tolerance for ambiguity		

Table 6.1. The Cognitive Domain. (*continued*)

Differentiating Characteristics	Examples of Related Needs	Organizational Patterns	Sample Classroom Strategies
An evaluative approach to themselves and others	To be exposed to people of varying ability and talent and to varying ways of seeing and solving problems	Flexible groupings with individualized learning available	Self-evaluation and cooperative evaluation experiences
	To set realistic, achievable short-term goals		Instruction and practice in goal setting, goal evaluation
	To develop skills in data evaluation and decision making		Introduction to models of decision making and practice in their use on real problems
Persistent, goal-directed behavior	To pursue inquiries beyond allotted time spans	Flexible time modules, individualized instruction, small support groups	Value clarification exercises (see Simon, Howe, and Kirschenbaum, 1972); self-chosen projects
	To set and evaluate priorities		

knowledge and assumptions to awareness, and to apply verbal ability and inquiry skills in the service of affective development.

The early appearance of social conscience that often characterizes gifted children signals an earlier need for development of a value structure and for the opportunity to translate values into social action. This can begin in the society of the classroom and should then be extended into the larger world, as appropriate to the child's increasing competence and widening concerns.

Sample classroom strategies suggested here have a heavy cognitive component. The discussion of each activity is essential in helping the students to process the personal meaning of their experiences cognitively. The teacher can be alert for opportunities to focus the discussion in ways that will draw upon higher cognitive processes, and thereby assist the children to a fuller integration of cognition and affect.

Educational planning for the affective development of gifted pupils, like the planning for cognitive development, must stem from the characteristics of the children to be served, and the special needs implied by those characteristics.

Differential Affective Characteristics of the Gifted

> Large accumulation of information about emotions that has not been brought to awareness
> Unusual sensitivity to the expectations and feelings of others.
> Keen sense of humor—may be gentle or hostile
> Heightened self-awareness, accompanied by feelings of being "different"
> Idealism and a sense of justice that appear at an early age
> Earlier development of an inner locus of control and satisfaction
> Advanced levels of moral judgment
> High expectations of self and others, which often lead to high levels of frustration with self, others, and situations
> Unusual emotional depth and intensity
> Sensitivity to inconsistency between ideals and behavior

Table 6.2 gives some examples of ways in which classroom organization and teaching strategies can relate to the affective characteristics and needs of gifted pupils.

Behavioral objectives in the affective domain have been organized by Krathwohl and his colleagues (1964) into the following hierarchy: awareness, receiving, responding, valuing, integration into a value structure, and characterization by a value. Program objectives appropriate to the affective characteristics and needs of gifted pupils may be thought of in the same conceptual framework.

Sample Program Provisions in the Affective Domain

A. *Awareness*

1. Opportunities to identify and name one's own emotions
2. Opportunities to identify one's own perceptual filters and defense systems and those of others
3. Opportunities to expand and to clarify awareness of the physical, social, and emotional environment

B. *Receiving*

1. Experiences and instruction in attitudes of receptivity and suspended judgment
2. Opportunities and support for actively seeking ideas and feelings from others

C. *Responding*

1. Opportunities and support for communicating personal expressions in a variety of ways
2. Opportunities to identify, establish, and participate in environments in which personal responses are invited, encouraged, and valued

D. *Valuing*

1. Opportunities and instruction in constructing and clarifying personal values
2. Opportunities and support for expressing personal values including caring, caring for, and caring about

E. *Integration into a value structure*

1. Opportunities to identify a variety of value systems
2. Opportunities to clarify short-term goals and examine them in relation to personal values and to achievability
3. Support for making a personal value system the foundation for career choice, including encouragement for discovering the student's own *vocation*, in the sense of *that which one is called to do*

III. The Physical Domain

People of highly developed intellectual ability may be unusually vulnerable to a characteristic "Cartesian split" between thinking and being, a lack of integration between mind and body. During school years, when the gifted student experiences large discrepancies between physical and intellectual development, the school may unintentionally encourage the student to avoid physical activity. If a child's intellectual peers are physically more advanced so as to make him or her feel physically inadequate, while physical peers are less intellectually stimulating and not within the child's friendship group, the usual competitive playground games may be neither inviting nor satisfying to the gifted student. If the physical development of gifted students is to be encouraged, programs should provide experiences that develop integration between mind and body in students with nonnormative developmental patterns (table 6.3).

Differential Physical Characteristics of the Gifted

Unusual discrepancy between physical and intellectual development
Low tolerance for the lag between their standards and their physical capacity
Cartesian split—can include neglect of physical well-being and avoidance of
    physical activity

Table 6.2.   The Affective Domain.

Differentiating Characteristics	Examples of Related Needs	Organizational Patterns	Sample Classroom Strategies
Large accumulation of information about emotions that have not been brought to awareness	To process the emotional meaning of experience cognitively	Individual learning center activities and small discussion groups	Task cards and group discussions based on *Feelings* by Polland (1975)
	To name one's own emotions		
	To identify one's own and others' perceptual filters and defense systems	Large group, small discussion groups	Awareness exercises in the first chapter of *Awareness* by Stevens (1971). After the teacher has led a sample activity or two, others can be put on task cards for student-led small group activity, in upper elementary or secondary groups.
	To expand and clarify awareness of the physical, social, and emotional environment	Large or small group or individual learning center activity	Physical environment: an exercise in finding your "spot" as in Castaneda (1972), pp. 18–25 After reading the pages, students try to find their spot, then write about or discuss their own process, how it felt to be in the different places they tried, the attributes of the place they selected, etc.
			Social environment: "One-way glasses" in *Toward Humanistic Education*, pp. 71–79 (Weinstein and Fantini, 1970)

Table 6.2. The Affective Domain. *(continued)*

Differentiating Characteristics	Examples of Related Needs	Organizational Patterns	Sample Classroom Strategies
			Emotional environment: "Magic Circle" method from the *Human Development Program* by Bessell and Palomares (1970)
	To clarify awareness of the needs and feelings of others	Can be a total class activity; requires a safe climate emphasizing respect for individuality	"Magic Circle" discussion about the magic box that has something in it to make every person happy. Children imagine what might be in the box for them and guess about what might be in the box for other children in the group, telling why they think that would make that particular child happy (Bessell and Palomares, *Human Development Program*, 1970).
Unusual sensitivity to the expectations and feelings of others	To learn to clarify the expectations of others	Large and small task-oriented groups	Out-of-focus slides, as described by Sonntag (1972, p. 6)
Keen sense of humor—may be gentle or hostile	To learn how behaviors affect the feelings and behavior of others	Group discussion in a climate that supports caring and honest exchange of feelings and ideas	"Silent Partners" in Sonntag (1972, p. 27)
Heightened self-awareness accompanied by feelings of being "different"	To learn to assert own needs and feelings nondefensively; to share self with others, for self-clarification	Large and small communications oriented groups	See Sonntag (1972), particularly "Teacher Intervention," pp. 31–35

Table 6.2. The Affective Domain. *(continued)*

Differentiating Characteristics	Examples of Related Needs	Organizational Patterns	Sample Classroom Strategies
Idealism and a sense of justice, which appear at an early age	To transcend negative reactions by finding values to which he or she can be committed	Small group discussions, grouping gifted students together	Activities drawn from *Values Clarification* by Simon, Howe, and Kirschenbaum (1972)
Earlier development of an inner locus of control and satisfaction	To clarify personal priorities among conflicting values To confront and interact with the value systems of others	Small group discussions; self-chosen groups	*Values Clarification*, Simon, Howe, and Kirschenbaum (1972)
Advanced levels of moral judgment	To receive validation for nonaverage morality	Discussion groups with adults or intellectual peers	Exercises in resolving moral dilemmas by Kohlberg (1972, 1974, 1976a, 1976b, 1977)
High expectations of self and others, which often lead to high levels of frustration with self, others, and situations	To learn to set realistic goals and to accept setbacks as part of the learning process	Small groups specifically organized to develop realistic goal setting and reality based self-concept	Self-esteem activities developed by Coopersmith (1975)
Unusual emotional depth and intensity	To find purpose and direction from personal value system To translate commitment into action in daily life	Participation in community social-action groups	Classroom examination of the opportunities for involvement offered by various community groups Out of classroom opportunity to work with group selected by the individual student
Sensitivity to inconsistency between ideals and behavior	To find a vocation that provides opportunity for actualization of student's personal value system, as well as an avenue for his or her talents and abilities	Out of classroom opportunity to interview persons in various careers about the opportunities for actualization of value systems offered by their career	Classroom discussion on ethical questions faced by persons in selected careers, and resolutions consistent with the student's value system

Table 6.3. The Physical Domain.

Differentiating Characteristics	Examples of Related Needs	Organizational Patterns	Sample Classroom Strategies
Unusual discrepancy between physical and intellectual development	To appreciate their physical capacities	Cluster groups of gifted pupils	Sensory awareness activities from *Sense Relaxation* by Gunther (1966)
			Body awareness activity, chapter 2, *Communications Skills*, Sonntag (1972)
			Activities to heighten awareness of the pleasures of having a healthy body, and of the means for health maintenance; *The Well Body Book* (Samuels and Bennett, 1973).
Low tolerance for the lag between their standards and their athletic skills	To discover physical activity as a source of pleasure	Physical education offered in a variety of structured, nonstructured, competitive, cooperative, and individual processes	*Sense Relaxation*, Gunther (1966)
	To find satisfaction in small increments of improvement	Small groups organized to learn and teach new physical activities	*Awareness Through Movement*, Feldenkrais (1972)
	To engage in noncompetitive physical activities	Individual and group opportunities for self-expression (through dance, movement, pantomime, etc.) in various areas of the curriculum	*Improvisation for the Theatre*, Spolin (1963)
			Music, Wampler (1973)

Table 6.3. The Physical Domain. *(continued)*

Differentiating Characteristics	Examples of Related Needs	Organizational Patterns	Sample Classroom Strategies
"Cartesian Split" can include neglect of physical well-being and avoidance of physical activity	To engage in activities leading to mind/body integration	Out of class time provided to explore the disciplines devoted to mind/body integration (Yoga, Judo, T'ai-chi Ch'uan, etc.)	Invite teachers or advanced students of these physical/philosophical disciplines to visit class and hold demonstrations
			Instruction in techniques of relaxation and tension reduction. *Sense Relaxation*, Gunther (1966)
	To develop a commitment to one's own physical well-being	Individual, small group, or large group	Develop a personal plan for meeting nutritional and activity needs; follow it, note effects, modify it, etc.
	To extend this concern to the social and political realm	Out of class time provided for community involvement	Identify current health needs of the community; examine the implications of current social and political policies for the health of the people in the community.

Sample program provisions in the physical domain.   Program provisions for gifted pupils to meet the needs of the physical domain can also be organized according to the following taxonomy:

A. *Awareness*

1. Experiences designed to heighten and clarify sensory awareness
2. Experiences designed to promote awareness of the student's own body and the creation of a positive body image
3. Experiences and information to heighten awareness of the pleasures of having a healthy body, and of the means for health maintenance and growth
4. Information and opportunities for inquiry into the clarification of physical responses to emotions

B. *Involvement*

1. Instruction and practice in techniques of relaxation and tension reduction
2. Opportunities for self-expression through movement, pantomime, dance, etc.
3. Opportunities to develop individual physical competence and experience the satisfaction of physical activity in ways chosen by the student from a wide range of structured and nonstructured, competitive, cooperative, and individual processes

C. *Integration*

1. Exposure to, and opportunities to learn, one of the disciplines devoted to mind/body integration: Yoga, Judo, T'ai-chi Ch'uan, etc.
2. Support for, and assistance in making, the care and development of one's own body a part of an individual life style
3. Opportunities to examine the implications of current social and political policies for the health of people in the community

IV. The Intuitive Domain

The intuitive function is involved in initiating or insightful acts and in creative activity. While this is the least defined area of human endeavor, it is probably the area that promises the most for the continuance and fulfillment of humankind. All other areas provide support for, and are supported by, this area of function. As each area evolves to higher levels, more of the intuitive and creative functions become available (table 6.4)

Differentiating Characteristics of the Gifted

Early involvement and concern for intuitive knowing, psychic and metaphysical ideas and phenomena

Open to experiences in this area; will experiment with psychic and metaphysical phenomena

Creativity apparent in all areas of endeavor

Acceptance and expression of a high level of intuitive ability, especially with the highly gifted

Table 6.4. The Intuitive Domain.

Differentiating Characteristics	Examples of Related Needs	Organizational Patterns	Sample Classroom Strategies
Early involvement and concern for intuitive knowing, psychic and metaphysical ideas and phenomena	Opportunities to converse meaningfully with philosophers and others on these ideas	An environment of trust and acceptance; independent study; mentors, guest experts, group experiences, and discussions	Small group meetings with experts to discuss and explore phenomena
	To recognize own intuitive energy and ability		Exercises on centering, relaxation, and meditation (Hendricks and Fadiman, 1975; Hendricks and Wills, 1975; Hendricks and Roberts, 1977)
	Guidance to develop and use intuitive energy and ability		Use of imagery, fantasy, and dreams
Open to experiences in this area; will experiment with psychic and metaphysical phenomena	Guidance in becoming familiar with, analyzing, and evaluating such phenomena	An environment where these ideas are valued	Lessons directed to use of psychic and intuitive energy

Table 6.4.   The Intuitive Domain. *(continued)*

Differentiating Characteristics	Examples of Related Needs	Organizational Patterns	Sample Classroom Strategies
	Should be provided a historical approach	Access to resources discussing phenomena throughout history	Controlled experiments investigating such phenomena Discussions of nonscientific evidence Independent study of brain research and psychic research relationship
Creativity apparent in all areas of endeavor	Guidance in evaluating appropriate uses of creative efforts Encouraging ongoing development of creative abilities	Flexible, open classroom; teacher acceptance of unusual products or ideas	Valuing activities dealing with results of the creative process Creativity exercises are in Beechhold (1971), Massialas and Zevin (1967), De Mille (1973), and Parnes (1967).
Acceptance and expression of a high level of intuitive ability, especially with the highly gifted understanding and acceptance of ability		A safe, accepting environment	Opportunities to use and develop abilities in a variety of subject areas (see activities on p. 268)

V. The Societal Domain

Society has unique needs for the services of unique individuals. While we would not wish that gifted education focus on societal needs at the expense of individual actualization, neither can education for the gifted disregard the importance of their mature social roles. Gifted students need direction in exploring the variety of opportunities for contributing what they have to offer society. They need conceptual frameworks to organize their experience of society (cf., Maslow's 1968 hierarchy of needs); and they need opportunities to develop those skills that will make it possible for them to have an effect on society. Educational programs should provide for the options, conceptual frameworks, and skills that underlie the effective social involvement of gifted students.

Differential Societal Characteristics of the Gifted

Strongly motivated by self-actualization needs
Advanced cognitive and affective capacity for conceptualizing and solving
     societal problems

Differential Social Expectations for the Gifted

Leadership
Solutions to social and environmental problems
Involvement with the metaneeds of society (e.g., justice, beauty, truth)

The needs of gifted pupils in the societal domain fall mainly into four categories: the need to be an effective member of a group; the need to understand what is going on in a group and to be able to influence the group process; the need to extend one's feeling of membership from family and small group to the community at large; the need to extend identification with one's community to identification with the human community. Program provisions in the societal domain can be organized according to this hierarchy:

Sample Program Provisions in the Societal Domain

A. *Membership*

1. Opportunities to participate in activities with a variety of groups (e.g., intellectual peers, varying age levels, varying ability levels, handicapped and nonhandicapped combinations)
2. Opportunities to identify and examine roles in group membership and their effect on this group
3. Opportunities to become aware of and practice methods and results of open communication
4. Opportunities to see the self in relation to others and the effect each has upon the other
5. Opportunities to examine and understand their own functioning within a group and to receive instruction in and opportunity to improve that function

Table 6.5. The Societal Domain .

Differentiating Characteristics	Examples of Related Needs	Organizational Patterns	Sample Classroom Strategies
Strongly motivated by self-actualization needs	Opportunities to follow divergent paths and pursue strong interests Help in understanding the demands of self-actualization	A trusting environment where self-esteem is supported and self-exploration valued and actively facilitated	Values clarification exercises (Kohlberg, 1972, 1974, 1976a, 1976b, 1977); magic circle activities (Bessell and Palomares, 1970); self-esteem activities (Coopersmith, 1975)
Advanced cognitive and affective capacity for conceptualizing and solving societal problems	Encounters with social problems Awareness of the complexity of problems facing society Conceptual frameworks for problem-solving procedures	Access to the community Flexible grouping allowing gifted to work together during part of the program Small group work	Visiting experts and community workers; small group field trips for information Debates, simulations, analysis of real problems Simulations; problem-solving models (Gallagher, 1975)
Leadership	Understanding of various leadership styles and practice in leadership skills	Integrated age and ability levels; cooperative planning and implementation of program	Leadership training groups; creating a government for the group; organizing and implementing social, cultural, or curricular programs
Solutions to social and environmental problems	Meaningful involvement in real problems	An environment where concern with social problems is valued; flexible programs permitting off-site involvement	Simulations; planning and implementing programs benefiting segments of the school community or the community at large
Involvement with the metaneeds of society, e.g., justice, beauty, truth	Exploration of the highest levels of human thought; application of this knowledge to today's problems	Independent study; flexible groupings; access to community	Great Books program; visiting experts; future studies

B. *Group process*

1. Opportunities to identify and examine a variety of leadership styles and their consequences
2. Opportunities to learn and apply leadership skills, including solicitation and use of counsel, advice, and criticism
3. Opportunities to develop, demonstrate, and communicate expertise in some field to colleagues
4. Opportunities to be sensitized to power issues and to explore the exercise and distribution of power

C. *Extended membership*

1. Opportunities to identify the problems of one's own social community—problem finding
2. Opportunities to develop possible and/or innovative solutions to community problems
3. Opportunities to function in cooperation with others in the community to implement solutions
4. Opportunities for recognition and respect of parent and community values

D. *Identification with humankind*

1. Opportunities for recognition of commonalities among human beings transcending natural or created boundaries
2. Opportunities for cognitive and affective understanding of human interdependence
3. Opportunities to mesh individual goals and needs with group and societal goals and needs
4. Opportunities for recognition of the possibility of conflict between the needs and goals of humanity and the personal and group needs and goals
5. Opportunities to develop a value system in which the long-term needs of humanity have priority

The intellectually gifted child characteristically differs from the average child in cognitive, affective, physical, intuitive, and societal behavior. These characteristic differences are the source of the special educational needs of gifted children. Methods, materials, and organizational patterns for educational programs should be clearly related to the needs and characteristics of the children in all five aspects of human development. The framework presented here is far from complete, and is offered in the hope that caring parents and educators will find it valuable as they seek to develop "qualitatively different" educational programs and experiences that will help to actualize the abilities of pupils with unusual capacities and unusual needs.

Differentiating Curriculum

In addition to beginning with the assessed needs of each gifted learner as discussed earlier in the chapter, and because those differentiated needs can commonly be found among many of the gifted, some general elements that help to define a differentiated curriculum can be discussed. These elements would include, but not be limited to, the following (Clark and Kaplan, 1981):

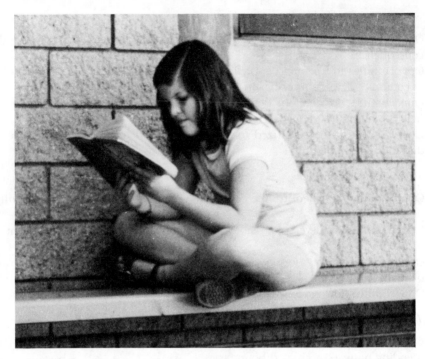

Differentiating the curriculum must allow for independence of thought and study.

- Accelerated or advanced content
- More complex understandings of generalizations, principles, theories, and the structure of the content area
- Abstract concepts and thought processes or skills
- Level and type of resources used to obtain information, acquire skills, and develop products
- Appropriation of longer/shorter time span for learning
- Generating new information and/or products
- Transfer of learning to new/different disciplines, situations, etc.
- Development of personal growth and sophistication in attitudes, appreciations, feelings, intuition
- Independence of thought and study

Individualizing the Program

In chapter 4, and again throughout the Hagen and Clark model, the importance of individualized instruction has been stressed. Because many things have been called individualized learning, not all of which are effective, what is meant by individualized learning in the context of this book needs to be discussed. Unless you understand not only what it is, but how it is begun, an individualized program model like the Cooperative Learning Environment would be impossible to implement.

In a recent study directed by Bloom (1981) it was found that of those persons studied who had achieved exceptional accomplishment of international note, their early instruction and a large part of their later instruction in their field of accomplishment was individualized. This was one of the identified differences between the instruction offered to the exceptionally accomplished and that found in the traditional schooling experience.

Individualization can be defined as a way of organizing learning experiences so that the rate, content, schedule, experiences, and depth of exploration available to all students stem from their assessed achievement and interests. Different programs have varying degrees of individualization. *Individual teacher diagnosis* and *prescriptive instruction* individualize the level and pace of instruction. When, in addition, the student becomes involved in the selection of goals, the instruction becomes more personalized. *Self-directed* or *independent study* needs to have all of the previously mentioned provisions as well as self-selection of learning activities and materials. *Total individualization* allows teacher and student to assess and select goals, learning materials, activities, and instructional techniques cooperatively. It also allows the student to self-pace, self-level, and self-evaluate, using the teacher as a consultant and resource. In this way, students can take advantage of their unique learning styles to enhance their creativity.

There are a number of strategies that can help you individualize. *Programmed learning* offers students a way to move at their own pace through skill-level learning. It includes individual assessment and allows students continuous feedback on work that is done at their own level. Programmed learning can free the teacher from much unnecessary drill work and allow the student to learn materials basic to higher learning or research by a self-checking procedure.

Instructional packages provide an excellent way for students to work individually or in small groups and be in charge of their learning. A learning activity or instructional package includes: an assessment or pretest procedure that permits students to discover their own level of need; multisensory resources and activities; and a self-evaluation or posttest component. The package gives students an excellent way to move through basic materials and new information. It should be self-paced and allow students to correct all their own mistakes prior to the teacher's evaluation of the learned information or skill.

Another structure often used to aid students in developing the skills for individualizing is the *learning contract*. It can be as simple as a statement of need or intent by the student, a description of what will be needed for accomplishing such a goal, and the agreed-upon evaluation procedures or criteria for deciding when the project or learning goal has been completed. Or it can be very complex, depending on its use and the student's ability to be self-directed. Usually the teacher and the learner cooperate in negotiating the learning contract; negotiation may even include the parents. Contractual decisions should be made after substantial assessment and the results have been discussed with the student. Cooperatively the teacher and the student (and sometimes the parent) must decide on the objectives, resources to be used, possible activities, reporting alternatives, and evaluation procedures for both self-assessment and teacher assessment. While contracts give a mutually agreed-upon base for beginning, they must always remain negotiable. Many factors, such as detours and side investigations, can cause the original plan to need modification. So long as both the teacher and the student agree, this can only enrich the experience. When we choose to individualize, we make a number of assumptions:

Students should assume some responsibility for their own learning.

Students should be helped to become independent learners.

Students have a right to learn at their own pace, through their preferred learning style, and at their own level of ability.

Knowledge students have is not held in common by the class, but by individuals in differing amounts.

A variety of materials allows students to exercise judgment. When everyone has the same material, learning ceases to be individualized. The greater the range of materials and experiences available, the greater is the range of learning opportunity for every individual.

Students should be graded in terms of their own achievement if grades must be given.

It is proper for schools to be concerned with the development of a student's self-esteem.

One of the most critical areas of concern in cognitive development is motivation. We have found that a very important way to bring out the motivation of students is to make them aware of their own power and to allow them to exercise it. Any way that a program or course can be structured to give more choice to the student uses that power. So often schools have rules that create the opposite effect.

Not all gifted students make choices easily. Structuring the choices will be necessary for those who have difficulty in order to guide them gradually into their own power. Others will be ready for responsible freedom. They should be given independence immediately. The following ideas have been found to work in allowing responsible choice:

Whatever the nonnegotiables are, whether mandated by the state, the district, or the school, let them be known. Discuss with the students the real consequences to you and to themselves of choice related to these nonnegotiables (for example, if the state requires the completion of a certain course of study, discuss how that can be accomplished and what will happen if it is not). If certain books are to be covered, discuss the time span necessary. Give students the information and choices in whatever areas are possible. One teacher found that by telling the students what the class requirements were and what other things could be done when they had finished, she and the students were able to work out a time span that got the required work completed in time to pursue the other material and projects. Before, students in her classes had moved slowly and unwillingly through only the required work.

If tests must be used for evaluation, give a choice between objective and subjective examination, between teacher written or student written tests. Often, even though you offer the same tests you have previously used, the element of choice creates more willing, more motivated students.

If tests are not required, contract with students to make a choice over a wide range of possible criteria to be used for evaluation. They can contract for a particular level of performance if grades are to be given.

Set up many ways of reaching the same learning goal. At secondary level, classrooms in English can become learning labs just as well as classrooms in chemistry. In the elementary class, the possibilities are limited only by the teacher's creativeness.

Crossgrading can be accomplished even in traditionally structured schools by developing a relationship between different age classes or nearby schools and allowing students extended passes to work with these students in their classrooms.

Make available off-school sites for those interested in working independently.

Make public and accessible the requirements for entry into the colleges and universities that your students will likely attend. Let students make choices about which of these sets of requirements most meets their needs.

Gifted students are interested in current topics that involve them and their personal welfare. Any new information, such as discoveries in brain research or physics, that can be shown to affect them and their world, are of great interest, especially if presented with all the unanswered questions and future challenges.

Interdisciplinary presentations are most requested by gifted students. One teacher with the proper background or a team from differing disciplines can make this approach available. Be aware that what the students are asking for is not tandem teaching, one instructor then the other, but a real team situation where the students can be a part of an interaction between disciplines.

Secondary departments might consider using an open, individualized approach that would allow more subject areas to be taught at higher levels. One school with a small faculty can offer five years of all basic language plus Latin, Russian, and Greek by teaching in an individualized pattern. Students can sign up for the language of their choice at their appropriate level. By the individualization model, they can receive instruction while others pursue their own choices during the same period. One period of typing could be individualized to accommodate many levels and instructional goals. A business teacher in my class recently developed a programmed typing manual to help her individualize such a class. This method of presenting instruction would work for all subject areas.

Dunn and Dunn (1975) present one of the best approaches to individualizing I have yet discovered. They provide a step-by-step approach to individualize a classroom successfully. Briefly, they suggest that you do the following:

1. Give students opportunities to build the skills needed for participation in individualized learning.
    — to make choices (choosing wisely leaves many options; choosing less wisely leaves fewer options, and only consequences can determine the value of the choice);
    — to self-evaluate;
    — to share.
2. Teach students the skills of learning in small groups
    — role playing;
    — peer teaching;
    — group analysis;
    — discussion.
3. Establish instructional areas that will support individualized learning
    — interest centers;
    — learning stations;

— media center;

— game area;

— quiet reading and study area;

— assessment center.

4. Develop student independence

— knowledge of resources, location, and use;

— alternative thinking in activities and in reporting.

5. Carefully assess students, curriculum, and resources.

6. Help class learn skills of cooperative assessment, goal setting, evaluation.

7. Let class assume more responsibility for planning and implementing the program.[1]

These steps are not easy. They require time and effort to be used successfully. However, if your goal is for independent, stimulated learners, you will find your efforts well rewarded.

Finally these eight shoulds and should nots can help you to clarify whether your curriculum is appropriately based on the commonly recognized needs of gifted learners (Clark and Kaplan, 1981).

The Shoulds and Should Nots of an Appropriately Designed Differentiated Curriculum

1. The curriculum *should* be planned and sequentially organized to include specific expectations for the acquisition of subject matter, mastery of skills, creation of products, and development of attitudes and appreciations related to self, others, and the environment.

   The curriculum *should not* be a potpourri of learning activities that are disjointed and haphazardly selected without reference to specified criteria.

2. The curriculum *should* place emphasis on the interdependence of subject matter, skills, products, and self-understanding within the *same* curricular structure.

   The curriculum *should not* focus on the attainment of cognitive competencies in isolation from the development of affective competencies. Nor should the curriculum focus on affective development without concern for cognitive growth.

3. The curriculum *should* include provisions to meet the need for some type of instructional pacing by any or all of the following means:

   a. Making it possible to accomplish a range of learning experiences in a shorter span of time using a continuous progress curriculum

   b. Assigning students to curricula at levels beyond those expected at the students' age/grade level

   c. Eliminating from the curricula what is already learned and substituting curricula more appropriate to student interest, abilities, and needs.

   The curriculum *should not* penalize students for being gifted or talented, through restricting their opportunities to learn by ignoring those characteristics that define their giftedness.

---

[1]From the book *EDUCATOR'S SELF-TEACHING GUIDE TO INDIVIDUALIZING INSTRUCTIONAL PRO-GRAMS* by Rita Dunn and Kenneth Dunn. © 1975 by Parker Publishing Company, Inc., West Nyack, New York 10994. Published by Parker Publishing Company, Inc., West Nyack, New York 10994.

4. The curriculum *should* allow for the expression of some aspect of the individual's interests, needs, abilities, and learning preferences. The curriculum *should* be organized to allow for some individualization and self-selection.

   The curriculum *should not* be without defined expectations and clearly expressed opportunities for teacher-directed as well as student-selected learning activities.

5. The curriculum *should* provide opportunities to learn to reconceptualize existing knowledge, to perceive things from various points of view, and to use information for new purposes or in new ways.

   The curriculum *should not* stress the accumulation of knowledge or reinforce mastery without simultaneously encouraging students to be productive thinkers.

6. The curriculum *should* provide learning experiences for students to address the unresolved issues and problems of society and apply personal and social data to analyze, clarify, and respond to such issues and problems.

   The curriculum *should not* focus only on knowledge of the world as it is, but should encourage the development of perceptions of the need to invent in order to restructure the world into what it ideally could be.

7. The curriculum *should* incorporate learning experiences that foster the development of the complex thought processes that encourage the creation of unique products and develop strategies of productive thought. The curriculum *should* teach both fundamental and higher-level thinking skills as integral parts of every learning experience.

   The curriculum *should not* overemphasize mastery of fundamental basic skills, nor should it exonerate gifted/talented students from mastering these. The curriculum *should not* ignore the development of fundamental or basic skills for the mastery of higher-level thinking skills.

8. The curriculum *should* provide opportunities for students to practice leadership and followership skills and appropriate and varied forms of communication skills and strategies.

   The curriculum *should not* be based on the assumption that gifted/talented students can assume positions of leadership without the development of skills and understandings that promote this end.

While this is a useful guide, you will always need to assess your gifted learners for their particular needs. They are your very best guide to an appropriate curriculum.

Models of Learning and Teaching Often Used in Developing Curriculum for the Gifted Learner

Bloom and Krathwohl   A number of conceptualizations of the learning process have influenced the development of curriculum in gifted education. They have provided structures that allow careful consideration of how learning may occur and how experiences may be designed to enhance growth in skills related to thinking and learning. One of the most often used is the *Taxonomy of Educational Objectives: Handbook I: Cognitive Domain*, edited by Bloom (1956). Table 6.6 presents and clarifies the taxonomy in ways that have been found useful in curriculum planning.

Table 6.6 Taxonomy Breakdown.

Area of Taxonomy	Definition	What Teacher Does	What Student Does	Process Verbs	
Knowledge	Recall or recognition of specific information	Directs Tells Shows Examines	Responds Absorbs Remembers Recognizes	define repeat list name label	memorize record recall relate
Comprehension	Understanding of information given	Demonstrates Listens Questions Compares Contrasts Examines	Explains Translates Demonstrates Interprets	restate describe explain identify report tell	discuss recognize express locate review
Application	Using methods, concepts, principles, and theories in new situations	Shows Facilitates Observes Criticizes	Solves problems Demonstrates use of knowledge Constructs	translate apply employ use practice shop	interpret demonstrate dramatize illustrate operate schedule

Table 6.6 Taxonomy Breakdown. *(continued)*

Area of Taxonomy	Definition	What Teacher Does	What Student Does	Process Verbs	
Analysis	Breaking information down into its constituent elements	Probes Guides Observes Acts as a resource	Discusses Uncovers Lists Dissects	distinguish calculate test contract criticize debate question solve analyze	appraise differentiate experiment compare diagram inspect inventory relate examine
Synthesis	Putting together constituent elements or parts to form a whole requiring original, creative thinking	Reflects Extends Analyzes Evaluates	Discusses Generalizes Relates Compares Contrasts Abstracts	compose propose formulate assemble construct set up manage	plan design arrange collect create organize prepare
Evaluation	Judging the values of ideas, materials, and methods by developing and applying standards and criteria	Clarifies Accepts Harmonizes Guides	Judges Disputes Develops criteria	judge evaluate compare score choose estimate predict	appraise rate value select assess measure

While the taxonomy is often used as a linear model, it can also be viewed as cyclic, with the highest level, evaluation, seen as producing new information that becomes knowledge and then moves through the entire process (figure 6.1).

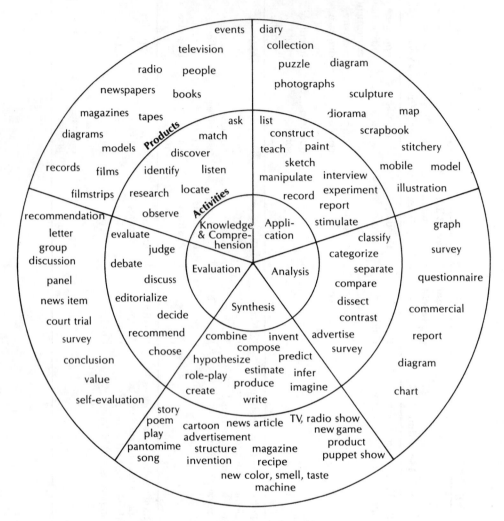

Figure 6.1.   Taxonomy Circle.[2]

Although one often hears that gifted learners should be working at the top levels of the taxonomy, such a statement can be quite misleading. It would not be possible for gifted students to analyze information that they do not understand. All students need to be exposed to experiences at all levels of the taxonomy. The emphasis in instruction makes the difference, as gifted students often bring a large amount of knowledge to class with them (see figure 6.2).

[2]The wheel in figure 6.1 was developed by my colleague, Barry Ziff, and a class of teachers of the gifted. They found it very useful in curriculum building.

Figure 6.2. Taxonomy of Educational Objectives—Affective Domain

Category	Subdivisions	Student Behavior to be Attained (Educational Objectives)	Category	Subdivisions	Student Behavior to be Attained (Educational Objectives)
1.0 Receiving	1.1 Awareness	Observes; recognizes, is aware of; develops sensitivity to	3.0 Valuing	3.1 Accepting a value	Develops a sense of responsibility, of kinship, of need for worship
Attending	1.2 Willingness to	Accepts others; develops a tolerance for. Listens carefully; recognizes persons as individuals		3.2 Preference for a value	Interest in enabling others; examines a variety of viewpoints; assumes active role in politics, literary organizations
	1.3 Controlled and selected attention	Discriminates; appreciates alertness to values; selects reading materials		3.3 Commitment	Displays a high degree of certainty, loyalty, faith in the power of reason
2.0 Responding	2.1 Acquiescence in responding	Willing to comply; observes rules and regulations	4.0 Organization	4.1 Conceptualization of a value	Establishes a conscious base for making choices. Identifies admired characteristics. Analyzes basic assumptions underlying codes of ethics and faith. Forms judgment as to responsibility of society to the individual and environment. Develops personal goals.
	2.2 Willingness to respond	Voluntarily seeks information, engages in variety of activities. Responds to intellectual stimuli; engages in research			
	2.3 Satisfactory in response	Finds pleasure in reading, listening, conversing, art, participation in groups			

Figure 6.2.   Taxonomy of Educational Objectives—Affective Domain *(continued)*

Category	Subdivisions	Student Behavior to be Attained (Educational Objectives)
4.0 Organization	4.2 Organization of a value system According to Edward Spranger values may be organized around the following: 1. Theoretical 2. Economic 3. Aesthetic 4. Social 5. Political 6. Religious	Examines role of democracy in conserving human and natural resources; accepts own potentialities and limitations realistically; views people as individuals, without prejudice; develops techniques for conflict management. Accepts responsibility for the future.
5.0 Characterization of a Value	5.1 Generalized set—the basic orientation which enables the individual to act consistently and effectively in a complex world	Readiness to reverse judgements or change behavior in light of evidence; to change one's mind and face facts: confidence in ability to succeed; solves problems in terms of what is rather than wishful thinking
	5.2 Characterization—one's personal philosophy of life demonstrated in behavior	Develops a code of behavior based on ethical principles consistent with democratic ideals: behavior which is consistent with beliefs

Source: Adapted from *Taxonomy of Educational Objectives: Handbook II: Affective Domain* by David R. Krathwohl et al. Copyright © 1964 by Longman Inc. Reprinted by permission of Longman Inc, New York.

Bloom was also involved in a second organization delineating a hierarchy of learning, the *Taxonomy of Educational Objectives: Handbook II: Affective Domain* (Krathwohl, Bloom, and Masia, 1964). The purpose of this list of objectives was to sequence behaviors that would indicate growth in the emotional area of function. As we saw on p. 201 those levels are awareness, receiving, responding, valuing, integration into a value structure, and characterization by a value.

One of the best things about working with gifted learners is that they enjoy these types of organizers. Not only can the teacher find them helpful in curriculum development, but the students can, after becoming familiar with the taxonomic structure, actually analyze and create curricular experiences at each level themselves.

Guilford and Meeker   Another major organizer used for development of curriculum in gifted education is the Structure of Intellect (SOI) Model (Guilford, 1967). The model (figure 6.3) provided psychology with a multifactor view of intelligence to replace the single factor view previously used.

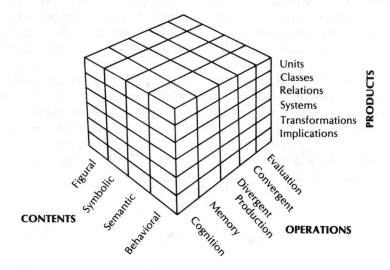

Figure 6.3.   Theoretical Model for Guilford's "Structure of Intellect."[3]

The factor analysis of numerous aptitude and ability tests provided the basis for this model. The division of intellectual abilities into three dimensions—contents, operations, and products—and their subdivisions gives this model the means to show interrelationships between human abilities (Guilford, 1967). Some educators, especially Meeker (1969), extend the use of the SOI Model to serve as a basis for a diagnostic-prescriptive tool in the teaching of thinking skills.

Meeker asserts that the use of the SOI Model provides a theory of intelligence to education, where previously one had not existed. By using the model for curriculum development, she believes that we can meet the educational needs of each child more adequately. Meeker has, therefore, developed assessment techniques that make use of the major tests of intelligence, the Stanford-Binet and the Weschler. These

---

[3]By J. P. Guilford, from *The Nature of Human Intelligence.* New York: McGraw Hill, 1967. Reprinted by permission.

tests can delineate the student's areas of strength and weakness that correspond with specific abilities on the SOI. The resulting profile of the student provides the basis for a curricular plan that may then be implemented by the use of materials developed by Meeker for classroom use.

While Meeker has made the SOI much more available to the classroom, the very success of her efforts may cause some teachers to restrict their planning to use of just these materials. We must be sure to include more than just activities of a cognitive nature in our total educational program. After all, the SOI is a theoretic model of intellectual abilities that, at best, only partially explains human functioning. While Meeker has made a valuable contribution, the SOI materials must be carefully integrated into a comprehensive educational plan that views intellectual ability as only one area of human functioning.

Bruner and Suchman   That any discipline could be taught at any age if the basic structure of the discipline were communicated in ways the child could understand was strongly believed by Bruner (1960). He urged educators to address themselves to the process of learning, to present science as the scientist would learn it. One educator who developed a strategy for doing just that was Richard Suchman.

Suchman (1961, 1962) developed an inquiry model from his understanding of the scientific model of thinking (figure 6.4). While it may oversimplify human thought by leaving out important areas, it is quite useful in teaching many important processes. Suchman's program gives students practice in solving problems, by establishing the properties of all objects or systems involved in the problem, finding which objects or systems are relevant to the problem, and discovering how they function in the solution. Sessions are designed to help students learn to formulate and test their own theories and to become aware of their own learning processes. The outcomes lead not so much to new answers, and never to right or wrong answers, but to new and more productive questions.

Figure 6.4.   A Visualization of the Inquiry Model.

Williams   An adaptation of the Guilford Model was developed by Williams (1979) for the purpose of combining cognitive and affective factors. The resulting three-dimensional model looks similar to the SOI cube and incorporates curriculum, teacher behaviors, and pupil behaviors. By use of these dimensions Williams believes that teachers can construct curriculum that can effectively cause pupils to think and feel creatively in any subject area.

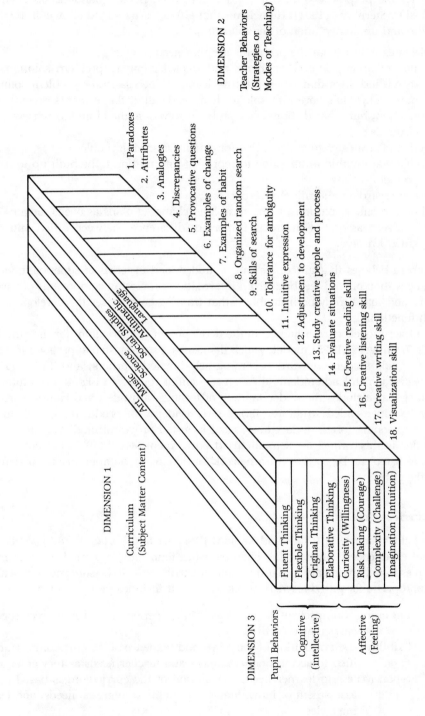

DIMENSION 2

Teacher Behaviors
(Strategies or
Modes of Teaching)

1. Paradoxes
2. Attributes
3. Analogies
4. Discrepancies
5. Provocative questions
6. Examples of change
7. Examples of habit
8. Organized random search
9. Skills of search
10. Tolerance for ambiguity
11. Intuitive expression
12. Adjustment to development
13. Study creative people and process
14. Evaluate situations
15. Creative reading skill
16. Creative listening skill
17. Creative writing skill
18. Visualization skill

DIMENSION 1

Curriculum
(Subject Matter Content)

Art
Music
Science
Social Studies
Arithmetic
Language

DIMENSION 3
Pupil Behaviors

Cognitive
(intellective)

Fluent Thinking
Flexible Thinking
Original Thinking
Elaborative Thinking

Affective
(Feeling)

Curiosity (Willingness)
Risk Taking (Courage)
Complexity (Challenge)
Imagination (Intuition)

An interesting theory that seeks to identify the components of cognitive giftedness for the purpose of improving differentiated curricular planning has been advanced by Sternberg (1981). He believes that gifted learners tend to excel in their access to and implementation of the following:

Decision as to just what the problems are that need solving

Selection of appropriate components and steps leading to problem solution. Research indicates that when intuitive leaps are necessary for problem solution, most individuals have available in their heads all of the elements necessary for solution, but what distinguishes problem solvers is the ability to retrieve these elements.

Selection of strategies to evolve a plan of action for solving problems

Learning ways within a discipline to represent information to be built up to use in problem solving

Decision regarding allocation of resources

Ability to monitor solutions, being flexible in changing plans as needs dictate. This was seen as one of the most important differences between gifted and nongifted learners.

Sternberg believes that giftedness can be understood in terms of superior functioning, activation of, and feedback from information processing components of various kinds, and that it may be trainable if that training emphasizes the development of such functioning.

Other models currently used in the development of curriculum for the gifted include Treffinger's (1975) model, which delineates a step-by-step approach for teachers to guide students toward becoming self-directed learners; and Taba's (1966) strategies, which lead students through sequential cognitive tasks to a resolution of conflict that includes the understanding of feelings, attitudes, and values. A rather complex, open-ended structure, Taba's gives evidence of producing growth in abstract reasoning (often declared as a goal in gifted programming). We should also mention in this context the Renzulli Triad Enrichment Model (1977) presented on p. 156, as it too can be used as a framework for developing an appropriate curriculum for the gifted.

A Curriculum Criteria Checklist

The following criteria (Clark and Kaplan, 1981) are appropriate for all good educational experiences; however, the characteristics found among gifted learners make them especially necessary to a differentiated curriculum. To be sure your curriculum is appropriate for gifted learners check to see if it includes provisions for:

1. Continuity—Comprehensive set of learning experiences that reinforces specific curricular objectives
2. Flexibility—Determination of the scope and sequence of the curriculum is modified to accommodate student and teacher needs as they emerge
3. Responsiveness to learner needs—Definition of the curriculum is based on an assessment of individual/group abilities, interests, needs, and learning styles.

4. Diversity—Provisions for alternative means to attain determined ends within a specified curricular framework
5. Integration—Integrative use of all abilities which include cognition, emotion, intuition, and mind/body into a single curriculum
6. Openness—Elimination of preset expectations that limit the learnings within the curricular framework
7. Independence—Provisions for some type(s) of self-directed learnings
8. Increasing levels of advanced abstraction and difficulty—Acceptance of the student's readiness to learn beyond traditional age/grade expectations and provisions for stimulating such readiness
9. Substantive learning—Inclusion of significant subject matter, skills, products, and awarenesses that are of consequence or of importance to the learner and the disciplines
10. Decision making—Provisions for students to make some appropriate/relevant decisions regarding what is to be learned and how it can be learned
11. Principles of learning—Inclusion of teaching practices that allow for motivation, practice, transfer of training and feedback
12. Creation/re-creation—Provisions to apply the creative process to improve, modify, etc. one's creations to challenge prevailing thought and offer more appropriate solutions
13. Interaction with peers and variety of significant others—Provisions to learn about and meet with individuals who share same and different gifts/talents
14. Value system—Inclusion of consistent opportunities to develop and examine personal and societal values and to establish a personal value system
15. Communication skills—Development of verbal, non-verbal systems and skills to dialogue, share, and exchange ideas
16. Commitment to society—Provisions to understand and relate to the society in which one lives and to find one's place in it

Studies comparing the learning styles of the gifted to nongifted learners (Price, et al., 1981) indicate that elementary and secondary gifted learners prefer less supervision in the learning setting; manipulative and active, real-life experiences to lectures, discussions, and tapes; and more small group, individual, and self-designed instructional opportunities.

Choice and Perceived Control

As we begin our discussion of strategies for teaching, let us be cautious about one item. During the past few years an impressive number of researchers in projects throughout the country have found that choice and the resulting perception of control are motivational variables that significantly affect children's academic achievement as well as their self-concept (Arlin and Whitley, 1978; Barnett and Kaiser, 1978; Calsyn, 1973; Matheny and Edwards, 1974; Stipek and Weisz, 1981; Thomas, 1980; Wang and Stiles, 1976). Interestingly it is not just the choice or control that is allowed children that makes the difference, but their perception of that choice. The possibilities for choice may be in the program, but unless children clearly see those alternatives and believe that they can really make a choice that will be acceptable, the positive effect will be missing.

One of the attributes of gifted learners is their early development of an internal locus of control. This means that they often do things for the pure pleasure of it. They can get very excited about learning new information, and they derive much satisfaction from discovering the solution to a problem. The term *locus of control* is used to express the idea that the perceived control can be located either within the child (as when a choice is made from the child's interest) or externally (as when a reward is given for making the choice). This is where gifted children show themselves to be characteristically different from the average learner. Gifted children are found to have more inner locus of control at a younger age than do average learners. It is one of the notable differences that needs to be considered when educational experiences are planned for the gifted. It is important to note that success in later life is in direct correlation to how much inner locus of control the individual has developed. This perception of responsibility for and control over one's life is the single most important condition for success, achievement, and a sense of well-being (Allen et al., 1974; Bar-Tal et al., 1980; Dweck and Goetz, 1978; Lao, 1970; Morrison and McIntyre, 1971; Phares, 1975).

Our schools have made use of external rewards, such as grades, prizes, gold stars, special privileges, threats, and punishments, without considering whether the child is intrinsically motivated or not. It has been established that the more the environment, either home or school, provides external controls, the greater will be the loss of the inner locus (Deci, 1975). Source of motivation is just what we who work with the gifted must notice. Greene (1974), Lepper, Greene, and Nisbett (1973), and others have found that, for children who have intrinsic motivation, an external reward system can be devastating. The child will no longer work for the joy or notice the satisfaction of accomplishment, but will focus on the learning task as a means to a different goal, the reward. Once the reward stops being offered, the task ceases to be worthwhile. For gifted learners this is most important. Not only do they have more inner control available earlier, they are more sensitive to the demands of the environment. They can, in fact, lose more of their perceived power faster than will the average learner. It then becomes important to plan an environment that builds inner locus and heightens the perception of choice. Development of intrinsic motivation and internal locus of control are important goals for gifted students to help them function positively in society and find personal satisfaction in whatever they choose to do. Be careful that unexamined practices of using rewards do not undermine this development.

Successful experiences are not enough. If children succeed, but believe that you gave them that success, it does not add to the perceived power. Likewise, failure can be viewed as positive if children believe by their own effort success would be possible. The world must be seen as able to be acted upon; it must not be viewed as a place where one is helpless and everything just happens to you. This perception is established very early, within the first two months. It is this perception that is one of the triggering mechanisms for developing higher levels of intelligence (De Charms, 1976; Gordon, 1977; Andrews and Debus, 1978).

How then can we plan an environment that works for the gifted child and increases a sense of perceived control? Here are some suggestions:

1. One critical factor is the structure of the program. It must be a complex structure that attempts to give every child alternatives at an appropriate level of choice. A flexible, responsive structure is important at home as well.

2. Incorporate lessons in making good choices and how to develop responsible choices. Children need a lot of practice in choosing.

3. The choices must be real; that is, any that are presented are equally acceptable to the teacher (or parent), and there is no hidden preference.

4. The situations for choice must come with a procedure for child developed alternatives to be considered whenever possible. "If you don't find what you want within what we suggest, what do you suggest?" becomes the question.

5. Teachers must believe that children can and should make the major part of the decisions about their learning experience. We are there to provide the organizers, the resources, and the structure to help the child be effective. Assignments can be given by teachers or parents, but the order and timing of the completion can be left to the child. It has been found that with even this much control children complete a significantly higher percentage of their assignments (Wang and Stiles, 1976). Children who participate in discussion groups, family councils, planning sessions for trips, committees, show far more satisfaction and responsible participation in the class or family (Sharan, 1980; Thomas, 1980; Stipek and Weisz, 1981).

6. Children need specific skills to make good choices. Some of these are: development of alternative thinking patterns, ability to build personal power through relaxation and tension reduction, imagery, intuitive strategies, and the ability to see and evaluate consequences.

7. Each child has irreducible dignity and can be helped to see that in self and others. Such experiences must be built into a home or school day. Demonstrations of caring cannot be left to chance.

8. One of the primary responsibilities of a faculty is to model effective interpersonal relationships and personal power. "If you want to see how it looks to be working toward effective growth," we must say to the child by our actions, "look at us, talk to us, we're trying too."

Homes and schools must be organized with flexibility and a structure that provides alternatives. Parents and teachers need to see themselves as the resources for ever widening, child initiated choice. Comfort with ambiguity, novel and open-ended situations is tremendously important. The behavior of all children is significantly influenced by their perceived locus of control. Success, achievement, and well-being come with personal power and the perception of inner control. Helping children develop their power is up to each of us, parents and teachers alike. For gifted children it is a matter of survival.

The Integrative Education Model: Using Brain/Mind Research in the Classroom

We have discussed general curricular models that are currently in use. The remainder of this chapter will acquaint you with an exciting new model being developed on the basis of the information available from brain/mind research. This research shows the physiological need for integrating learning experiences if we are to optimize the use of the very complex brain/mind system. The Integrative Education Model combines experiences of cognition with experiences in feelings or emotions, intuition, and physical sensing. All subject areas are presented through this integrative mode. Through this model each function of the brain is allowed to support the others, resulting in a very coherent, powerful learning experience. In the following pages we will explore each area of function separately and then through integrated activities.

Important for optimizing the learning experience is the discovery of the power of coherence in brain function. Different areas of the brain commonly function at different rates of speed, producing brain waves of differing velocity and frequency. When these differing rates are brought into coherence, the energy of the brain can be powerfully focused. Researchers are now investigating how to develop this coherence, and they report many unusual and exciting outcomes continuously. In our discussion of accelerated learning in chapter 10 we will describe one outcome that is especially relevant to the education of gifted learners.

Generally, it is important to design widely diverse curricula including such elements as guided imagery, dreams, mind/body integrative activities, and activities nurturing intuitive development. We must offer diversity in process and individualize our instruction if we are to effect the integration necessary for optimal development.

There are then some direct implications from these brain/mind data for change in the classroom:

Instead of:	**The New Data Demand:**
A focus on logical, rational thought as the center of educational experiences	A focus on an integration of all human functions including the logical, rational thought; the important avenues of sensing; the emotional, feeling functions; and the power of intuitive knowing. This focus assures use of the whole brain and optimizes the learner's ability to learn. This approach is known as the Integrative Model.
Using external tension for motivation and control	Use of relaxation and tension reduction to develop higher levels of learning, i.e., whole brain learning, as relaxation has been found to be the first step in thinking and synchronizing brain function.
Using the classroom environment as the container for the learning process	The use of the classroom environment as an important learning tool with color, sound, light, etc. contributing to the learning process, including the community and surrounding areas as part of the learning environment.

Instead of:	**The New Data Demand:**
A focus on group work	A focus on individual learning needs, styles and processes in small group or individual instruction as each individual was found to learn differently for physiological, psychological and emotional reasons.
A focus on set curriculum given to all	A focus on responsiveness to the interest and ability of each learner's choice as a powerful motivator in developing the curriculum. This need results from the influence of the limbic systems (the emotional trigger of the brain) on the ability of the brain to function optimally.
Knowledge of content the only necessary tool of the teacher and learner	Content communicated by cooperative processes annd interactions of the teacher and learner as both hemispheres of the brain must be involved for optimal learning to occur.
A focus on known facts being transferred from authorities	Encouragement of new ways of viewing facts, eliciting new questions and presentations of as yet unresolved issues which allows the learner to use higher cortical function.
A focus on controlling the student	A focus on empowering the student to be responsible for self, e.g., use of the inner locus of control which includes preparing the student for learning including relaxation, and anxiety reduction; discovering and changing negative attitudes and preconceptions regarding self and the learning experience; awareness of the suggestive impact of teacher words and attitudes; and teaching students about their learning resources and how to use them.

The Cooperative Learning Environment

An important part of the Integrative Education Model, the cooperative learning environment requires educators and parents to develop attitudes toward learning and views of gifted education that support optimal, integrated human growth. Skills of assessing, planning, and implementing individualized programs become important. The environment expands in meaning and usefulness. This type of structure has many titles and identifiers such as informal learning, natural learning, integrated day, and open education. The cooperative learning environment seems to describe the educational structure best.

The roots of this organizational plan are buried deeply in the work of Plato, Socrates, Froebel, Pestalozzi, Dewey, Montessori, Piaget, and numerous other innovative educators. Basically, it strives toward a unique learning experience for each individual. Participation is seen as necessary to learning, and involvement is encouraged to insure the assimilation of concepts. While the cooperative learning environment has a different format for each group of learners, there are some basic characteristics:

1. There is an open, respectful, and cooperative relationship among teachers, students, and parents that includes planning, implementing, and evaluating the learning experience.
2. The environment is more like a laboratory or workshop, rich in materials, with simultaneous access to many learning activities. The emphasis is on experimentation and involvement.
3. The curriculum is flexible and integrative. The needs and interests of the student provide the base from which the curriculum develops.
4. There is a minimum of total group lessons. Most instruction occurs in small groups or between individuals. Groups can be formed by teachers or students and will center around needs or interests.
5. The student is an active participant in the learning process. Movement, decision making, self-directed learning, invention, and inquiry are encouraged both inside and outside the classroom. Students may work alone, with a partner, or in groups. Peer teaching is important.
6. Assessment, contracting, and evaluation are all used as tools to aid in the growth of the student. Frequent conferences keep student, teacher, and parents informed of progress and provide guidance for future planning.
7. Cognitive, affective, physical, and intuitive activities are all valued parts of the classroom experience.
8. The atmosphere is one of trust, acceptance, and respect.

The cooperative learning environment is highly structured and presents a complex learning organization to the student. This environment has the ability to meet all learners at their present level of cognitive, emotional, social, physical, and intuitive development and to help them to move from that point. In this learning environment, gifted students can pursue interests in depth with a minimum of time limitations. They are no longer singled out, but they can be grouped flexibly with other students as their learning needs demand, or they can work individually whenever it is more appropriate. The gifted learner can function as a teacher, a challenged student, a researcher, an apprentice, a resident expert, or a learning manager. The classroom becomes more of a laboratory for learning and is more closely related to the real world. In fact, the student may often find projects and inquiries more profitably engaged in outside of the classroom in the larger community. You can find a large body of literature to help you understand the format and structure of this type of organization under any of its identifiers, so let us now look at this structure as it affects gifted individuals.

The Physical Environment

Gifted individuals often have the ability to integrate and synthesize information from many disciplines to develop new concepts or to enhance their understanding.

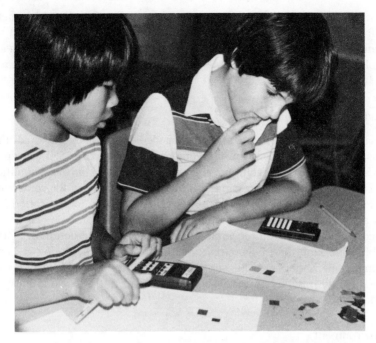

Structuring the classroom for cooperative learning.

In an open environment, the opportunity for this type of synthesis is available and even encouraged. Imagine a classroom. It has many activity areas and quiet, comfortable reading and study areas. Also, discussion areas are available to students and teacher/student groups. It has conference areas as well as large group spaces. Individual carrels are numerous. Space is provided by a greater use of floor and table surfaces, with movement facilitated by a minimum of desks and chairs. The walls display alternative activities and materials for self-directed study. Closets and cupboard doors provide media centers, and the use of many ways of learning is evident. At the beginning of the year, teacher-initiated activities and materials dominate; but by the end of the year, the environment will be representative of all the learners within. Gifted learners can structure this type of physical space to meet their unique abilities and levels of inquiry.

Movement in and out of the classroom to the library or other learning centers is not inhibited, and special grouping for specific interests is not uncommon. Pursuing any interest, however unusual, is not seen as odd by the other learners in this individualized setting. No one is asked to wait for the group to catch up or to do busy work to pass the time. Individual contracts and projects make it possible to learn at your own pace. The need the gifted learners often feel to pursue a subject in depth, to branch out into other related fields, or to stay with one inquiry for long periods of time are met without inhibiting the needs of others. There is adequate opportunity for the gifted to share their accomplishments by constructing a learning center to instruct others, conducting a seminar of other interested students, or meeting with a mentor for the challenge of expert advice and criticism. If the gifted student's needs cannot be met within the classroom, outside resources can be made available and arrangements made for field trips or apprenticeship programs. While these may also be arranged in a traditional classroom, the novelty of such arrangements and the exit from the classroom make re-entry a social problem for the gifted student. The richness of materials and opportunities make the cooperative learning environment a place where gifted individuals can meet their unique needs on a full-time basis.

Psychological Environment

In an environment where each student is considered a unique individual, the atypical needs of the gifted student cause no one to feel out of place. Self-concept can be developed in a realistic perspective with every person valued for those qualities he or she possesses. Accomplishments can be shared, and the value of the contributions of others can be experienced. Labels become unnecessary and identification inappropriate as a result of the system's continuous assessment.

Gifted students can gain recognition without seeming to dominate. They learn responsibility through the many opportunities provided for accepting responsibility for personal goals. Gifted students strengthen the inner locus of control by continuous encounters with the intrinsic values in learning from their own interest or from real need.

Social Environment

In a traditional classroom, the gifted student must often contend with the isolation that results from labeling. In a cooperative learning environment where labeling is unnecessary, such isolation occurs less frequently. Gifted youngsters have a need to seek out their intellectual peer group. They accomplish this easily when older and younger children can work together in a classroom with flexible grouping and freedom of movement. Any problems encountered in living together as a group can be resolved by the group to give a natural setting for the development of leadership skills.

The obvious benefits of a more flexible, open approach to learning have been verified (Bremer and Bremer, 1972; Hassett and Weisberg, 1972; Silberman, 1971; Stephens, 1974; and many others). The importance of this type of experience to the gifted is even more apparent. When offered alternative models, the gifted students and their parents overwhelmingly choose this model.

They encounter problems, however, in the transition from current programs for gifted education to the more extensive models. During transition, students, parents, teachers, and administrators need to work together to establish the kind of educational experience needed and most appropriate to the situation. Most parents of gifted students have successfully promoted a flexible, open learning environment with their own child for at least five years before the professional educator arrives. They have much information and ability to offer to the further educational program for their child through their familiarity with the open, individualized approach. The educator has alternatives and organizers to offer, as well as opportunities to broaden and deepen the student's experiences with living. The educator must direct the efforts and organize the opportunities for learning. This expertise will then bring focus and meaning to the experience in order to create a climate conducive to risk taking, exploration, and growth. The student offers unique information to the educational planning. Interest, level of skill, preferred methods, and style of learning are some of the necessary pieces of information that can be offered only by the student. Working together with the support of a capable administrator, this group can bring about a unique and useful educational program.

Too often, without proper planning, an organization that is called "open education" or "individualized learning" produces more chaos than openness or individualization. To insure against this, the transition should be treated as a slowly evolving process. Because most teachers, students, parents, and administrators have experienced learning in schools organized in the traditional way, some of their expectations may be hard to give up. They may believe that: learning occurs only in quiet rooms; everyone must learn from one book the same things at approximately the same time; and grading is the only way to show progress. Only as the skill of the teacher progresses, can the organization of an individualized environment progress. It will always be growing and becoming, as are the learners within.

Currently, this model takes many forms. School-within-a-school and alternative open schools draw gifted students and can be used to provide for their needs. They usually consist of four or more faculty members, drawn from different disciplines, who cooperatively team and integrate their disciplines in an open structure. Such programs are individualized, involving both students and parents in the educational decision making. Wherever found, open schools usually have a waiting list for entrance, for they are viewed favorably by gifted students and their parents alike. In some areas, entire schools use the open structure, while in others, only a resource room is presently available for this type of learning. Begin where you can; move slowly and knowledgeably. Your goal is to organize for learning that will better meet the atypical needs of gifted individuals. By individualizing education, we can better meet the needs of every learner.

Opening Classrooms for Growth—Eight Steps to the Cooperative Learning Environment:

1. Find out what provisions your district has made for meeting the needs of gifted learners.
2. Look at the needs gifted learners characteristically evidence (see chapter 2, p. 9), and discover how many your current district program strives to meet.
3. Do background reading, attend workshops, and/or take courses on gifted education and individualized education.
4. Develop a plan to change your present district program into what you would like it to be. Single out the steps you feel are necessary to expand or change your gifted program.
5. Discuss your plan with other parents, teachers, administrators, and your peer group. Modify your plans if needed.
6. Present your plan to another group—if you are a parent, to your principal; if you are a teacher, to parents; to whoever might be interested. Modify your plan if necessary.
7. Plan to inform all interested groups and solicit their cooperation and assistance.
8. You are now ready to begin the change. Move only as fast as you feel comfortable. Remember, this is a long-term plan, and you are providing a starting point for years of growth.

Responsive environments encourage a variety of interests.

These eight steps sound deceptively simple. They are not. Each step may take months to accomplish. Change is very difficult to bring about. Be satisfied with small increments that move in the planned direction. For some people, change is very threatening and for some, almost impossible. Seek out those who understand what you intend to do and its importance. You will need them for your own emotional support, as well as for aids to make the change happen. Only our efforts can better the education for gifted learners. If establishing good programs were easy, it would have been done by everyone long ago.

Structuring the Classroom Environment

The learning setting can facilitate or inhibit the learning program. The environment has far more impact than we previously assumed; it affects even the energy the student has to expend on learning goals. Although many factors could be stated to make up the learning environment, this discussion will concern itself primarily with the physical setting.

In an individualized program, the teacher must first develop a classroom with sufficient "people space." So many educational settings are overfilled with desks, tables, chairs, and equipment; space for people to move about, to group flexibly, to manipulate materials, and to actively participate in their own learning is restricted. People space can be obtained in a number of ways:

Take out furniture. In most learning environments, students do not need individual desks. If students are engaged in a variety of activities, rarely will everyone need to be sitting and writing at the same time. Writing can be done on the remaining tables, at centers, or on portable clipboards.

Each student's materials can be stored by use of racks, boxes or carton walls, or hall lockers.

Carpet some areas. Carpeted areas provide good group spaces and can be used for seating people quite flexibly. Carpet also reduces the noise of movement. Carpeting causes a room's atmosphere to become more interactive, less tense, and more pleasant. Students seem to show more pride in their surroundings and exercise care in the use of a carpeted facility. At the university, I teach a class that has several sections. I have noted with interest that when class takes place in the usual classroom of desks, board flooring, and sterile surroundings, there is far less discussion and interaction among the students than in the carpeted room that has pillows and floor spaces for seating. A different quality of learning occurs.

Use walls, windows, closets, and drawers for teaching areas. For example, a reclaimed teacher's desk makes a fine media center. The drawers provide space for storing projectors, films, slides, and filmstrips. The knee well makes a good projection area as it is somewhat protected from light. By sitting on the floor, a small group can participate quite effectively in a self-directed media presentation. Don't overlook the backs and insides of drawers, and the bottoms of tables for use as learning center areas. Can you imagine how much more interesting number facts become when third grade students must work them lying on the floor with a flashlight, reading them off the bottom of a table? Even in secondary and university settings, more flexible use of space would be beneficial.

Bring in comfortable, moveable furniture. A few comfortable pieces such as a couch or overstuffed chairs can provide reading and meeting spaces that will attract students. Floor pillows or small padded stools can provide highly flexible seating spaces also. In our university classroom these have made a significant instructional difference.

At first, the children may find it difficult to imagine how a classroom can be different. Let them help improve the learning environment by giving them a few options for changing their space. They will be more responsible and involved in using the classroom if they have a part in creating it.

Now that we have begun to look at the space in the classroom, let us think a moment about light and color. In Ismael's book (1973) on the effects of the environment, she suggests that soft lighting makes people less self-conscious and more receptive. When she tried it, she found interaction and cooperation among students increased. She felt a new sense of ease in teaching and communicating. Ott (1973) has found that natural light or full spectrum light is important to the proper use of human energy. Fluorescent light omits the needed ultraviolet rays, and pink fluorescent light increases irritability, hyper-aggressiveness, and negative feelings.

Color can be used for a variety of purposes. Heline (1969) gives the following information on our response to color.

1. Reds—stimulate and invigorate the physical body
2. Oranges—energize
3. Yellows—vitalize and accelerate mental activities
4. Greens—restful and soothing to the nervous system
5. Blues—inspirational, calming

By using color in relationship to the activity you are desirous of implementing, you may enhance the result.

Not all students have the same light and color preferences, so you may wish to vary the light intensity and color opportunities available and invite the students to use the environment as they feel best.

What about sound? Each of us has a differing need for silence and sound. Noise can be quite distracting; "busy people sound" is less so. Because the type of exciting, involved learning that we are discussing requires movement, we must consider the sound that this produces. Carpets help, easy flowing movement patterns within the room help, less furniture to move around helps. Sometimes, when students are not used to moving around and working on their own, they will need direction and advice from the teacher. This can create a source of noise if not handled well. Try creating a sign-up space such as an "I need you" list on the chalkboard where students can list their names when they need help in a project or lesson. Check the board and go to each individual, in order, as soon as possible. It works very well and reduces noise and frustration measurably.

The use of listening posts for films, slides, filmstrips, and video and audio tape systems is excellent to reduce noise. If students are to have free access to a lot of learning centers and media simultaneously, listening posts are essential. Not only lessons should be recorded on tape for student growth; natural sounds, such as water running in brooks, birds, ocean sounds, wind in trees, can be excellent contributions to the learning environment. Music can create different moods; can calm or inspire; some claim it heals. Whether played or heard, music has an important place in the learning environment. As you provided spaces for differing intensities of light, so too, must you provide for quiet, thoughtful activities and louder, busy learning.

Have you considered the structural designs with which you surround yourself and your students? The pyramid has intrigued humans for centuries. It seems to have some effect on the environment caused only by its shape. A great deal of literature discusses the properties of the pyramid. What about other shapes? The geodesic dome created by Buckminster Fuller, the spirals used by Frank Lloyd Wright, and all of the hexagons, pentagons, trapezoids, and spheres are claimed to affect those who live within them. We have lived so long in square and rectangular boxes; what effect would changing our space have? You may wish to explore this information with your class. There may be significant benefits to being more aware of the shape of our environment.

Temperature, quality of air, and odors all change the responses of learners. People differ in their needs along these dimensions. Plants and animals create a different climate in a classroom. In creating a learning environment, we might well be more aware of these factors.

The body has needs that, if met, can improve the entire learning ability of the student. Some people work well only when they have sufficient energy, and they need added fuel to maintain that level. Nuts, raisins, and vegetable sticks in bowls placed around the room can supply needed fuel. If you explain the purpose and allow students to be responsible for meeting their needs, you will find little misuse. Remembering Maslow's hierarchy of needs (see chapter 3, p. 121), we can understand why, if students do not fulfill their body needs, little energy is available for complex, higher level learning activities.

Teachers in classrooms that must be shared with other classes have a different and more difficult problem. For some elementary teachers, the environment belongs to them only part of the day; another teacher and another class move into the space regularly. In many departmentalized secondary schools, teachers change rooms each period. Many itinerant teachers of the gifted have no space that is really their own. While this situation creates more difficulties, they can be worked out. Design boxes that have all the props you will need for a center and create portable environments. We have developed very attractive "learning boxes" that visually add to the interest of the contents and can be used as part of the learning center itself. I have found that when I have to use a room for only certain periods, I need a good deal of portable equipment.

Look for storage room in closets or nearby offices to house your media equipment and materials. Try to get at least basic flexibility built into the rooms that you use, such as moveable tables and chairs, carpeted flooring, and attractive wall display areas. You may be able to share these latter areas with the other classes, although I have found that if my students and I are willing to arrange the displays, the other teachers are more than happy to let us. Let me inject one other small but important suggestion: after your class is over, return the furniture to its usual arrangement. I discovered that I could do anything in my classroom as long as the teacher following me did not have to put it back in its "proper" order. Oh yes, and while you are working out your way of sharing, start working toward changing the need to work this way. Convince scheduling or the administration of the importance of the environment to creating effective learning; keep trying to get your own space.

There is far more to consider in creating an environment for learning. It is beyond the scope of this book to do so. As you investigate your classroom, the following observations may be helpful. When you come into the classroom, do you feel good about being there? Does the environment seem pleasant, inviting, purposeful? Would you like to spend time there, given a choice? Try to see it from the student's viewpoint—does it still seem a good place to be? If you enjoy being there, you can be pretty sure the students will also. Of course, you could ask them.

Learning Centers

Another aid in structuring the environment for individualization is the use of learning centers, for they can serve many purposes. They can be set up as learning stations, as assessment centers, as game areas, as media centers, or as interest centers. They can be teacher-created, student-created, or the result of a cooperative venture. They may have a specific purpose or may be for exploration and discovery. They may develop content knowledge or process skills, or enrich either. They can be located anywhere in the room, using tables, desks, walls, doors, drawers, or whatever available for their function.

Pflum and Waterman (1974) conclude that every learning center, regardless of its purpose, must have the following components:

Directions (simple and clearly stated); they may be written or taped.

Purpose (as soon as the child gets to the center this should be obvious); not only must the children understand what the center is for, but also what is expected of them in it.

Content (this is why the center exists); the center can use manipulative materials, media, books, other people, etc., to communicate the content.

Activities (a variety of ways the children can apply what they have learned).

Evaluation (this is the way the children let you know what they learned); it can be very simple or an involved project; don't limit the evaluation procedures to testing alone; some centers do not require any evaluation other than the child's reaction to working there.

Some books to investigate for ideas and purposes for learning centers are: Allen, 1968; Christianson, 1969; Kahl and Gas, 1974; Kaplan, Kaplan, Madsen, and Taylor, 1973; Kaplan, Kaplan, Madsen, and Gould, 1975; and Voight, 1971.

Books for changing the educational environment and learning spaces in secondary schools include: Beach, 1977; James, 1968; Mason, 1972; and Truesdell and Newman, 1975.

In our previous discussion of the Integrative Education Program Model we defined each of the separate functions; thinking, feeling, sensing and intuition and stated the implications of their use (see pp. 159–162). When communicating such functions to students, it is important to make such abstract ideas as concrete as possible. Gifted learners especially appreciate knowing how and why something happens. The following are activities in each of the four areas that will aid in that understanding.

Learning to wonder, hypothesize, and experiment.

Strategies for Cognitive Development

This will be the most familiar area of brain function for both teachers and students alike. What may not be as familiar is the way in which this area of function can be strengthened by the use of the other brain functions such as physical sensing, affect, and intuition. While these activities will focus on cognitive development, the other functions will be seen to be integrated into this focus, providing accelerated learning, higher retention, and a more complex understanding. All of the strategies that follow can be adapted for use at the elementary or secondary levels.

Messing Around

Rationale: in all inquiry, there must be a period of time when the inquirer simply encounters the materials within the environment. Suchman (1961, 1962) believes that one of the primary functions of a teacher is to provide for these encounters. Such exploration is structured only by the properties of the materials and the experiences of the learner. During this activity, the learner begins to wonder, hypothesize, and experiment with ideas.

Time required: large blocks of uninterrupted time

Material needed: numerous components related to a specific principle, e.g., principle—electricity; components—batteries, cells, wire, light bulbs, circuit breakers, etc. Or you can use all material in a specific setting, such as tide pools and beach items. Books and equipment for research should be available.

Organizational pattern: freedom of movement; working singly, in teams, or in self-evolving small groups

Teaching function: provider, resource person, facilitator

Procedure: after setting up guidelines for movement, care of materials, and group structure, allow students to explore materials freely.

Evaluation: you may ask students to collect data on their observations, hypotheses, and conclusions throughout the experience (clipboards are good for mobile data collection) or have a group sharing at the end of the experience.

Inquiry

Rationale: to aid students to become independent in their thinking requires the development of many skills (making careful observations, asking good questions, alternative thinking, comparing, discovering relevant data, summarizing, and generalizing from data, to name a few). Inquiry sessions give students practice in these skills.

Time involved: forty-five minutes to an hour

Material needed: films, filmstrips, or materials to set up a dissonant event

Organizational pattern: the classroom must have resources, trust between students and teacher, and a sense of freedom for inquiry. The group should be seven to ten students, depending on age—the younger, the smaller the group.

Teaching function: the facilitator must have the ability to inquire; create classroom conditions that are accepting; clarify; probe for data, intent, prediction, and statements of theory; and be silent. (Teacher silence is critical in allowing students to think through the problem.)

Procedure: the facilitator sets up a dissonant event, either on film, tape, or by demonstration. For example, a film depicts two men sitting in a restaurant at identical tables placed next to each other. Both tables are set with exactly the same type of cloth and service. The waiter serves soup to the first man, then to the second. He notices a spot on the tablecloth at one table. Although the man is eating his soup, the water takes a hold of the edge of the tablecloth farthest from the diner and removes it in one motion without disturbing the man or the service at all. The other diner watches, is amazed, and decides to try the same thing at his table. He takes hold of the tablecloth on his table, just as the waiter did; but when removing the cloth, he causes all of the service to fall on the floor. This provides the focus for the inquiry. The students must now try to explain the event they observed and theorize about why the objects or systems functioned as they did. The rules for the session are:

1. Students must ask questions that can be answered yes or no.
2. Students, when recognized by the facilitator, may ask questions until they wish to yield. They indicate this by declaring that they "pass."
3. The facilitator does not answer statements of theories or questions attempting to gain approval for a theory (whether the facilitator accepts the theory or not).
4. Any student may test a theory at any time.
5. During inquiry, students are not allowed to discuss among themselves unless they call for a conference. This may be done at any time.
6. Inquirers may consult resources in the room at any time.

The inquiry continues until all theories are satisfactory to their originators. The facilitator then debriefs the session, helping the students to become aware of the processes they were using, what questions provided useful data, and how they might gain more information next time.

The following classroom inquiry problem related to a social studies unit on Africa. It was designed for fourth graders. The objective is for the children to bring forth their geographic and climatic knowledge about Africa to discover if they can apply this knowledge in a situation that appears unrelated to their study of Africa.

Figure 6.5.   A Classroom Inquiry Problem.

Problem Setting: Pretend the year is 2172 and you and your spaceship crew were on a 100-year outer space mission. You have all just awakened from your solar sleep three weeks prior to your reentry into the Earth's atmosphere and scheduled touchdown. You discover that your radio works, but you can't communicate with NASA. The lines are dead. You are worried about why NASA doesn't answer, but also you are worried about coordinating landing plans and instruments. Your spaceship has a manual on landing without NASA's help, but it has never been done that you know of. To complicate matters, two days before reentry you hit a terrific solar storm. Many of your instruments malfunction. Bravely, you and your crew prepare to land on Earth.

Miraculously, the landing was perfect. The crew is safe and alive. However, when you open the door of the spaceship, you realize you are not at the NASA landing strip in Nevada.

All your instruments that tell latitude and longitude, etc., broke during the storm. You must discover—

Focus Setting: "Where on Earth you are!"

Structuring: You instruct your crew to make a list of the things they see around them to help decide where they have landed. They agree to meet back at the ship in an hour to compare data.

I am going to tell you what was on the list briefly—it is your job to ask me more specific questions about the items listed so that later you can give opinions about where they are, from the information I have given and you have asked about.

The List:
1. landed on flat ground
2. miles in the distance emerald green looking mountains
3. a small river running (twenty feet wide) one-half mile from space ship
4. several large hawks circling above area from time to time
5. temperature about 85 degrees—sunny
6. a clump of trees near ship that look stunted but have leaves on them; another group of trees that look as if they were planted with their roots in the air instead of having leaves on their tops
7. the soil is rocky, but there is a lot of scrubby green plant life
8. snakes sighted
9. down by the river doglike paw marks
10. a group of small apelike creatures seen in rocky hills one and one-half miles from spaceship—probably baboons.
11. biggest find of all—houses sighted; constructed of materials found in area
12. people seen high up in hills through binoculars tending sheep

Figure 6.5.   A Classroom Inquiry Problem. *(continued)*

Accepting,	By asking more questions about the list I've read, you should be able to
Clarifying:	give an idea as to what:

1.   country they landed in
2.   time of year it is
3.   time of day
4.   type of life the inhabitants are living

Inquiry Session
Process Debriefing

Figure 6.5 is the format of the original inquiry session. Many modifications have been devised, and the strategy has been used for problem solving in science, social science, class discipline, and other subjects. Students can also be given opportunities to work on separate inquiry skills, such as asking good questions and finding irrelevant data, in short skill-development sessions. Through inquiry, students can become aware that truth still remains to be discovered.

Evaluation: through the debriefing period, the students may be helped to see their processes as less or more powerful and to find ways of improving their skills.

Other dissonant events:

a glass filled with water and a glass filled with alcohol look the same. Put an ice cube in each and different things happen. In this case only show the demonstration. Do not volunteer information on the contents of the glasses.

see the resource book with the *Inquiry Development Program* (1966).

Decision Making, Alternative Thinking

Rationale: gifted students will function in society as change agents, innovators, and reconstructionists. We believe that our societal problem solvers will come from this group. By being exposed to many ways of viewing problems, students may find better solutions. Give students experiences that allow them—

to become aware of bias in thinking, the difference between belief and fact,
to see that each conflicting viewpoint may be valid,
to see the importance of sources of information,
to experience the importance of cooperation and consensus in group action,
to seek many alternatives before deciding on solutions.

If we want to help our students make decisions on their own, we must present them with only the alternatives for which they can understand the consequences. If they cannot, they are not really making a choice. We must begin there and then gradually increase the number and complexity of the alternatives. In this way, our students will gain confidence in their abilities and become better decision makers (Jellison and Harvey, 1976).

Decision by Consensus

Time involved: approximately one hour

Material needed: instructions (figure 6.6), group summary and scoring sheets for each student (figure 6.7)

Figure 6.6. A Group Consensus Problem.

Instructions: You are a member of a space crew originally scheduled to rendezvous with a mother ship on the lighted surface of the moon. Due to mechanical difficulties, however, your ship was forced to land at a spot some 200 miles from the rendezvous point. During re-entry and landing, much of the equipment aboard was damaged and, since survival depends on reaching the mother ship, the most critical items available must be chosen for the 200-mile trip. Below are listed the fifteen items left intact and undamaged after landing. Your task is to rank order them in terms of their importance for your crew in allowing them to reach the rendezvous point. Place the number 1 by the most important item, the number 2 by the second most important, and so on through number 15, the least important.

Box of matches _____

Food concentrate _____

Fifty feet of nylon rope _____

Parachute silk _____

Portable heating unit _____

Two .45 calibre pistols _____

One case dehydrated Pet milk _____

Two 100-pound tanks of oxygen _____

Stellar map (of moon's constellation) _____

Life raft _____

Magnetic compass _____

Signal flares _____

First aid kit containing injection needles _____

Solar-powered FM receiver-transmitter _____

Five gallons of water _____

Organizational pattern: groups of five to seven, flexible grouping, responsive environment

Teaching function: modeling, encouraging student decision making in educational matters, facilitation of group exercises

Procedure: this is an exercise in group decision making. Your group is to employ the method of *group consensus* in reaching its decision. This means that the prediction for each of the fifteen survival items *must* be agreed upon by each group member before it becomes a part of the group decision. Consensus is difficult to reach. Therefore, not every ranking will meet everyone's *complete* approval. Try as a group to make each ranking one with which all group members can at least partially agree. Here are some guides to use in reaching consensus:

1. Avoid arguing for your own individual judgments. Approach the task on the basis of logic.
2. Avoid changing your mind only in order to reach agreement and avoid conflict. Support only solutions with which you are able to agree somewhat, at least.
3. Avoid "conflict-reducing" techniques such as majority vote, averaging, or trading in reaching decision.
4. View differences of opinion as helpful rather than as hindering in decision making.

Figure 6.7. Group Summary Sheet.

	Individual Predictions											Group Prediction
	1	2	3	4	5	6	7	8	9	10	11	
Box of matches												
Food concentrate												
50 ft. of nylon rope												
Parachute silk												
Portable heating unit												
Two .45 calibre pistols												
One case dehydrated pet milk												
Two 100 lb. tanks of oxygen												
Stellar map (of moon's constellations)												
Life raft												
Magnetic compass												
Signal flares												
First aid kit with injection needles												
Solar-powered FM receiver-transmitter												
5 gallons of water												

On the Group Summary Sheet (figure 6.7), place the individual ranking made earlier by each group member. Take as much time as you need in reaching your group decision.

Scoring instruction for decision by consensus: the prediction is that the group product will be more accurate than the average for the individuals. The lower the score, the more accurate. A score of "0" is a perfect score.

Figure 6.8. Key to Group Consensus Problem.

You are a member of a space crew originally scheduled to rendezvous with a mother ship on the lighted surface of the moon. Due to mechanical difficulties, however, your ship was forced to land at a spot some 200 miles from the rendezvous point. During re-entry and landing, much of the equipment aboard was damaged and, since survival depends on reaching the mother ship, the most critical items available must be chosen for the 200-mile trip. Below are listed the fifteen items left intact and undamaged after landing. Your task is to rank order them in terms of their importance for your crew in allowing them to reach the rendezvous point. Place the number 1 by the most important item, the number 2 by the second most important, and so on through number 15, the least important.

Little or no use on moon	15	Box of matches
Supply daily food required	4	Food concentrate
Useful in tying injured together, help in climbing	6	Fifty feet of nylon rope
Shelter against sun's rays	8	Parachute silk
Useful only if party landed on dark side	13	Portable heating unit
Self-propulsion devices could be made from them	11	Two .45 calibre pistols
Food, mixed with water for drinking	12	One case dehydrated Pet milk
Fills respiration requirement	1	Two 100-pound tanks of oxygen
A principal means of finding directions	3	Stellar map
CO_2 bottles for self-propulsion across chasms, etc.	9	Life raft
Probably no magnetic poles; useless	14	Magnetic compass
Distress call when line of sight possible	10	Signal flares
Oral pills or injection medicine valuable	7	First aid kit with injection needles
Distress signal transmitter, possible communication with mother ship	5	Solar-powered FM receiver-transmitter
Replenishes loss from sweating, etc.	2	Five gallons of water

Individual score: Individuals can score their own sheets. As you read aloud to the group the correct rank for each item (figure 6.8), they simply take the difference between their rank and the correct rank on that item and write it down. Do this for each item and add up these differences—*disregard* "+" and "−".

To get the average for all individuals, divide the sum of the individual scores by the number of individuals in the group. Compute the group score in the same way you computed each of the individual scores. If our hypothesis is correct, the group score will be lower than the average for all individuals.

Possible questions for the group:

1. Did the group really go by consensus? Or did we gloss over conflicts?
2. Did the group stay on the intellectual or task aspects or did we stop to examine our process to see how we could work more effectively?
3. How satisfied were we with the way the group worked? How efficient were we?

1	9
very poor	excellent

4. How satisfied are you (as members) with the group?
5. How much influence did you feel you had as an individual on the group decision?
6. Did the group listen to you? ignore you?
7. Did you stay involved in the exercise or did you give up?
8. In what ways could you change or improve your interaction with others?

Evaluation: debrief and discuss the NASA solutions with the class. Discuss the process of consensus.

The material in figures 6.5–6.8 was developed by the National Aeronautics and Space Administration for use in classrooms. By contacting the Educational Programs Officer at your nearest regional NASA Center, you can receive information on a variety of other educational programs and workshops available to teachers. New programs are made available as new technology is developed.

Simulation

While simulation develops cognitive abilities and understanding, it does so by the use of affective involvement. Simulation is the process of exploring a problem or idea by simulating or recreating the events within the classroom. It requires active participation on the part of the learner. The outcomes are decided by this participation. It has the advantages of—

bringing out a high degree of motivation;
leading the learner to inquiry and research;
using the skills of decision making, communication, persuasion, and resource allocation;
integrating curriculum areas;
developing a deeper level of understanding;
changing attitudes;
enhancing personal growth.

My only caution is in regard to the heavy emotional loading that often occurs. Although you may tell the students that they are simulating events, gaming, and role playing, a well-structured simulation may be so real that students will need help leaving their roles and looking at the process skills and information they have gained. For these reasons, you must debrief the sessions thoroughly.

Among the several types of simulations are board games, such as chess and Stocks and Bonds (3M Company). Paper and pencil exercises can also be designed as simulations. Environmental simulations can be accomplished by use of media equipment (e.g., geographical experiences or trips through body systems).

"Real life" simulations have the most impact (e.g., crises at the United Nations, power status of socioeconomic classes, or the signing of the Declaration of Independence). While a number of companies develop and sell simulations, they can also be structured and run by teachers and students. The following resources will aid you in developing simulations of your own: Boocock and Schild (1968); Sisk's *Teaching Gifted Children;* Taylor and Walford (1972); Zuckerman and Horn (1973); Seidner (1976).

Some of the organizations producing simulations are:

Project SIMILE, Western Behavioral Science Institute, 1150 Silverado, La Jolla, California 92037

Science Research Associates, Inc., 259 E. Erie Street, Chicago, Illinois 60611

Wiff 'n Proof, P.O. Box 71, New Haven, Connecticut 06501

Bibliotherapy

This term refers to the strategy of using books as tools to aid children in solving their problems, whether personal or educational. The strategy has been used to help develop a more positive self-concept, change attitudes and values, and to promote mental and emotional health. The use of this technique with gifted children has special advantages. It takes some of their strength areas, e.g., ability to conceptualize, to generalize, and to abstract, and allows them to use these strengths to support areas of need and personal growth. To begin such a program, the needs of the children to be served must be assessed. Then assistance should be sought for appropriate books to provide solutions for identified problems. A selection of appropriate alternatives should be made available. You may want to establish a file of such books as you discover them. Follow-up activities and discussions are an important part of such a program. For resources you may want to consider the Frasier and McCannon (1981) selection of books covering personal, social and educational/vocational problems.

A Mental Stretch: Integrating the Cognitive Function

Rationale: to experience the power of the cognitive ability to change a physical process

> *Time involved:* approximately five minutes
> *Materials needed:* none
> *Organizational pattern:* total class working individually with group instruction
> *Teaching role:* guiding the class through a directed activity
> *Procedures:* Ask the students to stand so that when they straighten their arm in front of them, to the side, and in back of them, they hit no one or no thing. Ask them to remain relaxed and comfortable with their feet slightly apart. They are to raise the right hand in front of them, palm open, thumb up, as in shaking hands. Allow the hand to swing away from the midline fully extended as far around to the back as they are comfortable going, turning the head as the hand moves. When they have gone as far as they can, ask them to look at what is directly beyond their

thumb and to remember what they see. Now return the arm to the forward position. Move the head to the left, the arm to the right, opening the space between right hand and turned head; return to front position, repeat five times. Again move head to left, but include hips swinging to left as the arm moves right; return; repeat five times. Starting from the forward position, follow the thumb with the eyes again to see how far you can comfortably move the arm behind you now. The students will find that they can move their arm much farther.

Now ask them to do the first step again with their left arm and find out how far they can move it to the left comfortably, remembering what they see beyond the thumb. Now ask the students to put their arm down, close their eyes, and just imagine that they are following the rest of the movements as you describe them exactly as before with the left arm moving left, head moving right, etc. Do not have them move, only think that they are moving. After the ten movements, ask them to open their eyes and really put their left arm in front of them and check out how far they can now move it to the back. Again the arm will move a lot farther.

Evaluation: This exercise makes concrete the idea that combining the cognitive function and the physical function allows us capability we may not have known we have. Our mental, cognitive process can affect our physical functioning. It is this understanding you can now evaluate.

Synectics

Rationale: Another approach to integrating the cognitive function with other functions of the brain is synectics, a strategy developed by W. J. J. Gordon (1961). The assumptions underlying this strategy are that learning is a combination of focusing, connection making, and application and that "to learn, students must respond to subject matter by focusing on important points, internalizing those points, expressing their comprehension, and sometimes creatively applying what they have learned. Effective internalization takes place when students connect the subject matter to something they already know about" (Gordon and Poze, 1980, p. 147).

Time involved: variable

Material needed: specific to the subject or demonstration

Organizational pattern: large or small groups

Teaching function: introducing terms and ideas, facilitating discovery, analyzing problems or ideas, and useful metaphors to express the paradox found in the problem or idea, and the communication of the solutions

Procedure: The ways these assumptions are realized in the curriculum or the problem-solving situation follow several steps and utilize analogy and metaphor as tools for learning. The first step is to discover within the concept to be learned or problem to be solved the paradox that exists at the core. For an example, Gordon shows that the concept of symbiosis has the paradox of double weakness, or that needs when taken together make for strength. Next, the student is asked to develop an analogy for the paradox. Gordon states that the very use of a connective analogy lends clarity and sophistication to expression of the concept. Later personal analogies are constructed by the students to clarify the concept further. This strategy allows children to work at their level of ability and can be used with a heterogeneously grouped class. Gifted students will produce creative extensions of the process, resulting from connection-making processes that were subliminal, which become conscious, explicit, and within their control.

Evaluation: use of the synectic techniques in solving other problems

Group Exploration

Rationale: Often by discussing with others and sharing interests, students can become more aware of different ideas and areas. It is also possible to set up situations where exploration as a group creates more data and excitement (such as demonstrations, group movement, group energy exchanges; these have more impact when more people participate).

Time involved: variable

Material needed: specific to the demonstration or often to the students

Organizational pattern: large group, with the possibility of breaking into smaller groups and then returning to large group discussion

Teaching function: group facilitator, demonstrator, occasional discussion leader; can be assumed by classroom teacher or student

Procedures:

Living Language

Students are divided into three groups. Each group is given a phrase and a rhythm; they say the phrase together in their group. The three groups are brought in and out of a chant by the teacher, as in singing rounds. Students are encouraged to say the phrase as directed with differing rhythms and emotions, starting and stopping at different places in the phrase. The result is an exploration of language as it comes alive. For many other examples of language orchestrations and grammar events, contact Toby Lurie, 1429 Page Street, Apt. E, San Francisco, California 94117.

Evaluation: self-evaluation of experience

Jigsaw groups

Small, independent learning groups where students cooperatively teach each other. If there is a single topic chosen, each student learns a portion of the material and then teaches that portion to the other group members while learning the remainder of the material from them. This procedure gives students differing points of view, a vested interest in and practice with open communication, and the development of interpersonal relations. Evaluation is on material learned and is done individually by examination or other mutually agreed upon method. Research on this strategy has shown that: it has positive interpersonal effects; cooperative groups perform better than competitive ones; students learn more than when in competition; attitudes toward school improve; there is a substantial improvement in the performance of minorities; and even in heterogeneously grouped classrooms, high ability students benefit (Blaney et al., 1976; Dunn and Goldman, 1966; Durrell et al., 1959; Lucker et al., 1976; Yuker, 1955).

Speakers

Rationale: By bringing experts from a variety of areas into a class, you give the students not only the chance to hear and ask questions, but also the opportunity to be exposed to fields of study through the enthusiasm of people actively engaged in creating and using that kind of knowledge.

Time involved: variable; weekly, to several times a year

Material needed: dynamic people, knowledgeable in their field

Organizational pattern: While these presentations can be made to the total group, it is often more successful to announce the speaker's subject in advance and invite interested students to sign up. Presentation would then be conducted in the discussion area of the room, while students who have no interest can work in other areas.

Teaching function: organizer, provider of related resource material for preparation and follow-up

Procedure: dependent on the speaker

Evaluation: optional, may serve as one of many resource experiences

Field Trips and Visitations

Rationale: a great deal of the world cannot be re-created inside a classroom. Students can learn naturally, in integrated ways in the setting of the specific events. For example, a trip to an island can provide experiences in math (arranging the trip, transportation, expenses, meals, etc.); science (climate, geology, astronomy, land and sea flora and fauna, navigation, food preservation and preparation, tide data, etc.); language (journal writing, communication with planning groups, letters to authorities requesting permission, etc.); social science (government jurisdiction and involvement, economics, ecology, etc.); and interpersonal relations. All of these and more have great built-in motivation.

Time involved: variable; one day, a series of visits, or a week-long journey

Material needed: transportation and financing; if camping, all necessary gear

Organizational pattern: adult to child ratio according to age and destination

Teaching function: pretrip planning and facilitation of arrangements; organization of trip; group leader and facilitator during trip; posttrip follow-up

Procedure: This will depend on the goals of the trip and should be decided in cooperation with the students and the parents.

Parents can take students to museums, concerts, and other places either during or after school hours. Torrance (1968) calls such provisions "time-outs." He believes strongly in such leave taking. Encouraging parents to become involved in school activities is important for both home and school. The students always benefit from this type of cooperation. Investigate the rules applying to field trips and parental responsibilities and rights. You may have options you didn't know you had. Just because it hasn't been done, doesn't mean it can't be.

Evaluation: journals; projects, films, and slides

Research Skills

Gifted students need a way to get to information and ideas far sooner than more typical learners. They must be able to move efficiently on their own into areas not yet explored. They need to become familiar with the skills of historical research, descriptive research, and experimental research as tools for future learning and thinking. Torrance and Myers (1962) report such a project as highly successful.

Other Possibilities

1. *Core curriculum:* In small groups, or individually, gifted students could take a particular period, concept, person, or object and, using it as a central theme, investigate the history, art and music, and social, cultural, economic, etc., conditions. By actually "living" through the creation of this person, object, period, or concept, the student will understand and appreciate inquiry far more.
2. *Seminar program:* Offers pupil assessment and individualized planning, open curriculum guides, and a variety of resource people. This program combines the use of independent study, advanced coursework, advanced placement in colleges, and special seminars for gifted students on an individual basis (Martinson, Hermanson, and Banks, 1972).
3. *Executive High School Internships:* a national program for high school juniors and seniors that allows them to serve, for a full semester, on sabbatical from regular classes, as interns to business executives and managers, government commissioners and administrators, newspaper editors, television producers and directors, hospital administrators, judges and attorneys, and directors of social service agencies and civic associations. In addition to Monday through Thursday placement, the students attend a Friday seminar on management, administration, and decision making. The program is managed by a local coordinator trained by the national parent organization, Executive High School internships of America, located in New York City (Hirsch, 1976).
4. *Publishing:* Gifted students should be encouraged to publish their work, either in established journals and magazines or in ones that are school or class-produced. Editing for publication teaches far more grammar, punctuation, and spelling than skill drilling and sentence diagramming.
5. *Resident expert:* Encourage all gifted students to become resident experts on the one area in which they are most interested. Call upon their expertise, let them help you and others in the school with problems in their area of knowledge.
6. *Conceptual frameworks and systems:* Be sure to expose gifted students to conceptual frameworks that you use to organize your thinking (e.g., Bloom, 1956). Encourage their participation in new problems—yours, theirs, the school's, and the community's—by the development of systems or conceptual frameworks. Be

sure there is a way for the students to share their creations. Example: a group of fifth- and sixth-grade students were studying the land use in their area. They obtained advice from architects, city planners, and engineers who paid regular visits to their classroom. After several months, one group devised a plan for development that excited them. Their teacher arranged for them to present their plan, with maps and graphs, to the Planning Board of the County. Later, the students were notified that a portion of their plan had been adopted. They received a commendation from the county for their work.

7. *High school, junior college, or university placement:* In many areass, high schools, junior colleges, and universities are making classes available to upper elementary gifted students. Some allow participation in regular classes, some in specially designed classes. In some cases, parents organize after school and weekend classes. These classes have saved many bored youngsters from giving up on a school as a place to learn.

Strategies for the Feeling or Affective Function

As we have seen, the brain makes special use of feelings or emotions in the learning process. When learning becomes separated from human values, the persons involved are alienated from each other and from themselves. Emotions are the gateway-triggering mechanism for higher cognitive function.

Strategies for affective development must be well integrated into the students' daily activities. Before using any of the activities that follow, the teacher must feel comfortable with them. Of all the areas, success of the strategies in the affective or feeling area depends most on the attitude and development of the teacher.

The ideas presented are not only useful for gifted students, but may be used in heterogeneous groupings. However, as in the cognitive area, the needs of the gifted are different—more intense, with more information on emotions to process, of broader concerns, etc. The gifted need opportunities to work with their intellectual peers in groups and, on other occasions, with groups of varying ages and abilities. Because these techniques concern human beings, there is no limit on the ages of the students participating. It will be necessary for teachers to adapt the presentation to their own particular group, whether it is at the elementary level or at the secondary level.

It has been said that all major decisions are made at a feeling level. As we saw earlier in the chapter, Krathwohl and his committee (1964) have organized affective learning into a taxonomy. This taxonomy and the material the committee developed for it may help you in organizing an affective curriculum for your students. Tomer (1981) suggests using the taxonomy as an organizer for developing a curriculum in the area of interpersonal communication.

Some activities that help students become aware of their emotional life follow. Be sure to take time to discuss these feelings with the students in an accepting manner. Often students are led to believe that some feelings are "wrong" or "bad." Help them to know that feelings just are. Once we recognize we have certain feelings, then we can decide what we want to do about the way they affect us and others. Try these activities:

For a day or a week list every incident and/or person that makes you mad (or happy, or scared, etc.). Discuss the list.

Do something nice for someone each day for a week. Tell how you felt doing it, when they knew, and when they didn't know that you had done it. List your feelings. Discuss what you found out.

When you feel especially angry (or happy, or anxious, etc.), write down where in your body you felt it (throat, head, stomach). Discuss.

Have children role play different situations while wearing glasses depicting various emotions. Find out how the situation would be different if you were angry, happy, felt cared for, were lonely, etc. Discuss differences in perception.

Valuing

As individual guides to living, values evolve and mature as experiences evolve and people mature through them. We will not be concerned with the particular value outcomes of any person's experience, but rather with the process used to develop values. It is important that our values work effectively and lead us to a satisfying, actualizing life. In this way, we form the moral character discussed by Kohlberg (see chapter 3, p. 112).

Valuing begins with the awareness of what values we now hold. Helping students to clarify their own values and to be aware of the values of others is the first step. First, encourage discussion of open-ended problems and positions on controversial issues. The next step provides knowledge of the process of decision making, knowing that each person is free to choose. The effects of expectations, responsibilities, and consequences must become a part of the information available to students.

Once their values have been affirmed, students need the opportunity to transform them into action, to experience them as an acknowledged part of their life. Change will come only from an examination of their own values and the way they work for them.

There are a number of resources on valuing available that will give you help in this area of your planning (Arnspiger et al.; Casteel and Stahl, 1975; Drews and Lepson, 1971; Elder, 1972; Harmin, 1973; Paulsen, 1974; Raths, Harmin, and Simon, 1966; Simon, Howe, and Kirschenbaum, 1972; and Simon, Kirschenbaum, and Fuhrmann, 1972).

Gifted students have need for some strategies that take their growing independence into consideration. They need more cooperative than authoritative guidance as they get older. Here is an idea for doing that:

Complaining Dyads

Students work with a partner and are instructed to take turns sharing all the unfair or misunderstood occasions they have experienced that day (or week). They are to be active listeners as their partner shares. This may not produce solutions for their problems, but it has a very calming effect and unloads a lot of the frustration and hostility.

For resources for strategies on awareness, see: Brooks (1974), Dinkmeyer (1969), Freed (1971), James and Jongeward (1973), Palomares (1972), Samples (1970), Schrank (1972), Sonntag (1972), and Stevens (1971).

Developing Open Communication

Communication between unique human beings arises as some kind of miracle. Open communication clearly conveys what is being felt and gives clear information to both giver and receiver. To achieve these goals, students must be aware of their real feelings and find a way to communicate them clearly. They must also be aware of how active listening affects the communication. To get the feeling and the words to match, the nonverbal and the verbal to convey the same message, is not easy. Students need lots of practice in meaningful situations with the chance to analyze what happened and try again. These activities are examples of techniques that will help.

Ways of Sharing Me

Have students select a partner. Sit in front of the partner and talk about five minutes. Share information about yourselves—who you are. Listen as your partner shares, and notice how this feels. After five minutes, close your eyes and remember the conversation. Notice how you feel about this person, what you know about the person, and what you think the person knows about you. Is that what you want your partner to know? Ask the partner to open his or her eyes and find another partner. Again they share themselves, but this time sit back-to-back, not looking, as they talk. After five minutes, ask them to close their eyes again and review the questions asked before. Compare how this situation was different (better, worse, etc.) from the first situation. Again, select a new partner; face each other and share without talking. Gesture or give any nonverbal clues. After five minutes, again close eyes, review, and compare with the other two situations. With a new partner, sit facing, no talking, no looking; only hands can be used for communication. After five minutes, review and compare. Discuss the entire experience. What kinds of information did you get? Was it different for the different ways? Which way was hardest, easiest? Whom do you feel you know better?

I'm Not Listening

Partners face each other; one role-plays an active nonlistener. One partner is to talk about something important to him or her, while the other partner does anything to indicate that he or she is not listening. The nonlistener may do anything except leave the room. After five minutes, switch roles. This is very powerful, so use only one-to-one dyads and watch the time. You may want to tell the students that this is going to be difficult, but to be effective, they must play their parts the best they can. Discuss feelings.

Backoff Space

On some issues students and teachers, as well as parents, often find that they hold different perceptions and different values. For some students this can create crisis situations. Often teachers and parents are not prepared for gifted students who do not share their view and who challenge their ideas and values. The parent or teacher may consider such differences as disrespectful or as a challenge to their authority. For teachers and parents who want to develop increasing understanding instead of alienation between themselves and the student, backoff space can be a useful tool. The teachers (or parents) first share with the students their own weaknesses or moods and discuss how the students can know when this is happening. For example, some days teachers are especially tired or are experiencing low energy, and they do not want to deal with a lot of extra problems—this is picked up by students through body posture and facial expressions. A teacher may be annoyed with a student's manner and not be able to listen further to complaints or "good" reasons and excuses—the student observes this from the tight lips and abrupt manner.

Once the teacher or parent and the students have discussed their own foibles, they agree to allow space for the other person and open communication of problems with dignity and caring—an understanding that when I'm not doing well you will give me space and I will do the same for you. When confrontations occur, both parties are committed to discuss, in private, the situation as they see it and to listen to the other person. Open communication respects the feelings of both parties and clarifies the situation. If both parties can arrive at a mutual agreement at that time, they do; if not, both agree to back off, and each gives the other time to cool off. Later discussion may prove more fruitful. The entire class shares this agreement for open communication and backoff space so that anyone can use it when needed and, at a point of confrontation, the other class members will be aware of the need to allow such a use of time by the teacher and the student. It is important for everyone to agree to participate with a high level of regard and for the technique not to be used punitively.

Assertion Training

Older students especially need assertion training. In the past, men and women have been caught between two exclusive ways of behaving—aggressiveness for men, passivity for women. To reverse these roles courted criticism and often rejection. For many people, neither stance was satisfying. With the identification of assertion as a possible alternative for both men and woman, communication can become more effective. *Assertion* is defined as communication that allows people to state their feelings and ideas clearly so that they may be considered in any decision making, and they take full responsibility for their decisions. While assertion does not promise that you always get your way, it does allow for open discussion, compromise, and far better understanding and relationships than the domineering, demanding role of the aggressive or the manipulative, martyr role of the passive.

One of the best ways to familiarize your students with the consequences of assertion, aggressiveness, and passivity is to set up open-ended situations and have the students in small groups (four to five) role play the various positions as they try to resolve the dilemma. You will find Alberti and Emmons (1970) and Phelps and Austin (1975) helpful in suggesting different techniques in assertion training.

Family Sculptures

As students begin to seek independence and consider establishing their own family units, they will need help in understanding the effects of family structures. They must understand how expectations we place on others control us as well as them and how responsibility functions (you can't give it; you can allow someone to take yours; you can't take it; others can allow you to take theirs). Satir has developed some powerful techniques for clarifying these two understandings. Her book *Peoplemaking* (1972) describes them and gives very useful information from her research with growth-producing family structures. I especially recommend the family sculptures technique. Your students physically assume positions portraying the common family structures. This statuelike positioning provides many insights into the dynamics of the relationships and their consequences. For some further resources for strategies in open communication, see Beier (1974), Clark (1974), Geldard (1968), Sisk (1975), and Stevens (1971).

Group Interaction

Students who have explored their concept of self and their interaction with others are now ready to function effectively in a group. These skills of group interaction can make student participation in a group more productive and more satisfying.

Inner-Outer Circle

Students select partners whose function will be to observe their participation in group discussion. One of the partners joins others in a circle. The observing partners position themselves where they can see their partner's face. The teacher gives the discussion group a topic that is controversial and/or meaningful to them. Observers are asked to watch their partners for any use of listening skills, responses, initiating activity, nonverbal communication, etc., that inhibits or facilitates the group discussion. After fifteen minutes, ask the discussants to join their partners for suggestions and observations of their participation in the group. Encourage the observers to give helpful suggestions also. After about ten minutes, ask the partners to change roles and give the new group a discussion topic. Repeat the process.

Trust Circles and Lines

End a class session with a trust-building activity. Have students sit on the floor, shoes off, shoulder-to-shoulder in a circle. One person stands in the center and all the others place their feet on this person's feet and ankles. Those in the circle now raise their hands and arms in front of them, ready to catch and pass the center person around the circle. When all in the circle are ready, the center person falls back into the circle with feet on the floor securely supported by all the other feet. By bending only at the knees and relaxing, the center person can be passed from hand-to-hand around the circle easily. Be sure students are close enough so that several will be supporting the center person at all times.

Another trust activity involves forming parallel lines so that one person can be passed down the row and back, shoulder high, very easily. The weight or height of the person is unimportant, as at least four pairs of hands will support him or her at all times. Both exercises provide the passed person with a sense of well-being and trust for the others. Try it yourself. Your students will enjoy your trust.

As resources for group interaction strategies, see: Galloway (1970), Gorman (1974), Johnson (1972), Otto (1973), Reihart (1970), and Schmuck and Schmuck (1971).

Developing Self-Esteem

To develop a positive view of ourselves, we must be given opportunities to experience ourself as a positive, loving person who is cared about and thought well of by others. The following strategies give students those opportunities. The time involved depends on the group response; however, it is important not to hurry such activities. The teaching function is to facilitate the establishment of a climate of trust, accep-

Building trust promotes a sense of well-being and respect for others.

tance, and caring. No materials are needed unless specified, and the organizational pattern is a small group, or at least a close, interactive group.

Appreciation Circle

An appreciation circle can be used to end a class session or as a morale builder. There are many variations, but the idea is to give students the opportunity to tell what they appreciate about each other. One structure would be to divide into groups of five and have one person remain silent as the others tell that person one thing they like or appreciate. Continue having a different person remain silent until all have participated. This is very powerful when larger groups or the whole class speak to one person at a time.

Name Game

At the beginning of the year, let the class become acquainted by ending a session with this game. All students sit in a circle. Beginning with the teacher, say your name and turn to the student on your right (or left). That student says his or her name and your name, the next student says his or her name, the second student's name, and your name. Continue around the circle. Even with thirty-five children participating, this works surprisingly well. Assure the children that they can ask a name if they forget. Few will need to.

Mural

Have students build a mural of things they like about themselves. The mural can consist of cutouts from magazines or objects and can be put together individually or as a class.

Here are some resources for strategies for building self-esteem: Briggs (1970), Brown (1971), Brown, Yeomans, and Grizzard (1975), Canfield and Wells (1976), Krippner and Blickenstaff (1970), Purkey (1970), Samples and Wohlford (1973), Satir (1972), Sonntag (1967), and Vogel (1974).

Strategies for Physical Integration

In addition to cognitive and affective development, gifted students must be given opportunities to integrate their minds with their physical bodies. In the past, schools have required only the development of the physical body as a separate entity. This development yields far more when integrated with the other functions.

Far back in recorded history humans talked of the need for balance in their lives. The ebb and flow of human energy has been central to many belief systems— the Yin/Yang of ancient China, the Ka of the ancient Egyptians, the Chi of the Eastern Indians, the Kaa of the American Indians, the Mana of the Hawaiians, and the circadian and biorhythm cycles of the Westerner. We are all affected by the differing amounts of energy available in our lives and by what inhibits or facilitates our energy supply. Researchers such as Selye (1956) and Pelletier (1977) present much information on how stress reduces our energy and on ways to move into energy-producing modes instead. Feldenkrais (1972), Gallwey (1974), Leonard (1975), Masters and Houston (1978), Schutz (1976), and Spino (1976), to name but a few, show us ways to integrate the mind and body, thereby promoting increased function and energy for all human systems. As important as this more total view of the human being is to all people, it is even more essential for the gifted person.

Early in school, the usual physical education curriculum can become boring to gifted youngsters. For many, body coordination does not keep pace with their accelerated mental development, thereby frustrating their expectations of performance. The patience required to drill and practice assures average youngsters of adequate physical performance in games and competitive activities. Youngsters more accustomed to moving rapidly through new ideas and challenges often lack that patience. When their physical performance falls short of the standards they set for themselves, when their opportunities for improvement come from repetitive activity, they often choose other alternatives, such as becoming ball monitors, judges, or umpires. They even seek excuses from doctors for such problems as asthma or they find leadership or teaching roles that allow them to use their cognitive ability to advantage.

It is not physical movement, but rather the traditional competitive system that creates the problem. Given the opportunity to structure their own physical education class, a group of gifted junior high school students turned to tennis, track events, and various mind/body integrating activities such as Yoga, T'ai-chi Ch'uan, and Aikido with enthusiasm.

Prior to the involvement in physical education classes in schools, most gifted children have no problem integrating physical and mental development. A rich fantasy life creates many opportunities for young gifted children to be physically active. They could use this same ability to continue their integrative development. In some schools and in professional sports, the use of fantasy has gained acceptance and is profitably used. Hendricks and Roberts (1977, p. 28) define fantasy as "the use of the natural ability of mental imagery to enhance performance or personal growth." They point out that the U.S. Olympic ski team, professional baseball and football teams, and highly successful track and field competitors have psychologists instruct them to use fantasy for improving performance. The tennis instruction methods of Gallwey (1974) exemplify how imagining or fantasizing correct performance actually changes the physical performance.

Dolle and Bardot (1979) reported confirmation of the importance of physical exercise on cognitive development as a result of their study exploring the influence of physical activity on mastery of cognitive structures in male and female adolescents (eleven-year-olds). They made over six times as much progress as did the controls, who also lacked the depth of understanding shown by the experimental group. The use of judo served as an integrative strategy in teaching the laws of physics.

Relaxation

Traditionally, Western culture has not valued relaxation; as a consequence, tension-related diseases dominate the illnesses of our bodies. If we are to integrate mind and body successfully, we must first learn to relax the body to allow cooperation with the mind's energy. At least six systems of relaxation are available: *Autogenics* (Schultz and Luthe, 1959), hypnotic suggestion, biofeedback, *Progressive Relaxation* (Jacobson, 1957), Yoga breathing, and meditation. Students would gain by exposure to several methods so that they might choose the one that works best for them.

Basic Body Relaxation

Begin basic body relaxation by asking students to sit or lie down comfortably. Use your own words for these ideas: "Close your eyes and get in touch with your breathing. Just notice; do not try to change your breathing. Allow it to happen. We each have our own rhythm of breathing. You will find that, as you notice, your breathing will begin to deepen, to become slower; soon you will be breathing with your whole body. . . . Now I am going to ask you to focus on some of the muscles throughout your body that may be holding tension. A muscle is supposed to tense, act, and relax. Sometimes all the tension is not released. Focus on the muscle across your forehead, just above your eyebrows and just below your hairline. This muscle may feel tight. As you breathe in, let air go into that area, and as you breathe out, let the tension out. . . . Now focus on your jaw muscles."

Continue talking your students through other muscles such as the muscles on either side of the neck, the shoulder muscles, the back muscles, down the legs, down the arms, letting all the tension flow out. Ask them to again be in touch with their breathing. Tell them that you will soon ask them to come back to their place in the room. Allow time for them to adjust. You might ask them to imagine what the room looked like when they closed their eyes, then imagine themslves back in the room. Tell them that when they are ready, they may open their eyes and return to the room. Allow time for them to come back. They may want to share their experience.

Physical Relaxation Techniques

It is useful to experience physical relaxation. While Autogenics and Progressive Relaxation both have a particular methodology, they use the basic concept of awareness of tension followed by relaxation. For example, you might say: "Close your right hand into a fist. Hold your arm perpendicular to the body, and push out as you tighten your fist. Continue until you feel discomfort, then suddenly let go completely, relaxing all of the arm and hand muscles. Now relax the arm one level further. Again further. Still further." This process can be used throughout the body.

For very young children, use this method:

Materials needed: One small, limp rag doll; recording of slow, quiet music

Procedure:

1. Have children sit on the floor around the teacher.
2. Teacher holds rag doll with both hands and shows the children how limp it is. She shakes it gently and calls their attention to the way its head, legs, and arms hang loosely.
3. Have children shake their hands and arms and let them hang limp. Do the same with the heads and bodies.
4. Play the record, and have children move around the room as if they were rag dolls.
5. Have children lie down. Go around to each one, lifting the arms and legs and letting them drop gently, saying: "Feel like a rag doll. Make your arms and legs heavy and floppy."

These resources provide information on relaxation: Bernstein and Borkover (1975), Hendricks and Roberts (1977), Hendricks and Wills (1975), Jacobson (1957), Pelletier (1977), Samuels and Bennett (1973), and Schultz and Luthe (1959).

Centering

The gifted can use another approach called *centering.* Useful not only for physical endeavors, but equally effective for intellectual and emotional balance, centering

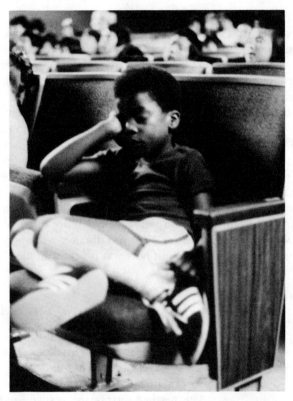

Relaxation is the first step toward integrating mind and body.

means the ability to relax, focus energy, and move with one's own natural rhythm. Nearly all human activity improves when one moves or acts from a centered position, as opposed to a fragmented or tense manner. Centering allows the integration of mind and body that results in synergistic thinking. It is exciting to have the feeling of being fully available, of discovering that solutions exist for problems you were not consciously processing. The concept of *centering* means combining the mind and body in such a way that we have total accessibility to our functioning. We become integrated, focused, and calm. Energy is readily available, and tasks are accomplished with grace and ease. We flow with nature and events. Centering nurtures.

If you were to draw a line from the top of your head to your toes, intersecting that line half way would put you at the gravity center of your body. It is here that the Chi or Ki of Eastern belief is found. From here we seek balance, peace, and concentration. By focusing at this point we can be physically centered, and from here we begin the centering process.

Next we relax and allow our awareness to move to this point in our physical body. From this point, we can use the ability of imagery now used by so many professional athletes. It is also from this center that we can begin the processes of healing, meditation, and other emotional and intuitive integrative techniques.

The *Centering Book* (Hendricks and Wills, 1975) and the *Second Centering Book* (Hendricks and Roberts, 1977) present activities and a rationale for developing our ability to center. One technique to show how being centered affects our movement is a game students of any age enjoy.

Standoff

Stand facing a partner. You should be close enough that your hands can touch each other's shoulders. Now bend your arms in front of you with your palms facing your partner. Your hands will be touching your partner's. Center yourself standing with your feet comfortably apart, knees slightly bent. You should feel heavy below your waist and light above. Without moving your feet, use your hands in forward or backward thrusts to unbalance or bring your partner out of center. Your partner will do the same to you. The first one who must step forward or back to maintain balance loses that round. One clue: when your partners thrust forward, give way, allowing them to come fully forward. Often this lack of confrontation will pull your partner out of center. If you both remain centered, you have a standoff. When this happens, it feels very much like a ballet. It's better than winning.

Don't view standoff as a game of strength, but as a game of centering and balance. This requires concentration. You will find out more about what unbalances you as you play with different partners. What you discover will apply not only to this game, but may tell you something about how you function in life.

Sensory Awareness

Sensory awareness is important in expanding the abilities of people. We are able to think or feel only about those objects or ideas brought into our awareness. We know gifted individuals have a heightened ability to use their senses. The following exercises will help them continue their growth in this important area. They require no materials unless specified and an organizational pattern of flexible grouping in a large, open area of the room. The teacher directs the activity and joins in when needed for correct numbers or when desired. Evaluation consists of a discussion of the students' experiences.

Visual Awareness

Rationale: the sense of sight is our first and most powerful interpreter of our environment. It provides a short cut for our concept processing and feedback for our personal and social development.

Do you see a change?
Time involved: twenty minutes, approximately

Procedure: Have students wander around the room in any direction. Ask them to stop and face the person closest to them. (Be sure everyone has a partner.) Ask them to look carefully at the person they are facing. After a few moments, ask the students to turn their back to their partner and change three things about their appearance (clothing, jewelry, hair, etc.). When all are ready, ask them to turn and face their partner and look for three things they have changed. If after a while any of the changes remains undiscovered, ask everyone to reveal their changes to their partner. Have all readjust their appearance and repeat from the beginning, finding new partners at least two more times.

Visual follow-the-leader
Time involved: fifteen to twenty minutes

Procedure: Have the group form a circle standing. Ask for three volunteers to step outside where they cannot hear or see the group. After the volunteers have left, explain to the group that they will follow a leader from their place in the circle. However, it is important that they do not look at the leader, but get their clues from others. Only a few should actually be looking at the leader. Ask for a volunteer leader; then, after the group has started, bring in one of the volunteers from outside the room. They must now find the leader visually. Repeat for each volunteer, with new leaders each time.

Tactile and Kinesthetic Awareness

Rationale: Simon (1974) has found that children are prohibited from touching each other or adults so early that, as we grow up, we have a problem he calls "skin hunger." Because of our human needs for tactile stimulation and to reduce our alienation from each other, Simon suggests that we find safe ways to allow people to explore their tactile and kinesthetic senses.

Whose hands?

Time involved: twenty minutes

Procedure: Divide the class in half. Form partners facing each other, standing in two concentric circles. Ask the students in the outside circle to remove all watches, bracelets, and rings, putting them in a safe place. Students on the inside of the circle now close their eyes and put their hands out in front of them with their palms up. Ask them not to open their eyes until you say so. Ask all students in the outside circle to go to any person except their partner and place their hands in the hands of that person. The inside circle students, still with eyes closed, are directed to feel the hands of the person in front of them. After several moments, ask the outside circle to go back to their partner. When all are in the original position, ask the students in the inside circle to open their eyes. The outside circle is now directed to extend their hands, and those on the inside are to locate the person they were facing by feeling the hands of those in the outside circle. After a while, help those who have not yet found their "hands" partner to do so. Now reverse roles and try it again.

Massage train (Simon, 1974)

Time involved: five to seven minutes

Procedure: Have students stand, facing counterclockwise in a single circle. Ask them to stand close enough to place their hands easily on the shoulders of the person in front of them and tell them to massage shoulders. End after a few minutes by slowly withdrawing hands from shoulders. Have everyone turn around and do this again to the person who just did it to them. Be sure you join in on this one.

Auditory Awareness

Rationale: Sight is such a powerful mediator of our experience that we do not develop our capacity to use our hearing as we should. Listening activities help to develop more of these abilities.

Listen without labeling

Time involved: five minutes

Procedure: After explaining our amazing hearing ability, ask the students to close their eyes and listen to the inside of themselves. Have them start by swallowing and follow that sound inside their bodies. Without labeling, what do they hear? After a while of listening inside, ask that they listen outside of themselves to sounds inside the room, then outside the room (the halls, room upstairs, the road by the school, etc.), and finally stretch to hear as far away as possible. Reverse the process, ending inside the room. Discuss what surprises they had.

Taped mysteries
Time involved: ongoing

Procedure: Tape familiar sounds around the house or school. Place cassette and recorder in an interest center with a listening post. Allow students to listen and try to identify sounds. Let students make their own sound mystery tapes to share with the rest of the class.

Awareness of Taste and Smell

Rationale: Again sight overrides the senses of taste and smell in interesting ways. By shutting out sight, familiar things become an adventure.

Tasty-turvy
Time involved: twenty minutes

Materials needed: cheese, breads (white, rye, wheat), and apples cut into pieces

Procedure: Have students form groups of two or three. Give each group an assortment of cheese, apple, and bread pieces. One student closes his or her eyes and is fed by the others. Sometimes request that the students hold their noses during feeding. Ask students to experiment with different combinations of foods (apple with cheese, bread with apple, etc.) After ten to fifteen minutes, discuss the experience. Be sure every person has an opportunity to be fed.

Have a sense-in: Students are invited to taste, smell, and feel all kinds of food and nonfood items, sometimes with sight, sometimes without, in a sense-in. They are required to use their senses to solve mysteries at different centers, such as: salt in a sugar bowl sitting on a C & H advertisement—use sight and feel and smell; cold mashed potatoes colored purple sitting in a snow cone cup with a small wooden spoon—use taste, sight, feel, and smell. The students can put together great centers once they understand the concept.

Strategies for Intuitive Development

The intuitive function has been the least recognized by educators. While the use of intuition can be shown to enhance the development of our other functions, until recently there has been no systematic concern for its development. Attitudes toward intuition seem to be changing. With the biological validation of differing brain functions, a new effort is being made to bring the right brain with its more holistic, integrative, inventive ways of knowing into the curriculum to provide a more balanced education. Breakthroughs in brain research and physics have caused reconsiderations of the very nature of reality. New information on the uses and nurture of human energy, meditation, personal space, fantasy, imagery, and dreams has much to offer educational programs for human learning. If, as Barbara Brown insists, all learning is subconscious, intuitive abilities need to be developed (Brown, 1974).

Nervousness, fear, and tension block even learned knowledge; the first step to releasing intuitive ability is to reduce tension (Assagioli, 1974; Roberts and Clark, 1976). Huxley (1962) also believes that intuitive ability can be developed. He views our cognitive ability as a conscious, active power and our intuitive ability as a complementary, receptive power. He states, "Both kinds of training are absolutely indispensable. If you neglect either you'll never grow into a fully human being" (p. 255).

Intuition is always available to us. There seem to be many reasons to develop this function. Clark (1977) gives us these three basic steps to developing our intuitive abilities: quiet the mind, focus attention, use a receptive attitude. These steps are very simple, but unless you as a teacher or parent allow time for these steps regularly, practice them yourself, and value the outcomes, they will not be developed. We are really talking about an attitude or a belief system, not a one-time exercise or strategy.

To begin, have the students sit quietly and comfortably. Ask them to relax and allow their minds to be very quiet. Be sure to explain that this is difficult, so that they won't be disappointed with themselves if they are not totally successful the first time. When a thought comes into their minds, ask them to allow it to be surrounded by a soft cloud and drift away. Try this for three to five minutes at first, gradually building up the skill to ten-minute periods. When this is possible for them, ask them to become quiet in their mind and then "see" a large screen inside their eyelids. Have them put a square on the screen, then a circle, now a triangle. In the triangle place numbers one at a time. Do this with several numbers. Now, on a blank screen, allow a picture to emerge. After a while ask them to open their eyes and share this picture by talking with a partner, drawing a picture, writing about it, and so on. This technique and variations of it will begin to develop powers of intuition. Purpose: to develop the skills of quieting the mind, focusing the attention, and being receptive.

At home, parents can begin by valuing and trusting their own intuition. How many times have you known, really known, how you wanted to do something, but, for whatever reason, allowed yourself to do it another, possibly more "sensible" way, only to discover later that your original idea would have proven far more workable? Trusting ourselves to know what is best for us is not easy. We often allow outside pressures to influence any use we might make of this type of knowledge. Begin by demonstrating the usefulness of your knowing as often as you can allow. Listen to yourself and act on that information more often. Then observe and discover your children's inner rhythms and ideas. Children are less out of touch with intuition than adults. They do not have to work as hard to regain their intuitive power. Find ways to draw out their ideas and show that you respect and value them. The inhibition of this ability begins when children find it ridiculed or devalued by those important to them.

As in other integrative work, we begin with relaxation and tension reduction. Use any of the relaxation techniques suggested earlier in this chapter.

Fantasy and Imagery

One of the most important components to developing intuitive ability is fantasy or imagery. Singer (1975) believes that fantasy may be the foundation for serenity and purpose in our lives. It plays a basic role in healthy development. He found that those who had trouble using fantasy to enrich their lives, or as a substitute for aggression, had serious problems. Children whose games are lacking in fantasy have trouble recalling facts and integrating events. In adolescence, these children are dependent on the external environment and may engage in antisocial, delinquent, and aggressive acts as a result of their inability to internalize humanistic attitudes. As adults, their problems increase and "their inner experiences seem less insistent than even the most irrelevant physical fact of their immediate environment" (Singer, 1976, p. 34). Alcoholism, obesity, and drug abuse may be the consequences of such impoverished inner life.

Yet it is easy to nurture the growth of fantasy. Parents and teachers can read to their children or tell stories to and with them. Sound effects and voice changes enhance the results. Making up plays, finishing open-ended stories, and playing pretending games all provide opportunities for development. Children need a climate that encourages the sharing of fantasies and allows them to become the basis for books, reports, poems, and journals.

Fantasy journeys can also be helpful. When guided, these can provide understandings in subject areas not available from factual reading. A high school teacher reported using fantasy as a tool for teaching history. After relaxing, the students were asked to go back in their imagination to the 1860s. They were told to see, taste, smell, and hear all that they could. After a time, the students were returned to the present and asked to write down everything they could remember. After compiling all the experiences into a class journal, the students were instructed to validate as much as they could by using library resources, texts, journals, and diaries written in that period. The results were an exciting learning experience that will long be remembered.

Electronics teachers can send the students as electrons through an entire circuit. Science teachers can guide the students, who imagine themselves to be red blood cells, through the circulatory system. I'm sure you can think of a myriad of uses for this technique. To read more about fantasy journeys and imagery, refer to Ahsen (1973), Castillo (1974), DeMille (1973), Hendricks and Roberts (1977), Masters and Houston (1972), Morris (1976), Rozman (1976), Samples (1976, 1977), and Singer (1975).

Cloud Watching

Have the students look at shapes such as those shown in figure 6.9. Suggest that these are clouds drifting overhead, and ask them to imagine what they "see." Remind them that everyone sees things differently. They might write a paragraph, make up a story, or draw a picture with their ideas. Purpose: to give students practice in using their imagination.

Dreams

We have not considered dreams as an educational tool, and yet we all dream. Dreams can be used for art projects, creative writing, as the content for research

Figure 6.9.   Clouds

surveys, or for self-understanding. Invite students to keep journals of their dreams. To help them remember dreams, they might keep a pad of paper by the bedside and write down key features immediately upon awakening. Ask them to tell themselves just before going to sleep that they want to remember their dreams. Hold group discussions of dreams, but avoid any interpretation. By reading articles about the dream work in the Senoi tribes and other books on dreams, you can be prepared to lead interesting and meaningful sessions using this powerful intuitive tool.

For books about dream work, see Downing (1973), Faraday (1972), Hendricks and Wills (1975), and Stewart (1969). Additionally, older students are fascinated by the history and future of parapsychological and metaphysical ideas. You may wish to use books such as Capra (1975), Hendricks and Fadiman (1975), Mishlove (1975), Ornstein (1973), Roberts (1974), Tayler (1972), and books by Castaneda, Krishnamurti, Ram Dass, and others.

Feeling Energy

The human being is only one of many forms of energy in the universe. The human system is surrounded by energy moving at varying rates of speed and with different intensity. You can help students become aware of their own field of energy and its effect on others.

By introducing the concept of field energy or biological auras (the energy extending from the human body seen by some people as color or light), we find that many children, even as late as school age, see colors and shapes of body energy or auras clearly. However, when they attempt to use this information, they are corrected or even censured and soon lose the ability through disuse (Peterson, 1975). In a study at UCLA, Hunt (1978) obtained what may be the first objective evidence of auras and field energy. Electronic measures verified the existence of changing fields and colors as observed by a person visually sensitive to such data. "The energy field described as aura has dynamic changes that coincide with emotional states, imagery, interpersonal relations, and the state of resiliency and plasticity of the connective tissue of the physical body" (p. 2), the report states. While these relation-ships have appeared in the literature of many ancient peoples, they can now be measured and are now, as Hunt states, "a fact not a subjective judgment" (p. 2). It is perhaps possible that we continue to pick up information from our environment intuitively that is above or below our normal range of sound or light receptive abil-ity. Though we do not process such information consciously, it may affect us. Chil-dren could be encouraged to develop this ability (Houston, 1977).

Hand Ball

After a relaxation exercise, ask the students to place their hands two to three inches apart, palms facing. Ask them to move their hands nearer together, then apart, until they can feel the energy between them. Some will feel it as heat, some as denser air. Maintaining this distance apart, move the hands in a parallel, circular motion with one hand preceding the other round and round, as your feet would move when ped-aling a bicycle. Now stop, and again feel the energy between the hands. Ask the stu-dents to give their "ball" of energy to the person seated next to them. Let them pass energy back and forth. Discuss the experience.

Personal space or space bubbles are other examples of human energy. Each of us has space surrounding us filled with our own energy and into which we feel com-fortable allowing few people. Exploring our own personal space gives us more infor-mation about our energy field.

Space Walking

Ask the students to walk around the room in any direction. Ask them to stop and face their nearest partner. (Be sure everyone has one partner.) Ask them to stand about two to three feet away from their partner. Partners now begin to slowly move toward each other. They should stop when they feel themselves in their partner's space. Have them back up and again walk forward. Again tell them to stop when they are in their partner's space. Have them turn around, both back up slowly until they feel the other, then stop. Move away and back up again. Change partners and do the procedure again. Ask students if they noticed any difference about how far each person could come before they felt uncomfortable. Does the space change? Ask them to explore this space with several other people, some they know well and some strangers or people they don't know too well. Discuss the experience.

Knowing Intuitively

Lady Bug (Chris Cenci, 1980)

Rationale: to allow the students to experience another way of knowing other than with the rational processes and to give them a concrete experience with the proc-esses of intuition

Time involved: twenty to thirty minutes, even longer if the students have a lot of interest in their experience and want to talk or write about it

Materials needed: a stuffed animal (we used a lady bug)

Organizational pattern: total class activity, teacher directed, individually experi-enced

Teaching role: guiding through the activity, facilitating follow-up discussions

Procedures: With the students seated (we prefer a circle), pass a stuffed toy around the group, asking the children to observe carefully. As it is being passed, guide them to look at its color, feel its texture, find out if it has an odor, notice all of its unique features. When all have handled the "lady bug" (or other stuffed toy or object), give it to one person to hide outside the room or somewhere the others cannot see. Once it is hidden, ask the children to close their eyes and remember all they can about the "lady bug" and notice how they feel. Ask them to become the lady bug. Ask them specific questions about where they are right now, reminding them that they were just hidden. Ask about what colors they sense are around them; The temperature; Is it light or dark? Are they over or under something? Are they on something hard or soft? Is there anything else they are aware of from where they are?

Ask the children to open their eyes; record their information on the board and ask them to do so at their seats. Ask the questions, again giving choices, e.g., how many felt cold? hot? saw light? darkness? red? blue?, etc. Now invite the children to follow the person who hid the "lady bug" and see just where it is. When they return, ask them to mark their paper with how many of their answers were "hits"—on target, or "not hits"—off target (do not say right or wrong). Remind them that, as with any other skill, intuition improves with practice. Allow them to discuss the experience, facilitating their further understanding.

Evaluation: The discussion will allow you to assess the understanding the students have developed of the function of intuition. (Chris Cenci has used this with very young children (two through five years old) and with fifth and sixth graders. I have used a similar activity substituting with peanuts, cookies, and other objects with adults.)

Telepathy Targets (Hendricks and Roberts, 1977)

Before a telepathy session, choose or ask students to bring in pictures to be used for targets. They should choose emotionally stimulating pictures that bring out strong reactions. Ask one student to act as a sender and seat him or her where the class cannot be seen. The sender selects a target picture and uses the following procedure:

Procedure: The activities on this card will help you send your picture to the rest of the class. You may do these in any order you wish. As you do these, keep the class in mind too.

1. Looking at the whole picture, what do you feel? Make that feeling stronger, if you can.
2. Pretend you are actually in the picture and can move around in it. In your mind, point out things to the class.
3. Imagine you are touching, tasting, or using your other senses on the objects in the picture.
4. If the picture shows something to do, imagine you are doing it with the rest of the class.
5. On a piece of paper, draw some of the things in the picture.
6. Can you think of something else to do? (Hendricks and Roberts, 1977, p. 171)

Have the class relax and begin to write down or draw ideas as they come to them. After a while, tell them to finish any idea they now have, then call in the sender and show the target picture. The sender may discuss what he or she did to help send the target to the class. Purpose: to improve the receptive abilities of the students in order to increase their ESP communication.

These then are the functions that we will integrate into a curriculum bringing into action the cognitive (higher cortex, left hemisphere) function; the physical sensing (motor area, sensory area, and lower brain stem) functions; feeling or emotional (limbic and right hemisphere) function; and the intuitive (prefrontal cortex and right hemisphere) function. Some environments are more supportive of integrative learning than are others. To bring together all that has been found to be most effective in optimizing the growth of high levels of intelligence, the Cooperative Learning Environment has been designed.

Elements of Integrative Education

The integration of the intellectual process of the brain/mind system is supported by the activities presented. These activities involve the elements found to be important to the integrative process, which are:

1. Relaxation, which reduces tension and allows more crosstalk between the hemispheres, more receptive and retentive information processing, and provides an aid to the total mind/body well-being. The brain does not function well under high anxiety conditions. Processing of data is slowed until pressure is removed (Hart, 1978).

2. Centering, which allows a focus of energy within a coherence of brain waves and an emotional balance

3. Imagery, a very powerful tool that brings into use one of the highest intellectual processes thought to be unique to humans; an example of the activity of the prefrontal lobe and the integrative use of the total mind/brain system

4. Verbal and physical affirmation, shown to be important to the earliest physical and intellectual growth of humans; clearly involved in emotional well-being and directed by the limbic area of the brain

5. Positive energy, effective in promoting nurturing biochemical exchanges between the limbic gateway and the higher cortical cells

6. Complex and challenging experiences, which lead to expansion of neural structures including increased dendritic and neuroglial growth, resulting in accelerated and more complex thought, especially within the neocortex, between the hemispheres, linking, and connecting the entire brain/mind system

    The human brain has little use for sequential presentation of material. A "logical" presentation of data is not facilitating. The brain works probabilistically, like an analog computer, and tends to deal in approximations (Hart, 1978).

7. Intuitive ability, activating the right hemisphere and prefrontal cortex areas, bringing forth the support of these less often acknowledged, but very important, areas of brain function and allowing for another way of knowing

As Carl Sagan stated, "mere critical thinking, without creative and intuitive insights, without the search for new patterns, is sterile and doomed. To solve complex problems in changing circumstances requires the activity of both cerebral hemispheres: the path to the future lies through the corpus callosum" (Sagan, 1977, pp.

190–191). Regardless of how giftedness expresses itself, integrative education can be used to optimize growth. Let us look at each specific way we have seen students express giftedness and see how integrative education could be used. When giftedness is expressed cognitively we have seen how integrative education can support its development, but what about when giftedness is expressed in academic ability, in creative behavior, in leadership, and through the visual and performing arts?

Developing Academic Ability

When giftedness is shown in this area, it will be important to assess the level of skill the student has already mastered. Gifted learners are commonly two to eight years ahead of their chronological age peers. Once assessed, the students should participate in individual conferences, acquainting them with their own profile of strength areas and the scope and sequence that is followed in those areas, allowing them to see the skills for which they are now ready and the possible future goals for which they might plan.

The needs of the gifted are not deficit needs, but rather needs for challenge in specific areas of strength. Just providing more of the same level of content will not fulfill this need; we must find ways to accelerate and enrich the concepts and processes in each content area of strength. The taxonomy developed by Bloom (1956) will allow us to assess our curricular planning and its appropriateness to the gifted student's profile. Generally, our main goal should be to go beyond mastery of standard content processes to develop with these students a greater understanding of the concepts underlying the content discipline. In both mathematics and science, we often find the computational and rational applications emphasized exclusively, so that the excitement found by the practicing mathematician or scientist is missing. Firing the imagination and creative ability of gifted students requires inclusion of the intuitive aspects of math and science. Only in this way can we help students view such subjects as dynamic, with real problems yet to be solved. These, after all, are the students who will contribute most to the expanding fields and disciplines. We must present them with an expanding, potentially limitless world view.

After assessing the peak areas or gifted needs of your students, you may wish to use a technique suggested by Tannenbaum to clarify your plans for differentiation of their content. Develop a grid with all of the content areas on one side and possible ways to modify the content across the top (see figure 6.10). Possible modifications could include those suggested by Tannenbaum: telescoping, that is, accelerating the content; expanding basic skills to include skills to produce as well as consume knowledge; prescribed augmentation, that is, modification directly related to the discipline; teacher-designated augmentation, finding new solutions, ways of mastering more complex, abstract ideas; out-of-school augmentation, that could include mentors, field experiences, etc. (Morgan, Tennant, and Gold, 1980). In addition, it is hoped that with what you now know you will include integrative experiences.

Sample Integrative Strategies in Academic Areas

History

Ask the students to close their eyes and with soft relaxing music playing guide them back in time to the period being studied. Give the students several minutes just to

Figure 6.10. Content Adjustment Chart

CONTENT AREAS	Telescope	Expand Basic Skills	Prescribed Augmentation	Teacher-Designed Augmentation	Out-of-School Augmentation
Language Arts					
Science					
Mathematics					
Social Sciences					
Arts					
Supplementary Content 1, Depending on Areas of Giftedness					
Supplement 2					
Supplement 3					

listen to the music and look around in this time frame. Then ask, "What do you see? Who is there? Are there people? What are they like? What are they doing, wearing, living in? Are there animals? Plants? What do you see, smell, hear?"

After several minutes, bring them gradually back to the room. Ask them to turn to one or two friends and discuss what they saw. Ask the group to record their experiences. Now introduce original materials, books, and journals from that period. Ask the students to compare and contrast their records with those from that period. Finally introduce the organization provided by the text you are using and allow them to note how all three sources compare. You will find the students much more interested in the material and more understanding of the reality experienced by those living in that time period.

Language Arts

Ask the students to close their eyes and imagine that they are on a hill in summer, lying on their backs and watching the clouds floating by in a blue sky. A biplane comes into view and begins to do some skywriting. It is writing their names. After completing the name, describe how the plane continues writing five words describing them around their names. When the last descriptive word is completed, bring them slowly back into the room and ask them to write the words on a piece of paper. Now ask the students to turn to their neighbor and write five words on their paper describing the neighbor. Give the students a few minutes to share the descriptions they are willing to share with their neighbor, then ask them to close their eyes.

Ask them to see themselves doing something they would feel comfortable doing right then in front of their neighbor. When they have done this, ask them to open their eyes and do what they saw themselves doing, taking turns with their partner. Now ask them to write on their paper five words describing how their partner did whatever he or she did, not what the partner did, but how the partner did it. Write words on the board given to you by the class: one list of words describing themselves or their partners, another list describing how their partners did the action requested. Now explain the differences between the lists and introduce the categories of adjectives and adverbs. This is an interesting way to present grammar and you will find that a high level of understanding and retention follows.

Academic areas such as mathematics, science, and social studies (including psychology, sociology, anthropology, economics, etc.) can be made exciting and appropriate for gifted learners by use of integrative experiences, use of the community, and outside experts. Encouraging research, survey, and field study techniques can make each discipline dynamic. It is the larger concepts, peopled by real participants, not just the involvement with the facts, that stimulates and challenges gifted learners. Allowing students to develop their own curriculum after they have been given conceptual frameworks such as Bloom's taxonomy is a good way to assure that they will be able to pursue their interests, as well as those the teacher feels are necessary.

Developing Creative Ability

In our discussion of creative behavior in chapter 1 we looked at the concept holistically, and a model using the four brain functions and synthesizing them as the highest expression of giftedness was presented. Strategies and conditions favoring developing of each aspect should allow teachers and parents to provide better for creative individuals and encourage more complete and balanced experiences in developing their creative behavior.

Strategies for Developing the Rational Aspects of Creativity

Creative Thinking Skills

Originality, fluency, flexibility, and elaboration can be increased by using the following activities suggested by Rob Russell. Although they were used at the junior high level, they can be adapted to elementary or secondary situations.

1. Give as many reasons as possible why . . . people wear clothes; x loves y but marries z; an elephant hunter meets an elephant in the jungle but doesn't shoot it.
2. Cut a pie into eight pieces with only three cuts.
3. What would it feel like to be a . . . misspelled wurd, last snow flake, trash can?
4. List all the things that come in twos.
5. List all the things that are . . . solid, flexible, colored . . . white, soft, edible. . . .
6. List all the attributes of . . . a banana, a belt, a window, an idea.
7. How could you use a vacuum cleaner to hold up a bank . . . a paper plate to stop a robbery?
8. What number . . . belongs to you, is you, is a mommy, is happy, is sad?
9. What are some unusual uses for a . . . tin can, newspaper (remember, be creative, not just practical)?
10. How could you improve a . . . bike, shoe, skate, coat, telephone . . .?
11. What would an elephant wish to be? A teacher? A school? A spider?
12. Given a stimulus word, students try to come up with a word that has an unusual connection to the first.
13. Given two distantly related words, students have to supply a third word that is related to the first two.
14. List as many impossibilities as you can.
15. Show children a picture of a situation.
    a. Have them ask all the questions they can about it (questions should be of the type that can't be answered just by looking at the picture).
    b. Have the students infer all the consequences of the situation.
    c. Have the students infer all the causes of the situation.
16. What would happen if . . . a person could become invisible at will, a hole were bored through the earth, the language of birds and animals could be understood by us, the days were twice as long, a person (or all people) could live forever, shadows suddenly came alive . . .?
17. Give students an answer and have them come up with as many problems as they can that have that solution.
18. Solve Mother Hubbard's problem.
19. What happened when the cow jumped over the moon?
20. Visualize this: . . . hard . . . red . . . snow . . . falling in one-half-inch cubes . . . playing music.

21. Visualize an animal. Pick out its outstanding characteristic. Get with two other students and make up a composite animal combining the characteristic of each of your animals. Draw a picture of it, give it a name, and write a story to explain why your animal did not make it onto the ark.

22. Finish these pictures in figure 6.11. What can you make?

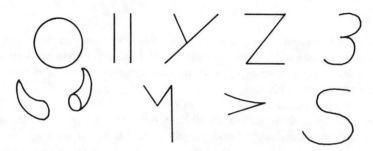

Figure 6.11.   Incomplete Pictures.

Brainstorming

Rationale: a greater fluency of ideas is believed to produce ideas of higher quality. This strategy allows groups to explore ideas without judgment or censure. All ideas receive acceptance and consideration. Unusual ideas or takeoffs from ideas already suggested are encouraged.

   Time involved: fifteen to thirty minutes. The session may last as long as the group continues to offer ideas. Follow-up activities may take another thirty minutes or could lead to a longer project.

   Material needed: none

   Organizational pattern: small group with a facilitator

   Teaching function: The teacher may serve as the group facilitator.

   Procedure: A focus for the group should be given and the rules of brainstorming stated:

1. No criticism allowed: all ideas are accepted.
2. Make your ideas as unusual as possible; give as many as you can.
3. Build on ideas you get from others.
4. No evaluation until the session is over

The facilitator lists all ideas on the board with no comment. Only after the fifteen-to-thirty-minute time period are the ideas discussed. The teacher may then help the group evaluate the ideas against a criterion for selection that they must devise. The ideas may serve as the basis for further development by individuals.

   Evaluation: the more ideas, the better. Be sure to use the ideas for a purpose; the outcomes should seem meaningful to the students. If you use real problems, they will have more meaning.

Trash Archeology

Have students collect waste baskets from at least three locations in the school at the end of the day. Treat the trash basket as an archeological dig and reconstruct the events throughout the day in that location, noting approximate times, events, possible antecedents, and outcomes, based on materials deposited in the trash basket. (Be sure that the people whose baskets are to be explored have given their permission. Some trash could be classified and reveal top secrets.) Purpose: To have students use creative thinking skills in an interesting way

Interest Centers

Rationale: Gifted students need opportunities to explore areas of their interest and become aware of areas not known to them. By establishing centers built around specific disciplines, and by covering, at various times, numerous areas of basic knowledge, both can be accomplished.

Time involved: ongoing, large blocks of time

Material needed: The centers should be open-ended and exciting, and they should provide understandings of how people in that field contribute to society; for example, an archeology center would incorporate instructions on organizing a dig, journals or books from famous digs, how the findings have changed our view of history, what experiences archeologists have, information on nearby sites now being excavated or worth excavation, films, tapes, etc.

Organizational pattern: open structure with simultaneous activity, freedom of movement, field trips available

Teaching function: Organize centers or help students organize center, resource person.

Procedure: students working at centers singly, in teams, or in small groups. The center provides the procedure to follow.

Evaluation: journals, projects, oral reports, conferences. In some cases, you may wish to have the student explore several interest centers without evaluation.

Other ideas for developing rational aspects of creativity can be found in Bruner and Dow (1967), Clymer and Wardeberg (1971), Covington, Crutchfield, and Davies (1967), Feldhusen, Treffinger, and Pine (1975), Gagné (1965), Gordon (1961), Hendrickson and Torrance (1961), Hopkins and Shapiro (1969), Kresse (1968), Myers and Torrance (1965), Parnes (1967), and Renzulli (1973).

Strategies for Developing the Feeling Aspects of Creativity

Who Are You?

Have students write the answer to the question "Who are You?" nine times on a piece of paper that only they will see. Either the teacher may repeat the question nine times, or the student can be given a paper with the question at the top. After the students have written the nine responses, ask them to look at each response carefully and cross off any such that, if they could not be that, they would still be themselves. Give students time to share any of their responses they wish with the group. Purpose: To get in touch with the uniqueness of the persons they are.

Experiencing the Now

Students form dyads and are instructed to converse with their partner about anything they wish as long as they do not refer to the past or the future. All of their focus must be on the present. After five to ten minutes, discuss the experience with the group. Purpose: To focus on awareness of the moment and to help them enrich their perception of themselves and their environment.

How Do You Feel?

Have students face a partner. They are not to talk, just to observe their partner while their partner observes them. Now ask them to close their eyes and notice how they are feeling . . . about themselves . . . about their partner. Now they open their eyes and again observe the partner. Ask them to discover anything they can about this partner. Is the person nervous? open? friendly? etc. Now ask them to close their eyes and again be in touch with their feelings about the experience. Once more observe the partner and try to communicate a particular idea or feeling nonverbally. Ask them to write down what they know about this person. After a while allow the partners to discuss with each other the observations and any of the written list they wish, sharing their feelings about the experience. Discuss the experience with the group. Purpose: To discover how congruent their feelings and expression of feelings are for each of them, to notice in what ways they protect themselves and how their feelings about the opinion and observation by others affects them.

Growth Groups

Not a single strategy, but a type of organized group that can nurture and support self-actualization, growth groups have the same characteristics and goals as those needed in the feeling aspect of creativity: individuality, well-integrated people, focus on higher levels of Maslow's needs hierarchy, openness, ability to change, confidence, sense of acceptance that allows and tolerates experimentation with new ideas, and responsiveness (Holleran and Holleran, 1976).

Any of the strategies for self-concept development and self-actualization would help in developing this aspect of creativity.

Strategies for Developing the Physical Sensing Aspect of Creativity

Creative Writing Pry-Mer

As a way of getting creative writing started, write the following categories across the top of the blackboard: Characters—Goals—Obstacles—Results. Ask the students to help you list ten items under each category, e.g.,

Character	Goals	Obstacles	Results
1. Wonder Woman	1. Wealth	1. Fire	1. A big bang
2. Abraham Lincoln	2. Moon flight	2. Stupidity	2. Elected President

When you have ten in each category, ask the students to take their own telephone number, drop the first three digits, and, using the last four digits, match the sequence to the numbers of the items in each of the four categories (e.g., if the phone number was 448-1121 the items would be Wonder Woman, wealth, stupidity, a big bang). They are now to write whatever story comes to their mind using their items. Have those who want to, share with the class. Purpose: To give students a way to experience their own creative ability, especially those who don't think they have any.

Creative Learning Centers

The visual, auditory, and kinesthetic-tactile are just some of the senses that can be developed in learning centers. You might also want various arts and craft centers, writing centers, and so on (see figure 6.12).

Other Activities (Jaime Tambara)

Make a famous sculpture using junk, and do the following:

Add a Texture. From magazines, cloth scraps, rubbings, think of words to describe these textures.

Squirt the Shirt! Use rubber bands or string to tie knots in your tee shirt. Squirt different colors of dye into the tied area. Allow dyes to soak into the shirt. Remove ties, unfold, hang to dry.

Puppet Parade! Take two soup bowls and cut one in half. Staple together. Create your own puppet, using paint, material scraps, colored paper, clay.

Drop-A-Dot Original. Cover the entire construction paper with water, using a brush. Load the brush with one watercolor and squeeze the color off onto the paper. Repeat with three more colors. Dry. List the different things you see in your design.

Figure 6.12.   Creative Learning Center.

Other Ideas For Developing Creative Talent (Maynard, 1970)

Arrange for children who are especially interested in one area of talent to watch, or
  better yet, work with an accomplished amateur or professional in that area.
Record the songs, poems, and stories that express a child's spontaneous response to
  life.
Provide lots and lots of materials to work with; avoid art materials that inhibit the
  child's imagination by imposing adult stereotypes of the way the world is supposed to be.
Let students help decorate the classroom.
Have students make and mail out greeting cards.

Also investigate Orff-Schulwerk as a way to bring out musical creativity.

Strategies for Developing Creativity Through Higher Levels of Consciousness

Movie Moods

One of the hardest things to do is to get students to let go of their habitual ways of
viewing the world so that they can perceive freshly and creatively. This exercise is a
great mood setter, and it works with any age group over third grade. Select three
films of approximately the same length. Try to get films with action or natural settings. Set up the films in your room so that you can run all at a time separately on
one wall. Have students face this wall, either in chairs or lying on the rug. Select one
sound track or a tape of music about the same length as the films. Turn off the
other sound tracks and show the films all at once. You will be amazed at how much
interrelationship the films have with each other and with the sound track. After-
wards, discuss with the students what they saw during the presentation. Be accepting of all comments. Now proceed to creative activities. Purpose: You will find a
very effective mood has been established. This exercise gives students a chance to let
go of their usual way of perceiving.

Coherence Corner

Materials needed: tape recorder; tapes of natural sounds, tranquil or classical music,
or relaxation exercises; listening post (see figure 6.13)
  Procedure: Direct students to sit or lie down comfortably, take ten to fifteen
minutes just to relax and imagine or meditate. Return to studies renewed.
  You will find other strategies for developing the feeling area of creativity in:
Hendricks and Roberts (1977), McConnell (1971), Osborn (1957), and Otto and
Mann (1971).

Developing Leadership Ability

Some of the characteristics commonly found in successful leaders (Judkins, 1900)
are—

above average intelligence;
skills of decision making;

Figure 6.13.   Thinking Space Relaxation Corner.

ability to deal with abstract concepts, future planning, time constraints;
a sense of purpose, direction;
flexibility, adaptability;
loyalty, responsibility;
self-confidence, knowledge of self;
perseverance;
tolerance, patience with people;
enthusiasm;
ability to express ideas in oral or written form clearly.

Opportunities to enhance any of these characteristics would be an important part of your leadership training program.

Although the literature presents no agreement on the best approach for leadership training, or even on what constitutes leadership, we shall discuss it as a set of skills that enable a group to reach its goals; maintain itself with mutual satisfaction; adapt to environmental change; and that allows individuals within the group to attain self-fulfillment. By this definition, leadership skills are mostly interpersonal and include flexibility, openness, and ability to organize. Leadership requires self-esteem, high values, and mature emotional development. Knowledge of group process and communication techniques strengthen the effectiveness of leadership. The characteristics found commonly with gifted children can, if given opportunities to develop, enhance any leadership role. In this context, the strategies presented in the affective domain will be of great benefit.

Leadership needs are often thought to be met by nominating class officers. That is only one type of leadership. It will be important for the gifted to become more involved in a system of evolving group leadership. When groups are encouraged to problem solve by using the skills and special abilities of all of the group members, gifted students will learn another, possibly more valuable, way of leading, that of sharing the leadership function. To learn more about developing leadership, see Arnold (1976), Csoka (1974), Cunningham and Gephart (1973), Fiedler (1967, 1971), Fleisham and Hunt (1973), Gibb (1969), Gowan and Demos (1962), Isaacs (1973), *Leadership: A Survey of Literature* (1976), Stogbill (1974), Stogbill and Coons (1957), and Yamamoto (1975).

Developing Ability in the Visual and Performing Arts

To develop abilities in the visual and performing arts the strategies must be specific to the art skill being developed and should be planned and implemented by an ac-

Creating the joy of music.

complished artist. While all children would benefit from exposure to enrichment in this area, only those teachers with advanced skills will be able to guide a student who shows giftedness through artistic ability.

While children who show their giftedness through expression in the visual arts are difficult to detect at the elementary level, such identification is important if the proper encouragement is to occur. A strategy to use for nurturing gifted artists within the classroom suggested by Chetelat (1981) is the station learning experience, where a child can investigate visual arts concepts with an emphasis on exploring in a more individual, independent, and accelerated manner. One such station devised by Chetelat contained three 18″ x 24″ wooden panels containing on each side reproductions of drawings and paintings of landscapes by great artists, art history books, and statements concerning advanced concepts to be read and studied. One panel contained a landscape by Van Gogh, the other side a landscape by Cezanne. The directions read:

> Look at landscape drawings by Van Gogh and Cezanne to discover ways that the artist used line to represent surface qualities found in nature. Use oil pastels to create a drawing of scenes in your community. Use line direction to emphasize contours of observed surfaces and use line to create textures and patterns on the surfaces of various objects in your drawing (p. 156).

Chetelat found his students enthusiastic about the station learning experience and advises that, when supervised by an art specialist, such an experience can be an effective way of providing for gifted artists within the classroom.

Some art educators believe that the most important thing that a teacher can do for artistically gifted children is to encourage them to maintain a sketchbook (Szekely, 1982). Such a book can serve to record observations, try out new ideas, develop technical skills, facilitate fanciful play, and most of all provide the growing artist with a place of privacy and freedom that has neither time pressures nor continuity. It is important that the sketchbook be chosen and retained by the artist as personal property. If there is to be an assigned format, it should be in a different book, one to be shared. Encouraging your students to keep their own sketchbooks is encouraging them to be their own art educators, encouraging the freedom, independence, and personal commitment of the accomplished artist.

To help children move from the consumer role in the arts to a creator role and to aid in the identification of those who are most able, programs must be developed to give experiences and understanding of how artistic products are created. An interdisciplinary thematic model including all areas of the arts was designed by Cohen (1981). The program focused the first year on opera and included visiting artists, singers, production personnel; visits to the orchestra and cast rehearsals and performances behind the scenes; tours; workshops and in-class projects. The children designed and built sets and props and worked on stage lighting. Some took parts in productions at theaters in the area. All learned at first hand about every aspect of opera production. "Art from the Inside Out" was an example of what is possible when children, artists, and teachers work cooperatively together.

Mary Hunter Wolf, long a leader in arts for the gifted, suggests that unusual talent can be uncovered by the use of exercises aimed at—

learning how to enter and share a learning community;
exploring and sharpening individual powers of concentration;

learning to own, release, and actualize one's imagination;
developing and sharpening environmental awareness.

As a result of using such exercises, gifted students will discover how to use themselves more effectively as learning instruments, the use of different learning styles and strategies to accomplish different tasks, and their own special interests and talents (Wolf, 1981). Many of these types of strategies can be found in the section on the Integrative Model in this chapter.

A specialized curriculum will not, in the view of Passow (1981), develop poets, musicians, etc., but should "activate and motivate the commitment and the development of the competencies and affective behaviors required for nurturing such talents" (p. 6).

Strategies for Enrichment

Many programs for the gifted provide only enrichment activities unrelated to any other needs of the gifted learner. The universe is so large and interesting that the introduction of new ideas could be endless. The structuring of some programs allows little time or continuity for other than enrichment experiences. *Enrichment* in this sense denotes experiences that are new, different, and usually unrelated to the total education program. While some very interesting programs have been built around enrichment ideas, such activities should not be allowed to provide the total differential program for gifted learners. The ideas that follow intend only to enrich a well planned program that assesses and meets the full range of gifted needs: cognitive, affective, physical, intuitive, and societal.

A project on propaganda and advertising. Students learn the basic techniques of propaganda and then analyze grocery and department store displays, newspaper ads, and television commercials for evidence of propaganda.

Weather prediction. By keeping records and consulting past records of weather and climatic conditions, students can use the laws of probability to predict the weather.

Planning and developing a planetarium. By careful study of known astronomical data, gifted students can design and build models of the planetary system that can be used for programs they conduct.

City redevelopment project. With outside consultative help, students can plan solutions for some of the city problems and present their ideas to appropriate government bodies.

Land and mountain measurement. Instruction and field trips with a licensed land surveyor give students a new view of math, geology, and land use planning and development.

Meet the author. After reading and discussing the works of authors, the class could invite these authors to teach a seminar on writing with a group of interested students.

The future and the laser. Experts work with students in their laboratory, sharing ideas for future uses of the laser.

Foreign exchange. Students in this country exchange with students in other countries for study.

Other possibilities. The gifted student could be encouraged to become a/an—

African Historian	Game Manufacturer
Alumni Detective	Holiday Historian
Animal Advisor	Language Etymologist
Animator	Philatelist
Bilingual Pal	Political Cartoonist
Class Curator	Resource Cart Organizer
Class Interviewer	Test Modernizer
Class Publisher	Unusual Fact Researcher
Exchange Ambassador	Weather Forecaster

The list never ends.

In this chapter we have looked at examples of strategies appropriate to meeting the needs of gifted learners in grades K–12, although many of these strategies will need to be adapted to fit your students. An overview of the characteristics and needs of gifted learners was presented, accompanied by suggestions for organizational patterns and sample strategies for meeting these needs. In view of the importance of differentiating and individualizing programs for gifted learners, some of the skills and methods needed for such development in the classroom have been discussed. The strategies were organized into areas for cognitive, academic, creative ability, leadership skill, and visual and performing arts to meet needs of children who show their giftedness in these various ways. Enrichment activities were also suggested. The Integrative Education Model was presented, and strategies for developing the functions of the model were given. It is through the integration of these functions that we can begin to develop more of the incredible potential of the human brain/mind system.

CHAPTER SEVEN

Secondary Schools
and
the Gifted Adolescent

Presented in the chapter for the reader are

- an overview of adolescence as a transition period for the gifted learner.
- a discussion of current programs available and possible structures for the gifted in secondary schools.
- suggestions for integrating learning in the secondary setting.

Intelligence can come only when there is freedom—freedom to think, to observe, to question.

Krishnamurti

The Gifted Adolescent

Adolescence is a particularly challenging period of growth. The following goals are often mentioned as the focus during this phase of life:

1. Achievement of independence
2. Discovery of identity as a person
3. Establishment of personal values and philosophy, both personal and social
4. Development of self-guidance, self-motivation, and self-esteem
5. Awareness of needs of others and how the self can contribute to meeting those needs
6. Exploration and acceptance of sexuality
7. Acknowledgment of intellectual power
8. Acquisition of life maintenance, career, and self-actualization skills
9. Development of meaningful interpersonal relationships
10. Exploration of reality structures by use of personal experiences

Our society seems to be organized to ignore and often actively inhibit the physical, mental, and emotional transitions from child to adult. In some cultures the transition is supported by ritual or is allowed to occur naturally as a useful phase of life. But in cultures like ours, achieving any meaningful place in the society must be delayed. Training for one's life work is continued well beyond puberty, and control of one's life is denied until well into the productive and creative phase of early adulthood. For many adolescents such practices have forced the creation of subcultures of teenagers with values, morals, and life styles that seek to depart from the accepted values and traditions of the established culture. Keniston (1975) suggests that many of the problems of this period are the result of the conflict in the youths' feelings of who they are and what society wants them to be. Many try to transform themselves, with resulting periods of introspection, drug use, and experimentation with various identities and roles. A teenager's future may be radically altered by the ways in which identity and meaning are sought during this transition period.

The gifted, the creative, and the talented adolescent may be better equipped in many ways to meet the biological and psychological challenges of this period. Their ability to conceptualize, to see alternatives, to seek out diverse patterns and relationships, to delay closure (which allows them a high degree of tolerance for ambiguity), and to express themselves in fulfilling ways will serve them well during this period of constant and often threatening change. But these very qualities that can lead to competence and power can bring to gifted, creative, and talented youth some unique problems.

There are few role models of their own age to emulate, and they seldom find peer guides, which can result in a feeling of isolation. Existing guidelines for the average teenager are often not applicable to their needs. For example, the question of overload: how much is too much extracurricular activity or attempted academic coursework? Often there is a lack of challenge, no chance to push to their limits, to make mistakes, to learn to cope. Since they can do so many things well how much exploring should they do? in how many areas? When should they begin to focus? make career choices? specialize?

Gifted girls are especially vulnerable during this period. Society gives adolescent girls mixed messages. More than ever before, they are urged to contribute their abilities and talents to society. More careers are open for their choosing, and higher levels within those careers are beginning to accept women. At the same time, the belief in male superiority still exists in many professions and sex role stereotyping still affects socialization and development at home and at school. Sex role differences are so evident by junior high years that girls begin a decline in achievement from the advantaged position they showed in elementary school (Maccoby and Jacklin, 1974). Fox (1981) tells us that these years are critical. If characteristics such as assertiveness, independence, leadership, and analytic and critical thinking are viewed by parents, teachers, and peers as masculine, the gifted girl will be forced to choose between being gifted and being feminine. Such a choice should never have to be made.

Adolescence may be the most frustrating time for youth and those who care about them, but it is also the best time for encouraging self-initiative, independence, and the growth of the creative mind. This period of reconstruction can be the beginning of personal excellence.

The Physical Transition

> Not since the fetal period and the first two years of life has the human body had as much change occurring to its physical structure so quickly. The development of sex organs and new hormonal balances add to the bewildering array of physical change to which the youth must adjust. Unlike during the period of infancy these changes occur with the full awareness of the young person who can observe with both joy and frustration the whole complex process (Craig, 1980).

Male high school students who show their giftedness in visual and performing arts have been found to differ significantly from average male students in their attitudes toward physical activity (Confessore and Confessore, 1981). Where the average youth preferred physical activities having a strong element of daring or requiring him to take chances, the talented youth preferred more aesthetic experiences, those that used the body as an instrument of expression. This was similar to the preference shown by the gifted female population, and was the activity least preferred by the average males. It was suggested that the affinity of males who show their giftedness in the arts for aesthetic experiences may cause others to view them as effeminate and that their low preference for any cathartic physical activity should be viewed seriously as a clue to further study of the problem of suicide and emotional disturbance among this population.

Often gifted students have been accelerated and now find themselves with a physically more mature peer group. This can result in more pronounced feelings of difference for gifted youth and they may retreat still further into activities of a cognitive nature. It is at this period that the proclivity for the separation of the activities of the mind and body are most evident and unless opportunities are provided for integration, a neglect and avoidance of physical pursuits may occur. By use of the gifted student's verbal and rational strength, an understanding of the dramatic changes that are occurring can be achieved and the need to integrate mind and body can be addressed.

The following suggestions will aid in this transition.
Provide for—

● Experiences designed to heighten and clarify sensory awareness
● Experiences designed to promote awareness of the student's own body and the creation of a positive body image
● Experiences and information to heighten awareness of the pleasures of having a healthy body, and of the means for health maintenance and growth
● Information and opportunities for inquiry into the clarification of physical responses to emotions
● Instruction and practice in techniques of relaxation and tension reduction
● Opportunities for self-expression through movement, pantomime, dance, etc.
● Opportunities to develop individual physical competence and experience the satisfaction of physical activity in ways chosen by the student from a wide range of structured and nonstructured, competitive, cooperative, and individual processes
● Exposure to and opportunities to learn one of the disciplines devoted to mind/body integration (Yoga, T'ai-chi, Ch'uan, etc.)
● Support for and assistance in making the care and development of one's own body a part of an individual life style
● Opportunities to examine the implications of current social and political policies for the health of people in the community

The Intellectual Transition

For most adolescents this is the beginning of Piaget's *formal operational thought*. Most youth now become capable of reasoning with alternative hypotheses, entertaining the possible and the probable in addition to the real and the concrete. While as many as 20 percent of the students of this age will not show a capability for this expansion of awareness, judgment, and insight (Neimark, 1975), the gifted student has been performing many such tasks for years and is now faced with an intolerable amount of repetition and conceptual stagnation.

It is quite common for schools to use the middle school grades to review and reintroduce concepts developed in the later elementary years. For gifted youth who were allowed to accelerate according to their needs and ability, such repetition is regressive. Even for those who have not had such opportunities the repetition of known concepts can create boredom and indifference to classroom achievement. The organization of most middle schools makes personalized instruction, which was found to be highly beneficial for the gifted student during the elementary years, difficult to continue. The student is now faced with discrete time blocks and segregated subject matter as most middle schools begin the practice of educational departmentalization.

The incidence of underachievement rises during this time. Boredom with school offerings, the need to challenge parental and teacher related values, desire for group acceptance combine to create the denial of academic ability. Girls, especially, will succumb to the conformity needs of this period.

Learning styles are also different between cognitively and academically gifted junior high school students and other students on at least five variables. Gifted students are less teacher motivated and more self-motivated; more persistent; prefer some sound to quiet during concentrated study; prefer visual, tactile, or kinesthetic to auditory modes of learning; and prefer to learn alone (Griggs and Price, 1980).

Suggestions for alleviating many of these problems are:

- Develop an academic core within the departmentalized setting where three periods may be combined with a team of two or three teachers. Gifted students can then be brought together for more appropriate instruction. Within such a core, flexible grouping can occur. Permitting able students to group for instruction at their level of need is far superior to the tracking plan employed by many middle and senior high school administrators, for it recognizes that the gifted student is not gifted in every subject and allows for appropriate curricular modifications and permits the advantages of mental peer interaction. Through the elective period choices, such a structure also allows broader exposure to students whose abilities may be in less academic areas.
- Use mentors to provide for the acceleration and depth of interest of gifted learners. Such specialized instructors can be found among the retired community, parents, and within the business community of any city or town.
- Use the resources of neighboring senior high schools, junior colleges and universities. Many universities have special provisions for middle grade students during summers in the regular courses where credits can be accumulated on an official university transcript. Some institutions of higher education offer specially designed programs to middle school talented and able learners in selected disciplines throughout the academic year.

Specifically within these frameworks gifted students need the following:

- Exposure to the environment and the culture, including aesthetic, economic, political, educational, and social aspects
- Exposure to, and opportunities to work with, peers, adults, and other students with expertise in the student's interest areas
- Advanced and/or unusual subject matter
- Experience in identifying data needs, establishing data organization, and data collection
- Opportunities to communicate and exchange ideas, information, and opinions in a variety of ways
- Instruction in developing original applications of knowledge and understandings, including hypothesizing and hypothesis testing
- Opportunities to examine and/or change/alter existing patterns physically and mentally
- Opportunities to identify and clarify standards of comparison and evaluation
- Instruction in, and opportunities to develop, data evaluation and decision-making skills
- Opportunities to evaluate personal choices in terms of available data, individual needs and goals, and choice consequences
- Opportunities to apply these ideas to real world situations

Social-Emotional Transitions

Acceptance, belonging, and self-esteem are the areas of critical concern to the maturing adolescent. Up to this point in time, modeling, guidance, rewards, and punishments have been used to give the young person an external value structure. During adolescence most young people are attempting to develop a personal value structure, their own moral system.

Giftedness gives special advantages and disadvantages to this process. While all adolescents can be characterized as intense and show rapid fluctuations in emotion and widely ranging mood swings (partly a result of biochemical changes that are occurring), the gifted confound this behavior by interspersing periods of unusual maturity and marvelous insight.

Bright adolescents appear to develop autonomy and time perspective faster than their average counterparts. And for gifted students who have in the past been threatening to teachers, a new assertion of independence during this period may result in verbal or sometimes even physical confrontation. Teachers least equipped to deal with this situation are those who see their role as one of authority that must be preserved. Those teachers who are successful in guiding the gifted adolescent can admit their own inadequacies and meet the gifted student as a person, for they care more about understanding problems or miscommunications than about being in charge.

The more typical adolescent admires those who are athletic or socially gregarious. If academic success is to be given approval by their peers, the gifted boy must be athletically able, often an impossible task for the student who is younger and less developed than his classmates. For both boys and girls good grades must be earned with seeming ease, for studious habits are often looked upon with suspicion and are often penalized. For girls intelligence is seen as too aggressive, masculine; for boys, too feminine.

Without guidance high levels of cognitive ability can be used to meet the youth's needs in ways that will prove to be socially destructive. Manipulation of others to gain personal goals is a skill too often found in these very able youngsters. Often the intense desire to know, to follow-up on concepts, to pursue ideas will result in a social insensitivity that can lead to rejection and isolation. Often large gaps between intellectual, physical, and emotional growth will need sorting out with adult help. It is important that nonjudgmental, open communication exist between teacher and student. Schools need to develop more expedient ways for the gifted to contact counselors and advisors. Too often, the intermediate and secondary systems with their departmentalization, administrative hierarchies, and large plants make immediate personal contact almost impossible. By the time a counseling session has been scheduled, with the proper hall passes and classroom permission secured, the student has given up on seeking help through the system. Overburdened counselors may be available only to disruptive or acting-out students. Gifted students complain that the counselor only relates to them for class scheduling or college preparation information. Some schools do recognize the problem; they set aside one day a week for counseling gifted students or run small counseling groups. Some have even developed a crisis contact system available to the gifted as well as to other students.

Gifted students can be helped to enjoy their differences, their uniqueness. They need to develop skills of individual competition, group cooperation, and trust. They need opportunities to work with students who are their intellectual peers and those with a variety of abilities. They can be taught to value their intellectual power and to use it to deal effectively with their emotions and their values. These are the students who can entertain new constructs of reality and who can envision more productive, higher levels of development for all humankind.

Suggestions for working with their emotional and social transition might include these:

- Opportunities to identify and name one's own emotions, perceptual filters, and defense systems and those of others
- Opportunities to expand and to clarify awareness of the physical, social, and emotional environment
- Experiences and instruction in attitudes of receptivity and suspended judgment
- Opportunities and support for actively seeking ideas and feelings from others
- Opportunities and instruction in constructing, clarifying, and expressing personal values
- Opportunities to clarify short-term goals and examine them in relation to personal values and to achievability
- Support for making personal values the foundation for career choice
- Opportunities to develop effective community membership by participating in activities with a variety of groups, examining roles in groups and the effect of those roles, practicing open communication, examining their own functioning within groups, and improving that function
- Opportunities to develop skills with group process including leadership skills and use of power
- Opportunities to develop commitment to groups and to larger community, including goals of humankind

Intuitive Transitions

Gifted youth have an early concern and interest in intuitive knowing. They need opportunities to converse meaningfully with philosophers and others who share their interest. Such inquiry can be made through independent study, with mentors, through group experiences led by guest experts, and through class discussions. It is important for gifted adolescents to be open to experiences in this area so that they may recognize their own intuitive energy and ability and how it contributes to their cognitive and emotional growth. They need guidance in becoming familiar with, analyzing, and evaluating such phenomena and should be provided with both the historical approach and the current body/mind data. As this dimension of creativity seems to be available to everyone but is to be found more active in the gifted and talented populations, guidance in evaluating appropriate uses of this type of creative effort should be available. The intuitive function is involved in initiating or insightful acts and in creative activity. It is an area that promises much for the fulfillment of humankind.

Peers in the school climate influence learning; in the case of creative students, their peer interactions do not seem to facilitate creative growth.

During adolescence classrooms must provide a safe place, but not overly limit risk taking and reaching beyond known paths. It is now that teachers become consultants and guides, and their past positions as authority figures and decision makers must be transformed. Knowing how to support without taking over, how to present consequences without removing choices, and how to provide structure without

An exciting alternative to traditional physical education.

limiting are some of the challenges faced by teachers of adolescents. For teachers of more sensitive gifted, talented, and creative adolescents, the challenge is even greater, and the significance of their success affects all of society.

Programs for the Gifted in Secondary Schools

Often those who plan the gifted program in the district concentrate on the elementary school structure and curriculum. Part of the reason for such omission of secondary levels can be found in the greater flexibility available in the elementary structure and time organization. Many of the needs created by the characteristics found among gifted learners—e.g., need for continuity, interdisciplinary content, delay of closure, flexible grouping to take advantage of peak learning areas, depth and diversity of interest, alternative learning styles and creative expression—can be more easily met in the elementary school organization. Other reasons are the limitations of the secondary structure in time given to each class and to each student because of the large number of students who must be served each day by each teacher and the limited interaction between faculty of the various disciplines. Though there are ways all of these problems can be resolved to provide appropriate programs for gifted learners, the largest barrier is the perception that program modification for gifted students is unnecessary in secondary schools. The assumption is that in a departmentalized setting students can choose programs that will meet their needs from the variety of courses offered. There may even be special honors classes available from which the gifted student can choose.

One often used practice that needs to be examined is the establishment of one or two advanced classes into which all gifted students are tracked regardless of their needs and abilities. Many high schools use special mathematics or science classes for this purpose. Such classes comprise the entire gifted program, and if students do not do well in mathematics or science, their identification as gifted comes under suspicion. We must offer the widest range of qualitatively different experiences we can devise, for this population is the most diverse in ability. Therefore, neither tracking nor a few special classes comprises a complete program that can meet the needs of gifted learners.

Silverman (1980) points out that while elementary gifted students may have relatively little involvement in the identification and planning procedures used in their program, secondary gifted students should be involved in both. In addition to more generally used identification procedures, she suggests the use of subject area examinations, preferably college level assessments; independent study proposals designed by the students; auditions and interviews; and self-nomination and self-selection.

Programs Found in Secondary Schools

Jordan (1973) believes that certain traits that can be found in gifted adolescents should define the programs planned at the secondary level; they are intellectualism, style, reflection, altruism, and idealism. As we look at the programs now found in secondary settings it will be well to see if such characteristics can be included.

The Advanced Placement Program

Available at approximately 20 percent of the secondary schools in the nation is the Advanced Placement Program (AP), a program of college-level courses and examinations sponsored by the College Entrance Examination Board in New York City. Usually planned for a full year, AP can take the form of an honors class, an advanced course, a tutorial, or an independent study. Such experiences are intended to be challenging, giving greater opportunity for individual progress and accomplishment. They often require more work, take more time, and go into greater depth than the usual high school course. AP examinations are given each year in the spring and result in credit or advanced placement in participating colleges and universities. In many universities a full year of college credit can be earned by AP work.

The Internationl Baccalaureate Program

Originating in Geneva, Switzerland, this program also demands a high level of subject mastery. The program is comprised of a two-year program outline, although it is quite flexible and a school is permitted to write its own program on the basis of the strengths and interests of the students involved. The resulting diploma is recognized by the major European universities and many American universities allow full college credit.

Core Curriculum

The time limits of classes in schools organized by subjects can be alleviated and the multidisciplinarity of subjects enhanced by the use of a core class organization. This approach allows two or three secondary teachers to block out multiple periods, usually two or three, each day during which flexible grouping and a cross-subject focus can be utilized. The usual student faculty ratio is maintained, but space is provided for the two or three groups that were formerly separate classes to meet as one group, with the two or three teachers forming an instructional team. The remainder of the students' schedules are as before, with electives chosen by the normal scheduling procedure.

Group Seminars

Another possibility for programming at the secondary level is the use of independently planned group seminars. An example of this type of structure for meeting the needs of gifted students at the secondary level is the Teacher/Advisor model. Students are allowed to ask any faculty member to serve as their gifted advisor. They then sign up for one period of gifted program time and arrange with their advisor how this period will be used. This is a highly individualized model wherein the gifted students may do directed independent study, cooperatively design seminars with their advisor to be conducted by either the student or the advisor, and/or take regular classes. Having a small area set aside as a gifted center helps to make this a socially, as well as academically, successful modification. Teacher acceptance of this plan is unusually high, and it provides for a wide choice of curriculum.

College and University Classes

Classes on college and university campuses are used successfully by many secondary schools. The assessment for such placement is the responsibility of the school district where the student is enrolled. This is frequently overlooked in programs that have limited offerings. Not all gifted students can benefit by attendance in such classes. Such a provision should not constitute the entire gifted program at the secondary level for all gifted students in that district. Placing students in advanced classes should be only part of a secondary gifted program.

Governor's Schools

Special schools have been successfully implemented at the secondary level. Notable has been the success of the various Governor's Schools. Eight states are providing the experience of a Governor's School for their gifted and talented learners. In six states the funding for all aspects of the program except transportation is provided by a combination of state and private resources. All of the programs are located on university campuses for full utilization of campus facilities. In some cases students are taught by university faculty. Many of the teachers are from secondary schools and are carefully selected. Student-teacher ratios are kept low. Grades are not awarded and university credit is not granted for completion of these programs.

The programs vary in length from four to six weeks and are in session only in the summer. They offer enrichment and acceleration in a variety of subject areas with different programs focusing on different areas. The students in some programs are as young as sixth graders, while in others the participation is limited to high school juniors and seniors. All participants are chosen from very carefully developed criteria (Karnes and Pearce, 1981).

The exception to the above profile is the new Governor's School in North Carolina, opened in September, 1980. It is the first public residential high school for highly able students in science and math. The school offers a full range of courses for eleventh and twelfth graders but emphasizes expanded course offerings in science and mathematics. Full costs of education and living expenses are provided by the state (Selby, 1980).

School-Within-a-School

Somewhat like a combination of core curriculum and special schools, the school-within-a-school approach allows gifted students to meet in a more flexible, integrated setting for their entire educational experience but utilizes the regular school facility and resources. Physically the students are located in a wing of the school or in bungalows on school grounds. As a separate unit they can pursue a curriculum that is accelerated and uses processes at a higher level of complexity than the regular secondary classroom can provide. Such a setting allows for more community and field experiences and flexibility of grouping without interrupting the overall school schedule. Many districts find such provisions especially attractive for the highly gifted or as a solution to low achieving gifted groups, as the cost is little more than offering another section of a regular class.

Mini-Courses

What would happen if all secondary teachers could teach only what they wanted to teach and the students were allowed to learn just what they wanted to learn? This was the question that started an interesting mini-course structure at a high school in the Los Angeles area. A group of teachers came together to find out. After securing permission to use a six-week time block, each teacher listed courses he or she most wanted to teach and how many weeks they would require. These were then scheduled under traditional categories such as history, biology, language, science, etc., with a descriptive, often creative title. Not surprisingly, most teachers found that their favorite themes fell within the area in which they were credentialed to teach. The students were then given the list of mini-courses and allowed to choose their favorites. As much as possible, first choices were honored with second choices used only when classes became too full. Classes that were not chosen were dropped. These mini-courses comprised only a part of each student's schedule and were fitted into the more traditional class schedule with other periods run as usual.

The results were exciting! The students and the teachers were highly motivated; the classes became far more creative, better attended, and more productive. The next time mini-courses were being scheduled, nearly twice as many faculty wanted to participate and students who had previously not wished to participate in the gifted program requested permission to sign up. The experiment might have eventually encompassed the entire school had there not been a change of administration, with a resulting return to more traditional and "manageable" scheduling procedures.

Radical acceleration as exemplified by the SMPY Program described on p. 152, mentor programs as discussed on p. 157, and programs for independent study as outlined on p. 158, can all be successfully implemented at the secondary level. At the very least, two interested teachers can combine their blocks of time and their students to create a laboratory setting where individualization, flexible grouping, and some cross-grading and interdisciplinary learning can occur.

In addition to the provisions described other options might include—

summer university courses, institutes, or programs for gifted learners;
curriculum acceleration and early graduation through competency testing and fast
    paced materials;
flexible scheduling (less regular class attendance);
interdisciplinary courses or themes;
community based career education and internships;
special-topic courses;
exchange student programs;
special study centers;
private schools for the gifted.

Special Problems in Evaluating Programs for Gifted in Secondary Schools

One source of evaluation of gifted programs in intermediate and high schools is the students themselves. Raspberry (1976) quotes a gifted student who left his junior high school because the environment

> Was not conducive to academic achievement. . . . In order to gain acceptance by
> the student body, one had to give some visible deference to either athletics, 'par-
> tying' or some form of rebellious activity. Those who excelled academically had
> to prove that they were 'all right.' The studious males ran the risk of being called
> 'sissy.' The studious females were definitely considered square. . . . Students make
> the difference, for students set the mood of the campus (pp. 36, 38)

In a 1958 study, Thistlewaite reports the 45 percent of the gifted students surveyed found their secondary programs either inadequate or having specific defects. My experiences with secondary programs for the gifted in the past ten years tell me that this percentage is still valid, perhaps even higher today. To make a videotape series at our university that would explore the feelings of gifted youths toward their programs, we selected gifted students from diverse racial, cultural, and socioeconomic backgrounds. The students most commonly complained that they were never challenged to use their abilities. They were often given more work, but usually of the same type used with typical learners. Even in situations where they were grouped with other gifted students for a small part of their program, they felt that the programs remained the same; only the people were different. Occasionally teachers worked with them to set up interesting educational experiences from which they could learn. These were the exceptions, however, and they expressed the belief that most of their teachers found them threatening and resented any special provisions made on their behalf.

The groups had suggestions for improving the situation. Most felt that a more open, flexible approach would have benefited them. One young woman, who experienced an individualized program for a couple of years in a language arts class, told of how much progress everyone had made and how interesting it was. "But the next year we had to go back into basic texts with our new teacher. We could use equipment like the controlled reader, but they set it at 400 words a minute and wouldn't let us change it. We were already reading 800 words per minute, but they didn't care. They said for our grade level, that was where we were supposed to be," she told us. One boy wanted to branch out and combine music, his first love, with math, history, and language. He suggested that such interdisciplinary study would be natural and would lead on and on to more exciting learning. He had just been dropped from the xx track classes (highly gifted) for gifted students because he felt the work was too boring and refused to do it. He was finding the x track (gifted) just as bad. All of these students expressed great appreciation for teachers who treated them like people and seemed to care how they felt. The students most pleased with their program came from an intermediate school where they were grouped together for three of their six periods in a cross-graded fifth through eighth grade, open structure. Their two-teacher team used the cooperative learning environment model and taught them all of their basic subjects. They were allowed to choose electives for the remaining periods from classes throughout the school. These students expressed none of the boredom and dissatisfaction of the others we interviewed.

Rice and Banks (1967) interviewed another group of junior and senior high school students regarding their opinions and recommendations for changes in their program. The findings will be given in some detail, for they are typical of comments found throughout the literature, in my work with gifted youth, and of teachers and coordinators with whom I have been in contact through our teacher training program.

In answer to a question on designing their own curriculum, the students wanted courses that would allow them to work at their own individual level of ability. They wanted more freedom in course selection and more flexibility in grade level placement. They divided their preference for the subjects offered equally among the sciences, mathematics, fine arts, foreign languages, and social sciences, with the request that the curriculum be culturally enriched and diversified. Students at the junior high school level requested interdisciplinary seminars. The students also asked that they be allowed to pursue courses in more depth, and that advanced placement and equivalency testing be made available.

In response to a question on opportunity for creative expression, the students requested more independence to create what they wanted instead of producing only what the school wanted. Girls expressed a greater need for more freedom of choice and creative outlets than did boys. In discussions of grouping, nearly all students favored some opportunity to learn with other gifted students; the highly gifted unanimously favored completely separate education. Students favored acceleration on a subject-by-subject basis, although they did not see it as taking the place of individualization. They gave preparation for formal education, emphasis on the use of the intellect, and promotion of social development and maturity as the top priority purposes for high school education.

In another survey of gifted fourteen-to-eighteen-year-olds in an affluent community in Los Angeles County (Stark, 1972), students gave the highest priority for their high school goals as preparation for: finding a career that would be interesting to them, being able to decide what vocation to follow, and being able to discover what special abilities they had. They felt their high school should teach more classes on how to live in the world. These students were interested in a career that would provide them with self-worth rather than high pay or security, and they preferred a job that would allow them to work with people rather than with data or things. They felt their greatest problem at school was overcoming boredom, and they wanted the chance to participate in a group that could discuss personal problems with an understanding adult. They desired an advanced program in which they could work alongside a professional in the actual environment. They believed that teachers could help them learn if the teachers were more interested in them as individuals. Although the population and the questionnaires differed from those of the Rice and Banks study, the ideas expressed by the students are surprisingly similar.

Students have not been the only ones to criticize the secondary programs for gifted students. In a four year follow-up study of gifted students in high school programs, Meeker (1968) found through measures of creativity, leadership, motor skills, grades, intelligence, and achievement that potentially brilliant achievers have been lost as a consequence of inadequate attention during the secondary school years. She blamed expectations and traditional departmentalized practices.

A study (Tremaine, 1979) comparing the attitudes, accomplishments and achievements of gifted high school students participating in a gifted program with gifted high school students who did not participate reported the following results: The gifted students—

earned higher GPAs,
took more advanced classes,
scored higher on SAT testing,
won significantly more scholarships and awards,
planned to attend a four-year university in far greater numbers,
expressed more positive attitudes toward school after graduation,
were involved and spent more time in school activities,
evaluated their teachers higher,
and enjoyed as many friends.

Tremaine feels that the contention that gifted programs result in snobbery, indifference, conceit, or any other negative quality cannot be validated by these data. In fact, they indicate that gifted programs in the secondary school make significant positive differences and are well worth the development and implementation effort.

Using Integrative Education in the Secondary Curriculum

All of the characteristics and needs of the gifted discussed in the last chapter are applicable to secondary as well as elementary students. Therefore, there remains the

Secondary students need differentiated, individualized curriculum experiences even more than before.

same need for differentiating and individualizing the curriculum. If anything, differentiation is more needed during adolescence, for it is during this period that the gifted pursue their independence and separate identity from their parents and their childhood values—sorting, testing, and validating their competence.

The philosophy of learning and teaching is also equivalent, as advances in brain/mind research make the same demands for change on the secondary teacher as they make on the elementary teacher. While the theories of cognitive development and the curricular models that attempt to facilitate them are important at the secondary level, the necessity of including and integrating other functions of feeling, intuition, and physical sensing are as critical to optimal learning and development in the secondary as they were at any other point in the growth of the gifted learner. The secondary teacher is asked to look again at chapter 6, with a view to adapting and translating the models and suggestions to fit his or her gifted learners. The description of the Integrative Education Model and its use of brain/mind research in the classroom does not change, nor does the environment in which it can best be implemented, whether at the elementary or secondary level. What does change is the way the implementation looks. Just as a decentralized laboratory setting in language arts looks different from this type of environment in science, so the individualized setting looks different when a school has a core curriculum or a six period day. The look may be different, but the same rules apply.

The secondary teacher is also asked to review the strategies given in chapter 6 to illustrate the four major brain functions, again with an eye to adapting when needed and re-creating for the specific group of learners. All of the strategies given have been used in some form with students from preschool through graduate school. The results have been most exciting! The elements of Integrative Education are not limited to any age group. However giftedness is expressed, the strategies given are useful.

Because the secondary schools are presently structured in a departmental format, strategies for integrative learning will be made within that format. Feel free to extend, expand, and invent, for the examples given are only suggestive of what might be done.

It is at the secondary level that real concern begins to be felt by gifted learners, their parents, and their teachers for academic performance. This is the point in an academic career when future opportunities may be facilitated or closed, depending upon the student's performance. Testing is often the measure of that performance and ways to improve a student's ability to perform on such tests may be quite interesting to that student.

We have seen in chapter 6 that relaxation is an important tool in optimizing learning. Not only will reduced tension allow more information to be processed more quickly, it will also allow the retrieval of more information more accurately. In a conversation with a secondary teacher regarding the use of relaxation in the classroom, I was told about a student who seemed to the teacher to be extremely able, who, however, almost always received low grades on written tests. The teacher began using guided fantasies prior to the administration of tests and found the students far less tense and the quality of the answers much improved. For the girl who had tested consistently low, the results were grades that went from C and D to grades of A and B. The teacher now teaches relaxation skills regularly and encourages the students to use such skills before any testing in which they must be involved. He tells the students that he cannot guarantee results, but that it has worked remarkably well for many students. He also informs them that the army is using similar techniques in their training programs. In addition to guided fantasy, the teacher informs me that during a test a break for the Massage Train (found on p. 267, chapter 6) revitalizes the students and aids their performance.

The following is the script of a guided imagery used by Tobias Manzanares of Garfield High School, Los Angeles, California, a secondary teacher.

A Guided Imagery for Secondary Students—An Aid in Test Taking

I would like you to take five cleansing breaths . . . inhale quietly through your nose . . . exhale quietly through your mouth. . . . Each time you exhale imagine that you are blowing tension out of your body. . . . Allow your eyes to close gently . . . feel your body soften as the tension leaves your muscles. . . . Allow any sounds that come into the classroom to float through your consciousness and back out again, you need not hold onto any of these sounds. . . . Again, another deep cleansing breath . . . and relax . . . this is a special time for you to find your center. . . . Imagine that you are lying on a hilltop watching clouds gently drifting across a vivid blue sky. . . . Feel the breeze blow through your hair . . . feel its coolness. . . . Watch as the clouds move into different shapes. . . . Notice how relaxed your body is . . . notice how comfortable you feel. . . .

Image yourself as you take the exam . . . notice the look of confidence on your face, a look that reflects the confidence in your ability to remember. Everything that you've ever heard is permanently recorded year after year in your brain. . . . The more relaxed you can become, the more you can remember, the greater the access to your incredible memory. . . . Notice the smile on your face as you mark the correct answers on your answer sheet and notice how comfortable your body feels.

When you're ready, return to the classroom and open your eyes. Remain relaxed and notice how you feel. You are now in a better mental state to perform well on your exam. Remember that smile of confidence as you begin and if you feel tension building, close your eyes for a moment, take a few cleansing breaths, and blow out the tension as you exhale. Half way through the exam we'll take a two minute break for a special treat that will help you with the last half of the test.

Using Integrative Education in Secondary Science Teaching

The following lessons have been successfully implemented by Tobias Manzanares in his high school biology class.

The Heart and the Human Circulatory System

Purpose: to facilitate the conceptualization of the human circulatory system and the movement of blood through that system; to reinforce the vocabulary relevant to the cardiovascular system

Time involved: One fifty-minute class period

Materials needed: Thirty red cards or pieces of construction paper; thirty blue cards; classroom furniture that is moveable

Procedure:

Step 1. Ask the students to draw the diagram of the circulatory system (see figure 7.1).

Step 2. Ask the students to visualize the room as a human body with the desks rearranged to represent the four-chambered heart in the center of the room. Ask for volunteers to represent the brain, the lungs, and the digestive tract. Direct them to the appropriate place in the room (body). With student help rearrange the desks to simulate the heart and the circulatory network.

Step 3. Distribute one red and one blue card to each of the remaining students (those not involved in the representation of the brain, the lungs, or the digestive tract). Instruct them that when they as red blood cells reach the lungs and become oxygenated, they will hold up the red card until they reach an organ using oxygen, where they will lower their red card and raise their blue card representing deoxygenated blood. The blue card will be held overhead until they reach the lungs to be recharged with oxygen.

Step 4. With the red card in their right hand and the blue card in their left, have students begin a walkthrough of the cycle using the following sequence: right atrium . . . right ventricle . . . pulmonary artery . . . lungs . . . pulmonary veins . . . left atrium . . . left ventricle . . . aorta . . . upper body (brain) or lower body (digestive tract) . . . superior vena cava or inferior vena cava . . . back again to the right atrium to complete the cycle and begin the next trip.

Step 5. Ask for a student volunteer to retrace the ten sequential steps. (Assist student volunteer as necessary.)

Superior Vena Cava
Pulmonary Artery
Lung
Inferior Vena Cava
Liver
Intestine
Kidney

Brain
Aorta
Pulmonary Artery
Left Pulmonary Vein
Lung
Heart
Stomach
Spleen
Kidney

Figure 7.1.   The Heart and Circulatory System

Step   6. Instruct the remaining students to fall in line behind the student leader and begin the first cycle, using the group as red blood cells. As the student red blood cells pass, remind the students representing the lungs to raise their right hands (red cards) . . . . as the students pass the student representing the brain and intestine, remind those students to lower the red cards and raise the blue cards . . . . instruct the student red blood cells to name out loud each of the ten structures as they pass these locations in the room.

Step   7. Stop the cycle. HEART ATTACK!!!

Step   8. At this point the brain can control the pace of circulation and the group can play with the various ideas affecting the speed of circulation (running, sleeping, yawning, meditation, watching a scary movie, etc.). Ask for volunteers to replace the students representing the brain, lungs, and intestines so those students can go through the process.

Step 9. Stop the process again and ask how long the students think it will take to go through one complete cycle. Record the guesses on the board and time one cycle. Ask the class to see if they can improve the time while still verbally indicating the name of the structure they are passing. On your mark . . . get set . . . go!

Step 10. Discuss the entire procedure after the class has returned the room to its usual order.

Phagocytosis

Purpose: to develop an understanding of the body's immune system through an integrative activity, and to reinforce the terminology used in the unit on the circulatory system.

Time involved: One fifty-minute class period

Materials needed: Handout of a drawing of the process of phagocytosis; classroom or outdoor area representing the human body

Figure 7.2.   Phagocytosis

Procedure:

Step 1. Students should record in their notebooks the diagram showing phagocytosis (figure 7.2) and should note the following:
   a. Many white blood cells are capable of phagocytizing, or eating, large numbers of invading microorganisms.
   b. Specialized cells in the liquid-filled spaces of your tissues are also capable of phagocytizing invading organisms, and are most effective in the specific region of a skin wound.
   c. If the infection moves into the body from the region of entrance, phagocytic cells residing in the lymph nodes will ingest the invaders. Additional phagocytic cells are found in the liver and spleen, should the infection reach the blood stream.

Step 2. Share with the class, so that everyone will be able to participate as either a part of a white blood cell or as a triad member representing an invading cell. Ask for volunteers to make three triads. Members of these triads can decide whether to be a virus or a bacterium.

Step 3. The remainder of the class links arms to form a closed circle representing a white blood cell. This group selects a member to act as the nucleus.

Step 4. Instruct the invading triads to leave the room momentarily and when they return to remember that they are invading the body (the room) through a wound, scratch, or any other method they may choose to describe. (Example: Giardia lambia is a protozoan that enters the body through contaminated drinking water.)

Step 5. Instruct the remaining group (white blood cell) that they are charged with the responsibility of protecting the body by ingesting and thus destroying the invading organisms.

Step 6. As the invading triads (arms linked) enter the room (body), instruct them to move at the speed of a microorganism (very slowly). Instruct the nucleus of the white blood cell to direct the action of the cell in the very best style and wisdom of a nucleus.

Step 7. Allow three to five minutes for the phagocyte to phagocytize. As an invading triad is ingested, instruct them to become part of the larger phagocyte by linking arms with that group.

Step 8. Stop the activity momentarily (after ingestion) to have the group focus on their feelings by asking the following questions . . . To the phagocyte: How did you feel as you attacked and ingested an invader? Did you have a sense of power? Did you feel a sense of responsibility? Success? To the invading triads: Did you feel a sense of exclusion relative to the bigger group? Did you feel differently after becoming part of the larger cell? What kinds of feelings were experienced upon penetration of the body?

Step 9. Have the class return to their seats and write a metaphor about their immune system.

Step 10. Conduct the following guide imagery to raise the students' awareness of their ability to assist their body's immune system, using imagery.

Allow your eyes to close gently . . . take five cleansing breaths, breathing quietly in through your nose and out through your mouth. . . . Become aware of your skin as a protective barrier completely surrounding your body. . . . Imagine yourself beginning to shrink in size until you are microscopic in dimension. . . . Imagine that you are a white blood cell floating down an endless river within your body. . . . Notice the body organs and structures from this new perspective, from the inside. . .

Become aware of the millions of other phagocytes who like you are charged with the responsibility of protecting the body from invading organisms. . . . Notice the enormous feeling of well-being that comes from being part of such an enormous and powerful group. . . . Become aware of a small number of cancer cells that have invaded the body and notice the immediate response of the phagocytes now mobilizing to destroy these invaders completely. . . . Notice the scene of the invasion as the cancer cells are rendered harmless by the action of these powerful phagocytes. . . . Notice the healthy color and glow return to the tissues in this scene as you and the other white blood cells move on in your protective responsibilities. . . . Begin now to grow larger and larger until you fill the physical frame of your body. . . . When you're ready, you may open your eyes and form triads to share your experiences during this imaging session.

Evaluation: The evaluation of both of these activities can be any of evaluative tools you would normally use. Manzanares has found that the students understand more clearly and will retain the information longer than with the usual teaching approaches.

Using Integrative Education in Secondary Social Science

American History—The Westward Movement

Purpose: To conceptualize and develop a better understanding of the life and the problems facing the native tribes of the American West and the migrating settlers during the Westward Movement.

Time involved: One fifty-minute period or broken up into several periods if more research is desired

Materials needed: Original journals or diaries of the time period written by those involved in the settlement of the American West, newspapers of that period, any other first hand data and artifacts from the historical period under investigation that can be obtained. If possible, a native American could be invited to speak to the group during this unit of study. Books written about this period of Western history should be made available. Student journals, tape recorders (optional)

Procedure:

Step 1.   Briefly describe the setting and time period to be introduced, the American Westward Movement.

Step 2.   Ask the students to get comfortable in their seats and gently close their eyes. Instruct them as follows: Breath deeply and slowly allow your body to relax. . . . Let all the tension flow out of your body. . . . Relax. . . . With each breath, you are allowing your body to become lighter, to expand, to slowly become all of the air in the room. . . . Gently let yourself rise slowly above your desk . . . above the room . . . rising gently, slowly above the school. . . . Imagine that you are now slowly moving through time and you are going backward about ten years . . . 50 years . . . 100 years . . . back to the time when the tribes of native Americans still lived in the Western United States. . . . You are now over the area of the United States that was the home of these tribes. . . . Look down. . . . What do you see?.. What is happening?. . . What are the people who live here doing?. . . How do they live?. . . What do they eat?. . . What are they wearing?. . . What do they do for fun?. . . Become one of the native people. . . . What are you doing?. . . Look out over the land. . . . You can see wagons moving slowly toward this spot. . . . How do you feel?. . . What are you concerned about?. . . What do you do?. . . Slowly rise above the tribal encampment. . . . Move toward the wagons of the settlers. . . . What are they doing?. . . Become one of the settlers. . . . How do you feel?. . . What are you concerned about?. . . What do you do?. . . Let yourself slowly rise above the wagons again. . . . Let yourself drift forward in time . . . slowly allow yourself to drift back into this room. . . . Notice how you feel here in this room and when you are ready, slowly, gradually open your eyes and return to the group. . . . When you are ready, open your eyes and choose two other people to share your experience.

Step 3.   Ask the students to share in triads, recording their experiences in their journals, in a group journal, or on the tape recorder (if one has been provided).

Step 4.   Ask each triad to use the original materials in the room to expand and authenticate their experiences. Use the other materials for comparison and record similarities and differences in all the sources.

Step 5.   Ask each triad to prepare a product relating their experiences and research to be shared with the class.

Step 6.   Ask for one triad to volunteer as the class historian and assemble the records or products of each triad into a class journal or display.

Step 7.   Ask each triad to share their most interesting information in whatever way they choose, allowing five minutes per triad (or whatever time is available).

Step 8.   Discuss with the total class the types of problems they felt each group might have, how they felt as a member of each group, and what solutions they felt each group might have tried. Discuss how their ideas related to the historical records. Which solutions might have had the best results? How does this situation seem to reflect events happening today? What are the similarities and the differences? Ask the students to take one emerging issue in today's world and develop possible solutions, either independently or with their triads, for presentation later in the week.

Evaluation: From the journals and position papers, the depth of understanding of the period will be evident. Use any evaluation tools you would normally choose.

Extension: If more than one time period is used, the students can be asked to role play a confrontation between the two groups and discuss the outcomes and consequences of the confrontation.

The content above was suggested by Ella Schroeder, teacher, Krantz Junior High School, El Monte, California.

Using Integrative Education in Secondary Language Teaching

A project conducted in the Los Angeles City Schools by Galyean (1976, 1979, 1980) for teaching foreign language to seventh- through eleventh-grade students included guided imagery, movement and art, fantasy, poetry, drama, music, and values clarification. Many of the curricular ideas used in the project can be found in the references cited.

Examples

When they are practicing tenses of verbs, have students close their eyes, breathe deeply, and take an imaginary journey to a significant event in their past. When they have explored the event, have them open their eyes, draw the event, and write about the experience in the foreign language they are practicing.

When they are learning the verb (to *love*), have students close their eyes and imagine themselves with five people they love. Have them tell each person why they are loved and then return, make a drawing of each person, and caption each with words from the foreign language.

Though we have discussed examples from only three of the possible academic areas found in the secondary school, all areas can be enhanced by the use of Integrative Education techniques.

In this chapter we have extended our concern for the education of gifted children into the adolescent years and specified programs and problems unique to the education of these students. While examples of integrative lessons presented to secondary gifted students have been given, those particularly interested in this population are asked to review chapter 6 and to adapt the integrative techniques to their classrooms. Do not allow the few examples given to limit the possibilities for your students. We are all creating new ways to include cognitive, affective, intuitive, and physical sensing functioning in all of the disciplines we teach. That is, of course, the joy of teaching.

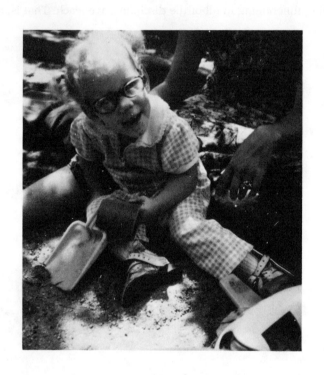

CHAPTER EIGHT

Areas of Concern in Gifted Education

This chapter presents discussions and information regarding

- labeling gifted learners.
- grading and its effect on gifted learners.
- underachieving gifted students.
- disadvantaged gifted students.
- culturally diverse gifted students.
- handicapped gifted learners.
- gifted females.
- career education for the gifted.

Children are not things to be molded, but people to be unfolded.

—Anonymous

The purpose of this chapter is to discuss and disseminate information on several areas within gifted education that have presented special problems. This chapter presents some suggestions for solutions and reports from programs that have been successful in remedying similar situations in their settings. This information should lead us to a clearer understanding of the nature of the problem. Mostly, in confronting issues that have not been successfully handled, we raise questions that only show our awareness that the problem exists. However, this can also be helpful, for as soon as we become aware of a problem, as soon as we can state a question clearly, we have begun the process that will lead us to the solution.

Here then is a discussion of concerns with labeling and grading gifted learners; underachieving, disadvantaged, culturally diverse, and handicapped gifted students; gifted females; and career education for the gifted.

You are sitting outside the principal's office waiting for the time of a previously arranged meeting to discuss the gifted program at her school. You begin to be aware of voices rising in volume inside. As the door opens, you hear clearly an angry, almost threatening statement, "Well, just what do you intend to do about it? You told me he was gifted!" The principal quietly comments, notices you, smiles, and finishes the conversation with the woman; still a little annoyed, the woman leaves. After joining the principal in her office, you learn that several weeks before, the woman's child had been identified for the gifted program. The parent had always wanted to be a musician and now felt that, if the child were gifted, he could become an accomplished violinist in no time. After three weeks, with the child totally uninterested in violin, the parent became very frustrated and when, finally, the violin teacher informed her that it would be best to stop the lessons, the parent came to the principal demanding that something be done.

Labeling Gifted Learners

Labeling students results in a change in parent and teacher expectations, as well as in the self-concept of the child. Often calls come to California State University, Los Angeles from parents who have just received a note from school that their child has been identified as gifted. The comment usually is "He (or she) was such a nice child. What do I do now?" Sometimes parents feel suddenly inadequate to guide their child's development once they know their child is "gifted." Sometimes the label results in very unreal expectations.

In high schools, labeling a student gifted can result in placement in every high track class, whether the student is advanced in that particular discipline or not.

An interesting, although frustrating, experience occurred at CSULA when we began a General Honors Program for students in their first two years who had shown a great deal of academic potential in high school. Immediately some professors began shifting their course presentation and requirements from basic information to synthesis of graduate level work. Those who did became very disappointed and angry at the students; they complained loudly against the program, all because of their expectations of "honors" students. Talking with them about student need or potential ability made no impression.

Labels create expectations. When using labels such as "gifted" or "honors," we must be very clear to state the precise meaning of the term, what it is and what it is not. Parents deserve more than an announcement of a new label for their child. We should arrange parent meetings to explain and answer questions regarding the concept of giftedness and its development at home and at school. We should communicate the meaning of giftedness and describe how the school experience will be different for the child after identification. Sending out additional information outlining ways the home can be involved in the further growth of the student would help.

When a school establishes a program for gifted learners, it should include inservice training for the entire faculty and staff regarding the meaning of giftedness and the importance of the new program. For the child's welfare and the success of the program, the school must work as a unit, and all of the personnel must see how the program will fit within the goals and structure of the school. Without such information, misunderstandings, hostility, and unnecessary obstructionism will be focused on the program, the responsible teacher, and the gifted child. As we saw earlier, teachers, administrators, and counselors often have very negative attitudes toward gifted students in most schools. Yet, by planning a program around the student's needs and purposefully communicating information on the program and giftedness in general, we can influence these attitudes to become favorable, even supportive.

If we label children gifted to improve their educational experience, then we have an obligation to keep the negative aspects of labeling from becoming the major effect.

> You attend a commencement program at a local high school. The senior class valedictorian, a lovely young woman, gives a pleasant, but not very insightful address. As the scholarships from local service organizations are announced, you notice that the students you know well from the Honors and Advanced Placement classes receive only a few awards. After the ceremony, you inquire of one of the students about the identity of the valedictorian, someone you had not known before. "Oh, she's a home economics major," you are told. "Her grade point average was higher than any of ours because we took all those accelerated classes." To your dismay, you discover this is also the reason the gifted students did not receive more of the service club special awards and scholarship money.

Grading Gifted Learners

To understand the problems in grading encountered by gifted students, we must first understand the problems inherent in the practice of grading itself. The practice of grading began as our society moved toward the goal of mass education. When it became impossible for school personnel to know each student and that student's ability, a system was devised to give a symbol, the grade, for each student's achievement. Individual ability disappeared into a more manageable, numerically manipulable representation of academic ability. Grades have been an integral part of schooling, indeed the major part, for more than half a century. Now it is difficult to conceive of schools functioning without them. Grading does not, however, contribute to the learning process and in many ways inhibits and impedes learning. Whatever reasons are given for continuing to use grading, it must be recognized as a force external to the student.

The reasons given for using grades (not evaluations, but grades) are these:

They provide a convenient communication of the student's academic progress to parents, administrators, other teachers, and the student.

They provide motivation for performance.

They help the school gain the cooperation of the parents in pursuing educational goals.

They establish an overall academic pattern of the student for other teachers, counselors, and administrators.

They establish data for educational research.

In the past fifty years a great deal of research has covered: the practice of grading; its effect on learning and on the learner; the merits of the practice; and the use of grades to predict future grades or success in life. You may find the results very interesting.

Grades Have No Inherent Stable Meaning and Are Low in Reliability

Grades are usually based on tests, observations, and performance as rated by the teacher. Tests are almost always subjectively constructed by the teacher, even when they are given and scored in an objective manner. Few teachers take the time needed or have learned the skills necessary to construct valid tests. Although observations made over time provide far more data than test scores, many teachers have not developed adequate observational skills; the observations they make are partly influenced by such things as their personal feelings about the student and the student's behavior, appearance, status, previous academic record, label, and so on (LaBenne and Greene, 1969; Reichstein and Pipkin, 1968; Rothney, 1955).

Teachers differ significantly in their interpretations of grades and in the standards they use. Even the philosophy of grading varies from teacher to teacher: some believe grades should show student effort; some grade on how much success a student has had in meeting a goal set by the teacher and student in consultation; some grade against an outside goal set up for the entire class or grade level. Many teachers grade according to a distribution dictated by the statistical representation of a normal population ("grading on the curve"). Although statisticians will quickly point out that the size of most classes makes the use of the curve technique totally inappropriate, it is, nevertheless, quite commonly used, especially in secondary and higher educational systems. Even with adaptations, this method of grading can be very unfair to the students and result in arbitrary and capricious grades (LaBenne and Greene, 1969; Pressey, 1925).

Researchers pointed out this variation in interpretation and its effect on grading in a number of studies where teachers from different classes, in some cases from different schools, were asked to grade the same papers. The range of grades on a single paper was extreme. Some more defensive teachers blamed the results on the material used, and they believed that the outcome would be different if papers and examinations from the more precise disciplines of math and science were used. If anything, the range in grades was even greater in the math and science studies. Even when graders have received intensive training to insure reliability, they disagree significantly. Such things as fatigue, personal values, neatness, organization, showing or not showing calculations all influence grading. Over a two-month period, teachers have been found to be inconsistent in remarking the same paper. And so it seems that variability in marks is not a function of the subject, but rather of the grader. While looking at what grades mean, we should mention that some teachers even use testing and test grades for punishment, e.g., the "pop quiz" to punish those who might not have studied (Dexter, 1935; Edwards, 1956; Rosenthal and Jacobsen, 1969; Starch and Elliott, 1912; Starch, 1913; Temple University, 1968; Tiegs, 1952).

Grades Do Not Predict Success in Careers, in Living, or in Level of Ability

Numerous studies continue to show little or no correlation between grades received in high school or college and future success in the world of work. There is only moderate correlation between test scores and grades with long-range academic performance and none with postacademic performance. Even in professions highly dependent on skills (e.g., engineering, teaching, physics) there is little relationship between grades and later success. The type of schools attended, the number of years of education and the people studied under and with all seem to have more correlation with success. The only predictive ability grades seem to have is on the basis of entry screening, where GPA is used for hiring, placement, or further study; but beyond this use as a screen, little correlation with job performance has been found. It has been pointed out that the GPA is an average or mean figure that flattens any high levels of achievement, leaving outstanding abilities hidden in some cases (Chansky, 1964; Drews, 1972; Hoyt, 1965; Lavin, 1965; Martin and Pacheres, 1962; Pallett, 1965; Wright, 1965).

For Most Students, Grades Do Not Motivate Learning

For a few successful students, grades provide the external motivation toward greater effort and achievement. A student who has experienced success repeatedly may be moved to perform for grades. Even with these students, we run the risk of lessening their intrinsic motivation and creating a reward situation that makes learning only a means, not a fulfilling or exciting pursuit in its own right. For less successful students, grades serve only to demean and debilitate their self-concept further. The research shows that downgraded students continue to fail.

Perrone and Male (1981) comment from their experience in interviews with high-achieving students that they "frequently dislike doing assignments and perceive a good grade not as recognition for what was produced but rather as payment for having endured such a painful or dull experience. Good grades may in fact lead good students to resent formal learning, while poor grades combined with a dislike of the learning task may lead poor achievers to abhor formal learning" (pp. 69–70).

Both those who are failing and others whose performance is mediocre will sometimes resort to failure-avoiding strategies such as false effort, academic cheating, or acting out in class to gain peer approval (Covington and Berry, 1976)

Intellectual ability may not be the determiner for the categorization of students that grading creates. Under the threat of grades, bright students balk at venturing into the unknown or trying any area in which they are not sure they will succeed. Boredom, irrelevant assignments, repetition, meaningless or unrealistic subject matter, and lack of opportunity to build skills all contribute to low grades. Grades have been shown to be poor indicators of student learning. Short term memorization, cheating, and other coping strategies result directly from grading practices; learning does not (Bowers, 1964; Chansky, 1962; Fala, 1968; Knowlton and Hamerlyneck, 1967; LaBenne and Greene, 1969). Researchers (Covington and Berry, 1976; Bidwell, 1973) have found that the excessive reliance on extrinsic rewards, the atmosphere of continual evaluation, and the fact that standards for success or failure are set by someone other than the student result in a breakdown in commitment and in self-regulated learning. When performance is exchanged for grades, many high achievers learn shortcuts to achievement rewards and learn to regard out-of-class learning as unrewarding (Doyle, 1978). Maehr and Stallings (1972) provide evidence that continuing motivation may be directly affected by the nature of evaluation procedures. They found that external evaluation, even though used to maintain or increase performance in the classroom, does so at the expense of negative effects on continued motivation.

Evaluation Without Grades Is Facilitating to the Learning Process

Allowing students the knowledge of their strengths and weaknesses while giving them support and opportunities to develop their skills is important to learning. Providing an environment where mistakes are valued as learning experiences promotes exploration and increases areas of knowledge. Reducing anxiety promotes long-term retention and higher quantities of knowledge gained. Evaluation, a continuous process, can use many sources for data collection. In evaluating, the teacher is the facilitator who helps the students discover their strengths and weaknesses and their interests and abilities, and who guides their growth toward greater fulfillment of their potential.

> The question is not how many of the "right" things the student remembered, what the student did to the subject, or how well he compared with others. It is rather how well did the student do in the things the teacher and student agreed were important, what the subject did to the student, and how he compared to his own goals and objectives (LaBenne and Greene, 1969, p. 87).

Gifted students have special problems with grading practices. When placed in homogeneously grouped classes, they earned significantly lower grades than when placed in heterogeneously grouped classes, although there were no differences between the groups on standardized achievement tests. These grades become a part of their permanent record, with notations about honors classes or special sections seldom made (Chansky, 1964; Hausdorff and Farr, 1965).

Gifted students in pullout classes often encounter grading practices that penalize them for missing class sessions while they attend their special class. One junior high student related that his math teacher not only held him responsible for material covered during the classes he missed, although he was working on second year algebra in his gifted class, but would explain assignments for the week and how he wanted them done while he was out of the room. When he returned and asked for the information, the teacher said, "You're gifted. Figure it out." One of the reasons for the criticism by gifted students and their parents of special classes and honor programs is the inequitable grading.

As evidenced in our vignette, students in high schools find scholarships, honors at graduation, and even membership in honor societies based on their grade point averages. I have, on several occasions, noted the frustration of gifted students passed over for special awards because of their attendance in the honors classes. In an attempt to correct the situation, some schools have adopted a grading policy that requires accelerated classes to give all students A's, or in some cases A's and B's. This becomes threatening to some teachers; and those who pride themselves in being "tough" will likely circumvent the rule by unreasonable assignments or pressure on students to transfer from their classes. It is important that accelerated classes be taught only by teachers who do not feel threatened by bright students.

Parents have often been the cause of schools keeping or reverting to grading practices. In many schools, we find teachers and administrators pleased by the conference method of evaluating. Although it is often more work, many teachers feel it more clearly reflects the student's achievements and is far more diagnostic in nature. However, they complain that the parents insist on knowing how their children compare to other children, rather than their strengths and weaknesses; what grade they received, rather than in what areas they should be guided.

In a survey taken of parents and teachers by the California Association for the Gifted, the following questions produced some interesting answers:

1. What grading practices are used in honors classes in your district or your school?

   In one district program no grades were given. 70 percent used a normal curve or traditional grading with several parents complaining that grades are used as motivators and require more work to obtain than the same grade in a regular class. Thirty percent make special provisions such as narrative reporting with grades, counseling during day-to-day evaluation, and detailed reporting of data from projects used for grades.

2. Do you feel that grading practices are a major consideration in whether students enroll in these classes?

   Better than half of the teachers and parents answering believed this to be a factor.

3. If you feel grading practices penalize gifted students or discourage involvement in honors classes, what provisions are being made to remedy the situation?

   In half the cases it was reported that either the local parent group or the individual parent recommended a change to the local School Board, with no results. Others had made no attempt to change the policy.

4. What would you recommend be done locally or statewide to alter grading procedures?

   Some suggestions: self-evaluation, grading on an individualized basis, conferencing, no grades in honors classes, weighted grades for honors classes, inservicing for parents and teachers on grading practices and policies, use of more comments, special notation of honors courses on the transcript.

Grades are quickly read, easy-to-manipulate symbols. In our ever growing school system, they provide a quick way to categorize and group children. However, grades are also unfair, misleading, meaningless in most cases, and damaging to the self-concept of both the bright and the less bright child. They create pressures and anxieties for both the teacher and the students. They neither motivate nor contribute to learning. They communicate information on a par with chance estimates; at best, what they say is neither explicit nor constructive. But for many parents and teachers alike, grades are the most important part of the school's responsibility.

Syphers (1972) tells of a teacher who wanted a different use to be made of the students' work and devised a way for students to do their own diagnoses. She displayed a checklist of common weaknesses and had the students organize and file sets of their papers. At regularly designated times, the students examined their papers to discover which mistakes they repeatedly made and why (due to carelessness, haste, lack of skill, misreading directions, etc.). She found that self-diagnosis created involvement on the part of the students in their own improvement and did not impose the stifling effects of grading. It also saved her a great deal of time. Even when you must ultimately record a grade, self-evaluation can be an important part of the process. It is possible to evaluate constructively and, if learning is our goal, the effort is really worth it.

I would like you to meet Rich. Rich attends a large integrated high school in the suburbs of a large city where the majority of the students come from middle-class families. He is athletic, good looking, and always well-dressed and well-groomed. His family has fairly traditional values and aspirations of achievement for their children. Rich, the third of five children, has an older brother and sister who were both high academic achievers. The father was a grade school dropout, but has worked his way from a dock loader to an office job with the firm. The mother was a high school graduate, and her family is from a decidedly higher social stratum than her husband's.

Although Rich has been identified as a gifted learner, he does not belong to the group of school leaders and achievers who determine school activities. Instead, he has chosen a peer group of underachievers like himself among whom he is considered a leader.

Rich is known to be very good at sports and is probably one of the best tennis players in his school, although he refuses to try out for the school tennis team.

Rich has been placed in advanced classes, although he maintains about a C average. His teachers often comment that he is not living up to his capability. Part of the reason for his low grades is his habit of putting off all assignments to the last minute and then doing only enough to get by. He is a good reader, has an exceptional vocabulary, and reads extensively in books unrelated to his school subjects. When Rich "tunes in" to a class, rarely, he can pull an A without any problem. But that is only when he gets excited about the class or the subject, as when he got into government last year and became so involved with politics, political systems, and strategies that he spent hours before and after school questioning the teacher about everything he knew. He ended up being picked to attend a model government conference in the state capital last summer, but now, with his new classes, he has "tuned out" again.

Although Rich is outgoing and open with his peers, he is extremely nervous and uncomfortable around authority figures, such as teachers. He lacks confidence in himself and is not very self-accepting. Once he was allowed to contract cooperatively with his teacher for a project in which he felt he would be interested. He set unrealistically high standards for himself, even though the teacher insisted that she would settle for far less. He procrastinated for weeks and then gave up the entire project saying, "If I can't do a good job on something, I just won't do it."

In trying to understand Rich and help him with his underachieving pattern, one of his teachers met with Rich and his family several times in their home. Although his father expressed the desire for Rich to attend college, he seemed to have a very negative attitude toward education. His father was very insistent on his son's strict obedience to the rules, seeing each act of compliance as a minor victory for himself and a defeat for his son. There was an obvious emotional gap between the father and son. Rich's father seemed to express only two attitudes toward him, indifference or hostility. He seemed totally incapable of responding to any of Rich's achievements, no matter how excellent. The teacher's effort to discuss the accomplishments Rich had made in the government class were met with stoney silence. It seemed as if there were actually a competition between the two, wherein the father hid his fear of losing behind demands for perfection and a refusal to recognize perfection should his son approach it. Thus, for Rich to attempt any new task meant risking almost certain reaffirmation of his inabilities, his self-believed worthlessness, and that would be even more traumatic should his efforts actually produce less than average grades or results. To fail became the one thing Rich could not allow. To quote Rich, "If I can't do a good job on something, I just won't do it."

Underachieving Gifted Students

Underachievement in gifted children is one of the most baffling, most frustrating problems a parent or teacher can face. You can see the child's possibilities, occasionally you're given a glimpse of the brilliance, but then it's gone, replaced by a wall of apathy or seeming unconcern. But all of this may be just a facade, for the underachiever may be even more frustrated than we are.

At least two types of underachievers have been designated. Those who underachieve only on occasion, as when a particularly difficult home problem erupts or a clash occurs with one particular teacher, are referred to as *situational underachievers*. They generally cause little real concern beyond getting help with the immediate problem.

Then there is the *chronic underachiever*, whose pattern recurs again and again, presenting a problem particularly resistant to remediation. In discussing this type of underachiever, keep in mind that the literature cautions us to be sure the underachievement is not of organic origin, by running the proper diagnostic tests for physical problems. If these measures do not indicate causation, then there are other places to look.

Lowther (1962) suggests that the term *underachiever* should be dropped as a label, for it is an inadequate and deceptively simple explanation of a very complex process. He suggests that it might be more useful to refer to *high, average,* or *low achievers,* for we would then need no explanatory implications, nor would our concern rest on any presumed ability-achievement relationship. Thorndike (1963) feels that there is no such thing as underachievement, because what is implied is a standard of expected achievement, and it would be more accurate to discuss this phenomenon as overprediction. In light of the complexity of the problem and what we now understand to be additional problems for the student caused by labeling, Lowther's suggestion should be kept in mind. There is, however, a growing body of data regarding the underachievement problem that we should consider.

We define here the underachieving gifted student as someone who has shown exceptional performance on a measure of intelligence and who, nevertheless, does not perform as well as expected for students of the same age on school related tasks. To show evidence of low performance, either achievement test scores or grades assigned by teachers could be used. Pippert and Archer (1963) reported that, when identifying by only comparing IQ with grades, they found twenty-one underachieving students, but when comparing IQ with achievement tests, they found nineteen underachievers in their population. Most important was the fact that only two of the forty children were found in both comparison groups!

While this is a limited definition of gifted underachievement, we cannot in good conscience use the "not performing up to capability" definition when we have no measures of capacity, innate or otherwise. The measure of achievement on intelligence tests and the evidence of performance on school related tasks should show a considerable amount of discrepancy. Underachievement becomes especially evident when you observe a student over time and find a noticeable pattern—when you see the special moments, the brilliance. To use any other criterion would create an unmanageable number of underachievers that would certainly include most of the gifted population, as they are so rarely challenged to use their ability. Whitmore (1980) reports that with this definition we may have 15–50 percent underachievers among the gifted population, though she feels that if the scores of all gifted students on individual aptitude tests were compared with their level of performance, we might find as many as 70 percent underachieving.

In a larger sense, everyone of us is underachieving, as we continue to use less than one-tenth of our brain's potential. Therefore, while we surely expect more of gifted third-grade students than we do of typical third-grade students, those who do not at least perform at an average level will be designated as *underachieving*.

Characteristics of Underachievers

You've met Rich. What about other underachievers? What are they like? The traits or characteristics of underachievers have been reported in many studies, although no one student would be expected to have all or even more than a few traits from this compilation. To complicate our identification of these children further, it has been noted that such children may be aggressive and act out their frustration by seeking attention negatively or they may withdraw and quietly allow their talents to waste away (Whitmore, 1980).

The following is a compilation of characteristics identified among underachievers (Bachtold, 1969; Combs, 1964; Gallagher, 1964; Gowan, 1957; Karnes et al., 1961; Kurtz and Swenson, 1951; Morgan, 1952; Morrow and Wilson, 1961; O'Shea, 1970; Pearlman, 1952; Perkins, 1965; Raph, Goldberg, and Passow, 1966; Roberts, 1960; Rust and Ryan, 1953; Shaw, 1964; Shaw and Black, 1960; Shaw and McCuen,

1960; Terman and Oden, 1947; Walsh, 1956; Wellington and Wellington, 1965; Whitmore, 1980);

A finding repeated in most studies is the low self-concept of underachievers. They are negative in their evaluations of themselves. Their feelings of inferiority may be demonstrated by distrust, indifference, lack of concern, and even hostility toward others. They believe no one likes them.

They often feel rejected by their family; they feel that their parents are dissatisfied with them.

Because of a feeling of helplessness, they may take no responsibility for their actions, externalizing conflict and problems.

They may show marked hostility toward adult authority figures and general distrust of adults.

They may have an autonomous focus, resistant to influence from teacher or parent.

They may feel victimized.

They often do not like school or their teachers and choose companions who have negative attitudes toward school, also.

They may seem rebellious.

Weak motivation for academic achievement has been noted, and they may lack academic skills.

They tend to have poor study habits, do less homework, frequently nap when trying to study, and leave more of their work incomplete.

They are less intellectually adaptive.

They are less persistent, less assertive, and show high levels of withdrawal in classroom situations.

They hold lower leadership status and are less popular with their peers.

They are often less mature than achievers (e.g., lack self-discipline, procrastinate, show unwillingness to complete tasks deemed unpleasant, have high distractibility, act highly impulsively, and are unwilling to face unpleasant realities).

They often show poor personal adjustment and express feelings of being restricted in their actions.

They may not have any hobbies, interests, or activities that could occupy their spare time.

They are often test phobic and have poor test results.

They tend to have lower aspirations than achievers and do not have a clear idea of vocational goals.

They are not able to think or plan future goals.

They tend to state their goals very late and often choose goals that are not in line with their major interests or abilities. Often the goals they adopt have been set for them.

In choosing a career, they show preferences for manual activities, business, sales occupations, or anything with a strong persuasive trend, over more socially concerned or professional occupations.

Causes for Underachievement

While reasons for underachievement are quite complex and must be individually assessed for each learner, some definite patterns of causation have been reported and seem to occur with great frequency.

The Personality of the Child

Whitmore (1980) has done a most thorough job of bringing together the findings that aid us in understanding the gifted underachiever. Though she admits that the research findings available at this time would indicate that the personality of under-achievers as described by the listed traits is certainly strongly involved in the problem of why they underachieve, she believes that such traits are only a part of the reason. There are, Whitmore states, internal pressures that influence the behaviors we observe, such as the gifted person's need for perfectionism, supersensitivity, and deficiency in social skills. There are, however, also external factors that may be equally at fault in creating this problem. From outside sources may come society's pressure to isolate one who is different, even if that difference would be beneficial to the group; the pressure of societal expectations, which intensify the problems of the perfectionism and sensitivity found within the gifted learner; and to all of these we may too often add the lack of appropriate educational provisions, which include inappropriate curriculum, a counterproductive instructional style and philosophy of the teacher, and the punitive social climate created by classroom peers.

Whitmore writes of the vulnerability that these pressures, both internal and external, create for the gifted learner and how the very characteristics typical of their high level of intelligence make it easy for them to feel rejected and valueless. She reports that parents and teachers often admit that children who learn quickly and think creatively tend to make them feel uncomfortable and that the child's endless questioning and verbalization cause them to feel irritated.

There is some indication that underachievement is a different problem for girls than for boys. Shaw and McCuen (1960) investigated patterns of underachievement of gifted students in grades 11 and 12. They found that male underachievers began getting lower grades than achievers in first grade; underachievement became significant by third grade and more apparent each following year. Female underachievers exceeded achievers in first through fifth grade and began their decline in sixth grade. The difference became most apparent in grade nine. For both groups, the data demonstrate that the problem of underachievement worsens each year between third and twelfth grades. Barrett (1957) found evidence of underachievement at least as early as fifth grade and found that low achievers consistently did poorly on tests of numerical and abstract reasoning. Some of my students have found that these scores are good predictors of success with disadvantaged populations.

Pierce and Bowman (1960) found that girls respond to dominant parents by achieving, while boys require freedom to achieve and are inhibited by authoritarian control. Roberts (1960) found underachieving girls to be more lacking in self-confidence, more suggestible, impulsive, and vacillating, and showing a greater external locus of control. Underachieving boys were more demanding, headstrong, rebellious, undependable, impatient, and indecisive. Bachtold (1969) found that underachieving girls in the fifth grade lacked self-confidence, were more excitable, and showed less self-control. Boys demonstrated less emotional stability, seriousness, and sensitivity.

In all the studies reported, the incidence of underachievement in males was at least twice that found in females. Whitmore reported that 90 percent of all referrals for placement in the Underachieving Gifted Program in Cupertino, California were male. It has been suggested that this results from the different expectations and opportunities provided by our society for females. Some gifted students, especially adolescent girls, feel that they risk unpopularity if they reveal their high academic ability. In many high school settings, academic achievement is not valued, and conformity is the yardstick of success.

Another cause of underachievement unique to gifted learners stems from their varied and numerous interests. They may, without proper guidance, extend their interests in too many areas, engage in too many activities, and be unable to set appropriate priorities. It is possible for gifted students to get involved in so many things that they do nothing well.

The Home and/or Parents

The literature indicates that the causes for underachievement can be found in the personality of the gifted child, in the home, and/or in the interaction between the children and the parents (Bricklin and Bricklin, 1967; Daniel, 1960; Kimball, 1953; McGillivray, 1964; Morrow and Wilson, 1961; Pierce and Bowman, 1960; Shaw and Black, 1960; Raph et al., 1966; and Wellington and Wellington, 1965). The families of underachievers differ in many ways from families of achieving students.

In families of high achieving students, often—

parents are more interested in their children;
the fathers are important life influences;
mothers are more responsible and independent;
parents have higher educational aspirations for their children;
parents are better educated;
families are smaller;
the student is often the first born or only child.

In families of underachieving students, often—

the student is more dependent on the mother;
the father is rejecting, domineering, gives little warmth or affection;
the relationship between father and daughter or father and son is negative or nonexistent;
parents set unrealistic goals for students, and the students imagine that they are only as valuable or "good" as their accomplishments;
parents allow achievement to go unrewarded;
the students identify less with their parents;
there are deep social and emotional problems in the family;
parents are less active and less supportive of students;
the student's achievements present a threat to the parents and their adult superiority;
parents are less sharing of ideas, affection, trust, or approval;
parents are more restrictive and severe in their punishment.

In some cases, the entire neighborhood devalues education and has caused some researchers to observe that low achieving, low socioeconomic students seem to fail not because of an initial lack of motivation to learn, but because basic learning processes learned in their own communities are not contiguous with those required for academic success (Bricklin and Bricklin, 1967; Brown, 1971; Fine, 1967; Kimball, 1953).

Coleman (1966), Gallagher (1964), and Kurtz and Swenson (1951) all found the causes for underachievement different with the disadvantaged and culturally diverse gifted student. They found that when underachievement occurs:

The subculture does not support academic achievement;
Academic activity is seen as "sissy" for boys and too aggressive for girls; the subculture supports sex role stereotypes.
Low aspirations for career goals center on mechanical or survival skills.
Educational goals are nonexistent.

The School

One source of underachievement mentioned less frequently than the home, although still of major importance, is that of the actual school situation. Whitmore (1980) suggests the schools may be not only a principle cause, but one that is most likely to yield to remediation. By changing the unproductive patterns traditionally found in all too many classrooms, we may prevent a large amount of the underachievement that we now observe. She states:

> Regardless of the extent to which innate personality characteristics may contribute to the development of the underachiever's problems, it seems much more useful for educators to examine how the environment might contribute to the child's difficulty and thereby be modified to help eliminate the problem.

> The actual causes of underachievement are a mixture of the student's characteristics . . . and a social environment that does not meet the personal needs of the child. Factors of the social environment that can contribute to the development of negative attitudes and underachieving behavior include external pressures of unrealistic expectations; emphasis on conformity and convergent thinking; a lack of rewards or the existence of social penalties for creativity and initiative; rigidity and inflexibility; excessive competition and criticism; and personally unrewarding curriculum and required activities (pp. 190–191).

Predominant in this causal cluster is the incompetent or insecure teacher. Evans (1965) has grouped the behaviors of teachers known to contribute to underachievement into the following types of teachers, who—

must maintain superiority in the field of knowledge;
impose unrealistic goals and standards (the perfectionist);
use threats, ridicule, warnings, and ultimatums; rarely show warmth or acceptance; are cold and impersonal;
are too easy; do not present a challenge;
have predictable, routine schedules; do not present a stimulating environment.

Bricklin and Bricklin (1967) and Fine (1967) also found poor teaching to be a major cause of underachievement in gifted students.

Closely related is the problem of poor work habits so many gifted students face upon meeting academic challenges (i.e., entering universities). After many years of learning in nonstimulating environments with little academic involvement, these students are required to perform with excellence. They find they do not have the basic knowledge, the academic tools or processes, or the habits of sustained inquiry to aid them. This problem may account for some of the large number of dropouts among gifted learners. Of the top 10 percent in the high school graduating class, it has been estimated that at least 27 percent did not continue their education. Of those who did, 70 percent lived in communities where attitudes toward college attendance were favorable. Of the boys, 85 percent continued, but only 64 percent of the girls did so (Kimball, 1953; Wright and Jung, 1959). Cassel and Coleman (1962) reported that only 7–10 percent of the students capable of college work actually attended. Douglass (1969) estimates that, of the 7.5 million dropouts in this decade, 10 percent (750,000) will have IQs in the top one-fourth of the population.

Remediation/Prevention

The earlier remediation for underachievement starts, the more effective it is; however, most reports on remediation look at secondary students. The availability of counseling at that level (which has been seen as a major intervention strategy) tries to rationalize this focus. Many of the projects yield disappointments both in the amount of change effected and in the time the change remained evident. Intervention during the elementary years, involving the entire family in a group counseling mode, has had the most and longest lasting impact (Bricklin and Bricklin, 1967; Fine, 1967; Gallagher, 1975; Satir, 1972; Shaw and Black, 1960; Shaw and McCuen, 1960; Shouksmith and Taylor, 1964).

Group counseling as an intervention strategy has been reported as successful in a number of studies:

Broedel (1958)—Adolescent gifted students who participated in group counseling made greater gains in reducing inappropriate behavior and raising grade point averages and in standardized achievement tests than uncounseled students.

Baymur and Patterson (1960)—Underachieving high school gifted students who participated in either individual or group counseling over a semester improved slightly in grades; the students in group counseling showed the most favorable results. A third group, after a one-time only pep talk about bringing up their grades, fell below the performance of the noncounseled control group. Unfortunately, parents and teachers too often use this very form of intervention just as unsuccessfully.

Ohlsen and Proff (1960)—Underachievers (eighth grade) improved in interpersonal relationships with peers, siblings, and parents and in acceptance of self in a group counseling situation that met twice a week for eight weeks. No improvement was made in academic performance or self-concept.

Shouksmith and Taylor (1964)—Researchers obtained positive results with preadolescent underachievers and their parents: eight of twelve were no longer underachievers in less than a year.

Other forms of counseling have also been studied:

Ewing and Gilbert (1967)—Researchers found that individual counseling improved the scholastic achievement of highly able underachieving students over noncounseled highly able underachieving students at the college level (freshmen). Effects seemed to have persisted into the next semester.

Perkins and Wicas (1971)—Counselors worked with bright underachieving ninth-grade boys alone, mothers alone, and mothers and sons simultaneously. All groups showed improvements in GPA.

Mallison (1972)—Intermediate gifted underachievers attended individual counseling, human relations, or academic groups for six months. Groups in human
relations and academic groups improved academically, but the human relations
group also improved in personal and social adjustment and maintained their
gains in the follow-up testing, while the academic group did not.

Shaw and Black (1960)—The researchers developed a family counseling model
that was quite successful. At the first several sessions, underachieving students
met with parents of other underachieving students to enable them to express
themselves openly. The parents expressed their views for half the period, the students the other half. After several sessions, the students then met with their own
parents for the remainder of the program.

In addition to counseling, some studies have investigated curricular and classroom organizational changes:

Goldberg (1959)—In a three-year program at the high school level, value was
found in grouping underachievers with other gifted students and placing them
with a supportive teacher. Goldberg emphasized the importance of the teacher in
the success of the project. She felt that, before any program could be implemented, an adequate educational, psychological, and social diagnosis of each
underachieving student was essential. At the end of the study, Goldberg drew the
following conclusions:

Academic underachievement appears to be a symptom of a variety of more basic personal and social problems.

Underachieving students who improved were able to identify with a teacher
who was consistently supportive and interested in them. The teacher helped
them acquire necessary skills missed earlier.

It was more effective to separate teaching and guidance functions (because of
grading).

Grouping underachievers together alone is unwise, although Whitmore's data
indicate that such grouping is quite productive. Grouping in regular classroom
by subject is not recommended.

Karnes, McCoy, Zehrbok, Wollershein, and Clarizio (1963)—Similarly, they found
that underachieving gifted pupils enrolled in homogeneously grouped gifted
classes made greater gains in academics, creativity, and perceived acceptance by
peers than underachieving gifted enrolled in heterogeneously grouped classes.

Purkey (1969)—Purkey reported on Project Self-Discovery, a program designed
to promote social and personal development among bright, underachieving
students. There were twelve chapters of reading and writing exercises dealing
with interpersonal relations, self-confidence, individual differences, feelings, and
self-discipline. While the material was designed to be used with groups or in
independent study, it is believed that a group guidance format would bring
about more significant differences than when used for an independent study,
correspondence-style format.

The Great Cities School Improvement Program—The program used such aids as
team teaching, parents in classrooms, different media, home visitation, and
workshops for teachers and parents.

The children in Whitmore's (1980, pp. 192, 193) program identified the following elements of their previous classroom environments, which they believed contributed significantly to the development of their underachievement.

Lack of genuine respect for each individual
A competitive social climate
Inflexibility and rigidity
Stress on external evaluation
The failure syndrome and criticism predominating
Adult/teacher control
An unrewarding curriculum

Whitmore believes that chronic underachievement by gifted students can be prevented by educational programs that allow these students to meet their needs. She also feels that early patterns of underachievement can be reversed through special education in elementary school. In her book she gives a detailed account of how effective classrooms can be developed. The similarity to the responsive, integrative environments we have discussed in chapters 4 and 6 is striking.

In 1973 Martinson warned that gifted children placed in regular classrooms may regress to the achievement level of their classmates, may become discipline problems as a result of boredom, and/or may withdraw to their own interests. She pointed out that there was evidence that students in the highest range of intellectual ability may have the greatest difficulty with adjustment in the regular classroom.

Both Whitmore and Pirozzo (1982) support the emphasis on a nonthreatening classroom environment where these children can engage in an extensive period of self-discovery. What seems to be indicated by these data is more special class placement, especially for the gifted underachiever. It may turn out to be, as Whitmore suggests, the least restrictive environment for the gifted child.

From the projects, the investigations, and the observations of teachers and parents, come the following suggestions for those who are concerned about the gifted underachiever.

If You Are a Parent:

1. Provide an intellectually stimulating, curiosity-producing atmosphere in your home.
2. Establish a close, mutually respectful relationship with your child.
3. Become role models of behavior you desire your child to have.
4. Be interested in your child's activities at home and at school.
5. Do not compare siblings; each child is unique.
6. Help your child establish effective time priorities.
7. Guide your children toward goals of their interest; do not set goals for them.
8. Make your demands and rules reasonable and mutual.
9. Show your affection, trust, and approval.
10. Support your child; get involved.

If You Are a Teacher or a Counselor:

1. Value achievements of high ability students.
2. Assess each student regularly, beginning in elementary school; know your students' profiles.
3. Provide opportunities for students to build their self-concept.
4. Create a learning environment: open, accepting, warm, intellectually challenging.

5. Give the underachiever an opportunity to focus on an area of ability, such as music, art, athletics.
6. Be available when help is needed; be sure to have conferences periodically about personal as well as academic matters.
7. Arrange group sessions with peers and with family.
8. Look for ways to meet individual needs (e.g., a place to study, tutorial help).
9. Involve parents in school activities.
10. Offer college and vocational guidance early.
11. If more than 15 percent of the gifted in your school are seriously underachieving, look carefully at your program.

Jerry had just moved into the neighborhood. This was the ninth move the family had made since Jerry started school five years ago. Jerry's father had just started another new job and the family had moved to join him, hoping that this time there would be enough money so that his mother wouldn't have to worry so much. There really wasn't much involved in moving as there weren't many things to move, a few dishes and pans, some blankets and clothes, his few books his mother had given him, his little sister's toys, and the family TV set. His father always rented furnished houses and although the furniture was far from new and there never was much of it, it never had to be moved.

The school Jerry now attends has a gifted class, and by the second week he was there, Jerry was invited to attend this special class. For the first time he found other children who were interested in a lot of the same things he liked; he could talk to them just as he talked to his mother. He had an unlimited number of books he could read, as there were shelves filled with books right in the classroom. He began working on a special project with another boy in his gifted class and began to find that he really liked his new school.

Although there was no space to study at home and the sound of the TV made what room there was difficult for any concentration, Jerry could go to his class early and stay late and often work at his friend's house. After only six months Jerry mastered skills far beyond his grade level and began exploring a lot of areas he had never even thought about. His teacher was really interested in his progress and shared her pleasure with his mother.

One day when Jerry was coming home he saw a rent-a-trailer in front of the house, and his father was loading their things into it. Jerry ran to find out what was happening. "We're leaving this dump. I'm going to the desert to work. A guy told me there was a lot of good jobs there. We don't have to tell no one. I don't care if we do owe rent. It'll serve that jerk right for charging us so much on this dump. Come on, Jerry, get it in gear. We'll be in the desert by morning."

Disadvantaged Gifted Students

First, we must clearly delineate the population we call *disadvantaged gifted students*. The terms *disadvantaged* and *culturally diverse* have often been used interchangeably in program reports, informational articles, and research reports. This practice is very misleading. While some children who are disadvantaged are also culturally diverse, many are not. And while some culturally diverse students are disadvantaged, again, many are not. In this discussion *disadvantaged* will mean being reared by poor, lower class parents out of the economic (instead of cultural) mainstream. This population seems characterized more by poverty than by cultural difference. In referring to *culturally diverse learners* we speak of any student (such as Rosa) whose rearing is more typical of a culture that differs significantly in values and attitudes from the dominant culture. These students have unique problems even when not reared in conditions of poverty.

A major problem encountered in providing for gifted students among the disadvantaged is the attitude, shared by teachers and parents alike, that giftedness could not exist in lower class populations. Such attitudes make identification very difficult. We have seen in chapter 2 that the nurture of intellectual ability depends more on child rearing patterns and attitudes than on social class or financial condition. For parents living in poverty, development of such facilitating conditions is not easy, but it is certainly not impossible. Because we have become aware of a gradual decline with age in measured intelligence among lower class students, several projects in infant development have sent teachers into lower class homes to teach parents how to use existing materials and resources to nurture their children. Such projects have met with success and important sibling carry-over. Many more projects have brought high risk children out of their downward cycle through preschool group intervention programs (see chapter 2).

Left to the educational opportunities available at existing schools in lower class areas, data show that the longer the children are in these schools, the further behind they become in achievement. Substandard performance is expected. Even if disadvantaged students begin school with relatively few problems, and their reading achievement is at grade level in the early grades, these students fall increasingly behind national reading norms. Although arithmetic achievement stays closer to national norms, these scores also fall as the student moves through the school system. Intelligence test scores go down in proportion to the time spent in school. Average drops of as much as 20 points in measured intelligence have been reported as disadvantaged students move through the grades (Coleman et al., 1966; Passow, Goldberg, and Tannenbaum, 1967; Pressman, 1969; Sexton, 1961). The fact is that, until recently, few gifted students have emerged from this population because no one thought to look.

Our first task is to make parents, teachers, principals, and boards of education aware that the gifted can be found in lower class homes. Then we must know how to identify them. In chapter 5 (p. 183) we reviewed the problems and alternate possibilities for identifying these gifted learners. Some traits of disadvantaged gifted learners that help with their identification (Baldwin, 1973; Farrell, 1973; McMillin, 1975; Torrance, 1964), where testing often fails, are observations of the following:

High mathematical abilities
Alertness, curiosity
Independence of action
Initiative, eagerness to do new things
Fluency in nonverbal communication
Imagination in thinking
Flexibility in approach to problems
Learning quickly through experience
Retaining and using ideas and information well
Showing a desire to learn in daily work

Originality and creativity in thinking
Responding well to visual media
Leadership ability in peer group
Responsible social behavior
Varied interests
Ability to generalize learning to other areas and to show relationships among appar-
    ently unrelated ideas
Resourcefulness, ability to solve problems by ingenious methods
Entrepreneurial ability, readily making money on various projects or activities
Imaginative story telling, language rich in imagery
Mature sense of humor
Responsiveness to the concrete

Once identified as gifted, these disadvantaged learners may be grouped with
more advantaged gifted students. Such grouping will aid them in many ways, but
only if the teacher is aware that the needs of these learners may be quite different. It
is unfair to expect lower class gifted children to be like middle and upper class
gifted children.

Some characteristics have been found to differentiate lower class gifted students
from the more advantaged students. Frierson (1965) showed that differences in attitudes and interests exist, although he found no evidence of physical or personality
differences. In interests and activities, upper status gifted differed from lower status
gifted in the quantity and quality of their reading, in their awareness of parental aspirations for college attendance, in their positive attitudes toward school, and in
their lower preference for competitive team sports. However, the personality patterns and interests of upper and lower status gifted children were more similar than
were the personality patterns and interests of lower status gifted and average children. Frierson also found that lower class children, placed in a special program
based on their giftedness by the second grade, differed markedly in achievement, attitudes, and aspirations from other lower class gifted children by the time they
reached the upper grades.

Houston (Goodall, 1972) found that, when asked to repeat a story to another
child who then repeats the story to the teacher, black lower class children do not
score as well on accuracy as do middle class Caucasian and black children. The
lower class children did score higher than the others on embellishing the story,
which, it was pointed out, would not give them high scores on intelligence tests.

Rohrer and Edmonson (1960) suggest some important differences in family
structures and values between lower and middle class families that put the learner
at a disadvantage. They have identified four major family patterns: Middle Class,
Matriarchy, Gang, and Nuclear.

Middle Class families hold values that view education as an important aspect of
life. When lower class families identify with this group and become upwardly mobile, these values take precedence over earlier religious, family, or political affilia-
tions. However, if the pattern of *Matriarchy*, mother and daughter aligned against
the world, is adhered to, there is a strong female dependency and male alienation
that is not conducive to intellectual growth or independent thinking. The equivalent
male pattern, the *Gang*, fosters aggressive independence, group secrecy and loyalty,
and exaggerated masculinity. As educational achievement is seen by the gang as a
feminine characteristic, alignment with such a pattern inhibits intellectual develop-

ment. The *Nuclear* family, as defined in the study, does develop respect for parent-hood, reliable employment, and family support. However, it is also characterized by suspicion and distrust of the outside world. Education is favored so long as it supports the unity of the family. If, as often is the case in higher education, discovery of different ideas and values brings the possibility of a different world view to the student, education may then be rejected. Any of these last three patterns would be antithetical to gifted development.

In a project conducted in the Los Angeles city schools to differentiate disadvantaged gifted learners from the regularly identified gifted learners (Arnold, 1974), the following classroom behaviors were noted among separate criteria (disadvantaged) gifted:

They exhibit greater dependence on the teacher for direction, which reduces their ability for self-directed activity.

They reason in a more step-by-step process.

They appear to have more patience in dealing with tasks not easily resolved.

The study also noted that parental involvement appeared to decrease from highly gifted, to regularly gifted, to special-criteria gifted.

Sisk (1973) states that the most serious deficiencies for this type of child are in cognitive functioning (e.g., the ability to observe and state sequences of events, to perceive cause and effect relationships, and to categorize); language skills (e.g., limited vocabularies and nonstandard grammar), and reading. She states, "The variations in responses are due in part to the individual's motivation and in part to the availability of adequate adult mediators who can help the child develop concepts with which to interpret his environment" (p. 5). These deficits may result in classroom behavior we seldom associate with gifted students: negative attitudes toward school, toward teachers, and toward their own achievement; inability to focus on long-term goals; and the use of violence in resolving problems. Baldwin (1973) notes that disadvantaged gifted students have seldom been exposed to books and magazines at home and have been "starved for verbal encounters" (p. 11). She also notes that, as with most underachievers, disadvantaged gifted students exhibit an external locus of control.

Riessman (1962) reports differences in learning style, which include: spatial—not temporal; physical—not aural; content centered—not form centered; inductive—not deductive. You can begin to see how difficult it would be to plan for only characteristically gifted children when disadvantaged gifted children are also in the program.

As we have seen in chapter 2, intellectual development is an important part of infant and early childhood education. For those children who could begin this actualization process only to have it limited or interrupted, intervention should occur as early as possible. However, most programs for the gifted, not to mention the disadvantaged gifted, do not begin until the middle elementary grades. There are a number of programs aimed at improving language skill in the disadvantaged population that would have a direct bearing on the giftedness of the student (e.g., McConnell, Horton, and Smith, 1969, whose preschool program for the disadvantaged showed significant gains; Deutsch and Deutsch, 1968; Schaefer and Aaronson, 1972). Other experimental projects, classes, and schools have focused on changing the language deficit problem, as well as other gaps in the education of the disadvantaged gifted. They come and go, usually not because of lack of success, but for lack of funding.

The literature contains many suggestions to consider when planning and implementing services for the disadvantaged gifted. Renzulli (1973) believes that there are two major factors to consider, the characteristics of the teacher and the relevancy of the curriculum. Teachers must enjoy working with these children and experience real personal satisfaction with their achievements and growth for the program to be successful. The curriculum must be involved with the immediate lives of the students. Renzulli defines relevant curriculum as "a set of experiences which deal with topics and issues that youngsters would talk about if given a free choice" (p. 443). When structured properly, these issues can be used to teach all the process skills and content information, while eliciting far more motivation and interest. Douglass (1969) points to four essential elements to include:

1. Greater flexibility in organization of the educational system, allowing for small learning groups and individualized instruction
2. An earlier start toward intervention in the limitations to intellectual development and socialization
3. Early apprenticeship so that lower class children can experience types of work other than the low paid, hard, demeaning work often engaged in by their parents
4. A more open, free, public, and universal educational system

Edmonds (1980) believes that schools can be developed to overcome the limitations of impoverished family environments. He and his Harvard colleagues have identified five elements as the key to urban, low-socioeconomic-area school success. A school's leadership, instructional emphasis and overall climate, how teachers imply what they expect, and how administrators use standardized testing results all affect student achievement. After conducting a needs assessment of the school, the Edmonds project provided help to bring it into positive alignment with the five elements for success. Through this procedure he improved the quality of many inner city New York schools.

In addition to her work in identifying the culturally diverse gifted learner (Baldwin, 1980), Baldwin (Boston, 1975) outlines programs and strategies necessary for the success of disadvantaged gifted learners. While many ideas are the same as those one would use to instruct advantaged gifted learners, a larger emphasis is given to the use of the community and models from the community as learning guides, organized experience programs, and creative teaching strategies. Unusual talents must be encouraged as the minds of these special learners are encouraged to expand.

Torrance (1975) has suggested the following approaches to programs for the gifted, which would make them more viable in meeting the needs of the disadvantaged gifted.

The curriculum should be designed to include the particular strengths of these students.

Unreasonable economic demands should be avoided.

Opportunities to help this group of children cope with and grow out of feelings of alienation must be provided.

Resources for study and information gathering must be made accessible.

The classroom should be organized to allow a lot of small group and team learning.

Mentors or sponsors should be developed.

By including the strengths and special needs of the disadvantaged in our curricular planning we can assure these children a better chance to grow with their giftedness.

Rosa is a lovely, dark haired girl who has lived with her Mexican-American family in the *barrio* all of her life. Her parents were raised in Mexico and came to Southern California to find a higher standard of living. They hold the traditional values of their culture and have found adapting to American values difficult. Throughout her high school career, Rosa has noticeably grown into a first rate student—curious, intelligent, constantly pursuing ideas and problems to ferret out original and creative solutions. She totally enjoys her scholastic ability. Rosa is quiet, poised, and self-confident. Her family provides her with strength and love and values her as a woman of their culture.

At the beginning of her senior year, the gifted coordinator suggested that she apply for scholarships to major universities throughout the country. She wrote to Stanford, Harvard, Yale, UC at Berkeley, and Columbia. When she received her scholarship offer from Stanford, everyone at school was excited. Then, when Harvard, Yale, and Berkeley also offered excellent scholarships, the entire faculty and all her friends were ecstatic. They all were anxious to see which one she would choose. What a fantastic opportunity! But then the gifted coordinator got the word. Rosa's father refused to allow her to go to college, any college. It was not right for women to be away from home unless they were married, and her place was with her family. Besides, what did she need a college degree for? She must start her family soon. Women had no business running around getting ideas put in their heads. The gifted coordinator talked to Rosa's father, and the principal and the family priest talked to him, but to no avail.

Then one day in May, Rosa came to school very disturbed and asked to see the gifted coordinator and one of her favorite teachers. As they sat down together, Rosa quietly, almost in whispers, with sadness brimming in her eyes and spilling softly down her cheeks, said that her father had issued an ultimatum. If she persisted in her foolishness of wanting to go to college, she would no longer be considered his daughter. She would have to move out of the house and never come back. Her beloved family would no longer claim her. He would forbid her mother, her brothers and sisters, even her grandmother and other relatives, to contact her or to receive her ever again. As far as the family would be concerned, she would not exist.

Rosa now sat looking very small as she lowered her head, and the momentary pause gave the others a chance to take in the finality and enormity of what she had said. Before anyone else could speak, she said, "I will leave this weekend." Now everyone spoke at once. Graduation was still a month away, the scholarships would not begin for three months after that. Where would she go; how would she live? Rosa sat looking very lost. Although she had thought of the questions herself, she had not worked out any answers. She only knew she had to be free to make her own choice. She had to decide for herself what her life was to be. To do that, she must leave home this weekend. The teacher, her own daughter in her mind, spoke first. "You will come live with me until you decide." And so it was that Rosa, who loved her family and loved the marvelous ability of her mind, was forced to give up one to have the other. Whether her father could be persuaded or time might change his resolve was known only to the future. For now, her loss was almost too great to bear.

Culturally Diverse Gifted Learners

Our educational system often penalizes children who are raised with significantly different values and attitudes from those found in the dominant culture. Subcultures can create conditions for their members that can be as limiting as those discussed for the disadvantaaged. If you add to cultural differences circumstances of poverty, the growing child risks alienation and very limited intellectual development. For example, it has been shown that unfavorable socialization experiences, unequal school opportunities, and obvious occupational discrimination all work together to lower the motivation and achievement of black children, especially boys, no matter how gifted they are. They attend school less regularly, they drop out in greater numbers, and their talents are more often lost (Bloom, Davis, and Hess, 1965; Dreger and Miller, 1960; Pettigrew, 1964).

However, in some subcultures, the reverse is true. Where the subculture's values and attitudes approximate those of the dominant culture, development is often facilitated. Cultural group support may enable the child to reach outstanding achievement.

Giftedness at the highest level can be found in every subcultural, racial, or ethnic group. However, the incidence of giftedness does differ from group to group. This difference results from differing values, attitudes, and opportunities. Groups also differ on other measures: those of cooperation, of production of certain kinds of talent, of spiritual leadership, and so on. What is valued in the culture is produced by the culture. In some instances the overlay of the problems of poverty makes it difficult to assess potential achievement in certain subcultures.

In subcultures that give the school the total responsibility for the education of their children and for the provision of models of adult achievement, painful disappointments cannot be avoided. The problems, and therefore the solutions, seem to lie partly with the family and its representation of the subculture, partly with the dominant society expressed through the people of the mainstream culture, and partly with the school as a translator of the dominant society's values and attitudes.

The United States has taken some pride, in the past, in being a "melting pot" for all nationalities and ethnic and racial groups, and as a haven for all religions. Our laws become more and more protective of rights to insure the equality of diverse groups. And yet the attitudes of the people within the groups are not always so open or so free. Often people are thought of as inferior, when actually they are only different. We have a long way to go to reach our goal of valuing each individual for his or her uniqueness. And yet the dream is there, and that, after all, is a very important part.

What responsibilities to that dream do the families within the subcultures have? The attitudes and skills for thinking and learning are established in the family, a base that forms the future of the children. The information is generalized and oversimplified regarding the contributions various subcultures make to the educational development of their children; yet it can show us trends that may help us as parents and teachers to be more aware of the preparation we make for these children. The data in table 8.1 came from studies of culturally diverse gifted children and may not be applicable to those who, in addition to their cultural difference, must deal with the limitations of poverty.

Table 8.1. Facilitating and Limiting Culturally Supported Attitudes and Abilities.

Subculture or Ethnic Group	Facilitating Culturally Supported Attitudes and Abilities Children Often Bring to the Learning Situation	Limiting Culturally Supported Attitudes and Abilities Children Often Bring to the Learning Situation
Japanese, Chinese, and other Asians (Coleman et al., 1966; Kitano, 1975; Klineberg, 1944)	Ability to listen, to follow directions Attitudes favoring education Respect for teachers and others Attitude toward discipline as guidance Serious and caring attitude toward their own development Tend to test at, or above, the norm on all tests of intelligence High achievement motivation Family unity, very supportive of child's achievement	Attitudes unfavorable to participation in discussion groups Little experience with independent thinking Strong valuing of conformity, which inhibits creative activity or divergent thinking Quiet manner, which may foster unrealistic expectations and inappropriate assessments Attitude of perfectionism, making using mistakes as learning experiences quite difficult Sex role differentiation—male more desirable and dominant sex Critical self-concept
Jewish (Adler, 1964; Barbe, 1953; Brill, 1956; Garrett, 1929; Hollingworth, 1942; Stodtbeck, 1958; Sumption, 1941; Terman and Oden, 1947; Witty, 1930)	Tendency to test high on all tests of intelligence, often registering very high scores Attitudes favoring education, personal improvement Very high achievement orientation Experience with independent thinking, abstract thinking, and problem solving Confidence, good self-concept Exposure to many ideas and content areas Highly verbal Belief that the world is orderly and can be rationally controlled Expectation that each child will leave home and achieve own contributing unit	Often overly competitive Perfectionist attitude that causes tension and frustration in learning new material Pressure to achieve from family sometimes excessive, especially with males

Table 8.1. Facilitating and Limiting Culturally Supported Attitudes and Abilities. *(continued)*

Subculture or Ethnic Group	Facilitating Culturally Supported Attitudes and Abilities Children Often Bring to the Learning Situation	Limiting Culturally Supported Attitudes and Abilities Children Often Bring to the Learning Situation
	Preference for individual rather than family credit for achievement Trend toward equality in family structure	
Black (Barbe, 1953; Gallagher, 1975; Garrett, 1947; Jenkins, 1950; Klineberg, 1944; Lawrie, 1969; Luckey, 1925; Miles, 1954)	Experience with independent action Self-sufficiency Imagination and humor Physical action oriented Middle class blacks accept as valid the values and attitudes of dominant society's middle class.	Limited experience with varied or extended language patterns Sex role stereotyping—sexes have defined roles, twice as many girls are identified gifted as boys, more black women employed than men Lower class blacks have problems that are typical of disadvantaged populations. Such problems are not a result of enculturation.
Mexican-American (Bernal, 1973; Aragon and Marquez, 1975)	Attitudes of cooperation Attitudes favoring education through high school Supportive family, community Affectionate, demonstrative parental relationship Unusual maturity and responsibility for their age Experience with giving advice and judgments in disputes, planning strategies, etc. Eagerness to try out new ideas Ability to initiate and maintain meaningful transactions with adults Facility for learning second language	Language of dominant culture often unfamiliar Attitudes depreciating education for family after high school, seen as unrealistic, especially for women Attitudes that differ on basic time, space reality; may cause misunderstandings Attitudes against competition make it difficult to succeed in some more traditional classrooms Sex role stereotyping—each sex expected to adhere to defined role Lack of experience with values of other cultures Emphasis on family over achievement and life goals of children

Every subculture and ethnic group instills both advantages and limiting attitudes in their children before they enter the school situation. The same can be said for every family from every area of the country, regardless of the culture. Families who want to help their children become all they can be need to be aware of any limiting practices in order to reduce them as much as possible. There is no reason to weaken the ties the child has with the culture. With awareness of what facilitates and what inhibits growth, families can find a way to strengthen the positive attitudes and abilities.

Strengths in some cultures could improve the functioning of others. For example, the achievement orientation of the Jewish culture combined with the cooperative spirit of the Mexican-American culture would enrich both groups. The possibilities are fantastic when we let go of the view of superior or inferior groups and notice that we are all just different.

Culturally diverse gifted children differ in many respects, but they do hold certain mental traits (Gallagher and Kinney, 1974) in common:

The ability to manipulate some symbol system held valuable in the subculture meaningfully
The ability to think logically, given appropriate data
The ability to use stored knowledge to solve problems
The ability to reason by analogy
The ability to extend or extrapolate knowledge to new situations or unique applications

Schools face the problem of deciding who is best qualified to teach gifted culturally diverse learners. Often we hear requests for teachers who understand intimately and deeply the culture of a particular group. At the same time, the same people often demand integrated classrooms, while expressing a need for cultural pluralism and exposure to the values of the dominant culture. Such demands place teachers in an impossible position. Few people have the experience or information to understand the values and attitudes of the dominant culture and even one additional subculture intimately. If we select a teacher for an integrated class because of upbringing in one subculture or ethnic group, how will the teacher relate to others in the class from other subcultures or to those from the dominant culture?

Wouldn't it be better to select teachers on the basis of their self-image, interest, concern, openness, desire to work with culturally diverse children, and teaching skill? Focusing on the qualities that create student success in a classroom seems a far better rationale for teacher selection than race or ethnic membership. Raising the awareness of all teachers and parents of the different needs of children from diverse cultural backgrounds should concern every teacher training and inservice education program. To have cultural diversity available in a classroom, why not have teams of culturally different teachers? The children can then truly benefit from seeing and experiencing a model interface of cultures. Think what both teachers and learners could gain from such experiences. The possibilities are unlimited.

Probably the most important and certainly the most far reaching unsettled questions were asked at one of the first conferences for studying the problems of culturally diverse gifted children (Gallagher and Kinney, 1974): Does our society really want cultural pluralism, or are we going to continue to insist on cultural assimilation? How do we plan to handle self-determinism and democratic ideals in the mode that we choose for our answer? What are the universal values, the common causes of all humanity? How can we reach the goals of human unity and love while still holding on to our own identities as culturally diverse beings?

These questions have no easy answers, and yet we must discuss them as parents, as teachers, as students, among ourselves, and all together. Many of the great thinkers, philosophers, and religious leaders have told of a unity for humankind that is like the waters of a river flowing into the cosmic oceans, mingling, coming together, and yet still maintaining their own essence and uniqueness. Perhaps the answer is not a choice, but an acceptance of reality as a oneness, a blending of dichotomies, with cohesion and separation available at the same time.

Parents, counselors and teachers who wish to work successfully with culturally diverse gifted learners will find help from the suggestions offered by Fraiser (1979) and Colangelo and Zaffrann (1981):

Use mentors to tutor culturally diverse students.
Help them to develop questioning, introspective attitudes.
Help them to understand and explore the problems they may face as they become upwardly mobile; as they try to align their cultural values with those of the dominant culture; as they try to develop their own individuality and establish their personal and cultural identity.
Help them to cope with peer pressures not to succeed, when they exist.
Help them to remediate any areas of skill that are lacking, especially limited language skills.
Give them opportunities to explore a variety of career options.

In response to the limiting conditions some cultures impose on their children seen in table 8.1, I would add:

Help them to deal with excessive pressures to succeed.
Help them to learn to value all persons regardless of cultural or sexual identity.
Give them opportunities to share their ideas, attitudes, and values.
Help them to learn of the strengths of each culture and the unity of all people.

Mike sat staring off into space, munching on a stick of high protein that was given in his class as a "reinforcer." He was seated at a desk alone, or as alone as you can be with fifteen students and two teachers and three teacher aides. The room was arranged so that each student was comparatively isolated, sometimes achieving this with the use of cardboard dividers between the desks. Rock music played in the background. This was a special class, and Mike had been sent here at the first of the year—seven months, four days, and two hours ago. He was selected because he was educationally handicapped, "passive-aggressive," the psychologist had said. He supposed he was; he sure wouldn't do the work in those dumb junior high classes, partly because the teachers were so "stupid" and partly because he'd already done all that stuff, for about three years running. Once, he remembered, in third grade there was this neat teacher who had let them all make a movie about a story by Shakespeare and had let some of the kids use her trig book for their math lessons. That was his best year, Mike thought.

"What are you doing, Mike?" came a voice close by. "Huh! Oh, nothing'," Mike responded. "Well, it will be checkup time in five minutes and I don't see much student behavior going on." Mike grunted at the teacher, shifted his slouch to a forward lean and picked up his pencil. The "task" before him, the completion of which would show "student behavior," was a work page out of a seventh grade workbook on basic science. Oh, they had taken it out of the book and clipped off the identifiers so that Mike, an eighth grader, wouldn't know it was baby work, but he knew. "Boy, they must think I'm really stupid," he groused, looking over the low level questions on the page. But he didn't bother to put in the answers; instead he reached over to a plant near his desk and deposited his protein stick wrapper in its pot.

"Take that out of there, Mike," came the voice again. "It's ok," Mike answered, "It's really an ash tray." Actually it was. Last month one of the "creativity projects" was to take a bunch of old ashtrays the teacher brought in and papier-mâché them into pots for these new plants. Of course Mike realized he was stretching a bit, but he was right. "I said take it out, now." Mike did and then made an elaborate and very grand passage to the waste basket and back to deposit the wrapper. It took fully three of the remaining minutes before "checkup time." On the way back, Mike managed very cleverly to start a fight between two other boys, who each thought the other responsible for the jabs and bumps they received. Mike looked the soul of innocence. One quickly executed swipe of his pencil completely dislocated the mast of a model ship the boy two tables back was assembling, then he slid back into his seat.

A little bell rang, checkup time was announced, and the teachers and aides hurried through the room giving check marks on cards presented by the students to redeem later that day for protein sticks, puzzles, and other prizes. One of the aides approached Mike, who now was sitting straight, feet on the floor, the perfect model of the attentive student. "You get one check for following directions," referring, Mike supposed, to his waste basket trip, "and one check for behaving like a student." Mike wasn't sure how she arrived at that assessment. "But Mike, I can't give you a check for work completed. You have another half hour now before lunch to finish your task." As she moved away, Mike slid back down into his seat, eyes glassy, staring off into space, and quietly began munching on another protein stick.

Oh yes, they all knew Mike tested around 165 IQ, but the gifted class wouldn't take him until he learned to behave like a student. In the regular class he was too disruptive and never accomplished anything, so here he was and they were going to have him complete his work successfully if it killed them.

Gifted Handicapped Learners

Gifted learners appear in every population of handicapped students with the obvious exceptions of the mentally retarded and severely developmentally disabled. Special classes for the deaf, the blind, the emotionally disturbed, the orthopedically handicapped, and the learning handicapped very often have among their students children who are also gifted. Mauser (1980) found that 2.3 percent of the learning disability children he tested in Illinois fell into the gifted range. An Office of Gifted and Talented Fact Sheet (1979) estimated that close to 300,000 children in the United States are both gifted and handicapped. Whitmore (1981) suggests that the figure may be as high as 540,000.

Until recently, little concern has been felt for these gifted children beyond the remediation of their handicapping condition. Children who are gifted and handicapped have need for special educational programming that can remediate any deficits in learning caused by their disability; accommodate the learning experience to minimize the impact of the disability (the condition with which the child was born) and any handicap (the degree to which the disability is allowed to interfere with the child's growth and function) it has created; provide opportunities for development of their special abilities; and challenge them to fuller utilization of their potential. Unfortunately, gifted programs often refuse to include the gifted handicapped learner.

The focus of special education teachers is often on the remediation needed by the child because of the presence of a disability. In a project developed by Eisenberg (1981) for the New York City schools, one of the outcomes was the realization of the teachers of the handicapped that their children could be extremely able. The belief had been that if the child were gifted, he/she would not be in a class for the handicapped. Their expectations had to be reassessed.

Karnes (1979) believes that special education teachers focus on the weakness and deficits of the handicapped because of their training and because they have little or no exposure to gifted education. Educators working with the gifted seldom understand the handicapped. Teachers who are well-trained and who are given adequate support will determine how much of the gifted potential each gifted handicapped learner will be allowed to meet. It has been suggested that such teachers develop the following competencies (Hegeman, 1981):

Knowledge of student abilities and disabilities and how these individual differences affect learning

Competence in methods of disability-related skills development and compensation

Adaptive strategies necessary for curricular modifications

Proficient and judicious use of devices, aids, technological equipment, and other resources and support services

Awareness of the psychological and counseling needs of the gifted handicapped student

Attitudes of cooperation with concerned staff, since teamwork is a necessary part of educational services for gifted handicapped students

Careful attention to the development of the students' social skills and relationships with both normal and disabled peers

Good interpersonal relations with parents, providing information, advice, and support

Realistic expectations in regard to both gifts and disabilities

Identification of the gifted handicapped learner will follow many of the same procedures of screening and multiple data collection that produce the best results in the gifted population. There are, however, some special considerations that must be made to alleviate the masking of the ability created by the disability. Pendarvis and Grossi (1980) present detailed procedures specific to each disability area, which should prove quite helpful.

Strategies and programs developed for the handicapped have tended to assume cognitive limits and often fail to provide opportunities for self-directed learning, creative self-expression, and exploration of the sciences and the arts—all of which are areas critical to programming for gifted learners (Whitmore, 1981). More collaboration between the teachers of the handicapped and the teachers of the gifted will be needed if the goals of both programs are to be made available to the gifted handicapped learner. Maker (1977) brought together some interesting data that can serve as a basis for such planning. She found that different disability groups differ in intellectual capacity, cognitive development, and self-concept.

The blind and visually impaired seem to be capable of the same ability levels as the sighted, but attain their maximum levels later. These students often show deficits in meaningful verbal memory. Maker interviewed some gifted visually handicapped people. Their suggestions included a desire for involvement in less protective, more integrated educational environments and more opportunities to explore the environment using their other, more operable senses. Maker noted a slower rate of development and difficulty dealing with abstractions among the deaf. Her deaf interviewees praised special separate schools. Learning disabled and emotionally disturbed students have diverse problems that reflect the wide array of characteristics under these designations. Problems of attention, perception, and ability to evaluate adequately were the most commonly found. For the physically handicapped, unless the condition is also related to mental retardation, the rate and type of cognitive processing would be comparable to the range of a normal population.

Maker examined the special problems that people who are both handicapped and gifted have in developing a positive self-concept. When the low self-esteem that develops around the disabling condition is combined with the often unrealistic expectations of the gifted learner, a level of dissonance between real and ideal self that adds greatly to the handicapped person's inability to relate and succeed can occur.

This initial drawing together of material showing some of the problems of the handicapped gifted in an educational system that often responds to categories instead of the individual learners has many excellent suggestions for the home and the school. In addition, Maker's book discusses programs for handicapped gifted and talented children and has a very useful section on organizations, agencies, and other resources. While Maker herself claims to raise more questions than she answers, her book, *Providing Programs for the Gifted Handicapped*, provides a valuable resource for those interested in this developing area of gifted education.

Those who work with the gifted need to become aware of what can be and is being done to promote services for the gifted handicapped learner so that their educational experience can work not only toward keeping the disability from becoming handicapping, but also toward actualizing the high potential of these students. The following are some indicators of progress in this direction:

Efforts to increase public awareness of the needs of gifted handicapped learners, to bring them to the atttention of local and state educational agencies, and to support advocacy in their behalf

Development of programs such as the New York City Program for Special Gifted Children in which regular and special educators work together to nominate, identify, and counsel students in special education who have exhibited above average to superior ability and to find appropriate placement for them, often within gifted classes

National conferences devoted to the problems of the handicapped gifted

More generic training for special education teachers so that they will be able to identify and plan for the gifted in their disability populations

Implementation of mainstream placement and the concurrent inservice in special
   education of general education teachers, making them more aware of the needs
   of gifted learners
Strong advocacy for gifted education from organizations whose historical role has
   been primarily associated with the handicapped, such as The Council of Exceptional Children
Sponsorship of national conferences for the study of problems of the gifted by such
   groups, such as a conference on culturally diverse gifted conducted by the Foundation for Exceptional Children
The establishment in institutions of higher learning of programs for training for
   leadership and teaching personnel in gifted education within the Departments
   of Special Education
Specialized graduate programs in the area of gifted handicapped, such as the one
   preparing teachers at the University of Denver
The existence and work of the Committee for the Gifted Handicapped of the Association for the Gifted in the Council for Exceptional Children
Programs for young gifted handicapped learners that explore early intervention,
   identification procedures, and programming strategies, such as the Retrieval
   and Acceleration of Promising Young Handicapped and Talented Program
   (RAPYHT) conducted at Chapel Hill, North Carolina (Karnes and Bertschi,
   1978; Karnes, 1979).

For those interested in further reading in the area of the gifted handicapped
learner, an excellent bibliography prepared by Dr. Elinor Katz, University of Denver,
should be of help to you.

The concern for gifted handicapped learners gives educators an opportunity
to appreciate the value of working in an interdependent, cooperative, collaborative style, for these children can be served no other way. The skills of the regular
classroom teacher, the special educator, the educator of the gifted, the parent, the
counselor/psychologist, the administrator, and the researcher are needed if these
children are to actualize their potential abilities.

Jane stood at the board between Tommy and her best friend Doris. As the
teacher pronounced each word, they wrote it on the board, carefully covering
their work until everyone was finished. When all the chalk was returned to the
chalk tray, the teacher spelled the word so that they could check their own work.
Doris had missed two already, and this time Tommy misspelled the word. Jane
noticed that the two of them nodded to each other and, although she wasn't
sure, she felt that they were excluding her. Four more words, and Doris missed
another one. Tommy missed the next one. Now it was obvious that she was being
excluded as Doris and Tommy exchanged gestures and looks of "I know how you
feel" and "Jane thinks she's so smart." Jane felt really uncomfortable. She really
liked Doris and Tommy; why did they have to act like that? There were only two
words left on the test when Jane decided that they would like her better if she
missed some words, too.

"Receive," said the teacher.

Jane carefully wrote r-e-c-i-e-v-e. Not too obvious, she thought. It wouldn't
help if they thought she missed on purpose. Everyone stood back. Tommy spelled
it just as she did. When the teacher read the right answer, Tommy noticed hers
was wrong and grinned at her encouragingly. She felt much better.

> "Commitment," said the teacher.
>
> C-o-m-m-i-t-t-m-e-n-t wrote Jane. Tommy got this one right. Both he and Doris looked sympathetically at Jane. Jane felt even better.
>
> "For those who have 100 percent on their test today," the teacher was saying, "I've got a special treat. The rest of you take out paper and pencil and write the words you missed correctly one hundred times." The teacher took the "good students" in tow, and off they went down the hall. Jane wanted to go too. After all, she knew those words. She wanted to tell Miss Jennings why she missed them, but that was silly. She'd never understand. After everyone left, Tommy and Doris began talking to her; she was obviously in their favor now. She thought a moment about the treat and wondered what it was, but as she heard comments around the room about the "smarty alecks," and the "prissy britches" who had just left, and as she looked again at her friends happily chatting with her included, she thought it was really worth it.

Gifted Females

Only recently has there been interest and effort spent on understanding the problems encountered by the gifted female in our society. The January 1977 supplement of the *National/State Leadership Training Institute Bulletin* featured attitudes of the past toward gifted women. Let us look at profiles of some of those noted.

After twenty-nine American medical schools rejected her, *Elizabeth Blackwell* (b. 1821) was accepted by New York's Geneva College because the student body voted in the "hen-medic" as a lark. She graduated at the head of the class. Barred from practicing in city hospitals, she opened a one-room dispensary in a New York slum that became the New York Infirmary for Women and Children.

Because "her presence would distract the male students," *Belva Lockwood* (b. 1830) was refused admittance to law school for two years. When she did complete the course, she had to petition the school's honorary president, U.S. President Ulysses S. Grant, to get her diploma. When denied access to federal courts to try cases, she persuaded Congress to pass a special bill. In 1879 she became the first woman to practice law before the U.S. Supreme Court.

Founder of ecology as a science, with specialities in water pollution, home economics, and consumer rights, *Ellen Swallow Richards* (b. 1842) was the first woman graduate of Massachusetts Institute of Technology. Also the first female faculty member at MIT, she was denied a doctorate by the narrow policies of the school. Smith College made her an honorary Doctor of Science at the age of sixty-nine, one year before her death.

One would like to think the experiences of these women are now considered ridiculous and that they simply couldn't happen today; however, a special issue of *Time* in 1972 published this advice: "If a woman wishes to become a college president, she is advised to become a nun" (p. 91). This was in response to the statistic given that only 1 percent of college presidents are women, and almost all of them are nuns. The same issue reported that, of all PhD's granted, only 13 percent go to women. A University of Minnesota Survey found female faculty salaries at 32 percent less than equal ranking males.

A friend of mine recently completed a doctorate at a well-known university. She received her diploma, which announced to the world that Mr._____ had completed *his* work . . ., etc. She returned the diploma for more appropriate wording.

Although one would like to think the current interest in women's rights and equality of opportunity would be reflected in the career data, the status of women actually declined between 1950 and 1970. In the 1940s women held 45 percent of all professional and technical jobs, but in 1970 the percentage dropped to 40 percent (Theodore, 1971). Two-thirds of women who work earn less than $10,000 a year; half are in jobs with no pensions; 80 percent occupy menial or semi-skilled jobs. While IQ bears a fairly close relationship to accomplishment among men, it bears essentially no relationship among women, with two-thirds of the women with IQs of 170 or above occupied as housewives or office workers. Many take jobs as back-up to men in power, receiving neither the credit nor the responsibility for their contributions (Dowling, 1981). More than one-third of all candidates for M.B.A. degrees are women, but only 5 percent of the executives in the top fifty American companies are women (*Time*, July 12, 1982).

Even in professions that are dominated by women, such as education, men comprise 80 percent of all elementary school principals, 96 percent of all junior high principals, and 99.9 percent of all school superintendents. Of all classroom teachers, 70 percent are women, yet for the same job, they make an average of $3,000 a year less than their male colleagues (*Time*, July 12, 1982). Schools of education are fairly equally staffed except for their departments of educational administration, which are often totally staffed with male professors. Also, from the enrollment figures in these departments, it seems that they accept as students an almost all-male population.

The famous Terman study of gifted children becoming adults followed the progress of only the men for information on careers because not enough women were expected to become professionals to make collection of data from them necessary. Later, when the women were not restricted from reports, it was found that 11 percent of the women were working in a professional job, while 45 percent of the men were so engaged. Although 70 percent of both men and women graduated from college, 13.8 percent of the men (compared to only 4 percent of the women) had taken a doctorate. Of the men, 47.7 percent earned over $10,000 a year, while only 6 percent of the women did so. The median earnings for the men were $9,640, for the women, $4,875 (Terman and Oden, 1959).

In this same study, some data appeared that raised questions about the loss of contributions of the gifted and talented women to society. Seven of the most talented writers in Terman's gifted group of children were girls, yet practically all the eminent adult writers were men. Carroll (1940) observed a similar contradiction in a follow-through study of artistic ability. While nearly all the eminent artists were men, the gifted girls, as a group, had been superior to the boys in artistic ability.

Why does this happen? If females have outstanding ability at one point in their lives, why not at another? To understand, we must look at society's expectations for women, the type of encouragement that is given, and the consequences of achievement for women.

In our dominant culture, and even more intensely in many subcultures, girl babies have an entirely different experience as a member of the family and the larger community than do boys. There is evidence that one of the most consistent determinants of parental expectations, perceptions, and organizers of behavior is the sex of their infant. This difference in expectation is evident even before the child is born. Parents prefer male offspring across a wide variety of cultures (Poffenberger and Poffenberger, 1973; Arnold et al., 1975). Hoffman (1977) found that in the United States there was a 2:1 preference for boys over girls. Among men the preference was 4:1. Couples are more likely to continue having children just to get a boy. Boys have a larger number of different toys, and twice as many toys as do girls (Rheinhold and Cook, 1975). The colors and the volume of sound surrounding them, the type of material used to clothe them, the toys given to them, the activities they are allowed to engage in, as well as the way they participate, are all very different.

From the beginning, girls are taught to be passive, accepting, nurturing. They are expected to enjoy quieter games and activities and not to take risks. They receive these messages from many places and many people in our society. Mothers encourage daughters to stay close by, to work with them. They buy irons and ironing boards, miniature kitchens, doll houses, tiny brooms, and baby dolls with cradles and bathinettes for them so they can imitate and learn the woman's role. Little boys are discouraged from playing with these "sissy" toys and, even when dolls are included for boys, they are "GI Joe" dolls or stuffed animals.

You can guess the sex of a baby just by walking into the nursery of most middle or upper class homes. The wallpaper, the mobiles, the choice of pictures and colors differ for boys and girls. The babies also receive different treatment within the nursery. Researchers have discovered that fathers and mothers both turn boy infants out toward the world and push them; little girls more often get hugged up close, face-to-face (Serbin and O'Leary, 1975).

Rubin, Provenzano, and Luria (1974) report interesting results from a study where parents were asked to describe their newborn first child within the first twenty-four hours. The infants were nearly identical in length and weight and all were healthy. The parents were given a list of opposite words and asked to choose ones that best described their infant. They believed the baby to be better coordinated, more alert, more attentive, bigger, and stronger if it was a boy. If a girl, the description included softer, finer featured, littler, and less attentive. Though the descriptions contradict the fact that physiologically girls are less vulnerable, nonetheless the stereotype held in every case.

In spite of their greater sturdiness and developmental maturity, female babies are handled less vigorously than are boy babies (Hoffman, 1972). The caregiver responds differently to crying from boys than from girls. Because they are comforted less and their crying is less often attended to, boy babies learn to become their own emotional caregiver, while girls learn to rely on others to meet their needs. Because her cries are often met with anxiety and concern, a girl learns to doubt her own competence.

This is the point at which parents begin inculcating their small daughters with the idea that so far as risk taking and the evaluation of their own safety are concerned, they should not trust themselves (Dowling, 1981, p. 109). Risk taking, self-trust, and independence are necessary to the development of high levels of intelligence. Studies show that bright girls consistently underestimate their own ability. The brighter the girl, the less expectation she has for intellectual success (Crandall, Katlovsky, and Preston, 1962).

As children enter school, more subtle, and some not so subtle, clues inculcate their role expectation. Preschool teachers reinforce the same type of behavior noted in the home. Little girls are allowed to stay near and are patted and spoken to quietly, while little boys are given directions for independent activity and sent on their way. Boys get more attention when they actively misbehave, and the teacher is more active in controlling them.

Boys actually learn more than girls because the teacher explains how things work and encourages them to try out toys and materials. Little girls are shown passively, as the teacher usually does the manipulation. Boys can explore and get involved in games and activities that are considered too rough for girls and from which, as girls, they are protected (Serbin and O'Leary, 1975).

In my childhood, I distinctly recall my father's aversion to my involvement in tree climbing. Our neighborhood was predominantly male, so my playmates were all tree climbers. There were dire consequences, both natural, as when I fell, and inflicted, as when I got caught, for my participation in this activity. Although I did not always escape undetected, I must admit that I was the best tree climber in the neighborhood. I could not only go higher, probably because I weighed less, but I also mastered the chicken house, the garage, and the neighbor's grape arbor. I never did think prohibiting me, while letting all those boys climb without any discouragement, was really fair. They didn't worry at all about getting caught.

Bardwick and Douvan (1971) theorize that little boys learn to cope with stress and switch to an independent mode by the age of two, while girls are actually kept from learning coping by having stress related situations mediated to the point of overprotection. The result is that passivity and a dependent orientation toward adults appear consistently in girls into adulthood (Dowling, 1981).

Serbin and O'Leary (1975) discovered that girls' actions have far less effect on their environment than do the actions of boys. The kind of help each receives, encouraging action for boys, passivity for girls, also seems to influence the development of their spatial and analytic reasoning. Boys learn to manipulate the environment openly, whereas girls must sit passively by and watch, manipulating covertly, out of frustration.

The preprimers and beginning readers given to school children express this same attitude. Recently, a student of mine surveyed the preprimers and beginning readers adopted for use in California schools to look for sexist materials. The results were amazing. She converted the especially biased pages into slides, and for over twenty minutes our class watched page after page build a stereotype of females that was demeaning, unrelentingly insipid, and totally incompetent. We watched Jane and Mother make lemonade to take out to Dick and Mike, who were building a neat doghouse. We saw Mother get ready to go on a shopping trip and put on earrings that did not match, an act that was discovered by Dick and Father with the comment, "Silly, silly Mother." At each crisis, we found we had to wait with Mother and Jane until Father came home to solve the problem. The final blow came when my student showed a slide of a page of occupations Dick was considering when he grew up. There were six columns of small print covering the page with a wide range of possible jobs. The next page was for Jane and showed the choices available to her. There were three very short columns with very large print. The first column read, "Nurse, Teacher, Mother, Secretary." The two other columns were equally imaginative.

Guttentag (1975) found that, by age five, most children are already sexists. They are convinced that boys are strong and fine and can do all sorts of interesting jobs, but that girls are weak and silly and best kept at home. By the fifth grade, it didn't matter for boys whether their mother was a homemaker or a doctor; the peer group pressures and media influences outweighed the example they got at home. Girls were not affected the same way. They responded to a course given in the fifth grade on sex roles by accepting the idea that women can enter a wide variety of jobs and combine work and family. The course also resulted in an increase in self-esteem for the older girls. Boys only expressed their traditional opinions more freely.

The literature on need achievement should give us some clues as to why girls start out so well, only to achieve in very small numbers. It should; however, it does not for the simple reason that, in the impressive and theoretically consistent body of data about the achievement motive, women have been left out altogether (Horner, 1969). In the few studies that include women, the results were so contradictory or confusing that they omitted women from future consideration. The *need to achieve* has been defined as an internalized standard of excellence, motivating the individual to do well in any achievement-oriented situation involving intelligence and leadership ability. We do know that women get higher test-anxiety scores than men, probably because a female who is motivated to achieve directly contradicts the role expectation of femininity. Horner states, "A bright woman is caught in a double bind. In testing and other achievement-oriented situations she worries not only about failure, but also about success" (p. 38). The solution for most women is to inhibit achievement motivation. Horner (1968) has done research on what she has termed the *motive to avoid success*. The results are most interesting:

Success inhibits social life for females; it enhances social life for males.
Women will fully explore their intellectual potential only when they do not need to compete.
Women block achievement even more when in competition with men.
Society holds the belief that it isn't ladylike to be too intellectual.
Most men treat the intelligent woman with distrustful tolerance at best, and outright prejudice at worst, if she pursues a career.

She found that the women in her study also equate intellectual achievement with loss of femininity and respond to success in one of three ways:

1. They show anxiety about becoming unpopular, unmarriageable, and lonely.
2. They feel guilt and despair, show doubt about their femininity or normality.
3. They deny the possibility that a mere woman can be successful.

Horner's original studies began in 1964, and in the 1970s she again looked at these issues, using as her population the "liberated" young women of the new women's movement era. She found an even higher portion of women showing fear of success, coping poorly or avoiding competition, and lowering their career expectations. The negative attitudes expressed by females had increased from 65 percent in 1964 to 88.2 percent in 1970 (Horner, 1972). This fear of success has been shown to intensify as girls move from seventh to tenth grade (Lavach and Lanier, 1975).

IQ can be found to correlate positively to boys' expectation for success and negatively to the success expectations of girls (Walberg, 1969). Girls seem to believe that if they succeed, it is luck; if they fail, it is their fault. Boys reverse this view for their successes and failures. It has been shown that teachers have contributed significantly to these views (Dweck et al., 1978). In the study, whenever a girl's work was evaluated negatively, it was always pointed out that the failure resulted from intellectual inadequacy; however, the feedback the boys received attributed failures to nonintellectual aspects of their performance, to their efforts or motivation.

Expectations of society also enter in to career decisions in other ways. To resolve the home/career conflict, women may choose to delay their education or the pursuit of appropriate career placement until after the family's needs have been mostly met and the children are less dependent, which has them beginning their career at an older age. Or they may choose an occupation, such as teaching or nursing, that is more compatible with the approved female role. These careers also meet the need of availability in most localities, as the primary decision of where the family will live will usually be the man's choice. If a more male-dominated career is chosen, the woman may work only part-time and choose specializations more compatible with the female role expectations (Wolleat, 1979).

One of the barriers to gifted women's becoming more involved in non-traditional careers is their lack of mathematics preparation. A study of 1,324 children in grades two through twelve found no significant differences between boys and girls in reported enjoyment of mathematics (Ernest, 1976). However, Ernest (1980) acknowledges that when mathematics becomes an optional course of study in high school, few girls enroll. Luchins and Luchins (1980) may have some of the reasons. They report that interviewing three hundred and fifty female members of the Association for Women in Mathematics and a smaller number of male mathematicians produced some interesting differences in career encouragement and discouragement received. Three times as many women reported being discouraged by teachers or advisers than did men, with the most marked discouragement occurring at the graduate level. The women mathematicians experienced all the stereotypic behaviors and comments we have noted earlier. They were told that boys do not like or are afraid of girls who are smart. They found that boys were given more support; less was expected of them as girls; they were advised to go into more traditional fields; their competence was questioned; and they had a problem being taken seriously. They encountered fewer offers, lower salary, and less advancement potential than equally or less qualified males. The women in this study had some suggestions for change if women are to be encouraged to pursue mathematics as a career:

Increase emphasis on precollege mathematics education for girls.
Teachers, counselors, and parents should encourage, not discourage, interest.
Treat girls as equal to boys in this area of study.
Provide female role models.
Provide awareness of career opportunities.
Change the conception of mathematics as a masculine domain.
Stress intuitive-recreational mathematics throughout school to dispel fear of the subject.

Fox, Brody, and Tobin (1980) have presented a number of useful ideas and programs, which could help to meet these concerns.

Rogers (1969) noted that achievement orientation is thought to prove maladaptive for girls because "highly motivated girls may never quite resign themselves to the routines of domestic life" (pp. 251–252). They could also create stress for their husbands by forcing them to fill the achievement needs they left unfilled, he says.

We know that gifted children tend to develop more quickly than more typical children, and we find that gifted girls usually develop even more quickly in the first few years. Connelly (1977) points out that this may cause devastating loneliness for sensitive girls of high potential. When these girls try to show their ability, they are accused of being bossy, unfeminine, and show-offs, so they tend to withdraw. Gifted girls are often considered aloof, conceited, and totally self-sufficient, and others do not feel comfortable with them. For this reason they may go through life with very few friends (Connelly, 1977). Average ability classmates and teachers who have not had a course in gifted education perceive gifted girls more negatively than they do gifted boys (Solano, 1977).

Add to this the observation that gifted girls more resemble gifted boys than nongifted girls on tests of interest, personality, and values. They demonstrate stronger academic and career interests and may be far more adversely affected by conflicts between their goals and the traditional role expectations of females in the society (Fox, 1977). In a comparison between older gifted women and nongifted women (Sears and Barbee, 1977), interesting differences were noted:

More gifted women were employed regardless of the marital status.
Of the gifted group, 67 percent had obtained college degrees as compared to 8 percent of the nongifted.
Husbands of gifted women had more education than those of the nongifted women.

Other comparisons have been made. Gifted girls who reject traditional feminine sex-typed behaviors have higher intellectual ability than those who accept the feminine stereotype (Kagan and Freeman, 1963), although there is reason to believe that gifted girls are not less interested in traditional feminine fields, but exhibit more interest in traditionally masculine domains (Fox, Pasternak, Peiser, 1976). In addition to the usual cognitive differences between gifted and nongifted females, the gifted can be distinguished by their more dominant career orientation, higher mathematical aptitudes and interests, less traditional sex role orientation, and their greater need to achieve (Wolleat, 1979).

Maccoby (1966) found that any differences persisting until high school show girls ahead of boys on intellectual tasks. However, in high school girls begin to fall behind in some areas, and beyond high school their productivity and accomplishment drops off rapidly.

As recently as 1970, it was stated that women can expect sex discrimination on being admitted to almost any college. In an effort to change this problem, a federal judge ordered the University of Virginia to admit all women students who met normal admission requirements. Some universities, such as those in North Carolina and Georgia, still limit the number of women by declaring that women must live on campus in dormitories that are limited in number. There is no such requirement for male students (Joesting, 1970).

The National/State Leadership Training Institute on the Gifted and the Talented, January, 1977 supplement on gifted females states:

> With the objective of ending sex discrimination in American education, Title IX, which is part of the Education Amendment of 1972, became effective July 21, 1975. The approximately 16,000 public school systems and 2,700 post-secondary institutions affected were urged to consider Title IX as an opportunity to ensure equal opportunity in education. (p. 2)

My involvement with the implementation of Title IX provisions tells me that attitudes are changing: however, the awareness of the need for change is still very low.

Even after breaking the barrier of college admittance, women who earn baccalaureate degrees are less than half as likely as men to earn a graduate degree, despite the fact that, on the average, they have better undergraduate records (Jencks and Riesman, 1968). Nearly half of all bachelor's and master's degrees, approximately one-fourth of the professional degrees in medicine and law, and 14 percent of the doctorates awarded in 1979 went to women. The doctorates earned were primarily in the fields of home economics, foreign languages, and library science. There was, however, an increase in doctorates earned even in more nontraditional fields such as law and medicine (National Center for Education Statistics, 1979). In the 1980–81 school year the Association of American Medical Colleges reports that 26 percent of the total enrollment were women, a record. However, no woman yet heads a medical school, only 10 percent of the nation's physicians are women, women trail far behind in admission to training programs in surgery, ophthalmology, allergies, and ear, nose, and throat specializations. If they specialize at all, women are expected to be in pediatrics, psychiatry, radiology, anesthesia, or pathology (*Los Angeles Times*, 12 July 1981).

Another type of discrimination exists for those women in the sciences. Candace Pert was denied a Lasker Award for her research on brain peptide-opiate relationships, with the award given to a man. Jocelyn Bell failed to receive the Nobel prize for her discovery of pulsars; the award went to the professor for whom she worked at the time of her discovery (*Science News*, April 21, 1979).

With such family and educational experience in a culture that "characterizes women as inconsistent, emotionally unstable, lacking in a strong superego, weaker, nurturant rather than productive, intuitive rather than intelligent and—if they are at all normal—suited to the home and family. . . . If she knows her place (the home) she is really a quite lovable, loving creature, happy and childlike" (Weisstein, 1969, p. 58), what about the gifted woman's career?

Joesting (1970) relates a story of a young preteen who attempted to get a paper route only to be refused on the grounds that there are too many job hazards for girls. Joesting believes that vocational counseling should begin at the junior high school level, because it is there that gifted girls begin to be "shuttled" into stereotypic jobs (nurse instead of doctor, legal secretary instead of lawyer, etc.)

As with achievement motivation research, career development theory is derived almost entirely from research on males (Mattheis, 1972). Rogers (1969) finds that general society and individual families spend less money and effort to provide girls with the adequate education required for good jobs.

As we have seen from chapter 1, differences in ability between men and women may be rooted in biological differences that are established in the brain during prenatal life, shown in later differences in brain organization, and enhanced by hormones throughout the life span (Levy, 1980). How the sexes differ genetically in the way their brain develops, how the outside environment modifies this development, and how much we as parents and educators can affect the development of brain organization are questions now being asked and studied by those in the neurosciences. The next ten years will be most interesting as these questions begin to be answered.

Some of the differences were summarized by Block (Nova, 1980) into seven major areas:

1. Aggression—Boys are far more aggressive, as expressed in play, fighting behavior, preference for more adventurous and aggressive films and stories, and in greater competition.
2. Activity—Boys play outside more, more actively, with more variety, and find it harder to stay still.
3. Curiosity and exploratory behavior—Boys want to know how things work and they engage in more exploratory activities than girls.
4. Impulsivity—Boys find it more difficult to resist temptation, distractions, risk taking, and becoming involved in dangerous situations.
5. Importance of social relationships—Girls are more nurturant from an early age and express concern for the welfare of the group, they cooperate and compromise more, are more empathic. Girls have fewer, but more intimate, intense relationships.
6. Self-concept—Males view themselves as more powerful, having more control over events in the world, and believe that they make a difference. They see themselves as more effective, more ambitious, more assertive, and more able to make things happen.
7. Achievement-related behaviors—Males expect to do better than females and set higher levels of aspiration for themselves. Females tend to underestimate their performances and are less confident. Males blame failure on external circumstances and take credit for their successes. Females reverse this view.

From this summary it is evident that whether primarily caused by biological differences, environmental differences, or an interaction of both, these differences do not favor independent, successful achievement for girls.

What Can Be Done?

There are few studies of women, much less of gifted women. Connelly (1977) has the following comments on some areas that might be researched and developed:

Teaching women how to establish their credentials
Teaching how to cope with anger
Teaching to use power effectively, assertiveness
Investigating networking, a source of peer contacts, for women since the "old boy" tie seems to be a fact of life among men
Help with personal development and self-actualization even when the woman is not meeting society's role expectations for females.

Wolleat (1979) suggests that a counseling program should be designed to insure gifted females with both personal and academic resources so that they may develop their abilities more fully. Such a program should include—

deliberate psychological education, including examination of forces that facilitate and inhibit their achievement;
dual (male/female) career-decision making, which has the family at the center;
an all-female career day;

mentors, successful role models;

support groups;

support for self-concept development, nontraditional interests, coping with success.

Callahan (1980, p. 20) suggests that the curriculum could do the following:

1. Provide activities that require females to practice visual-spatial problem solving from a young age.
2. Provide role models of gifted women engaging in successful problem-solving activities.
3. Provide activities that teach gifted girls the impact they can have on their own destinies, i.e., help them develop an internal locus of control.
4. Provide opportunities for gifted females to interact with successful, attractive feminine role models in a variety of professions.
5. Provide activities that encourage women to establish their own personal goals.
6. Set equivalent standards and criteria for reinforcement for males and females.

Fox (1977) concludes that there are five major areas of concern for future research and program planning that become evident from the existing evidence on sex differences. By investigation of these areas, both gifted boys and gifted girls will benefit.

1. Sex role stereotypes
2. Homogeneous grouping
3. Acceleration of learning and appropriate content for the gifted
4. Need for early identification and planning
5. Counseling for gifted learners

It doesn't seem that the secure, self-sufficient, successful, self-actualizing gifted woman is commonly found in and supported by our society. Groth (1975) observes that the pattern for men's success is a straight, conventional one, encouraged by society. Women's pattern is far more complicated, when even success can bring failure.

The interview with the group of highly gifted high school seniors was being video-taped for use in a teacher education class. They had covered most of the usual issues when the interviewer asked, "What do you plan to do when you graduate? What do you think you want to do with your life?" A couple of students mentioned college, although they weren't sure why. It just seemed to be the expected next step. A very pretty young woman spoke up, "I don't know, the way school is and everything. I'm really not interested in anything we've done. There's such pressure to fit into a mold, especially for women, you know. I just don't know. Maybe I'll travel a year and write. I still like to write, not in English class, but for myself. But right now I just want to get away from school, it's such a drag. I really feel dull and bored."

When you looked at her pretty, young face, so serious, so tired looking, so depressed, you really had to wonder what had disillusioned her, "turned her off" so completely. The group was quiet then, and you could tell they knew what she was feeling. They all wondered what was next, and no one seemed happy about the prospects.

Career Education for the Gifted

Since the convening of the National Invitational Seminars on Career Education for Gifted and Talented Students at the University of Maryland on October 15, 1972, career education for the gifted has drawn the attention of educators, researchers, and government agencies. Hoyt and Hebeler (1974) reported the contributions of this and a subsequent conference. The following discussion summarizes some of these contributions.

Although we can find a variety of definitions and objectives for career education in the schools, most definitions include—

availability of information and experience on the world of work to all students from K–14 and beyond if desired;
provision of occupational skills and related knowledge and skills;
development of attitudes conducive to occupational responsibility;
development of personal and interpersonal skills, valuing, and communication and decision-making skills;
awareness of consumer issues and consumer rights;
relevancy of school studies to preparation for gainful and satisfying employment.

It has been pointed out that career education is not intended to displace liberal arts curricula, but rather to strengthen the student's motivation for pursuing such education. While some fear that overemphasis on vocational training may subvert the broader goals of education, the belief expressed by those espousing career education is that education that does not contain future goals for the learners becomes irrelevant. It is true that career education and career guidance should be available to all students. What is not true is that all students should be presented with the same options, asked to process the same information, or proceed through the same decision-making steps (Herr and Watanabe, 1979). There must be individualized programming and resources available.

All students may experience some of these concerns regarding their career choices (Hoyt and Hebeler, 1974):

Worker alienation is widespread as a result of (a) the fragmentation and repetitive nature of some jobs; (b) the number of unskilled workers in an increasingly complex job market; (c) rapid change in skills required; (d) inflexibility of systems and people who are not equipped for change.
Current life expectancy and rapidly changing demands of society make several occupations in a lifetime an increasing reality.
Relationships between education and the occupational society are increasing.
Students also show evidence of alienation to their school curricula.
Fragmentation and repetition can be seen in school organization and are partially responsible for worker alienation among teachers, counselors, and school administrators.

Gifted and talented students, in addition, may encounter the following problems in establishing their careers (Hoyt and Hebeler, 1974; Herr and Watanabe, 1979; Rodenstein, Pfleger, and Colangelo, 1977):

They possess multiple talents and interests that complicate career choices.
High expectations of parents, teachers, themselves, and society operate as pressures and restrict their choice.

The length of training for most professional careers preferred by many gifted students is long, requiring an early vocational decision and long-term commitment. Newland (1976) states that the "brighter the individual, the later his decision regarding the specific area of commitment should be made" (p. 146).

Career as a life style: gifted tend to regard their work as a means of self-expression and build a life-style around it, becoming consumed by work-related activities.

Social isolation results from interests that are too different from those of their peers.

There is a lack of adult role models who have the intelligence or creative ability of the gifted student in the area of interest.

Problems faced by women seeking careers in our society are of special concern to nearly all gifted females.

To aid in understanding a commitment to career education, Hoyt and Hebeler give the following definitions to clarify what have been felt to be misconceptions in this field:

Work—the conscious effort aimed at producing benefits for one's self and/or for others

Career—the totality of work that one does in his or her lifetime

Education—the totality of formal, informal, and incidental processes through which an individual learns

Vocation—one's primary work role at any given point in time

Occupation—one's primary work role in the world of paid employment

Leisure—activities that an individual pursues when not engaged in his or her vocation

Career education—the total effort of public education and the community to help all individuals become familiar with the values of a work-oriented society, to integrate those values into their personal value systems, and to implement those values in their lives in such a way that work becomes possible, meaningful, and satisfying to each individual (pp. 43–46)

Feldhusen and Kollof (1979) suggest a three-stage model of career education that includes instructional activities to enhance and develop creative thinking, problem-solving skills, project abilities, exploratory reading, and independent learning capacity. The model provides a framework for instructional planning for gifted learners. Stage 1 focuses on basic thinking skills and is characterized by short span activities. Stage 2 introduces creative thinking and problem-solving strategies that stress the process of fact finding, problem finding, idea finding, solution finding, and acceptance finding. While guidance is still provided by the teacher, the student is involved in implementing the problem-solving process. It is at this stage that the child begins self-study and is guided toward self-understanding. At stage 3 the student gets guidance and encouragement from the teacher, but independently proceeds to research and complete a project. Gifted learners will not be content to be given the factual data, nor merely to observe someone involved in a career that interests them. The mentor relationship is encouraged by Feldhusen and Kollof (1979) to provide a role model and a guide for meaningful career exploration. From printed materials and visiting professionals, the gifted child can begin to explore career possibilities. Career mentors provide the next step in career exploration, with an in-depth involvement on site, an example of third level exploration. The Purdue three stage model can be used in a regular classroom, in a resource room, or in a special class.

Moore (1979, p. 20) believes that the main purpose of career education is to provide gifted students with skills and attitudes necessary for "changing with change," including these:

Basic academic skills
Decision making, job seeking, and job holding skills
Good work habits

More specifically related to gifted and talented students are these:

Exploration skills to assist with all other future career decisions
Skills for developing occupations
Abilities to cope with a number of different and/or interrelated occupational skills
The ability to move freely between occupations with the least amount of resistance
    and restrictions

In a survey of teachers of the gifted, career counselors, principals, and college professors in Illinois (Ford and Ellis, 1979), the most frequently mentioned practices were the use of community resource persons, field trips, and guidance and counseling. Abraham (1976) suggests that competent counseling can direct individuals into new fields that they might not have considered, encourage delaying a decision until major possibilities are known, help the student to understand parental pressures and to facilitate scholarship opportunities.

There is evidence that the results of career education programs for gifted and talented are worth the effort. In a post-high school follow-up of participants and nonparticipants of a career education program for gifted and talented, the students were asked which high school experiences had the greatest impact on them. Among the participants the career education program received 53.33 percent; extracurricular activities received 33.3 percent, with only one student's selecting a regular course. No one from either group mentioned advanced courses, enrichment activities, or the school counseling program (Colson, 1980).

Finally, Hoyt and Hebeler (1974) suggest the following program guidelines:

1. Career education programs, as with other programs for gifted learners, should begin with consideration of their special needs and characteristics.
2. Decision-making skills should be included.
3. Provisions must include actual involvement in the community and the world of work.
4. Care should be taken to discover and enrich the talented student's career potential as well as that of the gifted.

Torrance (1976) suggests that gifted students need to learn about the future:

> We need to help them invent alternative futures, evaluate these alternative futures, improve these alternatives and make choices about them that will make a difference in the kind of world we shall have (p. 143).

Futurists describe shifts in our occupational focus from agricultural to industrial to service (Little, 1973). Resources were located primarily in the land, and the dominant figure in society was the landowner. The focus then moved to business, and the businessperson became the dominant figure. Now scientists and researchers assume a major role, as the focus shifts to knowledge and technology (Bell, 1972). Maruyama (1975) optimistically identifies the following positive changes in emphasis that society is making: from competition to interdependence; from efficiency to esthetics and ethics; from conquering nature to living in harmony with nature. Many believe the future will require more cooperation, more recycling and conservation, more creativity, and more interdependence.

We must be careful that the career education does not focus on careers that may become obsolete by the time our students move into the world of work. We must be sensitive to shifts in the needs of this area and focus our efforts on such future preparatory issues as: comfort with change; access to information; skills of creative thinking, problem solving, and forecasting; effective communication, personal competence, and self-esteem; and the background needed to understand modern humans and their environment.

Singer (1974) finds that the student's image of the future influences the achievement of that student in the present. If the belief in the future is a positive one, if the student can envision personal success, academic achievement will be high and school will have meaning for that student. When the future focus is weak or negative, poor achievement, maladaptive behavior, and dropping out of school may result. The study of futures can be intriguing to gifted students.

Activities to Develop Awareness of Career Possibilities

1. Ask students to bring to class the "Help Wanted" section of their newspaper. In small groups, compile the following information:
   Identify the kinds of job opportunities that now exist.
   What differences are there in job opportunities for men and for women?
   What kinds of qualifications and training are required?
   Discuss.
2. Watch for job roles on television during one week and note the different jobs presented.
   By whom are they filled? (e.g., men, women, older, younger, minorities, etc.)
   What kinds of qualifications do you notice the job holders having?
3. Write a list of job categories on the board (e.g., Agricultural, Business, Banking, Body and Fender, Computing, Data Processing, Clerical, Craftsman, Dental, Drafting, Electronics, Engineering, Firefighting, Florists, Graphic Arts, Health, Home Economics, Hotel/Restaurant, Law Enforcement, Repairperson).
   Ask students to write down as many names of people who fit in these categories as they can in three minutes. Now ask them to go over their lists to see how many are men, women, minorities, etc.
   Discuss.
4. Using a current issue of a newspaper, working in small groups, list societal problems that are not yet solved. Discuss possible solutions and what jobs these solutions might create. What jobs might no longer exist if the problems are solved? Discuss the group's findings with the class.

In this chapter, we have briefly explored eight problems currently being researched in gifted education: labeling, grading practices, underachievement, disadvantaged gifted, culturally diverse gifted, handicapped gifted, gifted females, and career education for the gifted. The intent was to create an awareness of the problems in the hope that such awareness might foster increased efforts toward solutions, both in the home and at school.

CHAPTER NINE

Teachers of the Gifted at School and at Home

This chapter presents material concerning teachers of the gifted at school, those who support their work, and parents, who are the teachers of the gifted at home. The chapter covers

- the abilities, values, and characteristics necessary to be an effective teacher of the gifted learners at school.
- presenting gifted education to classroom teachers, administrators, and parents through university programs and other inservice opportunities.
- the need for support systems, when establishing effective gifted education and for a teacher's unique teaching style within the school system.
- other personnel within the school system, such as administrators and counselors, and their role in gifted programs.
- the need for establishing parent organizations.
- inservice experiences for parents of gifted learners.
- the importance of parents as resources.
- living with gifted children.

No man can reveal to you aught but that which already lies half asleep in the dawning of your knowledge.

The teacher . . . gives not of his wisdom but rather of his faith and his lovingness.

If he is indeed wise he does not bid you enter the house of his wisdom, but rather leads you to the threshold of your own mind.

Kahlil Gibran

Some years ago at a conference sponsored by the American Educational Research Association, David Aspy presented the results of a research project on factors differentiating effective teachers from less effective ones. I was most impressed to hear that one factor counts far more than any other, the teacher's self-concept. The high self-esteem of a teacher, Aspy related, correlates with student success in the classroom; no other factor shows such a significant correlation (Aspy, 1969). On the same panel, William Brookover stated that the teacher's attitude toward self and others is more important to classroom success than techniques, practices, and materials, and that accepting one's self made one more accepting of others. When he suggested that the development of self-concept might be more important in teacher education than methodology, I was truly amazed (Brookover, 1969).

It was not that I had difficulty in integrating such data into my view of reality, for my experience in working with teachers supported everything they said. What was amazing was, and still is, that if this is true, why are there no selection criteria, no courses in the teacher training institutions, and no qualifications in the hiring practices of school districts that relate to this critical factor? Since that time, our institution has developed coursework for generating positive teacher self-concept, and a few other institutions and districts have become concerned with this issue in teacher preparation. It remains a low priority for most, however, and still does not influence screening, teacher selection, or hiring practices to any great degree. In part, we can understand, for there is a lack of acceptable standardized instruments to measure a person's self-concept. Academic achievement scores and grade point averages are still considered "safer" and are more acceptable in the educational decision-making process. Measureability has been a controlling factor for a long time now.

Almost everyone agrees that the teacher has the most significant influence on a learning environment. Many factors influence the learning of a student, but within the classroom situation, the teacher is of critical importance. In a survey of people working in gifted programs, Renzulli (1968) found that they ranked the teacher highest as a factor critical to the success of the programs. They considered both selection and training of teachers as major issues. Anderson and Kennedy (1932) long ago stated that the mental attitude of the teacher most influenced the atmosphere of the classroom. Gallagher, Aschner, and Jenne (1967) found intellectual productivity in school directly related to the teacher's style, expectation, and response pattern. Web (1971) believes that his data show that the way teachers behave, not what they know, is the most important issue in the transmission of the teaching-learning exchange. It seems apparent that those who wish to provide optimal learning situations for gifted students will be concerned about the characteristics, values, self-concepts, and training of the teachers who implement gifted programs.

Surprisingly, few states have any requirements beyond the regular teaching credentials for teachers of the gifted. Even worse, few institutions, districts, or state departments of education provide pre- or inservice experiences in gifted education. The National/State Leadership Training Institute on Gifted and Talented has made one of the most impactful contributions in this area. By setting up summer institutes and national conferences, they have begun to make people in every state aware of this critical training need and have provided models and expertise for changing what was a desolate picture. Much still remains to be done, for we already know that attitudes of teachers, counselors, and administrators change favorably toward the gifted when they have participated in some gifted education. If we are ever to provide opportunities that will allow gifted children to develop their potential, we must have sensitive, knowledgeable teachers both at school and in the home.

Teachers of the Gifted—At School

Abilities, Values, and Characteristics

Few educational decisions have as much influence on the gifted program as teacher selection. If we believe the lists of characteristics offered by researchers and writers in this field, we would need to find a person who is so outstanding and exemplary that few gifted programs could exist. Some believe that the teachers of gifted students must be brilliant and highly gifted to keep ahead of their students. Others want them learned and wise, with extraordinary insights and a depth of understanding of their subject or field that comes with years of living and teaching. Some would require the teacher to be an accomplished counselor, a profound philosopher, and an active community leader.

After reading the lists, one has the impression that only a Shakespearean sonnet could do them justice. At the least, those employed to select such a teacher must be totally overwhelmed. To complicate matters, there are teachers who have only a few of the characteristics commonly listed, who are exciting and productive in the classroom; others have many of the characteristics, but they are cold, arrogant boors who communicate little of value to their students. We should look at those traits that seem not just desirable, but most essential. We can find clues to effective characteristics and attitudes from those who work in gifted programs, from researchers, and from the students themselves.

One especially significant body of data derives from projects Arthur Combs (1969; Combs, et al., 1974) developed, which resulted in an innovative teacher education program at the University of Florida (Wass et al., 1974). Validation for Combs's work has also come from Usher and Hanke (1971) at the University of Northern Colorado and numerous doctoral studies. These studies concluded by identifying the differences between effective and ineffective teachers (Combs, 1969):

A. General frame of reference that emphasizes—
   internal rather than external,
   concern with people rather than things,
   meaning rather than facts or events,
   the value of authenticity,
   immediacy in causation of behavior,
   a phenomenological or perceptual orientation rather than a behavioristic one.

B.   Effective teachers tend to perceive other people and their behavior as—
     able rather than unable,
     friendly rather than unfriendly,
     worthy rather than unworthy,
     internally rather than externally motivated,
     dependable rather than undependable,
     helpful rather than hindering.
C.   Effective teachers tend to perceive themselves as—
     with people rather than apart from people,
     able rather than unable,
     dependable rather than undependable,
     worthy rather than unworthy,
     wanted rather than unwanted.
D.   Effective teachers tend to perceive the teaching task as—
     freeing rather than controlling,
     larger rather than smaller,
     revealing rather than concealing,
     involved rather than uninvolved,
     encouraging process rather than achieving goals.

Another clue comes from Iannon and Carline (1971) in their conclusion that teachers who have qualities of spontaneity, acceptance, creativity, and self-realization can most effectively help develop human potential. Aspy (1969) concurs in his request for accepting, supportive, facilitating teachers. Flanders (1960) adds the need for teachers to have the ability to provide several support and organizational structures for students and to be sensitive as to when their use is appropriate.

Aspy and Roebuck (1972) investigated the relationship between teachers' classroom behavior and students' level of cognitive functioning. They found that teachers whose students attained cognitive levels beyond memory and recognition provided significantly higher levels of positive regard than those whose students stayed at that level. Only the levels of positive regard were significantly different between groups of teachers. Positive regard is directly facilitative of higher cognitive functioning within the instructional situation, concluded these researchers.

Insecure, insensitive, sarcastic teachers not only do not facilitate learning, they have a marked negative effect on the quality and quantity learned, as well as on the student's self-esteem (Aspy, 1969; Webb, 1971).

Another way to look at facilitating learning is to specify the results we wish to obtain and the teacher behaviors and attitudes that have been shown to achieve these results best. The following compilation reported by Gordon (Welch, Richards, and Richards, 1973) uses the research of Amidon and Flanders (1961), Anderson and Brewer (1946), Brown (1968), Ober (1970), Soar (1970), and Severy and Davis (1971).

Promoting (and Inhibiting) Characteristics of Effective/Affective Teachers

That Promote Growth of THE INQUIRING MIND:
1.   Involve the pupil in incomplete situations.
2.   Lead the pupil to a question or problem that puzzles.

3. Ask the kind of question that is not readily answerable by a study of the "lesson."
4. Permit the pupil to suggest additional or alternative answers.
5. Encourage the pupil to guess or hypothesize about the unknown or untested.
6. Entertain even wild or far-out suggestions by pupils.
7. Ask the pupil to support answers or opinions by providing evidence.
8. Provide material and time for the pupil to develop ideas.
9. Ask "How would you predict?" questions.
10. Make "If, then" statements.

That Promote Growth of SELF-RESPECT:
1. Move freely among the pupils.
2. Engage in positive redirection, attend pupils closely, give individual attention.
3. Praise, smile, laugh, nod, show authentic feelings.
4. Admit errors openly.
5. Listen to each pupil's opinion.
6. Use group discussion to allow feelings to be expressed, to solve problems.
7. Have the pupil write stories about self.
8. Take time for activities in developing self-esteem.
9. Tell the pupils about their work.
10. Plan and evaluate cooperatively.

That Inhibit Growth of SELF-RESPECT:
1. Humiliate pupils as a form of control.
2. Punish pupils for showing anger.
3. Require pupils to line up.
4. Require pupils to work only on specific instructions from the teacher.
5. Ignore pupils.

That Promote Growth in RESPECT FOR OTHERS:
1. Ask pupils to help others.
2. Help pupils to solve problems of disturbing others.
3. Ask the class to discuss differences in people.
4. Discuss controversial issues with the class.
5. Ask the class about how they think others might feel.
6. Use value clarification techniques.
7. Encourage social interchange and cooperation.

That Promote Growth of SENSE OF COMPETENCE, Aiding Self-Esteem:
1. Have pupils find their own information.
2. Provide the time and opportunity for pupils to use special aids, language aids, tape recorders, learning centers, etc.
3. Tell the pupils when they have done a good job.
4. Allow pupils space to display their own work.
5. Give alternative ways of working when a pupil shows a lack of interest or frustration.
6. Keep a record of work accomplished (visibly and cooperatively).
7. Give fewer directions, less criticism, less lecturing; encourage participation.

*That Promote Growth of the SENSE OF RESPONSIBILITY FOR ONE'S OWN CON-
DUCT:*
1. Have pupils make their own analysis of subject matter.
2. Have pupils find detailed facts and information on their own.
3. Have pupils work independently on what concerns them.
4. Encourage self-discipline on the part of the pupil.
5. Withhold judgment on pupil's behavior or work.
6. Encourage the pupil to put his or her ideas to a test.
7. Evaluate the work of different pupils by different standards, cooperatively.
8. Use self-evaluation.

That Inhibit Growth of the SENSE OF RESPONSIBILITY:
1. Allow no discussion.
2. Make all the rules and decisions.
3. Tell pupils to raise their hands, wait their turn, and stay in their seats.
4. Help pupils only when they raise their hands for help.

*That Promote Growth of the SENSE OF COMMITMENT (Encourage pupils to engage
in the following behaviors with peers and others):*
1. Showing concern.
2. Advising, suggesting, or interpreting.
3. Comforting or reassuring.
4. Fixing something.
5. Protecting, warning, defending.
6. Getting help for somebody else, helping another accomplish a task, or helping
   out in distress.
7. Offering needed help.

Students also provide a source of information on effective teaching strategies,
attitudes, and characteristics. Schaefer (1970) found that the creative high school
girls in his sample specified the following traits as indicative of outstanding teachers
they had had:

Enthusiasm for subject taught, ability to make a subject come alive
Personal interest in the student and belief in his/her ability
Sincerity and honesty, especially in acknowledging personal mistakes or information
    gaps
A good listener who encourages students to express themselves
Likeable, warm, kind, concerned

Johnson (1976) asked 1,800 students five to eighteen years old, from kindergarten through high school in the Philadelphia area, to answer two sets of questions.
One set asked what made a teacher good and what teachers did to help them learn;
the other questioned what teachers did that made it hard to learn. A partial summary will show a surprising consistency with the other data we have previously
mentioned. Johnson tells us that the children pointed to nearly the same teacher behaviors whether they were young or older, high or low achieving, from economically
deprived or affluent areas.

These teacher traits helped them learn:

Paying attention to their needs, listening to them
Understanding their problems, communicating
Sharing their successes, making them feel important
Treating them openly, fairly, and with respect
Humor and pleasant nature, being real and authentic

Overall, the affective qualities were more important to the students than the cognitive traits, and the personal, human qualities outweighed concerns with methods, materials, and curriculum. They found it hard to learn from teachers who—

yelled at them, embarrassing them;

made unreasonable demands;

used physical restraint and punishment, "many commonly used management devices" (e.g., staying in at recess or after school, writing as punishment, standing in the corner, hitting or slapping);

acted condescending; as one student put it, "They talk down to you even if you're taller;"

acted "real phony."

The above practices distinguish effective teachers in regular educational settings. They should be the basis for choosing teachers who will work with the gifted. Certain specific qualities have also been shown to make good teachers of the gifted.

Some writers suggest that we specify characteristics of teachers according to what is effective with different types of gifted children (e.g., disadvantaged, underachieving, creative). They advise different selection and training depending on the subgroup involved. In my experience, this would not only be impractical and needlessly restrictive, but a disadvantage for both the teacher and the program. Few programs are so specialized that such subgrouping would be feasible. In most groups of gifted children, all subgroups are duly represented.

A possible exception might be in the area of the visual and performing arts. As we have seen, this is an area that requires a level of accomplishment that many of us have not acquired to make the role of teacher of use to the student who shows giftedness in this area. As one student so wisely observed, "Every teacher is different; his or her talents, skills and interests vary. To be most beneficial, the teacher should perceive not only the needs of the individual student, but his or her own capability to fill those needs" (Dubner, 1980).

A major study (Bishop, 1968) used student selection of the "most successful" teachers of high school gifted programs, results of teacher and student questionnaires, teacher interviews, teacher academic records and testing scores. Bishop offers the following conclusions: while not differing in sex, marital status, type of undergraduate institution attended, highest degree held, course work preparation, and extent of association with professional organizations, the teachers judged effective by intellectually gifted, high achieving students did differ from teachers not so identified. Effective teachers—

were more mature, experienced teachers;

were mentally superior;

pursued intellectual avocations;

had high achievement needs;

pursued intellectual growth;
showed more favorable attitudes toward students, were sensitive and empathetic;
were more student centered in their teaching approach;
assumed a more systematic, orderly, and businesslike classroom approach;
were more stimulating, imaginative, well-grounded, and enthusiastic toward the
    subject and teaching;
supported special educational provisions for gifted students.

In a recent study (Kathnelson and Colley, 1982) students, six to sixteen years of
age, in a special project for gifted and highly able learners, were asked to record descriptions of what they would like an ideal teacher to do as a teacher and as a person. The results showed the following:

Student Responses Regarding Desirable Characteristics in Teachers of the Gifted

A. Items mentioned 50 percent of the time:
    1. Someone who understands them
    2. Someone who has a sense of humor
    3. Someone who can make learning fun
    4. Someone who is cheerful
B. Items mentioned 30 percent of the time:
    1. Someone who supports and respects them
    2. Someone who is intelligent
    3. Someone who is patient
    4. Someone who is firm with them
    5. Someone who is flexible
C. Items mentioned occasionally (5–10 percent of the time):
    1. Someone who knows the subject
    2. Someone who explains things carefully
    3. Someone who is skilled in group processes

The teachers and parents chose "knowledge of nature and need of gifted," "skill
in developing self-concept," and "skills in integrating the cognitive, affective, sensory
and intuitive abilities" as top priorities in their ranking of professional competencies
for the teachers of gifted. They listed "understands, accepts, respects, trusts and
likes self;" "supports, respects, trusts and is sensitive to others;" and "is open to new
ideas, flexible" as the top priorities for personal attributes. The project was a summer school that used the Integrative Education Model as its philosophical and instructional base, so the emphasis among parents choosing the school and faculty
teaching at the school would be on goals associated with this educational approach.

Lindsey (1980) presents us with a synthesis of what is known to be preferred in
the personal characteristics and teaching behaviors of those who are successful in
their work with gifted learners.

Personal Characteristics
    Understands, accepts, respects, trusts, and likes self; has outstanding ego
        strength
    Is sensitive to others, less concerned with self; supports, respects, trusts others

Is above average intellectually; exhibits an intellectual style of conceptualizing, generalizing, creating, initiating, relating, organizing, imagining

Is flexible, open to new ideas

Has intellectual interests, literary and cultural

Desires to learn, increase knowledge; has high achievement needs

Is enthusiastic

Is intuitive, perceptive

Is committed to excellence

Feels responsible for own behavior and consequences

Personal-Professional Predispositions

To guide rather than to coerce or pressure

To be democratic rather than autocratic

To focus on process as well as product

To be innovative and experimental rather than conforming

To use problem-solving procedures rather than jump to unfounded conclusions

To seek involvement of others in discovery rather than give out answers

Teaching Behaviors

Develops a flexible, individualized program

Creates a warm, safe, and permissive atmosphere

Provides feedback

Uses varied strategies

Respects personal self-images and enhances positive ones; respects personal values

Respects creativity and imagination

Stimulates higher-order mental processes

Respects individuality and personal integrity (Lindsey, 1980, pp. 13, 14).

Whitmore (1980) believes that the most critical factor in developing appropriate educational experiences for gifted children is the teachers involved. Some of the qualities she would ask the teacher of the gifted to possess are: a person who models the traits and life-style of a scholar, challenges the student to think at higher levels, and who stimulates interest and independent pursuits; one who is compatible to the need for flexibility, increasing self-direction, reduction of pressure, opportunities for self-expression. Such a person must have superior organization skills; enjoy energetic, inquiring minds; and understand the needs of gifted children.

The above qualities do make good teachers, and students prefer them. Some of the characteristics may even be unique preferences of gifted students. We cannot be sure which are desirable for all students and which are necessary for only the gifted. It is my belief that there are specific abilities, attainable by many teachers, that are necessary if they are to provide effective programs for gifted learners. For example, a teacher does not need to be highly intelligent to work effectively with the gifted learner, but that teacher should definitely value intelligence, understand its implications, and know how to nurture it. Not all teachers will have or will desire to acquire the abilities listed here, but it is possible for many to do so. Teachers for gifted programs should be selected on the basis of such abilities.

Specifically, teachers must develop these abilities if they are to be effective with gifted learners:

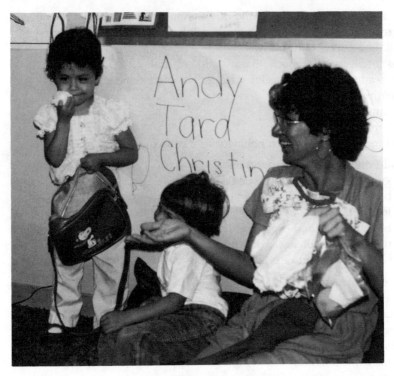

A teacher of the gifted must be authentic, congruent, and humane as a deep personal commitment.

1. A knowledge and understanding of the cognitive, social, and emotional characteristics, needs, and problems found in gifted students as a result of their atypical mental development
2. The ability to develop a flexible, individualized, enriching curriculum appropriate to meeting the individual gifted pupil's needs and nurturing group interaction
3. The ability to create an environment in which the gifted can use their strengths, explore their personal and interpersonal development, risk new areas of thought and action, feel challenged, and actually be more of who they are
4. The ability to teach the gifted learner the skills of higher level cognitive thinking, integration of mind and body, self-actualization, intuitive development, and self-evaluation
5. The ability to nurture creativity in all its aspects of thinking, feeling, intuiting, and expressing talent through products
6. The ability to encourage in gifted learners a sense of social awareness and commitment to humanity and to their environment, and a respect for the worth and dignity of others
7. The ability to relate well to colleagues and parents of gifted learners and to conduct professional meetings for their benefit

To develop such traits requires an uncommon amount of ability to—

empathize and inspire;

tolerate ambiguity; be open, flexible, and innovative;

share enthusiasm, a love of learning, and a joy of living;

be authentic, congruent, and humane as a deep personal commitment;

be alert, knowledgeable, and informed;

value intelligence, intuition, diversity, and uniqueness in self and others;

value change, growth, and self-actualization for self and others.

The research of the following persons supports the need for these abilities: Baldwin (1977); Bishop (1968); Drews (1972); Freehill (1975); Gallagher, Aschner, and Jenne (1967); Lyon (1975); Newland (1976); Rogers (1969); Rogge (1970); Strang (1960); Ward (1961); and Wilson (1958).

Knowing the traits that, when present, prevent teachers from encouraging the development we are seeking in gifted students is also important. Torrance (Gowan, Demos, and Torrance, 1967) found the following characteristics present among teachers who could not apply one or more accepting, supporting principles used in his study:

> authoritarian, defensive, dominated by time, insensitive to their pupils' intellectual and emotional needs, lacking in energy, pre-occupied with their information giving functions, intellectually inert, disinterested in promoting initiative and self-reliance in their pupils, pre-occupied with disciplinary matters, and unwilling to give much of themselves in the teaching-learning compact (p. 162).

Frasier and Carland (1980) felt that it was also important to understand the relationship that exists between regular classroom teachers and teachers of the gifted. From a survey of a national sample of teachers and program directors, they discovered that some of the factors viewed as important in the development of a positive relationship were: having strong administrative support; communicating goals and objectives of the gifted program, the selection procedures, and the student's performance while in the program; and provision for inservice for all teachers. Factors judged least important were that teachers of the gifted have the same number of students as the teacher of the regular classroom and that the teacher of the gifted work along with the regular classroom teacher in developing appropriate curricula. As these relationships have a lot to do with how well the gifted program can be implemented and the amount of success that can be achieved by gifted students, these factors could be valuable clues to all who wish to serve gifted learners.

Elizabeth Drews (1976) reminds us,

> The teacher's task is to inspire and release. . . . The teachers who have the greatest appeal to the gifted are those who combine two characteristics. First of all, they must know a great deal, and their knowledge should extend to the far reaches of their subjects. (Those who are themselves excited learners can communicate this feeling to their students.) Second, they must have a superlative ability to relate to others. For the gifted as well as for all students, the creative teacher is one who has faith in young people and loves students, who is cooperative and kind, who is democratic and considerate. Such teachers act on the belief that all human beings are naturally good and have transcendent potentiality. With such values and guidance, the student can make the most fundamental decisions—choices of life-style and world view—as well as the minute-to-minute choices of which most people actually remain unaware. . . .

Let us all recognize that gifted children have great insights from the beginning and that our task as teachers is the Socratic one of leading out the creative and letting them be where, as Rousseau, Wordsworth, and Thoreau divined, they can discover what in truth they already know (p. 28).

Teacher Education and Certification

The seven specific abilities of teachers necessary for effectively working with gifted students (p. 372) provide a base of competency toward which teacher educators can instruct and state agencies can certify. Basing a teacher education program, either preservice or inservice, on the seven competencies insures that those who acquire such education have at least the basic requirements for providing quality programs for gifted learners. There is no way to insure success in classrooms; however, opportunities can be provided for teachers to gain an awareness and an experiential background in these areas that have been shown to increase their effectiveness in gifted programs. There are many ways for teachers to gain these competencies, from district sponsored workshops and conferences to an intensive involvement in a university teacher education program leading to a credential or a graduate degree. This discussion details two of the many models that could be used and, in addition, briefly looks at some other alternatives.

College and University Programs: Preservice and Inservice

At least 140 colleges and universities in more than forty states currently offer some type of program to teachers wishing to specialize in the teaching of the gifted learner (Hultgren, 1982). The programs may offer only one or two courses periodically or there may be an entire multi-course program leading to a degree and/or credential in the gifted specialization, with the M.A. degree programs the most commonly found. Several surveys have indicated that many courses offered do not lead to degrees or credentials, are nearly all at the graduate level of study, and require the candidate to have a teaching credential and some previous teaching experience (Lindsey, 1980).

While it seems that more universities and colleges are developing programs addressing the needs of teachers of the gifted, there are some further concerns that must be addressed. In a survey of practitioners in the field, a list of areas not adequately addressed by the university programs they attended emerged. Included in this list were: lack of knowledge of leadership skills, counseling for the gifted, career options for gifted, cultural differences, educational technological developments, needs of underachievers, parent/community relations and resources. The university personnel surveyed were concerned about the lack of opportunities in many of the areas also. One of the highest rated deficiencies on preparation programs was the lack of supervised practicum experience. Both at the teaching and administrative levels, opportunities for practicum experience were seen to be inadequate or missing in far too many programs (Hultgren, 1982).

State-mandated certification is favored by both a large percentage of university program directors and practitioners (Hultgren, 1982). Of the state consultants reporting (forty), 70 percent favored certification requirements, though in a 1979 survey only ten states reported any certification requirements in effect, with ten more initiating movement toward future certification (Karnes, 1981). Those not favoring such requirements cited lack of established teacher competencies and the limited number of college and university teacher education programs. Some practitioners feel that such a mandate would cause inconvenience to them due to the need to add more requirements, especially in areas where programs in education of the gifted are largely unavailable. Administrators are often concerned about a loss of autonomy were such requirements to become law. However, most educators feel that the advantages of having well-trained professionals far outweigh the disadvantages (Hultgren, 1982).

In 1981 a set of professional standards for training programs in gifted education were recommended jointly by a special task force on teacher education from The Association for the Gifted (TAG) and a committee on professional training from the National Association for Gifted Children (NAGC) (Seeley, 1981). The purposes for such standards were reported to be:

1. In gifted/talented child education—Establishing standards encourages the continued growth of our field. Standards provide a basis for communication and reciprocity among programs, and for continued dialogue relative to the nature of training in our evolving field. Providing an impetus for continued improvement of professional programs would also promote the advancement of the field.
2. For Institutions—Adopting standards for approved programs performs a crucial function on this level: ensuring a minimum university commitment to professional training. By "institutionalizing" programs, we are eliminating much of the "patched on" quality which is unfortunately beginning to characterize many higher education programs. Institutionalization and program approval move us closer to permanence.
3. In training programs—It is not the purpose of standards to guarantee that graduates have mastered particular skills. However, professional standards would ensure that trainees at various levels have been exposed to essential information in theoretical and applied contexts (p. 165, 166).

The six standards recommended were:

I. Admission and Selection Criteria—The institution should publish specific criteria for admission to programs at each degree level. These criteria should include cognitive and affective evidence obtained from multiple sources and should be congruent with stated program philosophy and goals.
II. Curriculum and Competence Areas—Training programs should establish a coherent, comprehensive and discernible curriculum that addresses the major areas of gifted education as well as related studies. The curriculum should address theory, practice, and research in each of these areas.
III. Degree Programs—Degree programs with a major emphasis in gifted education should be offered only at the graduate level and should be differentiated from each other appropriate to level (i.e., master's, specialist, doctoral).
IV. Faculty for Graduate Programs—Faculty members with major teaching responsibilities in graduate programs should hold the doctorate with advanced study in gifted child education, or have competence in the field as demonstrated by

significant research, writing or leadership in gifted education. Faculty members who conduct the advanced programs should be engaged in scholarly activity that supports their specialization in the field, and have experience which relates directly to gifted/talented child education.

V.   Administrative Structure: Staffing—The faculty for advanced programs should include at least one full-time doctoral-level person who holds an appropriate degree or has demonstrated competence, and at least three persons who hold the doctorate in fields which directly support the degree programs.

VI. Administrative Structure: Evaluation—The program's mission and course offerings should be reviewed regularly. The results of this evaluation should be used in program modification and improvement efforts. Systematic opportunities should be provided for student and faculty input into program administration, review and planning.

VII. Resources and Facilities—Institutions that offer graduate programs in gifted education should assure adequate human and material resources and facilities to implement their prescribed course of study (pp. 166–168).

The adoption of such standards will allow the specialization of gifted education to build from a base of excellence and professional quality.

The Environment

Lindsey (1980), in reviewing studies of institutions in which student values show the most change during their university years, found that these characteristics were shared commonly: "relationships between students and faculty were close; it was expected that ideas would be questioned, differences of opinion would be examined, and persons would be held accountable for their decisions; the instructional strategies emphasized dialogue, discussion, debate, and inquiry" (p. 27).

In our university over eight years ago, it was determined that, to facilitate human learning, a more flexible, more nurturing environment would be needed for the teacher/learners in the gifted education program. It would be far easier, went the thinking, to teach appropriate education for gifted learners if it matched the type of education that the teacher/learners experienced during their program. With this in mind, a plan was developed to equip one room in the University instructional unit with carpet, tables, floor pillows, comfortable furniture, listening posts, and other media equipment necessary for establishing learning centers. The walls were painted a warm color, and attractive posters were hung. Later, an additional room was similarly equipped. With this environment available, in addition to on site environments within elementary and secondary schools, the teacher/learners could experience how a cooperative learning environment operates by learning in one.

An important part of the climate of any teacher education environment is the ability and attitude of the teacher educator. Those who teach teachers must themselves possess the attributes, knowledge, and skills essential for optimizing learning and developing individual potential. The program should allow all who participate to learn in a structure and with the teaching and evaluation strategies they are being asked to create. Those processes we value in gifted education must be modeled in the university classroom. The characteristics and competencies appropriate for a teacher of the gifted must be evident in the teacher of that teacher.

Teacher education classes can be exciting learning experiences.

The Course Work

Although the number and regularity of offerings vary, according to surveys (Zettel, 1980; Hultgren, 1982) the overall content of courses on education of the gifted is similar in most institutions involved in gifted education programs. Most commonly offered is a course that explores the education and psychology of the gifted individual; introduces the concept of giftedness; and includes definition, identification, characteristics, etiology, and nurture. Many institutions also offer a course in methods and curriculum for teaching gifted learners. Other areas that may be found as part of programs leading to degrees or credentials in education of the gifted are: measurement and testing, leadership principles and practices, affective development, creative behavior, classroom management, advanced studies, research methods, and administrative provisions. Practicum experiences are rated as essential by both practitioners and university trainers; yet 37 percent of universities offering programs in gifted education offer no practicum experiences in teaching the gifted learner, and 76 percent offer no administrative practicum (Hultgren, 1982). In the same sample, 61 percent of the practitioners assessed had no practicum in teaching and 80 percent had no administrative practicum, although one-third engaged in administration of gifted programs. Universities offering higher degrees rather than just occasional coursework offered more practicum experience.

We have seen that attitudes of teachers are influenced favorably toward gifted learners if they have had even one course in education of the gifted (Weiner and O'Shea, 1963). It has also been noted that the major part of the educational experience of most gifted students is planned and implemented by the regular classroom teacher, and yet we find information regarding gifted learners and their needs rare in the general offerings for teachers. Most of the courses with information on understanding giftedness are offered at the graduate level and to students taking them in pursuit of a higher degree in this area of specialization.

Competency Based Programs

Programs that list competencies or skills to be developed by perspective teachers have many advantages: the competency approach is systematic, it is process oriented, and it is designed by and communicated to those in the particular setting.

To develop a competency based program for training teachers of the gifted Lindsey (1980) suggests four basic steps:

Step 1   Define the knowledge, skills, and attitudes to be achieved. Each university will have a list particularly meaningful to them. In Hultgren's study (1982) twenty-four competencies were selected and among them the following were considered most essential:

Knowledge of nature and needs of gifted
Skill in promoting higher cognitive thinking abilities and questioning techniques
Ability to develop methods and materials for the gifted
Knowledge of affective/psychological needs of the gifted
Skill in facilitating independent research and study skills
Ability to develop creative problem solving
Skill in individualizing teaching techniques
Knowledge of approaches to extend and enrich subject areas
Ability to teach a group of gifted students (a supervised experience)

Our university has developed competencies based upon the seven abilities necessary for effective teaching with gifted children listed on page 372. Lindsey (1980) suggests that we consider at least three areas in which competencies should be developed: what a teacher needs to be, to know, and to be able to do. The unifying theme is the development of the wholeness of the person.

Step 2   Design alternative strategies for helping different students achieve the listed competencies. Just as we believe the best way for gifted children to reach their potential is through educational programs that are individualized with varied opportunities, so too should teacher preparation programs be planned to allow each teacher to identify and meet his or her own needs and interests appropriately.

Step 3   Evaluate the degree to which the competencies are met, allowing for a variety of evaluative procedures. Evaluation is not synonymous with examination, and it has been my experience that far more learning and change occur when a variety of data—such as student projects, papers, journals, observations, case studies, task sheets, book and journal reviews, media productions—provide the means for evaluation.

Step 4   Feedback the results into all elements of the system. Finally, Lindsey (1980, pp. 43–45) suggests these questions as a guide for assessing the quality of each teacher education program:

Are the goals of the program made explicit?

Are the opportunities the program provides for students consistent with the stated goals?

Is the program dynamic rather than static?

Are those who design and operate the program effective models?

Are those who have a stake in the program significantly involved in its designing, implementation, and evaluation?

Are adequate resources available and productivity used?

Does the institutional environment stimulate expectancies and achievement?

Does the program provide continuity between practice and theory?

Does the program provide both social and independent experience?

A national survey of teacher competencies for the education of gifted and talented children was conducted during the spring of 1978 (Seeley, 1979). The respondents, representing universities and colleges, principals, and teachers, ranked the following competencies in order of perceived importance with little disagreement between groups. Competencies considered most important were: higher cognitive teaching and questioning; curriculum modification strategies; special curriculum development strategies; diagnostic prescriptive teaching skills; student counseling strategies. As the purpose of the study was the establishment of a teacher certification regulation, the data were summarized into the following recommendations:

1. Teachers specifically assigned to teach gifted and talented children should hold a master's degree in the field.
2. State certification and endorsement standards should be mandatory, with provisions for a permissive phase-in until sufficient qualified professionals are available.
3. Information concerning gifted and talented children should be a part of every teacher's training.
4. One to two years of successful teaching experience should be required of teachers before assignment to gifted and talented special programs.
5. Teachers of gifted and talented children should have a strong content area emphasis in their background.
6. Teachers should have a variety of special competencies for teaching gifted children (p. 13).

Further Inservice Models

A number of other inservice models have been used. Among them have been summer institutes, district sponsored conferences and workshops, meetings with consultants, demonstration classes, and centers. We found it especially effective for gifted students to attend for half a day at the morning demonstration classes. Teacher/learners working with them attended in the morning and met with consultants in the afternoon. This enabled the consultants to demonstrate the strategies and materials with the gifted students in the morning as the teacher/learners observed. They got together to explore the ideas in detail during the afternoon. In planning inservice experiences, the same competencies should serve as the base, just as they do in the more extensive credential and degree programs.

Most district conferences and inservice workshops have one abiding weakness: their overemphasis on strategies and "how to do its." Teachers need to be aware of effective techniques to use with gifted children; however, if they are never exposed to a deeper understanding of the needs and problems of these children, they will never learn to generate activities appropriate to themselves and to the atypical learners with whom they work daily. What does one do after having attended the workshop on "101 Creative Activities for Gifted Learners" on the one hundred and second day? Our teachers deserve better than the dependency and confusion that result from total reliance on these workshops and conferences.

Of course, the opposite is also true. Inservice programs that give nothing but theoretical background with little or no participation can result in little or no change in the classroom. Inservice for classroom teachers should be offered in a total context of theory and practice, designed not only to teach strategies, but to show in what way the strategies meet the needs of gifted learners. Teachers of the gifted must themselves understand the nature of these learners and the needs they have. Through personal experience, they should be shown many alternatives to meeting gifted needs. The competency base provides this more complete and useful framework.

For descriptions of other programs that may be helpful in your planning, see Gear (1974), Maker (1975), Renzulli (1973), and Sisk (1975).

Support Systems

The teacher of the gifted, especially if she or he is creative, innovative, effective, and successful, will quite likely find some unexpected consequences of that success. Many of our more traditional schools resist change and reward conformity. In such a system, the person who deviates, who does not follow the usual procedures, is neither valued nor supported and, in many cases, is not even tolerated easily. Many subtle pressures maintain the system as it is and discourage new ideas. For example, teachers who innovate more open structuring may find that they are left to eat alone in the teachers' lunchroom. Teachers who start new programs find their students reprimanded for being outside of class and disturbing others, even when such activities were part of the classroom program and were being carried out in the agreed-on manner. When such a teacher requests help, other teachers may refuse or point out that, if the "rules" were being followed, they wouldn't need "so much help." Any deviation from the value structure of some teachers may be met with censure, backbiting, and unpleasant confrontations.

I believe that innovating teachers should present the changes as inoffensively as possible, remain aware of any imposition their practices may have on others, and keep from becoming defensive and retaliatory in behavior. Teachers who are not part of the regular faculty, but hired as special teachers, have an even more difficult problem. You must be aware that your very presence says to some teachers "I am here to do what you can't. I'm a special teacher." For some, that is very threatening. You will need to focus on establishing good interpersonal communications with the entire faculty. And no matter how caring you are, it may not work.

Such experiences can certainly take the joy out of teaching and create loneliness, frustration, and the inclination to give up even ideas you have shown to be effective.

Some teachers leave the profession rather than have such dissention become part of their everyday lives.

Other solutions besides conforming or quitting exist. Establish a support system and use it. It is neither weak nor unworthy to need support in your attempt to create an effective learning situation for your students. Support systems can be built in many ways:

1. Watch for those teachers who are interested in what you are doing, invite them into your room, share your materials and ideas, ask them for their opinions, share.
2. Be sure to take every opportunity to let the entire faculty know they are welcome at any time to visit, participate, share ideas, or have the children work with yours.
3. Discuss what you are doing with the principal and other administrators. Keep administration informed and invite their participation. But be careful of making presentations before the entire faculty. Many may be there only because they were required to attend and will view the proceeding as a put-down of what they are doing. Unexpected attacks may follow such a presentation, no matter how good it is.
4. Include parents whenever possible. If they are informed, they will provide tremendous support. Parents have the power to establish or close a program. Make sure they know your goals and are involved in their implementation.
5. Custodians and office clerks can provide invaluable support. They have knowledge about systems and how to make them work that can never be learned from those "in charge."
6. Attend workshops, conferences, and university classes that present training in the areas of your interest and in innovative approaches. Meet others, exchange phone numbers, and then call them when you need sympathetic, understanding discussions. Near the end of each class I teach, we discuss the problem of support. The students exchange addresses and phone numbers so that they know there are always knowledgeable, caring people out there, should they need them.

Don't minimize the need for support systems. Many people cannot handle change. Once you accept that fact and know that it really isn't you, it's just the institutional apathy in your way, you can then go about your job of providing the best education you know how to gifted children. They, after all, will be your best support system. Purposefully include in your life supportive, nurturing people. Whatever you do, don't quit. We need you.

Administrative Support

Administrative support is as important to success as a well-chosen teacher. We often find that such support is withheld only because of lack of information. The coordinator must stay in close touch with the school principal, the superintendent, and the members of the school board. Don't wait until they have questions or you have a problem; prepare a package of information to leave with them, make an appointment, and present the program to them in detail. Some of the areas you must be sure to cover are these:

Who the gifted are and why they need special programs
The types of program experiences you have, or would like to plan
What your program offers that is not already being provided
How it will be staffed, scheduled, equipped
What it will cost, and how it will be paid for
How it will be evaluated
How your program will benefit the entire school or district
Ways in which parents will be involved
How the persons or groups to whom you are speaking are needed, and the role they
    will play in the success of the program.

Finally, find out what they want from the program, and be prepared to answer any
questions they may have.

Involve the administrative personnel in your program planning and evaluation
as much as possible. Several years ago, one of my students took over the coordinator
role of a district near Los Angeles. Not only was very little happening in gifted education within this district, but a great deal of negative feeling pervaded the area
from experiences with previous programs for the gifted. The new coordinator used
her first year to gain the administration's confidence, change attitudes, and establish
support for the structure she was developing. She carefully assessed the needs of
each principal, the superintendent, and the school board members.

At times, she called me to discuss a particularly untractable or negative stance
she had confronted. The university offered a six-week course in the evening to parents, teachers, and administrators at a site in their district on education of the
gifted. In the spring, the coordinator arranged a three-day retreat conference. Using
teams and facilitators, those attending planned the district program. She involved
all levels of the educational structure. The participants had time to discuss problems
and correct misunderstandings. By beginning this way, the program had excellent
results. The program has continued to build and is now one of the strongest, most
effective gifted programs in the state. You may wish to look at the possibilities of a
similar cooperative effort for your district. Informed, involved administration makes
quality education for gifted learners possible. Be sure to give your administration the
opportunity to become informed and involved.

Counselors and Psychologists as Support Personnel

Most gifted students, especially in secondary programs, perceive the counselor as a
program scheduler. Sometimes they experience the counselor as a tester or evaluator.
Unfortunately, gifted learners are too often given this limited view of the educational
staff member who could provide them with a valuable, even in some instances, critical service.

A number of years ago, my own son in junior high had for several semesters
complained about his dull, repetitive math class. I became aware that, if something
were not done, his interest in math, previously a true fascination, would be completely gone. I phoned the school counselor to arrange an appointment to discuss
the problem. After identifying myself and the problem as I perceived it, I asked for
consultation time. "I don't recall any problem we have had," said the counselor, "Let
me pull his file." After a pause, he returned to the phone to assure me that there
was no problem and an appointment would not be necessary.

I repeated my perception of the problem, assuring him that I realized that my son was not a behavior problem, but that I felt he did need help. I suggested that I would be agreeable to let him attend math classes at the nearby high school if that were considered feasible, but in any case, I would like an opportunity to explore the issue. "Well, we don't use acceleration. Our policy is against it except in rare cases. We have lots of students here as smart as your son. I don't see any purpose in a conference. He is not a problem, is doing excellent work, and his file shows that he is well-adjusted. I'll call you if we see any problem in the future." End of conversation. I was not at all assertive at that point in my life and was unsure of the value of pursuing the matter further. My son did drop his math interest and, although he might have done so in any case, I will always wonder. My work over the years that followed convinces me that gifted children who are not "problems" very often get little, if any help from school counselors.

When a counselor or guidance staff member becomes involved in the program for gifted learners, the results and benefits are very exciting, not only to the gifted students, but to their teachers and parents as well. Borgers and Treffinger (1979) admonish counselors to consider three basics to any effective counseling program: (1) counselors must be sensitive to any internal or external force that limits individual potential; (2) to meet such individual needs, they must provide a variety of services; and (3) they need to be "developmental and proactive rather than remedial and reactive" (p. 240).

A counselor can provide students with preventive and informational consultation, crisis intervention, and ongoing process or self-discovery counseling. Rather than wait for a problem to occur, the counselor should inform gifted students of such things as graduation needs, career counseling, and alternative choices for future planning (e.g., whether to go on to college immediately or work or travel for a year first). The counselor has access to resources that are not known to the student, the teacher, or the parents.

Gifted students have many problems to which they could find their own solution if given just a little help from an effective counselor. Gowan and Demos (1964) found that gifted students at all levels, elementary through secondary, profit greatly by having a counselor available as soon as problems arise. The same observation is true of gifted university undergraduates. Rothney and Koopman (1958) believe gifted students can be very independent in counseling situations and can evaluate information with their counselor very effectively. Moore (1960) states that gifted students profit more from counseling than their more average classmates. Vargiu (1971) sums up by saying that:

> With relatively little help gifted students can learn to become more in touch with all their personality aspects and develop them further, in a balanced, harmonious and effective way. They can be helped to solve their inner conflicts, and to coordinate and integrate their personality through discovery of a stable center of identity and awareness from which to function in the world (p. 2).

Gifted students and those who work with them (Gowan and Demos, 1964; Newland, 1976; Rothney and Koopman, 1958; Zaffrann and Colangelo, 1977) most often mention the students' need to—

discuss what is happening to them in their classroom, in their program, and in their personal lives;

find ways to communicate effectively with their teachers and parents;

discuss questions of identity, roles, relationships, and self-concept;

discover their special abilities and vocational choices, selecting from an overwhelming number of interests and abilities;

develop study habits, overcome underachievement patterns;

develop effective self-expression and communication;

develop personal standards of conduct; discuss frustration over discrepancy between
   ideals or intellectual conception of performance and physical ability to realize
   performance level that is high enough to meet their expectations.

Immediacy of contact is the major element of crisis intervention counseling that
must be available. Many students complain that, when they want to get help from a
school counselor, the procedure is so cumbersome and time consuming that they
seldom persevere. In her work, Newman (1967) emphasizes the necessity for available and continuing support of the counseling staff. She favors on-the-spot, as opposed to scheduled, seminars for staff consultations. Extending this approach to students could create some scheduling problems. However, the present situation in
many schools must be looked at carefully to make some decisions regarding priorities of services. If gifted students benefit so much from crisis intervention counseling, they must be able to get it.

Counselors should provide a third service for gifted students: process, or personal growth consultation. Some programs use small counseling groups that meet
weekly for support and discussion of personal problems. The adult counselor facilitates, but also encourages students to give their ideas. Group members assist in clarifying problems and presenting solutions. Even if they cannot agree on a solution,
having the opportunity to discuss the problem with sympathetic listeners often helps
them to alleviate the crisis, allowing the student to try alternative ideas for coping.
Such a group can serve as a peer counselor training experience at the same time. Often, a group session is more beneficial to the student than an individual session.

In addition to problem solution, a growth group structured as a learning experience can provide a safe place for gifted students to explore areas of communication, self-concept, assertion, and other strategies to facilitate personal and interpersonal growth. Gifted students will be able to interact with other students who have
many of the same problems and are more of a peer group than students found at
their grade level. Teachers trained and experienced in guidance procedures may provide these functions. Whether through a counselor or a teacher, this type of guidance
must be available to the gifted throughout their academic careers. Sanborn (1979)
declares the need for counseling and guidance activities to be designed "to help children learn about their own qualities and to attempt to relate these qualities to opportunities open to them both in the present and in the future" (p. 159). In turn, the
counselor must make use of this knowledge to help the school better understand the
student so that more appropriate and meaningful educational opportunities can be
planned.

The Counseling and Personnel Services Clearinghouse in a recent *Highlight*
(Winter, 1982) suggests that counselors coordinate a system-wide needs assessment
with gifted learners to determine counseling program goals unique to their population. While every group of gifted learners differs, problems and issues often found
are these:

Positive self-concept may be difficult to maintain because of excessive self-criticism and sensitivity to criticism from others. Gifted students may experience a split self-concept because of the conflict between superior ability and the need to be "one of the gang."

Great frustration may occur in gifted students with subjects or situations they cannot handle. They are unaccustomed to this experience and think they should know all the answers. As a result, they may not know how to ask for help when they need it.

Greater sensitivity and perceptiveness may result in acute negative responses to lack of genuineness, warmth and understanding, or to an uncomfortable situation.

Values and attitudes are likely to be divergent, different from the "norm." This can make it difficult for them to find true peers. It can also complicate career/vocational choices and pursuits.

Gifted students are not necessarily aware of their own abilities. They may not have had the opportunity to do truly outstanding work because they have not been fully challenged in the classroom. Both academic and career/vocational decisions can be seriously misguided.

Gifted students may have intense single interests and fail to apply themselves in other areas of school and social life. They may have poor and inefficient study habits.

Gifted girls often face socialization conflicts and lack good role models. Personal and social problems can result, as well as underachievement in school and career/vocation.

Gifted cultural and racial minorities may lack family support, appropriate role models, and social/economic access to particular careers or vocations.

The wider interests and multiple superior abilities of gifted students often require a broader range of career areas for exploration and selection (p. 2).

For the teacher of the gifted, the counselor may provide help in identification and with assessment profiles. A helpful consulting service would make suggestions for placement and how to meet needs best. A counselor could train teachers to use strategies and procedures they might otherwise not know. Teachers often encounter problems that require professional guidance; they should be able to seek the help of their colleagues. Often such mutual support between teacher and counselor is missing or is turned into a competitive situation, each needing to show the other that he or she is more effective. In such situations, everyone loses. Each member of the team in a gifted program has valuable skills. No one needs to use rank or professional one-upmanship to prove the importance of one's service; each function is critical.

For the parents of gifted learners, the counselor can provide information, understanding, and guidance. In crisis situations, a counselor can set up one of the most effective approaches ever developed for finding solutions to family problems, the family therapy group. So many student problems can be solved only when all the family members are aware of their responsibility for the problem and the need the student has for their support. Family therapy groups have been extremely productive.

When districts choose not to have a full-time coordinator, the counselor must take on coordinating tasks as well. A number of counseling approaches have worked well with gifted students. Gowan and Demos (1964) found a preference for a less directive approach.

Teachers of the Gifted—At Home: Parents

The beginning of this book emphasized how important parents are to actualizing the giftedness of each child. Throughout the book, we have seen how parents and the home play a significant part in every phase of a child's growth and influence the outcome of every educational decision. I am firmly convinced that the home is the true cradle of eminence. Whatever we find in our world that we would like to change, we must begin at the starting place with parenting. Some have tried to show that other influences are equally or even more important; however, they have yet to account for the powerful effects of motivation, self-image, and attitudes toward self and others—the factors that find their definition in the home.

What a parent is, even before conceiving the child, profoundly influences the child's physical, emotional, social, intuitive, and cognitive abilities. What a parent does, all of the decisions and actions the parent makes, follow directly from who and what the parent is. Our society would never think of allowing damage and misuse to happen to our highways, our food, our financial arrangements, even our political and professional institutions; yet we refuse to interfere in the gross misuse of our children. If we were to care for our children, all of our children, in ways we already know, we would abundantly increase the population of children who could actualize their potential to the degree we now designate as gifted. Giftedness may be more "normal" than the behaviors and abilities we now call typical.

The teacher in the home begins the process of human actualization, maintains and supports it, and allows this unique essence to become known while continually nourishing it with love. Anything less is unthinkable. There is no one way to nurture. As parents, we grow as the child grows; we make mistakes. Not all of our actions are the finest, nor even always what we know we are capable of, but rather than feel guilt, we feel joy in our learning. We try again, and we do better at our next chance. There are times when we feel inadequate to the task, frustrated by our inabilities, our lack of patience and energy.

We need to continue to value our own growth, to challenge ourselves in each area of our functioning to be more of who we are. We must find more ways to allow our growing children their own uniqueness, not limited by our perception of the world, but free to teach us their views. And between us, we should continually nurture and value love for ourselves, for each other, and for that of us that exists in all things. If we do all this, we have done enough, for it is incomparable. With this great respect and appreciation for parenting, the section of this book that deals with our present world comes to an end. As it began with concern for parenting, it is fitting that it should end with parenting.

Organizing for Cooperation

As children move into the school system, with their environment and their opportunities no longer as closely controlled by the home, parents often begin to feel powerless. They may be unaware that they have ways to influence what is happening to their child. When confronted with a situation that they know is not appropriate or that could even be damaging to their child's welfare, they may react as I did when my son was in need—trust that the school knows best and do nothing. Some parents of gifted children (fewer, I'm sure, than their public image suggests) attempt to change what is happening by complaining, attacking those they feel to be responsible, and creating only enough conflict and pressure to make everyone defensive.

There is a better way. Fortunately, both parents and school personnel want what is best for the child—at least, what they perceive to be best. The most effective way to change or correct a bad situation is not by direct confrontation, in most instances, but by an organized, knowledgeable, cooperative effort. If there must be winners and losers, too often the child is one of the losers, no matter who wins.

The first step is to organize, even before a problem crops up. Join with other parents of gifted children in your school or your district. Such organizations have accomplished many goals. As your child finds the school experience different than others find it, you as parents will find your experience with your child differs from the more typical parental experiences. Review the characteristics and unusual needs your gifted child has as a result of heightened mental ability, and you will begin to understand why your role as a parent is also unusual. It helps to meet with other parents who are experiencing themselves and their children in ways similar to yours. When a group of parents of gifted children organizes, they find such understanding, and even relief, in their sharing of common concerns and experiences.

Once your group begins to meet, you will easily find people willing to share information on educating gifted children. They can inform you of what is known about giftedness, the identification procedures used in your district, the gifted program in which your child participates, and answers to many questions you will have. They will tell you of many alternatives and possibilities for providing quality education both at home and at school. You will now be in a position to help change inadequate or unfair practices in your schools. Many teachers, administrators, and school board members are anxious to make changes, try more challenging programs, or end detrimental practices. However, they do not want to go against the wishes of the community. It is, after all, your school; these are your children.

As a group, you should present informed support for the practices you prefer for your children, not only showing what is wrong, but presenting other alternatives. By suggesting positive changes, you will be far more able to resolve the problems. If no one needs to defend, each can spend that energy constructing. Organize first, then become informed. With so many resources (e.g., people, books, classes, conferences) available, becoming informed will not be difficult. I have found that most people who are committed to gifted education are very interesting and generous. You may find learning about giftedness more fascinating than you thought.

One note of caution—gifted children often have gifted parents who exhibit all the same characteristics and who have some of the same independent, divergent natures. Organizing such groups may take a bit of doing; diverse opinions must be expected and allowed. For information on how others have organized groups of parents of gifted children write to: the ERIC Clearinghouse on Handicapped and Gifted Children, Council for Exceptional Children, 1920 Association Drive, Reston, Virginia 22091. The same group publishes two very useful handbooks (Delp and Martinson, 1974; Kaufmann, 1976) that can be obtained at minimal cost. Two other very useful books that you will find helpful are by Hall and Skinner (1980) and the American

Association for Gifted Children (1980) and were written for the Perspectives on Gifted and Talented Education project directed by Abraham Tannenbaum.

Often groups of parents of gifted provide out-of-school experiences for their children when changes do not occur in the schools as fast as they had hoped. A parent group in California, the Gifted Children's Association, offers an extensive curriculum after school and on Saturdays. They house their program on junior college campuses, charge a small tuition to cover the cost of hiring professors and teachers, print and distribute the schedule of offerings, and handle, fees and registration. Their brochures would rival any college extension program.

Informed groups can also schedule field trips to enrich the learning of their children. Many educational trips that single families would not find accessible are available to groups. Factories; museums; dress rehearsals of concerts; plays and ballets; tours of industries, professional groups, and businesses; archeological digs; and historical events can all be experienced by your group. The possibilities are limitless, but be careful not to spend all your energy outside of the school system, with none left for changing what is happening to your child all day, five days a week.

Parent Inservice

It is equally important for teachers in the home to understand the needs of gifted children and how to meet these needs as it is for teachers in the schools. I have often given five- to eight-week parent inservice courses that help parents better understand the problems of the school, the program, and their gifted children. Among other things, we discuss alternative programs and strategies to use both at home and at school to build self-concept and open communication and to develop all four areas of functioning: thinking, feeling, sensing, and intuiting. I will outline the sessions here so that you might know what we do as you consider inservicing the parents of gifted in your organization. The gifted coordinator will often provide such a course or hire someone to present it. If not, you may wish to bring your resources together, using your parent organization as the coordinating or planning group. We use the following five sessions:

1. Understanding Giftedness—Who are the gifted? How do you nurture giftedness?
2. Emotional and Social Development of the Gifted—Developing self-esteem, values, and creativity
3. Meeting the Needs of the Gifted—Program alternatives, differential curriculum, learning and challenges, integrating all four areas of learning, and evaluation
4. Effective Teachers at Home and at School—The nurturing home, growth, families, communication, the teacher in the classroom as a part of the learning community
5. What Can You Do Now?—Planning with the school, student-parent-teacher interaction, legislative possibilities and provisions, becoming active in your community for gifted education

Parents As Resources

Parents can cooperate with the schools in providing quality education for their gifted learners in many ways. One way is to offer their services as teachers. If the classroom is individualized and/or organized into centers, a parent can create and implement a center for a given period of time. For example, in a school near our campus, a kindergarten teacher assesses the interests, occupations, and abilities of the parents of the children in her class each year. She invites them to share something they are especially good at with a small group of children in a learning center for three days. She has had language centers, construction centers, baking centers, black history centers, Cinco de Mayo centers, and numerous others. The parents are much more involved in the classroom, provide many other needed services, and enrich the learning experience for everyone. Often parents will be comfortable sharing with a few children, even when they would never consider "teaching" the entire class.

Parents can also provide materials, help with construction when changing the classroom environment, run individualized learning labs in subjects such as reading or math, and provide transportation, additional supervision sources, and arrangements for field trips. Some parents enjoy organizing other parents to make all of the above suggestions possible. It is important that teachers ask for the help they need and not waste parental talent on busy work. Parents can make important contributions to classroom learning if both teacher and parents take the responsibility to initiate and carry out such involvement.

At the very least, parents should be involved in planning and evaluation conferences with their child and the teacher. Each of these persons has something unique to contribute to the data needed for good educational decision making. Such involvement is at the heart of The Integrative Education Model discussed in chapter 4 (p. 159).

Parents can make a significant impact in the area of legislation. Most of the provisions for special education at the state and federal levels have been enacted because of the efforts of groups of parents. Parents must stay informed about bills and legislative action and let their elected representatives know what they want. Government officials are asked to resolve many problems. It is very easy for them to feel that the needs of gifted students, if they know of them at all, have very low priority. Teachers and other school personnel cannot influence the boards of education, the state superintendents, the governors, and the legislators with anywhere near the effectiveness that parents can. In sheer numbers, parents have the advantage. You as parents truly have the power in our school systems. Be aware of it. Use it for the benefit of your children.

I have found the following suggestions useful as a parent and as a teacher. Many of them came from other parents or from students, and some my children taught me. If you live with gifted children:

1. Create open communication that is available from birth on. Set aside a special time for each child to have you to him/herself, to be interested in her/him alone, to be listened to nonjudgmentally, to share ideas. Don't wait for problems or decision-making times. I personally used the time I tucked each child in bed, sitting down each evening for ten to thirty minutes, with all our attention available to each other. Also try the family council described in chapter 3 (p. 126).
2. Do what you like doing and include the child, as well as doing things in which the child is interested.
3. Permit the children their own individuality, and enjoy them for who they are, not what you would like them to be.

4. Respect your child and allow the child as much dignity as you would a friend.
5. Allow your children to make lots of decisions, and consult them on issues affecting them whenever you believe they can understand the consequences.
6. Don't confuse the IQ with the child; the child is much more.
7. Help the child understand and deal with his or her belonging and conformity needs. Often, especially for girls, the pressure is very great; they must feel it's really all right to be different.
8. Help children with their need for perfectionism and what that does to their self-image. Serve as an example of how hard it is to accept your own mistakes, and show them how you keep trying. Let them feel your acceptance of them as people. Help them set realistic standards and not hold everyone up to them.
9. Arrange back-to-nature times, quiet together and apart times; value reflection and daydreaming.
10. Help your child set time and energy priorities. Too often the world is so exciting for these children that they seem to need to do everything at once.
11. Help them appreciate individual differences, both in themselves and in others.
12. Instruct by your actions more than your words. If you want your child to be an avid reader, you will probably need to be one. Other interests develop this way, too.
13. Don't insist that every project have closure before other things can happen. Often, what the child wanted or needed to learn from an experience occurs before the project is "finished." Sometimes other fascinating areas just have to be explored before the project can be finished properly. Otherwise, you may end up with a few finished projects and a turned-off child.
14. Be careful about supporting teachers when they are doing stupid things (e.g., a homework assignment of fifty problems all on a concept that your child mastered two years ago, or the insisting, under threat of low grades, on completion of an overnight project even when your child is playing in a special concert that evening). You should plan a conference with the teacher and be sure the situation is understood. If the teacher remains unreasonable, you have a right to discuss your perception with the principal. There is little value in obedience at any cost.
15. Provide a safe place. At times, your child will find being different very difficult. Neither the teacher nor the child's friends will always understand, and your child will need a place where it is safe to be who he or she is.
16. Enjoy living with your child! Your life together will be a great adventure! Children are not comparable, so value each for what each offers. As parents, we are truly blessed to be able to become so intimately involved with such marvelous people, our children.

In this chapter, we have discussed abilities, values, attitudes, and characteristics of effective teachers of the gifted at home and at school. The teacher is the most significant influence on the learning environment at school. We have identified general differences between effective and ineffective teachers. In addition, we have looked at the abilities every teacher of gifted learners should develop. To develop them, both preservice and inservice teacher education must be provided. For classroom teachers to become more effective, especially in situations requiring change and innovation, they will need to establish a support system. Among suggestions to aid in such development, we looked at the possible contributions of administrators, counselors, and guidance personnel. However, the gifted program must be made known to them and provision for their services planned if they are to be used properly.

The parents of the gifted (their teachers at home) were encouraged to organize, to become informed, and to work cooperatively with school personnel to provide the best possible education for their children. We looked at some of the services parents can provide and suggested ways to live effectively with the gifted. As we began the book by showing the importance of parenting, so we bring the current information in the book to an end by recognizing parents as the most valuable teachers of the gifted.

CHAPTER TEN

The Amazing Possibilities Ahead

This chapter introduces the reader to some of the future influences on gifted education, which include

- ideas of physicists and philosophers on reality, and our connectedness.
- developments in brain research that are expanding our concept of who we are and what we can become.
- better understanding of our growing self, especially as shown in the use of early learning, biofeedback, and superlearning techniques.
- the link between integrative education and transpersonal learning.
- parapsychology and psi research, and their relationship to our understanding of our intuitive abilities.
- the importance of future studies in our search for optimal realities for each of us.

> Your belief system explains only what your limits are—not what *the* limits are.
> Belief systems limit experience. Impossible things are things you don't believe in.
>
> James Fadiman

We are living in a most interesting and exciting time. As each year passes, more astounding discoveries are being made. More amazing thoughts are being discussed. More beliefs are being jiggled. The results are an overwhelming excitement, a constant rethinking of old structures, dramatic reassessment and realignment of who we are, why we are, and where we are. If I had lived during the Renaissance, I could not have felt more excited about the changes appearing in every facet of life. Though I'm sure that that period was very special and the people then would have found themselves in awe of their circumstances, they should be here now!

What we will share in this chapter will only touch on some of the contributing events, and much of what we will discuss will be only theories, best guesses, clues to what lies ahead. But already what can be seen tells us that we are not just looking at how we may better use the resources we now have, both human and material; we are redefining our reality, our meaning, and our connection to the universe. We may find ourselves not only a wondrous part of the creation, but an intimate part of the creating.

The Joining

As we explore the new areas of scientific thought that affect us as guides to the intellect of ourselves and others, we must first give up the need for dichotomies. It no longer seems possible to believe one truth or one view; the operable word has become *and*. This can be seen in so many places and is being seen by so many of our best minds. In physics it is now necessary to believe that everything is both waves and particles. In human understanding we are asked to reconcile two paths, the rational, empirical path of science and the inner path of the intuition and imagination. Each of us is asked to see him- or herself as being and becoming. Even our classrooms are places of the integration of polarities of knowing. Without a need for right/wrong, true/false, we are free to examine a few of these bigger, more wonderfully outrageous ideas and those who ask us to entertain them.

A part of the "way the world is" has been the idea that entropy exists; that is, all of the matter and energy in the universe is gradually being reduced to an ultimate state of inert uniformity. Now we are asked to see such events not as a reduction in organization, but as a catalyst of complexity or increasing order. Ilya Prigogine (1980), a Belgian chemist and Nobel Prize winner, believes that everything is alive and these living systems periodically become so disrupted by disharmony that they appear to fall apart. What is really happening is that the turbulence has led to a transition, a movement toward a higher level of organization. The more the turbulence, the more complex will be the restructuring; the more complex a structure becomes, the more often it will go into apparent disharmony. The part I like best is that a seemingly small number or critical mass can create enough disharmony that even huge systems and institutions will be forced to change.

Think what that can mean to those involved in gifted education at every level. A small, creative and committed group of educators can indeed have an effect on even such a large system as the institution of education in today's society. Prigogine speaks of examples such as biological systems, black holes, chemical reactions, brains, cultures, and social arrangements all being similarly affected. He calls such systems "dissipative structures," and because such structures cannot accommodate entropic disorder beyond a critical point, they suddenly reconfigure themselves into more highly ordered systems that can accommodate the increased entropy. In such a view, all systems become open to fluctuation and to innovation. With such a view, there can be no prediction other than the constant movement toward higher being.

One of the complex systems that is affected by Prigogine's theory is the human brain. To add to the theory of "dissipative structure," we now have two very impressive thinkers asking us to see it also as a hologram. A hologram, you remember, can reconstruct a three-dimensional picture from a process involving interference waves of light and can reconstruct such a picture from any fragment of its surface. The brain is considered such an instrument by David Bohm (1980), an English physicist and mathematician, and a protégé of Albert Einstein; and Karl Pribram (1977), a neurophysiologist and respected researcher from Stanford University. Together they conclude that not only is the brain a hologram, but it interprets for us in a holographic way the larger hologram, the universe. This means that the brain is far more complex than we now imagine and that it operates in dimensions as yet unknown, possibly beyond time and space. Our brains construct "concrete" reality by interpreting frequencies from other dimensions, allowing us to feel at home in whatever level we can understand. "We were beginning to find in our laboratories that the brain was actually responding to vibrations," commented Pribram (Tarrytown Group, 1982).

Bohm asks that we cease to think of reality as made up of independent fragments. "The notion that all these fragments are separately existent is evidently an illusion, and this illusion cannot do other than lead to endless conflict and confusion. Indeed, the attempt to live according to the notion that the fragments are really separate is, in essence, what has led to the growing series of extremely urgent crises that is confronting us today" (pp. 1, 2).

Fritjof Capra (1982), a physicist at the Lawrence Berkeley Radiation Laboratory, expands on these ideas and finds in his pursuit of the atomic and subatomic world that the universe is interdependent and involved in cyclical change. He believes that the seemingly separate objects we have thought to exist in our world are in reality patterns in an inseparable cosmic process, which are intrinsically dynamic, continually changing into one another, holistic, and ecological. Capra sees this view of reality affecting all forms of social organizations and institutions.

Notions of common sense, inductive reasoning, and speed of light as an upper limit of information transfer may also be changing. Bernard d'Espagnet (1979), a French physicist, has reported some interesting findings that support Pribram's view of vibrations and Capra's sense of an inseparable, holistic universe. His research is showing a mysterious linkage between the properties of subatomic particles separated by a considerable distance. His data seem to imply that all objects constitute an indivisible whole. He believes that the concept of an independently existing reality is remote from everyday experience.

Physicist Geoffrey Chew (Ferguson, 1982) states that physics is "evolving beyond attempts to isolate phenomena, reproduce experimental results and make clear distinctions between separate aspects of the world. Viewing the universe as a collection of pieces is no longer tolerable" (p. 1).

This linking, this indivisibility affects the way we view learning. According to a new theory by Rupert Sheldrake (Sheldrake, 1981), these invisible organizing fields create a "morphic resonance" that affects an entire species. "Whenever one member of a species learns a new behavior, the causative field for the species is changed. These fields have no energy, but are causative because they serve as blueprints for form and behavior. For example, if a human being learns to do a task that no other person has ever done before, humans everywhere else in the world should be able to learn the task more easily, in the absence of any known type of physical connection or communication." Such a theory again supports the idea of a holographic reality.

While more centered on the brain as the mediating system, the theory proposed by William Gray, a Massachusetts psychiatrist, also has important implications for human learning. "Feelings may be the organizers of the mind and personality. Finely tuned emotions may form the basis of all we know" (Ferguson, 1982, p. 1). According to this new theory, feelings form the underlying structure of thought, with emotion serving as the key to memory, recognition, and generation of new ideas. Gray believes that humans are more intelligent than other species because they have a richer supply of emotional nuances available to them. This results from the larger human forebrain and the more extensive connections between the frontal lobe and the limbic system. Gray says,

> I had important confirmation in Einstein's repeated statement that ideas come to him first in the form of vague and diffuse bodily sensations that gradually refined themselves into exact and reproduceable feeling-tones. Only when this process was completed could Einstein mathematically define the new concept (p. 4).

Paul LaViolette (Ferguson, 1982), a systems theorist, combined Prigogine's theory and Gray's theory to explain how the brain physically processes new ideas. "Mental events—sensations, perceptions, feelings, emotions—are encoded and processed by the brain as if they were AM/FM neuroelectric waveforms" (p. 1). The encoded waveforms are then amplified into thoughts while they recycle between the limbic and cortical systems. A higher degree of intelligence then means a higher degree of caring.

According to Gray and LaViolette, the brain uses feelings to structure information. Abstract information may be so hard to recall because it is cut off from feelings. Often, even after a decade of exploration of affective or feeling education, the cognitive or rational learning mode is most highly valued. The irony is that the efficiency of learning is prevented by ignoring feelings. Integration of emotion and cognition is far more efficient, more easily and rapidly dealt with, contends Gray.

One of the leaders in gifted education, John C. Gowan, has, during the past decade, been exploring the area of creativity in a way that has opened for him areas to be explored beyond those usually assigned to this field of inquiry. While some have been satisfied to limit their inquiry to the realm of creative problem solving and creative thinking, Gowan has begun to discuss and theorize in areas he refers to as those of increasing order. This seems to indicate a tie to Prigogine's theory of the ever increasing complexity of higher levels of organization, or, if you will, increasing order. Gowan writes of the operations of these levels of increasing order and attempts to describe, organize, and map this new territory (Gowan, 1980). With his help and that of others such as those found in this chapter, we may indeed, as

Gowan suggests, "illuminate the Divinity which resides in each of us and make it blossom like a rose" (p. XV).

A very special person who took this idea of a holographic universe one step further and through delightful analogies has left us with quite a lot to think about was Itzhak Bentov. Having been with him only once, I was very surprised by the loss I felt and continue to feel at his death in the DC-10 crash in Chicago in 1979. I suppose this is the mark of a master teacher, for he was truly that. He could take very abstract and difficult concepts and with humor help me to understand many levels of meaning. I continue to read his books (Bentov, 1977, 1982) and continue to wonder and to learn. He seems to tickle the mind with his comments, for example:

> Everything in the entire universe, including our bodies, is made of this cosmic substance. We contain atoms from the most distant galaxies and are thus connected to the whole universe (1982, p. 5).

> The universe is a hologram or interference pattern in which all parts are interconnected, containing information about each other and thus about the entire universe. . . . Each individual human consciousness is part of that hologram; therefore, by projecting one's consciousness into the Universal Mind in a heightened state of awareness, one can obtain knowledge about the whole universe. . . . It also follows that the thoughts of all human beings are interconnected, affecting each other and in turn affecting the entire universe. Whatever one thinks or does becomes part of the universal hologram (1982, p. 6).

> In short, consciousness in a vibratory state manifests as our familiar matter, from which the different forms that we see around us are made. The table, the flowers, the scent of the flowers, and our bodies are all made of rapidly vibrating consciousness (1982, p. 11).

> If we take a chicken egg and attach electrodes to the two ends, we discover that it reflects the structure of the universe. . . . Every seed in nature, whether plant or animal, has a similar current running along its axis, creating an electromagnetic field around the seed (1982, pp. 31, 32).

> I suggest, therefore that our brain is not the *source* of thought but a thought *amplifier*. As we have seen, it takes a tiny impulse, magnifies it for us, and only then does it become a thought. It appears that the thought does not originate within the brain; rather, the brain picks up the tiny impulses implanted there . . . (1977, p. 86).

Margaret Mead was concerned about global interdependence and an emerging world culture (Houston, 1977). She believed that we have now reached an age when the planet must be mutually shared. We are, she felt, on the brink of a planetary integration that will provide "opportunities for human and cultural potentiation of a scale and depth never known before" (p. 58). However, such wholeness would need to be seen in a framework of preserving human differences and individual uniqueness. In such a vision, the smallest actions of each of us affect the reality of us all. Although this view may seem impossibly optimistic, Mead assures us that "what seemed impossible to accomplish yesterday is a shared activity of thousands tomorrow" (p. 58). It requires only the development of the ideas.

Life-styles and belief systems change, dichotomies no longer exist, and time and space have another dimension. Reality is seen as an outward projection of internal thoughts, feelings, and expectations. Energy is the connector, the center, the basis of all matter, and consciousness forms reality. It is this progression that we make available as we present opportunities to our students that allow the integration of body and mind. As science continues to validate this interconnected view of reality, Western pragmatists will join Eastern mystics, and all humans will benefit. Human potential, as yet unknown, will have the chance to develop.

Teilhard de Chardin (1959) predicted that the future of consciousness is to become more complex, more inclusive. He too believed that we are evolving toward a harmonious interrelationship, a single entity, one that will not diminish all of its parts but enhance our individuality, making each of us more truly what we are. He spoke of love as the elemental energy drawing the whole towards its culmination and fulfillment. This vision has been shared by philosophers and educators throughout the ages.

While all of the foregoing are just theories, I remind you that theories are all we have in constructing our reality and ordering our thoughts. They are the best explanations their originators have for what is happening. Observations and "facts" are also theories that we accept and have decided to use to help us understand our world and ourselves in it. It may be, as Bentov says, that "we are all part of this great hologram called Creation which is everybody else's SELF. . . . You create your own reality. It's all a cosmic play, and there is nothing but *you*!" (1982, p. 85).

Brain Research: Extending the Learning About You

Within the past few years, technology has been vastly improving our ability to understand how our brain functions, leading to a better understanding of how we, as human beings, learn. Curiously the more we are discovering, the more we can validate the ancient wisdoms that have come to us from Chinese, Hindu, Egyptian and other age-old teachings.

One example is the work of the Japanese inventor, Hiroshi Motoyama, who has designed the Apparatus for Measuring the Functioning of the Meridians and Corresponding Internal Organs (AMI). The AMI can distinguish disorders of organs and specific disease tendencies. Used by the government in Japan to screen employees during a required medical exam, the AMI tests have indicated that energy flowing in and out of the meridians can interact with the meridian energy of other persons. This energy does not travel through the nervous system. Instead it is conducted electrolytically via connective tissue emitting signals near the surface of the body. The energy points correspond to the locations or the Hindu *chakras*, or energy centers, and the Chinese acupuncture meridians. It is most interesting to find validation for the often experienced notion that each human energy field influences others in its vicinity. Motoyama's work was reported in the *Brain/Mind Bulletin* (Ferguson, 1981).

Another interesting view of how we function is coming from the use of the magnetoencephalogram (MEG), which has allowed researchers to map the brain at work. This instrument is giving researchers a clearer understanding of the link between higher mental processes (such as understanding the meaning of words) and underlying brain activity. The MEG works by detecting the extremely small magnetic fields associated with the movement of ions into and out of the brain cells. The MEG has the advantage of needing only to be placed next to the head without touching it and is relatively impervious to signals from anywhere other than precisely where it is focused. The MEG permits the detailing of the intricacies of the brain at work, while minimizing interference with its natural activity (Zimmerman, 1982).

Another exciting new technological breakthrough is the invention of the nuclear magnetic resonance scanner (NMR), literally a new kind of window to the interior of the brain and the entire body. Previously used diagnostic tools, such as the computerized axial tomography scanner (CAT) and the positron emission tomography scanner (PET), have involved the use of ionizing radiation that can be injurious to the patient and to the operator. The NMR requires no x-rays or other harmful material, as it works by use of harmless magnets and a radio-frequency energy about a billion times weaker than that of visible light. By sensing the exchange of atoms between molecules in chemical reactions, NMR can literally watch physiological processes in action, including the brain and its natural rhythms (Wingerson, 1982).

Brain research is also opening up new fields of inquiry that already ask us to stretch, or in some cases change, our belief systems about how we function.

Chronopsychology is the mind/body study involving daily (circadian) and other temporal cycles and the effects of biological rhythms on physical, cognitive, and emotional aspects of human behavior. Results of research in this new field have shown that—

Short-term memory is less effective in the afternoon, as long-term memory improves;

Reading speed declines during the day; comprehension increases;

Birth most commonly occurs at 4 A.M., death at 6 A.M.;

Activity phases of most circadian rhythms peak in early afternoon, rest phases shortly after midnight;

Levels of hormones change, mood swings, cell division, pulse rate, blood pressure, body temperature all fluctuate.

Circadian timetables influence learning, effectiveness of medication, immune responses, and susceptibility to disease. The recorded fluctuations in intellectual performance over the day are sufficiently great to account for the difference between an A, B, or C grade on tests (Ferguson, 1981).

The possibility of learning to strengthen the immune system of the body mentally has received validation from the experiments of Ader and Cohen of the University of Rochester in New York (Wingerson, 1982b). Their work, along with that of others throughout the United States and Canada, has opened a new field of investigation in how the brain affects the ability of the immune system to fight off disease, *psychoneuroimmunology.*

David Loye (1982) tells us that individuals with balanced brain hemisphere dominance apparently are better predictors than persons with strong dominance in a single hemisphere. Acting as the executive, the frontal lobes monitor differences of right and left brain input, then decide what is the true composite nature of the future and how it is to be lived.

Other interesting findings in brain research are these:

Male sex hormones (androgens) may affect the ability to visualize and manipulate objects mentally, key components of mathematical skills widely considered to be more innate to males than females (Hier and Crowley, 1982).

Mature nervous systems form new synapses in response to changes in the environment, intense muscle activity, variations in hormone levels, and prolonged drug treatment (Cottman and Nieto-Sampedro, 1982).

The stream of consciousness is activated when 100 million synapses are simulta-neously engaged in quantum interactions. This type of information begins to pro-vide a physical definition of consciousness. There is even the possibility that translocation, the transporting of oneself instantly to a new location, may be pos-sible, as there is such a precedent in the quantum effect known as *tunneling* (Ferguson, 1982c).

Memory drugs, experimentally used to improve performance on memory tasks, have been found to give results significantly higher than 'chance. Originating in Belgium, piracetam has been researched in Europe for over five years and is in test status in the United States. It has been found effective in improving the recall of students and in treating disorders of senility. Researchers believe its effective-ness results from its ability to aid integrative activities in the brain (Ferguson, 1977).

Early Learning: Pondering When and How Giftedness Begins

How early do we begin to learn? At what point does the environment begin to inter-act with the genetic programs we carry? Just what does have an effect on us? How much does the early experience have to do with giftedness, optimal development? with personality? with who we turn out to be? In chapter 2 we discovered how very critical the first years of life are if we are to use the potential with which we are born. It has been suggested that giftedness is the result of an appropriate and nur-turing interaction between the child and the environment. Researchers are now looking at just what such an environment should contain and when it begins to im-pact the growth and development of the child. The following data are the result of inquiry into the fetal period, the life of the unborn child. Although there are ques-tions unanswered and controversies unresolved, the findings are clearly provocative. That we may learn to optimize the opportunities for all children, let us review and consider.

Quoting research from many sources, Verny (1981) has shown the fetus to be a hearing, sensing, feeling being. By the fourth month the unborn child can frown, squint, and grimace. By the fifth month the child is sensitive to touch. At four or five months the unborn child reacts to sounds and melodies; Vivaldi and Mozart cause the child to relax, Beethoven and Brahms stimulate movement. It has been reported that the fetus hears clearly from the sixth month in utero and can be seen to move in rhythm to the mother's speech. In 1980, for the first time, scientists managed to record sounds from within the amniotic sac of a mammal. Using a sheep embryo, the experiment showed that external sounds, including conversation, are clearly audible. From these and other results on fetal hearing, it is now concluded that the auditory experience of the unborn child is more significant than was previously thought (Armitage, 1980).

By five months the fetus is very sensitive to light. If a light is shone on the mother's stomach, the child will look the other way or show a startled reaction, re-ports Verny. By the seventh or eighth month the neural circuits of the fetus are as advanced as a newborn's, and the cerebral cortex is mature enough to support con-sciousness. Memory may begin somewhere between the sixth and the eighth month.

An area of concern to many of the prenatal researchers influences the self-esteem and security feelings of the infant. Attitudes of the mother seem to be picked up clearly by the infant in utero by the sixth or seventh month. Some researchers feel that the mother's attitude toward the child has the single greatest effect on the well-being and future welfare of the unborn. Even when the mother pretends to be pleased with the pregnancy, but deeply resents or rejects the baby, the baby knows the true feelings and reacts to them. Intense stress or prolonged discomfort in the life of the mother is deeply felt by the infant she is carrying. Studies indicate that anxious and troubled children result from unrelieved anxiety experienced by the mother during the pregnancy (Scott, 1973, 1977; Huttunen and Niskanen, 1978; Verny, 1981).

Bonding after birth seems to be a continuation of the bonding process begun in the womb. The last two or three months before birth are important for establishment of affectional ties that can be carried into the hours and days immediately after birth. Study after study shows that happy, content women are far more likely to have bright, outgoing infants. The when and the how of optimal development, the beginning of giftedness, must be seen as occurring prior to birth. Intelligence is partially dependent on the life of the unborn child.

Further Possibilities in Human Learning—Superlearning

Certain elements, independently used, have positively affected learning and have been reported in the educational literature during the past decade: the critical influence of teachers and their personalities; the importance of supportive, responsive, stimulating environments; the reduction of tension and anxiety in the learning interaction; the need for a variety of approaches; the need for a change of pace in the presentation of material. In Bulgaria, a teacher/researcher by the name of Georgi Lozanov (1977) has been putting such information together and has, through numerous experiments, developed a system he calls *Suggestopedia* that not only accelerates the learning process, but dramatically increases the retention factor. Lozanov bases the Suggestopedia system on three principles: joy and the absence of tension, oneness of the conscious and unconscious, and suggestive interaction.

To assure the first principle, a relaxed ambience is developed using tension reduction and relaxation techniques. Any practice that would produce anxiety, stress, fear of failure, or humiliation for the learner must be discontinued. The student is encouraged to view learning as a pleasant activity, one he or she will enjoy, with results easily obtainable. The second principle is developed by the use of music (generally classical) chosen for this purpose. Dramatic skits and psychodrama may also be used to heighten the awareness of wholeness or oneness. Lozanov (1977) states,

> Oneness of the conscious and the unconscious (or totality) requires that the learning process be so organized that it uses not only the reactions and the conscious functions of the learner's personality, but also his unconscious authority. . . . It raises consciousness in the wider sense of behavior and motivation to a higher level (p. 3).

The third principle can be met only by a sensitive, nonthreatening, caring teacher. The part the teacher plays and the attitude emanating from this instructor-supporter-facilitator are critical.

The Suggestopedia system of accelerated learning has produced some impressive results: students show significant improvement in memory; they cover material that, under former educational methodology and situations, took over a year to learn, in two to three months with a higher level of retention. Recent research shows that Suggestopedia can be used in every discipline, for the students benefit by feelings of harmony, restfulness, pleasant emotions, and the calling forth and combining of all the mental, physical, and psychic reserves. Racle (1977) reports that this type of instruction is not only "many times more efficacious" than other teaching methods, but "much more humane and much less burdensome for the studying individual" (p. 2).

Many countries, including the United States, and also the United Nations Educational Service (UNESCO), are interested and involved in research of the possibilities of accelerated learning. Conferences, workshops, pamphlets, and journal articles have begun to disperse information about this exciting new practice. To learn more, you may contact The Society for Suggestive-Accelerative Learning and Teaching, Inc., 2740 Richmond Ave., Des Moines, Iowa 50317.

Other thoughts toward optimizing learning:

> Relaxed concentration facilitates learning; performance equals potential minus self-interference (Gallwey, 1976).

> Human beings experience numerous states of waking consciousness without full awareness of the potentials and abilities unique to each state. Educators must be about the business of teaching this awareness (Roberts, 1982).

> Individual biases toward attending to or ignoring stimuli can be measured soon after birth. Infants at high risk, related to differences in reading ability, for example, can be diagnosed in time to remediate their problem (Ferguson, 1981).

> Computerized video games may have major implications for the future of learning. Eventually they may be directed by brainwave biofeedback. They are highly interactive and provide immediate response. Games are now being developed to feature realistic simulation experiences that reward original, creative thinking (Adkins, 1982).

> Synchronization of the hemispheres may allow greater intuitive learning. Such synchronization may be self-taught by the use of biofeedback instrumentation (Millay, 1981).

> Biofeedback is proving to be a valuable tool for optimizing learning. Though it has long been recognized that nearly all organs and parts of the human body generate electrical current, only after the discovery of biofeedback techniques did we find that this electrical activity is within our control. And more than just an internal generation is possible.

Dr. Elmer Green, founder of the Biofeedback and Psychophysiology Center at Menninger Foundation, tells us that biofeedback uses an approach to self-regulation in human beings that means getting immediate, ongoing information about one's own biological processes or conditions, e.g., heart action, temperature, brain-wave activity, blood pressure, or muscle tension, and using the information to change and control voluntarily the specific process or response being monitored. He suggests that you must visualize what you want the body to do, tell it to do it, and then relax and let it happen. The biofeedback instrument only allows you to observe the change. The process does nothing to the person; rather it is a tool for releasing that person's potential (Pew, 1979).

During biofeedback, the electrical energy of the body is turned into a source of electrical power. It seems that only a fraction of the electrical power we develop as our bodies function is actually used. Most of this energy emanates from the body and dissipates into the environment around us. Some researchers have tapped this source of electrical energy and made its existence dramatically real by using body energy to light displays, power sound devices, and even run electric trains (Brown, 1974). Brown feels that staggering amounts of energy are untapped and wasted constantly because we have not yet learned how to harness this never-ending master resource. She envisions using bioenergy as a source of electrical energy to run computers and other powered devices or as a sophisticated communications system.

Discovery of the techniques of biofeedback has provided us with important information and insights into the functioning of our human system. Biofeedback techniques can be as simple as looking into a mirror or as complex as the monitoring of sophisticated electronic devices. Any object or material that provides information about the body's systems can be called a biofeedback device. Biofeedback is important to education because it can give us information on how our biosystem functions and on abilities about which we have been previously unaware. Already many psychologists and educators are finding a multitude of uses for this tool. Kamiya, Haight, and Jampolsky (1975) use biofeedback to remove learning blocks, but not to manipulate or gain control of behavior, calling this process "personal biology." Reportedly, it has had much effect on student self-image, on improvement in focus of attention, emotional stability, communications, and reading skills. There have also been reports of reduction in anxiety and hyperactive behavior in students (French, 1978). These reports show that biofeedback has been used in a college physiology course, as part of the training of student nurses and with the developmentally disabled, all with results showing significant gains in learning. "Feedback display systems have evolved from clicks, beeps and flashing red lights into multi-dimensional color video and concert quality musical tones. Children can affect the race of turtles across a video screen by increasing their production of alpha brainwaves" (French, 1978, p. 2). Relaxation exercises learned in biofeedback training helped University of Wisconsin football players to cut their injuries and win more games; they improved from a 60 percent win record to a 90 percent win record after training (Pew, 1979).

Mulholland (1973) believes there is tremendous potential for biofeedback in education, but that there exists a pronounced communication gap between the two areas. He believes educators could use biofeedback in at least three ways: to enhance self-awareness, self-exploration, and self-control; to accentuate processes conducive to learning and to diminish those that impede learning; and to strengthen a specific skill. The attending process could be facilitated by self-regulating biofeedback units, insuring better attention during learning. Learning could also be facilitated by training students to be more in control of their emotional states, for we know that emotions have as much effect on learning as attention. With biofeedback training, students could become aware of the physiological states associated with pleasant feelings and train themselves to use such states to reduce states of anxiety, fear, or anger that tend to impede learning. By intelligent and creative application of current research in biofeedback, Mulholland believes that the educational community will achieve a major professional advance.

Students can participate in researching these new body data. By bringing resources and practitioners to class, you can open this fascinating area for your students. Once they understand the concept, they will find methods and materials in common use from which they can gain more biofeedback information. For more biofeedback information, see Brown (1974); DiCara (1970); Lang (1970); Shapiro, Tursky, Gershon, and Stern (1969); Stearn (1976); and Taylor and Bongar (1976).

Brown (1974) believes that with biofeedback we now have a way to observe different types of learning. She sees biofeedback as an important step toward the realization of the truly integrated, responsible learner:

> Physical and mental attitudes more suitable for learning could be learned more readily as well as improvement of their attention span by their own volition. Feedback could initiate in Western education something that it has lacked since the time of Plato—a holistic education, an education of mind and body together so that finally the student might truly be educated in terms of that ancient but futuristic motto: mens sana in corpore sano (p. 388).

A true education of mind and body now seems available. In 1981, Frank Farley, then President of the American Educational Research Association, in his address to the conference said,

> Education in the year 2000 will be radically altered by emerging conceptions of what the brain can do and what we can do to the brain. Discoveries in brain research demand many radical changes.

Some of those changes we have discussed; some are yet ahead to amaze us.

Integrative Education: Creating Transpersonal Learning

As we discovered in chapters 4 and 6, there is a way to use the elements from these new approaches and the implications of the brain research in the classroom. It is called Integrative Education. Barzakov (Ferguson, 1982) reports from his work that all things in the environment including colors, sounds, textures, rhythms, shapes, objects, other persons, and the appearance and syntax of a text are significant in the learning process. We optimize the learning process when emotional, physical, mental, and intuitive energies are presented harmoniously. The mind does not perceive just bits and pieces, but is constantly weaving a large pattern from our experiences. "If you feed the brain properly, there is practically nothing it isn't capable of learning," states Barzakov. He believes that our best learning and performance come from the hidden teacher/artist within each of us. This inner teacher is one of the basic elements of the Integrative approach (see pages 159 and 231).

Abraham Maslow, mentioned in chapter 3 (p. 121), developed a hierarchy of human needs that has much to say to educators. At the highest level, level 5, Maslow placed self-actualization. Subsequent writing, just prior to his death in 1970, showed his thinking regarding a higher, sixth level that would go beyond self-actualization into a state he referred to as *transcendence*. This would be the level of interconnectedness, the state of oneness with the universe that would include and use all of human functioning at its highest actualization. Writers, psychologists, and philosophers since Maslow's death have developed the basis for a new psychology, *Transpersonal*, that builds on his work on self-actualization and includes the concept of transcendence. This concern in psychology has begun to touch education.

With the same values and concerns, the area of integrative education has begun to take root. The thoughts of East and West are coming together in a climate of acceptance.

Coming together can be seen as the central theme of this book, the model on which its structure is based, a coalescing of thinking, feeling, sensing, and intuiting functions. While approaches may differ, those involved in integrative education are seeking to unite the logical with the mystical, the analytical with the intuitive. As transpersonal psychology seeks a more inclusive vision of human reality, including areas of human experience not yet explored, integrative education attempts to translate this vision into the realization of more and more aspects of human potential. The results will be a greater connectedness within and among people, a greater sense of wholeness, of purpose, of inner direction, and outer responsible caring.

As integrative education becomes more accepted and practiced, we will find more curricula that include relaxation and development of integrative abilities. Guided fantasies and dreams, recognition and use of altered states of consciousness, and centering activities will develop more of our intuitive abilities. As this chapter suggests, there are new possibilities for expanding even those areas of human learning we have always been using. All this and more lie ahead as we seek to bring all of our knowledge, feelings, talents, and creativity into the classroom in the service of actualizing and transcending. Integrative education promises this, and it is also the message of this book.

Parapsychology, Psi, and Our Intuitive Awareness

There was a time when information about fields of energy surrounding the body, out-of-body experiences, healing energy, the influence of magnetic energy from outside this planet, and the results of unexplained human abilities was labeled as fraudulent, unnatural, absurd, or worse. Some still choose not to believe such phenomena exist. But for several decades, such information has been under scientific investigation. The findings of psi research have begun to coalesce with the research findings of the hard sciences. For those who must have physical proof to believe in the existence of such phenomena, their need is now being met. All of these inquiries are fascinating and surely add to or modify our view of reality, making any phase of this research valuable content for the education of human beings. In this brief discussion, we will mention only a few of the directions parapsychology and psi research are taking to extend the abilities available to humans.

> Views of Tiller (Ferguson, 1973), an American scientist, on characteristics of psychoenergetic phenomena are not compatible with the more limited laws of conventional science. He reports that the energy fields seem to be different, that there is a level of substance that is dominantly magnetic with an organizing, rather than disorganizing, tendency as temperature increases. At the physical level, he notes a hologram of energy that acts as a force envelope around the organized substances. He, too, comments on the interconnectedness between all things in the universe.
>
> Krippner (Chance, 1973) has conducted experimental work on telepathy, precognition, dreams, and out-of-body experiences, and other psi phenomena. He is convinced that all these occurrences are available and evident in all human beings and can be explained by natural biological and physical forces. Understand-

ing them requires only that we take a more holistic view of the universe. He feels we can no longer continue to hold onto a simplistic cause and effect notion of human behavior. He believes that while scientific methodology must change, our basic understanding of nature will only be enhanced. He expresses the belief that altered states of consciousness, psychic phenomena, and many types of creativity will be found to be closely linked to right brain function.

Interest in healing energy is creating a plethora of books and conferences on the subject. Thelma Moss, UCLA researcher, has used Kirlian photography to capture some provocative pictures of the actual energy that healers send (Mishlove, 1975). Her work follows years of Kirlian study by Russian scientists (Ostrander and Schroeder, 1970). Krieger (1976) of New York University discovered that hemoglobin levels of patients could be changed positively by the therapeutic touch of nurses trained to "touch with the intent to heal" (p. 2). She feels the discovery is highly significant, as hemoglobin can be considered a valid index of the body's basic metabolism. She taught this procedure to thirty-two RNs with results that had a probability of chance occurrence of only one in a thousand. Frank (1977) of Johns Hopkins has commented to his colleagues in a speech that, although he is convinced that healing power does exist, it can never be evaluated clearly enough for full acceptance by Western scientists.

Kraft (O'Connell, 1976) feels that the intuitive and the psychic are the same thing and are part of the consciousness of all humans. Among others who have made similar observations, Mishlove (1975) notes Carl Jung, Jerome Bruner, Albert Einstein, Isaac Newton, Pythagoras, Plato, and Goethe.

Businessmen like Ray Kroc (McDonald's) and David Mahoney (Chair, Norton Simon) in the tradition of J. P. Morgan and Cornelius Vanderbilt take great pride in their intuitive "hunches." Chief executives of some of the biggest corporations in our nation make their corporate decisions on more than feasibility studies, risk-reward ratios, and cost analysis figures. A measurable correlation has been shown to exist between the company's profitability and the boss's precognitive ability. While often depicted as a wholly analytical creature, in reality, says Mintzberg of McGill University's Faculty of Management, the corporate executive is a holistic, intuitive thinker constantly relying on hunches to cope with problems far too complex for rational analysis. There is even a company, Williams Inference Service of New York, that sells educated hunches or "disciplined intuition" to major corporations (Rowan, 1979).

Kasatkin, a Russian doctor who has spent his life studying the value of dreams for diagnosis and treatment of illness, believes he has clear evidence that dreams inform us of our upcoming illness while we sleep. Different illnesses show defined brain patterns and produce recurrent and typical dreams that begin to repeat a month or more before the illness could be diagnosed any other way. He states,

"One has to remember that the sensitivity of the outer layer of the brain is very high, much higher than that of any other part of the brain. I call it the dream band. It is a thick skin around the brain, with about sixteen million nerve cells. We have found that the pain centers inside the brain do not pick up deviations as quickly as the cells on the outer layer. Its more sensitive cells monitor what is happening in your mind and body and react to the minutest deviation from normal conditions. The danger then is registered in these outer layers. It becomes a vivid dream as you sleep, indirectly issuing an early warning of coming illness. Different areas of the 'dream band' handle specific illnesses" (Gris and Dick, 1978, p. 317).

Vilenskaya of the Bio-Information Department of the Popov Group, Moscow's parapsychology center, has reported an investigation of "optical sensitivity of the human skin to record images, both by direct contact and at a distance" (Gris and Dick, 1978). Experiments have demonstrated that with proper training students can be taught to identify the color and form of images by touch or near-touch; identify hidden objects; and pinpoint magnetic fields. Results of this training have been noted to be 60–90 percent accurate. The process is referred to as *Dermo-Optical Perception* (DOP). This is seen as a great benefit to the blind, and further experiments are involved in teaching the blind to read using these techniques. Chinese paranormal research is also involved in exploring these techniques (Krippner, 1981).

A 1981 report to the congress urged a serious assessment of psi research in the United States. The report cited over 150 areas of potential study. Among them were:

Medicine—advancing the use of mind-initiated cures
Business—applying psychic ability to executive decision making
Investigation—detecting emotional imprints of past events that provide clues for
    archaeological and detective work
Defense—exploiting the obvious implications of one's ability to identify distant
    sites and affect sensitive instruments or other humans
Weather modification, earthquake prediction, and nutrition

For further information, contact the House Committee on Science and Technology, Survey Chairman, Representative Don Fuqua, House of Representatives Office Bldg., Washington, D.C. 20515.

While parapsychology and psi research are in themselves fascinating, their real value lies, in part, in their ability to point out inadequacies in our current belief systems. This type of information, and even the development of these types of abilities, provide one more link in the exploration of human potential.

Studying the Future: Creating an Optimal Reality

Throughout history there have been those people and those moments that have brought dramatic change to all who followed. Today it is becoming increasingly evident that such times are occurring with greater frequency and the need for gifted people to bring vision to these times is of foremost concern. How can we who are most concerned with the nurture of gifted people help provide the experiences and the tools, the attitudes and the commitment they will need to optimize our future? That is the mission of a group of educators who are increasing in number and organizational strength each year. Their academic discipline is most commonly called "Future Studies" and deals with the process of change, alternative thinking, choice, self-concept, values, and the development of optimistic images of the future. A futurist must deal comfortably with uncertainties, open-ended situations, and vastly divergent possibilities. Cornish (1977), a futurist with the World Future Society, believes it imperative that we study the future in order that we may: (1) forecast crises so that they may be averted; (2) assist in deciding the future we want; (3) be prepared to live in a changing world; (4) discover a format for working together cooperatively; (5) contribute to and participate in the furtherance of science and thought; (6) encourage more creativity; (7) increase the motivation to learn; (8) provide for the development of a well-balanced and integrated personal value structure and philosophy of life; and (9) provide a means for recreation and fun.

In underscoring our need to include the study of the future, Goodlad (Silvernail, 1980) states

> Other generations believed that they had the luxury of preparing their children to live in a society similar to their own. Ours is the first generation to have achieved the Socratic wisdom of knowing that we do not know the world in which our children will live (p. 17).

Undoubtedly all children will need the attitudes, skills and information that would result from the future studies curricula, but for the gifted there are some special benefits and some special responsibilities involved. One of the most obvious reasons for the involvement in gifted education comes from the needs and characteristics of the gifted themselves. The interdisciplinary nature will appeal to children who think in diverse ways and who see unusual relationships. The higher levels of thinking will meet needs these children do not often find met in their educational experiences. The challenge of delving into unknown areas will appeal to the gifted of all ages, and the support for self-actualization, creative thinking, and value exploration will further the search for higher values that is characteristic in so many gifted individuals. It seems that the correlation between the needs of the gifted and the goals of the future studies programs are significant and meaningful.

The curriculum of future studies can be quite varied. Silvernail (1980) suggests that a futuristic curriculum contain the following components: (1) basic skills, both the traditional 3 R's and new skills such as skill in humanistic processes, cross-disciplinary understandings, computer language, research skills, anticipatory skills of seeing relationships and taking action on evaluated data, skills based on cross-cultural and multiethnic insights, and change skills; (2) study of the future that would include examination of the past and emerging issues and developing creative plans for action; (3) self-concept; (4) self-actualization, the exploration and planning for personal futures; and (5) valuing.

In a study reported by Wooddell, Fletcher, and Dixon (1982), the curriculum was organized around three aims or areas of competency to be developed in the students: a futures perspective that involved the "recognition and valuing of an interest in the future and a concern for how actions and decisions can affect individual and collective futures;" self-actualization, as described by Maslow (1954); "futuring competencies, involving those abilities to locate, process and evaluate information, to make decisions, to solve problems and systematically to consider alternative futures" (p. 26). The content for the program was eclectic and covered a wide range of subjects. In this study the gifted groups showed higher scores on all the instruments given and even the gifted in the control group outscored the nongifted in the experimental group receiving the future studies curriculum. The gifted in the experimental group outperformed the control group on measures of self-actualization and inner locus of control, with the control group showing actual declines in this area. Gifted students had a significantly higher futures perspective than the nongifted; however it was noted that the gains made by the nongifted in the experimental group, having started the program at a lower level, were greater.

A program in future studies that began operation during the early 1970s and now involves over 75,000 gifted students in grades four through twelve throughout the United States is Torrance's Future Problem Solving Program (Torrance et al., 1980; Torrance, 1981). The Program consists of a year-long curriculum project and a local, state, and national interscholastic team and individual competition. Its goal is to provide experiences that will allow gifted students to make a constructive difference in the future through development of creative problem-solving skills; skills of teamwork, cooperation, and communication; an international sense; and through enlarging, enriching more accurate images of the future. The Program has established statewide and national networks of interaction of students and teachers interested in future studies and in affecting the world of the future. For more information, write to Future Problem Solving Program, Nebraska Department of Education, Lincoln, Nebraska.

The methods and materials developed for future studies curricula are exciting and guaranteed to motivate students of all ages. Some examples are:

> Future System's Innovative Learning Series (Kauffman, 1980): Its games and exercises involve the student in consequences and side effects of various actions, future problem finding, seeing the total or holistic view, alternative thinking, and in seeing and evaluating interrelationships.

> The Future Wheel and the Cross Impact Matrix (Bleedorn, 1976, 1980): Involving exercises on thinking process, these are two usable techniques for bringing futuristic perspectives and processes into K–12 classrooms.

> Scenarios (Torrance, 1980) are developed by studying the available information about a problem, selecting an alternative, and then imagining what might result as a consequence of following that alternative. It is commonly used by futurists in military and government agencies in creating national and international policies. Scenario writing can be used in every subject area and can be clearly related to real life situations.

> Films, audiotapes, games, and simulations: *World Future Society Catalog, 1979* is a catalog compiled by the World Future Society, which lists valuable resources for future studies curricula. Examples of games listed: *Space Future*, a game involving missions into space that stresses the cooperative approach to solving problems and settling other planets; *Earth Game*, another cooperative game that involves the students in problems of the planet; *Future Shock*, a game of the effects of rapid change in our lives.

Torrance (1981) summarizes the importance of future studies in the gifted curriculum:

> Perhaps the most important challenge in educating gifted, talented, and creative students for the future is to help them acquire a positive image of the future—especially a positive image of their own future careers. Positive images of the future seem to have a powerful and magnetic force. Our future images draw on us and energize us. They give us the courage and will to take important initiatives to 'make a difference' in the future (pp. 45–46).

In this chapter we have looked briefly at some exciting possibilities on the horizon. The almost unbelievable ideas of the physicists and philosophers blend views of reality that change our relationship to each other and to our universe and speak to us of the unlimited potential of which we are an integral part. As we seek to optimize the use of that potential it becomes critical to look more closely and more knowledgeably at the human brain, how it works, and the part it plays in the creation of our reality. As brain researchers explore this inner world we find more and more links to our total connectedness.

If we are to develop the human brain/mind system optimally, we must understand our own development, beginning prior to our birth, proceeding through the important periods of early learning, and climaxing in the efficient and effective use of the total brain/mind system we are calling *Integrative Education,* a lifelong way to actualize our transpersonal self. Biofeedback, computers, and techniques of Suggestopedia are but some of the techniques that can enhance this actualization.

Psi research continues to be an area of fascination as it continues to extend the range of human ability and empower each of us beyond the limits by which we believed we were bound. Studying the future can bring the excitement of all we have discussed in this chapter directly into the classroom, where the gifted among us can learn the skills, develop the attitudes, and find the freedom so necessary to dreaming the dreams, seeing the visions, and translating them into a future where all humankind can realize their place in the universe.

Giftedness is, for now, a way of speaking about and defining a few who are intellectually able. When we have integrated our focus, changed and extended our view of reality, and established the underlying connectedness of each to all, we will then have a new meaning of giftedness. The gifted, the talented, and the creative will then be merged, and we will truly be *GROWING UP GIFTED: DEVELOPING THE POTENTIAL OF CHILDREN AT HOME AND AT SCHOOL.*

SECTION THREE

Resources

APPENDIX

Annotated List of Standardized Tests Used with Gifted Students*

Brief descriptions of the following tests will be given:

Tests of Intelligence

Individual

    Leiter International Performance Scale
    Peabody Picture Vocabulary Test
    Slosson Intelligence Test (SIT)
    Stanford-Binet Intelligence Scale (S-B)
    Wechsler Intelligence Scale for Children (WISC)

Group

    California Test of Mental Maturity (1963 rev.)
    Goodenough-Harris Drawing Test
    The Lorge-Thorndike Intelligence Test
    Otis Lennon Mental Ability Test

Tests of Achievement

    California Achievement Tests (1957 ed.; 1963 Norm)
    Metropolitan Achievement Tests
    SRA Achievement Series
    SRA High School Placement Test
    Stanford Achievement Test
    Other tests for Educational Assessment (e.g., Standardized reading tests and Specialized tests)

Tests: Personal-Social

Nonprojective

    California Psychological Inventory 1969, age 13+

---

*The information given in this Appendix has been compiled from Oscar Buros (Ed.). *Mental Measurement Yearbooks.* Vols. I and II. Seventh edition (1972), Sixth edition (1965), and Fifth edition (1959). Published by Gryphon Press, Highland Park, New Jersey.

Minnesota Multiphasic Personality Inventory (Rev. ed.)
Personal Orientation Inventory

Test of Creativity

Torrance Tests of Creative Thinking (Verbal & Figural)

Individual Tests of Intelligence

Leiter International Performance Scale—C. H. Stoelting Co.

Description: An individual nonverbal scale for ages 2–18; is most suitable for children 3–8. It gives both an MA and IQ. It has no time limits. Tests ability to learn at the lower levels rather than acquired skills, perceptual organization, and discrimination.

Test is administered by showing picture cards and pantomiming directions. Child chooses matching blocks. Tasks range from matching colors and completing forms, to completing patterns, design, and classification of objects.

The IQ equivalency of the 98 percent score on the Leiter is 127.

Background: Developed by R. Leiter and G. Arthur 1936–1955, ages 2–18, revised in 1948, and adapted by G. Arthur 1952–1955, ages 3–8.

Standardized on 289 children from middle-class, midwestern, metropolitan background. Few or none of the nonverbal children for whom it was designed were in the group.

Usability: Validity is based on correlations with other individual IQ tests, S-B (.69–.93) and WISC (.79–.80) for the Arthur adaptation. No tests of predictive validity reported.

It is suggested that it is especially useful for testing children with speech and hearing difficulties, foreign born, cross-cultural and bilingual children, and shy or withdrawn children.

Use by experienced clinician advised.

Peabody Picture Vocabulary Test

American Guidance Service, Inc.
Publishers Bldg.
Circle Pines, Mn. 55014

Description: An untimed individual test with two forms, A and B, for ages 2.5–18. It gives a percentile rank, MA, or IQ score. It is designed to measure verbal intelligence.

Test is administered by reading stimulus words to a subject who is viewing a card where several line drawings are shown. The subject then indicates which picture best illustrates the word given. It takes approximately 15 minutes to give.

Background: Developed by Lloyd M. Dunn 1959. Standardized on 4,012 white children and youths in and around Nashville, Tennessee. Only younger children were given the test individually.

Usability: Validity based on correlations with Form B and California Test of Mental Maturity (.58), S-B (MA .70–.80), and WISC (.75–.80). Form B and Henmon-Nelson Test of Mental Ability (.61). Content validity is well established. Reliability is moderate.

The test is simple to administer and score.

Caution is advised in using this test for judgments of intelligence because it is a very short, restricted sample of behavior, only one of the many aspects of intelligence. It does not require a trained examiner.

Slosson Intelligence Test (SIT)—Slosson Educational Publications

Description: A brief individual test of intelligence designed to be used with infants from two weeks through adults (27 years). There are no time limits.

Gives a ratio IQ score. Testing and scoring take 10–30 minutes and can be used by relatively untrained examiners. Infant testing items assess postural control and locomotion. Between 2 and 4 years, the emphasis is on language skills. Above 4 years, all questions are presented verbally and require spoken responses. Content includes mathematical reasoning, vocabulary, auditory memory, and information.

Background: Developed by R. Slosson 1961–1963. Based in part on the Stanford-Binet Intelligence Scale (Third Revision) and Gesell Developmental Schedules. The standardization sample was 701 children and adults from rural and urban populations in New York State. The sample included both gifted and retarded children. Age, sex, ethnic groups, socioeconomic backgrounds are not mentioned.

Usability: Validity is based on correlations with S-B (.90–.98) and WISC (.60). A correlation of .70 with the Cattell Infant Intelligence Scale is reported for the infant section.

The SIT is best used as a screening device and should be used with caution where diagnostic decisions or special class placement is required. The heavy emphasis on language skills makes it a difficult test for disadvantaged or culturally different children, especially at the preschool level.

Stanford-Binet Intelligence Scale (S-B)—Third Revision

Houghton Mifflin Co.
110 Tremont St.
Boston, Mass. 02107

Description: An individual test of mental activities that are known as general intelligence for ages 2 and over. There are few time limits, and when there are, they are generous enough for most subjects to respond. Verbal, nonverbal, and performance items are found in the Binet battery. The test is given orally, scored manually, and the complete test takes 60–90 minutes to administer.

1. The language category consists of evaluating vocabulary (maturity, extent, quality) and comprehension.
2. Memory evaluation is divided into subtests of meaningful, nonmeaningful, and visual memory.

3. Conceptual thinking deals with abstract thinking in activities involving generalizing and assuming an "as if" position, among others.
4. Verbal and nonverbal reasoning ability is tested by items of absurdity and pictorial and orientation problems, for example. Logical relations, discrimination ability, and analysis and synthesis function in this area.
5. Numerical reasoning includes arithmetic problems demanding ability to concentrate and generalize.
6. The visual motor category tests manual dexterity, eye-hand coordination, and perception of spatial relations.
7. Social intelligence evaluates social maturity and judgment. Social comprehension is also reflected in the reasoning category.

Expectancies at various age levels:

1. At the early age level (2–5), 85% of the items measure visual motor capacities, nonverbal reasoning, social intelligence, and language functions. The other test skills are not developed at this age. The child's world consists of common objects, and his understanding includes knowing why we have cars, tests, and books. His visual motor ability includes building blocks, stringing beads, copying a circle and a straight line. Persistence is a factor here.
2. The middle age children have a memory for stories and designs and are developing abstract reasoning and conceptual thinking. Verbal descriptions and definitions are required. Arithmetic skills are measured by block counting and making change; visual motor skills require copying a diamond, paper cutting, and maze tracing.
3. Adolescents are tested in verbal reasoning, memory, and social intelligence, among other items. Knowing subtleties of their world, right and wrong, and social customs is expected.
4. Postadolescent testing is dominated by language functions and conceptual thinking. Reasoning, comprehension, and analysis and generalization ability are evaluated.

The IQ equivalency of the 98% score of the Stanford-Binet is 132.

Background: The Stanford-Binet is a revision made in 1916 by Lewis Terman, an American psychologist at Stanford University, of an intelligence scale developed in France in 1906 by Binet and Simon. Terman used the test to identify children for his longitudinal study of giftedness that began in 1921.

The first revision (1916) introduced the concept of the IQ, ratio of mental age to chronological age.

The second revision (1937) was made by Terman and Merrill. It corrected for problems of administration and scoring and added variety that enhanced interest. Two forms were in use, Forms L & M.

The third revision (1960) combined the best subtests of the two previous forms into L-M Form, checked standardization, and continued to improve administration and scoring. The deviation method of scoring was introduced.

Standardization of the first revision was done on 1,000 children and 400 adults found in and around the Stanford area. The second revision was standardized on 3,184 native born white persons ages 1½ to 18 years of age, equally divided between male and female. Seventeen communities, both rural and urban, in widely separated states represented the geographical distribution. In the third revision, this same group was used. School age subjects' records from three states, California, Massachusetts, and New Jersey, were obtained for information needed for scale revision, and individuals from California of various ages and from a background of diverse occupational categories (fathers) were selected for comparison with the 1937 standardization group.

Usability: The Stanford-Binet is believed to be a valid test for assessing general intelligence.

For nearly seventy years, the Binet has been used in the U.S. It meets the criteria for construct validity by testing what is generally agreed is intelligence. Many other tests use the Binet as a basis for assessing their construct validity (e.g., Wechsler).

The Binet for many years has demonstrated its predictive validity. Those with high I.Q.'s have usually been successful in our educational system and professional world.

The Stanford-Binet appears to be a reliable test with test retest correlations ranging from .83 to .98.

Low socioeconomic groups and culturally diverse children score low or low average, generally, which may be partially the result of the low loading in the Binet of visual perception, visual memory, and rote learning. Knowing that the standardized sample was all white and of a higher socioeconomic level than the general population makes criticism of the test's use with these groups worth considering.

The Binet is appropriately chosen when information about a subject's general mental adaptability is desired. It is important to remember that separate aspects of mentality and perspective are best measured by using other test forms that diagnose particular areas of strengths and weaknesses. The Binet does have an advantage over other tests in covering the low range and the extremes.

This test requires a trained examiner.

Wechsler Intelligence Scale for Children (WISC)

Psychological Corporation
304 East 45th St.
New York, N.Y. 10017

Description: An individual test of mental activities, which are known as general intelligence, for ages 5–15. The WISC gives 15 scores, divided into two scales: *verbal*—information, comprehension, arithmetic, similarities, vocabulary, digit span (optional), total; *performance*—picture completion, picture arrangement, block design, object assembly, mazes (optional), coding, total, and total score MA and IQ scores given. The complete test takes 40–60 minutes.

The IQ equivalency of the 98% score on the WISC is 131.

There is a Spanish edition available.

Background: Developed by David Wechsler, 1949. The record booklet was slightly revised in 1958. The test abandons the concept of mental age found in the Stanford-Binet Intelligence Scale and uses instead a score derived from comparing the child with a sample of the same age peers. While this allows equal means (100) and standard deviations (15) at all age levels, it puts particular stress on the selection of standardization groups. With only 100 boys and 100 girls chosen to represent each age group, the sampling of very bright children is quite limited. The population was reported as white, American children for the original standardization sample.

Usability: The major appeal of the test is in its separate verbal and performance scales and in its individual subtests. These provide a pattern that may be used when making educational program decisions. Research on score patterns has yielded little to confirm and much to challenge such definitive usage. The test has reliability coefficients of .88–.96 for the Verbal Scale and .86–.90 for the Performance Scale. The validity, when compared to the Stanford-Binet, is fairly high at .8 + and differs little in its ability to predict academic attainment. As this test does not discriminate either the extremes of age 5–6 years and 14–15 years or of intelligence, its sensitivity in testing gifted children is quite limited.

This test requires a trained examiner.

Group Intelligence Tests

California Test of Mental Maturity (CTMM)—1963 Revision

California Test Bureau
Division of McGraw-Hill Book Company
Del Monte Research Park,
Monterey, Ca. 93940

Description: A group test of abilities basic to learning, problem solving, and responding to new situations for K–adult. Test is organized around five factors: logical reasoning, spatial relationships, numerical reasoning, verbal concepts, and memory; presented at six levels: 0. grades K–1.0, 48–58 minutes; 1. grades 1.5–3, 63–75 minutes; 2. grades 4–6, 83–93 minutes; 3. grades 7–9, 83–93 minutes; 4. grades 9–12, 81–91 minutes; 5. grades 12–16 and adults, 81–91 minutes. Levels 2 through 5 are machine scorable. Deviation IQ, MA, and performance scores, stanines, Intellectual Status Index, and Anticipated Achievement Grade Placements can be obtained.

Background: Developed by E. Sullivan, W. Clark, and E. Tiegs in 1936. Has been revised several times, with the latest revision done in 1963. The 1963 standardization sample included classes from 253 schools, representing 7 geographical regions and 49 states.

Usability: Nearly all reliability data are on the Short Form of this test. Validity is again correlative with S-B (.66–.74), with California Achievement Test (.79–.84), others in high .70s and .80s.

It is suggested that it be used primarily at middle and upper levels, as the lower levels lack reliability. The Short Form of the test takes less time and may provide just as adequate a measure.

Goodenough-Harris Drawing Test (GHDT)

   Harcourt, Brace, Jovanovich
   757 3rd Ave., Test Dept.
   New York, N.Y. 10017

Description: A test for children aged 3–15 asks the child to make a picture of a man, a woman, or of self that is then evaluated for accuracy of observation and the development of conceptual thinking. The test takes about five or ten minutes to administer and is then scored by checking the drawing against scorable items and points given in the manual. It may be administered either individually or to groups. Raw scores are converted to standard scores, with a mean of 100 and a standard deviation of 15. A table is provided for converting standard scores to percentiles.

Background: The Draw-A-Man Test was originally published in 1926 by Florence Goodenough. In 1963, Dale B. Harris published the results of an extensive revision of the Draw-A-Man Test, redeveloping the scoring criteria; changed from mental age ratio to the deviation IQ concept; introduced a quality drawing score; and restandardized the test. He also introduced the Draw-A-Woman Test. The new standardization sample was composed of 2,975 children between the ages of 5 and 15 years, representative of the occupational distribution of the U.S. in 1950 and found in a few major geographical areas.

Usability: Due to improved scoring instructions, the reliability is usually over .90. Correlatives between GHDT and the Stanford-Binet, WISC, and other intelligence tests are reported as significant and substantial. The major validity derives from the evidence obtained from the item analysis procedures followed in developing the scales. Caution in interpretation of the scale is advised. GHDT is a quick, nonverbal test of intellectual maturity recommended especially for preschool children and those with language handicaps.

The Lorge-Thorndike Intelligence Tests, Multi-Level Edition

   Houghton Mifflin Co.
   110 Tremont St.
   Boston, Mass. 02107

Description: A group test of intelligence that uses test material that is both verbal and nonverbal in grades 3–15. The test is meant to test abstract intelligence, i.e., the ability to work with ideas and relationships. The test provides a verbal IQ (for higher levels) and a nonverbal IQ, with provisions for a composite IQ score if it is desired. All IQ scores are deviation IQ's, and median IQ's for each age group are presented. The administration takes a little over an hour. Separate answer sheets are used and machine scoring is available.

Background: The test was developed in 1954 by Irving Lorge and Robert L. Thorndike and was revised in 1966 by Lorge, Thorndike, and Elizabeth Hagen. It was originally standardized on 136,000 children in 22 states. The communities were selected for varied socioeconomic levels and attributes. The revision standardization data were obtained from some 600 pupils per grade in 14 school systems enrolled in the Iowa Basic Skills Testing Program.

Usability: The test is considered a power test and is timed. The manual reports high correlations with tests of achievement (.60–.70) and moderate to high with tests of intelligence. Nonverbal scores do not seem as effective as verbal scores in predicting school achievement. The verbal battery also shows better reliability (.83–.91; nonverbal .80–.88). This test is reported to be a widely used, well-constructed and presented series of tests.

Otis-Lennon Mental Ability Test

Harcourt, Brace, Jovanovich
757 3rd Ave., Test Dept.
New York, N.Y. 10017

Description: A group intelligence test, which is timed and claims to be a power measure for grades K–12. Scores may be given as deviation IQ's, as age and grade percentile ranks showing the pupils' standing in the national sample, and as stanines. The Otis-Lennon seeks to test the verbal-educational aspects of mental abilities, not the practical-mechanical, and items measure broad reasoning abilities involving manipulation of ideas. The test has six levels: grades K, 1–1.5, 1.6–3.9, 4–6, 7–9, and 10–12.

Background: The test was first published by Arthur Otis as the Otis Quick-Scoring Mental Ability Tests in 1936. It was revised in 1970 by Otis and Roger T. Lennon and republished under its new name. The standardization sample was chosen to represent the U.S.A.'s educational system and not the population at large. All 50 states were represented, and socioeconomic factors were considered.

Usability: The test is timed and is considered a power measure. The three lower levels of the test require no reading, and minimal competency in reading ability is required for the other test levels, with a few exceptions. The test correlates adequately with other general scholastic aptitude measures. The test results must be interpreted carefully for children with other than normal backgrounds and motivation. The test has an insufficient range at some levels, making the measurement of exceptionally high or low ability difficult. This test predicts scholastic success because it is a direct measure of scholastic ability. It may be used by teachers, counselors, or other professional educators.

Tests of Achievement

California Achievement Tests

California Test Bureau
Del Monte Research Park
Monterey, Ca. 93940

Description: A group achievement test series in five levels: Lower Primary (grades 1–2), administration 89–110 minutes; Upper Primary (grades 2.5–4.5), adm. 124–145 minutes; Elementary (grades 4–6), 160–175 minutes, machine scored; Junior High (grades 7–9), 178–190 minutes, machine scored; Advanced (grades 9–14), 178–190 minutes, machine scored. Scores in reading vocabulary, reading comprehension, reading total, arithmetic reasoning, arithmetic fundamentals, arithmetic total, mechanics of English, spelling, language total, total handwriting. Student profile sheets available. Usually administered in two sessions. Scores may be converted to grade placement scores, percentile rank, standard scores, and stanines. Intended as diagnostic tests.

Background: Developed by Ernest W. Tiegs and Willis W. Clark, 1934 as Progressive Achievement Tests. Revised in 1950 and 1957, with new norms established in 1963. Standardization was last done in 1963, with over 15,000 students representing 49 states by seven geographic regions and from all grades 1–12.

Usability: Validity of content must be varied in light of the curriculum of the schools using the test. The correlation between subtests of this battery and those of the Stanford Achievement Test and the Metropolitan Achievement Tests are uniformly high and indicate that all of these tests may be measuring similar skills.

The examiner need only be familiar with the manual and instructions for administration. The manual also provides suggestions for interpretation of the scores.

This test is recommended for schools that want to focus their achievement measurement and diagnosis on the traditional, fundamental skills and content areas of reading, arithmetic, and language (English).

Metropolitan Achievement Tests

Harcourt, Brace, Jovanovich
757 3rd Ave., Test Dept.
New York, N.Y. 10017

Description: A group achievement test series at six levels
Primary I Battery: Grade 1.5 Primary Battery I consists of four tests: *Word Knowledge* measures sight vocabulary, or word recognition ability; *Word Discrimination* measures ability to select an orally presented word from among a group of printed words with similar sound elements; *Reading* measures ability to comprehend sentences and passages of paragraph length; *Arithmetic Concepts and Skills* provides a comprehensive measure, independent of reading ability, of the student's mastery of essential concepts, ability to solve verbal problems, and ability to perform addition and subtraction exercises. 85–115 minutes, 4 sessions.
Primary II Battery: Grade 2 Primary II Battery consists of five tests: *Word Knowledge* measures word recognition and understanding; *Word Discrimination* measures ability to select an orally presented word from among a group of printed words with similar sound elements; *Reading* measures ability to comprehend sentences and passages of paragraph length; *Spelling* is a measure of spelling ability; *Arithmetic* provides a comprehensive measure, independent of reading ability, of the student's mastery of essential concepts, ability to solve verbal problems, and ability to perform addition and subtraction exercises. 100–125 minutes, 4 sessions.

Elementary Battery: Grades 3–4 Elementary Battery consists of seven tests: *Word Knowledge* is a vocabulary test; *Word Discrimination* measures ability to select a word needed to complete a sentence from among several words of similar sound elements; *Reading* measures reading comprehension through a series of reading selections, each followed by several questions; *Spelling* is a measure of spelling ability; *Language,* in two parts, evaluates language usage and punctuation and capitalization skills; *Arithmetic Computation* is a measure of skill in the four fundamental arithmetic operations; *Arithmetic Problem Solving and Concepts,* in two parts, measures ability to solve verbal problems and understanding of important concepts. 147–177 minutes, 5 sessions.

Intermediate Battery: Grades 5–6, Partial Battery, 11 scores—those above, plus: *Language*—parts of speech, study skills; *Social Studies*—study skills. 197–227 minutes, 5 sessions. Complete Battery—all above, plus *Social Studies* information, *Science.* 237–267 minutes, 5 sessions. All intermediate batteries machine scorable.

Advanced Battery: Grades 7–9. Partial Battery—same as Intermediate Partial plus *Language*—kinds of sentences, 207–237 minutes, 5 sessions. Complete Battery —same as intermediate partial battery, plus *Language*—kinds of sentences. 247–277 minutes, 5 sessions.

High School Battery: Grades 9–12, 11 scores: *Reading; Spelling; Language*—language study skills; *Social Studies*—study skills, vocabulary, information; *Mathematics*—computation and concepts, analysis, and problem solving; *Science*—concepts and understandings, information. 282–316 minutes. Machine scorable.

Background: Developed by ten prominent psychologists (including Gertrude Hildreth) in 1931–1962. The latest revisions were made in 1971. The authors reviewed the goals of education, textbooks, and courses of study on essential skills. These data provided the basis for their selection of items, and the tests were developed to reflect materials to which students are believed to be most commonly exposed. National norms are provided, although test users are encouraged to develop their own local norms, stanines, and percentile ranks.

Usability: The test was designed to measure achievement on what was determined to be the material to which students were most commonly exposed. It reflects the emphasis schools place on rote learning of information and skills, and therefore does not measure higher cognitive processes. The tests at all levels make possible the measure of superior achievement, although measurement of poor learners is generally inadequate.

Directions for administration and scoring are detailed and clear. A trained examiner is not needed.

SRA Achievement Series

Science Research Associates, Inc.
259 East Erie Street
Chicago, Illinois 60611

Description: A group test of achievement that measures performance in arithmetic, reading, and language arts in separate subtests or a multilevel edition for grades 4–9 that additionally includes social science and work-study skills. It offers a program for testing basic skills in grades 1–9.

Reading (Grades 1–2, 3–4, 4–9): Comprehension and vocabulary scores, plus an area score are given for all batteries. The 1–2 battery gives two additional subtest scores:

1. *Verbal-Pictorial Association* (1–2 battery only): Measures the ability to understand the meaning of written words, phrases, and sentences.
2. *Language Perception* (1–2 battery only): Measures ability to understand central themes and main ideas, draw logical conclusions, and retain significant details. Test selections are from fiction, biography, science, and social studies.
3. *Vocabulary:* Measures ability to understand the meaning of words in context.

Arithmetic (Grades 1–2, 3–4, 4–9): The arithmetic test, included in all batteries, gives three subtest scores, plus an area score:

1. *Reasoning:* Measures understanding of logical and mathematical steps that lead to the solution of arithmetic problems presented in story form.
2. *Concepts:* Requires the student to translate verbal statements into mathematical principles.
3. *Computation:* Covers the use of four basic computational processes applied to whole numbers, fractions, and decimals.

Language Arts (Grades 1–2, 3–4, 4–9): At all levels punctuation, capitalization, and usage are measured.

Science (Grades 4–9): Included are questions on general science, biology, astronomy, geology, physics, and chemistry.

Social Studies (Grades 4–9): Includes questions on geography, history, government, and economics.

In Science and Social Studies, items are at the factual level, measuring recall rather than understanding or application of information. In basic areas the emphasis is on development of understanding and application of learning.

There is also available the SRA High School Placement Test for entering ninth-grade students which covers educational ability, achievement in reading, language art, mathematics, social studies, and science.

Background: This test was developed in 1954 by Louis P. Thorpe, D. W. Lefever, and R. A. Naslund. The latest of its three revisions was made in 1969. The standardization group was heavily parochial and included a large number of very small schools. The test was developed from studies of elementary school curricula.

Usability: The test is well-written and appropriate to its goals. The directions for administration are clear and adequate. The series compares favorably with other series of its type. It is one of the few batteries that include tests of beginning reading skills at the primary level. It is reported to be one of the most valid and reliable achievement batteries currently available.

Standard Achievement Tests

Harcourt, Brace, Jovanovich
757 3rd Ave., Test Dept.
New York, N.Y. 10017

Description: This achievement test battery is the earliest of its kind and the most widely used. The test is divided into:

Primary I Battery (Grades 1.5–2.4): Subtests in word reading, paragraph meaning, vocabulary, spelling, word study skills, and arithmetic.

Primary 2 Battery (Grades 2.5–3.9): Subtest in word reading, paragraph meaning, vocabulary, spelling, word meaning skills, science and social studies concepts, languages, and arithmetic concepts.

Intermediate 1 Battery (Grades 4.0–5.4): Subtests in word reading, paragraph meaning, vocabulary, spelling, word study skills and arithmetic. Subtest added—arithmetic applications.

Intermediate 2 Battery (Grades 5.5–6.9): Subtest in word reading, paragraph meaning, vocabulary, spelling, and arithmetic.

Advanced Battery (Grades 7.0–9.9): Same as above with omission of word meaning subtest.

Also available are—SAT: High School Arts and Humanities Test; SAT: High School Basic Battery; Stanford Early School Achievement Test (Grades K–12).

Background: This test battery was developed in 1923 by T. L. Kelley, R. Madden, E. F. Gardner, and H. C. Rudman. Its latest revision was in 1968.

Usability: The tests are most widely used for evaluation purposes. They are sometimes given for predictive purposes in place of course grades, teachers' ratings, and in selecting students for special programs. There are no available data comparing SAT to the Metropolitan, the California Achievement, or others.

Other Tests for Educational Assessment

1. *Comprehensive Tests of Basic Skills*
    California Test Bureau
    Division of McGraw-Hill Book Company
    Del Monte Research Park
    Monterey, Ca. 93940

Four tests are available:
Level 1—Grades 2.5–4; *Level 2*—Grades 4–6; *Level 3*—Grades 6–8; *Level 4*—Grades 8–12.

Subtests for vocabulary, comprehension, and certain study skills are included.

2. *Iowa Every-Pupil Test of Basic Skills*
    Houghton Mifflin Company
    110 Tremont Street
    Boston, Mass. 02107

Elementary—Grades 3–5; *Advanced*—Grades 5–9

Test A: Silent Reading Comprehension (measures vocabulary and paragraph comprehension); *Test B:* Work Study Skills (tests skills in map reading and use of indexes, references, and the dictionary); *Test C:* Basic Language Skills; *Test D:* Basic Arithmetic Skills.

When tests A and B are used together, specific diagnosis in reading can be made. Taken as a battery, these four tests can be useful when assessment of performance in the four basic skill areas is needed. Four forms for each test are available: *L, M, N, O.*

Standardized reading tests

1. *Silent Reading Diagnostic Tests*
   Lyons and Carnahan, Educational Division
   407 East 25th Street
   Chicago, Ill. 60616

The tests yield a profile of 11 subtest scores. Subtests are presented in a single test booklet, and provision is made for plotting a graphic profile based upon the test data. Subtests included are: Word Recognition, Recognition of Words in Context, Recognition of Reversible Words in Context, Word Recognition Techniques: Visual Analysis—Locating Usable Elements, Word Recognition Techniques: Visual Analysis—Syllabication, Word Recognition Techniques: Visual Analysis—Locating the Root Words, Phonetic Knowledge: General Word Elements, Rhyming Words, Letter Sounds, and Word Synthesis.

These tests can be used by the classroom teacher without extensive clinical training, as the administration is uncomplicated and scoring procedure straightforward. The diagnostic scores derived from the subtests are in word recognition and word analysis techniques. Tests are intended for use in grades 3–6.

2. *Gilmore Oral Reading Test* (new edition)
   Harcourt, Brace, Jovanovich
   757 3rd Avenue, Test Department
   New York, N.Y. 10017

Test consists of 10 paragraphs of increasing difficulty, designed for analyzing oral reading performance of pupils in *grades 1–8.* Separate record booklets provide a convenient means of scoring for the examiner to record errors, reading time, and answers to comprehension questions. Norms for accuracy, comprehension, and rate of oral reading are provided. Four forms are available, *A, B, C, D.* The test is very useful and can serve as a model for teachers who want to devise informal oral tests of their own. Comprehension is tested after oral reading—a procedure that may be considered a limitation.

3. *Spache Diagnostic Reading Scales*
   California Test Bureau
   Division of McGraw-Hill Book Company
   Del Monte Research Park
   Monterey, Ca. 93940

The battery includes 3 word recognition lists, 22 reading passages of graduated difficulty, and 6 supplementary phonics tests. *Scales* are of three purposes: to estimate the pupil's instructional reading level; to reveal the pupil's method of attack and analysis; and to evaluate the pupil's sight vocabulary.

Specialized tests

1. *Learning Methods Test*
   Mills Center
   1512 East Broward Avenue
   Fort Lauderdale, Fla. 33310

Designed to aid teachers in determining the individual student's ability to learn new words under four different procedures: 1. the visual method; 2. the phonic or auditory method; 3. the kinesthetic or tracing method; or 4. the combined method, where equal stress is placed upon visual, auditory, and kinesthetic methods.

Procedure is simple: ten words are taught to the subject by each of the four methods over a period of four consecutive days. A delayed recall score is computed to indicate the best teaching method for the individual.

2. *Marianne Frostig Developmental Test of Visual Perception*
   Follett Educational Corporation
   1010 West Washington Blvd.
   Chicago, Ill. 60607

Test was constructed to assess children's ability in five areas of visual perception believed by Frostig to be most relevant to school performance. Five subtests assess eye-hand coordination, figure-ground discrimination, form constancy, position in space, and spatial relations. Certain of the subtests scores have been found to be related to reading performance.

3. *Bender Visual Motor Gestalt Test*
   Psychological Corporation
   304 East 45th Street
   New York, N.Y. 10017

Test designed to measure children's visual motor development and is used by some psychologists to gain insight into child's mental development and language abilities. Test is comprised of nine designs, which are copied by the student. The drawings are then judged for distortion, rotation, perseveration, and other factors.

4. *Harris Test of Lateral Dominance*
   Psychological Corporation
   304 East 45th Street
   New York, N.Y. 10017

Set of tests designed to measure hand, eye, and foot dominance to reveal direction confusion as related to reading problems.

5. *Educational Evaluation of Preschool Children*—by Else Haeussermann. Based on "Developmental Potential of Preschool Children" by Haeussermann. New York, N.Y., Grune and Stratton, 1958.

The developmental age of the child as determined by this test relates well to the MA determined by the WISC and Stanford-Binet.

6. *Chicago Non-Verbal Test*
    Psychological Corporation
    304 East 54th Street
    New York, N.Y. 10017

Tests: Personal-Social

California Psychological Inventory (CPI)

> Consulting Psychologists Press, Inc.
> 577 College Ave.
> Palo, Alto, Ca. 94306

Description: The CPI consists of 480 items, all of which are presented in a true-false format. Its goal is to measure character traits that arise from interpersonal life and may predict social behavior (e.g., leadership, social maturity, college attendance, academic achievement, etc.). It is designed to be used with persons 13 years of age or older. The results come in 18 scores, which include: dominance, sociability, self-acceptance, responsibility, etc.

Background: The CPI was developed in 1956 by Harrison G. Gough. The latest revision of the test was in 1969. The norm group of 13,000 people, over one-half women, includes machine operators, military personnel, prison inmates, and medical students.

Usability: Except for research, the usability is limited.

Minnesota Multiphasic Personality Inventory (MMPI)

> Psychological Corporation
> 304 East 45th St.
> New York, N.Y. 10017

Description: A nonprojective personality test designed for persons 16 years of age or over. It yields 14 scores, including: depression, masculinity and femininity, test taking attitude, paranoia, etc. It can be given as an individual or as a group test. With 566 items, it is the largest inventory on the market.

Background: Developed in 1942 by S. R. Hathaway and C. McKinley. Latest revision was in 1967. The norming population was all white.

Usability: The foremost instrument in objective clinical assessment. Caution must be exercised in using MMPI with blacks, as they differ significantly from whites in their response patterns. Those with limited education and rural residence also raise questions regarding applicability. This instrument is most often used to determine the nature and degree of emotional upset with adolescents and adults. The MMPI interpreter must be quite sophisticated, and the test is only valid when given by an expert.

Personal Orientation Inventory—Educational and Industrial Testing Service

Description: An instrument developed to measure values, attitudes, and behavior relevant to Maslow's concept of the self-actualized person by self-report. The test may be used with grades 9–16 and adults. Measures are given on: *inner directed* (the ability to value and be guided by internal motivation rather than external pressure), *time competence* (the ability to live in the present without being limited by past events and future uncertainties), *self-actualizing values, existentiality, feeling reactivity, spontaneity, self-regard, self-acceptance, awareness, nature of man, synergy, acceptance of aggression, and capacity for intimate contact.* On each item, subjects are asked to choose the most personally representative two statements, which represent extreme points of view. This is one of the few tests of personality that focus directly on sound functioning rather than the presence or absence of pathology.

Background: Developed by Everett L. Shostrom in 1962 with revisions made in 1968. All normative data in the manual are based toward the college student population, and the profile sheet given reflects norms of 2,607 entering college freshmen. Some information is given on business supervisors, Peace Corps volunteers, high school students, and others.

Usability: The content validity is reported to be quite good. A number of studies indicate that these scales effectively measure feelings, values, and attitudes appropriate to Maslow's concept of self-actualization. As this concept is one of becoming, high scores do not necessarily indicate that the subjects are using all their self-actualizing capabilities. While this test cannot be utilized by itself for assessment of educational data, it should be a very useful tool. The reliability coefficients range from .55 to .85, with only three subscales reported below .70.

Tests of Creativity

Torrance Tests of Creative Thinking (TTCT)

Personnel Press, Inc.
191 Spring St.
Lexington, Mass. 02173

Description: A test of creativity based on Guilford's Structure of the Intellect that may be given individually or in groups. The intent is to identify process abilities necessary for operating creatively. It may be used from kindergarten through college. The test is divided into verbal and figural subtests, with scores given for fluency, flexibility, originality, and elaboration in each area. Examples of the verbal activities:

1. *Ask and Guess.* Designed to reveal the ability to formulate hypotheses concerning cause and effect.
2. *Product Improvement.* Ways to improve a toy.
3. *Unusual Uses.* How many ways a product can be used.
4. *Unusual Questions.* Designed to test divergent ability.
5. *Just Suppose.* Predicting outcomes for unusual situations (45–60 minutes). Examples of the figural activities: a. *Picture Construction*, b. *Picture Completion*, c. *Repeated Figures* (30–45 minutes). Scores are to be converted to T scores, and percentile ranks are not available.

Background: This test was developed by Paul E. Torrance in 1966 and had minor revisions made in 1970. The standardization group was 118 fifth graders in St. Croix, Wisconsin.

Usability: There is a controversy regarding the kinds of processes the tests are attempting to identify and especially regarding criteria used to validate the results (e.g., quality of the response is not considered in scoring). Whether this test can be considered a valid test of creativity is dependent on the definition of creativity one uses. Studies of content validity and ability of the test to predict adult creative achievement are still being conducted. At this time, Torrance believes that the TTCT alone is not an adequate predictor. Reliability data range from .50 to .93. There appears to be an overlap of the abilities being measured and those commonly assessed on intelligence tests. The test may be administered by anyone. The major problem is in whether measures of fluency, flexibility, and originality can be considered measures of creativity. The directions for administering and scoring are clear and direct.

REFERENCES

Abraham, W. Counseling the gifted. *Focus on Guidance*, 1976 *9* (1), 1–12.

Adkins, L. Video games could revolutionize the way we learn and teach. *Brain/Mind Bulletin*, 1982. 7(12), 2.

Adler, M. Ethnology of a group of gifted children. *Gifted Child Quarterly*, 1964, *5*, 40–41.

Ahsen, A. *Eidetic behavior*. Yonkers-on-Hudson, N.Y.: Eidetic, 1973.

Ainsworth, M. Individual differences in strange situation behavior of one-year-olds. In H. Schaffer (Ed.), *Origins of human relations*. New York: Academic Press, 1974.

Alberti, R., & Emmons, M. *Your perfect right: A guide to assertive behavior*. San Luis Obispo, Ca.: Impact, 1970.

Alexander, P., & Skinner, M. The effects of early entrance on subsequent social and academic development: A follow-up study. *Journal for the Education of the Gifted*, 1980 *3* (3), 147–150.

Alexander, R. An historical perspective on the gifted and talented in art. *Studies in Art Education*, 1981, *22* (2), 38–48.

Allen, G., Giat, L., & Cherney, R. Locus of control, test anxiety and student performance in a personalised instruction course. *Journal of Educational Psychology*, 1974, *66*, 968–973.

Allen, R. W. Grouping through learning centers. *Childhood Education*, 1968, *45*, 200–203.

Allport, G. *Becoming*. New Haven: Yale University Press, 1955.

Alvino, J., McDonnel, R., & Richert, S. National survey of identification practices in gifted and talented education. *Exceptional Children*, October, 1981, *48*, (2), 124–132.

American Association for Gifted Children. *Reaching out, advocacy for the gifted and talented*. New York: Teachers College Press, 1980.

Amidon, E., & Flanders, N. The effects of direct and indirect teacher influence on dependent-prone students learning geometry. *Journal of Educational Psychology*, 1961, *52*, 286–291.

Anderson, H. H. Creativity as personality development. In. H. H. Anderson (Ed.), *Creativity and its cultivation*. New York: Harper & Row, 1959.

Anderson, H. H. On the meaning of creativity. In F. Williams (Ed.), *Creativity at home and in school*. St. Paul, Minn.: Macalester Creativity Project, 1968.

Anderson, H. H., & Anderson, G. A cross-national study of children: A study of creativity and mental health. In I. J. Gordon (Ed.), *Human development*. Chicago: Scott, Foresman, 1965.

Anderson, H. H., & Brewer, J. E. *Effects of teacher dominative and integrative contacts on children's classroom behavior* (Studies for Teachers' Classroom Personalities II). Palo Alto Ca.: Stanford University Press, 1946.

Anderson, K. (Ed.). *Research on the academically talented student.* Washington, D.C.: National Education Association, 1960.

Anderson, L. *Assessing affective characteristics in the schools.* Boston: Allyn and Bacon, Inc., 1981.

Anderson, M. The relations of psi to creativity. *Journal of Parapsychology,* 1962, *26,* 277–292.

Anderson, V. V., & Kennedy, W. M. *Psychiatry in education.* New York: Harper, 1932.

Andrews, E. G. The development of imagination in the preschool child. *University of Iowa Studies of Character,* 1930, *3* (4), 1–64.

Andrews, F. Social and psychological factors which influence the creative process. In I. Taylor, & J. Getzels (Eds.), *Perspectives in creativity.* Chicago: Aldine Publishing Company, 1975, 117–145.

Andrews, G., & Debus, R. Persistence and the causal perception of failure: Modifying cognitive attributions. *Journal of Educational Psychology,* 1978, *70,* 154–166.

Aragon, J., & Marquez, L. Spanish-speaking component. In J. Miley, I. Sato, W. Luché, P. Weaver, J. Curry, & R. Ponce (Compilers), *Promising practices: Teaching the disadvantaged gifted.* Ventura, Ca.: Ventura County Superintendent of Schools, 1975.

Arlin, M., & Whitley, T. Perceptions of self-managed learning opportunities and academic locus of control: A causal interpretation. *Journal of Educational Psychology,* 1978, *70,* 988–992.

Armitage, S. Newborns can learn to call for mother's voice and prefer it. *Brain/Mind Bulletin,* 1980, *5* (17), 1.

Arnold, A. (Ed.). *Programs for gifted: Research abstracts 1973-1974.* Los Angeles: Los Angeles City Unified School District, 1974.

Arnold, A. (Chair) *Leadership: A survey of literature.* Los Angeles, Ca.: Los Angeles Unified School District, Instructional Planning Division, 1976.

Arnold, R., Bulatao, R., Buripakdi, C., Chin, B., Fawcett, J., Iritani, T., Lee, S., & Wu, T. *The value of children: Introduction and comparative analysis (Vol. 1).* Honolulu: East-West Population Institute, 1975.

Arnspiger, V., Rucker, W., Brill, J., & Blanchette, Z. *Human values series.* Austin, Tex.: Steck-Vaughn.

Asimov, I. *The human brain.* Boston: Houghton Mifflin, 1965.

Aspy, D. *Self theory in the classroom.* Paper presented at the annual meeting of the American Educational Research Association, Los Angeles, February 1969.

Aspy, D., & Bahler, J. The effect of teacher's inferred self concept upon student achievement. *The Journal of Educational Research,* 1975, *68,* 386–389.

Aspy, D., & Roebuck, F. An investigation of the relationship between student levels of cognitive functioning and the teacher's classroom behavior. *Journal of Educational Research,* 1972, *65* (8), 365–368.

Assagioli, R. *The act of will.* New York: Viking, 1973.

Ausubel, D. P. Cognitive structure: Learning to read. *Education,* 1967, *87,* 544–548.

Bachtold, L. Interpersonal values of gifted junior high school students. *Psychology in the Schools,* 1968, *5,* 368–370.

Bachtold, L. Personality differences among high ability underachievers. *The Journal of Educational Research,* 1969, *63,* 16–18.

Backman, M. Patterns of mental abilities: Ethnic, socioeconomic, and sex differences. *American Educational Research Journal*, 1972, *9*, 1–12.

Baldwin, A. *Identifying the disadvantaged.* Paper presented at the First National Conference on the Disadvantaged Gifted, Ventura, Ca., March 1973.

Baldwin, A. Instructional planning for gifted disadvantaged children. In B. Boston (Ed.), *Gifted and talented: Developing elementary and secondary school programs.* Reston, Va.: Council for Exceptional Children, 1975.

Baldwin, A. Seven keys in program planning for gifted and talented. *Roeper City and County School Parent Communication*, 1977, *2*, 3–6.

Baldwin, A. The Baldwin Identification Matrix, its development and use in programs for the gifted child. Paper presented at the Convention of the Council for Exceptional Children, Philadelphia, Pa., April, 1980.

Barbe, W. *A follow-up study of graduates of special classes for gifted children.* Unpublished doctoral dissertation, Northwestern University, 1953.

Barbe, W. Differentiated guidance for the gifted. *Education*, 1954, *74*, 306–311.

Barbe, W. Evaluation of special classes for gifted. *Exceptional Children*, 1955, *22*, 60–62.

Barbe, W. *One in a thousand—A comparative study of moderately and highly gifted elementary school children.* Columbus, Ohio: Ohio State Department of Education, 1964.

Barbe, W. *Psychology and education of the gifted.* New York: Appleton-Century-Crofts, 1965.

Barbe, W., & Renzulli, J. (Eds.), *Psychology and education of the gifted (2nd ed.)* New York: Irvington Publishing, 1975.

Bardwick, J., & Douvan, E. Ambivalence: The socialization of women. In V. Gornick and B. Moran (Eds.), *Woman in sexist society.* New York: Basic Books, 1971.

Barnett, M., & Kaiser, D. The relationship between intellectual-achievement responsibility attributions and performance. *Child Study Journal*, 1978, *8*, 209–215.

Barrett, H. The intensive study of thirty-two gifted children. *Personnel and Guidance Journal*, 1957, *36*, 192–194.

Barron, F. *Creative person and creative process.* New York: Holt, Rinehart & Winston, 1969.

Bar-Tal, D., Kfir, D., Bar-Zohar, Y., & Chen, M. The relationship between locus of control and academic achievement, anxiety, and level of aspiration. *British Journal of Educational Psychology*, 1980, *50*, 53–60.

Bayley, N. On the growth of intelligence. *American Psychologist*, 1955, *10*, 805–818.

Bayley, N. Behavioral correlates of mental growth: Birth to thirty-six years. *American Psychologist*, 1968, *23*, 1–17.

Bayley, N., & Schaefer, E. S. Correlations of maternal and child behaviors with the development of mental abilities: Data from the Berkeley Growth Study. *Monographs of the Society for Research in Child Development*, 1964, *29* (6, Whole No. 97).

Baymur, F., & Patterson, C. Three methods of assisting underachieving high school students. *Journal of Counseling Psychology*, 1960, *7*, 83–90.

Beach, D. *Reaching teenagers: Learning centers for the secondary classroom.* Santa Monica, Ca.: Goodyear, 1977.

Beadle, M. *A child's mind.* Garden City, N.Y.: Doubleday, 1970.

Beck, J. *How to raise a brighter child.* New York: Trident, 1967.

Becker, W. Consequences of different kinds of parental discipline. In M. Hoffman & L. Hoffman (Eds.), *Review of child development research* (Vol. 1). New York: Russell Sage Foundation, 1964.

Beckwith, C. Relationships between attributes of mothers and their infants' I.Q. scores. *Child Development*, 1971, *42*, 1083–1097.

Beechhold, H. *The creative classroom: Teaching without textbooks.* New York: Charles Scribner's Sons, 1971.

Beier, E. Nonverbal communication—How we send emotional messages. *Psychology Today*, 1974, *8* (5), 53–56.

Bell, D. *The coming of post-industrial society: A venture in social forecasting.* New York: Basic Books, 1972.

Bentov, I. *Stalking the wild pendulum: On the mechanics of consciousness.* New York: E. P. Dutton, 1977.

Bentov, I., with Bentov. M. *A cosmic book: On the mechanics of creation.* New York: E. P. Dutton, 1982.

Berliner, D. Tempus educare. In P. Peterson and H. Walberg (Eds.), *Research on teaching: Concepts, findings, and implications.* Berkeley, Ca.: McCrutchan Publishing Corporation, 1979, 120–135.

Bernal, E. *Mexican American perceptions of child giftedness in three Texas communities.* Paper presented at The First National Conference on the Disadvantaged Gifted. Ventura, Ca., March 1973.

Bernal, E. The identification of gifted Chicano children. In A. Baldwin, G. Gear, & L. Lucity (Eds.), *Educational planning for the gifted.* Reston, Va.: the Council for Exceptional Children, 1978.

Bernstein, D., & Borkover, T. *Progressive relaxation training: A manual for the helping professions.* Champaign, Ill.: Research Press, 1975.

Bessell, H., & Palomares, U. *Methods in human development, theory manual (1970 rev.). San Diego, Ca.: Human Development Training Institute, 1970.*

Bidwell, C. The social psychology of teaching. In R. Travers (Ed.), *Second handbook of research on teaching.* Chicago: Rand McNally, 1973.

Binet, A. The education of intelligence. In P. Torrance & W. White (Eds.), *Issues and advances in educational psychology.* Itasca, Ill.: F. E. Peacock, 1969.

Binet, A., & Simon, T. [*The development of intelligence in children (the Binet-Simon Scale)*] (E. Kite, trans.). New York: Arno Press, 1973. (Originally published, 1916).

Birch, H., & Gussow, J. *Disadvantaged children.* New York: Harcourt, Brace & World, 1970.

Birnbaum, M. Educational problems of rural education for the gifted. In B. Johnson (Ed.) *Ideas for urban/rural gifted/talented.* Ventura, Ca.: Office of the Ventura County Superintendent of Schools, National/State Leadership Training Institute on the Gifted/Talented, 1977.

Birns, B., & Golden, M. Prediction of intellectual performance at three years from infant test and personality measures. *Merrill-Palmer Quarterly*, 1972, *18*, 53–58.

Bish, C., & Fliegler, L. Summary of research on the academically talented student. *Review of Educational Research*, 1959, *39*, 408–450.

Bishop, W. Successful teachers of the gifted. *Exceptional Children*, 1968, *34*, 317–325.

Blakemore, C. Developmental factors in the formation of feature extracting neurons. In F. O. Schmidt & F. G. Warden (Eds.), *The neurosciences: Third study program.* Cambridge: MIT Press, 1974, 31–41.

Blancher-Dixon, J., & Turnbull, A. A pre-school program for gifted-handicapped children. *Journal for the Education of the Gifted*, 1978, *1* (2), 15–22.

Blaney, N., Stephan C., Rosenfield, D., Aronson, E., & Sikes, J. *Interdependence in the class-room: A field study.* Unpublished manuscript, University of Texas at Austin, 1976.

Bloom, B. (Ed.). *Taxonomy of educational objectives. Handbook I: Cognitive domain.* New York, David McKay, 1956.

Bloom, B. *Stability and change in human characteristics.* New York: John Wiley & Sons, 1964.

Bloom, B. The role of gifts and markers in the development of talent. *Exceptional Children.* 1982, *48* (6), 510–522.

Bloom, B., Davis, A., & Hess, R. *Compensatory education for cultural deprivation.* New York: Holt, Rinehart & Winston, 1965.

Bloom, B., & Sosniak, L. Talent development vs. schooling. *Educational Leadership*, 1981, *39* (2), 86–94.

Bodmer, W., & Cavalli-Sforza, L. Intelligence and race. *Scientific American*, 1970, *223* (4), 19–29.

Boehm, L. The development of conscience: A comparison of American children of different mental and socioeconomic levels. *Child Development*, 1962, *33*, 575–590.

Bogen, J. Some educational aspects of hemispheric specialization. *UCLA Educator*, 1975, *17* (2), 24–32.

Bohm, D. *Wholeness and the implicate order.* Boston: Routledge & Kegan, 1980.

Boocock, S., & Schild, E. *Simulation games in learning.* Beverly Hills, Ca.: Sage, 1968.

Bordan, R., & Schuster, D. The effects of suggestion, synchronized breathing and orchestrated music on the acquisition and retention of Spanish words. *SALT Journal*, 1976, *1* (1), 27–40.

Bordie, J. Language tests and linguistically different learners: The sad state of the art. *Elementary English*, 1970, *47*, 814–828.

Borg, W. *An evaluation of ability grouping.* U.S. Department of Health, Education and Welfare, Office of Education, Cooperative Research Project No. 577. Logan, Utah: Utah State University, 1964.

Borgers, S., & Treffinger, D. Creative talent: Implications for counselors. In N. Colangelo & R. Zaffrann (Eds.), *New voices in counseling the gifted.* Dubuque, Iowa: Kendall/Hunt Publishing Company, 1979.

Borland, J. Teacher identification of the gifted: A new look. *Journal for the Education of the Gifted*, September 1978, *2* (1), 22–32.

Bortner, M. (Ed.). *Cognitive growth and development—essays in honor of Herbert G. Birch.* New York: Brunner/Mazel, 1979.

Bower, R., Broughton, J., & Moore, M. Assessment of intention in sensorimotor infants. *Nature*, 1970, *228*, 679–681.

Bowers, W. *Student dishonesty and its control in college.* New York: Bureau of Applied Behavioral Science, 1964.

Bradley, R., & Caldwell, B. Early home environment and changes in mental test performance in children from 6 to 30 months. *Developmental Psychology*, 1976, *12*, 93–97.

Braga, J. L. Analysis and evaluation of early admission to school for mentally advanced children. *Journal of Educational Research*, 1969, *63*, 103–106.

Braga, J. Early admission: Opinion vs. evidence. *The Elementary School Journal*, 1971, *72*, 35–46.

Branscomb, A. (Chair) *Commerce Technical Advisory Board recommendations on learning environments for innovation*, a report of the CTAB to Jordan J. Baruch, Assistant Secretary for Productivity, Technology and Innovation, U.S. Department of Commerce, May, 1980.

Brazelton, T. B., & Als, H. Four early stages in the development of mother-infant interaction. *Psychoanalytic Study of the Child*, 1979, *34*, 349–369.

Breidenstine, A. The educational achievement of pupils in differentiated and undifferentiated groups. *Journal of Experimental Education*, 1936, *5*, 91–135.

Bremer, J., & Bremer, A. *Open education: A beginning*. New York: Holt, Rinehart & Winston, 1972.

Bricklin, B., & Bricklin, P. *Bright child—poor grades: The psychology of underachievement*. New York: Delacorte, 1967.

Briggs, D. *Your child's self-esteem; The key to his life*. Garden City, N.Y.: Doubleday, 1970.

Brierley, J. *The growing brain*. Windsor, Great Britain: NFER, 1976.

Brill, M. Studies of Jewish and non-Jewish intelligence. *Journal of Educational Psychology*, 1956, *47*, 302–309.

Broedel, J. *A study of the effect of group counseling on the academic performance and mental health of underachieving gifted adolescents*. Ann Arbor: University of Michigan Press, 1958.

Brookover, W. *Self and school achievement*. Paper presented at the annual meeting of the American Educational Research Association, Los Angeles, February 1969.

Brookover, W., LePere, J., Hamachek, D., Thomas, S., & Erickson, E. *Self-concept of ability and school achievement* (Vol. 11). USOE Cooperative Research Report, Project No. 1636. East Lansing: Michigan State University, 1965.

Brooks, C. *Sensory awareness*. New York: Viking, 1974.

Brown, B. *The experimental mind in education*. New York: Harper & Row, 1968.

Brown, B. *New mind, new body. Biofeedback: New directions for the mind*. New York: Harper & Row, 1974.

Brown, E. *Underachievement—A case of inefficient cognitive processing*. Address to the American Educational Research Association, New York, February 1971.

Brown, G. *Human teaching for human learning: An introduction to confluent education*. New York: Viking, 1971.

Brown, G., Yeomans, T., & Grizzard, L. *The live classroom: Innovations through confluent education and Gestalt*. New York: Viking, 1975.

Bruch, C. Modification of procedures for identification of the disadvantaged gifted. *The Gifted Child Quarterly*, 1971, *15*, (4), 267–272.

Bruner, J. *The process of education*. Cambridge, Mass.: Harvard University Press, 1960.

Bruner, J. The course of cognitive growth. *American Psychologist*, 1964, *19*, 1–15.

Bruner, J. *Toward a theory of instruction*. New York: W. W. Norton, 1968.

Bruner, J., & Dow, P. *Man: A course of study; a description of an elementary social studies curriculum.* Cambridge, Mass.: Education Development Center, 1967.

Bruner, J. Organization of early skilled action. *Child Development*, 1973, *44*, 1–11.

Bryden, M. Laterality effects in dichotic listening: Relations with handedness and reading ability in children. *Neuropsychologia*, 1970, *8*, 443–450.

Bucke, R. *Cosmic consciousness* (6th ed.). New York: E. P. Dutton, 1929.

Buell, S., & Coleman, P. Quantitative evidence for selective dendritic growth in normal human aging but not in senile dementia. *Brain Research*, 1981, *214* (1), 23–41.

Bull, B., & Wittrock, M. Imagery in the learning of verbal definitions. *British Journal of Educational Psychology*, 1973, *43*, 289–293.

Buros, O. (Ed.). *Mental measurement yearbook* (Vols. I & II, 5th ed.). Highland Park, N.J.: Gryphon, 1959.

Buros, O. (Ed.). *Mental measurement yearbook* (Vols. I & II, 6th ed.). Highland Park, N.J.: Gryphon, 1965.

Buros, O. (Ed.). *Mental measurement yearbook* (Vols. I & II, 7th ed.). Highland Park, N.J.: Gryphon, 1972.

Caffee, B. The Arkadelphia secondary gifted and talented program. *G/C/T*, 1981, *17*, 55–57.

Callahan, C. The gifted girl: An anomaly? *Roeper Review*, 1980, 2 (3), 16–20.

Callaway, W. R. A holistic conception of creativity and its relationship to intelligence. *The Gifted Child Quarterly*, 1969, *13*, 237–241.

Callaway, W. R. Modes of biological adaptation and their role in intellectual development. *The Galton Institute Monograph Series*, 1970, *1* (1), 1–34.

Calsyn, R. *The causal relationship between self-esteem, a locus of control and achievement: A cross-lagged panel analysis.* Unpublished doctoral dissertation. Northwestern University, 1973.

Cancro, R. (Ed.). *Intelligence: Genetic and environmental influences.* New York: Grune & Stratton, 1971.

Canfield, J., & Wells, H. *100 ways to enhance self-concept in the classroom.* Englewood Cliffs, N.J.: Prentice-Hall, 1976.

Capra, F. *The Tao of physics.* Berkeley, Ca.: Shambhala, 1975.

Capra, F. *The turning point: Science, society, and the rising culture.* New York: Simon and Schuster, 1982.

Carew, J. *Environmental stimulation: A longitudinal observational study of how people influence the young child's intellectual development in his everyday environment.* Paper presented at the annual meeting of the American Educational Research Association, San Francisco, April 1967.

Carroll, H. *Genius in the making.* New York: McGraw-Hill, 1940.

Cass-Beggs, B. *Your baby needs music—A music sound book for babies up to two years old.* New York: St. Martin's Press, 1978.

Cassel, R., & Coleman, J. A critical examination of the school dropout, reluctant leader, and abler non-college student problem. *NEA Secondary School Principal's Bulletin*, 1962, *46*, 60–65.

Cassel, R., & Haddox, G. Comparative study of leadership test scores for gifted and typical high school students. *Psychological Report*, 1959, *5*, 713–717.

Castaneda, C. *Journey to Ixtlan: The lessons of Don Juan.* New York: Simon & Schuster, 1972.

Casteel, J., & Stahl, R. *Value clarification in the classroom: A primer.* Pacific Palisades, Ca.: Goodyear, 1975.

Castillo, G. *Left-handed teaching.* New York: Praeger, 1974.

Cattell, R. *The culture-free intelligence test.* Champaign, Ill.: Institute for Personality Assessment and Testing, 1949.

Cattell, R. The structure of intelligence in relation to the nature—nurture controversy. In R. Cancro (Ed.). *Intelligence genetic and environmental influences.* New York: Grune & Stratton, 1971.

Cenci, C. "Lady Bug": An activity developed for the New Age School, Summer, 1980, Los Angeles, California.

Chall, J., & Mirsky, A. (Eds.). *Education and the brain: The seventy-seventh yearbook of the National Society for the Study of Education,* Part II. Chicago: The University of Chicago Press, 1978.

Chance, P. Parapsychology is an idea whose time has come. *Psychology Today,* 1973, *7,* 105–116.

Chansky, N. The x-ray of the school mark. *The Educational Forum,* March 1962, 347–352.

Chansky, N. A note of the grade point average in research. *Educational and Psychological Measurement,* 1964, *24,* 95–99.

Chess, S. Why some bright children have trouble in school. *Parents Magazine,* 1971, *46,* 42–43; 85; 89–90.

Chetelat, F. Visual arts education for the gifted elementary level art student. *Gifted Child Quarterly,* 1981, *25* (4), 154–158.

Childs, R. A comparison of the adaptive behavior of normal and gifted five and six year old children. *Roeper Review,* 1981, *4* (2), 41–43.

Chomsky, N. *Cartesian linguistics.* New York: Harper & Row, 1966.

Christiansen, T., & Livermore, G. A comparison of Anglo American and Spanish American children on the WISC. *Journal of Social Psychology,* 1970, *81,* 9–14.

Christianson, B. Learning centers that work. *Instructor,* 1969, *79,* 135.

Chukovsky, K. *From two to five.* Berkeley: University of California Press, 1966.

Clark, B., & Kaplan, S. *Improving differentiated curricula for the gifted/talented.* Los Angeles: California Association for the Gifted, 1981.

Clark, F. Building intuition. In G. Hendricks & T. Roberts, *The second centering book.* Englewood Cliffs, N.J.: Prentice-Hall, 1977.

Clark, H. The power of positive speaking: It takes longer to understand no. *Psychology Today,* 1974, *8* (4), 102–111.

Clarke-Stewart, K. Interactions between mothers and their young children: Characteristics and consequences. *Monographs of Society for Research in Child Development,* 1973, *38,* (No. 153).

Clymer, T., & Wardeberg, H. *Skills handbook: To turn a stone.* Lexington, Mass.: Ginn & Co., 1971.

Cohen, E. The arts from the inside out: Developing a performing arts curriculum. *G/C/T,* 1981, *20,* 38–42.

Colangelo, N., & Lafrenz, N. Counseling the culturally diverse gifted. *Gifted Child Quarterly,* 1981, *25* (1), 27–30.

Colangelo, N., & Zaffrann, R. Special issues in counseling the gifted. *Counseling and Human Development,* 1979, *11* (5), 1–12.

Cole, H. Process curricula and creativity development. *Journal of Creative Behavior,* 1969, *3,* 243–259.

Coleman, J. The adolescent subculture and academic achievement. *American Journal of Sociology,* 1960, *65,* 337–347.

Coleman, J. *The adolescent society.* New York: Free Press of Glencoe, 1962.

Coleman, J., Campbell, E., Hobson, C., McPartland, J., Mood, A., Weinfeld, F., & York, R. *Equality of educational opportunity.* Washington, D.C.: U.S. Government Printing Office, 1966.

Colson, S. The evaluation of a community-based career education program for gifted and talented students as an administrative model for an alternative program. *Gifted Child Quarterly,* 1980, *24* (3), 101–106.

Colvin, S. What infant prodigies teach educators. *Illustrated World,* 1915, *24,* 47–52.

Combs, A. W. (Ed.). *Perceiving, behaving, becoming.* Yearbook of the Association for Supervision and Curriculum Development, Washington, D.C.: The National Education Association, 1962.

Combs, A. W. Florida studies in the helping professions. *Social Science Monograph,* 1969, No. 37. Gainesville: University of Florida Press.

Combs, A. W., Blume, R. A., Newan, A. J., & Wass, H. L. *The professional education of teachers: A perceptual view of teacher preparation* (2nd ed.). Boston: Allyn & Bacon, 1974.

Combs, A. W., & Snygg, D. *Individual behavior* (Rev. ed.). New York: Harper & Row, 1959.

Combs, C. Perception of self and scholastic underachievement in the academically capable. *Personnel and Guidance Journal,* 1964, *43,* 47–51.

Confessore, G., & Confessore, S. Attitudes toward physical activity among adolescents talented in the visual and performing arts. *Journal for the Education of the Gifted,* 1981, *4* (3), 261–269.

Connelly, M. Gifted girls and gifted women. *Roeper City and County School Quarterly,* 1977, *12,* 12–13.

Coopersmith, S. *The antecedents of self-esteem.* San Francisco: W. H. Freeman, 1967.

Coopersmith, S. *Developing motivation in young children.* San Francisco: Albion, 1975.

Cornish, E. *The study of the future.* Washington, D.C.: World Future Society, 1977.

Cottman, C., & Nieto-Sampedro, M. Brain function, synapse renewal and plasticity. *Annual Review of Psychology,* 1982, *33,* 371–401.

Council for Exceptional Children. *The nation's commitment to the education of gifted and talented children and youth; Summary of findings from a 1977 survey of states and territories.* Reston, Va.: Council for Exceptional Children, 1978.

Covington, M., & Beery, R. *Self-worth and school learning.* New York: Holt, Rinehart & Winston, 1976.

Covington, M., Crutchfield, R., & Davies, L. *Teacher's guide to the productive thinking program: General problem-solving.* Educational Innovations, Box 9248, Berkeley, Ca. 1967. (16 self-instructional lessons.)

Cox, C. The early mental traits of three hundred geniuses. In L. Terman (Ed.), *Genetic studies of genius* (Vol. II). Stanford, Ca.: Stanford University Press, 1926.

Craig, G. *Human development* (2nd ed.). Englewood Cliffs, N.J.: Prentice Hall, Inc., 1980.

Crandall, V., Katkovsky, W., & Preston, A. Motivational and ability determinants of young children's intellectual achievement behaviors. *Child Development*, 1962, *33*, 643–661.

Crutchfield, R. Nurturing the cognitive skills of productive thinking. In L. Rubin, *Life skills in school and society.* Washington, D.C.: Association for Supervision and Curriculum Development, National Education Association, 1969.

Csoka, L. A relationship between leader intelligence and leader rated effectiveness. *Journal of Applied Psychology*, 1974, *59*, 43–47.

Cunningham, L., & Gephart, W. (Eds.). *Leadership—The science and the art today.* Itasca, Ill.: F. E. Peacock, 1973.

Damm, V. Creativity and intelligence: Research implications for equal emphasis in high school. *Exceptional Children*, 1970, *36*, 565–569.

Daniel, R. Underachievement of superior and talented students. In B. Shertzer (Ed.), *Working with superior students.* Chicago: Scientific Research Associates, 1960.

Darwin, D. *On the origin of species.* London: Murray, 1859.

Das, J., Kirby, J., & Jarman, R. Simultaneous and successive syntheses: An alternate model for cognitive abilities. *Psychological Bulletin*, 1975, *82*, 87–103.

Davies, A. The perceptual maze test in a normal population. *Perceptual and Motor Skills*, 1965, *20*, 287–293.

Davis, A., & Eells, K. *Davis-Eells games.* New York: Harcourt, Brace & World, 1953.

Davis, G. In frumious pursuit of the creative person. *The Journal of Creative Behavior*, 1975, *9*, 75–87.

Davis, G., Manske, M., & Train, A. *Training creative thinking.* Madison, Wis.: Occasional paper No. 6, Research and Development Center for Learning and Re-education, The University of Wisconsin, 1967.

DeCharms, R. *Enhancing motivation: Change in the classroom.* New York: Halsted, 1976.

Deci, E. *Intrinsic motivation.* New York: Plenum Press, 1975.

Delisle, J., Reis, S., & Gubbins, E. The revolving door identification and programming model. *Exceptional Children*, 1981, *48* (2), 152–156.

Delp, J., & Martinson, R. *The gifted and talented: A handbook for parents.* Reston, Va.: Council for Exceptional Children, 1974.

DeMille, R. *Put your mother on the ceiling.* New York: Viking, 1973.

Dennis, W. Causes of retardation among institutional children: Iran. *Journal of Genetic Psychology*, 1960, *96*, 47–59.

Dennis, W., & Dennis, M. The effect of restricted practice upon the reaching, sitting and standing of two infants. *Journal of Genetic Psychology*, 1935, *47*, 21–29.

Dennis, W., & Najarian, P. Infant development under environmental handicap. *Psychology Monograph*, 1957, *71* (7, Whole No. 436), 1–13.

Desmond, M., Rudolph, A., & Phitaksphraiwan, P. The transitional care nursery: A mechanism of a preventive medicine. *Pediatric Clinics of North America*, 1966, *13*, 651–668.

d'Espagnet, B. The quantum theory and reality. *Scientific American*, 1979, *241* (5), 158–181.

Deutsch, C., & Deutsch, M. Brief reflections on the theory of early childhood enrichment programs. In R. Hess & R. Bear, *Early education*. New York: Aldine, 1968.

Dexter, E. The effect of fatigue or boredom on teacher's marks. *Journal of Educational Research*, 1935, *28*, 664–667.

DiCara, L. *Biofeedback and self control*. Chicago: Aldine, 1970.

Dinkmeyer, D. *Developing understanding of self and others*. Circle Pines, Minn.: American Guidance Service, 1969. (A kit of materials)

Dirks, J., & Quarfoth, J. Selecting children for gifted classes: Choosing for breadth vs. choosing for depth. *Psychology in the Schools*, 1981, *18* (4), 437–449.

Dobzhansky, T. *Heredity and the nature of man*. New York: New American Library, 1964.

Doherty, E., & Evans, L. Independent study process: They can think, can't they? *Journal for the Education of the Gifted*, 1981, *4* (2), 106–111.

Doktor, R., & Bloom, D. Selective lateralization of cognitive style related to occupation as determined by EEG alpha asymmetry. *Psychophysiology*, 1977, *14*, 385–392.

Dolle, J., & Bardot, A. Learning judo and cognitive development: Understanding the laws of physics through judo. *Psychologie Francaise*, 1979, *24* (2), 97–109.

Doman, G. *How to teach your baby to read*. New York: Random House, 1964.

Domino, G. Maternal personality correlates of son's creativity. *Journal of Consulting and Clinical Psychology*, 1969, *33*, 180–183.

Douglass, J. *Strategies for maximizing the development of talent among the urban disadvantaged*. Paper presented at the annual meeting of the Council for Exceptional Children, Denver, April 1969.

Dowling, C. *The Cinderella complex*. New York: Summit Books, Simon & Schuster, 1981.

Downing, J. *Dreams and nightmares*. New York: Harper & Row, 1973.

Doyle, W. Classroom tasks and student abilities. In P. P. Peterson & H. Walbert (Eds.). *Conceptions of teaching*. Berkeley, Ca.: McCutchan, 1978.

Dreger, R., & Miller, K. Comparative psychological studies of Negroes and whites in the United States. *Psychological Bulletin*, 1960, *57*, 361–402.

Drevdahl, J. Factors of importance for creativity. *Journal of Clinical Psychology*, 1956, *12*, 21–26.

Drews, E. M. The four faces of able adolescents. *Saturday Review*, 1963, *46*, 68–71.

Drews, E. M. *The creative intellectual style in gifted adolescents* (Vols. I, II & III). E. Lansing, Mich.: Michigan State University, 1964, 1965, 1966.

Drews, E. M. *Learning together: How to foster creativity, self-fulfillment and social awareness in today's students and teachers*. Englewood Cliffs, N.J.: Prentice-Hall, 1972.

Drews, E. M. Leading out and letting be. *Today's Education*, 1976, *65*, 26–28.

Drews, E. M., & Knowlton, D. The being and becoming series for college-bound students. *Audiovisual Instruction*, 1963, *8*, 29–32.

Drews, E. M., & Lepson, L. *Values and humanity*. New York: St. Martin's, 1971.

Dreyer, A., & Wells, M. Parental values, parental control in young children. *Journal of Marriage and Family*, 1966, *28*, 83–88.

Dubner, F. Thirteen ways of looking at a gifted teacher. *Journal for the Education of the Gifted*, 1980, *3* (3), 143–146.

Dubos, R. Biological individuality. *The Columbia Forum*, 1969, *12* (1), 5–9.

Dubrowsky, W. Gifted children benefit from learning to be self-accepting. *Gifted Child Quarterly*, 1968, *12*, 85–88.

Dunn, B. *The effectiveness of teaching early reading skills to two-to-four-year-old children by television*. Unpublished doctoral dissertation, University of California, Los Angeles, 1969.

Dunn, L. *Exceptional children in the schools* (2nd ed.). New York: Holt, Rinehart & Winston, 1973.

Dunn, R., & Dunn., K. *Educator's self-teaching guide to individualizing instructional programs*. West Nyack, N.Y.; Parker, 1975.

Dunn, R., & Goldman, M. Competition and noncompetition in relationship to satisfaction and feelings toward own-group and non-group members. *Journal of Social Psychology*, 1966, *68*, 299–311.

Durden, W. The Johns Hopkins program for verbally gifted youth. *Roeper Review: A Journal on Gifted Education*, 1980, *3* (2), 34–37.

Durden-Smith, J. Male and female—Why? *Quest*, October 1980, 15–19; 93–98.

Durkin, D. *Children who read early*. New York: Teachers College Press, 1966.

Durrell, D., Scribner, H., McHugh, W., Manning, J., & Rockfort, G. Adapting instruction to the learning needs of children in the intermediate grades. *Journal of Education*, 1959, *142*, 1–78.

Dweck, C., Davidson, W., Nelson, S., & Enna, B. Sex differences in learned helplessness. *Developmental Psychology*, 1978, *14*, 268–276.

Dweck, C., & Goetz, T. Attributions and learned helplessness. In J. Harvey, W. Ickes, & R. Kidd (Eds.). *New directions in attribution research* (Vol. 2). Hillsdale, N.J.: Erlbaum, 1978.

Eccles, J. *The understanding of the brain*. New York: McGraw-Hill Book Co., 1973.

Edmonds, R. Inner-city schools can be effective. *Report on Education Research*, November 12, 1980.

Edwards, B. *An experiment in perceptual skills in drawing*. Unpublished doctoral dissertation, University of California, Los Angeles, 1976.

Edwards P. The use of essays in selection at 11 plus: Essay marking experiments: Shorter and longer essays. *British Journal of Educational Psychology*, 1956, *26*, 128–136.

Eisenberg, D. Handicapped children can be gifted too, say educators. *Education of the Handicapped*, December 1981.

Eisenman, R., & Schussel, N. Creativity, birth order and preference for symmetry. *Journal of Consulting Clinical Psychology*, 1970, *34*, 275–280.

Elder, C. *Making value judgments: Decisions for today*. Columbus: Charles E. Merrill, 1972.

Elkind, J. The gifted child with learning disabilities. *The Gifted Child Quarterly*, 1973, *17*, 96–97.

Ellinger, B. *The home environment and the creative thinking abilities of children*. Unpublished doctoral dissertation, Ohio State University, 1964. *Dissertation Abstracts International*, 1965, *25* (6), 6308. (Order No. 65-3850)

Ellis, M. & Scholtz, G. *Activity and play of children*. Englewood Cliffs, N.J.: Prentice Hall, 1978.

Ellison, R., Abe, C., Fox, D., & Coray, K. Using biographical information in identifying artistic talent. *Gifted Child Quarterly*, Winter, 1976, *20* (4), 402–413.

Emde, R., & Robinson, J. The first two months: Recent research in developmental psychobiology and the changing view of the newborn. In J. Noshpitz & J. Call (Eds.), *Basic handbook of child psychiatry*. New York: Basic Books, 1976.

Engelmann, T., & Engelmann, S. *Give your child a superior mind*. New York: Simon & Schuster, 1966.

Epstein, H. Growth spurts during brain development: Implications for educational policy and practice. In J. Chall & A. Mirsky (Eds.), *Education and the brain, the seventy-seventh yearbook of the National Society for the Study of Education, part II*. Chicago: University of Chicago Press, 1978, 343–370.

Erikson, E. *Childhood and society*, New York: Norton, 1950 (Rev. 1964).

Erikson, E. *Identity, youth and crisis*. New York: W. W. Norton, 1968.

Ernest, J. Mathematics and sex. *American Mathematical Monthly*, 1976, *83* (8), 595–614.

Ernest, J. Is mathematics a sexist discipline? In L. Fox, L. Brody, & D. Tobin, (Eds.) *Women and the mathematical mystique*. Baltimore: The Johns Hopkins University Press, 1980.

Ertl, J. Intelligence testing by brain waves. *Mensa Bulletin*, 1968, *110*, 3–6.

Evans, E. Pupil underachievement, are we responsible? *Instructor*, 1965, 75, 25–42.

Ewing, T., & Gilbert, W. Controlled study of the effects of counseling on the scholastic achievements of students of superior ability. *Journal of Counseling Psychology*, 1967, *14*, 235–239.

Fadiman, J. *The mind can do anything*. Talk presented to the Mind Can Do Anything Conference, San Rafael, Ca., 1976.

Fala, M. *Dunce cages, hickory sticks and public evaluations: The structure of academic authoritarianism*. Madison, Wisc.: The Teaching Assistant Association, University of Wisconsin, 1968.

Falbo, T., & Cooper, C. Young children's time and intellectual ability. *Journal of Genetic Psychology*, 1980, *137* (2), 299–300.

Fantz, R. The origin of form perception. *Scientific American*, 1961, *204*, 66–72.

Fantz, R. Visual perception from birth as shown by pattern selectivity. *New Issues in Infant Development, New York Academy of Sciences Annals*, 1965, *118* (21), 793–814.

Faraday, A. *Dream power*. New York: Coward, McCann & Geoghegan, 1972.

Farrell, P. *Teacher involvement in identification*. Paper presented at the First National Conference on the Disadvantaged Gifted, Ventura, Ca., March 1973.

Fearn, L. Individual development: A process model in creativity. *The Journal of Creative Behavior*, 1976, *10*, 55–64.

Feldenkrais, M. *Body and mature behavior*. New York: International Universities Press, 1949.

Feldenkrais, M. *Awareness through movement*. New York: Harper & Row, 1972.

Feldhusen, J., Denny, T., & Condon, C. Anxiety, divergent thinking and achievement. *Journal of Educational Psychology*, 1965, *56*, 40–45.

Feldhusen, J., & Klausmeier, H. Anxiety, intelligence and achievement in children of low, average and high intelligence. *Child Development*, 1962, *33*, 403–407.

Feldhusen, J., & Kollof, M. An approach to career education for the gifted. *Roeper Review*, 1979, 2 (2), 13–16.

Feldhusen, J., Treffinger, D., & Pine, P. *Teaching children how to think* (Teacher's ed.) Technical Report (NIE-G-74-0063), National Institute of Education, 1975.

Feng, G., & Wilkerson, H. *T'ai-Chi: A way of centering and I Ching.* New York: Macmillan, 1969.

Ferguson, M. *The brain revolution.* New York: Taplinger, 1973.

Ferguson, M. Bohm sees hologram as model for new description of reality. *Brain/Mind Bulletin*, 1977a, 2 (16), 2.

Ferguson, M. Memory drug piracetam now being researched in U.S. *Brain/Mind Bulletin*, 1977b, 2 (16), 3

Ferguson, M. 'Mind mirror' EEG identifies states of awareness. *Brain/Mind Bulletin*, 1977c, 2 (30), 1–2.

Ferguson, M. Chronopsychology links brain function to cycles. *Brain/Mind Bulletin*, 1981, 7 (1), 1, 3.

Ferguson, M. Electronic device reads acupuncture meridians. *Brain/Mind Bulletin*, 1981, 7 (2), 1 & 2.

Ferguson, M. New theory: Feelings code, organize thinking. *Brain/Mind Bulletin*, 1982, 7 (6), 1, 2.

Ferguson, M. Subatomic physics may offer models for consciousness, psi. *Brain/Mind Bulletin*, 1982, 7 (10), 1, 3.

Ferguson, M. Optimallearning: Orchestrating best performance. *Brain/Mind Bulletin*, 1982, 7 (8), 1, 2.

Ferguson, M. The new reality: interacting approximations. *Brain/Mind Bulletin*, 1982, 7 (10), 1, 2.

Fiedler, F. *A theory of leadership effectiveness.* New York: McGraw-Hill, 1967.

Fiedler, F. Validation and extension of the contingency model of leadership effectiveness: A review of empirical findings. *Psychological Bulletin*, 1971, 76, 128–148.

Fincher, J. (Ed.). *The brain mystery of matter and mind. The Human Body Series.* Washington, D.C.: U.S. News Books, 1981.

Findley, W., & Bryan, M. *Ability grouping 1970. Status, import, and alternatives.* Athens, Ga.: Center for Educational Improvement, University of Georgia, 1971.

Fine, B. *Stretching their minds.* New York: E. P. Dutton, 1964.

Fine, B. *Underachievers—How they can be helped.* New York: E. P. Dutton, 1967.

Fischer, D., Hunt, D., & Randhawa, B. Empirical validity of Ertl's brain-wave analyzer. *Educational and Psychological Measurement*, 1978, 38 (4), 1017–1030.

Flanders, N. A. *Teacher influence—Pupil attitudes and achievement* (Final report, University of Minnesota Project No. 397). Washington, D.C.: U.S. Department of Health, Education and Welfare, Cooperative Research Program 1960.

Fleisham, E., & Hunt, J. (Eds.). *Current developments in the study of leadership.* Carbondale: Southern Illinois University Press, 1973.

Flescher, I. Anxiety and achievement of intellectually gifted and creatively gifted children. *Journal of Psychology*, 1963, 56, 251–268.

Ford, B., & Ellis, J. Career education: A continuing need of Illinois gifted students. *Journal for the Education of the Gifted*, 1979, 2 (3), 153–156.

Fowler, W. Cognitive learning in infancy and early childhood. *Psychology Bulletin*, 1962a, *59*, 116–152.

Fowler, W. Teaching a two-year-old to read: An experiment in early childhood learning. *Genetic Psychology Monograph*, 1962b, *66*, 181–283.

Fowler, W. The concept of the gifted child and the preschool years. *The Gifted Child Quarterly*, 1963, 7, 102–105.

Fox, L. Sex differences: Implications for program planning for the academically gifted. In J. Stanley, W. George, & C. Solano (Eds.), The gifted and the creative: A fifty-year perspective. Baltimore: The Johns Hopkins University Press, 1977.

Fox, L. Instruction for the gifted: Some promising practices. *Journal for the Education of the Gifted*, Fall 1981, 4 (3), 246–254.

Fox, L., Brody, L., & Tobin, D. (Eds.). *Women and the mathematical mystique*. Baltimore: The Johns Hopkins University Press, 1980.

Fox, L., Pasternak, S., & Peiser, N. Career-related interests of adolescent boys and girls. In D. Keating (Ed.), *Intellectual talent: Research and development*. Baltimore: The Johns Hopkins University Press, 1976.

Fox, L., & Turner, L. Gifted and creative females in the middle school years. *American Middle School Education*, 1981, 4 (1), 17–23.

Frank, J. Talk to annual meeting of the National Institute for the Psychotherapies in New York, reported in *Brain/Mind Bulletin*, 1977, 2 (15).

Frasier, M. Counseling the culturally diverse gifted. In N. Colangelo & R. Zaffrann (Eds.), *New voices in counseling the gifted*. Dubuque, Iowa: Kendall/Hunt Publishers, 1979.

Frasier, M., & Carland, J. A study to identify key factors that affect the establishment of a positive relationship between teachers of the gifted and regular classroom teachers. Journal for the Education of the Gifted, 1980, 3 (4), 225–227.

Frasier, M., & McCannon, C. Using bibliotherapy with gifted children. *Gifted Child Quarterly*, 1981, 25 (2), 81–85.

Freed, A. *TA for kids*. Los Angeles: Jalmar, 1971.

Freed, A. *TA for tots*. Los Angeles: Jalmar, 1973.

Freehill, M. Teachers for the gifted. In B. Boston (Ed.), *A resource manual of information on educating the gifted and talented*. Reston, Va.: Council for Exceptional Children, 1975.

Freehill, M. Foreword. In B. Johnson (Ed.) *Ideas for urban/rural gifted/talented*. Ventura, Ca.: Office of the Ventura County Superintendent of Schools, National/State Leadership Training Institute on the Gifted/Talented, 1977.

French, D. Microcomputers revolutionizing biofeedback; California school districts develop curricula. *Brain/Mind Bulletin*, 1978, 4 (1), 2.

Frierson, E. Upper and lower status gifted children: A study of differences. *Exceptional Children*, 1965, 32, 83–90.

Fromm, E. The creative attitude. In H. H. Anderson, *Creativity and its cultivation*. New York: Harper & Row, 1959.

Fund for the Advancement of Education. *They went to college early*. Education Report No. 2. New York: The Fund for the Advancement of Education, 1957.

Gagné, R. *The conditions of learning.* New York: Holt, Rinehart & Winston, 1965.

Gallagher, J. Social status of children related to intelligence propinquity and social perception. *Elementary School Journal,* 1958, *58,* 225–231.

Gallagher, J. *Teaching the gifted child.* Boston: Allyn & Bacon, 1964.

Gallagher, J. *Research summary on gifted child education.* Springfield, Ill.: Office of the Superintendent of Public Instruction, 1966.

Gallagher, J. *Teaching the gifted child* (2nd ed.). Boston: Allyn & Bacon, 1975.

Gallagher, J., Aschner, M., & Jenne, W. Productive thinking of gifted children in classroom interaction. CEC Research Monograph Series B, 1967, *B-5,* 1–103.

Gallagher, J., & Crowder, T. The adjustment of gifted children in the regular classroom. *Exceptional Children,* 1957, *23,* 306–312; 317–319.

Gallagher, J., & Kinney, L. (Eds.). *Talent delayed—talent denied, the culturally different gifted child—A conference report.* Reston, Va.: The Foundation for Exceptional Children, 1974.

Galloway, C. *Teaching is communication* (Bulletin No. 29). Washington, D.C.: The Association for Student Teaching, 1970.

Gallwey, W. *The inner game of tennis.* New York: Random House, 1974.

Galton, F. *Hereditary genius: An inquiry into its laws and consequences.* London: Macmillan, 1869.

Galyean, B. *Language from within.* Los Angeles: Prism, 1976.

Galyean, B. *The confluent teaching of foreign languages, ESEA Title IV-C project year-end reports.* Los Angeles City Unified Schools, Los Angeles, California, 1977–1980.

Galyean, B. *A confluent language program for K-3, NES LES students, ESEA Title IV-C project, year-end reports.* Los Angeles City Unified Schools, Los Angeles, California, 1978–1981.

Galyean, B. *The effects of guided imagery activities on various behaviors of one class of low achieving students.* Research paper. Los Angeles: Ken-Zel, 1979.

Gardner, J. The development of object identity in the first six months of infancy. Paper presented at the Biennial Meeting of the Society of Research in Child Development, Minneapolis, 1971.

Garrett, H. Jews and others. *The Personnel Journal,* 1929, *7,* 341–348.

Garrett, H. Negro-white differences in mental ability in the United States. *Scientific Monthly,* 1947, *65,* 329–333.

Gazzanega, M. Review of the split brain. *UCLA Educator,* 1975, *17* (2), 9–12.

Gear, G. *Teaching the talented program: A progress report.* Storrs, Conn.: University of Connecticut, 1974.

Gear, G. *Effects of the training program, Identification of the potentially gifted on teacher's accuracy in the identification of intellectually gifted children.* Unpublished doctoral dissertation, University of Connecticut, 1976.

Gear, G. Effects of training on teachers' accuracy in the identification of gifted children, *The Gifted Child Quarterly,* Spring 1978, *22* (1), 90–97.

Geldard, F. Body English. *Psychology Today,* 1968, *2* (7), 43–68.

Gesell, A., Halverson, H., Thompson, H., Ilg, F., Castner, B., Ames, L., & Amatruda, C. *The first five years of life: A guide to the study of the preschool child.* New York: Harper, 1940.

Getzels, J., & Jackson, F. Family environment and cognitive style: A study of the sources of highly intelligent and highly creative adolescents. *American Sociological Review*, 1961, *26*, 351–359.

Getzels, J., & Jackson, F. *Creativity and intelligence.* New York: John Wiley & Sons, 1962.

Gibb, C. *Leadership: Selected readings.* Baltimore, Md.: Penguin, 1969.

Goertzel, V., & Goertzel, M. *Cradles of eminence.* Boston: Little Brown, 1962.

Gold, M. *Education of the intellectually gifted.* Columbus, Ohio: Charles E. Merrill, 1965.

Goldberg, M. A three year program at DeWitt Clinton High School to help bright underachievers. *High Points*, 1959, *41*, 5–35.

Goldberg, M., Passow, A., Justman, J., & Hage, G. *The effects of ability grouping.* New York: Bureau of Publications, Columbia University, 1965.

Goldstein-Jackson, K. *Experiments with everyday objects; Science activities for children, parents, and teachers.* Englewood Cliffs, N.J.: Prentice-Hall, Inc., 1978.

Goleman, D. A new computer test of the brain. *Psychology Today*, 1976, *9* (12), 44–48.

Goodall, K. Tie line: Who's bright, two approaches. *Psychology Today*, 1972, 5 (11), 24–26.

Goodman, D. Learning from lobotomy. *Human Behavior*, 1978, (1), 44–49.

Gordon, D. Children's beliefs in internal-external control and self-esteem as related to academic achievement. *Journal of Personality Assessment*, 1977, *41*, 383–386.

Gordon, I. *Baby learning through baby play.* New York: St. Martin's, 1970.

Gordon, W. *Synetics: The development of creative capacity.* New York: Harper & Row, 1961.

Gordon, W., & Poze, T. SES Synectics and gifted education today. *Gifted Child Quarterly*, 1980, *24* (4), 147–151.

Gorman, A. *Teachers and learners: The interactive process of education* (2nd ed.). Boston: Allyn & Bacon, 1974.

Gowan, J. C. Dynamics of the underachievement of gifted students. *Exceptional Children*, 1957, *24*, 98–102.

Gowan, J. C. What makes a gifted child creative? *The Gifted Child Quarterly*, 1965, *9*, 3–6.

Gowan, J. C. *Development of the creative individual.* San Diego, Ca.: Robert R. Knapp, 1972.

Gowan, J. C. *The education of gifted youth.* Paper presented at the First National Conference on the Disadvantaged Gifted, Ventura, Ca., March 1973.

Gowan, J. C. *The development of the psychedelic individual.* Buffalo, N.Y.: Creative Education Foundation, 1974.

Gowan, J. C. *Trance, art, and creativity.* Buffalo, N.Y.: Creative Education Foundation, 1975.

Gowan, J. C. *Operations of increasing order.* Westlake Village, Ca.: Gowan, 1980.

Gowan, J. Introduction. In J. Gowan, J. Khatena, & E. P. Torrance, *Creativity: Its educational implications,* (2nd ed.). Dubuque, Iowa: Kendall/Hunt Publishing Company, 1981.

Gowan, J. C., & Demos, G. D. *How to enhance effective leadership.* Long Beach: California State College, 1962.

Gowan, J. C., & Demos, G. D. *The education and guidance of the ablest.* Springfield, Ill.: Charles C. Thomas, 1964.

Gowan, J. C., Demos, G. D., & Torrance, E. P. (Eds.), *Creativity: Its educational implications.* New York: John Wiley & Sons, 1967.

Grace, H. A., & Booth, N. R. Is the gifted child a social isolate? *Peabody Journal of Education*, 1958, *35*, 195–196.

Grant, W. V., & Lind, C. G. *Digest of education statistics* (1976 ed.). Washington, D.C.: U.S. Government Printing Office, 1977.

Granzin, K., & Granzin, W. Peer group choice as a device for screening intellectually gifted children. *The Gifted Child Quarterly*, 1969, *13* (3), 189–194.

Greene, D. *Immediate and subsequent effects of differential reward systems on intrinsic motivation in public school classrooms.* Unpublished doctoral dissertation, Stanford University, 1974.

Grier, J., Counter, S., & Shearer, W. Prenatal auditory imprinting in chickens. *Science*, 1967, *155*, 1692–1693.

Griffiths, R. *A study of imagination in early childhood and its function in mental development.* London: K. Paul, Trench, Trubner, 1945.

Griggs, S., & Price, G. A comparison between the learning styles of gifted versus average suburban junior high school students. *Roeper Review*, 1980, *3* (1), 7–8.

Gris, H., & Dick, W. *The new Soviet psychic discoveries.* Englewood Cliffs, N.J.: Prentice-Hall, 1978.

Groth, N. Success and creativity in male and female professors. *The Gifted Child Quarterly*, 1975, *19*, 328–335.

Guilford, J. P. The structure of intellect. *Psychological Bulletin*, 1956, *53*, 267–293.

Guilford, J. P. Three faces of intellect. *American Psychology*, 1959, *14*, 469–479.

Guilford, J. P. *The nature of human intelligence.* New York: McGraw-Hill, 1967.

Gunther, B. *Sense relaxation below your mind.* New York: Collier Books, 1966.

Guttentag, M. *Undoing sex stereotypes.* New York: McGraw-Hill, 1975.

Hadley, D. *Effects of classroom anxiety on creativity.* Paper presented at a meeting of the Council of Exceptional Children, Denver, April 1969.

Hagen, E. *Identification of the gifted.* New York: Teachers College Press, 1980.

Hagen, J., & Clark, B. *Unusual capacity-unusual needs.* Paper presented at the second Conference of the World Council for Gifted, San Francisco, July 1977.

Haggard, E. Socialization, personality and academic achievement in gifted children. *School Review*, 1957, *65*, 388–414.

Hall, E., & Skinner, N. *Somewhere to turn: Strategies for parents of the gifted and talented.* New York: Teachers College Press, 1980.

Hallman, R. The commonness of creativity. *Educational Theory*, 1963, *13*, 132–136.

Halpin, G., Payne, G., & Ellett, C. Biographical correlates of the creative personality: Gifted adolescents. *Exceptional Children*, 1973, *39*, 652–653.

Handler, P. (Ed.). *Biology and the future of man.* New York: Oxford University Press, 1970.

Harmin, M. *Making sense of our lives.* Niles, Ill.: Argus Communications, 1973. (A multimedia kit).

Harrington, D. Creativity, analogical thinking, and muscular metaphors. *Journal of Mental Imagery*, 1980, *4* (2), 13–23.

Harris, T. *I'm OK: You're OK.* New York: Harper & Row, 1967.

Hart, L. *How the brain works.* New York: Basic Books, 1975.

Hart, L. The new "brain" concept of learning. *Phi Delta Kappan*, 1978, *59* (6), 393–396.

Hart, L. Brain, language, and new concepts of learning. *Educational Leadership*, 1981, *39*, 443–445.

Hassett, J., & Weisberg, A. *Open education: Alternative within our tradition*. Englewood Cliffs, N.J.: Prentice-Hall, 1972.

Hausdorff, H., & Farr, S. The effects of grading practices on the marks of gifted sixth grade children. *Journal of Educational Research*, 1965, *59*, 169–172.

Haynes, H., White, B., & Held, R. Visual accommodation in the human infant. *Science*, 1965, *148*, 528–530.

Hegeman, K. *A position paper on the education of gifted-handicapped children*. For the Committee for the Gifted-Handicapped of the Association for the Gifted, Council for Exceptional Children, Reston, Virginia, 1981.

Heline, C. *Color and music in the new age*. Oceanside, Ca.: New Age Press, 1969.

Hendricks, G. *The family centering book: Awareness activities the whole family can do together*. Englewood Cliffs, N.J.: Prentice-Hall, 1979.

Hendricks, G., & Fadiman, J. *Transpersonal education: A curriculum for feeling and being*. Englewood Cliffs, N.J.: Prentice-Hall, 1975.

Hendricks, G., & Roberts, T. *The second centering book*. Englewood Cliffs, N.J.: Prentice-Hall, 1977.

Hendricks, G., & Wills, R. *The centering book*. New York: Prentice-Hall, 1975.

Hendrickson, P., & Torrance, E. *Just suppose* (Forms A & B). Minneapolis, Minn.: Bureau of Educational Research, University of Minnesota, 1960, 1961.

Herr, E., & Watanabe, A. Counseling the gifted about career development. In N. Colangelo and R. Zaffrann (Eds.). *New voices in counseling the gifted*. Dubuque, Iowa: Kendall/Hunt Publishing Company, 1979.

Herrmann, N. The creative brain. *Training and Development Journal*, 1981, *35* (10), 10–16.

Hess, R., & Shipman, V. Early experience and the socialization of cognitive modes in children. *Child Development*, 1965, *36* (2), 869–887.

Heyns, O. *Abdominal decompression: A monograph*. Johannesburg: Witwatersrand University Press, 1963.

Hier, D., & Crowley, W. Spatial ability in androgen-deficient men. *New England Journal of Medicine*, 1982, *306* (20), 1202–1205.

Hilliard, P. *Identifying gifted minority children through the use of non-verbal test*. Unpublished doctoral dissertation, Yeshiva University, 1976.

Hirsch, S. Executive high school internship a boon for the gifted and talented. *Teaching Exceptional Children*, 1976, *9* (1), 22–23.

Hobson, J. High school performance of underage pupils initially admitted to kindergarten on the basis of physical and psychological examinations. In W. George, S. Cohn, & J. Stanley (Eds.), *Educating the gifted: Acceleration and enrichment*. Baltimore: Johns Hopkins University Press, 1979.

Hoffman, L. Early childhood experiences and women's achievement motives. *Journal of Social Issues*, 1972, *28*, 129–155.

Hoffman, L. Changes in family roles, socialization and sex differences. *American Psychologist*, 1977, *32*, 644–658.

Hoffman, L., & Hoffman, M. (Eds.). *Review of child development research* (Vol. 1). New York: Russell Sage Foundation, 1964.

Hoffman, L., & Hoffman, M. (Eds.). *Review of child development research* (Vol. 2). New York: Russell Sage Foundation, 1966.

Holland, J. Some limitations of teacher ratings as predictors of creativity. *Journal of Educational Psychology*, 1959, *50*, 219–223.

Holland, J. Creative and academic performance among talented adolescents. *Journal of Educational Psychology*, 1961, *52*, 136–147.

Holland, W. Language barrier as an educational problem of Spanish-speaking children. *Exceptional Children*, 1960, *27*, 42–50.

Holleran, B., & Holleran, P. Creativity revisited: A new role for group dynamics. *The Journal of Creative Behavior*, 1976, *10*, 130–137.

Hollingworth, L. *Gifted children*. New York: Macmillan, 1926.

Hollingworth, L. *Children above 180 IQ*. Yonkers-on-Hudson, N.Y.: World Books, 1942.

Hopkins, L., & Shapiro, A. *Creative activities for the gifted child*. Palo Alto, Ca.: Fearon, 1969.

Horner, M. *Sex differences in achievement motivation and performance in competitive and non-competitive situations*. Unpublished doctoral dissertation, University of Michigan, 1968.

Horner, M. Fail: Bright women. *Psychology Today*, 1969, *3* (6), 36–38; 62.

Horner, M. Toward an understanding of achievement related conflicts in women. *Journal of Social Issues*, 1972, *28*, 157–175.

Houston, J. Margaret Mead at seventy-five. *Saturday Review*, February 5, 1977a, *6* 58.

Houston, J. *Re-seeding America*. Paper presented at the annual meeting of the American Humanistic Psychologists, Berkeley, Ca., August 1977b.

Houston, S. (Reported in Tie Line). *Psychology Today*, 1972, *5* (11), 24–26.

Hoyt, K., & Hebeler, J. (Eds.). *Career education for gifted and talented students*. Salt Lake City, Utah: Olympus, 1974.

Hoyt, P. *The relationship between college grades and adult achievement* (ACT Research Report No. 7). Iowa City: American College Testing Program, 1965.

Hughes, H. The enhancement of creativity. *Journal of Creative Behavior*, 1969, *3* (2), 73–83.

Hultgren, H. Competencies for teachers of the gifted. Doctoral dissertation, University of Denver, 1982. *Dissertation Abstracts International*, 1982.

Hunt, J. McV. *Intelligence and experience*. New York: Ronald Press, 1961.

Hunt, J. McV., & Kirk, G. Social aspects of intelligence: Evidence and issues. In R. Cancro (Ed.), *Intelligence genetic and environmental influences*. New York: Grune & Stratton, 1971.

Hunt, V. A study of structural integration from neuromuscular, energy-field and emotional approaches. Unpublished study from the Department of Kinesiology, University of California, Los Angeles, 1977. Reported by M. Ferguson, Electronic evidence of auras, chakras in UCLA study. *Brain/Mind Bulletin*, 1978, *3* (9), 1–2.

Huttunen, M., & Niskanes, P. Prenatal loss of father and psychiatric disorders. *Archives of General Psychiatry*, 1978, *35*, 429–31.

Huxley, A. *Island*. New York: Harper & Row, 1962.

Iannon, R. V., & Carline, J. L. A humanistic approach to teacher education. *The Journal of Teacher Education*, 1971, *22*, 429–433.

Inquiry Development Program. Chicago, Ill.: Science Research Association, Inc., 1966.

Isaacs, A. Giftedness and leadership. *The Gifted Child Quarterly*, 1973, *17*, 103–112.

Isaacson, R. *The limbic system*. New York: Plenum Press, 1974.

Ismael, C. *The healing environment*. Millbrae, Ca.: Celestial Arts, 1973.

Jackson, N., Famiglietti, J., & Robinson, H. Kindergarten and first grade teachers' attitudes toward early entrants, intellectually advanced students and average students. *Journal for the Education of the Gifted*, Winter 1981, *4* (2), 132–142.

Jacobs, J. Effectiveness of teacher and parent identification of gifted children as a function of school level. *Psychology in the Schools*, 1971, *8*, 140–142.

Jacobson, E. *You must relax*. New York: McGraw-Hill, 1957.

James, C. *Young lives at stake: The education of adolescents*. New York: Schocken Books, 1968.

James, M., & Jongeward, D. *Born to win*. Reading, Mass.: Addison-Wesley, 1973.

Jeffrey, W. The developing brain and child development. In M. Wittrock (Ed.), *The brain and psychology*. New York: Academic Press, 1980.

Jellison, J., & Harvey, J. Give me liberty: Why we like hard positive choices. *Psychology Today*, 1976, *9* (10), 47–49.

Jencks, C., & Riesman, D. Where graduate schools fail. *Atlantic Monthly*, 1968, *221*, 49–55.

Jenkins, M. Intellectually superior Negro youth: Problems and needs. *Journal of Negro Education*, 1950, *19*, 322–332.

Jensen, A. How much can we boost IQ and scholastic achievement? *Harvard Educational Review*, 1969, *39* (1), 1–24.

Jensen, A. The heritability of intelligence. In P. Rosenthal (Ed.), *Annual editions: Readings in human development*. Guilford, Conn.: Dushkin, 1974.

Jerison, H. Evolution of the brain. In M. Wittrock, (Ed.), *The human brain*. Englewood Cliffs, N.J.: Prentice-Hall, Inc., 1977.

Jersild, A. *In search of self*. New York: Bureau of Publications, Teachers College, Columbia University, 1952.

Joesting, J. Future problems of gifted girls. *The Gifted Child Quarterly*, 1970, *14*, 82–90.

John E. Brain mechanisms of memory. In J. McGaugh (Ed)., *Psychobiology: Behavior from a biological perspective*. New York: Academic Press, 1971.

Johnson, B. *Ability, achievement and bilingualism: A comparative study involving Spanish-speaking and English-speaking children at the sixth grade level*. Unpublished doctoral dissertation, University of Maryland, 1962.

Johnson, B. (Ed.). *National/State Leadership Training Institute on the Gifted and the Talented Bulletin* (Gifted Female Supplement). Ventura, Ca.: Ventura County Superintendent of Schools, January 1977.

Johnson, D. *Reaching out: Interpersonal effectiveness and self-actualization*. Englewood Cliffs, N.J.: Prentice-Hall, 1972.

Johnson, G., & Kirk, S. Are mentally handicapped children segregated in regular grades? *Exceptional Children*, 1950, *17*, 65–68.

Johnson, M. I think my teacher is a. . . . *Learning,* 1976, 4, 36–38.

Jones, R. *Fantasy and feeling in education.* New York: New York University Press, 1968.

Jourard, S. *The transparent self: Self-disclosure and well-being.* Princeton, N.J.: D. Van Nostrand, 1964.

Judkins, P., Jr. Certain criteria lead toward leadership. In *A new generation of leadership: Education for the gifted in leadership.* N/S-LTI-G/T Brief No. 4, Ventura, Ca. Office of the Ventura County Superintendent of Schools.

Jung, C. *Psychological types.* New York: Harcourt, 1933.

Jung, C. (Ed.). *Man and his symbols.* New York: Dell, 1964.

Justman, J. Personal and social adjustment of intellectually gifted accelerants and non-accelerants in junior high schools. *School Review,* 1953, *61,* 468–478.

Justman, J. Academic achievement of intellectually gifted accelerants and non-accelerants in junior high school. *School Review,* 1954, *62,* 142–150.

Justman, J., & Wrightstone, J. Expressed attitudes of teachers towards special classes for intellectually gifted children. *Educational Administration and Supervision,* 1956, *42,* 141–148.

Kagan, J. On cultural deprivation. In D. Glass (Ed.), *Environmental influences: Third of a series on biology and behavior.* New York: Rockefeller University Press and the Russell Sage Foundation, 1968.

Kagan, J. *Change and continuity in infancy.* New York: John Wiley & Sons, 1971.

Kagan, J., & Freeman, M. Relation of childhood intelligence, maternal behaviors, and social class to behavior during adolescence. *Child Development,* 1963, *34,* 899–911.

Kagan, J., & Lewis, M. Studies of attention in the human infant. *Merrill-Palmer Quarterly,* 1965, *11,* 95–127.

Kagan, J., & Moss, H. *Birth to maturity: A study in psychological development.* New York: John Wiley & Sons, 1962.

Kahl, D., & Gas, B. *Learning centers in the open classroom.* Encino, Ca.: International Center for Educational Development, 1974.

Kamiya, J., Haight, M., & Jampolsky, G. *A biofeedback study in high school.* Paper presented at a meeting of the Biofeedback Research Society in Monterey, Ca., 1975.

Kanigher, H. *Everyday enrichment for gifted children at home and school.* Ventura, Ca.: Office of the Ventura County Superintendent of Schools, 1977.

Kaplan, S. *Providing programs for the gifted and talented: A handbook.* Ventura, Ca.: Office of the Ventura County Superintendent of Schools, 1974.

Kaplan, S., Kaplan, J., Madsen, S., & Gould, B. *A young child experiences.* Pacific Palisades, Ca.: Goodyear, 1975.

Kaplan, S., Kaplan, J., Madsen, S., & Taylor, B. *Change for children.* Pacific Palisades, Ca.: Goodyear, 1973.

Karmel, B., & Maisel, E. A neuronal activity model for infant attention. In L. Cohen & P. Salapatek (Eds.), *Infant perception: From sensation to cognition: Basic visual processes* (Vol. 1). New York: Academic Press, 1975.

Karnes, M. Young handicapped children can be gifted and talented. *Journal for the Education of the Gifted,* 1979, 2 (3), 157–172.

Karnes, F., & Collins, E. Teacher certification in the education of the gifted: an update. *Journal for the Education of the Gifted.* 1981, 4 (2), 123–131.

Karnes, M., & Bertschi, J. Identifying and educating gifted/talented nonhandicapped and handicapped preschoolers. *Teaching Exceptional Children*, 1978, *10* (4), 114–119.

Karnes, M., McCoy, G., Zehrbok, R., Wollershein, J., & Clarizio, H. The efficacy of two organizational plans for underachieving intellectually gifted children. *Exceptional Children*, 1963, *29*, 438–446.

Karnes, M., McCoy, G., Zehrbok, R., Wollershein, J., Clarizio, H., Costin, C., & Stanley, L. *Factors associated with underachievement and overachievement of intellectually gifted children.* Champaign, Ill.: Champaign Community Unit Schools, Department of Special Services, 1961.

Karnes, F., & Pearce, N. Governors' honors programs: A viable alternative for the gifted and talented. *G/C/T*, 1981, *18*, 8–11.

Kathnelson, A., & Colley, L. Personal and professional characteristics valued in teachers of the gifted. Unpublished paper presented at California State University, Los Angeles, Los Angeles, California, 1982.

Katz, I., Roberts, S., & Robinson, J. Effects of difficulty, race of administrator and instructions on Negro digit-symbol performance. *Journal of Personality and Social Psychology*, 1965, *70*, 53–59.

Katz, I., Robinson, J., Epps, E., & Wally, P. Effects of race of experimenter and test vs. neutral instructions on expression of hostility in Negro boys. *Journal of Social Issues*, 1964, *20*, 54–59.

Kaufmann, F. *Your gifted child and you.* Reston, Va.: The Council for Exceptional Children, 1976.

Kavett, H., & Smith, W. Identification of gifted and talented students in the performing arts. *G/C/T*, September/October 1980, *14*, 18–20.

Keniston, K. Youth as a stage of life. In R. Havinghurst & P. Dreyer (Eds.). *Youth: 74th Yearbook of the NSSE.* Chicago: University of Chicago Press, 1975.

Kennell, J., Jerauld, R., Wolfe, H., Chesler, D., Kreger, N., McAlpine, W., Steffa, N., & Klaus, M. Maternal behavior one year after early and extended post-partum contact. *Developmental Medicine and Child Neurology*, 1974, *16*, 172–179.

Kennell, J., & Klaus, M. Early mother-infant contact: Effects on the mother and the infant, *Bulletin of the Menninger Clinic*, 1979, *43* (1), 69–78.

Khatena, J. Some problems in the measurement of creative behavior. *Journal of Research and Development in Education*, 1971, *4*, 71–80.

Killian, J., & Hughes, L. A comparison of short forms of the Intelligence Scale for Children—Revised in the screening of gifted referrals. *The Gifted Child Quarterly*, Spring 1978, *22* (1), 111–115.

Kimball, B. Case studies in educational failure during adolescence. *American Journal of Orthopsychiatry*, 1953, *23*, 406–415.

Kimura, D. Functional asymmetry of the brain in dichotic listening. *Cortex*, 1967, *3*, 163–178.

King, M. Biofeedback boosts students' self-concept. *Brain/Mind Bulletin*, 1977, 2 (17), 1.

Kitano, H. Cultural diversity and the exceptional child. In J. Miley, I. Sato, W. Luché, P. Weaver, J. Curry, & R. Ponce (Eds.), *Promising practices: Teaching the disadvantaged gifted.* Ventura, Ca.: Ventura County Superintendent of Schools, 1975.

Klausmeir, H. Learning and human abilities. New York: Harper & Row, 1971.

Klineberg, O. (Ed.). *Characteristics of the American Negro.* New York: Harper & Bros., 1944.

Kneller, G. *The art and science of creativity.* New York: Holt, Rinehart & Winston, 1965.

Knowlton, J., & Hamerlyneck, L. Perception of deviant behavior: A study of cheating. *Journal of Educational Psychology,* 1967, *58,* 379–385.

Koestler, A. *The act of creation.* New York: Macmillan, 1964.

Koestler, A. *The ghost in the machine.* London: Hutchinson & Co., 1968.

Kohlberg, L. Development of moral character and moral ideology. In M. Hoffman & L. Hoffman (Eds.), *Review of child development research* (Vol. 1). New York: Russell Sage Foundation, 1964.

Kohlberg, L. Understanding the hidden curriculum. *Learning,* 1927b, *1* (2), 10–14.

Kohlberg, L. *First things: Social development—grades 2 to 5.* New York: Guidance Associates, 1974.

Kohlberg, L. *Relationships and values: Grades 7 to 9.* New York: Guidance Associates, 1976a.

Kohlberg, L. *Values in a democracy: Grades 9 to 12.* New York: Guidance Associates, 1976b.

Kohlberg, L. *Universal values in America: Grades 9 to 12.* New York: Guidance Associates, 1977.

Korner, A., & Grobstein, R. Visual alertness as related to soothing in neonates: Implications for maternal stimulation and early deprivation. *Child Development,* 1966, *37,* 867–876.

Kough, J. Administrative provisions for the gifted. In B. Shertzer (Ed.), *Working with superior students.* Chicago: Science Research Association, 1960.

Krantz, B. *Multi-dimensional screening device for the identification of gifted/talented children.* Grand Forks, North Dakota: Bureau of Educational Research and Services, The University of North Dakota, 1978.

Krashen, S. The left hemisphere. *UCLA Educator,* 1975, *17* (2), 17–23.

Krathwohl, D., Bloom, B., & Masia, B. *Taxonomy of educational objectives. Handbook II: Affective domain.* New York: David McKay, 1964.

Krech, D. Psychoneurobiochemeducation. *Phi Delta Kappan,* 1969, *L,* 370–375.

Krech, D. Don't use the kitchen sink approach to enrichment. *Today's Education,* 1970, *59,* 30–32.

Kresse, F. *Materials and activities for teachers and children: A project to develop and evaluate multimedia kits for elementary schools* (Vols. I & II). Washington, D.C.: USOE Final Report, Project No. 5-0710, 1968.

Krieger, D. Therapeutic touch affects hemoglobin. *Brain/Mind Bulletin,* 1976, *1* (2), 2.

Krippner, S. The ten commandments that block creativity. *The Gifted Child Quarterly,* 1967, *11,* 144–151.

Krippner, S. Consciousness and the creative process. *The Gifted Child Quarterly,* 1968, *12* (3), 141–157.

Krippner, S. Parapsychologists make historic trip to investigate psi research in China. *Brain/Mind Bulletin,* 1981, *6* (17), 2.

Krippner, S., & Blickenstaff, R. The development of self-concept as part of an art workshop for the gifted. *The Gifted Child Quarterly,* 1970, *14* (3), 163–166.

Krishnamurti, J. *Think on these things.* New York: Harper & Row, 1964.

Kurtz, J., & Swenson, E. Factors related to overachievement and underachievement in schools. *School Review,* 1951, *59,* 472–480.

Kurtzman, K. A study of school attitudes, peer acceptance, and personality of creative adolescents. *Exceptional Children*, 1967, *34* (3), 157–162.

LaBenne, W., & Greene, B. *Educational implications of self-concept theory.* Pacific Palisades, Ca.: Goodyear Publishing, 1969.

Lamaze, F. *Painless childbirth: Psychoprophylactic method* (L. Celestin, trans.). Chicago: Henry Regnery, 1970.

Landry, R. *Bilingualism and creative abilities.* Fargo, N.D.: North Dakota State University, 1968.

Lang, P. Autonomic control. *Psychology Today*, 1970, *4* (5), 37–86.

Lao, R. Internal-external control and competent and innovative behavior among Negro college students. *Journal of Personal Social Psychology*, 1970, *14*, 263–270.

Lavin, D. *The prediction of academic performances.* New York: Russell Sage Foundation, 1965.

Lavach, J., & Lanier, H. The motive to avoid success in 7th, 8th, 9th and 10th grade high-achieving girls. *Journal of Educational Research*, 1975, *68*, 216–218.

Lawrie, J. Making it the hardest way. *Psychology Today*, 1969, *3*, 29–31; 60.

Laycock, F., & Caylor, J. Physiques of gifted children and their less gifted siblings. *Child Development*, 1964, *35*, 63–74.

Lazlow, A., & Nelson, P. Testing the gifted child in the elementary school. *Gifted Child Quarterly*, 1974, *18*, 152–162.

Leadership: A survey of literature. Los Angeles City Schools, Instructional Planning Division: Program for Gifted, 1976.

Leaverton, L., & Herzog, S. Adjustment of the gifted child. *Journal for the Education of the Gifted*, Spring 1979, *2* (3), 149–152.

LeBoyer, F. *Birth without violence.* New York: Random House, 1975.

Lehane, S. *The creative child, how to encourage the natural creativity of your preschooler.* Englewood Cliffs, N.J.: Prentice-Hall, 1979.

Lehane, S. *Help your baby learn: 100 Piaget-based activities for the first two years of life.* Englewood Cliffs, N.J.: Prentice-Hall, 1976.

Lehman, E., & Erdwins, C. The social and emotional adjustment of young, intellectually-gifted children. *Gifted Child Quarterly*, Summer 1981, *25* (3), 134–137.

Lehman, H. *Age and achievement: American Philosophical Society Memoirs* (Vol. 33). Princeton, N.J.: Princeton University Press, 1953.

Leiter, R. The Leiter adult intelligence scale. *Psychological Service Center Journal*, 1951, *3*, 185–236.

Lenneberg, E. *Biological foundations of language.* New York: John Wiley & Sons, 1967.

Leonard, G. *The ultimate athlete.* New York: Viking, 1975.

Lepper, M., Greene, D., & Nisbett, R. Undermining children's intrinsic interest with extrinsic rewards. *Journal of Personality and Social Psychology*, 1973, *28* (1), 129–137.

Lerner, G., & Libby, W. *Heredity, evolution, and society.* San Francisco: Freeman, 1976.

Lessinger, L., & Martinson, R. The use of the California Psychological Inventory with gifted pupils. *Personnel and Guidance Journal*, 1961, *39*, 572–575.

Levine, S. Infantile experience and resistance to physiological stress. *Science*, 1957, *126*, 405.

Levine, S. Stimulation in infancy. *Scientific American*, 1960, *202*, 80–86.

Levy, J. *The baby exercise book for the first fifteen months.* New York: Pantheon Books, 1975.

Levy, J. Cerebral asymmetry and the psychology of man. In M. Wittrock (Ed.), *The brain and psychology.* New York: Academic Press, 1980.

Levy, J., & Reid, M. Work reported in right-hemisphere language function may exist only in split-brain subjects. *Brain/Mind Bulletin,* 1975, *1* (2), 1.

Lewis, H. *Opening windows into the future.* Winston-Salem, N.C.: The Governor's School of North Carolina, 1970.

Lewis, M. State as an infant-environment interaction: An analysis of mother-infant behavior as a function of sex. *Merrill-Palmer Quarterly,* 1972, *18,* 95–121.

Lewis, M., & Rosenblum, L. *The effect of the infant on its caregiver.* New York: Wiley, 1974.

Liberty, P., Jones, R., & McGurie, C. Age-mate perception of intelligence, creativity and achievement. *Perceptual Motor Skills,* 1963, *16,* 194.

Lickona, T. How to encourage moral development. *Learning,* 1975, *5* (7), 37–43.

Lightfoot, G. *Personality characteristics of bright and dull children.* Contributions to Education (No. 969). New York: Teachers College, Columbia University, 1951.

Lindsey, M. *Training teachers of the gifted and talented.* New York: Teachers College Press, 1980.

Lipsitt, L., Mustaine, M., & Zeigler, B. Effects of experience on the behavior of the young infant. *Neuropadiatrie,* 1976, *8,* 107–133.

Little, D. Post-industrial society and what it may mean. *The Futurist,* 1973, *7,* 259–262.

Lorenz, K. Innate bases of learning. In K. Pribram (Ed.), *On the biology of learning.* New York: Harcourt, Brace & World, 1969.

Lowther, M. What is over- and under-achievement? *The University of Michigan School of Education Bulletin,* 1962, *34,* 105–108.

Loye, D. People with balanced brains better forecasters. *Brain/Mind Bulletin,* 1982, 7 (3), 1.

Lozanov, G. A general theory of suggestion in the communications process and the activation of the total reserves of the learner's personality. *Suggestopaedia-Canada,* 1977, *1,* 1–4.

Luchins, E., & Luchins, A. Female mathematicians: A contemporary appraisal. In L. Fox, L. Brody, and D. Tobin (Eds.), *Women and the mathematical mystique.* Baltimore: The Johns Hopkins University Press, 1980.

Lucito, L. Independence-conformity behavior as a function of intellect: Bright and dull children. *Exceptional Children,* 1964, *31,* 5–13.

Lucker, G., Rosenfield, D., Sikes, J., & Aronson, E. Performance in the interdependent classroom: A field study. *American Educational Research Journal,* 1976, *13* (2), 115–123.

Luckey, B. Racial differences in mental ability. *Scientific Monthly,* 1925, *22,* 245–248.

Lurie, T. *Conversations and constructions.* San Francisco: Journeys into Language, 1978.

Lyon, H. *Realizing our potential.* Paper given at the First World Conference on Gifted Children, London, England, September 1975.

Maccoby, E. *The development of sex differences.* Stanford: Stanford University Press, 1966.

Maccoby, E., & Jacklin, C. *The psychology of sex differences.* Stanford, Ca.: Stanford University Press, 1974.

MacKinnon, D. The creativity of architects. In C. W. Taylor (Ed.), *Widening horizons in creativity.* New York: John Wiley & Sons, 1964.

MacKinnon, D. Personality and the realization of creative potential. *American Psychologist,* 1965, *20,* 273–281.

Mac Lean, P. A mind of three minds: Educating the triune brain. In J. Chall and A. Mirsky, (Eds.), *Education and the brain,* the seventy-seventh yearbook of the National Society for the Study of Education, Part II. Chicago, Ill.: University of Chicago Press, 1978.

Maehr, M., & Stallings, W. Freedom from external evaluation. *Child Development,* 1972, *43,* 177–185.

Maggio, E. *Psychophysiology of learning and memory.* Springfield, Ill.: Charles C Thomas, 1971.

Maker, J. *Training teacher for the gifted and talented: A comparison of models.* Reston, Va.: The Council for Exceptional Children, 1975.

Maker, J. *Providing programs for the gifted handicapped.* Reston, Va.: The Council for Exceptional Children, 1977.

Mallinson, T. *Gifted underachievers.* Toronto: Ontario Board of Education, Research Department, 1972.

Malone, C. *Identification of educationally deprived gifted kindergarten children.* Unpublished doctoral dissertation, United States International University, 1974.

Malone, C., & Moonan, W. Behavioral identification of gifted children. *The Gifted Child Quarterly,* 1975, *19* (4), 301–306.

Mann, H. How real are friendships of gifted and typical children in a program of partial segregation? *Exceptional Children,* 1957, *23,* 199–201.

Marano, H. Biology is one key to the bonding of mothers and babies. *Smithsonian,* 1981, *11* (11), 60–68.

Marland, S., Jr. *Education of the gifted and talented.* Report to the Congress of the United States by the U.S. Commissioner of Education. Washington, D.C.: U.S. Government Printing Office, 1972.

Martin, P. *Experiment in depth.* London: Routledge & Kegan Paul, 1955.

Martin, R., & Pacheres, J. Good scholars not always the best. *Business Week,* February 24, 1962, 77–78.

Martindale, C. What makes creative people different. *Psychology Today,* 1976, *9* (2), 44–50.

Martinson, R. *Educational programs for gifted pupils.* Sacramento: California State Department of Education, 1961.

Martinson, R. Research on the gifted and talented: Its implications for education. In S. Marland, Jr., *Education of the Gifted and Talented.* Report to the Congress of the United States by the U.S. Commissioner of Education, Washington, D.C.: U.S. Government Printing Office, March 1972.

Martinson, R. Children with superior cognitive abilities. In L. Dunn (Ed.), *Exceptional children in the schools.* New York: Holt, Rinehart & Winston, 1973.

Martinson, R. *The identification of the gifted and talented.* Ventura, Ca.: Office of the Ventura County Superintendent of Schools, June 1974.

Martinson, R. Hermanson, D., & Banks, G. An independent study-seminar program for the gifted. *Exceptional Children,* 1972, *35* (5), 421–426.

Martyn, K. *The social acceptance of gifted students.* Unpublished doctoral dissertation, Stanford University, 1957.

Maruyama, M. Post-industrial logic. In A. Spekke (Ed.), *The next 25 years: Crisis and opportunity.* Washington, D.C.: World Future Society, 1975.

Marzollo, J., & Lloyd, J. *Learning through play.* New York: Harper & Row, 1972.

Maslow, A. *Motivation and personality.* New York: Harper & Row, 1954.

Maslow, A. Creativity in self-actualizing people. In H. Anderson (Ed.), *Creativity and its cultivation.* New York: Harper & Row, 1959.

Maslow, A. *Toward a psychology of being.* New York: Van Nostrand, 1962.

Maslow, A. *Toward a psychology of being* (2nd ed.). New York: Van Nostrand Reinhold, 1968.

Maslow, A. *The farther reaches of human nature.* New York: Viking, 1971.

Mason, E. *Collaborative learning.* New York: Schocken Books, 1972.

Massialas, B., & Zevin, J. *Creative encounters in the classroom.* New York: John Wiley & Sons, 1967.

Masters, R., & Houston, J. *Mind games.* New York: Viking, 1972.

Masters, R., & Houston, J. *Listening to the body.* New York: Delacorte, 1978.

Matheny, K., & Edwards, C. Academic improvement through an experimental classroom management system. *Journal of School Psychology,* 1974, *12,* 222–232.

Mattheis, D. Career education: What it is and what it seeks to accomplish. Paper presented at Career Education Conference, Edmund, Okla., 1972. In K. Hoyt & J. Hebeler (Eds.), *Career education for gifted and talented students.* Salt Lake City: Olympus Publishing, 1974.

Mauser, A. LD in gifted children. *ACLD Newsbriefs,* 1980, *130,* 2.

May, R. *Man's search for himself.* New York: W. W. Norton, 1953.

May, R. The nature of creativity. In H. Anderson (Ed.), *Creativity and its cultivation.* New York: Harper & Row, 1959.

May, R. *Psychology and the human dilemma.* Princeton, N.J.: D. Van Nostrand, 1967.

Maynard, F. How to raise a more creative child. *Woman's Day,* January 1970, 33–68.

McCall, R. Qualitative transitions in behavioral development in the first two years of life. In M. Bornstein & W. Kessen (Eds.), *Psychological development from infancy: Image to intention.* New York: John Wiley & Sons, 1979.

McCandless, B. Relation of environmental factors to intellectual functioning. In H. Stevens & R. Heber (Eds.), *Mental retardation.* Chicago: University of Chicago Press, 1964.

McClelland, D. Do IQ tests measure intelligence? In P. Rosenthal (Ed.), *Annual editions: Readings in human development.* Guilford, Conn.: Dushkin, 1974.

McConnell, F., Horton, K., & Smith, B. Language development and cultural disadvantagement. *Exceptional Children,* 1969, *35,* 597–606.

McConnell, R. *ESP: A curriculum guide.* New York: Simon & Schuster, 1971.

McGillivray, R. Differences in home background between high-achieving and low-achieving gifted children: A study of one hundred grade eight pupils in the City of Toronto Public Schools. *Ontario Journal of Educational Research,* 1964, *6,* 99–106.

McGuinness, B., & Pribram, K. The origins of sensory bias in the development of gender differences in perception and cognition. In M. Bortner (Ed.), *Cognitive growth and development: Essays in honor of Herbert G. Birch.* New York: Brunner/Mazel, 1979.

McKenna, A. The role of the adult in infant speech. *Enfance,* 1978, *1,* 5–12.

McMillin, D. *Separate criteria: An alternative for the identification of disadvantaged gifted.* Paper presented at the National Teacher Institute on Disadvantaged Gifted, Los Angeles, May 1975.

McNeill, D. Developmental psycholinguistics. In F. Smith & G. Miller (Eds.), *The genesis of language.* Cambridge, Mass.: M.I.T. Press, 1966.

Mead, M. The gifted child in the American culture today. *Journal of Teacher Education,* 1954, *5* (3), 211–214.

Mednick, S., & Mednick, M. *Examiner's manual: Remote Associates Test.* Boston: Houghton Mifflin, 1967.

Meeker, M. Differential syndromes of giftedness and curriculum planning: A four year follow-up. *Journal of Special Education,* 1968, *2,* 185–194.

Meeker, M. *The structure of intellect: Its use and interpretation.* Columbus, Ohio: Charles E. Merrill, 1969.

Meltzoff, A., & Moore, M. Imitation of facial and manual gestures by human neonates. *Science,* 1977, *198,* 75–78.

Mensch, I. Rorschach study of the gifted child. *Exceptional Children,* 1950, *17,* 8–14.

Mercer, J., & Lewis, J. *Parent interview manual: System of multicultural pluralistic assessment.* New York: Psychological Corporation, 1977.

Mercer, J., & Lewis, J. Using the *System of Multicultural Pluralistic Assessment (SOMPA)* to identify the gifted minority child. In A. Baldwin, G. Gear, & L. Lucito (Eds.), *Educational planning for the gifted.* Reston, Va.: Council for Exceptional Children, 1978.

Mercer, J., & Smith, J. *Subtest estimates of the WISC full scale IQs for children.* Rockville, Md.: National Center for Health Statistics, 1972.

Miles, C. Gifted children. In L. Carmichael (Ed.), *Manual of child psychology.* New York: John Wiley & Sons, 1954.

Millay, J. Bilateral synch: Key to intuition? *Brain/Mind Bulletin,* 1981, *6* (9), 1; 3.

Millay, J. In a talk given at the New Age School, S. Pasadena, Ca., June 1981.

Miller, R. Social status and socio-empathetic differences among mentally superior, mentally typical and mentally retarded children. *Exceptional Children,* 1956, *23,* 114–119.

Mills, B. Attitudes of decision-making groups toward gifted children and public school programs for the gifted. Unpublished doctoral dissertation, UCLA, 1973. *Dissertation Abstracts International,* 1973, *34,* 1739–1740.

Mischel, W., & Baker, N. Cognitive appraisals and transformations in delay behavior. *Journal of Personality and Social Psychology,* 1975, *31,* 254–261.

Mishlove, J. *The roots of consciousness. Psychic liberation through history, science, and experience.* New York: Random House, 1975.

Mitchell, B. An update on the state of gifted/talented education in the U.S. *Phi Delta Kappan,* 1982, *64* (5), 357–358.

Mitchell, P., & Erickson, D. The education of gifted and talented children: A status report. *Exceptional Children,* 1978, *45* (1), 12–16.

Moffit, A. Consonant cue perception by twenty-to-twenty-four-week-old infants. *Child Development,* 1971, *42,* 717–731.

Moore, B. A model career education program for gifted disadvantaged students. *Roeper Review,* 1979, *2* (2), 20–22.

Moore, G. D. Counseling the gifted child. *School Review*, 1980, *68*, 63–70.

Moore, O. K. Orthographic symbols and the preschool child. In E. Torrance (Ed.), *Creativity*. Minneapolis: University of Minnesota Press, 1961.

Moore, O. K. Personal letter to J. S. Chall. In J. S. Chall, *Learning to read: The great debate*. New York: McGraw-Hill, 1967.

Moore, T. Language and intelligence: A longitudinal study of the first eight years. Part 1. Patterns of development in boys and girls. *Human Development*, 1967, *10*, 88–106.

Morgan, H. A psychometric comparison of achieving and nonachieving college students of high ability. *Journal of Consulting Psychology*, 1952, *16*, 292–298.

Morgan, H., Tennant, C., & Gold, M. *Elementary and secondary level programs for the gifted and talented*. New York: Teachers College Press, 1980.

Morris, J. Meditation in the classroom. *Learning*, 1976, *5* (4), 22–27.

Morris, V. *Existentialism in education*. New York: Harper & Row, 1966.

Morrison, A., & McIntyre, D. *Schools and socialization*. Baltimore: Penguin, 1971.

Morrow, W., & Wilson, R. Family relations of bright high achieving and underachieving high school boys. *Child Development*, 1961, *32*, 501–510.

Moustakas, C. *Creativity and conformity*. New York: Van Nostrand Reinhold, 1967.

Mulholland, T. It's time to try hardware in the classroom. *Psychology Today*, 1973, *7*, 103–104.

Murphy, J., Dauw, D., Horton, R., & Friedian, A. Self-actualization and creativity. *Journal of Creative Behavior*, 1976, *10*, 39–44.

Murphy, L. Infants' play and cognitive development. In M. Piers (Ed.), *Play and development*. New York: W. W. Norton, 1972.

Muson, H. Moral thinking, can it be taught? *Psychology Today*, 1979, *12* (9), 48–68; 92.

Myers, R. E., & Torrance, E. P. *Invitations to speaking and writing creatively*. Lexington, Mass.: Ginn & Co., 1965.

Nebes, R. Man's so-called "minor" hemisphere. *UCLA Educator*, 1975, *17*, 13–16.

Neimark, E. Longitudinal development of formal operational thought. *Genetic Psychology Monograph*, 1975, *91*, 175–225.

Nevin, D. Seven teenage math prodigies take off from Johns Hopkins on the way to advanced degrees. *Smithsonian*, 1977, *8* (7), 76–82.

Newland, T. E. *The gifted in socioeducational perspective*. Englewood Cliffs, N.J.: Prentice-Hall, 1976.

Newman, R. *Psychological consultation in the schools: A catalyst for learning*. New York: Basic Books, 1967.

Nichols, R. Parental attitudes of mothers of intelligent adolescents and creativity of their children. *Child Development*, 1964, *35*, 1041–1049.

Nova. *The pinks and the blues*. Broadcast by Public Broadcasting System in September, 1980.

Ober, R. Reciprocal category system. *Journal of Research and Development in Education*, 1970, *4*, 34–51.

O'Connell, M. Intuitive and psychic identical, Kraft stresses at New York seminar. *Brain/Mind Bulletin*, 1976, *1* (10), 2.

Ohlsen, M., & Proff, C. *The extent to which group counseling improves the academic and personal adjustment of underachieving, gifted adolescents* (Cooperative Research Project, No. 623). Washington, D.C.: U.S. Office of Education, 1960.

Ohnmacht, F. Achievement, anxiety, and creative thinking. *American Educational Research Journal*, 1966, *3*, 131–138.

Olton, R. A self-instructional program for developing productive thinking skills in 5th & 6th grade children. *Journal of Creative Behavior*, 1969, *3* (1), 16–25.

Ornstein, R. *The psychology of consciousness*. San Francisco: W. H. Freeman, 1972.

Ornstein, R. Right and left thinking. *Psychology Today*, 1973a, *6*, 87–92.

Ornstein, R. (Ed.). *The nature of human consciousness*. New York: Viking, 1973b.

Osborn, A. *Applied imagination*. New York: Scribner, 1957.

O'Shea, A. Low achievement syndrome among bright junior high school boys. *Journal of Educational Research*, 1970, *63*, 257–262.

Ostrander, S., & Schroeder, L. *Psychic discoveries behind the iron curtain*. Englewood Cliffs, N.J.: Prentice-Hall, 1970.

Ott, J. *Health and light: The effects of natural and artificial light on man and other living things*. Old Greenwich, N.Y.: Devin-Adair, 1973.

Otto, H. *Group methods to actualize human potential*. Beverly Hills, Ca.: Holister Press, 1973.

Otto, H., & Mann, J. (Eds.). *Ways of growth: Approaches to expanding awareness*. New York: Pocket Books, 1971.

Owen, G., Fram, K., Garry P., Lower, J., & Lubin, A. *A study of nutritional status of preschool children in the United States*, 1974, *53*, Part II, Supplement, 597–646.

Oyle, I. *The healing mind*. Millbrae, Ca.: Celestial Arts, 1975.

Painter, G. *Teach your baby*. New York: Simon & Schuster, 1971.

Pallett, J. *Definition and predictions of success in the business world*. Unpublished doctoral dissertation, University of Iowa, 1965.

Palomares, U. *Magic circle*. La Mesa, Ca.: Human Development Training Institute, 1972.

Palomares, U., & Johnson, L. Evaluation of Mexican American pupils for EMR classes. *California Education*, 1966, *3* (8), 27–29.

Parmelee, A., & Sigman, M. Development of visual behavior and neurological organization in pre-term and full-term infants. In A. Pick (Ed.), *Minnesota symposia on child psychology* (Vol. 10). Minneapolis: University of Minnesota Press, 1976.

Parnes, S. Education and creativity. *Teachers College Record*, 1963, *64*, 331–339.

Parnes, S. *Creative behavior guidebook*. New York: Charles Scribner's Sons, 1967.

Passow, A. *Education for gifted children and youth: An old issue—a new challenge*. Ventura, Ca.: Ventura County Superintendent of Schools Office, 1980.

Passow, A. The four curricula of the gifted and talented: Toward a total learning environment. *G/C/T*, 1981, *20*, 2–7.

Passow, A., Goldberg, M., & Tannenbaum, A. (Eds.). *Education of the disadvantaged: A book of readings*. New York: Holt, Rinehart & Winston, 1967.

Paulsen, W. *Deciding for myself*. Minneapolis, Minn.: Winston Press, 1974. (A multi-media kit)

Payne, D., Halpin, W., Ellet, C., & Dale, J. General personality correlates of creative personality in academically and artistically gifted youth. *Journal of Special Education*, 1971, *9*, 105–108.

Pearlman, S. *An investigation into the problems of academic underachievement among intellectually superior college students*. Unpublished doctoral dissertation, Columbia University, 1952.

Pegnato, C., & Birch, J. Locating gifted children in junior high schools: A comparison of methods. *Exceptional Children*, 1959, *25*, 300–304.

Pelletier, K. *Mind as healer, mind as slayer.* New York: Delacorte, 1977.

Pendarvis, E., & Grossi, J. Designing and operating programs for the gifted and talented handicapped. In J. Jordan & J. Grossi (Eds.), *An administrator's handbook on designing programs for the gifted and talented.* Reston, Va.: Council for Exceptional Children, 1980.

Perkins, H. Classroom behavior and underachievement. *American Educational Research Journal*, 1965, *2*, 172.

Perkins, J., & Wicas, E. Group counseling bright underachievers at 9 Florida high schools. *Gifted Child Quarterly*, 1971, *18*, 273–278.

Perrone, P., & Male, R. *The developmental education and guidance of talented learners.* Rockville, Md.: Aspen Publications, 1981.

Peterson, J. Extrasensory abilities of children, an ignored reality? *Learning*, 1975, *4*, 10–14.

Pettigrew, T. *A profile of the Negro American.* Princeton, N.J.: Van Nostrand, 1964.

Pew, T. Biofeedback seeks new medical uses for concept of yoga. *Smithsonian*, 1979, *10* (9), 106–114.

Pflum, J., & Waterman, A. *Open education: For me?* Washington, D.C.: Acropolis Books, 1974.

Phares, E. *Locus of control in personality.* Morristown, N.J.: General Learning Press, 1975.

Phelps, S., & Austin, N. *The assertive woman.* San Luis Obispo, Ca.: Impact, 1975.

Piaget, J. [*The origins of intelligence in children*] (M. Cook, trans.). New York: International Universities, 1952. (Originally published, 1936.)

Piaget, J. *The construction of reality in the child.* New York: Basic Books, 1954.

Piaget, J. [*The moral judgment of the child*] (M. Gabin, trans.). New York: Free Press, 1965. (Originally published, 1932.)

Pierce, J., & Bowman, P. Motivation patterns of high school students. *Cooperative Research Monograph No. 2: The Gifted Student* (OE-35016). Washington, D.C.: U.S. Office of Education, 1960, 33–66.

Pietsch, P. *Shufflebrain.* Boston: Houghton Mifflin, 1981.

Pines, M. "Good Samaritans at age two?" *Psychology Today,* June 1979, *13* (1), 66–77.

Pines, M. A head start in the nursery. *Psychology Today,* September 1979, *13* (4), 56–68.

Pines, M. What produces great skills? Specific pattern is discerned. *New York Times*, March 30, 1982, Science Time.

Pippert, R., & Archer, N. A comparison of two methods for classifying underachievers with respect to selected criteria. *Personnel and Guidance Journal*, 1963, *41*, 788–791.

Pirozzo, R. Gifted underachievers. *Roeper Review*, 1982, *4* (4), 18–21.

Pizzamiglio, L., & Cecchini, M. Development of the hemispheric dominance in children from 5 to 10 years of age and their relations with the development of cognitive processes. *Brain Research*, 1971, *31*, 363–364.

Plowman, P., & Rice, J. *Final report: California Project Talent.* Sacramento: California Department of Public Instruction, 1967.

Podgoretskaya, N. A study of spontaneous logical thinking in adults. *Soviet Psychology*, 1979, *17* (3), 70–84.

Poffenberger, T., & Poffenberger, S. The social psychology of fertility in a village in India. In J. Fawcett (Ed.), *Psychological perspectives on population*. New York: Basic Books, 1973.

Polland, B. *Feelings: Inside you and out loud, too*. Millbrae, Ca.: Celestial Arts, 1975.

Porteus, S. *Porteus maze test: Fifty years' application*. Palo Alto, Ca.: Pacific Books, 1965.

Prescott, J. Alienation of affection. *Psychology Today*, December 1979, *13* (7), 124.

Pressey, S. Fundamental misconceptions involved in current marking systems. *School and Society*, 1925, *21*, 736–738.

Pressey, S. Concerning the nature and nurture of genius. *Science*, 1955, *31*, 123–129.

Pressey, S. The nature and nurture of genius. In J. French (Ed.), *Educating the gifted child*. New York: Holt, Rinehart & Winston, 1964.

Pressman, H. Schools to beat the system: Can we open the gates of the ghetto and let the children out? *Psychology Today*, 1969, *2*, 58–63.

Pribram, K. The brain. *Psychology Today*, 1971, *5*, 44–48; 88–90.

Pribram, K. *Languages of the brain: Experimental paradoxes and principles in neuropsychology*. Englewood Cliffs, N.J.: Prentice-Hall, 1971.

Pribram, K. Primary reality may be frequency realm. *Brain/Mind Bulletin*, 1977, *2*, 1–3.

Price, G., Dunn, K., Dunn, R., & Griggs, S. Studies in students' learning styles. *Roeper Review*, 1981, *4* (2), 38–40.

Prichard, A., & Taylor, J. *Accelerating learning: The use of suggestion in the classroom*. Novato, Ca.: Academic Therapy Publications, 1980.

Prigogine, I. *From being to becoming*. San Francisco, Ca.: Freeman, 1980.

Provence, S., & Lipton, R. *Infants in institutions: A comparison of their development with family-reared infants during the first year of life*. New York: International Universities Press, 1962.

Purkey, W. Measured and professed personality characteristics of gifted high school students and analysis of their congruence. *The Journal of Educational Research*, 1966, *3*, 99–103.

Purkey, W. Project self discovery: Its effect on bright but underachieving high school students. *The Gifted Child Quarterly*, 1969, *13*, 242–246.

Purkey, W. *Self-concept and school achievement*. Englewood Cliffs, N.J.: Prentice-Hall, 1970.

Racle, G. Documents: Research Institute of Suggestology, Sofia, Bulgaria, 1971. *Suggestopaedia-Canada*, 1977, *2*, 1–3.

Radcliffe, S., & Hatch, W. *Advanced standing. New Dimensions in Higher Education* (No. 8). Washington, D.C.: U.S. Government Printing Office, 1961.

Ramaseshan, P. *The social and emotional adjustment of the gifted*. Unpublished doctoral dissertation, University of Nebraska, 1957.

Raph, J., Goldberg, M., & Passow, A. *Bright underachievers*. New York: Teachers College Press, Columbia University, 1966.

Raspberry, W. What about elitist high schools? *Today's Education*, 1976, *65*, 36–39.

Raths, L., Harmin, M., & Simon, S. *Values and teaching*. Columbus: Charles E. Merrill, 1966.

Reichstein, K., & Pipkin, R. A study of academic justice. *The Law and Society Review*, 1968, *2*, 259–276.

Reid, M. Cerebral lateralization in children: An ontogenetic and organismic analysis. Doctoral dissertation, University of Colorado, 1980.

Reihart, R. *Selfawareness through group dynamics.* Dayton, Ohio: George A. Pflaum, 1970.

Renzulli, J. Identifying key features in programs for the gifted. *Exceptional Children*, 1968, *35*, 217–221.

Renzulli, J. *Graduate study in special education of the gifted and talented.* University of Connecticut, Department of Educational Psychology, 1973a. (Mimeographed)

Renzulli, J. *New directions in creativity.* New York: Harper & Row, 1973b.

Renzulli, J. Talent potential in minority group students. *Exceptional Children*, 1973c, *39* (6), 437–444.

Renzulli, J. Identifying key features in programs for the gifted. In W. Barbe & J. Renzulli (Eds.), *Psychology and education of the gifted.* New York: Irvington Publishing, 1975.

Renzulli, J. *A guidebook for evaluating programs for the gifted and talented.* Ventura, Ca.: Office of the Ventura County Superintendent of Schools, 1975b.

Renzulli, J. The enrichment triad model (Part I). *The Gifted Child Quarterly*, Fall 1976, *20* (3), 303–326.

Renzulli, J. *The enrichment triad model: A guide for developing defensible programs for the gifted and talented.* Mansfield Center, Conn.: Creative Learning Press, 1977.

Renzulli, J., & Hartman, R. Scale for rating behavioral characteristics of superior students. *Exceptional Children*, 1971, *38* (3), 243–248.

Renzulli, J., Hartman, R., & Callahan, C. Teacher identification of superior students. *Exceptional Children*, 1971, *38* (3), 221–224.

Renzulli, J. "What makes giftedness?" Reexamining a definition. *Phi Delta Kappan*, 1978, *60*, 180–184; 261.

Renzulli, J. *What makes giftedness: A Reexamination of the definition of the gifted and talented.* Ventura, Ca.: Ventura County Superintendent of Schools Office, 1979a.

Renzulli, J. (Ed.). *Sample instruments for the evaluation of programs for the gifted and talented.* Storrs, Conn.: Bureau of Educational Research, 1979b.

Renzulli, J., & Ward, V. *Diagnostic and evaluative scales for differential education for the gifted.* Storrs, Conn.: University of Connecticut, 1969.

Restak, K. *The brain: The last frontier.* New York: Doubleday, 1979.

Reynolds, M. (Ed.). *Early school admission for mentally advanced children.* Reston, Va.: Council for Exceptional Children, 1962.

Rheingold, H., & Cook, K. The contents of boys' and girls' rooms as an index of parent behavior. *Child Development*, 1975, *46*, 459–463.

Rhodes, M. An analysis of creativity. *Phi Delta Kappan*, 1961, *42*, 305–310.

Rice, J., & Banks, G. Opinions of gifted students regarding secondary school programs. *Exceptional Children*, 1967, *34* (4), 269–272.

Riessman, F. *The culturally deprived child.* New York: Harper & Row, 1962.

Rimm, S., & Davis, G. GIFT: An instrument for the identification of creativity. *Journal of Creative Behavior*, 1976, *10* (3), 178–182.

Roberts, H. *Factors affecting the academic underachievement of bright high school students.* Unpublished doctoral dissertation, University of California, Los Angeles, 1960.

Roberts, J. *The education of oversoul #7.* Englewood Cliffs, N.J.: Prentice-Hall, 1973.

Roberts, J. *The nature of personal reality.* Englewood Cliffs, N.J.: Prentice-Hall, 1974.

Roberts, T. Consciousness meets education at UC Berkeley. *Brain/Mind Bulletin*, 1982, 7 (12), 1.

Roberts, T., & Clark, F. Transpersonal psychology in education. In G. Hendricks & J. Fadiman (Eds.), *Transpersonal education*. Englewood Cliffs, N.J.: Prentice-Hall, 1976.

Rodenstein, J., Pfleger, L., & Colangelo, N. Career development of gifted women. *The Gifted Child Quarterly*, 1977, *21*, 340–358.

Rogers, C. Toward a theory of creativity. In H. H. Anderson (Ed.), *Creativity and its cultivation*. New York: Harper & Row, 1959.

Rogers, C. *On becoming a person*. Boston: Houghton Mifflin, 1961.

Rogers, C. *Freedom to learn*. Columbus, Ohio: Charles E. Merrill, 1969.

Rogers, D. (Ed.). *Issues in adolescent psychology*. New York: Appleton-Century Crofts, 1969.

Rogge, W. *IMPACT Session IV: Change: Risks, groups, processes*. Paper presented at the annual meeting of the Council of Exceptional Children, Chicago, April 1970.

Rohrer, J., & Edmondson, M. (Eds.). *The eighth generation*. New York: Harper & Row, 1960.

Rorvik, D., & Heyns, O. *Decompression babies*. New York: Dodd, Mead, 1973.

Rose, S. Environmental effects on brain and behavior. In K. Richardson and D. Spears (Eds.), *Race, culture and intelligence*. Hardmondsworth: Penguin, 1972.

Rosenberg, B., & Sutton-Smith, B. Sibling age spacing effects upon cognition. *Developmental Psychology*, 1969, *1*, 661–668.

Rothenberg, A. Creative contradictions. *Psychology Today*, 1979, *13* (1), 55–62.

Rosenthal, R. *Pygmalion in the classroom: Teacher expectation and pupil's intellectual development*. New York: Holt, Rinehart & Winston, 1968.

Rosenthal, R., & Jacobsen, L. *Pygmalion in the classroom: Self-fulfilling prophecies and teacher expectations*. New York: Holt, Rinehart & Winston, 1969.

Rosenzweig, M. Environmental complexity, cerebral change and behavior. *American Psychologist*, 1966, *21*, 321–332.

Rothney, J. *Evaluating and reporting pupil progress*. Washington, D.C.: National Educational Association, 1955.

Rothney, J., & Koopman, N. Guidance of the gifted. In N. Henry (Ed.), *Education of the gifted. Fifty-seventh yearbook* (Part II). National Society of Secondary Education, Chicago: University of Chicago Press, 1958.

Rowan, R. Those business hunches are more than blind faith. *Fortune*, 1979, *99*, 110–114.

Rozman, D. *Meditation for children*. Millbrae, Ca.: Celestial Arts, 1976.

Rubenzer, R. Identification and evaluation procedures for gifted and talented programs. *The Gifted Child Quarterly*, Summer 1979, *23* (2), 304–316.

Rubin, J., Provenzano, F., & Luria, Z. The eye of the beholder: Parents' views on sex of newborns. *American Journal of Orthopsychiatry*, 1974, *44*, 512–519.

Rugg, H. *Images and imagination*. New York: Harper & Row, 1963.

Runions, T. The Mentor Academy Program: Educating the gifted/talented for the 80's. *Gifted Child Quarterly*, 1980, *24* (4), 152–157.

Rust, J., & Lose, B. Screening for giftedness with the Slosson and the Scale for Rating Behavioral Characteristics of Superior Students. *Psychology in the Schools*, 1980, *17* (4), 446–451.

Rust, R., & Ryan, F. The relationship of some Rorschach variables to academic behavior. *Journal of Personality*, 1953, *21*, 441–456.

Rutherford, G. *An attitudinal survey of teachers toward gifted education.* Paper presented at California State University, Los Angeles, Department of Special Education, August 1977.

Sagan, C. *Broca's brain.* New York: Random House, 1974.

Sagan, C. *The dragons of eden.* New York: Random House, 1977.

Salk, L. The role of the heartbeat in the relations between mother and infant. *Scientific American*, 1973, *288*, 24–29.

Samples, B. *Essence I & II.* Reading, Mass.: Addison-Wesley, 1970. (Two classroom kits for awareness activities)

Samples, B. Learning with the whole brain. *Human Behavior*, 1975, *4*, 18–23.

Samples, B. *The metaphoric mind: A celebration of creative consciousness.* Reading, Mass.: Addison-Wesley, 1976.

Samples, B. Mind cycles and learning. *Phi Delta Kappan*, 1977, *58*, 688–692.

Samples, B., Charles, C., & Barnhart, D. *The wholeschool book: Teaching and learning late in the 20th century.* Reading, Mass.: Addison-Wesley, 1977.

Samples, B., & Wohlford, B. *Opening: A primer for self-actualization.* Reading, Mass.: Addison-Wesley, 1973.

Samuels, M., & Bennett, H. *The well body book.* New York: Random House, 1973.

Sanborn, M. Differential counseling needs of the gifted and talented. In N. Colangelo & R. Zaffrann (Eds.), *New voices in counseling the gifted.* Dubuque, Iowa: Kendall/Hunt Publishing Company, 1979.

Satir, V. *Peoplemaking.* Palo Alto, Ca.: Science & Behavior Books, 1972.

Sattler, J. Racial "experimenter effects" in experimentation, testing, interviewing, and psychotherapy. *Psychological Bulletin*, 1970, *73* (2), 137–160.

Saunders, R. Art education for the gifted. *Roeper Review*, 1982, *4* (3), 7–10.

Scarr-Salapatek, S. Comment on individual and group differences in I.Q. In P. Rosenthal, (Ed.), *Annual editions: Readings in human development.* Guilford, Conn.: Dushkin, 1974a.

Scarr-Salapatek, S. *Genetic determinants of infant development: An overstated case.* Paper presented to the Psycho-Biology Symposium: The Importance of Infancy, American Association for the Advancement of Science, San Francisco, February 1974b.

Schaefer, C. E. A psychological study of 10 exceptionally creative adolescent girls. *Exceptional Children*, 1970, *36* (6), 431–441.

Schaefer, E., & Aaronson, M. Infant education pre-school project: Implementation and implications of a home tutoring program. In R. Parker (Ed.), *The pre-school in action: Exploring early childhood programs.* Boston: Allyn & Bacon, 1972.

Schaefer, E., & Marcus, M. Self-stimulation alters human sensory brain responses. *Science*, 1973, *181*, 175–177.

Scheibel, M., & Scheibel, A. Some neural substrates of postnatal development. In M. Hoffman & L. Hoffman (Eds.), *Review of child development research* (Vol. 1.). New York: Russell Sage Foundation, 1964.

Schmuck, R., & Schmuck, P. *Group process in the classroom.* Dubuque, Iowa: William C. Brown, 1971.

School Staffing Survey 1969-70. Washington, D.C.: Department of Health, Education, and Welfare, U.S. Office of Education.

Schrank, J. *Teaching human beings: 101 subversive activities for the classroom.* Boston: Beacon Press, 1972.

Schulte, F. Excitation, inhibition, and impulsive conduction in spinal motoneurones of preterm, term and small-for-dates newborn infants. In R. J. Robinson (Ed.), *Brain and early behavior: Development in the fetus and infant.* New York: Academic Press, 1969, 87–109.

Schulz, J., & Luthe, W. *Autogenic training: A psychophysiological approach to psychotherapy.* New York: Grune & Stratton, 1959.

Schutz, W. Education for the body. In G. Hendricks & J. Fadiman (Eds.), *Transpersonal education: A curriculum for feeling and being.* Englewood Cliffs, N.J.: Prentice-Hall, 1976.

Schwartz, G., & Shapiro, D. (Eds.). *Consciousness and self-regulation* (Vol. 1). New York: Plenum, 1976.

Scientific American. *The brain.* San Francisco, Ca.: Freeman, 1979.

Scott, J. Critical period in behavioral development. *Science*, 1962, *138* (3544), 949–953.

Seagoe, M. Some learning characteristics of gifted children. In R. Martinson, *The identification of the gifted and talented.* Ventura, Ca.: Office of Ventura County Superintendent of Schools, 1974.

Sears, P., & Barbee, A. Career and life satisfactions among Terman's gifted women. In J. Stanley, W. George, & C. Solano (Eds.), *The gifted and the creative: A fifty-year perspective.* Baltimore: The Johns Hopkins University Press, 1977.

Seeley, K. Competencies for teachers of gifted and talented children. *Journal for the Education of the Gifted.* 1979, *3* (1), 7–13.

Seeley, K. Professional standards for training programs in gifted education. *Journal for the Education of the Gifted*, 1981, *4* (3), 165–168.

Seidner, C. Teaching with simulations and games. In N. Gage (Ed.), *The psychology of teaching methods: The seventy-fifth yearbook of the National Society on the Study of Education*, 1976, 217–251.

Selby, C. Science as the 'fourth R'—basic and also beautiful. *Science Digest*, S 1980, *88*, 44–47.

Selye, H. *The stress of life.* New York: McGraw-Hill, 1956.

Serbin, L., & O'Leary, K. How nursery schools teach girls to shut up. *Psychology Today*, 1975, *9*, 57–58; 102–103.

Severy, L., & Davis, K. Helping behavior among normal and retarded children. *Child Development*, 1971, *4*, 1017–1031.

Sexton, P. *Education and income.* New York: Viking, 1961.

Shapiro, D., Tursky, B., Gershon, E., & Stern, M. Effects of feedback and reinforcement on the control of human systolic blood pressure. *Science*, 1969, *163*, 588–590.

Sharan, S. Cooperative learning in small groups: Recent methods and effects on achievement, attitudes, and ethnic relations. *Review of Educational Research*, 1980, *50* (2), 241–271.

Shaw, M. Definition and identification of academic underachievers. In J. French (Ed.), *Educating the gifted* (Rev. ed.). New York: Holt, Rinehart & Winston, 1964.

Shaw, M., & Black, D. The reaction to frustration of bright high school underachievers. *California Journal of Educational Research*, 1960, *11*, 120–124.

Shaw, M., & McCuen, J. The onset of academic underachievement in bright children. *Journal of Educational Psychology*, 1960, *51*, 103–108.

Sheldon, W., & Manolakes, G. Comparison of the Stanford-Binet, Revised Form L and the California Test of Mental Maturity (S-Form). *Journal of Educational Psychology*, 1954, *45*, 499–504.

Sheldrake, R. A new science of life. *New Scientist*, 1981, *90* (1256), 749; 766–768.

Shostrom, E. An inventory for the measurement of self-actualization. *Educational and Psychological Measurement*, 1964, *24*, 207–218.

Shouksmith, G., & Taylor, J. The effect of counseling on the achievement of high ability pupils. *British Journal of Educational Psychology*, 1964, *34*, 51–57.

Silberman, C. *Crisis in the classroom*. New York: Random House, 1971.

Silverman, L. Secondary programs for gifted students. *Journal for the Education of the Gifted*, 1980, *4* (1), 30–42.

Silvernail, D. Gifted education for the 80's and beyond: A futuristic curriculum model for the gifted child. *Roeper Review*, 1980, *2* (4), 16–18.

Simon, S. Please touch! How to combat skin hunger in our schools. *Scholastic Teacher*, 1974, *105*, 22–25.

Simon, S., Howe, L., & Kirschenbaum, H. *Values clarification*. New York: Hart Publishers, 1972.

Simon, S., Kirschenbaum, H., & Fuhrmann, B. *An introduction to values clarification*. New York: J.C. Penney, 1972.

Simonov, P. Emotions and creativity. *Psychology Today*, 1970, *4* (3), 51–55; 77.

Simpson, R., & Martinson, R. *Educational programs for gifted pupils*. Sacramento, Ca.: California State Department of Education, 1961.

Singer, B. The future-focused role image. In A Toffler (Ed.), *Learning for tomorrow*. New York: Vintage, 1974.

Singer, J. *The inner world of day dreaming*. New York: Harper & Row, 1975.

Singer, J. Fantasy: The foundation of serenity. *Psychology Today*, 1976, *10* (2), 32–37.

Sisk, D. *Teaching gifted children*. Developed in conjunction with a Federal Grant from Title V, Section 505. Project Director, James Turner, South Carolina. (Florida component)

Sisk, D. *Developing teacher mediators/teacher training for disadvantaged gifted*. Paper presented at the First National Conference on the Disadvantaged Gifted, Ventura, Ca., March 1973.

Sisk, D. Communication skills for the gifted. *The Gifted Child Quarterly*, 1975a, *19*, 66–68.

Sisk, D. Teaching the gifted and talented teacher: A training model. *The Gifted Child Quarterly*, 1975b, *19*, 81–88.

Skeels, H. Adult status of children with contrasting early life experiences. *Monographs of the Society for Research in Child Development*, 1966, *31* (3).

Skeels, H., & Dye, H. A study of the effects of differential stimulation on mentally retarded children. *Proceedings of American Association on Mental Deficiency*, 1959, *44*, 114–136.

Skeels, H., Updegraff, R., Wellman, B., & Williams, H. A study of environmental stimulation: An orphanage preschool project. *University of Iowa Studies in Child Welfare*, 1938, *15* (4), 28; 264.

Skodak, M., & Skeels, H. A final follow-up study of one hundred adopted children. *Journal of Genetic Psychology*, 1949, *74–75*; 85–125.

Sluckin, W. *Imprinting and early learning*. Chicago, Ill.: Aldine, 1965.

Smith, R. The relationship of creativity to social class. *United States Office of Education Cooperative Research Project* (No. 2250). Pittsburgh: University of Pittsburgh, 1965.

Soar, R. Research findings from systematic observation. *Journal of Research and Development in Education*, 1970, *4*, 116–122.

Solano, C. Teacher and pupil stereotypes of gifted boys and girls. *Talents and Gifts*, 1977, *19*, 4–8.

Sonntag, J. Sensitivity training with gifted children. *The Gifted Child Quarterly*, 1967, *13* (1), 51–57.

Sonntag, J. *Communications and relatedness: A curriculum guide for mentally gifted minors*. Sacramento, Ca.: California State Department of Education, 1972.

Sontag, L., Baker, C., & Nelson, V. Mental growth and personality development: A longitudinal study. *Monograph of Sociological Research in Child Development*, 1958, *23* (2, Whole No. 68).

Spino, M. *Beyond jogging: The innerspaces of running*. Millbrae, Ca.: Celestial Arts, 1976.

Spolin, V. *Improvisations for the theatre*. Evanston, Ill.: Northwestern University Press, 1963.

Springer, S., & Deutsch, G. *Left brain, right brain*. San Francisco, Ca.: W. H. Freeman & Co., 1981.

Sroufe, L. A. Socioemotional development. In J. Osofsky (Ed.), *Handbook of infant development*. New York: John Wiley & Sons, 1979.

Standing, E. *The Montessori revolution in education*. New York: Schocken, 1966.

Stanley, J. The case for extreme educational acceleration of intellectually brilliant youths. In J. Gowan, J. Khatena, & E. P. Torrance (Eds.), *Educating the ablest, a book of readings*, (2nd ed.). Itasca, Ill.: F. E. Peacock Publishers, Inc., 1979.

Stanley, J., Keating, D., & Fox, L., (Eds.). *Mathematical talent: Discovery, description, and development*. Baltimore: Johns Hopkins University Press, 1974.

Starch, D. Reliability of grading work in mathematics. *School Review*, 1913, *21*, 254–295.

Starch, D., & Elliott, E. Reliability of grading of high school work in English. *School Review*, 1912, *20*, 442–457.

Stark, M. *Results of a questionnaire given to 152 high school gifted students*. Paper presented at California State University, Los Angeles, 1972.

Stearn, J. *The power of alpha thinking*. New York: William Morrow, 1976.

Steele, J. *Instructional climate in Illinois gifted classes*. Springfield, Ill.: Illinois State Office of the Superintendent of Public Instruction, Dept. of Program Planning for Gifted, 1969.

Stein, M. *Survey of the psychological literature in the area of creativity with a view toward needed research*. U.S. Office of Education Cooperative Research Project #E-3. New York: New York University, 1962.

Stephens, L. *The teacher's guide to open education*. New York: Holt, Rinehart & Winston, 1974.

Sternberg, R. A componential theory of intellectual giftedness. *Gifted Child Quarterly*, 1981, *25* (2), 86–93.

Stevens, J. *Awareness: Exploring, experimenting, experiencing*. Moab, Utah: Real People Press, 1971.

Stevenson, H., Hale, G., Klein, R., & Miller, L. Interrelations and correlates in children's learning and problem solving. *Monographs of the Society for Research in Child Development*, 1968, *33*.

Stewart, E. Learning styles among gifted/talented students: Instructional technique preferences. *Exceptional Children*, 1981, *48* (2), 134–138.

Stewart, K. Dream theory in Malaya. In C. Tart (Ed.), *Altered states of consciousness: Book of readings*. New York: John Wiley & Sons, 1969.

Stipek, D., & Weisz, J. Perceived personal control and academic achievement. *Review of Educational Research*, 1981, *51* (1), 101–137.

Stodtbeck, F. Family interaction values and achievement. In D. McClelland (Ed.), *Talent and society*. Princeton, N.J.: Van Nostrand Reinhold, 1958.

Stogbill, R. *Handbook of leadership: A survey of theory and research*. New York: Free Press, 1974.

Stogbill, R., & Coons, A. (Eds.). *Leader behavior; its description and measurement* (No. 88). Columbus, Ohio: Bureau of Business Research, Ohio State University, 1957.

Stone, L., Smith, H., & Murphy, L. (Eds.), *The competent infant: Research and commentary*. New York: Basic Books, 1973.

Stott, D. Follow-up study from birth of the effects of prenatal stresses. *Developmental Medicine and Child Neurology*, 1973, *15*, 770–787.

Stott, D. Children in the womb: The effects of stress. *New Society*, 1977, *40*, 329–331.

Strang, R. Gifted adolescents, views of growing up. *Exceptional Children*, 1956, *23*, 10–15; 20.

Strang, R. *Helping your gifted child*. New York: E. P. Dutton, 1960.

Suchman, J. R. Inquiry training: Building skills for autonomous discovery. *Merrill Palmer Quarterly of Behavior and Development*, 1961, *7*, 147–169.

Suchman, J. R. *The elementary school training program in scientific inquiry*. Urbana, Ill.: University of Illinois Press, 1962.

Sumption, M. *Three hundred gifted children*. Yonkers-on-Hudson, N.Y.: World Book, 1941.

Superka, D. Approaches to values education. *Science Education Consortium Newsletter*, November 1974.

Syphers, D. *Gifted and talented children: Practical programming for teachers and principals*. Arlington, Va.: The Council for Exceptional Children, 1972.

Szekely, G. The artist and the child—A model program for the artistically gifted. *Gifted Child Quarterly*, 1981, *25* (2), 67–72.

Szekely, G. Creative learning and teaching of the gifted through sketchbooks. *Roeper Review*, 1982, *4* (3), 15–17.

Taba, H. *Teaching strategies and cognitive functioning in elementary school children* (USOE Cooperative Research Project #2404). San Francisco: San Francisco State College, 1966.

Tannenbaum, A. *Adolescent attitudes toward academic brilliance*. New York: Bureau of Publications, Teachers College, Columbia University, 1962.

Tan-Willman, C., & Gutteridge, D. Creative thinking and moral reasoning of academically gifted secondary school adolescents. *Gifted Child Quarterly*, Fall 1981, *25* (4), 149–153.

Tarjan, G. Some thoughts on sociocultural retardation. In H. C. Haywood (Ed.), *Socio-cultural aspects of mental retardation*. New York: Appleton-Century-Crofts, 1970.

Tayler, T. *Altered states of awareness: Readings from Scientific American*. San Francisco: W. H. Freeman, 1972.

Taylor, C. W. (Ed.). *Research conference on the identification of creative scientific talent*. Salt Lake City: University of Utah Press, 1956.

Taylor, C. W. Identifying the creative individual. In E. P. Torrance (Ed.), *Creativity: Proceedings of the second Minnesota conference on gifted children*. Minneapolis: Center for Continuation Study, 1959.

Taylor, C. W. Clues to creative teaching: The creative process and education. *Instructor*, 1963, *73*, 4–5.

Taylor, C. W., & Williams, F. E. *Instructional media and creativity*. New York: John Wiley & Sons, 1966.

Taylor, I. Psychological sources of creativity. *Journal of Creative Behavior*, 1976, *10*, 193–202.

Taylor, J., & Walford, R. *Simulation in the classroom*. Baltimore: Penguin Books, 1972.

Taylor, L., & Bongar, B. *Clinical applications in biofeedback therapy*. Los Angeles: Psychology Press, 1976.

Taylor, L., Tom, G., & Ayers, M. *Electromyometric biofeedback therapy*. Los Angeles: Biofeedback and Advanced Therapy Institute, Inc., 1981.

Teilhard de Chardin, P. *The divine milieu*. New York: Harper & Row, 1959.

Temple University. *Report of the college of education ad hoc committee on grading systems*. Philadelphia, 1968.

Terman, L. *The measurement of intelligence*. Boston: Houghton Mifflin Co., 1916.

Terman, L. Mental and physical traits of a thousand gifted children. In L. Terman (Ed.), *Genetic studies of genius* (Vol. I). Stanford: Stanford University Press, 1925.

Terman, L. The discovery and encouragement of exceptional talent. *American Psychologist*, 1954, *9*, 221–230.

Terman, L., & Oden, M. The gifted child grows up. In L. Terman (Ed.), *Genetic studies of genius* (Vol. IV). Stanford: Stanford University Press, 1947.

Terman, L., & Oden, M. The gifted group at mid-life; thirty-five year's follow-up of the superior child. In L. Terman (Ed.), *Genetic studies of genius* (Vol. V). Stanford University: Stanford University Press, 1959.

Teyler, T. An introduction to the neurosciences. In M. Wittrock (Ed.), *The human brain*. Englewood Cliffs, N.J.: Prentice-Hall, 1977.

Theodore, A. *The professional woman*. Cambridge, Mass.: Schenkman Publishing Company, 1971.

Thinking Caps: Materials for gifted: Cognitive, affective, psychomotor skills and activities. Box 7239, Phoenix, Az. 85011.

Thistlewaite, D. How the talented student evaluates his high school. *School Review*, 1958, *66*, 164–168.

Thomas, A., Hertzig, I., & Fernandez, P. Examiner effect in IQ testing of Puerto Rican working-class children. *Measurement and Evaluation in Guidance*, 1971, 4 (3), 172–175.

Thomas, J. Agency and achievement: Self-management and self-regard. *Review of Educational Research*, 1980, *50* (2), 213–240.

Thompson, R., Berger, T., & Berry, S. An introduction to the anatomy, physiology, and chemistry of the brain. In M. Wittrock (Ed.), *The brain and psychology*. New York: Academic Press, 1980.

Thorndike, R. L. *The concepts of over and underachievement*. New York: Bureau of Publications, Teachers College, Columbia University, 1963a.

Thorndike, R. L. The measurement of creativity. *Teachers College Record*, 1963b, *64*, 422–424.

Thorndike, R. L. Mr. Binet's test 70 years later. *Educational Researcher*, 1975, 4 (5), 3–6.

Tiegs, E. Educational diagnosis. *Educational Bulletin* (No. 18). Monterey, Ca.: California Testing Bureau, 1952.

Time, 1972, *99*, 25–103.

Tomer, M. Human relations in education—A rationale for a curriculum in inter-personal skills for gifted students—grade K–12. *Gifted Child Quarterly*, 1981, 25 (2), 94–97.

Torrance, E. P. The Minnesota studies of creative thinking in the early school years. *University of Minnesota Research Memorandum* (No. 59-4). Minneapolis, Minn.: University of Minnesota Bureau of Educational Research, 1960.

Torrance, E. P. *Guiding creative talent*. Englewood Cliffs, N.J.: Prentice-Hall, 1962.

Torrance, E. P. *Education and the creative potential*. Minneapolis, Minn.: University of Minnesota Press, 1963.

Torrance, E. P. Education and creativity. In C. W. Taylor (Ed.), *Creativity: Progress and potential*. New York: McGraw-Hill, 1964a.

Torrance, E. P. *Rewarding creative behavior*. Englewood Cliffs, N.J.: Prentice-Hall, 1964b.

Torrance, E. P. *Torrance Tests of Creative Thinking: Norms-technical manual*. Princeton, N.J.: Personnel Press, 1966.

Torrance, E. P. Creativity and its educational implications for the gifted. *The Gifted Child Quarterly*, 1968a, 12 (2), 67–78.

Torrance, E. P. A longitudinal examination of the fourth grade slump in creativity. *The Gifted Child Quarterly*, 1968b, 12 (4), 195–199.

Torrance, E. P. Creative positives of disadvantaged children and youth. *The Gifted Child Quarterly*, 1969, 13 (2), 71–81.

Torrance, E. P. Future careers for gifted and talented students. *Gifted Child Quarterly*, 1976, 20, 142–156.

Torrance, E. P. Creatively gifted and disadvantaged gifted students. In J. Stanley, W. George, & C. Solano (Eds.), *The gifted and the creative: A fifty-year perspective*. Baltimore: The Johns Hopkins University Press, 1977.

Torrance, E. P. Cross-cultural studies of creative development in seven selected societies. In J. Gowan, J. Khatena, & E. P. Torrance (Eds.), *Creativity: Its educational implications*, second edition. Dubuque, Iowa: Kendall/Hunt Publishing Company, 1981, 89–97.

Torrance, E. P., Blume, B., Maryanopolis, J., Murphey, F., & Rogers, J. *Teaching scenario writing*. Lincoln, Neb.: Future Problem Solving Program, Nebraska Department of Education, 1980.

Torrance, E. P., & Myers, R. Teaching gifted elementary pupils research concepts and skills. *Gifted Child Quarterly*, 1962, 6, 1–16.

Torrance, E. P., & Torrance, J. P. Educating gifted, talented and creative students for the future. *American Middle School Education*, 1981, 4 (1), 39–46.

Treffinger, D. Teaching for self-directed learning: A priority for the gifted and talented. *The Gifted Child Quarterly*, 1975, 19 (1), 46–59.

Tremaine, C. Do gifted programs make a difference? *The Gifted Child Quarterly*, 1979, 23 (3), 500–517.

Trotter, R. Self-image. *Science News*, 1971, *100*, 130–131.

Trowbridge, A. Evolution of triune brain consciousness. *Man-Environment Systems*, 1978, 8 (3), 105–112.

Truesdell, B., & Newman, J. Can jr. highs make it with wide open spaces? *Learning*, 1975, *4* (3), 74–77.

Usher, R., & Hanke, J. Third force in psychology and college teacher effectiveness research at the University of Northern Colorado. *Colorado Journal of Educational Research*, 1971, *10*, 2.

Uzgiris, I. C., & Hunt, J. McV. *An instrument for assessing infant psychological development.* Mimeograph paper. Urbana: University of Illinois, Psychological Department Laboratory, 1966.

Van Duyne, J., & D'Alonzo, B. Amount of verbal information and ear differences in 5- and 6-year-old boys and girls. *Perceptual and Motor Skills*, 1976, *43*, 31–39.

Van Horn, M., & Hanson, R. *Leading creative participation.* Unpublished article, 1975.

Van Tassel, J. Evaluation of gifted programs. In J. Jordan & J. Grossi (Eds.), *An administrator's handbook on designing programs for the gifted and talented.* Reston, Va.: Council for Exceptional Children, 1980.

Vare, J. Moral education for the gifted: A confluent model. *The Gifted Child Quarterly*, Fall 1979, *23* (3), 487–499.

Vargiu, S. *Psychosynthesis case studies: Three gifted adolescents.* Redwood City, Ca.: Psychosynthesis Institute, 1971.

Vermilyea, J. Common sense in the identification of gifted and talented students who need alternative programming. *G/C/T*, January/February 1981, *16*, 11–14.

Vernon, P. *Intelligence: Heredity and environment.* San Francisco: Freeman, 1979.

Verny, T. *The secret life of the unborn child.* New York: Summit Books, 1981.

Vogel, J. Learning and self-esteem. *Learning*, 1974, *2* (7), 68–72.

Voight, R. *Invitation to learning: The learning center handbook.* Washington, D.C.: Acropolis Books, 1971.

Vygotsky, L. [*Thought and language*] (E. Hanfmann & G. Vakar, Eds. and trans.). New York: Wiley, 1962.

Vygotsky, L. The problem of age-periodization of child development (trans. M. Zender & B. Zender) *Human Development*, 1974, *17*, 24–40.

Waber, D. Biological substrates of field dependence: Implications of the sex difference. *Psychological Bulletin*, 1977, *84*, 1076–1087.

Waber, D. Sex differences in mental abilities, hemispheric lateralization and rate of physical growth at adolescence. *Developmental Psychology*, 1977, *13*, 29–38.

Wachs, T. *The measurement of early intellectual functioning: Contributions from developmental psychology.* Paper presented at American Association on Mental Deficiency, San Francisco, May 1969.

Wachs, T. Utilization of a Piagetian approach in the investigation of early experience effects: A research strategy and some illustrative data. *Merrill-Palmer Quarterly*, 1976, *22*, 11–30.

Walberg, H. Physics, femininity, and creativity. *Developmental Psychology*, 1969, *1*, 47–54.

Wallach, M., & Kogan, N. *Cognitive originality, physiognomic sensitivity and defensiveness in children.* Durham: Duke University, 1965.

Wallas, G. *The art of thought.* London: C. A. Watts, 1926.

Walsh, A. *Self-concepts of bright boys with learning difficulties.* New York: Teachers College Press, Teachers College, Columbia University, 1956.

Wampler, M. *Music: A curriculum guide for mentally gifted minors.* Sacramento, Ca.: California State Department of Education, 1973.

Wang, M., & Stiles, B. An investigation of children's concept of self-responsibility for their school learning. *American Educational Research Journal,* 1976, *13,* 159–179.

Ward, V. *Educating the gifted: An axiomatic approach.* Columbus, Ohio: Charles E. Merrill, 1961.

Wass, H., Blume, R., Combs, A., & Hedges, W. *Humanistic teacher education: An experiment in systematic curriculum innovation.* Fort Collins, Colo.: Shields, 1974.

Watson, G. Some personality differences in children related to strict or permissive parental discipline. *Journal of Psychology,* 1957, *44,* 227–249.

Web, D. Teacher sensitivity: Affective impact on students. *The Journal of Teacher Education,* 1971, *22,* 455–459.

Webb, R. Concrete and formal operations in very bright six to eleven year olds. *Human Development,* 1974, *17,* 292–300.

Weiner, J. Attitudes of psychologists and psychometrists toward gifted children and programs for the gifted. *Exceptional Children,* 1968, *34,* 354.

Weiner, J., & O'Shea, H. Attitudes of university faculty, administrators, teachers, supervisors, and university students toward the gifted. *Exceptional Children,* 1963, *30* (4), 163–165.

Weinheimer, S. How to teach your child to think: A conversation with Jean Piaget, the "giant in the nursery." *Redbook,* March 1972, 96–97; 118; 120.

Weinhold, B. Transpersonal communication in the classroom. In G. Hendricks & J. Fadiman (Eds.), *Transpersonal education.* Englewood Cliffs, N.J.: Prentice-Hall, 1976.

Weinstein, G., & Fantini, M. *Toward humanistic education: A curriculum of affect.* New York: Praeger, 1970.

Weiss, M. *Free for baby and mother: An encyclopedia of things available to parent and child at no cost.* South Brunswick, N.J.: A. S. Barnes, 1972.

Weiss, P., & Gallagher, J. The effects of personal experience on attitudes toward gifted education. *Journal for the Education of the Gifted,* 1980, *3* (4), 194–197.

Weisstein, N. Woman as nigger. *Psychology Today,* 1969, *3,* 20–22; 58.

Welch, I., Richards, F., & Richards, A. *Educational accountability: A humanistic perspective.* Fort Collins, Colo.: Shields, 1973.

Wellington, C., & Wellington, J. *The underachiever: Challenges and guidelines.* Chicago: Rand McNally, 1965.

Wellman, B. Iowa studies on the effects of schooling. *Yearbook of the National Society on Studies in Education,* 1940, *39,* 377–399.

Wescott, G., & Woodward, J. Locating the not so obvious gifted. *G/C/T,* November/December 1981, *20,* 11.

White, B. *The first three years of life.* Englewood Cliffs, N.J.: Prentice-Hall, 1975.

White, B., & Castle, P. Visual exploratory behavior following postnatal handling of human infants. *Perceptual & Motor Skills,* 1964, *18,* 497–502.

White, B., & Watts, J. *Experience and environment* (Vol. I). Englewood Cliffs, N.J.: Prentice-Hall, 1973.

White, M. The case of specifically designed education for the gifted. *Gifted Child Quarterly,* 1970, *14,* 159–162.

Whitmore, J. *Giftedness, conflict, and underachievement.* Boston: Allyn and Bacon, 1980.

Whitmore, J. Gifted children with handicapping conditions: A new frontier. *Exceptional Children*, 1981, *48* (2), 106–114.

Williams, F. (Ed.). *Creativity at home and in school.* St. Paul, Minn.: Macalester Creativity Project, 1968.

Williams, F. Models for encouraging creativity in the classroom. In J. Gowan, J. Khatena, & E. P. Torrance (Eds.), *Educating the ablest, a book of readings.* Itasca, Ill.: F. E. Peacock Publishers, Inc., 1979.

Wilson, F. T. The preparation of teachers for the education of gifted children. In B. Henry (Ed.), *Education for the gifted, 57th yearbook* (Part II). National Society for the Study of Education, Chicago: University of Chicago Press, 1958.

Wingerson, L. A window on the body. *Discover*, 1982, *3* (4), 85; 86; 88.

Wingerson, L. Training the mind to heal. *Discover*, 1982, *3* (5), 80–82; 85.

Witelson, S. Sex and the single hemisphere. *Science*, 1976, *193*, 425–427.

Witters, L., & Vasa, S. Programming alternatives for educating the gifted in rural schools. *Roeper Review*, 1981, *3* (4), 22–24.

Wittrock, M., Beatty, J., Bogan, J., Gazzaniga, M., Jerison, H., Krashen, S., Nebes, R., & Teyler, T. *The human brain.* Englewood Cliffs, N.J.: Prentice-Hall, 1977.

Wittrock, M. Learning and the brain. In M. Wittrock (Ed.), *The brain and psychology.* New York: Academic Press, 1980.

Wittrock, M. *The brain and psychology.* New York: Academic Press, 1980.

Witty, P. A study of one hundred gifted children. *Bulletin of Education*, 1930, *2* (7).

Witty, P. Some considerations in the education of gifted children. *Educational Administration and Supervision*, 1940, *26*, 512–521.

Witty, P. (Ed.). *The gifted child.* Boston: Heath, 1951.

Wodtke, K. Some data on the reliability and validity of creative tests at the elementary school level. *Educational and Psychological Measurement*, 1964, *24*, 399–408.

Wolf, M. The CITE approach to innovative education. *Roeper Review*, 1981, *4* (2), 33–34.

Wolleat, P. Guiding the career development of gifted females. In N. Colangelo & R. Zaffrann (Eds.), *New voices in counseling the gifted.* Dubuque, Iowa: Kendall/Hunt Publishing Company, 1979.

Wooddell, G., Fletcher, G., & Dixon, T. Futures study for the adolescent gifted: A curriculum evaluation. *Journal for the Education of the Gifted*, 1982, *5* (1), 24–33.

Worcester, D. *The education of children above average mentality.* Lincoln, Neb.: University of Nebraska Press, 1955.

World Future Society. *World Future Society catalog*, 1979. (4916 St. Elmo Ave. (Bethesda), Washington, D.C. 20014.)

Wright, P. *Enrollment for advanced degrees* (E-5401-63, Circular No. 786). Washington, D.C.: Office of Education, U.S. Department of Health, Education and Welfare, 1965.

Wright, W., & Jung, C. Why capable school students do not continue their schooling. *Bulletin of the School of Education*, Indiana University, 1959, *35* (1).

Yamamoto, J. *Leadership skill development syllabus.* Los Angeles: Los Angeles City Schools, Instructional Planning Division, 1975.

Yamamoto, K. Creative thinking: Some thoughts on research. *Exceptional Children*, 1964, *30*, 403–410.

Yamamoto, K. Effects of restriction of range and test unreliability on correlation between measures of intelligence and creative thinking. *British Journal of Educational Psychology*, 1965, *35*, 300–305.

Yarrow, L. Research in dimensions of early maternal care. *Merrill Palmer Quarterly*, 1968, *9*, 101–114.

Yarrow, L., Rubenstein, J., Pedersen, F., & Jankowski, J. Dimensions of early stimulation and their differential effects on infant development. *Merrill-Palmer Quarterly*, 1972, *18*, 205–218.

Yarrow, L., Rubenstein, J., & Pedersen, F. *Infant and environment. Early cognitive and motivational development.* New York: Halsted, 1973.

Yuker, H. Group atmosphere and memory. *Journal of Abnormal and Social Psychology*, 1955, *51*, 17–23.

Zaffrann, R., & Colangelo, N. Counseling with gifted and talented students. *The Gifted Child Quarterly*, 1977, *20*, 305–321.

Zimmerman, J. MEG gets inside your head. *Psychology Today*, 1982, *16* (4), 100.

Zoccolotti, P., & Oltman, P. Field dependence and lateralization of verbal and configurational processing. *Cortex*, 1978, *14*, 155–163.

Zuckerman, D., & Horn, R. *The guide to simulations/games for education and training.* Lexington, Mass.: Information Resources, 1973.

SUBJECT INDEX

AUTHOR INDEX

get piano teacher
write to magazine address
Betsy - retest?
✓ Carolyn - data to